WASHINGTON CAMPING

TOM STIENSTRA

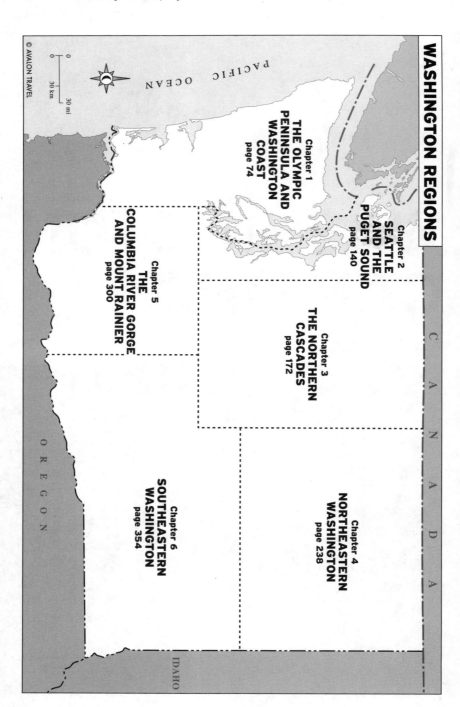

WASHINGTON REGIONS

Chapter 1
THE OLYMPIC
PENINSULA AND
WASHINGTON
COAST
page 74

Chapter 2
SEATTLE
AND THE
PUGET SOUND
page 140

Chapter 5
THE
COLUMBIA RIVER GORGE
AND MOUNT RAINIER
page 300

Chapter 3
THE NORTHERN
CASCADES
page 172

Chapter 6
SOUTHEASTERN
WASHINGTON
page 354

Chapter 4
NORTHEASTERN
WASHINGTON
page 238

PACIFIC OCEAN

OREGON

IDAHO

CANADA

© AVALON TRAVEL

0   30 mi
0   30 km

Contents

How to Use This Book
ABOUT THE CAMPGROUND PROFILES
The campgrounds are listed in a consistent, easy-to-read format to help you choose the ideal camping spot. If you already know the name of the specific campground you want to visit, or the name of the surrounding geological area or nearby feature (town, national or state park, forest, mountain, lake, river, etc.), look it up in the index and turn to the corresponding page. Here is a sample profile:

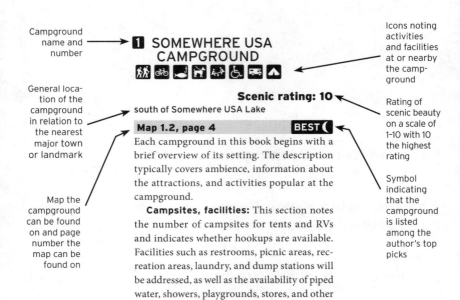

Campground name and number →

Icons noting activities and facilities at or nearby the campground

General location of the campground in relation to the nearest major town or landmark →

Map the campground can be found on and page number the map can be found on →

1 SOMEWHERE USA CAMPGROUND

Scenic rating: 10

south of Somewhere USA Lake

Rating of scenic beauty on a scale of 1-10 with 10 the highest rating

Map 1.2, page 4   **BEST (**

Symbol indicating that the campground is listed among the author's top picks

Each campground in this book begins with a brief overview of its setting. The description typically covers ambience, information about the attractions, and activities popular at the campground.

Campsites, facilities: This section notes the number of campsites for tents and RVs and indicates whether hookups are available. Facilities such as restrooms, picnic areas, recreation areas, laundry, and dump stations will be addressed, as well as the availability of piped water, showers, playgrounds, stores, and other amenities. The campground's pet policy and wheelchair accessibility is also mentioned here.

Reservations, fees: This section notes whether reservations are accepted, and provides rates for tent sites and RV sites. If there are additional fees for parking or pets, or discounted weekly or seasonal rates, they will also be noted here.

Directions: This section provides mile-by-mile driving directions to the campground from the nearest major town or highway.

Contact: This section provides an address, phone number, and website, if available, for the campground.

ABOUT THE ICONS

The icons in this book are designed to provide at-a-glance information on activities, facilities, and services available on-site or within walking distance of each campground.

- 🏔 Hiking trails
- 🚲 Biking trails
- 🏊 Swimming
- 🎣 Fishing
- 🛶 Boating
- 🚣 Canoeing and/or kayaking
- ⛷ Winter sports

- ♨ Hot springs
- 🐾 Pets permitted
- 🛝 Playground
- ♿ Wheelchair accessible
- 🚐 RV sites
- ⛺ Tent sites
- 5️⃣ 5 Percent Club

ABOUT THE SCENIC RATING

Each campground profile employs a scenic rating on a scale of 1 to 10, with 1 being the least scenic and 10 being the most scenic. A scenic rating measures only the overall beauty of the campground and environs; it does not take into account noise level, facilities, maintenance, recreation options, or campground management. The setting of a campground with a lower scenic rating may simply not be as picturesque that of as a higher rated campground, however other factors that can influence a trip, such as noise or recreation access, can still affect or enhance your camping trip. Consider both the scenic rating and the profile description before deciding which campground is perfect for you.

MAP SYMBOLS

⋯⋯⋯	Expressway	(80)	Interstate Freeway	✗	Airfield
⋯⋯⋯	Primary Road	(101)	U.S. Highway	✈	Airport
⋯⋯⋯	Secondary Road	(21)	State Highway	○	City/Town
========	Unpaved Road	[66]	County Highway	▲	Mountain
⋯⋯⋯⋯	Ferry	⬮	Lake	⬥	Park
▬ ▪ ▬ ▪	National Border	⬭	Dry Lake	)(	Pass
──-───	State Border	⬮	Seasonal Lake	◉	State Capital

ABOUT THE MAPS

This book is divided into chapters based on major regions in the state; an overview map of these regions precedes the table of contents. Each chapter begins with a map of the region, which is further broken down into detail maps. Campgrounds are noted on the detail maps by number.

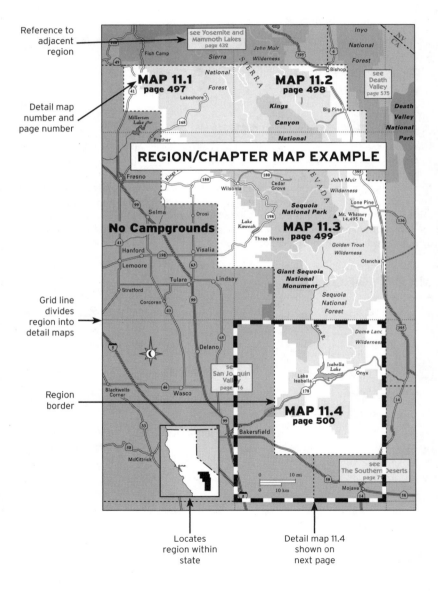

Reference to adjacent region

Detail map number and page number

Grid line divides region into detail maps

Region border

Locates region within state

Detail map 11.4 shown on next page

REGION/CHAPTER MAP EXAMPLE

MAP 11.1 page 497

MAP 11.2 page 498

MAP 11.3 page 499

MAP 11.4 page 500

No Campgrounds

see Yosemite and Mammoth Lakes page 432

see Death Valley page 575

see San Joaquin Valley page 516

see The Southern Deserts page 7

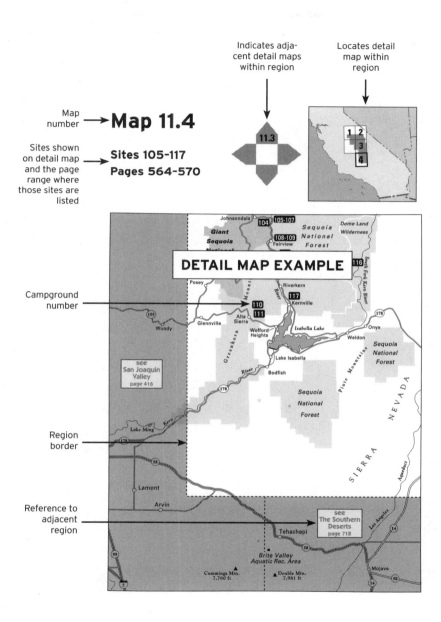

Indicates adja-
cent detail maps
within region

Locates detail
map within
region

Map
number ──► **Map 11.4**

Sites shown
on detail map ──► **Sites 105-117**
and the page **Pages 564-570**
range where
those sites are
listed

1 2
3
4

11.3

DETAIL MAP EXAMPLE

Johnsondale 104 105-107 Sequoia Dome Land
Giant 108-109 National Wilderness
Sequoia Fairview Forest
National

Campground
number

Posey 116

Riverkern
110 117
111 Kernville

155 Alta
Sierra
Woody Glennville Wofford Isabella Lake 178 Onyx

see Heights Weldon Sequoia
San Joaquin Lake Isabella National
Valley Forest
page 416 178 Bodfish

Sequoia

Region National
border Forest

Lake Ming Kern River NEVADA

128 SIERRA

58

Lamont Aqueduct

Reference to
adjacent Arvin see
region The Southern
Deserts Los Angeles 14
Tehachapi page 718

58

99 Brite Valley
Aquatic Rec. Area Mojave

Cummings Mtn. Double Mtn. 14 58
7,760 ft 7,981 ft

INTRODUCTION

Author's Note

When my family and friends throughout Washington heard I was writing this book, they all instantly hated me! They figured their favorite spots would be revealed to all. But after reading the book, they don't hate me anymore (except for this one cousin). That is because they have discovered, as I have, that Washington is filled with beautiful, little-used campgrounds that are perfect jump-off points for adventure—and there are hundreds of outstanding destinations, in addition to their sprinkling of personal favorites.

Looking for *mystery?* There are hundreds of hidden, rarely used campgrounds listed and mapped in this book that most people have never dreamed of. *Excitement?* At many of them, you'll find the sizzle with the steak: the hike to a great lookout or the big fish at the end of your line. *Fun?* The Camping Tips section of this book can help you take the futility out of your trips and put the fun back in. Add it up, put it in your cash register, and you can turn a camping trip into the satisfying adventure it's meant to be, whether it's just an overnight quickie or a month-long expedition.

Going on a camping trip can be like trying to put hiking boots on an octopus. You've tried it too, eh? Instead of a relaxing and fun trip full of adventure, it turns into a scenario called "You Against the World." You might as well try to fight a volcano. But it doesn't have to be that way, and that's what this book is all about. If you give it a chance, the information herein can remove the snarls, confusion, and occasional, volcanic temper explosions that keep people at home, locked away from the action.

It's estimated that 95 percent of American vacationers use only 5 percent of the country's available recreation areas. With this book, you can leave the herd, wander, and be free. You can join the inner circle, the Five Percenters who know the great hidden areas used by so few people. To join the Five Percent Club, take a hard look at the maps for the areas you wish to visit and the corresponding campground listings. As you study the camps, you'll start to feel a sense of excitement building, a feeling that you are about to unlock a door and venture into a world that is rarely viewed. When you feel that excitement, act on it. Parlay that energy into a great trip.

The campground maps and listings can serve in two ways: 1) If you're on the road late in the day and you're stuck for a spot for the night, you can likely find one nearby; or 2) if you are planning a trip, you can tailor a vacation to fit exactly into your plans rather than heading off and hoping—maybe praying—it turns out all right.

For the latter, you may wish to obtain additional maps, particularly if you are venturing into areas governed by the U.S. Forest Service or Bureau of Land Management. Both are federal agencies that offer low-cost maps detailing all hiking trails, lakes, streams, and backcountry camps reached via logging roads. The Resource Guide at the back of this book details how to obtain these and other maps.

Backcountry camps listed in this book are often in primitive and rugged settings but provide the sense of isolation that you may want from a trip. They also provide good jump-off points for backpacking trips, if that's your calling. These camps are often free, and I have listed hundreds of them.

At the other end of the spectrum are the developed parks for RVs. They offer a home away from home, with everything from full hookups to a grocery store and laundry room. Instead of isolation, an RV park provides a place to shower and get outfitted for food and clean clothes. For RV cruisers, it's a place to stay in high style while touring the area. RV

KEEP IT WILD

"Enjoy America's country and leave no trace." That's the motto of the Leave No Trace program, and I strongly support it. Promoting responsible outdoor recreation through education, research, and partnerships is its mission. Look for the Keep It Wild Tips, developed from the policies of Leave No Trace, throughout the Camping Tips portion of this book. This copyrighted information has been reprinted with permission from the Leave No Trace Center for Outdoor Ethics. For more information or materials, please visit www.LNT.org or call 303/442-8222 or 800/332-4100.

parks range in price, depending on location, and an advance deposit may be necessary in summer.

Somewhere between the two extremes are hundreds and hundreds of campgrounds that provide a compromise: beautiful settings and some facilities, with a small overnight fee. Piped water, vault toilets, and picnic tables tend to come with the territory. Fees for these sites are usually in the $10-35 range, with the higher-priced sites located near population centers. Because they offer a bit of both worlds, they are in high demand. Reservations are usually advised, and at state parks, particularly during the summer season, you can expect company. This doesn't mean you need to forgo them in hopes of a less confined environment. For one thing, most state parks have set up quotas so that visitors don't feel as if they've been squeezed in with a shoehorn. For another, the same parks are often uncrowded during the off-season and on weekdays.

Before your trip, you'll want to get organized, and that's when you must start putting boots on that giant octopus. The trick to organization for any task is breaking it down to its key components and then solving each element independent of the others. Remember the octopus. Grab a moving leg, jam on a boot, and make sure it's on tight before reaching for another leg. Do one thing at a time, in order, and all will get done quickly and efficiently.

Now you can become completely organized for your trip in just one week, spending just a little time each evening on a given component. Getting organized is an unnatural act for many. By splitting up the tasks, you take the pressure out of planning and put the fun back in.

As you might figure, this is not a hobby for me, as it is for some part-time writers who publish books. This is my full-time job. Because I spend up to 200 days a year in the field, I understand how seriously people take their fun, what they need to know to make their trips work, as well as their underlying fears that they might get stuck for the night without a spot. I get tons of emails and letters, and I read each one carefully. These have been of great benefit. In the process, I have incorporated dozen of suggestions from readers to make this book they want it to be. Your comments and questions are always welcome and appreciated. As a full-tome outdoors writer, the question I am asked more than any other is: "Where are you going this week?"

All of the answers are in this book.

Best Campgrounds

Can't decide where to stay? Here are my picks for the best Washington campgrounds in seven different categories.

BEST(Most Scenic

Fort Flagler State Park, The Olympic Peninsula and Washington Coast, page 92.
Kalaloch, The Olympic Peninsula and Washington Coast, page 98.
Pacific Beach State Park, The Olympic Peninsula and Washington Coast, page 99.
Fay Bainbridge Park, The Olympic Peninsula and Washington Coast, page 117.
Moran State Park Ferry-In, Seattle and the Puget Sound, page 150.
Turn Island Marine State Park Boat-In, Seattle and the Puget Sound, page 152.
Camano Island State Park, Seattle and the Puget Sound, page 162.
Panorama Point, The Northern Cascades, page 180.
Harts Pass Walk-In, The Northern Cascades, page 193.
Kamloops Island, Northeastern Washington, page 263.

BEST(Families

Lena Lake Hike-In, The Olympic Peninsula and Washington Coast, page 105.
Kitsap Memorial State Park, The Olympic Peninsula and Washington Coast, page 115.
KOA Lynden/Bellingham, Seattle and the Puget Sound, page 147.
Bay View State Park, Seattle and the Puget Sound, page 158.
Leavenworth/Pine Village KOA, The Northern Cascades, page 228.
Ellensburg KOA, The Northern Cascades, page 235.
Curlew Lake State Park, Northeastern Washington, page 260.
Shore Acres Resort, Northeastern Washington, page 284.
Henley's Silver Lake Resort, The Columbia River Gorge and Mount Rainier, page 307.
Yakima Sportsman State Park, Southeastern Washington, page 360.

BEST(Fishing

Coppermine Bottom, The Olympic Peninsula and Washington Coast, page 98.
West Beach Resort Ferry-In, Seattle and the Puget Sound, page 150.
Doe Island Marine State Park Boat-In, Seattle and the Puget Sound, page 151.
Pearrygin Lake State Park, The Northern Cascades, page 199.
Chopaka Lake, Northeastern Washington, page 245.
Conconully State Park, Northeastern Washington, page 252.
Rock Lakes, Northeastern Washington, page 254.
Long Lake, Northeastern Washington, page 265.
Offut Lake Resort, The Columbia River Gorge and Mount Rainier, page 306.
Mossyrock Park, The Columbia River Gorge and Mount Rainier, page 312.
Silver Lake Motel and Resort, The Columbia River Gorge and Mount Rainier, page 314.
Potholes State Park, Southeastern Washington, page 361.

BEST❰ Hiking

Campbell Tree Grove, The Olympic Peninsula and Washington Coast, page 108.
Moran State Park Ferry-In, Seattle and the Puget Sound, page 150.
Silver Fir, The Northern Cascades, page 177.
Beaver Plant Lake Hike-In, The Northern Cascades, page 192.
Harts Pass Walk-In, The Northern Cascades, page 193.
Mount Spokane State Park, Northeastern Washington, page 295.
Lower Falls, The Columbia River Gorge and Mount Rainier, page 338.
Beacon Rock State Park, The Columbia River Gorge and Mount Rainier, page 345.

BEST❰ Waterfalls

Wallace Falls State Park Walk-In, The Northern Cascades, page 208.
Denny Creek, The Northern Cascades, page 212.
Silver Falls, The Northern Cascades, page 218.
Douglas Falls, Northeastern Washington, page 275.
Ohanapecosh, The Columbia River Gorge and Mount Rainier, page 325.
Lower Falls, The Columbia River Gorge and Mount Rainier, page 338.
Palouse Falls State Park, Southeastern Washington, page 363.

BEST❰ Waterfront Campgrounds

Lena Lake Hike-In, The Olympic Peninsula and Washington Coast, page 105.
Coho, The Olympic Peninsula and Washington Coast, page 108.
Skokomish Park at Lake Cushman, The Olympic Peninsula and Washington Coast, page 111.
Lake Sylvia State Park, The Olympic Peninsula and Washington Coast, page 114.
Birch Bay State Park, Seattle and the Puget Sound, page 145.
Larrabee State Park, Seattle and the Puget Sound, page 156.
Maple Grove, The Northern Cascades, page 180.
Pearrygin Lake State Park, The Northern Cascades, page 199.
Twenty-Five Mile Creek State Park, The Northern Cascades, page 220.
Lake Chelan State Park, The Northern Cascades, page 224.
Sun Lakes-Dry Falls State Park, Northeastern Washington, page 288.
Spring Canyon, Northeastern Washington, page 290.

BEST❰ Wildlife-Viewing

Bear Creek, The Olympic Peninsula and Washington Coast, page 83.
Ocean City State Park, The Olympic Peninsula and Washington Coast, page 100.
Birch Bay State Park, Seattle and the Puget Sound, page 145.
Larrabee State Park, Seattle and the Puget Sound, page 156.
Pearrygin Lake State Park, The Northern Cascades, page 199.
Napeequa Crossing, The Northern Cascades, page 217.
Lake Wenatchee State Park, The Northern Cascades, page 222.
Palmer Lake, Northeastern Washington, page 247.
Haag Cove, Northeastern Washington, page 268.
Big Meadow Lake, Northeastern Washington, page 272.

Camping Tips

SLEEPING GEAR

On an eve long ago in the mountain pines, my dad, brother, and I had rolled out our sleeping bags and were bedded down for the night. After the pre-trip excitement, a long drive, an evening of trout fishing and a barbecue, we were like three tired doggies who had played too much.

But as I looked up at the stars, I was suddenly wide awake. I was still wired. A half hour later? No change. Wide awake.

And as little kids can do, I had to wake up ol' Dad to tell him about it. "Hey, Dad, I can't sleep."

After the initial grimace, he said: "This is what you do. Watch the sky for a shooting star and tell yourself that you cannot go to sleep until you see at least one shooting star. As you wait and watch, you will start getting tired, and it will be difficult to keep your eyes open. But tell yourself, you must keep watching. Then you'll start to really feel tired. When you finally see a shooting star, you'll go to sleep so fast you won't know what hit you."

Well, I tried it that night and I don't even remember seeing a shooting star, I went to sleep so fast.

It's a good trick, and along with having a good sleeping bag, ground insulation, maybe a tent, or a few tricks for bedding down in a pickup truck or RV, you can get a great night's sleep on every camping trip.

More than 20 years after that camping episode with my dad and brother, we made a trip to the planetarium at the Academy of Sciences in San Francisco to see a show. The lights dimmed, and the ceiling turned into a night sky, filled with stars and a setting moon. A scientist began explaining the phenomena of the heavens.

After a few minutes, I began to feel drowsy. Just then, a shooting star zipped across the planetarium ceiling. I went into such a deep sleep, it was like I was in a coma. I didn't wake up until the show was over, the lights were turned back on, and the people were leaving.

Feeling drowsy, I turned to see if Dad had liked the show. Oh yeah? Not only had he gone to sleep too, but he apparently had no intention of waking up, no matter what. Just like a camping trip.

Sleeping Bags

The first rule of a good nights' sleep is that you must be dry, warm and safe. A good sleeping bag can help plenty. A sleeping bag is a shell filled with heat-retaining insulation. By itself, it is not warm. Your body provides the heat, and the sleeping bag's ability to retain that heat is what makes it warm or cold.

The cheap cotton bags are heavy, bulky, cold, and, when wet, useless. With other options available, their function is limited. Anybody who sleeps outdoors or backpacks should choose otherwise. Use a sleeping bag filled with down or one of the quality poly-fills. Down is light, warm, and aesthetically pleasing to those who don't think camping and technology mix. If you choose a down bag, be sure to keep it double wrapped in plastic garbage bags on your trips to keep it dry. Once it's wet, you'll spend your nights howling at the moon.

The polyfiber-filled bags are not necessarily better than those filled with down, but they can be. Their one key advantage is that even when wet, some poly-fills can retain up to 85 percent of your body heat. This allows you to sleep and get valuable rest even in miserable conditions. In my camping experience, no matter how lucky you may be, there will come a time when you will get caught in an unexpected, violent storm and everything you've got will get wet, including your sleeping bag. That's when a poly-fill bag becomes priceless. You have one and can sleep. Or you don't have one and suffer. It is that simple. Of the synthetic fills, Quallofil made by DuPont is the industry leader.

But just because a sleeping bag uses a

KEEP IT WILD TIP 1: CAMP WITH CARE

1. Choose an existing, legal site. Restrict activities to areas where vegetation is compacted or absent.
2. Camp at least 75 steps (200 feet) from lakes, streams, and trails.
3. Always choose sites that won't be damaged by your stay.
4. Preserve the feeling of solitude by selecting camps that are out of view when possible.
5. Don't dig trenches or build structures or furniture.

high-tech poly-fill doesn't necessarily make it a better bag. There are other factors.

The most important are a bag's temperature rating and weight. The temperature rating of a sleeping bag refers to how cold it can get outside before you start actually feeling cold. Many campers make the mistake of thinking, "I only camp in the summer, so a bag rated at 30 or 40°F should be fine." Later, they find out it isn't so fine, and all it takes is one cold night to convince them of that. When selecting the right temperature rating, visualize the coldest weather you might ever confront, and then get a bag rated for even colder weather.

For instance, if you are a summer camper, you may rarely experience a night in the low 30s or high 20s. A sleeping bag rated at 20°F would be appropriate, keeping you snug, warm, and asleep. For most campers, I advise bags rated at 0 or 10°F.

But guess how the companies come up with their temperature ratings? Usually it's a guy like me field-testing a bag before it is commercially released, and then saying, "Well, it got down to 40°F and I was pretty warm." So they rate it at 30 degrees. Obviously, testers can have different threshold levels for cold, while others base their ratings on how much fill is used.

If you buy a poly-filled sleeping bag, try not to leave it squished in your stuff sack between camping trips. Instead, keep it on a hanger in a closet or use it as a blanket. One thing that can reduce a poly-filled bag's heat-retaining qualities is if the tiny hollow fibers that make up the fill lose their loft. You can avoid this with proper storage.

The weight of a sleeping bag can also be a

key factor, especially for backpackers. When you have to carry your gear on your back, every ounce becomes important. Sleeping bags that weigh just 2-3 pounds are available, although they are expensive. But if you hike much, it's worth the price to keep your weight to a minimum. For an overnighter, you can get away with a 4- or 4.5-pound bag without much stress. However, bags weighing five pounds and up should be left back at the car.

I have several sleeping bags; they range from a seven-pounder that feels like a giant sponge to a three-pounder. The heavy-duty model is for pickup-truck camping in cold weather and doubles as a blanket at home. The lightweight bag is for expeditions.

Insulation Pads

Even with the warmest sleeping bag in the world, if you just lay it down on the ground and try to sleep, you will likely get as cold as a winter cucumber. That is because the cold ground will suck the warmth right out of your body. The solution is to have a layer of insulation between you and the ground. For this, you can use a thin Insulite pad, a lightweight Therm-a-Rest inflatable pad, a foam pad or mattress, an airbed, or a cot. Here is a capsule summary of each:

Insulite pads: They are light, inexpensive, roll up quickly for transport, and can double as a seat pad at your camp. The negative side is that in one night, they will compress, making you feel like you are sleeping on granite. But they are light and they help keep you warm in the wilderness.

Therm-a-Rest pads: These are a real

luxury for wilderness travel because they do everything an Insulite pad does, but they also provide a cushion. The negative side is that they are expensive by comparison, and if they get a hole in them, they become worthless without a patch kit. Most wilderness campers carry one "bonus item"—and a full-length Therm-A-Rest is often what they choose.

Foam mattresses, air beds, and cots: These are excellent for car campers. The new line of air beds, especially the thicker ones, are outstanding and inflate quickly with an electric motor inflator that plugs into a power plug or cigarette lighter in your vehicle. Foam mattresses are also excellent; I think they are the most comfortable of all, but their size precludes many from considering them. I've found that cots work great, too. I've always had one and they're great for drive-in tent sites. For camping in the back of a pickup truck with a camper shell, the cots with three-inch legs are best, of course. Here's the trick: Put a blanket over the sleeping surface, then add a Therm-A-Rest pad; you need insulation to keep the cold air beneath you from sucking out the warmth.

A Few Tricks

When surveying a camp area, the most important consideration should be to select a good spot for sleeping. Everything else is secondary. Ideally, you want a flat area that is wind-sheltered and on ground soft enough to drive stakes into. Yeah, and I want to win the lottery, too.

Sometimes, the ground will have a slight slope to it. In that case, always sleep with your head on the uphill side. If you sleep parallel to the slope, every time you roll over, you'll find yourself rolling down the hill. If you sleep with your head on the downhill side, you'll get a headache that feels as if an ax is embedded in your brain.

When you've found a good spot, clear it of all branches, twigs, and rocks, of course. A good tip is to dig a slight indentation in the ground where your hip will fit. Since your body is not flat, but has curves and edges, it will not feel comfortable on flat ground. Some people even get severely bruised on the sides of their hips when sleeping on flat, hard ground. For that reason alone, they learn to hate camping. What a shame, especially when the problem is solved easily with a Therm-a-Rest pad, foam insulation, an air bed, or a cot.

After the ground is prepared, throw a ground cloth over the spot, which will keep much of the morning dew off you. In some areas, particularly where fog is a problem, morning dew can be heavy and get the outside of your sleeping bag quite wet. In that case, you need overhead protection, such as a tent or some kind of roof, like a poncho or tarp with its ends tied to trees.

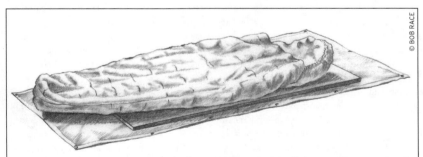

© BOB RACE

Even with the warmest sleeping bag in the world, if you just lay it down on the ground and try to sleep, you will likely get as cold as a winter cucumber. That is because the cold ground will suck the warmth right out of your body. The solution? A sleeping pad.

A Great Nights' Sleep

Some people sleep seven, eight hours at camp, but it comes in 10 installments. They keep waking up. They wake up and half their body is paralyzed. Heh, heh, heh. They can't get comfortable. To solve this, practice camp-style sleeping at home until you get it perfect. At home, you have flexibility and complete control over your sleeping surface. Get it right. Get it just how you like it.

For wilderness travel, my bonus item is an extra inflatable pillow; that's right, I carry two, not one. I inflate them about half full. It puts my head at a perfect comfort zone for deep sleep. Whatever it takes, know how to get a great night's sleep and your entire trip has the chance to feel epic, no matter what you do.

Tents and Weather Protection

All it takes is to get caught in the rain once without a tent and you will never go anywhere without one again. A tent provides protection from rain, wind, and mosquito attacks. In exchange, you can lose a starry night's view, though some tents now even provide moon roofs.

A tent can be as complex as a four-season, tubular-jointed dome with a rain fly or as simple as a tarp roped up to a tree. They can be as cheap as a $10 tube tent, which is nothing more than a hollow piece of plastic, or as expensive as a $500 five-person deluxe expedition, multi-room dome. They vary greatly in size, price, and assembly time. For those who camp infrequently and want to buy a tent without paying much, off-brand models are available at considerable price discounts. My experience in field-testing outdoor gear, though, is that cheap tents often rip at the seams if subjected to regular use. If you plan on getting a good one, plan on doing plenty of shopping and asking lots of questions. With a little bit of homework, you can get the right answers to these questions:

Will It Keep Me Dry?

On many one-person and two-person tents, the rain fly does not extend far enough to keep water off the bottom sidewalls of the tent. In a driving rain, water can also drip from the rain fly and onto those sections of the tent. Eventually, the water can leak through to the inside, particularly through the seams.

You must be able to stake out your rain fly so it completely covers all of the tent. If you are tent shopping and this does not appear possible, then don't buy the tent. To prevent potential leaks, use a seam water-proofer, such as Seam Lock, a glue-like substance that can close potential leak areas on tent seams. For large umbrella tents, keep a patch kit handy. Coleman tents, by the way, are guaranteed to keep campers dry.

Another way to keep water out of your tent is to store all wet garments outside the tent, under a poncho. Moisture from wet clothes stashed in the tent will condense on the interior tent walls. If you bring enough wet clothes into the tent, by the next morning you'll feel as if you're camping in a duck blind.

How Hard Is It to Put Up?

If a tent is difficult to erect in full sunlight, you can just about forget it at night, especially the first night out if you arrive late to camp. Some tents can go up in just a few minutes, without requiring help from another camper. This might be the kind of tent you want.

The way to compare put-up times when shopping for tents is to count the number of connecting points from the tent poles to the tent and the number of stakes required. The fewer, the better. Think simple. My two-person-plus-a-dog tent has seven connecting points and, minus the rain fly, requires no stakes. It goes up in a few minutes.

My bigger family tent, which has three rooms with walls (so we can keep our two kids isolated on each side if necessary), takes about a half hour to put up. That's without anybody's help. With their help, add about 15 minutes. Heh, heh.

Another factor is the tent poles themselves. Always make sure the poles are connected by

© SABRINA YOUNG

Tents vary in complexity, size, and price. Be sure to buy the one that's right for you.

an interior bungee cord. It takes only an instant to convert them to a complete pole.

Some outdoor shops have tents on display on their showroom floors. Before buying the tent, have the salesperson take the tent down and put it back up. If it takes him more than five minutes, or he says he doesn't have time, then keep looking.

Is It Roomy Enough?

Don't judge the size of a tent on floor space alone. Some tents that are small on floor space can give the illusion of roominess with a high ceiling. You can be quite comfortable and snug in them.

But remember that a one-person or two-person tent is just that. A two-person tent has room for two people plus gear. That's it. Don't buy a tent expecting it to hold more than it is intended to.

How Much Does It Weigh?

If you're a hiker, this becomes the preeminent question. If it's much more than six or seven pounds, forget it. A 12-pound tent is bad enough, but get it wet and it's like carrying a

piano on your back. On the other hand, weight is scarcely a factor if you camp only where you can take your car. My dad, for instance, used to have this giant canvas umbrella tent that folded down to a neat little pack that weighed about 500 pounds.

Family Tents

It is always worth spending the time and money to buy a tent you and your family will be happy with.

Many excellent family tents are available from Cabela's, Coleman, Eureka!, North Face, Remington, and Sierra Designs. Guide-approved expedition tents for groups cost more. Here is a synopsis of some of best tents available:

Cabela's Two- or Three-Room Cabin

800/237-4444

www.cabelas.com

This beautiful tent features two to three rooms, a 10- by 16-foot floor available in different configurations with removable interior walls. Three doors mean everybody doesn't tromp through the center room for access to the side rooms. It will stand up to wind, rain, and frequent use.

COLEMAN MODIFIED DOME

800/835-3278

www.coleman.com

Coleman Modified Dome tents are available in six different single- and multi-room designs. The pole structure is unique, with all four upright poles and one ridgepole shock-corded together for an integrated system that makes setup extremely fast and easy. Yet, because of the ridgepole's engineering, the tent has passed tests in high winds. Mesh panels in the ceiling are a tremendous plus for ventilation.

COLEMAN WEATHERMASTER

800/835-3278

www.coleman.com

The Weathermaster series features tents with multiple rooms, walls, and ample headroom, and they are guaranteed to keep rain out. The 17- by 9-foot model sleeps six to eight, has a 76-inch ceiling, and has zippered dividers. Since the dividers are removable, you can configure the tent in multiple layouts. The frame is designed with poles adjustable to three different heights to accommodate uneven ground.

KELTY

800/423-2320

www.kelty.com

Kelty offers top-of-the-line tents based on a sleek dome profile. This is a great package, with mesh sides, tops, and doors, along with a full awning fly and coverage for weather protection. Clip sleeves and rubber-tipped poles for easy slide during setup are nice bonuses.

REI

800/423-2320

www.rei.com

REI has 94 backpacking tents and 27 tents available for car camping, including their own designs as well as those from other manufacturers. A great backpacking tent for two is the REI

Half Dome 2 Plus. The Eureka Copper Canyon 6 is one of the better family values.

Bivouac Bags

If you like going light or solo, and choose not to own a tent at all, a bivy bag or tarp can be the way to go. Bivy is short for bivouac bag and pronounced "bivvy" as in dizzy, not "bivy" as in ivy, and can provide the extremely lightweight weather protection you require. A bivy bag is a water-repellent shell in which your sleeping bag fits. It is light and tough, and for some is the perfect alternative to a heavy tent. My own bivy weighs 31 ounces and cost around $250; it's made by OR (Outdoor Research), and I just plain love the thing on expeditions. On the downside, however, some say it can be a bit difficult getting settled just right in it, and others say they feel claustrophobic in such close quarters. Once you get used to a bivy, spend a night in a tent; the tent will feel like a room at the Mirage. For me, not a problem.

The idea of riding out a storm in a bivy can be quite worrisome for some. You can hear the rain hitting you, and sometimes even feel the pounding of the drops through the bivy bag. For some, it can be unsettling to try to sleep under such circumstances. On the other hand, I've always looked forward to it. In cold weather, a bivy also helps keep you warm. I've had just one miserable night in mine. That was when my sleeping bag was a bit wet when I started the night. By the middle of the night, the water was condensing from the sleeping bag on the interior walls of the bivy, and then soaking the bag, like a storm cycle. The night hit only about 45°F but I just about froze to death anyway. Otherwise, I've used it on more than 100 expeditions with great results: warm, dry quarters and deep, restful sleeps by night, and a pack lightened without carrying a tent by day.

Many long-distance hikers are switching to light tarps in the continuing mission to minimize weight. They work great in rain and the spacious feel beneath them is fantastic. You just need a tree to tie to and soft enough ground for stakes, so they don't work above tree line. Tarps are great, except when there are bug problems; then you need some kind of mosquito netting. A bivy or tent solves that, of course.

Pickup Truck Campers

If you own a pickup truck with a camper shell, you can turn it into a self-contained campground with a little work. This can be an ideal way to go: It's fast, portable, and you are guaranteed a dry environment.

But that does not necessarily mean it is a warm environment. In fact, without insulation from the metal truck bed, it can be like trying to sleep on an iceberg. The metal truck bed will get as cold as the air temperature, which is often much colder than the ground temperature. Without insulation, it can be much colder in your camper shell than it would be on the open ground.

When I camp in my rig, I use a large piece of foam for a mattress and insulation. The foam measures four inches thick, 48 inches wide, and 76 inches long. It makes for a bed as comfortable as anything one might ask for. In fact, during the winter, if I don't go camping for a few weeks because of writing obligations, I sometimes will throw the foam on the floor, lay down the old sleeping bag, light a fire, and camp right in my living room. It's in my blood, I tell you. Airbeds and cots are also extremely comfortable and I've used both many times. Whatever you choose, just make sure you have a comfortable sleeping unit. Good sleep makes for great camping trips.

RVs

The problems RVers encounter come from two primary sources: lack of privacy and light intrusion.

The lack of privacy stems from the natural restrictions of where a land yacht can go. Without careful use of the guide section of this book, owners of RVs can find themselves in parking-lot settings, jammed in with plenty of neighbors. Because RVs often have large picture windows, you lose your privacy, causing some late nights; then, come daybreak, light intrusion forces an early wake up. As a result, you get shorted on your sleep.

The answer is to carry inserts to fit over the inside of your windows. These close off the outside and retain your privacy. And if you don't want to wake up with the sun at daybreak, you don't have to. It will still be dark.

Many campgrounds and RV parks enforce a quiet time. If that is important to you, make sure you don't end up somewhere where a quiet time is optional.

HIKING AND FOOT CARE

We had set up a nice little camp in the woods, and my buddy, Foonsky, was strapping on his hiking boots, sitting against a big Douglas fir.

"New boots," he said with a grin. "But they seem pretty stiff."

We decided to hoof it down the trail for a few hours, exploring the mountain wildlands that are said to hide Bigfoot and other strange creatures. After just a short while on the trail, a sense of peace and calm seemed to settle in. The forest provides the chance to be purified with clean air and the smell of trees, freeing you from all troubles.

But it wasn't long before a look of trouble was on Foonsky's face. And no, it wasn't from seeing Bigfoot.

"Got a hot spot on my toe," he said.

Immediately, we stopped. He pulled off his right boot, then his sock, and inspected the left side of his big toe. Sure enough, a blister had bubbled up, filled with fluid, but hadn't popped. From his medical kit, Foonsky cut a small piece of moleskin to fit over the blister and taped it to hold it in place. In a few minutes we were back on the trail.

A half hour later, there was still no sign of Bigfoot. But Foonsky stopped again and pulled off his other boot. "Another hot spot." On the little toe of his left foot was another small blister, over which he taped a Band-Aid to keep it from further chafing against the inside of his new boot.

In just a few days, ol' Foonsky, a strong, 6-foot-5, 200-plus-pound guy, was walking around like a sore-hoofed horse that had been loaded with a month's worth of supplies and ridden over sharp rocks. Well, it wasn't the distance that had done Foonsky in; it was those blisters. He had them on eight of his 10 toes and was going through Band-Aids, moleskin, and tape like a walking emergency ward. If he'd used any more tape, he would've looked like a mummy from an Egyptian tomb.

If you've ever been in a similar predicament, you know the frustration of wanting to have a good time, wanting to hike and explore the area where you have set up a secluded camp, only to be held up by several blisters. No one is immune—all are created equal before the blister god. You can be forced to bow to it unless you get your act together.

What causes blisters? In almost all cases, it is the simple rubbing of a foot against the rugged interior of a boot. That can be worsened by several factors:

1. A very stiff boot or one in which your foot moves inside as you walk, instead of a boot that flexes as if it were another layer of skin.

2. Thin, ragged, or dirty socks. This is the fastest route to blisters. Thin socks will allow your feet to move inside your boots, ragged socks will allow your skin to chafe directly against the boot's interior, and dirty socks will wrinkle and fold, also rubbing against your feet instead of cushioning them.

3. Soft feet. By themselves, soft feet will not cause blisters, but in combination with a stiff boot or thin socks, they can cause terrible problems. The best way to toughen up your feet is to go barefoot. In fact, some of the biggest, toughest-looking guys you'll ever see, from Hells Angels to pro football players, have feet that are as soft as a baby's butt. Why? Because they never go barefoot and don't hike much.

The Perfect Boot

Every hiker eventually conducts a search for the perfect boot in the mission for ideal foot comfort and freedom from blisters. While there are many entries in this search—in fact, so many that it can be confusing—there is a way to find that perfect boot for you.

To stay blister-free, the most important factors are socks and boot flexibility. If there is

© SABRINA YOUNG

Hiking shoes are perfect for short treks to day-long trips.

KEEP IT WILD TIP 2:
KEEP THE WILDERNESS WILD

1. Let nature's sound prevail. Avoid loud voices and noises.
2. Leave radios and tape players at home. At drive-in camping sites, never open car doors with music playing.
3. Careful guidance is necessary when choosing any games to bring for children. Most toys, especially any kind of gun toys with which children simulate shooting at each other, shouldn't be allowed on a camping trip.
4. Control pets at all times or leave them with a sitter at home.
5. Treat natural heritage with respect. Leave plants, rocks, and historical artifacts where you find them.

---

any foot slippage from a thin sock or a stiff boot, you can rub up a blister in minutes. For instance, I never wear stiff boots and I sometimes wear two fresh sets of SmartWools.

My search for the perfect boot included discussions with the nation's preeminent long-distance hikers, Brian Robinson of Mountain View (7,200 miles in 2001) and Ray Jardine of Oregon (2,700 miles of Pacific Crest Trail in three months). Both believe that the weight of a shoe is the defining factor when selecting hiking footwear. They both go as light as possible, believing that heavy boots will eventually wear you out by forcing you to pick up several pounds on your feet over and over again.

It is absolutely critical to stay away from very stiff boots and thin socks. Always wear the right style boots for what you have in mind and then protect your feet with carefully selected socks. If you are still so unfortunate as to get a blister or two, it means knowing how to treat them fast so they don't turn your walk into a sore-footed endurance test.

Selecting the Right Boots

The first time we did the John Muir Trail, I hiked 400 miles in three months; that is, 150 miles in a two-month general-training program, then 250 miles in three weeks from Mount Whitney to Yosemite Valley. In that span, I got just one blister, suffered on the fourth day of the 250-miler. I treated it immediately and suffered no more. One key is wearing

the right boot, and for me, that means a boot that acts as a thick layer of skin that is flexible and pliable to my foot. I want my feet to fit snugly in them, with no interior movement.

There are four kinds of hiking footwear, most commonly known as: 1. Hiking boots; 2. Hunting boots; 3. Mountaineering boots; 4. Athletic shoes. Select the right one for you or pay the consequences.

One great trick when on a hiking vacation is to bring all four, and then for each hike, wear different footwear. This has many benefits. By changing boots, you change the points of stress for your feet and legs, greatly reducing soreness and the chance of creating a hot spot on a foot. It also allows you to go light on flat trails and heavy on steep trails, where additional boot weight can help with traction in downhill stretches.

HIKING BOOTS

Lightweight hiking boots are basically Gore-Tex walking shoes. They are designed for day walks or short backpacking trips and look like rugged, lightweight athletic shoes, designed with a Gore-Tex top for lightness and a Vibram sole for traction. These are perfect for people who like to walk but rarely carry a heavy backpack. Because they are flexible, they are easy to break in, and with fresh socks, they rarely cause blister problems. Because they are light, general hiking fatigue is greatly reduced. Like many, I've converted over 100 percent to them.

On the negative side, because hiking boots are light, traction can be far from great on steep, gravelly surfaces. In addition, they provide less than ideal ankle support, which can be a problem in rocky areas, such as along a stream where you might want to go trout fishing.

Regardless of the distance you anticipate, they are the footwear of choice. My personal preference is Merrell's, but New Balance, Salomon, Asolo, Zamberlan, Vasque, and others make great hiking boots. Many of the greatest long-distance hikers in America wear trail running shoes.

HUNTING BOOTS

Hunting boots are also called backpacking boots, super boots, or wilderness boots. They feature high ankle support, deep Vibram lug sole, built-in orthotics and arch support, and waterproof exterior.

They have fallen out of favor among campers and backpackers. On the negative side, hunting boots can be quite hot, weigh a ton, and if they get wet, take days to dry. Because they are heavy, they can wear you out. Often, the extra weight can add days to long-distance expeditions, cutting into the number of miles a hiker is capable of on a daily basis.

They are still popular among mountaineers who hunt. Their weight and traction make them good for trekking off-trail or for carrying heavy packs because they provide additional support. They also can stand up to hundreds of miles of wilderness use, constantly being banged against rocks and walked through streams while supporting 200 pounds.

My favorite hunting boot is made by Mendl, out of Germany. I have also used Danner, Cabela's and RedWing.

MOUNTAINEERING BOOTS

Mountaineering boots are identified by midrange tops, laces that extend almost as far as the toe area, and ankle areas that are as stiff as a board. The lack of "give" is what endears them to mountaineers. Their stiffness is preferred when rock-climbing, walking off-trail

on craggy surfaces, or hiking along the edge of streambeds where walking across small rocks can cause you to turn your ankle. Because these boots don't give on rugged, craggy terrain, they reduce ankle injuries and provide better traction.

The drawback to stiff boots is that if you don't have the proper socks and your foot starts slipping around in the boot, blisters will inevitably follow. If you just want to go for a walk or a good tromp with a backpack, then hiking shoes or hunting boots will serve you better.

Vasque makes my favorite mountaineering boots for rock climbing.

AT THE STORE

There are many styles, brands, and price ranges to choose from. If you wander about comparing all their many features, you will get as confused as a kid in a toy store.

Instead, go into the store with your mind clear about what you want, find it, and buy it. If you want the best, expect to spend $85-200 for hiking boots, $100-250 for hunting boots, $250-300 for mountaineering boots. If you go much cheaper, well, then you are getting cheap footwear.

This is one area where you don't want to scrimp, so try not to yelp about the high cost. Instead, walk into the store believing you deserve the best, and that's exactly what you'll pay for.

You don't always get what you pay for, though. Once, I spent $200-plus on some hunting boots that turned out to be miserable blister-makers and I had to throw them out. Even after a year of trying to get my money's worth, I never felt they worked right on the trail. Adios. Move on to what works.

If you plan to use the advice of a shoe salesperson, first look at what kind of boots he or she is wearing. If the salesperson isn't even wearing boots, then their advice may not be worth much. Most people I know who own quality boots, including salespeople, wear them almost daily if their jobs allow, since boots are the best footwear available. However, even these well-meaning folks can offer sketchy advice. Plenty of hikers claim to wear the world's greatest boot! Instead of asking how great the boot is, ask, "How many blisters did you get when you hiked 12 miles a day for a week?"

Enter the store with a precise use and style in mind. Rather than fish for suggestions, tell the salesperson exactly what you want, try two or three brands of the same style, and always try on both boots in a pair simultaneously so you know exactly how they'll feel. If possible, walk up and down stairs with them. Are they too stiff? Are your feet snug yet comfortable, or do they slip? Do they have that "right" kind of feel when you walk?

If you get the appropriate answers to those questions, then you're on your way to blister-free, pleasure-filled days of walking.

Socks

People can spend so much energy selecting the right kind of boots that they virtually overlook wearing the right kind of socks. One goes with the other.

Your socks should be thick enough to cushion your feet as well as fit snugly. Without good socks, you might tie your bootlaces too tight—and that's like putting a tourniquet on your feet. You should have plenty of clean socks on hand, or plan on washing what you have on your trip. As socks are worn, they become compressed, dirty, and damp. If they fold over, you'll rub up a blister in minutes.

My companions believe I go overboard when it comes to socks, that I bring too many and wear too many. But it works, so that's where the complaints stop. So how many do I wear? Well, it varies. On day hikes, I have found a sock called a SmartWool that makes my size 13s feel as if they're walking on pillows. I often wear two of them; that is, two on each foot. Several manufacturers now produce socks that are the equivalent of SmartWools, but are a lot less expensive. SmartWool socks and other similar socks are a synthetic composite. They can partially wick moisture away from the skin.

Some hikers wear multiple socks and it works for them—a comfortable cotton-poly blend sock on the interior and wool sock on the exterior. This will cushion your foot, provide that just-right snug fit in your boot, and give you some additional warmth and insulation in cold weather. It is critical to keep the interior sock clean. If you wear a sock over and over again, it will compact, lose its cushion, and start wrinkling or folding over while you hike and a blister will be born.

Do not wear thin cotton socks. Your foot can get damp and mix with dirt, which can cause a hot spot to start on your foot. Eventually, you get blisters, lots of them.

Inner Sole

If you are like most folks, the bottoms of your feet are rarely exposed and can be quite soft. You can take additional steps in their care. The best tip is keeping a fresh inner sole footpad in your boot. I prefer Dr. Scholl's gel pad or the equivalent. Some new inner soles can be slippery for a few days, which, if your foot slides around while you're hiking, can cause blisters. Just like new boots and new socks, they need to be broken in before an expedition.

Another cure for soft feet is to get out and walk or jog on a regular basis before your camping trip. On one trip on the Pacific Coast Trail, I ran into the long-distance master Jardine. He swore that going barefoot regularly is the best way to build up foot strength and arch support, while toughening up the bottom of your feet.

If you plan to use a foot pad and wear two heavy socks, you will need to use these items when sizing boots. Do not buy shoes if you're wearing thin cotton socks; wear the socks you're planning to wear when hiking, insert the inner sole, and then see how they feel. That's the only right way to size a hiking boot.

Treating Blisters

The key to treating blisters is fast work at the first sign of a hot spot. If you feel a hot spot, never keep walking, figuring that the problem will go away or that you will work through it. Wrong! Stop immediately and go to work.

Before you remove your socks, check to see if the sock has a wrinkle in it, a likely cause of the problem. If so, either change socks or pull them tight, removing the tiny folds, after taking care of the blister.

To take care of the blister, forget Moleskin. (They changed how they manufacture it and I've found it will slide off the blister while hiking.) Instead, use "Second Skin," which adheres over the top of the blister and does not dislodge. For small blisters, Band-Aids can do the job, but these have to be replaced daily, and sometimes with even more frequency. At night, clean your feet and sleep without socks. That will allow your feet to dry and heal.

Tips in the Field

Three other items that can help your walking are an Ace bandage, a pair of gaiters, and hiking poles.

For sprained ankles and twisted knees, an Ace bandage can be like an insurance policy to get you back on the trail and out of trouble. In many cases, a hiker with a twisted ankle or sprained knee has relied on a good wrap with a four-inch bandage for the added support to get home. Always buy the Ace bandages that come with the clips permanently attached, so you don't have to worry about losing them.

Gaiters are leggings made of Gore-Tex that fit from just below your knees, over your calves, and attach under your boots. They are of particular help when walking in damp areas or in places where rain is common. As your legs brush against ferns or low-lying plants, gaiters deflect the moisture. Without them, pants can get soaked wet in short order.

Many hikers would never hit the trail without hiking poles. Personally, they are not for me; I like to hike in rhythm and keeping my arms swinging effortlessly. I don't like to have to watch where I'm putting my poles all the time. But for those who have trouble with footing, a cranky knee or ankle, or want the upper body workout, poles can be a good fit. If it floats your boat, bring 'em.

Another tip: Should your boots become wet, never try to force-dry them. Some well-meaning folks will try to dry them quickly at the edge of a campfire, or at home, actually put the boots in an oven. While this may dry the boots, it can also loosen the glue that holds them together, ultimately weakening them until one day they fall apart in a heap.

A better bet is to treat the leather so the boots become water-repellent. Silicone-based liquids are the easiest to use and least greasy of the treatments available.

A final tip is to have another pair of lightweight shoes or moccasins that you can wear around camp and, in the process, give your feet the rest they deserve.

CLOTHING AND WEATHER PROTECTION

What started as an innocent pursuit of the perfect campground evolved into one heck of a predicament for Foonsky and me.

We had parked at the end of a logging road and then bushwhacked our way down a canyon to a pristine trout stream. On my first cast—a little flip into the plunge pool of a waterfall—I caught a 16-inch rainbow trout, a real beauty that jumped three times. Magic stuff.

Then, just across the stream, we saw it: The Perfect Camping Spot. On a sandbar on the edge of the forest, there lay a flat spot, high and dry above the river. Nearby was plenty of downed wood collected by past winter storms that we could use for firewood. And, of course, this beautiful trout stream was bubbling along just 40 yards from the site.

But nothing is perfect, right? To reach it, we had to wade across the river, although it didn't appear to be too difficult. The cold water tingled a bit, and the river came up surprisingly high, just above the belt. But it would be worth it to camp at The Perfect Spot.

Once across the river, we put on some dry clothes, set up camp, explored the woods, and fished the stream, catching several nice trout for dinner. But late that afternoon, it started raining. What? Rain in the summertime? Nature makes its own rules. By the next morning, it was still raining, pouring like a Yosemite waterfall from a solid gray sky.

That's when we noticed The Perfect Spot wasn't so perfect. The rain had raised the river level too high for us to wade back across. We were marooned, wet, and hungry.

"Now we're in a heck of a predicament," said Foonsky, the water streaming off him.

Getting cold and wet on a camping trip with no way to warm up is not only unnecessary and uncomfortable, it can be a fast ticket to hypothermia, the number one killer of campers in the woods. By definition, hypothermia is a condition in which body temperature is lowered to the point that it causes illness. It is particularly dangerous because the afflicted are usually unaware it is setting in. The first sign is a sense of apathy, then a state of confusion, which can lead eventually to collapse (or what appears to be sleep), then death.

You must always have a way to get warm and dry in short order, regardless of any conditions you may face. If you have no way of getting dry, then you must take emergency steps to prevent hypothermia. (See the steps detailed in *First Aid and Insect Protection* in this chapter.)

But you should never reach that point. For starters, always have spare sets of clothing tucked away so no matter how cold and wet you might get, you have something dry to put on. On hiking trips, I always carry a second set of clothes, sealed to stay dry, in a plastic garbage bag. I keep a third set waiting back at the truck.

If you are car camping, your vehicle can cause an illusory sense of security. But with an extra set of dry clothes stashed safely away, there is no illusion. The security is real. And remember, no matter how hot the weather is when you start your trip, always be prepared for the worst. Foonsky and I learned the hard way.

So both of us were soaking wet on that sandbar. With no other choice, we tried holing up in the tent for the night. A sleeping bag with Quallofil or another polyester fiberfill can retain warmth even when wet, because the fill is hollow and retains its loft. So as miserable as it was, the night passed without incident.

The rain stopped the next day and the river dropped a bit, but it was still rolling big and angry. Using a stick as a wading staff, Foonsky crossed about 80 percent of the stream before he was dumped, but he made a jump for it and managed to scramble to the riverbank. He waved for me to follow. "No problem," I thought.

It took me 20 minutes to reach nearly the same spot where Foonsky had been dumped. The heavy river current was above my belt and pushing hard. Then, in the flash of an instant, my wading staff slipped on a rock. I teetered in the river current and was knocked over like a bowling pin. I became completely submerged. I went tumbling down the river, heading right toward the waterfall. While underwater, I looked up at the surface, and I can remember how close it seemed yet how out of control I was. Right then, this giant hand appeared, and I grabbed it. It was Foonsky. If it weren't for that hand, I would have sailed right over the waterfall.

My momentum drew Foonsky right into the river, and we scrambled in the current, but I suddenly sensed the river bottom under my knees. On all fours, the two of us clambered ashore. We were safe.

"Thanks, ol' buddy," I said.

"Man, we're wet," he responded. "Let's get to the rig and get some dry clothes on."

The Art of Layering

The most important element for enjoying the outdoor experience in any condition is to stay dry and warm. There is no substitute. You must stay dry and you must stay warm.

Thus comes the theory behind layering, which suggests that as your body temperature fluctuates or the weather shifts, you simply peel off or add available layers as needed—and have a waterproof shell available in case of rain.

The introduction of a new era of outdoor clothing has made it possible for campers to turn choosing clothes into an art form. Like art, it's much more expensive than throwing on a pair of blue jeans, a T-shirt, and some flannel, but, for many, it is worth the price.

KEEP IT WILD TIP 3: TRAVEL LIGHTLY

1. Visit the backcountry in small groups.
2. Below tree line, always stay on designated trails.
3. Don't cut across switchbacks.
4. When traveling cross-country where no trails are available, follow animal trails or spread out with your group so no new routes are created.
5. Read your map and orient yourself with landmarks, a compass, and an altimeter. Avoid marking trails with rock cairns, tree scars, or ribbons.

In putting together your ideal layering system, there are some general considerations. What you need to do is create a system that effectively combines elements of breathability, durability, insulation, rapid drying, water repellence, wicking, and wind resistance, while still being lightweight and offering the necessary freedom of movement, all with just a few garments.

The basic intent of a base layer is to manage moisture. Your base layer will be the first article of clothing you put on and the last to come off. Since your own skin will be churning out the perspiration, the goal of this second skin is to manage the moisture and move it away from you. The best base layers are made of bicomponent knits, that is, blends of polyester and cotton, which provide wicking and insulating properties in one layer.

The way it works is that the side facing your skin is water-hating, while the side away from your skin is water-loving; thus, it pulls or "wicks" moisture through the material. You'll stay dry and happy, even with only one layer on, something not possible with old single-function weaves. The best include Capilene, Driclime, Lifa, Polartec 100, and Thermax. The only time that cotton should become a part of your base layer is if you wish to keep cool, not warm, such as in a hot desert climate where evaporative cooling becomes your friend, not your enemy.

Stretch fleece and microdenier pile also provide a good base layer, though they can be used as a second layer as well. Microdenier pile can be worn alone or layered under or over other pieces; it has excellent wicking capability as well as more windproof potential.

The next layer should be a light cotton shirt or a long-sleeved cotton/wool shirt, or both, depending on the coolness of the day. For pants, many just wear blue jeans when camping, but blue jeans can be hot and tight, and once wet, they tend to stay that way. Putting on wet blue jeans on a cold morning is a torturous way to start the day. A better choice is pants made from nylon with detachable leggings; these are light, have a lot of give, and dry quickly. If the weather is quite warm, nylon shorts that have some room to them can be the best choice. My preference is for The North Face dark-green expedition hiking shorts.

Finally, you should top the entire ensemble off with a thin, windproof, water-resistant layer. You want this layer to breathe, yet not be so porous that rain runs through it. Patagonia's Velocity shell is one of the best; its outer fabric is treated with DWR (Durable Water Repellent finish) and the coating is by Goretex. Patagonia, Marmot, and The North Face and others all offer their own versions. Though condensation will still build up inside, it manages to get rid of enough moisture.

Note: It is critical to know the difference between "water-resistant" and "waterproof." (This is covered under the *Rain Gear* section in this chapter.)

But hey, why does anybody need all this fancy stuff just to go camping? Fair question. You don't have to opt for this aerobic-function fashion statement. It is unnecessary on many camping trips. The fact is that you must be ready for anything when you venture into the outdoors. The new era of outdoor clothing works, and it works better than anything that has come before. Regardless of what you choose, weather should never be a nuisance or cause discomfort. There is no such thing as bad weather, so the saying goes, only bad gear.

Hats

Another word of advice: Always pack along a warm hat for those times when you need to seal in warmth. You lose a large percentage of heat through your head. At night in cold weather, I wear a skullcap. During the day, I almost always wear a wide-brimmed hat, something like those that the legendary outlaws wore 150 years ago. There's actually logic behind it: My hat is made of waterproof canvas, is rigged with a lariat (it can be cinched down when it's windy), and has a wide brim that keeps the tops of my ears from being sunburned. If you're outside a lot, do not wear baseball hats—the tops of your ears will burn to a red crisp. Years ago, that's how an old friend of mine lost his ears to skin cancer.

HEAD LIGHT

I've tried many head lights and the Trail Torch Hat Light is my favorite by a mile (www.halibut. net). It comes with five white and green LED lights in a horizontal row that clips under the bill of your hat. For the best option, order the set with three green lights (for night vision) and two white lights. (At night you'll look like a jet coming in for a landing.)

Vests and Parkas

In cold weather, you should take the layer system one step further with a warm vest and a parka jacket. Vests are especially useful because they provide warmth without the bulkiness of a parka. The warmest vests and parkas are either filled with down or Quallofil, or they are made with a cotton/wool mix. Each has its respective merits and problems. Down fill provides the most warmth for the amount of weight, but becomes useless when wet, closely resembling a wet dishrag. Quallofil keeps much of its heat-retaining quality even when wet, but it is expensive. Vests made of cotton/wool mixes are the most attractive and also are quite warm, but they can be as heavy as a ship's anchor when wet.

Sometimes, the answer is combining a parka with a vest. One of my best camping companions wears a good-looking cotton/wool vest and a parka filled with Quallofil. The vest never gets wet, so weight is not a factor.

Rain Gear

One of the most miserable nights of my life was on a camping trip for which I hadn't brought my rain gear or a tent. Hey, it was early August, the temperature had been in the 90s for weeks, and if anybody had said it was going to rain, I would have told him to consult a brain doctor. But rain it did. And as I got wetter and wetter, I kept saying to myself, "Hey, it's summer, it's not supposed to rain." Then I remembered one of the 10 commandments of camping: Forget your rain gear and you can guarantee it will rain.

To stay dry, you need some form of water-repellent shell. It can be as simple as a $5 poncho made out of plastic or as elaborate as a $300 Gore-Tex jacket-and-pants set. What counts is not how much you spend, but how dry you stay.

The most important thing to realize is that waterproof and water-resistant are completely different things. In addition, there is no such thing as rain gear that is both waterproof and breathable. The more waterproof a jacket is, the less it breathes. Conversely, the more breathable a jacket is, the less waterproof it becomes.

If you wear water-resistant rain gear in a sustained downpour, you'll get soaked. Water-resistant rain gear is appealing because it breathes and will keep you dry in the light stuff, such as mist, fog, even a little splash from a canoe paddle. But in rain? Forget it.

So what is the solution?

I've decided that the best approach is a set of fairly light but 100 percent-waterproof rain gear. I recently bought a hooded jacket and pants from Coleman, and my assessment is that it is the most cost-efficient rain gear I've ever had. All I can say is, hey, it works: I stay dry, it doesn't weigh much, and it didn't cost a fortune.

The absolute best foul weather gear made is by Simms, both jacket and bib. While it is expensive, you will stay dry and warm in any condition but that in which you need a survival suit.

You can also stay dry with any of the waterproof plastics and even heavy-duty rubber-coated outfits made for commercial fishermen. But these are uncomfortable during anything but a heavy rain. Because they are heavy and don't breathe, you'll likely get soaked anyway (that is, from your own sweat), even if it isn't raining hard.

On backpacking trips, I still stash a super-lightweight, water-repellent slicker for day hikes and a poncho, which I throw over my pack at night to keep it dry. But, otherwise, I never go anywhere—*anywhere*—without my rain gear.

Some do just fine with a cheap poncho, and note that ponchos can serve other uses in addition to a raincoat. Ponchos can be used as a ground tarp, as a rain cover for supplies or a backpack, or can be snapped together and roped up to trees in a pinch to provide a quick storm ceiling if you don't have a tent. The problem with ponchos is that in a hard rain, you just don't stay dry. First your legs get wet, then they get soaked. Then your arms follow the same pattern. If you're wearing cotton, you'll find that once part of the garment gets wet, the water spreads until, alas, you are dripping wet, poncho and all. Before long, you start to feel like a walking refrigerator.

One high-cost option is to buy a Gore-Tex rain jacket and pants. Gore-Tex is actually not a fabric, as is commonly believed, but a laminated film that coats a breathable fabric. The result is lightweight, water-repellent, breathable jackets and pants. They are perfect for campers, but they cost a fortune.

Some hiking buddies of mine have complained that the older Gore-Tex rain gear loses its water-repellent quality over time. However, manufacturers insist that this is the result of water seeping through seams, not leaks in the jacket. At each seam, tiny needles have pierced the fabric, and as tiny as the holes are, water will find a way through. An application of Seam Lock, especially at major seams around the shoulders of a jacket, can usually fix the problem.

If you don't want to spend the big bucks for Gore-Tex rain gear but want more rain protection than a poncho affords, a coated nylon jacket is the compromise that many choose. They are inexpensive, have the highest water-repellency of any rain gear, and are warm, providing a good outer shell for your layers of clothing. But they are not without fault. These jackets don't breathe at all, and if you zip them up tight, you can sweat a river.

My brother Rambob gave me a nylon jacket before a mountain-climbing expedition. I wore that cheap special all the way to the top with no complaints; it's warm and 100 percent waterproof. The one problem with nylon comes when temperatures drop below freezing. It gets so stiff that it feels as if you are wearing a straitjacket.

There's one more jacket-construction term to know: DWR, or Durable Water-Repellent finish. All of the top-quality jackets these days are DWR-treated. The DWR causes water to bead on the shell. When the DWR wears off, even a once-waterproof jacket will feel like a wet dishrag.

Also note that ventilation is the key to coolness. The only ventilation on most shells is often the zipper. But waterproof jackets need additional openings. Look for mesh-backed pockets and underarm zippers, as well as cuffs, waists, and hems that can be adjusted to open wide. Storm flaps (the baffle over the zipper) that close with hook-and-loop material or snaps let you leave the zipper open for airflow into the jacket.

Other Gear

What are the three items most commonly

forgotten on a camping trip? A hat, sunglasses, and lip balm.

A hat is crucial, especially when you are visiting high elevations. Without one you are constantly exposed to everything nature can give you. The sun will dehydrate you, sap your energy, sunburn your head, and in worst cases, cause sunstroke. Start with a comfortable hat. Then finish with sunglasses, lip balm, and sunscreen for additional protection. They will help protect you from extreme heat.

To guard against extreme cold, it's a good idea to keep a pair of thin ski gloves stashed away with your emergency clothes, along with a wool ski cap, or a skull cap. The gloves should be thick enough to keep your fingers from stiffening up, but pliable enough to allow full movement so you don't have to take them off to complete simple tasks, like lighting a stove. An alternative to gloves is glovelets, which look like gloves with no fingers. In any case, just because the weather turns cold doesn't mean that your hands have to.

FOOD AND COOKING GEAR

It was a warm, crystal clear day, a perfect day for skydiving. That was exactly the case for my old pal Foonsky, who had never before tried the sport. But a funny thing happened after he jumped out of the plane and pulled on the rip cord: His parachute didn't open.

In total free fall, Foonsky watched the earth below getting closer and closer. Not one to panic, he calmly pulled the ripcord on the emergency parachute. Again, nothing happened. No parachute, no nothing.

The ground was getting ever closer, and as he tried to search for a soft place to land, Foonsky detected a small object shooting up toward him, growing larger as it approached. It looked like a camper.

Figuring this was his last chance, Foonsky shouted as they passed in midair, "Hey, do you know anything about parachutes?"

The other fellow just yelled back as he headed off into space, "Do you know anything about lighting camping stoves?"

Well, Foonsky got lucky and his parachute opened. As for the other guy, well, he's probably in orbit like a NASA weather satellite. If you've ever had a mishap while lighting a camping stove, you know exactly what I'm talking about.

When it comes to camping, all gear is not created equal. Nothing is more important than lighting your stove easily and having it reach full heat without feeling as if you're playing with a short fuse to a miniature bomb. If your stove does not work right, your trip can turn into a disaster, regardless of how well you have planned the other elements. In addition, a bad stove will add an underlying sense of foreboding to your day. You will constantly have the inner suspicion that your darn stove is going to foul up again.

Camping Stoves

If you are buying a camping stove, remember this one critical rule: Do not leave the store with a new stove unless you have been shown exactly how to use it.

Know what you are getting. Many stores that specialize in outdoor recreation equipment now staff experienced campers/employees who will demonstrate the use of every stove they sell. While they're at it, they'll also describe the stoves' respective strengths and weaknesses.

An innovation by Peak 1 is a two-burner butane-powered backpacking stove that allows you to boil water and heat a pot of food simultaneously. While that has long been standard for car campers using Coleman's legendary camp stove, it was previously unheard of for wilderness campers in high-elevation areas. It's a fantastic stove.

The standard Coleman car camping stove, the green one with the two burners, is a legend around the world. Electronic ignition has solved all the old lighting problems.

A stove that has developed a cult-like following is the little Sierra, which burns small twigs and pinecones, then uses a tiny battery-driven fan to develop increased heat and

© SABRINA YOUNG

Stoves are available in many sizes and burn a variety of fuels.

cooking ability. It's an excellent alternative for long-distance backpacking trips, as it solves the problem of carrying a fuel bottle, especially on expeditions for which large quantities of fuel would otherwise be needed. Some tinkering with the flame (a very hot one) is required, and they are legal and functional only in the alpine zone where dry wood is available. Also note that in years with high fire danger, the U.S. Forest Service enacts rules prohibiting open flames, and fires are also often prohibited above an elevation of 10,000 feet.

The MSR Whisperlite is an icon among backpackers. I've gone through several of them. It uses white gas in a separate fuel container so you can easily monitor fuel consumption. The one flaw is the connector links from the fuel line. After a few years of heavy use, they can develop leaks; ignite and you've got meltdown.

For heavy, long-term use, ease of cleaning the burner is the most important. If you camp often, especially with a smaller stove, the burner holes will eventually become clogged. Some stoves have a built-in cleaning needle: a quick twist of the knob and you're in business. Others require disassembly and a protracted cleaning session using special tools. If a stove is difficult to clean, you will tend to put off the tiresome chore, and your stove will sputter and pant while you watch that pot of water sitting there, staying cold.

Before making a purchase, have the salesperson show you how to clean the burner head. Except in the case of large, multi-burner family-style camping stoves, which rarely require cleaning, this run-through can do more to determine the long-term value of a stove than any other factor.

Fuels for Camping Stoves

White gas and butane have long been the most popular camp fuels, but a newly developed fuel could dramatically change that.

LPG (liquid petroleum gas) comes in cartridges for easy attachment to a stove or lantern. At room temperature, LPG is delivered in a combustible gaseous form. When you shake the cartridge, the contents sound liquid; that is because the gas liquefies under pressure, which is why it is so easy to use. Large amounts of fuel can be compressed into small canisters.

The following summaries detail the benefits and drawbacks of other available fuels:

Butane: You don't have to worry about explosions when using stoves that burn bottled butane fuel. Butane requires no pouring, pumping, or priming, and butane stoves are the easiest to light. Just turn a knob and light—that's it. On the minus side, because it comes in bottles, you never know precisely how much fuel you have left. And when a bottle is empty, you have a potential piece of litter. (Never litter. Ever.)

The other problem with butane is that it just plain does not work well in cold weather or when there is little fuel left in the cartridge. Since you cannot predict mountain weather in spring or fall, you might wind up using more fuel than originally projected. That can be frustrating, particularly if your stove starts wheezing when there are still several days left to go. In addition, with most butane cartridges, if there is any chance of the temperature falling below freezing, you often have to sleep with the cartridge to keep it warm. Otherwise, forget about using it come morning.

Butane/Propane: This blend offers higher octane performance than butane alone, solving the cold temperature doldrums somewhat. However, propane burns off before butane, so there's a performance drop as the fuel level in the cartridge lowers.

Coleman Max Performance Fuel: This fuel offers a unique approach to solving the consistent burn challenge facing all pressurized gas cartridges: operating at temperatures at or below 0°F. Using a standard propane/butane blend for high-octane performance, Coleman gets around the drop-off in performance other cartridges experience by using a version of fuel injection. A hose inside the cartridge pulls liquid fuel into the stove, where it vaporizes—a switch from the standard approach of pulling only a gaseous form of the fuel into a stove. By drawing liquid out of the cartridge, Coleman gets around the tendency of propane to burn off first and allows each cartridge to deliver a

consistent mix of propane and butane to the stove's burners throughout the cartridge's life.

Denatured alcohol: Though this fuel burns cleanly and quietly and is virtually explosion-proof, it generates much less heat than pressurized or liquid gas fuels.

Kerosene: Never buy a stove that uses kerosene for fuel. Kerosene is smelly and messy, generates low heat, needs priming, and is virtually obsolete as a camp fuel in the United States. As a test, I once tried using a kerosene stove. I could scarcely boil a pot of water. In addition, some kerosene leaked out when the stove was packed, ruining everything it touched. The smell of kerosene never did go away. Kerosene remains popular in Europe only because most campers there haven't yet heard much about white gas. When they do, they will demand it.

Primus Tri-Blend: This blend is made up of 20 percent propane, 70 percent butane, and 10 percent isobutane and is designed to burn with more consistent heat and efficiency than standard propane/butane mixes.

Propane: Now available for single-burner stoves using larger, heavier cartridges to accommodate higher pressures, propane offers the very best performance of any of the pressurized gas canister fuels.

White gas: White gas is the most popular camp fuel in the United States because it is inexpensive and effective—not to mention, sold at most outdoor recreation stores and many supermarkets. It burns hot, has virtually no smell, and evaporates quickly when spilled. If you are caught in wet, miserable weather and can't get a fire going, you can use white gas as an emergency fire starter; however, if you do so, use it sparingly and never on an open flame.

White gas is a popular fuel both for car campers who use the large, two-burner stoves equipped with a fuel tank and a pump and for hikers who carry a lightweight backpacking stove. On the latter, lighting can require priming with a gel called priming paste, which some people dislike. Another problem with white gas is that it can be extremely explosive.

As an example, I once almost burned my

KEEP IT WILD TIP 4: CAMPFIRES

1. Fire use can scar the backcountry. If a fire ring is not available, use a lightweight stove for cooking.
2. Where fires are permitted, use existing fire rings away from large rocks or overhangs.
3. Don't char rocks by building new rings.
4. Gather sticks from the ground that are no larger than the diameter of your wrist.
5. Don't snap branches of live, dead, or downed trees, which can cause personal injury and also scar the natural setting.
6. Put the fire "dead out" and make sure it's cold before departing. Remove all trash from the fire ring and sprinkle dirt over the site.
7. Remember that some forest fires can be started by a campfire that appears to be out. Hot embers burning deep in the pit can cause tree roots to catch fire and burn underground. If you ever see smoke rising from the ground, seemingly from nowhere, dig down and put the fire out.

beard completely off in a mini-explosion while lighting one of the larger stoves designed for car camping. I was in the middle of cooking dinner when the flame suddenly shut down. Sure enough, the fuel tank was empty, and after refilling it, I pumped the tank 50 or 60 times to regain pressure. When I lit a match, the sucker ignited from three feet away. The resulting explosion was like a stick of dynamite going off, and immediately the smell of burning beard was in the air. In a flash, my once thick, dark beard had been reduced to a mass of little, yellow, burned curlicues.

My error? After filling the tank, I forgot to shut the fuel cock off while pumping up the pressure in the tank. As a result, the stove burners were slowly emitting the gas/air mixture as I pumped the tank, filling the air above the stove. Then, strike a match from even a few feet away and ka-boom!

Building Fires

One summer expedition took me to the Canadian wilderness in British Columbia for a 75-mile canoe trip on the Bowron Lake Circuit, a chain of 13 lakes, six rivers, and seven portages. It is one of the greatest canoe trips in the world, a loop that ends just a few hundred feet from its starting point. But at the first camp at Kibbee Lake, my stove developed a fuel leak at the base of the burner, and the nuclear-like

blast that followed just about turned Canada into a giant crater.

As a result, we had to complete the final 70 miles of the trip without a stove, cooking instead on open fires each night. The problem was compounded by the weather. It rained eight of the 10 days. Rain? In Canada, raindrops the size of silver dollars fall so hard they actually bounce on the lake surface. We had to stop paddling a few times to empty the rainwater out of the canoe. At the end of the day, we'd make camp and then face the critical decision: either make a fire or go to bed cold and hungry.

Equipped with an ax, at least we had a chance for success. Although the downed wood was soaked, I was able to make my own fire-starting tinder from the chips of split logs; no matter how hard it rains, the inside of a log is always dry.

In miserable weather, matches don't stay lit long enough to get tinder started. Instead, we used either a candle or the little waxlike fire-starter cubes that remain lit for several minutes. From those, we could get the tinder going. Then we added small, slender strips of wood that had been axed from the interior of the logs. When the flame reached a foot high, we added the logs, their dry interior facing in. By the time the inside of the logs had caught fire, the outside was drying from the heat. It wasn't long before a royal blaze was brightening the rainy night.

That's a worst-case scenario, and I hope you will never face anything like it. Nevertheless, being able to build a good fire and cook on it can be one of the more satisfying elements of a camping trip. At times, just looking into the flames can provide a special satisfaction at the end of a good day.

However, never expect to build a fire for every meal or, in some cases, even to build one at all. Many state and federal campgrounds have been picked clean of downed wood. During the fire season, the danger of forest fires can force rangers to prohibit fires altogether. In either case, you must use your camp stove or go hungry.

But when you can build a fire and the resources for doing so are available, it will enhance the quality of your camping experience. Of the campgrounds listed in this book, those where you are permitted to build fires will usually have fire rings. In primitive areas where you can make your own fire, you should dig a ring eight inches deep, line the edges with rock, and clear all the needles and twigs in a five-foot radius. The next day, when the fire is dead, you can scatter the rocks, fill over the black charcoal with dirt, and then spread pine needles and twigs over it. Nobody will even know you camped there. That's the best way I know to keep a secret spot a real secret.

When you start to build a campfire, the first thing you will notice is that no matter how good your intentions, your fellow campers will not be able to resist moving the wood around. Watch. You'll be getting ready to add a key piece of wood at just the right spot, and your companion will stick his mitts in, confidently believing he has a better idea. He'll shift the fire around and undermine your best-thought-out plans.

So I enforce a rule on camping trips: One person makes the fire while everybody else stands clear or is involved with other camp tasks, such as gathering wood, getting water, putting up tents, or planning dinner. Once the fire is going strong, then it's fair game; anyone adds logs at his or her discretion. But in the early, delicate stages of the campfire, it's best to leave the work to one person.

Before a match is ever struck, you should gather a complete pile of firewood. Then, start small, with the tiniest twigs you can find, and slowly add larger twigs as you go, crisscrossing them like a miniature tepee. Eventually, you will get to the big chunks that produce high heat. The key is to get one piece of wood burning into another, which then burns into another, setting off what I call the chain of flame. Conversely, single pieces of wood set apart from each other will not burn.

On a dry summer evening at a campsite where plenty of wood is available, about the only way you can blow the deal is to get impatient and try to add the big pieces too quickly. Do that and you'll get smoke, not flames, and it won't be long before every one of your fellow campers is poking at your fire. It will drive you crazy, but they just won't be able to help it.

Cooking Gear

I like traveling light, and I've found that all I need for cooking is a pot, small frying pan, metal pot grabber, fork, knife, cup, and matches. If you want to keep the price of food low and also cook customized dinners each night, a small pressure cooker can be just the ticket. (See *Keeping the Price Down* in this chapter.) I store all my gear in one small bag that fits into my pack. If I'm camping out of my four-wheel-drive rig, I can easily keep track of the little bag of cooking gear. Going simple, not complicated, is the key to keeping a camping trip on the right track.

You can get more elaborate by buying complete kits with plates, a coffeepot, large pots, and other cookware, but what really counts is having a single pot that makes you happy. It needs to be just the right size, not too big or small, and stable enough so it won't tip over, even if it is at a slight angle on a fire, filled with water at a full boil. Mine is just six inches wide and 4.5 inches deep. It holds better than a quart of water and has served me well for several hundred camp dinners.

The rest of your cook kit is easy to complete. The frying pan should be small, light-gauge aluminum, and Teflon-coated, with a fold-in handle so it's no hassle to store. A pot grabber is a great addition. This little aluminum gadget clamps to the edge of pots and allows you to lift them and pour water with total control and without burning your fingers. For cleanup, take along a plastic scrubber and a small bottle filled with dish soap, and you're in business.

A sierra cup, a wide aluminum cup with a wire handle, is an ideal item to carry because you can eat out of it as well as use it for drinking. This means no plates to scrub after dinner, so washing up is quick and easy. In addition, if you go for a hike, you can clip its handle to your belt. Some people bring a giant cup called a "Fair Share." In expeditions where food has to be rationed, they manage to get a lot more than their "fair share" because a cup of food looks so small in these giant vessels.

If you opt for a more formal setup, complete with plates, glasses, silverware, and the like, you can end up spending more time preparing and cleaning up after meals than enjoying the country you are exploring. In addition, the more equipment you bring, the more loose ends you will have to deal with, and loose ends can cause plenty of frustration. If you have a choice, go simple.

Remember what Thoreau said: "A man is rich in proportion to what he can do without."

Food and Cooking Tricks

On a trip to the Bob Marshall Wilderness in western Montana, I woke up one morning, yawned, and said, "What've we got for breakfast?"

The silence was ominous. "Well," finally came the response, "we don't have any food left."

"What!?"

"Well, I figured we'd catch trout for meals every other night."

On the return trip, we ended up eating wild berries, buds, and, yes, even roots (not too tasty). When we finally landed the next day

at a suburban pizza parlor, we nearly ate the wooden tables.

Running out of food on a camping trip can do more to turn reasonable people into violent grumps than any other event. There's no excuse for it, not when figuring meals can be done precisely and with little effort. You should not go out and buy a bunch of food, throw it in your rig, and head off for yonder. That leaves too much to chance. And if you've ever been really hungry in the woods, you know it's worth a little effort to guard against a day or two of starvation. Here's a three-step solution:

1. Draw up a general meal-by-meal plan and make sure your companions like what's on it.

2. Tell your companions to buy any specialty items (such as a special brand of coffee) on their own and not to expect you to take care of everything.

3. Put all the food on your living room floor and literally plan out every day of your trip, meal by meal, putting the food in plastic bags as you go. That way, you will know exact food quotas and you won't go hungry.

Fish for your dinner? There's one guarantee as far as that goes: If you expect to catch fish for meals, you will most certainly get skunked. If you don't expect to catch fish for meals, you will probably catch so many they'll be coming out of your ears. I've seen it a hundred times.

Keeping the Price Down

"There must be some mistake," I said with a laugh. "Whoever paid $750 for camp food?"

But the amount was as clear as the digital numbers on the cash register: $753.27.

"How is this possible?" I asked the clerk.

"Just add it up," she responded, irritated.

Then I started figuring. The freeze-dried backpack dinners cost $6 apiece. A small pack of beef jerky went for $2, the beef sticks for $0.75, granola bars for $0.50. Multiply it all by four hungry men, including Foonsky.

The dinners alone cost close to $500. Add in the usual goodies—candy, coffee, dried fruit, granola bars, jerky, oatmeal, soup, and

Tang—and I felt as if an earthquake had struck when I saw the tab.

A lot of campers have received similar shocks. In preparation for their trips, campers shop with enthusiasm. Then they pay the bill in horror.

Well, there are solutions, lots of them. You can eat gourmet-style in the outback without having your wallet cleaned out. But it requires do-it-yourself cooking, more planning, and careful shopping. It also means transcending the push-button, I-want-it-now attitude that so many people can't leave behind when they go to the mountains.

Now when Foonsky, Mr. Furnai, Rambob, and I sit down to eat such a meal, we don't call it "eating." We call it "hodgepacking" or "time to pack your hodge." After a particularly long day on the trail, you can do some serious hodgepacking.

If your trip is a shorter one, say for a weekend, consider bringing more fresh food to add some sizzle to the hodge. You can design a hot soup/stew mix that is good enough to eat at home.

Start by bringing a pot of water to a full boil, and then add pasta, ramen noodles, or macaroni. While it simmers, cut in a potato, carrot, onion, and garlic clove, and cook for about 10 minutes. When the vegetables have softened, add in a soup mix or two, maybe some cheese, and you are just about in business. But you can still ruin it and turn your hodge into sludge. Make sure you read the directions on the soup mix to determine cooking time. It can vary widely. In addition, make sure you stir the whole thing up; otherwise, you will get those hidden dry clumps of soup mix that taste like garlic sawdust.

How do I know? Well, it was up near Kearsage Pass in the Sierra Nevada, where, feeling half-starved, I dug into our nightly hodge. I will never forget that first bite—I damn near gagged to death. Foonsky laughed at me, until he took his first bite (a nice big one) and then turned green.

Another way to trim food costs is to make your own beef jerky, the trademark staple of campers for more than 200 years. A tiny packet of beef jerky costs $2, and for that 250-mile expedition, I spent $150 on jerky alone. Never again. Now we make our own and get big strips of jerky that taste better than anything you can buy.

For a crew of four, you can get by with two freeze-dried dinners that you cook right in the container pouch. Liam Furniss discovered that by adding a separate bonus pack of garlic-seasoned mashed potatoes, which cook in 90 seconds; everybody has plenty of food. That goes even for his dad Mo, with his gigantic, crater-of-the-moon "Fair Share" cup.

You can supplement your eats with sweets, nuts, freeze-dried fruits, and drink mixes. In any case, make sure you keep the dinner menu varied. If you and your buddies look into your dinner cups and groan, "Ugh, not this again," you will soon start dreaming of cheeseburgers and french fries instead of hiking, fishing, and finding beautiful campsites.

If you are car camping and have a big ice chest, you can bring virtually anything to eat and drink. If you are on the trail and don't mind paying the price, the newest freeze-dried dinners provide another option.

Some of the biggest advances in the outdoors industry have come in the form of freeze-dried dinners. Some of them are almost good enough to serve in restaurants. Sweet-and-sour pork over rice, tostadas, Burgundy chicken—it sure beats the poopy goop we used to eat, like the old soupy chili-mac dinners that tasted bad and looked so unlike food that consumption was nearly impossible, even for my dog, Rebel. Foonsky usually managed to get it down, but just barely.

To provide an idea of how to plan a menu, consider what my companions and I ate while hiking 250 miles on California's John Muir Trail:

Breakfast: instant soup, oatmeal (never get plain), one beef or jerky stick, coffee or hot chocolate.

Lunch: one beef stick, two jerky sticks, one

HOW TO MAKE BEEF JERKY IN YOUR OWN KITCHEN

Start with a couple of pieces of meat: lean top round, sirloin, or tri-tip. Cut them into 3/16-inch strips across the grain, trimming out the membrane, gristle, and fat. Marinate the strips for 24 hours in a glass dish. The fun begins in picking a marinade. Try two-thirds teriyaki sauce, one-third Worcestershire sauce. You can customize the recipe by adding pepper, ground mustard, bay leaf, red wine vinegar, garlic, and, for the brave, Tabasco sauce.

After a day or so, squeeze out each strip of meat with a rolling pin, lay them in rows on a cooling rack over a cookie sheet, and dry them in the oven at 125°F for 12 hours. Thicker pieces can take as long as 18-24 hours.

That's it. The hardest part is cleaning the cookie sheet when you're done. The easiest part is eating your own homemade jerky while sitting at a lookout on a mountain ridge. The do-it-yourself method for jerky may take a day or so, but it is cheaper and can taste better than any store-bought jerky.

—*my thanks to Jeff Patty for this recipe*

granola bar, dried fruit, half cup of pistachio nuts, Tang, one small bag of M&Ms.

Dinner: instant soup, one freeze-dried dinner (split between two people), one milk bar, rainbow trout.

What was that last item? Rainbow trout? Right! Unless you plan on it, you can catch them every night.

Trout Dinner

If all this still doesn't sound like your idea of a gourmet but low-cost camping meal, well, you are forgetting the main course: rainbow trout. Remember: If you don't plan on catching them for dinner, you'll probably land more than you can finish in one night's hodgepacking.

Some campers go to great difficulties to cook their trout, bringing along frying pans, butter, grills, tinfoil, and more, but all you need is some seasoned salt and a campfire.

Rinse the gutted trout, and while it's still wet, sprinkle on a good dose of seasoned salt, both inside and out. Clear any burning logs to the side of the campfire, then lay the trout right on the coals, turning it once so both sides are cooked. Sound ridiculous? Sound like you are throwing the fish away? Sound like the fish will burn up? Sound like you will have to eat the campfire ash? Wrong on all counts. The fish cooks perfectly, the ash doesn't stick, and

after cooking trout this way, you may never fry again.

If you can't convince your buddies, who may insist that trout should be fried, then make sure you have butter to fry it in, not oil. Also make sure you cook them all the way through, so the meat strips off the backbone in two nice, clean fillets. The fish should end up looking like one that Sylvester the Cat just drew out of his mouth—only the head, tail, and a perfect skeleton.

FIRST AID AND INSECT PROTECTION

Mountain nights don't get any more perfect, I thought as I lay in my sleeping bag.

The sky looked like a mass of jewels and the air tasted sweet and smelled of pines. A shooting star fireballed across the sky, and I remember thinking, "It just doesn't get any better."

Just then, as I was drifting into sleep, a mysterious buzz appeared from nowhere and deposited itself inside my left ear. Suddenly awake, I whacked my ear with the palm of my hand, hard enough to cause a minor concussion. The buzz disappeared. I pulled out my flashlight and shined it on my palm, and there, lit in the blackness of night, lay the squished intruder: a mosquito, dead amid a stain of blood.

Satisfied, I turned off the light, closed my

KEEP IT WILD TIP 5: SANITATION

If no refuse facility is available:
1. Deposit human waste in "cat holes" dug 6-8 inches deep. Cover and disguise the cat hole when finished.
2. Deposit human waste at least 75 paces (200 feet) from any water source or camp.
3. Use toilet paper sparingly. When finished, carefully burn it in the cat hole, then bury it.
4. If no appropriate burial locations are available, such as in popular wilderness camps above tree line in granite settings, then all human refuse should be double-bagged and packed out.
5. At boat-in campsites, chemical toilets are required. Chemical toilets can also solve the problem of larger groups camping for long stays at one location where no facilities are available.
6. To wash dishes or your body, carry water away from the source and use small amounts of biodegradable soap. Scatter dishwater after all food particles have been removed.
7. Scour your campsites for even the tiniest piece of trash and any other evidence of your stay. Pack out all the trash you can, even if it's not yours. Finding cigarette butts, for instance, provides special irritation for most campers. Pick them up and discard them properly.
8. Never litter. Never. Or you become the enemy of all others.

eyes, and thought of the fishing trip planned for the next day. Then I heard them. It was a squadron of mosquitoes making landing patterns around my head. I tried to grab them with an open hand, but they dodged the assault and flew off. Just 30 seconds later, another landed in my left ear. I promptly dispatched the invader with a rip of the palm.

Now I was completely awake, so I got out of my sleeping bag to retrieve some mosquito repellent. But en route, several of the buggers swarmed and nailed me in the back and arms. After I applied the repellent and settled snugly again in my sleeping bag, the mosquitoes would buzz a few inches from my ear. After getting a whiff of the poison, they would fly off. It was like sleeping in a sawmill.

The next day, drowsy from little sleep, I set out to fish. I'd walked but 15 minutes when I brushed against a bush and felt a stinging sensation on the inside of my arm, just above the wrist. I looked down: A tick had his clamps in me. I ripped it out before he could embed his head into my skin.

After catching a few fish, I sat down against a tree to eat lunch and just watch the water go by. My dog, Rebel, sat down next to me and stared at the beef jerky I was munching as if it were a T-bone steak. I finished eating, gave

him a small piece, patted him on the head, and said, "Good dog." Right then, I noticed an itch on my arm where a mosquito had drilled me. I unconsciously scratched it. Two days later, in that exact spot, some nasty red splotches started popping up. Poison oak. By petting my dog and then scratching my arm, I had transferred the oil residue of the poison oak leaves from Rebel's fur to my arm.

When I returned home, Foonsky asked me about the trip.

"Great," I said. "Mosquitoes, ticks, poison oak. Can hardly wait to go back."

"Sorry I missed out," he answered.

Mosquitoes, No-See-Ums, and Horseflies

On a trip to Canada, Foonsky and I were fishing a small lake from the shore when suddenly a black horde of mosquitoes could be seen moving across the lake toward us. It was like when the French army looked across the Rhine and saw the Wehrmacht coming. There was a buzz in the air. We fought them off for a few minutes, then made a fast retreat to the truck and jumped in, content the buggers had been foiled. But in some way still unknown to us, the mosquitoes gained entry to the truck. In 10 minutes, we squished 15 of them as they attempted to plant their oil drills into our skins. Just outside the truck, the black horde waited for us to make a tactical error, such as rolling down a window. It finally took a miraculous hailstorm to squelch the attack.

When it comes to mosquitoes, no-see-ums, gnats, and horseflies, there are times when there is nothing you can do. However, in most situations, you can muster a defense to repel the attack.

When under heavy attack by mosquitoes, the first key is to wear clothing too heavy for them to drill through. Expose a minimum of skin, wear a hat, and tie a bandanna around your neck, preferably one that has been sprayed with repellent. If you try to get by with just a thin cotton T-shirt and nylon shorts, you will be declared a federal mosquito sanctuary.

So, first, your skin must be well covered, with only your hands and face exposed. Second, you should have your companion spray your clothes with repellent. (I prefer Deep Woods Off!) Third, you should dab liquid repellent directly on your skin.

At night, the easiest way to get a good sleep without mosquitoes buzzing in your ear is to sleep in a bug-proof tent. If the nights are warm and you want to see the stars, new tent models are available that have a skylight covered with mosquito netting. If you don't like tents on summer evenings, mosquito netting rigged with an air space at your head can solve the problem. Otherwise, prepare to get bitten, even with the use of mosquito repellent.

A newer option is a battery-powered, clip-on mosquito repellent made by Off! that is also portable. It includes a canister that lasts 12 hours and a small fan, so you can set right next to you. That's right, you don't spray it on.

If your problems are with no-see-ums or biting horseflies, then you need a slightly different approach. No-see-ums are tiny black insects that look like nothing more than a sliver of dirt on your skin. Then you notice something stinging, and when you rub the area, you scratch up a little no-see-um. The results are similar to mosquito bites, making your skin itch, splotch,

and, when you get them bad, swell. In addition to using the techniques described to repel mosquitoes, you should go one step further.

The problem is that no-see-ums are tricky little devils. Somehow, they can actually get under your socks and around your ankles, where they will bite to their hearts' content all night long while you sleep, itch, sleep, and itch some more. The best solution is to apply a liquid repellent to your ankles, then wear clean socks.

Horseflies are another story. They are rarely a problem, but when they get their dander up, they can cause trouble you'll never forget.

Always wear sunglasses when you hike. If you enter an area with flies, the moisture from your eyes will attract them. The sunglasses will keep them from getting in your eyes.

On one trip, Foonsky and I were paddling a canoe along the shoreline of a Lake Quesnel in British Columbia. This giant horsefly, about the size of a fingertip, started dive-bombing the canoe. After 20 minutes, it landed on Foonsky's thigh. He immediately slammed it with an open hand, then let out a blood-curdling "Yeeeee-ow!" that practically sent ripples across the lake. When Foonsky whacked it, the horsefly had somehow turned around and bit him on the hand, leaving a huge red welt.

In the next 10 minutes, that big fly strafed the canoe on more dive-bomb runs. I finally got my canoe paddle, swung it as if it were a baseball bat, and nailed that horsefly as if I'd hit a home run. It landed about 15 feet from the boat, still alive and buzzing in the water. While I was trying to figure what it would take to kill this bugger, a large rainbow trout surfaced and snatched it out of the water, finally avenging the assault.

If you have horsefly or yellow jacket problems, you'd best just leave the area. One, two, or a few can be dealt with. More than that and your fun camping trip will be about as fun as being roped to a tree and stung by an electric shock rod.

On most trips, you will spend time doing everything possible to keep from getting bitten by mosquitoes or no-see-ums. When your attempts fail, you must know what to do next, and fast, especially if you are among those ill-fated campers who get big, red lumps from a bite inflicted from even a microscopic mosquito.

A fluid called After Bite or a dab of ammonia should be applied immediately to the bite. To start the healing process, apply a first-aid gel (not a liquid), such as the one made by Campho-Phenique.

DEET

What is DEET? You're not likely to find the word DEET on any repellent label. That's because DEET stands for N,N diethyl-m-toluamide. If the label contains this scientific name, the repellent contains DEET. Despite fears of DEET-associated health risks and the increased attention given natural alternatives, DEET-based repellents are still acknowledged as by far the best option when serious insect protection is required.

On one trip, I had a small bottle of mosquito repellent in the same pocket as a Swiss army knife. Guess what happened? The mosquito repellent leaked a bit and literally melted the insignia right off the knife. DEET will also melt synthetic clothes. That is why, in bad mosquito country, I'll expose a minimum of skin, just hands and face (with full beard), apply the repellent only to my cheeks and the back of my hands, and perhaps wear a bandanna sprinkled with a few drops as well. That does the trick, with a minimum of exposure to the repellent.

"NATURAL" REPELLENTS

Are natural alternatives a safer choice than DEET? Some are potentially hazardous if ingested, and most are downright painful if they find their way into the eyes or onto mucus membranes. For example, pennyroyal is perhaps the most toxic of the essential oils used to repel insects and can be deadly if taken internally. Other oils used include cedarwood, citronella, and perhaps the most common, eucalyptus and peppermint.

How effective are natural repellents? The average effective repelling time of a citronella product appears to range from 1.5-2 hours, so it must be reapplied to be effective.

What other chemical alternatives are there? Another line of defense against insects is the chemical permethrin, used on clothing, not on skin. Permethrin-based products are designed to repel and kill arthropods or crawling insects, making them a preferred repellent for ticks. The currently available products remain effective—repelling and killing chiggers, mosquitoes, and ticks—for two weeks and through two launderings.

Ticks

Ticks are nasty little vermin that will wait in ambush, jump on unsuspecting prey, and then crawl to a prime location before filling their bodies with their victim's blood.

I call them Dracula bugs, but by any name they can be a terrible camp pest. Ticks rest on grass and low plants and attach themselves to those who brush against the vegetation (dogs are particularly vulnerable). Typically, they can be found no more than 18 inches above ground, and if you stay on the trails, you can usually avoid them.

There are two common species of ticks. The common coastal tick is larger, brownish in color, and prefers to crawl around before putting its clamps on you. The feel of any bug crawling on your skin can be creepy, but consider it a forewarning of assault; you can just pick the tick off and dispatch it. The coastal tick's preferred destination is usually the back of your neck, just where the hairline starts. The other species, the wood tick, is small and black, and when he puts his clamps in, it's immediately painful. When a wood tick gets into a dog for a few days, it can cause a large red welt. In either case, ticks should be removed as soon as possible.

If you have hiked in areas infested with ticks, it is advisable to shower as soon as possible, washing your clothes immediately. If you just leave your clothes in a heap, a tick can crawl out and invade your home. They like warmth, and one way or another, they can end up in your bed. Waking up in the middle of the night with a tick crawling across your chest can be unsettling, to put it mildly.

Once a tick has its clampers in your skin, you must determine how long it has been there. If it has been a short time, the most painless and effective method for removal is to take a pair of sharp tweezers and grasp the little devil, making certain to isolate the mouth area, then pull him out. Reader Johvin Perry sent in the suggestion to coat the tick with Vaseline, which will cut off its oxygen supply, after which it may voluntarily give up the hunt.

If the tick has been in longer, you may wish to have a doctor extract it. Some people will burn a tick with a cigarette or poison it with lighter fluid, but neither is advisable. No matter how you do it, you must take care to remove all of the tick, especially its clawlike mouth.

The wound, however small, should then be cleansed and dressed. First, apply liquid peroxide, which cleans and sterilizes, and then apply a dressing coated with a first-aid gel, such as First-Aid Cream, Campho-Phenique, or Neosporin.

Lyme disease, which can be transmitted by the bite of a deer tick, is rare but common enough to warrant some attention. To prevent tick bites, some people tuck their pant legs into their hiking socks and spray tick repellent, called Permamone, on their pants.

The first symptom of Lyme disease is a bright red, splotchy rash that develops around the bite area. Other possible early symptoms include headache, nausea, fever, and/or a stiff neck. If any of these happen, or if you have any doubts, you should see your doctor immediately. If you do get Lyme disease, don't panic. Doctors say it is easily treated in the early stages with simple antibiotics. If you are nervous about getting Lyme disease, carry a small plastic bag with you when you hike. If a tick manages to get his clampers into you, put the tick in the plastic bag after you pull it out. Then give it to your doctor for analysis to see if the tick is a carrier of the disease.

During the course of my hiking and camping career, I have removed ticks from my skin hundreds of times without any problems. However, if you are worried about ticks, you can buy a tick removal kit from any outdoors store. These kits allow you to remove ticks in such a way that their toxins are guaranteed not to enter your bloodstream.

If you are particularly wary of ticks or perhaps even have nightmares of them, wear long pants that are tucked into your socks, as well as a long-sleeved shirt tucked securely into your pants and held with a belt. Clothing should be light in color, making it easier to see ticks, and tightly woven so ticks have trouble hanging on. On one hike with my mom, Eleanor, I brushed more than 100 ticks off my blue jeans in less than an hour, while she did not pick up a single one on her polyester pants.

Perform tick checks regularly, especially on the back of the neck. The combination of DEET insect repellents applied to the skin and permethrin repellents applied directly to clothing is considered to be the most effective line of defense against ticks.

Poison Oak

After a nice afternoon hike, about a five-miler, I was concerned about possible exposure to poison oak, so I immediately showered and put on clean clothes. Then I settled into a chair with my favorite foamy elixir to watch the end of a baseball game. But the game went on for hours, 18 innings; meanwhile, my dog, tired from the hike, went to sleep on my bare ankles.

A few days later, I had a case of poison oak. My feet looked as though they had been on fire and put out with an ice pick. The lesson? Don't always trust your dog, give him a bath as well, and beware of extra-inning ball games.

You can get poison oak only from direct contact with the oil residue from the plant's leaves. It can be passed in a variety of ways, as direct as skin-to-leaf contact or as indirect as leaf to dog, dog to sofa, sofa to skin. Once you have it, there is little you can do but feel horribly itchy. Applying Caladryl lotion or its equivalent can

poison oak

help because it contains antihistamines, which attack and dry the itch.

My pal Furniss offers a tip that may sound crazy but seems to work. You should expose the afflicted area to the hottest water you can stand, then suddenly immerse it in cold water. The hot water opens the skin pores and gets the "itch" out, and the cold water then quickly seals the pores.

In any case, you're a lot better off if you don't get poison oak to begin with. Remember that poison oak can disguise itself. In the spring, it is green; then it gradually turns reddish in the summer. By fall, it becomes a bloody, ugly-looking red. In the winter, it loses its leaves altogether and appears to be nothing more than the barren, brown sticks of a small plant. However, at any time and in any form, its contact with skin can quickly lead to infection.

Some people are more easily afflicted than others, but if you are one of the lucky few who aren't, don't cheer too loudly. While some people can be exposed to the oil residue of poison oak with little or no effect, the body's resistance can gradually be worn down with repeated exposure. At one time, I could

practically play in the stuff and the only symptom would be a few little bumps on the inside of my wrist. Now, more than 15 years later, my resistance has broken down. If I merely brush against poison oak now, in a few days the exposed area can look as if it were used for a track meet.

So regardless of whether you consider yourself vulnerable or not, you should take heed to reduce your exposure. That can be done by staying on trails when you hike and making sure your dog does the same. Remember, the worst stands of poison oak are usually brush-infested areas just off the trail. Also protect yourself by dressing so your skin is completely covered, wearing long-sleeved shirts, long pants, and boots. If you suspect you've been exposed, immediately wash your clothes and then wash yourself with aloe vera, rinsing with a cool shower.

And don't forget to give your dog a bath as well.

Sunburn

The most common injury suffered on camping trips is sunburn, yet some people wear it as a badge of honor, believing that it somehow enhances their virility. Well, it doesn't. Neither do suntans. Too much sun can lead to serious burns or sunstroke.

Both are easy enough to avoid. Use a high-level sunscreen on your skin, apply lip balm, and wear sunglasses and a hat. If any area gets burned, apply first-aid cream, which will soothe and provide moisture to the parched skin.

The best advice is not to get even a suntan. Those who tan are involved in a practice that can eventually ruin their skin and possibly lead to cancer.

Giardia and Cryptosporidium

You have just hiked in to your backwoods spot, you're thirsty and a bit tired, but you smile as you consider the prospects. Everything seems perfect—there's not a stranger in sight, and you have nothing to do but relax with your pals.

You toss down your gear, grab your cup, dip it into the stream, and take a long drink of that ice-cold mountain water. It seems crystal pure and sweeter than anything you've ever tasted. It's not till later that you find out it can be just like drinking a cup of poison.

Whether you camp in the wilderness or not, if you hike, you're going to get thirsty. And if your canteen runs dry, you'll start eyeing any water source. Stop! Do not pass Go. Do not drink.

By drinking what appears to be pure mountain water without first treating it, you can ingest a microscopic protozoan called *Giardia lamblia*. The ensuing abdominal cramps can make you feel like your stomach and intestinal tract are in a knot, ready to explode. With that comes long-term diarrhea that is worse than even a bear could imagine.

Doctors call the disease giardiasis, or giardia for short, but it is difficult to diagnose. One friend of mine who contracted giardia was told he might have stomach cancer before the proper diagnosis was made.

Drinking directly from a stream or lake does not mean you will get giardia, but you are taking a giant chance. There is no reason to assume such a risk, potentially ruining your trip and enduring weeks of misery.

A lot of people are taking that risk. I made a personal survey of campers in the Yosemite National Park wilderness, and found that roughly only one in 10 was equipped with some kind of water-purification system. The result, according to the Public Health Service, is that an average of 4 percent of all backpackers and campers suffer giardiasis. According to the Parasitic Diseases Division of the Center for Infectious Diseases, the rates range from 1 percent to 20 percent across the country.

But if you get giardia, you are not going to care about the statistics. "When I got giardia, I just about wanted to die," said Henry McCarthy, a California camper. "For about 10 days, it was the most terrible thing I have ever experienced. And through the whole thing, I kept thinking? I shouldn't have drunk that water, but it seemed all right at the time.'"

That is the mistake most campers make. The stream might be running free, gurgling over

Always filter water before drinking.

boulders in the high country, tumbling into deep, oxygenated pools. It looks pure. Then in a few days, the problems suddenly start. Drinking untreated water from mountain streams is a lot like playing Russian roulette. Sooner or later the gun goes off.

SteriPEN

We would never do another wilderness trip without one and I keep mine with me all the time. By using UV light, the SteriPEN destroy viruses, bacteria and protozoa (like Giardia) that can make you sick. Dip your water bottle in a cold stream, purify the water with the UV light in under two minutes, and drink all the cold, clean mountain water you can. It's like having a cooler full of ice-cold water with you all the time. On expeditions of more than four days, make sure you bring extra batteries.

Filters

Handheld filters are getting more compact, lighter, easier to use, and often less expensive. Having to boil water or endure chemicals that leave a bad taste in the mouth has been all but eliminated.

With a filter, you just pump and drink. Filtering strains out microscopic contaminants, rendering the water clear and somewhat pure. How pure? That depends on the size of the filter's pores—what manufacturers call pore-size efficiency. A filter with a pore-size efficiency of one micron or smaller will remove protozoa, such as *Giardia lamblia* and cryptosporidium, as well as parasitic eggs and larva, but it takes a pore-size efficiency of less than 0.4 micron to remove bacteria. All but one of the filters recommended here do that.

A good backcountry water filter weighs less than 20 ounces, is easy to grasp, simple to use, and a snap to clean and maintain. At the very least, buy one that will remove protozoa and bacteria. (A number of cheap, pocket-sized filters remove only *Giardia lamblia* and cryptosporidium. That, in my book, is risking your health to save money.) Consider the flow rate, too: A liter per minute is good.

All filters will eventually clog—it's a sign that they've been doing their job. If you force water through a filter that's becoming difficult to pump, you risk injecting a load of microbial nasties into your bottle. Some models can be back-washed, brushed, or, as with ceramic elements, scrubbed to extend their useful lives. And if the filter has a pre-filter to screen out the big stuff, use it: It will give your filter a boost in mileage, which can then top out at about 100 gallons per disposable element. Any of the filters reviewed here will serve well on an outing into the wilds, providing you always play by the manufacturer's rules.

First Need Deluxe: The filter pumps smoothly and puts out more than a liter per minute. The 15-ounce First Need Deluxe from General Ecology does something no other handheld filter will do: It removes protozoa, bacteria, and viruses without using chemicals. Such effectiveness is the result of a fancy three-stage matrix system. The First Need has been around since 1982. Additional cartridges mean you just replace the cartridge, not the entire unit. If you drop the filter and unknowingly crack the cartridge, all the little nasties can get through. A small point worth noting.

Basic Designs Ceramic: It clogs quickly and therefore is not a good choice for long trips. The Basic Designs Ceramic Filter Pump weighs eight ounces and is as stripped-down a filter as you'll find. The pump is simple, easy to use, and quite reliable. The ceramic filter effectively removes protozoa and bacteria, making it ideal and cost effective for backpacking—but it won't protect against viruses. Also, the filter element is too bulbous to work directly from a shallow water source; as with the PentaPure, you'll have to decontaminate a pot, cup, or bottle to transfer your unfiltered water.

Katadyn Hiker Pro: The Katadyn effectively removes protozoa and bacteria. I found it challenging to put any kind of power behind the pump's tiny handle, and the filtered water comes through at a paltry half-liter per minute. It also requires more cleaning than most filters—though the good news is that the element is made of long-lasting ceramic.

MSR MiniWorks: The 14-ounce MiniWorks looks similar to the more expensive WaterWorks, and, like the WaterWorks, is fully field-maintainable, while guarding against protozoa, bacteria, and chemicals. It attaches directly to a standard one-quart Nalgene water bottle. Takes about 90 seconds to filter that quart.

MSR WaterWorks II Ceramic: At 17.4 ounces, the WaterWorks II isn't light. You get a better flow rate (90 seconds per liter), an easy pumping action, and—like the original Mini Filter—a long-lasting ceramic cartridge. This filter is a good match for the person who encounters a lot of dirty water—its three-stage filter weeds out protozoa, bacteria, and chemicals. The MSR can be completely disassembled in the field for troubleshooting and cleaning.

SweetWater WalkAbout: The WalkAbout is perfect for the day hiker or backpacker who obsesses on lightening the load. The filter weighs just 8.5 ounces, is easily cleaned in the field, and removes both protozoa and bacteria: a genuine bargain. There are some trade-offs, however, for its diminutiveness. Water delivery is a tad slow at just under a liter per minute, but filter cartridges are now good for up to 100 gallons.

The big drawback with filters is that if you pump water from a mucky lake, the filter can clog in a few days. Therein lies the weakness. Once plugged up, it is useless, and you have to replace it or take your chances. One trick to extend the filter life is to fill your cook pot with water, let the sediment settle, then pump from there. As an insurance policy, always have a spare filter canister on hand.

Boiling Water

Except for water filtration, this is the only treatment that you can use with complete confidence. According to the federal Parasitic Diseases Division, it takes a few minutes at a rolling boil to be certain you've killed *Giardia lamblia*. At high elevations, boil for 3-5 minutes. A side benefit is that you'll also kill other dangerous bacteria that live undetected in natural waters.

But to be honest, boiling water is a thorn for most people on backcountry trips. For one thing, if you boil water on an open fire, what should taste like crystal-pure mountain water tastes instead like a mouthful of warm ashes. If you don't have a campfire, it wastes stove fuel. And if you are thirsty *now,* forget it. The water takes hours to cool.

The only time boiling always makes sense, however, is when you are preparing dinner. The ash taste will disappear in whatever freeze-dried dinner, soup, or hot drink you make.

Water-Purification Pills

I bring water-purification pills for back-up use only. They are cheap and, in addition, they kill most of the bacteria, regardless of whether you use iodine crystals or potable aqua iodine tablets. The problem is they just don't always kill *Giardia lamblia,* and that is the one critter worth worrying about on your trip. That makes water-treatment pills unreliable and dangerous.

Another key element is the time factor. Depending on the water's temperature, organic content, and pH level, these pills can take a long time to do the job. A minimum wait of 20 minutes is advised. Most people don't like waiting that long, especially when they're hot and thirsty after a hike and thinking, "What the heck, the water looks fine."

And then there is the taste. On one trip, my water filter clogged and we had to use the iodine pills instead. It doesn't take long to get tired of iodine-tinged water. Mountain water should be one of the greatest tasting beverages of the world, but the iodine kills that.

No Treatment

This is your last resort and, using extreme care, can be executed with success. Michael Furniss, the renowned hydrologist, has shown me the difference between safe and dangerous water sources.

When I was in the Boy Scouts, I remember

a scoutmaster actually telling me if you could find water running over a rock for at least five feet, it was a guarantee of its purity. Imagine that. What we've learned is that the safe water sources are almost always small springs in high, craggy mountain areas. The key is making sure no one has been upstream from where you drink. We drink untreated water only when we can see the source, such as a spring.

Furniss mentioned that another potential problem in bypassing water treatment is that even in settings free of *Giardia lamblia,* you can still ingest other bacteria that cause stomach problems.

Hypothermia

No matter how well planned your trip might be, a sudden change in weather can turn it into a puzzle for which there are few answers. Bad weather or an accident can set in motion a dangerous chain of events.

Such a chain of episodes occurred for my brother Rambob and me on a fishing trip one fall day just below the snow line. The weather had suddenly turned very cold, and ice was forming along the shore of the lake. Suddenly, the canoe became terribly imbalanced, and, just that quickly, it flipped. The little life vest seat cushions were useless, and using the canoe as a paddleboard, we tried to kick our way back to shore where my dad was going crazy at the thought of his two sons drowning before his eyes.

It took 17 minutes in that 38-degree water, but we finally made it to shore. When they pulled me out of the water, my legs were dead, not strong enough even to hold up my weight. In fact, I didn't feel so much cold as tired, and I just wanted to lie down and go to sleep.

I closed my eyes, and my brother-in-law, Lloyd Angal, slapped me in the face several times, then got me on my feet and pushed and pulled me about.

In the celebration over our making it to shore, only Lloyd had realized that hypothermia was setting in. Hypothermia is the condition in which the temperature of the body is lowered to the point that it causes poor reasoning, apathy, and collapse. It can look like the afflicted person is just tired and needs to sleep, but that sleep can be the first step toward a coma.

Ultimately, my brother and I shared what little dry clothing remained. Then we began hiking around to get muscle movement, creating internal warmth. We ate whatever munchies were available because the body produces heat by digestion. But most important, we got our heads as dry as possible. More body heat is lost through wet hair than any other single factor.

A few hours later, we were in a pizza parlor replaying the incident, talking about how only a life vest can do the job of a life vest. We decided never again to rely on those little flotation seat cushions that disappear when the boat flips.

We had done everything right to prevent hypothermia: Don't go to sleep, start a physical activity, induce shivering, put dry clothes on, dry your head, and eat something. That's how you fight hypothermia. In a dangerous situation, whether you fall in a lake or a stream or get caught unprepared in a storm, that's how you can stay alive.

After being in that ice-bordered lake for almost 20 minutes and then finally pulling ourselves to the shoreline, we discovered a strange thing. My canoe was flipped right-side up and almost all of its contents were lost: tackle box, flotation cushions, and cooler. But remaining were one paddle and one fishing rod, the trout rod my grandfather had given me for my 12th birthday.

Lloyd gave me a smile. "This means that you are meant to paddle and fish again," he said with a laugh.

Getting Unlost

I could not have been more lost. There I was, a guy who is supposed to know about these things, transfixed by confusion, snow, and hoofprints from a big deer.

I discovered that it is actually quite easy to get lost. If you don't get your bearings, getting found is the difficult part. This occurred on a wilderness trip where I'd hiked in to a remote lake and then set up a base camp for a deer hunt.

"There are some giant bucks up on that rim," confided Mr. Furnai, who lives near the area. "But it takes a mountain man to even get close to them."

That was a challenge I answered. After four-wheeling it to the trailhead, I tromped off with pack and rifle, gut-thumped it up 100 switchbacks over the rim, then followed a creek drainage up to a small but beautiful lake. The area was stark and nearly treeless, with bald granite broken only by large boulders. To keep from getting lost, I marked my route with piles of small rocks to act as directional signs for the return trip.

But at daybreak the next day, I stuck my head out of my tent and found eight inches of snow on the ground. I looked up into a gray sky filled by huge, cascading snowflakes. Visibility was about 50 yards, with fog on the mountain rim. "I better get out of here and get back to my truck," I said to myself. "If my truck gets buried at the trailhead, I'll never get out."

After packing quickly, I started down the mountain. But after 20 minutes, I began to get disoriented. You see, all the little piles of rocks I'd stacked to mark the way were now buried in snow, and I had only a smooth white blanket of snow to guide me. Everything looked the same, and it was snowing even harder now.

Five minutes later, I started chewing on some jerky to keep warm, then suddenly stopped. Where was I? Where was the creek drainage? Isn't this where I was supposed to cross over a creek and start the switchbacks down the mountain?

Right then, I looked down and saw the tracks of a huge deer, the kind Mr. Furnai had talked about. What a predicament: I was lost and snowed in and seeing big hoofprints in the snow. Part of me wanted to abandon all safety and go after that deer, but a little voice in the back of my head won out. "Treat this as an emergency," it said.

The first step in any predicament is to secure your present situation, that is, to make sure it does not get any worse. I unloaded my rifle (too easy to slip, fall, and have a misfire),

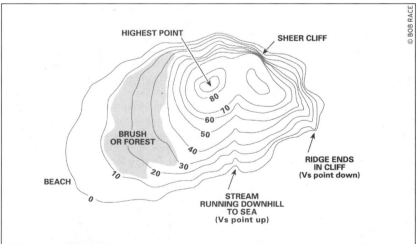

HIGHEST POINT

SHEER CLIFF

© BOB RACE

80
70
60
50
40
30
20
10
0

BRUSH OR FOREST

BEACH

RIDGE ENDS IN CLIFF (Vs point down)

STREAM RUNNING DOWNHILL TO SEA (Vs point up)

The **topographical map** is easier to read than many believe. Lines close together mean steep gradients; lines farther apart mean gentle gradients; V-shaped sets of lines pointing to higher elevations mean gulleys or stream-beds; V-shaped sets of lines pointing to lower elevations mean ridges.

© SABRINA YOUNG

Rock cairns (small piles of rocks) can act as directional signs to keep you from getting lost.

took stock of my food (three days' worth), camp fuel (plenty), and clothes (rain gear keeping me dry). Then I wondered, "Where the hell am I?"

I took out my map, compass, and altimeter, then opened the map and laid it on the snow. It immediately began collecting snowflakes. I set the compass atop the map and oriented it to north. Because of the fog, there was no way to spot landmarks, such as prominent mountaintops, to verify my position. Then I checked the altimeter, which read 4,900 feet. Well, the elevation at my lake was 5,320 feet. That was critical information.

I scanned the elevation lines on the map and was able to trace the approximate area of my position, somewhere downstream from the lake, yet close to a 4,900-foot elevation. "Right here," I said, pointing to a spot on the map with my finger. "I should pick up the switchback trail down the mountain somewhere off to the left, maybe just 40 or 50 yards away."

Slowly and deliberately, I pushed through the light, powdered snow. In five minutes, I suddenly stopped. To the left, across a 10-foot

depression in the snow, appeared a flat spot that veered off to the right. "That's it! That's the crossing."

In minutes, I was working down the switchbacks, on my way, no longer lost. I thought of the hoofprints I had seen, and now that I knew my position, I wanted to head back and spend the day hunting. Then I looked up at the sky, saw it filled with falling snowflakes, and envisioned my truck buried deep in snow. Alas, this time logic won out over dreams.

In a few hours, now trudging through more than a foot of snow, I was at my truck at a spot called Doe Flat, and next to it was a giant, all-terrain U.S. Forest Service vehicle and two rangers.

"Need any help?" I asked them.

They just laughed. "We're here to help you," one answered. "It's a good thing you filed a trip plan with our district office in Gasquet. We wouldn't have known you were out here."

"Winter has arrived," said the other. "If we don't get your truck out now, it will be stuck here until next spring. If we hadn't found you, you might have been here until the end of time."

They connected a chain from the rear axle of their giant rig to the front axle of my truck and started towing me out, back to civilization. On the way to pavement, I figured I had gotten some of the more important lessons of my life. Always file a trip plan and have plenty of food, fuel, and a camp stove you can rely on. Make sure your clothes, weather gear, sleeping bag, and tent will keep you dry and warm. Always carry a compass, altimeter, and map with elevation lines, and know how to use them, practicing in good weather to get the feel of it.

And if you get lost and see the hoofprints of a giant deer, well, there are times when it is best to pass them by.

CATCHING FISH, AVOIDING BEARS, AND HAVING FUN

Feet tired and hot, stomachs growling, we stopped our hike for lunch beside a beautiful little river pool that was catching the flows from a long but gentle waterfall. My brother Rambob passed me a piece of jerky. I took my boots off, then slowly dunked my feet into the cool, foaming water.

I was gazing at a towering peak across a canyon when suddenly, Wham! There was a quick jolt at the heel of my right foot. I pulled my foot out of the water to find that, incredibly, a trout had bitten it.

My brother looked at me as if I had antlers growing out of my head. "Wow!" he exclaimed. "That trout almost caught himself an outdoors writer!"

It's true that in remote areas trout sometimes bite on almost anything, even feet. On one high-country trip, I caught limits of trout using nothing but a bare hook. The only problem is that the fish will often hit the splitshot sinker instead of the hook. Of course, fishing isn't usually that easy. But it gives you an idea of what is possible.

America's wildlands are home to a remarkable abundance of fish and wildlife. Deer browse with little fear of man, bears keep an eye out for your food, and little critters, such as squirrels and chipmunks, are daily companions. Add in the fishing, and you've got yourself a camping trip.

Your camping adventures will evolve into premium outdoor experiences if you can work in a few good fishing trips, avoid bear problems, and occasionally add a little offbeat fun with some camp games.

Trout and Bass

He creeps up on the stream as quietly as an Indian scout, keeping his shadow off the water. With his little spinning rod he'll zip his lure within an inch or two of its desired mark, probing along rocks, the edges of riffles, pocket water, or wherever he can find a change in river habitat. Rambob is trout fishing, and he's a master at it.

In most cases, he'll catch a trout on his first or second cast. After that, it's time to move up the river, giving no spot much more than five minutes' due. Stick and move, stick and move,

stalking the stream like a bobcat zeroing in on an unsuspecting rabbit. He might keep a few trout for dinner, but mostly he releases what he catches. Rambob doesn't necessarily fish for food. It's the feeling that comes with it.

You don't need a million dollars' worth of fancy gear to catch fish. What you need is the right outlook, and that can be learned. That goes regardless of whether you are fishing for trout or bass, the two most popular fisheries in the United States. Your fishing tackle selection should be as simple and clutter-free as possible.

At home, I've got every piece of fishing tackle you might imagine, more than 30 rods and many tackle boxes, racks and cabinets filled with all kinds of stuff. I've got one lure that looks like a chipmunk and another that resembles a miniature can of beer with hooks. If I hear of something new, I want to try it and usually do. It's a result of my lifelong fascination with the sport.

But if you just want to catch fish, there's an easier way to go. And when I go fishing, I take that path. I don't try to bring everything. It would be impossible. Instead, I bring

brother Rambob's big Almanor trout

a relatively small amount of gear. At home, I scan my tackle boxes for equipment and lures, make my selections, and bring just the essentials. Rod, reel, and tackle will fit into a side pocket of my backpack or a small carrying bag.

So what kind of rod should be used on an outdoor trip? For most camper/anglers, I suggest the use of a light, multi-piece spinning rod that will break down to a small size. The lowest-priced, quality six-piece rod on the market is the Daiwa 6.5-foot pack rod, number 6752, which is made of a graphite/glass composite that gives it the quality of a much more expensive model. And it comes in a hard plastic carrying tube for protection. Other major rod manufacturers, such as Fenwick, offer similar premium rods. It's tough to miss with any of them.

The use of graphite/glass composites in fishing rods has made them lighter and more sensitive, yet stronger. The only downside to graphite as a rod material is that it can be brittle. If you rap your rod against something, it can crack or cause a weak spot. That weak spot can eventually snap under even light pressure, like setting a hook or casting. Of course, a bit of care will prevent that from ever occurring.

If you haven't bought a fishing reel in some time, you will be surprised at the quality and price of micro spinning reels on the market. The reels come tiny and strong, with rear-control drag systems. Among others, Abu, Cardinal, Shimano, Sigma all make premium reels. They're worth it. With your purchase, you've just bought a reel that will last for years and years.

The one downside to spinning reels is that after long-term use, the bail spring will weaken. As a result, after casting and beginning to reel, the bail will sometimes not flip over and allow the reel to retrieve the line. Then you have to do it by hand. This can be incredibly frustrating, particularly when stream fishing, where instant line pickup is essential. The solution is to have a new bail spring installed every few years. This is a cheap, quick operation for a tackle expert.

You might own a giant tackle box filled with lures but, on your fishing trip, you are better off to fit just the essentials into a small container. One of the best ways to do that is to use the Plano Micro-Magnum 3414, a tiny two-sided tackle box for trout anglers that fits into a shirt pocket. In mine, I can fit 20 lures in one side of the box and 20 flies, split-shot weights, and snap swivels in the other. For bass lures, which are bigger, you need a slightly larger box, but the same principle applies.

There are more fishing lures on the market than you can imagine, but a few special ones can do the job. I make sure these are in my box on every trip. For trout, I carry a small black Panther Martin spinner with yellow spots, a small gold Kastmaster, a yellow Roostertail, a gold Z-Ray with red spots, a Super Duper, and a Mepps Lightning spinner.

You can take it a step further using insider's wisdom. My old pal Ed "the Dunk" showed me his trick of taking a tiny Dardevle spoon, spray painting it flat black, and dabbing five tiny red dots on it. It's a real killer, particularly in tiny streams where the trout are spooky.

The best trout catcher I've ever used on rivers is a small metal lure called a Met-L Fly. On days when nothing else works, it can be like going to a shooting gallery. The problem is that the lure is nearly impossible to find. Rambob and I consider the few we have remaining so valuable that if the lure is snagged on a rock, a cold swim is deemed mandatory for its retrieval. I've been able snag about five of these and they only get pulled out when fishing turns into Mission Impossible.

For bass, you can also fit all you need into a small plastic tackle box. I have fished with many bass pros, and all of them actually use just a few lures: twist-tail grubs, Senkos, Brush Hog, a white spinner bait, a surface plug called a Zara Spook, and AC plug. At times, like when the bass move into shoreline areas during the spring, shad minnow imitations like those made by Rebel or Rapala can be dynamite. My favorite is the one-inch, blue-silver Rapala. Every spring as the lakes begin to warm and the fish snap out of their winter doldrums, I like to float and paddle around in my small raft. I'll cast that little Rapala along the shoreline and catch and release hundreds of bass, bluegill, and sunfish. The fish are usually sitting close to the shoreline, awaiting my offering.

Fishing Tips

There's an old angler's joke about how you need to think like a fish. But if you're the one getting zilched, you may not think it's so funny.

The irony is that it is your mental approach, what you see and what you miss, that often determines your fishing luck. Some people will spend a lot of money on tackle, lures, and fishing clothes, and that done, just saunter up to a stream or lake, cast out, and wonder why they are not catching fish. The answer is their mental outlook. They are not attuning themselves to their surroundings.

You must live on nature's level, not your own. Try this and you will become aware of things you never believed even existed. Soon you will see things that will allow you to catch fish. You can get a head start by reading about fishing, but to get your degree in fishing, you must attend the University of Nature.

On every fishing trip, regardless of what you fish for, try to follow three hard-and-fast rules:

1. Always approach the fishing spot so you will be undetected.

2. Present your lure, fly, or bait in a manner so it appears completely natural, as if no line was attached.

3. Stick and move, hitting one spot, working it the best you can, then moving to the next.

APPROACH

No one can just walk up to a stream or lake, cast out, and start catching fish as if someone had waved a magic wand. Instead, give the fish credit for being smart. After all, they live there.

Your approach must be completely undetected by the fish. Fish can sense your presence through sight and sound, though these factors are misinterpreted by most people. By sight, fish rarely actually see you; more often, they see your shadow on the water or the movement of your arm or rod while casting. By sound, they

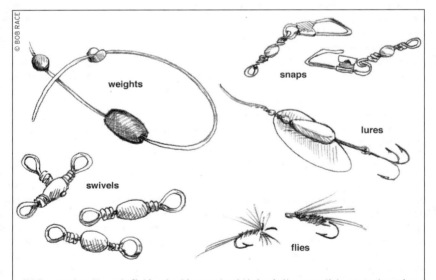

© BOB RACE

weights

snaps

lures

swivels

flies

While camping, the only **fishing tackle** you should bring is the essentials: several varying weights, about 20 lures, and about 20 flies, splitshot, and snap swivels. These should all fit into a container just bigger than a deck of cards.

don't necessarily hear you talking, but they do detect the vibrations of your footsteps along the shore, a rock being kicked, or the unnatural plunking sound of a heavy cast hitting the water. Any of these elements can spook them off the bite. In order to fish undetected, you must walk softly, keep your shadow off the water, and keep your casting motion low. All of these key elements become easier at sunrise or sunset, when shadows are on the water. At midday, the sun is at its peak, causing a high level of light penetration in the water. This can make the fish skittish to any foreign presence.

Like a hunter, you must stalk the spots. When my brother Rambob sneaks up on a fishing spot, he is like a burglar sneaking through an unlocked window.

PRESENTATION

Your lure, fly, or bait must appear in the water as if no line were attached, so it looks as natural as possible. My pal Mo Furniss has skin-dived in rivers to watch what the fish see when somebody is fishing.

"You wouldn't believe it," he said. "When the lure hits the water, every trout within 40 feet, like 15, 20 trout, will do a little zigzag. They all see the lure and are aware something is going on. Meanwhile, onshore the guy casting doesn't get a bite and thinks there aren't any fish in the river."

If your offering is aimed at fooling a fish into striking, it must appear as part of the natural habitat, like an insect just hatching or a small fish looking for a spot to hide. That's where you come in.

After you have sneaked up on a fishing spot, you should zip your cast upstream and start your retrieval as soon as it hits the water. If you let the lure sink to the bottom and then start the retrieval, you have no chance. A minnow, for instance, does not sink to the bottom, then start swimming. On rivers, the retrieval should be more of a drift, as if the "minnow" is in trouble and the current is sweeping it downstream.

When fishing on trout streams, always hike and cast upriver and retrieve as the offering drifts downstream in the current. This is effective because trout will sit almost motionless, pointed upstream, finning against the current. This way, they can see anything coming their direction, and if a potential food morsel arrives, all they need to do is move over a few inches, open their mouths, and they've got an easy lunch. Thus, you must cast upstream.

Conversely, if you cast downstream, your retrieval will bring the lure from behind the fish, where he cannot see it approaching. And I've never seen a trout that had eyes in its tail. In addition, when retrieving a downstream lure, the river current will tend to sweep your lure inshore to the rocks.

FINDING SPOTS

A lot of anglers don't catch fish, and a lot of hikers never see any wildlife. The key is where they are looking.

The rule of the wild is that fish and wildlife will congregate wherever there is a distinct change in the habitat. This is where you should begin your search. To find deer, for instance, forget probing a thick forest, but look for where it breaks into a meadow or a clearcut has splayed a stand of trees. That's where the deer will be.

In a river, it can be where a riffle pours into a small pool, a rapid plunges into a deep hole and flattens, a big boulder in the middle of a long riffle, a shoreline point, a rock pile, a submerged tree. Look for the changes. Conversely, long, straight stretches of shoreline will not hold fish—the habitat is lousy.

On rivers, the most productive areas are often where short riffles tumble into small oxygenated pools. After sneaking up from the downstream side and staying low, you should zip your cast so the lure plops gently into the white water just above the pool. Start your retrieval instantly; the lure will drift downstream and plunk into the pool. Bang! That's where the trout will hit. Take a few more casts and then head upstream to the next spot.

With a careful approach and lure

© BOB RACE

The rule of the wild is that wildlife will congregate wherever there is a distinct change in habitat. To find where fish are hiding, look where a riffle pours into a small pond, where a rapid plunges into a deep hole and flattens, and around submerged trees, rock piles, and boulders in the middle of a long riffle.

presentation and by fishing in the right spots, you have the ticket to many exciting days on the water.

Of Bears and Food

The first time you come nose-to-nose with a bear can make your skin quiver.

Even the sight of mild-mannered black bears, the most common bear in America, can send shock waves through your body. They weigh 250-400 pounds and have large claws and teeth that are made to scare campers. When they bound, the muscles on their shoulders roll like ocean breakers. But in California, you don't have to be scared of them. They aren't interested in you, just your food.

Bears in camping areas are accustomed to sharing the mountains with hikers and campers. They have become specialists in the food-raiding business. As a result, you must be able to bear-proof your camp or be able to scare the fellow off. Many campgrounds provide bear- and raccoon-proof food lockers. In most wilderness areas, bear-proof food canisters are required. Never leave your food or trash in your car!

Bear-proof food canisters are so effective in wilderness areas at Yosemite, Kings Canyon-Sequoia, and Mount Whitney that I never see bears on trips there anymore—they've given up on backpackers. Instead, they head to the drive-in campgrounds where they can walk right in and often find food sitting out on top of picnic tables.

No problem. Use the bear-proof food lockers. The bear will just move on to the next site on his daily mooching round.

Food Hangs

If you are staying at one of the backpack sites listed in this book, it is unlikely that there will be food lockers available. Your car will not be there, either. The solution is to make a bear-proof food hang, suspending all of your food wrapped in a plastic garbage bag from a rope in midair, 10 feet from the trunk of a tree and 20 feet off the ground. (Counterbalancing two bags with a rope thrown over a tree limb is very

© CESLO DINIZ/123RF.COM

Use bear-proof containers to protect your campsite.

GRIZZLY BEAR TERRITORY

If you are hiking in a wilderness area in Canada or Alaska that may have grizzlies, it is necessary to wear bells on your pack. That way the bear will hear you coming and likely get out of your way. Keep talking, singing, or maybe even debating the country's foreign policy, but do not fall into a silent hiking vigil. And if a breeze is blowing in your face, you must make even more noise (a good excuse to rant and rave about the government's domestic affairs). Noise is important because your smell will not be carried in the direction you are hiking. As a result, the bear will not smell you coming.

If a bear can hear you and smell you, it will tend to get out of the way and let you pass without your knowing it was even close by. The exceptions are if you are carrying fish or lots of sweets in your pack or if you are wearing heavy, sweet deodorants or makeup. All of these are bear attractants.

effective, but finding an appropriate limb can be difficult.)

The food hang is accomplished by tying a rock to a rope, then throwing it over a high but sturdy tree limb. Next, tie your food bag to the rope and hoist it in the air. When you are satisfied with the position of the food bag, tie off the end of the rope to another tree. In an area frequented by bears, a good food bag is a necessity—nothing else will do.

I've been there. On one trip, my pal Foonsky and my brother Rambob left to fish. I was stoking up an evening campfire when I felt the eyes of an intruder on my back. I turned around and saw a big bear heading straight for our camp. In the next half hour, I scared the bear off twice, but then he got a whiff of something sweet in my brother's pack.

The bear rolled into camp like a truck, grabbed the pack, ripped it open, and plucked out the Tang and the Swiss Miss. The 350-pounder then sat astride a nearby log and lapped at the goodies like a thirsty dog drinking water.

Once a bear gets his mitts on your gear, he considers it his. I took two steps toward the pack, and that bear jumped off the log and galloped across the camp right at me. Scientists say a man can't outrun a bear, but they've never seen how fast I can go up a granite block with a bear on my tail.

Shortly thereafter, Foonsky returned to find

me perched on top of the rock and demanded to know how I could let a bear get our Tang. It took all three of us, Foonsky, Rambob, and me, charging at once and shouting like madmen, to clear the bear out of camp and send him off over the ridge. We learned never to let food sit unattended.

The Grizzly

When it comes to grizzlies, well, my friends, you need what we call an attitude adjustment. Or that big ol' bear may just decide to adjust your attitude for you, making your stay at the park a short one.

Grizzlies are nothing like black bears. They are bigger, stronger, have little fear, and take what they want. Some people believe there are many different species of this critter, such as Alaskan brown, silvertip, cinnamon, and Kodiak, but the truth is they are all grizzlies. Any difference in appearance has to do with diet, habitat, and life habits, not speciation. By any name, they all come big.

The first thing you must do is determine if there are grizzlies in the area where you are camping. That can usually be done by asking local rangers. If you are heading into Yellowstone or Glacier National Park, or the Bob Marshall Wilderness of Montana, well, you don't have to ask. They're out there, and they're the biggest and potentially most dangerous critters you could run into.

One general way to figure the size of a bear is from his footprint. Take the width of the footprint in inches, add one to it, and you'll have an estimated length of the bear in feet. For instance, a nine-inch footprint equals a 10-foot bear. Any bear that big is a grizzly. In fact, most grizzly footprints average about 9-10 inches across, and black bears (though they may be brown in color) tend to have footprints only 4.5-6 inches across.

Most encounters with grizzlies occur when hikers fall into a silent march in the wilderness with the wind in their faces, and they walk around a corner and right into a big, unsuspecting grizzly. If you do this and see a big hump just behind its neck, don't think twice. It's a grizzly.

And then what should you do? Get up a tree, that's what. Grizzlies are so big that their claws cannot support their immense weight, and thus they cannot climb trees. And although young grizzlies can climb, they rarely want to get their mitts on you.

If you do get grabbed, every instinct in your body will tell you to fight back. Don't believe it. Play dead. Go limp. Let the bear throw you around a little. After a while, you'll become unexciting play material and the bear will get bored. My grandmother was grabbed by a grizzly in Glacier National Park and, after a few tosses and hugs, was finally left alone to escape.

Some say it's a good idea to tuck your head under his chin, since that way the bear will be unable to bite your head. I'll take a pass on that one. If you are taking action, any action, it's a signal that you are a force to be reckoned with, and he'll likely respond with more aggression. And bears don't lose many wrestling matches.

What grizzlies really like to do, believe it or not, is to pile a lot of sticks and leaves on you. Just let them, and keep perfectly still. Don't fight them; don't run. And when you have a 100 percent chance (not 98 or 99) to dash up a nearby tree, that's when you let fly. Once safely in a tree, you can hurl down insults and let your aggression out.

In a wilderness camp, there are special precautions you should take. Always hang your food at least 100 yards downwind of camp and get it high; 30 feet is reasonable. In addition, circle your camp with rope and hang the bells from your pack on it. Thus, if a bear walks into your camp, he'll run into the rope, the bells will ring, and everybody will have a chance to get up a tree before ol' griz figures out what's going on. Often, the unexpected ringing of bells is enough to send him off in search of a quieter environment.

You see, more often than not, grizzlies tend to clear the way for campers and hikers. So be smart, don't act like bear bait, and always have a plan if you are confronted by one.

My pal Foonsky had such a plan during a wilderness expedition in Montana's northern Rockies. On our second day of hiking, we started seeing scratch marks on the trees 13-14 feet off the ground.

"Mr. Griz made those," Foonsky said. "With spring here, the grizzlies are coming out of hibernation and using the trees like a cat uses a scratch board to stretch the muscles."

The next day, I noticed Foonsky had a pair of track shoes tied to the back of his pack. I just laughed.

"You're not going to outrun a griz," I said. "In fact, there's hardly any animal out here in the wilderness that man can outrun."

Foonsky just smiled.

"I don't have to outrun a griz," he said. "I just have to outrun you!"

Fun and Games

"Now what are we supposed to do?" the young boy asked his dad.

"Yeah, Dad, think of something," said another son.

Well, Dad thought hard. This was one of the first camping trips he'd taken with his sons and one of the first lessons he received was that kids don't appreciate the philosophic release of mountain quiet. They want action and lots of it. With a glint in his eye, Dad searched around the camp and picked up 15 twigs, breaking them so each was four inches long.

He laid them in three separate rows, three twigs in one row, five twigs in another, and seven in the other.

"OK, this game is called 3-5-7," said Dad. "You each take turns picking up sticks. You are allowed to remove all or as few as one twig from a row, but here's the catch: You can pick only from one row per turn. Whoever picks up the last stick left is the loser."

I remember this episode well because those two little boys were my brother Bobby, as in Rambobby, and I. And to this day, we still play 3-5-7 on campouts, with the winner getting to watch the loser clean the dishes. What I have learned in the span of time since that original episode is that it does not matter what your age is: Campers need options for camp fun.

Some evenings, after a long hike or ride, you feel too worn out to take on a serious romp downstream to fish or a climb up to a ridge for a view. That is especially true if you have been in the outback for a week or more. At that point, a lot of campers will spend their time resting and gazing at a map of the area, dreaming of the next day's adventure, or just take a seat against a rock, watching the colors of the sky and mountain panorama change minute by minute. But kids in the push-button video era, and a lot of adults too, want more. After all, "I'm on vacation. I want some fun."

There are several options, such as the 3-5-7 twig game, and they should be just as much a part of your trip planning as arranging your gear.

For kids, plan on games, the more physically challenging the competition, the better. One of the best games is to throw a chunk of wood into a lake and challenge the kids to hit it by throwing rocks. It wreaks havoc on the fishing, but it can keep kids totally absorbed for some time. Target practice with a wrist-rocket slingshot—firing rocks at small targets, like pinecones set on a log—is also all-consuming for kids.

You can also set kids off on little missions near camp, such as looking for the footprints of wildlife, searching out good places to have a "snipe hunt," picking up twigs to get the evening fire started, or having them take the water purifier to a stream to pump some drinking water into a canteen. The latter is an easy, fun, yet important task that will allow kids to feel a sense of equality they often don't get at home.

For adults, the appeal should be more to the intellect. A good example is star and planet identification, and while you are staring into space, you're bound to spot a few asteroids or shooting stars. A star chart can make it easy to find and identify many distinctive stars and constellations, such as Pleiades (the Seven Sisters), Orion, and others from the zodiac, depending on the time of year. With a little research, this can add a unique perspective to your trip. You could point to Polaris, one of the most easily identified of all stars, and note that navigators in the 1400s used it to find their way. Polaris, of course, is the North Star and is at the end of the handle of the Little Dipper. Pinpointing Polaris is quite easy. First find the Big Dipper and then find the outside stars of the ladle of the Big Dipper. They are called the "pointer stars" because they point right at Polaris.

A tree identification book can teach you a few things about your surroundings. It is also a good idea for one member of the party to research the history of the area you have chosen and another to research the geology. With shared knowledge, you end up with a deeper love of wild places.

Another way to add some recreation into your trip is to bring a board game, a number of which have been miniaturized for campers. The most popular are chess, checkers, and cribbage. The latter comes with an equally miniature set of playing cards. And if you bring those little cards, that opens a vast set of other possibilities. With kids along, for instance, just take three queens out of the deck and you can play Old Maid.

But there are more serious card games, and they come with high stakes. Such occurred on one high-country trip where Foonsky, Rambob, and I sat down for a late-afternoon game of poker. In a game of seven-card stud, I caught a straight on the sixth card and felt like a dog licking on a T-bone. Already, I had bet several Skittles and peanut M&Ms on this promising hand.

Then I examined the cards Foonsky had face up. He was showing three sevens, and acting as happy as a grizzly with a pork chop—or a full house. He matched my bet of two peanut M&Ms, then raised me three SweetTarts, one Starburst, and one sour apple Jolly Rancher. Rambob folded, but I matched Foonsky's bet and hoped for the best as the seventh and final card was dealt.

Just after Foonsky glanced at that last card, I saw him sneak a look at my grape stick and beef jerky stash.

"I raise you a grape stick," he said.

Rambob and I both gasped. It was the highest bet ever made, equivalent to a million dollars laid down in Las Vegas. Cannons were going off in my chest. I looked hard at my cards. They looked good, but were they good enough?

Even with a great hand like I had, a grape stick was too much to gamble, my last one with 10 days of trail ahead of us. I shook my head and folded my cards. Foonsky smiled at his victory.

But I still had my grape stick.

Old Tricks Don't Always Work

Most people are born honest, but after a few camping trips, they usually get over it.

I remember some advice I got from Rambob, normally an honest soul, on one camping trip. A giant mosquito had landed on my arm and he alerted me to an expert bit of wisdom.

"Flex your arm muscles," he commanded, watching the mosquito fill with my blood. "He'll get stuck in your arm, then he'll explode."

For some reason, I believed him. We both proceeded to watch the mosquito drill countless holes in my arm.

Alas, the unknowing face sabotage from their most trusted companions on camping trips. It can arise at any time, usually in the form of advice from a friendly, honest-looking face, as if to say, "What? How can you doubt me?" After that mosquito episode, I was a little more skeptical of my dear old brother. Then the next day, when another mosquito was nailing me in the back of the neck, out came this gem:

"Hold your breath," he commanded. I instinctively obeyed. "That will freeze the mosquito," he said, "then you can squish him."

But in the time I wasted holding my breath, the little bugger was able to fly off without my having the satisfaction of squishing him. When he got home, he probably told his family, "What a dummy I got to drill today!"

Over the years, I have been duped numerous times with dubious advice:

On a grizzly bear attack: "If he grabs you, tuck your head under the grizzly's chin; then he won't be able to bite you in the head." This made sense to me until the first time I saw a nine-foot grizzly 40 yards away. In seconds, I was at the top of a tree, which suddenly seemed to make the most sense.

On coping with animal bites: "If a bear bites you in the arm, don't try to jerk it away. That will just rip up your arm. Instead, force your arm deeper into his mouth. He'll lose his grip and will have to open it to get a firmer hold, and right then you can get away." I was told this in the Boy Scouts. When I was 14, I had a chance to try it out when a friend's dog bit me as I tried to pet it. What happened? When I shoved my arm deeper into his mouth, he bit me three more times.

On cooking breakfast: "The bacon will curl up every time in a camp frying pan. So make sure you have a bacon stretcher to keep it flat." As a 12-year-old Tenderfoot, I spent two hours looking for the bacon stretcher until I figured out the camp leader had forgotten it. It wasn't for several years that I learned that there is no such thing.

On preventing sore muscles: "If you haven't hiked for a long time and you are facing a rough climb, you can keep from getting sore muscles in your legs, back, and shoulders by practicing the 'Dead Man's Walk.' Simply let your entire body go slack, and then take slow, wobbling steps. This will clear your muscles of lactic acid, which causes them to be so sore after a rough hike." Foonsky pulled this one on me. Rambob and I both bought it and tried it while we were hiking up Mount Whitney, which requires a 6,000-foot elevation gain in six miles. In one 45-minute period, about 30 other hikers passed us and looked at us as if we were suffering from some rare form of mental aberration.

Fish won't bite? No problem: "If the fish are not feeding or will not bite, persistent anglers can still catch dinner with little problem. Keep casting across the current, and eventually, as they hover in the stream, the line will feed across their open mouths. Keep reeling and you will hook the fish right in the side of the mouth. This technique is called 'lining.' Never worry if the fish will not bite, because you can always line 'em." Of course, heh, heh, heh, that explains why so many fish get hooked in the side of the mouth.

On keeping bears away: "To keep bears away, urinate around the borders of your campground. If there are a lot of bears in the area, it is advisable to go right on your sleeping bag." Yeah, surrrrrre.

On disposing of trash: "Don't worry about packing out trash. Just bury it. It will regenerate into the earth and add valuable minerals." Bears, raccoons, skunks, and other critters will dig up your trash as soon as you depart, leaving one huge mess for the next camper. Always pack out everything.

Often the advice comes without warning. That was the case after a fishing trip with a female companion, when she outcaught me two to one, the third such trip in a row. I explained this to a shopkeeper, and he nodded, then explained why.

"The male fish are able to detect the female scent on the lure, and thus become aroused into striking."

Of course! That explains everything!

Getting Revenge

I was just a lad when Foonsky pulled the old snipe-hunt trick on me. It took nearly 30 years to get revenge.

You probably know about snipe hunting. The victim is led out at night in the woods by a group, and then is left holding a bag.

"Stay perfectly still and quiet," Foonsky explained. "You don't want to scare the snipe. The rest of us will go back to camp and let the woods settle down. Then when the snipe are least expecting it, we'll form a line and charge through the forest with sticks, beating bushes and trees, and we'll flush the snipe out right to you. Be ready with the bag. When we flush the snipe out, bag it. But until we start our charge, make sure you don't move or make a sound or you will spook the snipe and ruin everything."

I sat out there in the woods with my bag for hours, waiting for the charge. I waited, waited, and waited. Nothing happened. No charge, no snipe. It wasn't until well past midnight that I figured something was wrong. When I finally returned to camp, everybody was sleeping.

Well, I tell ya, don't get mad at your pals for the tricks they pull on you. Get revenge. About 25 years later, on the last day of a camping trip, the time finally came.

"Let's break camp early," Foonsky suggested to Mr. Furnai and me. "Get up before dawn, eat breakfast, pack up, and be on the ridge to watch the sun come up. It will be a fantastic way to end the trip."

"Sounds great to me," I replied. But when Foonsky wasn't looking, I turned his alarm clock ahead three hours. So when the alarm sounded at the appointed 4:30am wake-up time, Mr. Furnai and I knew it was actually only 1:30am.

Foonsky clambered out of his sleeping bag and whistled with a grin. "Time to break camp."

"You go ahead," I answered. "I'll skip breakfast so I can get a little more sleep. At the first sign of dawn, wake me up, and I'll break camp."

"Me, too," said Mr. Furnai.

Foonsky then proceeded to make some coffee, cook a breakfast, and eat it, sitting on a log in the black darkness of the forest, waiting for the sun to come up. An hour later, with still no

---

KEEP IT WILD TIP 6: PLAN AHEAD AND PREPARE

1. Learn about the regulations and issues that apply to the area you're visiting.
2. Avoid heavy-use areas.
3. Obtain all maps and permits.
4. Bring extra garbage bags to pack out any refuse you come across.

---

sign of dawn, he checked his clock. It now read 5:30am. "Any minute now we should start seeing some light," he said.

He made another cup of coffee, packed his gear, and sat there in the middle of the night, looking up at the stars, waiting for dawn. "Anytime now," he said. He ended up sitting there all night long.

Revenge is sweet. Before a fishing trip at a lake, I took Foonsky aside and explained that the third member of the party, Jimbobo, was hard of hearing and very sensitive about it. "Don't mention it to him," I advised. "Just talk real loud."

Meanwhile, I had already told Jimbobo the same thing. "Foonsky just can't hear very good."

We had fished less than 20 minutes when Foonsky got a nibble.

"GET A BITE?" shouted Jimbobo.

"YEAH!" yelled back Foonsky, smiling. "BUT I DIDN'T HOOK HIM!"

"MAYBE NEXT TIME!" shouted Jimbobo with a friendly grin.

Well, they spent the entire day yelling at each other from the distance of a few feet. They never did figure it out. Heh, heh, heh.

That is, I thought so, until we made a trip salmon fishing. I got a strike that almost knocked my fishing rod out of the boat. When I grabbed the rod, it felt as if Moby Dick were on the other end. "At least a 25-pounder," I said. "Maybe bigger."

The fish dove, ripped off line, and then bulldogged. "It's acting like a 40-pounder," I announced, "Huge, just huge. It's going deep. That's how the big ones fight."

Some 15 minutes later, I finally got the "salmon" to the surface. It turned out to be a coffee can that Foonsky had clipped on the line with a snap swivel. By maneuvering the boat, he made the coffee can fight like a big fish.

This all started with a little old snipe hunt years ago. You never know what your pals will try next. Don't get mad. Get revenge.

CAMPING OPTIONS
Boat-In Seclusion

Most campers would never think of trading in their cars, pickup trucks, or RVs for a boat, but people who go by boat on a camping trip enjoy virtually guaranteed seclusion and top-quality outdoor experiences.

Camping with a boat is a do-it-yourself venture in living under primitive circumstances. Yet at the same time, you can bring along any luxury item you wish, from giant coolers, stoves, and lanterns to portable gasoline generators. Weight is almost never an issue.

Many outstanding boat-in campgrounds in beautiful surroundings are available. The best are on the shores of lakes accessible by canoe or skiff, and at offshore islands reached by saltwater cruisers. Several boat-in camps are detailed in this book.

If you want to take the adventure a step further and create your own boat-in camp, perhaps near a special fishing spot, this is a go-for-it deal that provides the best way possible to establish your own secret campsite. But most people who set out freelance style forget three critical items for boat-in camping: a shovel, a sunshade, and an ax. Here is why these items can make a key difference in your trip:

Shovel: Many lakes and virtually all reservoirs have steep, sloping banks. At reservoirs

Claim your own boat-in island.

subject to drawdowns, what was lake bottom in the spring can be a campsite in late summer. If you want a flat area for a tent site, the only answer is to dig one out yourself. A shovel gives you that option.

Sunshade: The flattest spots to camp along lakes often have a tendency to support only sparse tree growth. As a result, a natural shield from sun and rain is rarely available. What? Rain in the summer? Oh yeah, don't get me started. A light tarp, set up with poles and staked ropes, solves the problem.

Ax: Unless you bring your own firewood, which is necessary at some sparsely wooded reservoirs, there is no substitute for a good, sharp ax. With an ax, you can almost always find dry firewood, since the interior of an otherwise wet log will be dry. When the weather turns bad is precisely when you will most want a fire. You may need an ax to get one going.

In the search to create your own personal boat-in campsite, you will find that the flattest areas are usually the tips of peninsulas and points, while the protected back ends of coves are often steeply sloped. At reservoirs, the flattest areas are usually near the mouths of the feeder streams and the points are quite steep. On rivers, there are usually sandbars on the inside of tight bends that make for ideal campsites.

Almost all boat-in campsites developed by government agencies are free of charge, but you are on your own. Only in extremely rare cases is piped water available.

Any way you go, by canoe, skiff, or power cruiser, you end up with a one-in-a-million campsite you can call your own.

Desert Outings

It was a cold, snowy day in Missouri when 10-year-old Rusty Ballinger started dreaming about the vast deserts of the West.

"My dad was reading aloud from a Zane Grey book called *Riders of the Purple Sage*," Ballinger said. "He would get animated when he got to the passages about the desert. It wasn't long before I started to have the same feelings."

That was in 1947. Since then Ballinger has spent a good part of his life exploring the West, camping along the way. "The deserts are the best part. There's something about the uniqueness of each little area you see," Ballinger said.

"You're constantly surprised. Just the time of day and the way the sun casts a different color. It's like the lady you care about. One time she smiles, the next time she's pensive. The desert is like that. If you love nature, you can love the desert. After a while, you can't help but love it."

A desert adventure is not just an antidote for a case of cabin fever in the winter. Whether you go by RV, pickup truck, car, or on foot, it provides its own special qualities.

If you go camping in the desert, your approach has to be as unique as the setting. For starters, don't plan on any campfires, but bring a camp stove instead. And unlike in the mountains, do not camp near a water hole. That's because an animal, such as a badger, coyote, or desert bighorn, might be desperate for water, and if you set up camp in the animal's way, you may be forcing a confrontation.

In some areas, there is a danger of flash floods. An intense rain can fall in one area, collect in a pool, then suddenly burst through a narrow canyon. If you are in its path, you could be injured or drowned. The lesson? Never camp in a gully.

"Some people might wonder 'What good is this place?'" Ballinger said. "The answer is that it is good for looking at. It is one of the world's unique places."

CAMP ETHICS AND POLITICS

The perfect place to set up a base camp turned out to be not so perfect. In fact, according to Doug Williams of California, it did not even exist.

Williams and his son, James, had driven deep into Angeles National Forest, prepared to set up camp and then explore the surrounding area on foot. But when they reached their destination, no campground existed.

"I wanted a primitive camp in a national forest where I could teach my son some basics," said the senior Williams. "But when we got there, there wasn't much left of the camp, and it had been closed. It was obvious that the area had been vandalized."

It turned out not to be an isolated incident. A lack of outdoor ethics practiced by a few people using the unsupervised campgrounds available on national forestland has caused the U.S. Forest Service to close a few of them and make extensive repairs to others.

"There have been sites closed, especially in Angeles and San Bernardino National Forests in Southern California," said David Flohr, regional campground coordinator for the U.S. Forest Service. "It's an urban type of thing, affecting forests near urban areas, and not just Los Angeles. They get a lot of urban users and they bring with them a lot of the same ethics they have in the city. They get drinking and they're not afraid to do things. They vandalize and run. Of course, it is a public facility, so they think nobody is getting hurt."

But somebody is getting hurt, starting with the next person who wants to use the campground. And if the ranger district budget doesn't have enough money to pay for repairs, the campground is then closed for the next arrivals. Just ask Doug and James Williams.

In an era of considerable fiscal restraint for the U.S. Forest Service, vandalized campgrounds could face closure instead of repair. Williams had just a taste of it, but Flohr, as camping coordinator, gets a steady diet.

"It starts with behavior," Flohr said. "General rowdiness, drinking, partying, and then vandalism. It goes all the way from the felt-tip pen things (graffiti) to total destruction, blowing up toilet buildings with dynamite. I have seen toilets destroyed totally with shotguns. They burn up tables, burn barriers. They'll burn up signs for firewood, even the shingles right off the roofs of the bathrooms. They'll shoot anything, garbage cans, signs. It can get a little hairy. A favorite is to remove the stool out of a toilet building. We've had people fall in the open hole."

The National Park Service had similar problems some years back, especially with rampant littering. Park Director Bill Mott responded by creating an interpretive program that attempts to teach visitors the wise use of natural areas,

KEEP IT WILD TIP 7: RESPECT OTHER USERS

1. Horseback riders have priority over hikers. Step to the downhill side of the trail and talk softly when encountering horseback riders.
2. Hikers and horseback riders have priority over mountain bikers. When mountain bikers encounter other users even on wide trails, they should pass at an extremely slow speed. On very narrow trails, they should dismount and get off to the side so hikers or horseback riders can pass without having their trip disrupted.
3. Mountain bikes aren't permitted on most single-track trails and are expressly prohibited in designated wilderness areas and all sections of the Pacific Crest Trail. Mountain bikers breaking these rules should be confronted and told to dismount and walk their bikes until they reach a legal area.
4. It's illegal for horseback riders to break off branches that may be in the path of wilderness trails.
5. Horseback riders on overnight trips are prohibited from camping in many areas and are usually required to keep stock animals in specific areas where they can do no damage to the landscape.

and to have all park workers set examples by picking up litter and reminding others to do the same.

The U.S. Forest Service has responded with a similar program, making brochures available that detail the wise use of national forests. The four most popular brochures are titled: "Rules for Visitors to the National Forest," "Recreation in the National Forests," "Is the Water Safe?" and "Backcountry Safety Tips." These include details on campfires, drinking water from lakes or streams, hypothermia, safety, and outdoor ethics.

Flohr said even experienced campers sometimes cross over the ethics line unintentionally. The most common example, he said, is when campers toss garbage into the outhouse toilet, rather than packing it out in a plastic garbage bag.

"They throw it in the vault toilet bowls, which just fills them up," Flohr said. "That creates an extremely high cost to pump it. You know why? Because some poor guy has to pick that stuff out piece by piece. It can't be pumped."

At most backcountry sites, the U.S. Forest Service has implemented a program called "Pack it in, pack it out," even posting signs that remind all visitors to do so. But a lot of people don't do it, and others may even uproot the signs and burn them for firewood.

On a trip to a secluded lake near Carson Pass in the Sierra Nevada, I arrived at a small, little-known camp where the picnic table had been spray painted and garbage had been strewn about. A pristine place, the true temple of God, had been defiled.

Getting Along with Fellow Campers

The most important thing about a camping, fishing, or hunting trip is not where you go, how many fish you catch, or how many shots you fire. It often has little to do with how beautiful the view is, how easily the campfire lights, or how sunny the days are.

Oh yeah? Then what is the most important factor? The answer: The people you are with. It is that simple.

Who would you rather camp with? Your enemy at work or your dream mate in a good mood? Heh, heh. You get the idea. A camping trip is a fairly close-knit experience, and you can make lifetime friends or lifelong enemies in the process. That is why your choice of companions is so important. Your own behavior is equally consequential.

Yet most people spend more time putting

together their camping gear than considering why they enjoy or hate the company of their chosen companions. Here are 10 rules of behavior for good camping mates:

1. **No whining:** Nothing is more irritating than being around a whiner. It goes right to the heart of adventure, since often the only difference between a hardship and an escapade is simply whether or not an individual has the spirit for it. The people who do can turn a rugged day in the outdoors into a cherished memory. Those who don't can ruin it with their incessant sniveling.

2. **Activities must be agreed upon:** Always have a meeting of the minds with your companions over the general game plan. Then everybody will possess an equal stake in the outcome of the trip. This is absolutely critical. Otherwise they will feel like merely an addendum to your trip, not an equal participant, and a whiner will be born (see number one).

3. **Nobody's in charge:** It is impossible to be genuine friends if one person is always telling another what to do, especially if the orders involve simple camp tasks. You need to share the space on the same emotional plane, and the only way to do that is to have a semblance of equality, regardless of differences in experience. Just try ordering your mate around at home for a few days. You'll quickly see the results, and they aren't pretty.

4. **Equal chances at the fun stuff:** It's fun to build the fire, fun to get the first cast at the best fishing spot, and fun to hoist the bagged food for a bear-proof food hang. It is not fun to clean the dishes, collect firewood, or cook every night. So obviously, there must be an equal distribution of the fun stuff and the not-fun stuff, and everybody on the trip must get a shot at the good and the bad.

5. **No heroes:** No awards are bestowed for achievement in the outdoors, yet some guys treat mountain peaks, big fish, and big game as if they are prizes in a trophy competition. Actually, nobody cares how wonderful you are, which is always a surprise to trophy chasers.

What people care about is the heart of the adventure, the gut-level stuff.

6. **Agree on a wake-up time:** It is a good idea to agree on a general wake-up time before closing your eyes for the night, and that goes regardless of whether you want to sleep in late or get up at dawn. Then you can proceed on course regardless of what time you crawl out of your sleeping bag in the morning, without the risk of whining (see number one).

7. **Think of the other guy:** Be self-aware instead of self-absorbed. A good test is to count the number of times you say, "What do you think?" A lot of potential problems can be solved quickly by actually listening to the answer.

8. **Solo responsibilities:** There are a number of essential camp duties on all trips, and while they should be shared equally, most should be completed solo. That means that when it is time for you to cook, you don't have to worry about me changing the recipe on you. It means that when it is my turn to make the fire, you keep your mitts out of it.

9. **Don't let money get in the way:** Of course everybody should share equally in trip expenses, such as the cost of food, and it should be split up before you head out yonder. Don't let somebody pay extra, because that person will likely try to control the trip. Conversely, don't let somebody weasel out of paying a fair share.

10. **Accordance on the food plan:** Always have complete agreement on what you plan to eat each day. Don't figure that just because you like Steamboat's Sludge, everybody else will, too, especially youngsters. Always, always, always check for food allergies, such as nuts, onions, or cheese, and make sure each person brings his or her own personal coffee brand. Some people drink only decaffeinated; others might gag on anything but Burma monkey beans.

Obviously, it is difficult to find companions who will agree on all of these elements. This is why many campers say that the best camping buddies they'll ever have are their mates, who know all about them and like them anyway.

OUTDOORS WITH KIDS

How do you get a youngster excited about the outdoors? How do you compete with the television and remote control? How do you prove to a kid that success comes from persistence, spirit, and logic, which the outdoors teaches, and not from pushing buttons?

The answer is in the Ten Camping Commandments for Kids. These are lessons that will get youngsters excited about the outdoors and that will make sure adults help the process along, not kill it. I've put this list together with the help of my own kids, Jeremy and Kris, and their mother, Stephani. Some of the commandments are obvious, some are not, but all are important:

1. Take children to places where there is a guarantee of action. A good example is camping in a park where large numbers of wildlife can be viewed, such as squirrels, chipmunks, deer, and even bears. Other good choices include fishing at a small pond loaded with bluegill or hunting in a spot where a kid can shoot a .22 at pinecones all day. Boys and girls want action, not solitude.

2. Enthusiasm is contagious. If you aren't excited about an adventure, you can't expect a child to be. Show a genuine zest for life in the outdoors, and point out everything as if it is the first time you have ever seen it.

3. Always, always, always be seated when talking to someone small. This allows the adult and child to be on the same level. That is why fishing in a small boat is perfect for adults and kids. Nothing is worse for youngsters than having a big person look down at them and give them orders. What fun is that?

4. Always *show* how to do something, whether it is gathering sticks for a campfire, cleaning a trout, or tying a knot. Never tell—always show. A button usually clicks to "off" when a kid is lectured. But kids can learn behavior patterns and outdoor skills by watching adults, even when the adults are not aware they are being watched.

5. Let kids be kids. Let the adventure happen, rather than trying to force it within some preconceived plan. If they get sidetracked watching pollywogs, chasing butterflies, or sneaking up on chipmunks, let them be. A youngster can have more fun turning over rocks and looking

at different kinds of bugs than sitting in one spot, waiting for a fish to bite.

6. Expect short attention spans. Instead of getting frustrated about it, use it to your advantage. How? By bringing along a bag of candy and snacks. Where there is a lull in the camp activity, out comes the bag. Don't let them know what goodies await, so each one becomes a surprise.

7. Make absolutely certain the child's sleeping bag is clean, dry, and warm. Nothing is worse than discomfort when trying to sleep, but a refreshing sleep makes for a positive attitude the next day. In addition, kids can become quite scared of animals at night. A parent should not wait for any signs of this, but always play the part of the outdoor guardian, the one who will take care of everything.

8. Kids quickly relate to outdoor ethics. They will enjoy eating everything they kill, building a safe campfire, and picking up all their litter, and they will develop a sense of pride that goes with it. A good idea is to bring extra plastic garbage bags to pick up any trash you come across. Kids long remember when they do something right that somebody else has done wrong.

9. If you want youngsters hooked on the outdoors for life, take a close-up photograph of them holding up fish they have caught, blowing on the campfire, or completing other camp tasks. Young children can forget how much fun they had, but they never forget if they have a picture of it.

10. The least important word you can ever say to a kid is "I." Keep track of how often you are saying "Thank you" and "What do you think?" If you don't say them very often, you'll lose out. Finally, the most important words of all are: "I am proud of you."

PREDICTING WEATHER

Foonsky climbed out of his sleeping bag, glanced at the nearby meadow, and scowled hard.

"It doesn't look good," he said. "Doesn't look good at all."

I looked at my adventure companion of 20 years, noting his discontent. Then I looked at the meadow and immediately understood why: *"When the grass is dry at morning light, look for rain before the night."*

"How bad you figure?" I asked him.

"We'll know soon enough, I reckon," Foonsky answered. *"Short notice, soon to pass. Long notice, long it will last."*

When you are out in the wild, spending your days fishing and your nights camping, you learn to rely on yourself to predict the weather. It can make or break you. If a storm hits the unprepared, it can quash the trip and possibly endanger the participants. But if you are ready, a potential hardship can be an adventure.

You can't rely on TV weather forecasters, people who don't even know that when all the cows on a hill are facing north, it will rain that night for sure. God forbid if the cows are all sitting. But what do you expect from TV?

Foonsky made a campfire, started boiling some water for coffee and soup, and we started to plan the day. In the process, I noticed the smoke of the campfire: It was sluggish, drifting and hovering.

"You notice the smoke?" I asked, chewing on a piece of homemade jerky.

"Not good," Foonsky said. "Not good." He knew that sluggish, hovering smoke indicates rain.

"You'd think we'd have been smart enough to know last night that this was coming," Foonsky said. "Did you take a look at the moon or the clouds?"

"I didn't look at either," I answered. "Too busy eating the trout we caught." You see, if the moon is clear and white, the weather will be good the next day. But if there is a ring around the moon, the number of stars you can count inside the ring equals the number of days until the next rain. As for clouds, the high, thin ones—called cirrus—indicate a change in the weather.

We were quiet for a while, planning our strategy, but as we did so, some terrible things happened: A chipmunk scampered past with his tail high, a small flock of geese flew by very low, and a little sparrow perched on a tree limb quite close to the trunk.

"We're in for trouble," I told Foonsky.

"I know, I know," he answered. "I saw 'em, too. And come to think of it, no crickets were chirping last night either."

"Damn, that's right!"

These are all signs of an approaching storm. Foonsky pointed at the smoke of the campfire and shook his head as if he had just been condemned. Sure enough, now the smoke was blowing toward the north, a sign of a south wind. *"When the wind is from the south, the rain is in its mouth."*

"We'd best stay hunkered down until it passes," Foonsky said.

I nodded. "Let's gather as much firewood now as we can, get our gear covered up, then plan our meals."

"Then we'll get a poker game going."

As we accomplished these camp tasks, the sky clouded up, then darkened. Within an hour, we had gathered enough firewood to make a large pile, enough wood to keep a fire going no matter how hard it rained. The day's meals had been separated out of the food bag so it wouldn't have to be retrieved during the storm. We buttoned two ponchos together, staked two of the corners with ropes to the ground, and tied the other two with ropes to different tree limbs to create a slanted roof/shelter.

As the first raindrop fell with that magic sound on our poncho roof, Foonsky was just starting to shuffle the cards.

"Cut for deal," he said.

Just as I did so, it started to rain a bit harder. I pulled out another piece of beef jerky and started chewing on it. It was just another day in paradise.

Weather lore can be valuable. Here is the list I have compiled over the years:

When the grass is dry at morning light,
Look for rain before the night.
Short notice, soon to pass.
Long notice, long it will last.

When the wind is from the east,
'Tis fit for neither man nor beast.
When the wind is from the south,
The rain is in its mouth.
When the wind is from the west,
Then it is the very best.

Red sky at night, sailors' delight.
Red sky in the morning, sailors take warning.

When all the cows are pointed north,
Within a day rain will come forth.

Onion skins very thin, mild winter coming in.
Onion skins very tough, winter's going to be very rough.

When your boots make the squeak of snow,
Then very cold temperatures will surely show.

If a goose flies high, fair weather ahead.
If a goose flies low, foul weather will come instead.

Small signs provided by nature and wildlife can also be translated to provide a variety of weather information:

A thick coat on a woolly caterpillar means a big, early snow is coming.

Chipmunks will run with their tails up before a rain.

Bees always stay near their hives before a rainstorm.

When the birds are perched on large limbs near tree trunks, an intense but short storm will arrive.

On the coast, if groups of seabirds are flying a mile inland, look for major winds.

If crickets are chirping very loudly during the evening, the next day will be clear and warm.

If the smoke of a campfire at night rises in a thin spiral, good weather is assured for the next day.

If the smoke of a campfire at night is sluggish, drifting and hovering, it will rain the next day.

CAMPING GEAR CHECKLIST

COOKING GEAR

- Camp stove and fuel
- Dish soap and scrubber
- Fire-starter cubes
- Heavy-duty paper plates
- Ice chest and drinks
- Itemized food, separated by groups
- Knife, fork, cup
- Large, heavy-duty garbage bags
- Matches stored in resealable (such as Ziploc) bags
- One lighter for each camper
- Paper towels
- Plastic spatula and stir spoon
- Pot grabber or pot holder
- Salt, pepper, spices
- Two pots and no-stick pan
- Water jug or lightweight plastic "cube"

Optional Cooking Gear

- Aluminum foil
- Ax or hatchet
- Barbecue tongs
- Can opener
- Candles
- Dustpan
- Grill or hibachi
- Plastic clothespins
- Tablecloth
- Whisk broom
- Wood or charcoal for barbecue

CLOTHING

- Cotton/canvas pants
- Gore-Tex parka or jacket
- Gore-Tex rain pants
- Lightweight, breathable shirt
- Lightweight fleece jacket
- Medium-weight fleece vest
- Polypropylene underwear
- Rain jacket and pants, or poncho
- Sunglasses
- Waterproofed, oilskin wide-brimmed hat

Optional Clothing

- Gloves
- Shorts
- Ski cap

HIKING GEAR

- Backpack or daypack
- Hiking boots
- Fresh bootlaces
- Innersole or foot cushion (for expeditions)
- Moleskin and medical tape
- SmartWool (or equivalent) socks
- Water-purification system

Optional Hiking Gear

- Backup lightweight shoes or moccasins
- Gaiters
- Water-repellent boot treatment

SLEEPING GEAR

- Ground tarp
- Sleeping bag
- Tent or bivy bag
- Therm-a-Rest pad

Optional Sleeping Gear

- Air bed
- Cot

- Catalytic heater
- Foam pad for truck bed
- Mosquito netting
- Mr. Heater and propane tank (for use in pickup truck camper shell)
- Pillow (even in wilderness)
- RV windshield light screen
- Seam Lock for tent stitching

FIRST AID

- Ace bandage
- After-Bite for mosquito bites (before you scratch them)
- Aspirin
- Biodegradable soap
- Caladryl for poison oak
- Campho-Phenique gel for bites (after you scratch them)
- Mosquito repellent
- Lip balm
- Medical tape to affix pads
- Neosporin for cuts
- Roller gauze
- Sterile gauze pads
- Sunscreen
- Tweezers

Optional First Aid

- Athletic tape for sprained ankle
- Cell phone or coins for phone calls
- Extra set of matches
- Mirror for signaling
- Thermometer

RECREATION GEAR

- All required permits and licenses
- Fishing reel with fresh line
- Fishing rod

- Knife
- Leatherman tool or needle-nose pliers
- Small tackle box with flies, floats, hooks, lures, snap swivels, and splitshot

Optional Recreation Gear

- Backpacking cribbage board
- Deck of cards
- Folding chairs
- Guidebooks
- Hammock
- Mountain bike
- Reading material

OTHER NECESSITIES

- Duct tape
- Extra plastic garbage bags
- Flashlight and batteries
- Lantern and fuel
- Maps
- Nylon rope for food hang
- Spade for cat hole
- Toilet paper
- Toothbrush and toothpaste
- Towelettes
- Wristwatch

OTHER OPTIONAL ITEMS

- Altimeter
- Assorted bungee cords
- Binoculars
- Camera with fresh battery and digital card or film
- Compass
- Feminine hygiene products
- GPS unit
- Handkerchief
- Notebook and pen

If there is a ring around the moon, count the number of stars inside the ring, and that is how many days until the next rain.

If the moon is clear and white, the weather will be good the next day.

High, thin clouds, or cirrus, indicate a change in the weather.

Oval-shaped lenticular clouds indicate high winds.

Two levels of clouds moving in different directions indicate changing weather soon.

Huge, dark, billowing clouds, called cumulonimbus, suddenly forming on warm afternoons in the mountains mean that a short but intense thunderstorm with lightning can be expected.

When squirrels are busy gathering food for extended periods, it means good weather is ahead in the short term, but a hard winter is ahead in the long term.

And God forbid if all the cows are sitting down....

THE OLYMPIC PENINSULA AND WASHINGTON COAST

© NATALIA BRATSLAVSKY/123RF

Vast, diverse, and beautiful, the Olympic Peninsula is like no other landscape. Water borders the region on three sides: the Pacific Ocean to the west, the Strait of Juan de Fuca to the north, and the inlets of Hood Canal to the east. At its center are Olympic National Park and Mount Olympus, with rainforests on its slopes feeding rivers and lakes that make up the most dynamic river complex in America. Almost every one of these rivers provides campsites, often within walking distance of prime steelhead fishing spots. A series of stellar campgrounds ring the perimeter foothills of Mount Olympus, both in Olympic National Park and at the state parks and areas managed by the Department of Natural Resources. Your campsite can be your launch pad for adventure—just be sure to bring your rain gear.

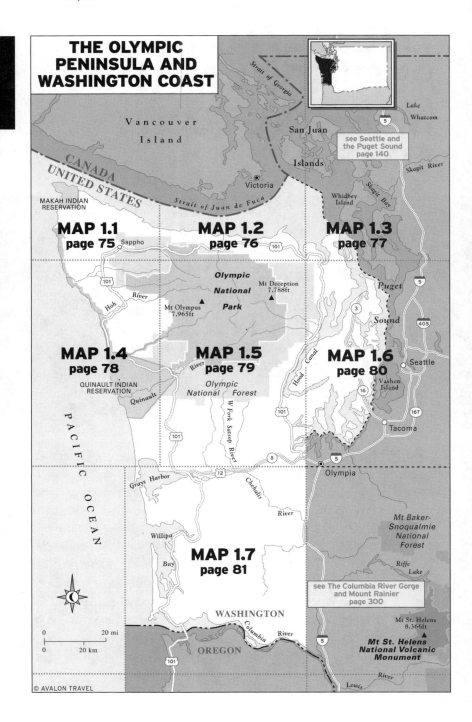

THE OLYMPIC PENINSULA AND WASHINGTON COAST

Vancouver Island

Strait of Georgia

San Juan Islands

see Seattle and the Puget Sound page 140

Lake Whatcom

Skagit River

Victoria

Strait of Juan de Fuca

Whidbey Island

Skagit Bay

CANADA
UNITED STATES

MAKAH INDIAN RESERVATION

MAP 1.1
page 75   Sappho

MAP 1.2
page 76

MAP 1.3
page 77

Olympic National Park

Mt Deception 7,788ft

Puget

Mt Olympus 7,965ft

Sound

Hoh River

Seattle

MAP 1.4
page 78

QUINAULT INDIAN RESERVATION

Quinault

MAP 1.5
page 79

Olympic National Forest

River

W Fork Satsop River

Hood Canal

MAP 1.6
page 80

Vashon Island

Tacoma

PACIFIC OCEAN

Grays Harbor

Chehalis

River

Olympia

Mt Baker-Snoqualmie National Forest

Willapa

Bay

MAP 1.7
page 81

Riffe Lake

see The Columbia River Gorge and Mount Rainier page 300

WASHINGTON

Columbia   River

Mt St. Helens 8,366ft

Mt St. Helens National Volcanic Monument

0   20 mi
0   20 km

OREGON

River

Lewis

© AVALON TRAVEL

Map 1.1

**Sites 1-7
Pages 82-84**

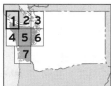

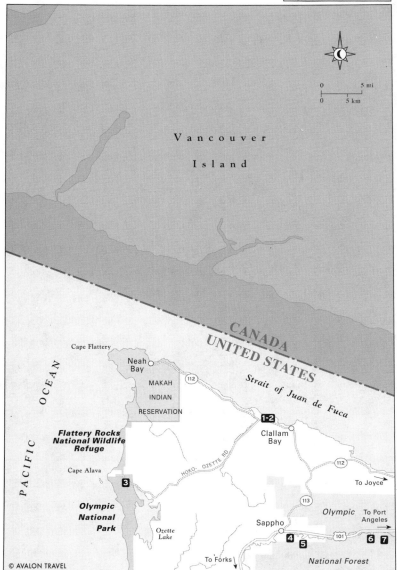

Vancouver
Island

0   5 mi
0   5 km

CANADA
UNITED STATES

Cape Flattery

Neah
Bay

MAKAH

INDIAN

RESERVATION

Strait of Juan de Fuca

1-2

Clallam
Bay

*Flattery Rocks
National Wildlife
Refuge*

HOKO-OZETTE RD

Cape Alava

PACIFIC OCEAN

3

*Olympic
National
Park*

Ozette
Lake

Sappho

4 **5**

To Forks

To Joyce

Olympic   To Port
Angeles

6 **7**

101

National Forest

© AVALON TRAVEL

Map 1.2

Sites 8-20
Pages 85-90

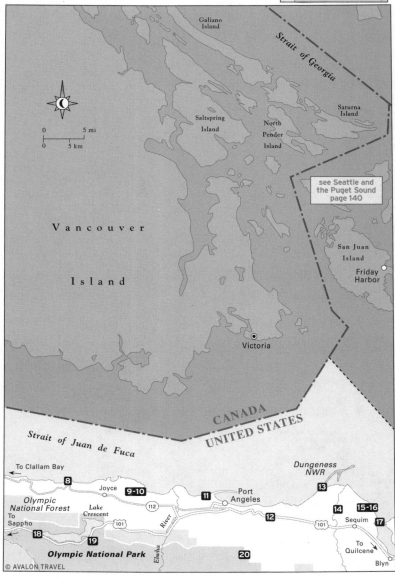

Map 1.3

Sites 21-25
Pages 91-93

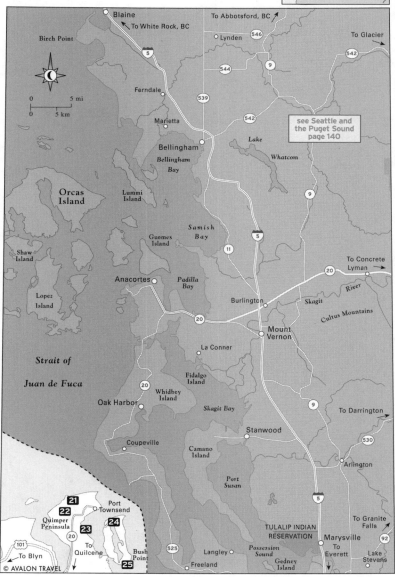

1.2

1.6

Blaine

To White Rock, BC

To Abbotsford, BC

Birch Point

Lynden   546

To Glacier

5

544

9

542

Ferndale

539

Marietta

542

Lake

see Seattle and
the Puget Sound
page 140

Bellingham

*Bellingham
Bay*

Whatcom

*Orcas
Island*

Lummi
Island

9

*Samish
Bay*

*Shaw
Island*

Guemes
Island

5

11

To Concrete
Lyman

20

*Lopez
Island*

Anacortes

*Padilla
Bay*

River

Burlington   Skagit

Cultus Mountains

20

Mount
Vernon

La Conner

9

Strait of

Juan de Fuca

*Fidalgo
Island*

To Darrington

20

Whidbey
Island

Oak Harbor

Skagit Bay

Stanwood

530

Coupeville

Camano
Island

Arlington

*Port
Susan*

5

To Granite
Falls

21

Port
Townsend

22

24

TULALIP INDIAN
RESERVATION   Marysville

92

*Quimper
Peninsula*

23

101

20

To
Quilcene

Bush
Point

525

Langley

*Possession
Sound*

To
Everett

Lake
Stevens

To Blyn

© AVALON TRAVEL

25

Freeland

*Gedney
Island*

Map 1.4

Sites 26-43
Pages 93-100

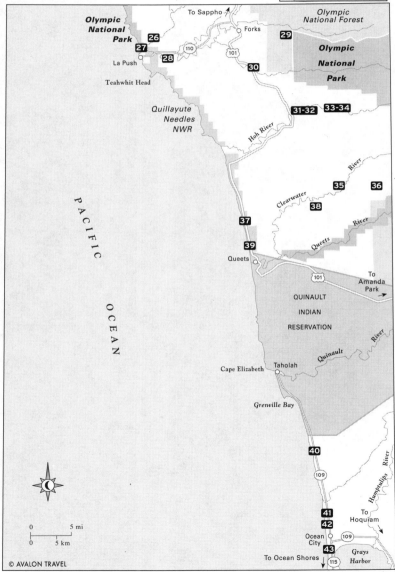

Map 1.5

Sites 44-72
Pages 101-114

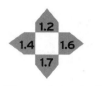

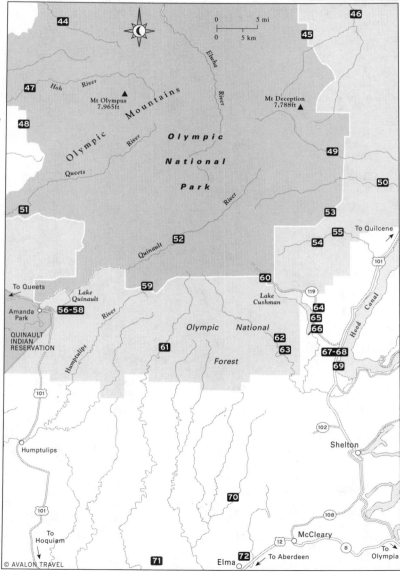

Map 1.6

**Sites 73-89
Pages 115-124**

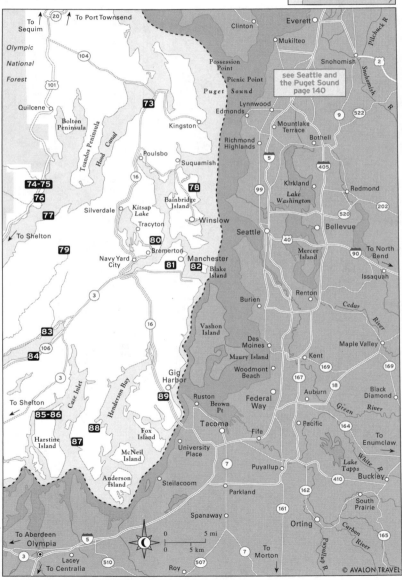

© AVALON TRAVEL

Map 1.7

Sites 90-117
Pages 124-137

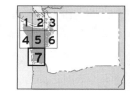

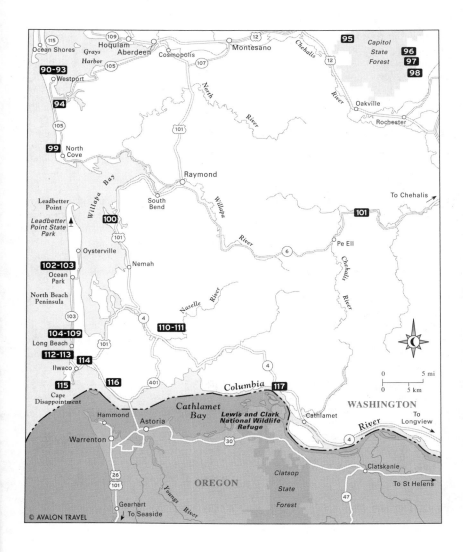

1 VAN RIPER'S RESORT

Scenic rating: 7

on Clallam Bay in Sekiu

Map 1.1, page 75

Part of this campground hugs the waterfront and the other part sits on a hill overlooking the Strait of Juan de Fuca. Most sites are graveled, many with views of the strait. Other sites are grassy, without views. Note that some of the campsites are rented for the entire summer season. Hiking, fishing, and boating are among the options here, with salmon fishing being the principal draw. The beaches in the area, a mixture of sand and gravel, provide diligent rock hounds with agates and fossils.

Campsites, facilities: There are 100 sites with full or partial hookups (30 amps) for tents or RVs of any length. Some sites are pull-through. A mobile home, a house, and 12 motel rooms are also available. Picnic tables are provided; fire rings and cable TV are available at some sites. Restrooms with flush toilets and showers, drinking water, a dump station, firewood, and ice are available. A store, café, and coin laundry are located within one mile. Boat docks, launching facilities, and rentals are available. Leashed pets are permitted; no pets are allowed in cabins or other buildings.

Reservations, fees: Reservations are not accepted for campsites. Sites are $35 per night. Open April-September. Some credit cards are accepted.

Directions: From Port Angeles, take U.S. 101 west and drive 41 miles to Sappho Junction and Highway 113. Continue north on Highway 113 for nine miles to a fork with Highway 112. Take Highway 112 for two miles to Sekiu and Front Street. Turn right and drive 0.25 mile to the resort on the right.

Contact: Van Riper's Resort, 280 Front Street, Sekiu, 360/963-2334, www.vanripersresort.com.

2 MASON'S OLSON RESORT

Scenic rating: 5

in Sekiu

Map 1.1, page 75

Olson's Resort is large with full services, and the nearby marina is salmon-fishing headquarters. In fact, the resort caters to anglers, offering all-day salmon-fishing trips and boat moorage. Chartered trips can be arranged by reservation. A tackle shop, cabins, houses, and a motel are also available. Other recreation options include hiking, boating, and beachcombing for agates and fossils.

Campsites, facilities: There are 55 sites for tents or RVs of any length (no hookups), 45 sites for tents or RVs of any length (full hookups), 7 camping cabins, 6 motel rooms, and 7 houses available (3 are waterfront). Picnic tables are provided, and fire rings are available at most sites. Restrooms with flush toilets and showers, drinking water, a dump station, coin laundry, convenience store, bait and tackle, and ice are available. Boat docks, launching facilities, boat rentals, bait, tackle, fish-cleaning station, and gear storage are also available on-site. A restaurant is within walking distance. Some facilities are wheelchair accessible. Leashed pets are allowed, with certain restrictions.

Reservations, fees: Reservations are required for the motel and cabins, but are not accepted for campsites. RV sites are $40 per night, tent sites are $30 per night. Boat launch is $15 (daily moorage is $1 per foot). Some credit cards are accepted. Open year-round.

Directions: From Port Angeles, drive 41 miles west on U.S. 101 to Sappho Junction and Highway 113. Continue north on Highway 113 for nine miles to a fork with Highway 112. Take Highway 112 for two miles to Sekiu and Front Street. Turn right and drive one block to the resort on the right.

Contact: Mason's Olson Resort, 444 Front Street, Sekiu, 360/963-2311.

3 OZETTE

Scenic rating: 6

on Lake Ozette in Olympic National Park

Map 1.1, page 75

Many people visit this site located on the shore of Lake Ozette just a few miles from the Pacific Ocean. Set close to a trailhead road and ranger station, with multiple trailheads nearby, this camp is a favorite for both hikers and boaters and is one of the first to fill in the park.

Campsites, facilities: There are 15 sites for tents or RVs up to 21 feet long. Picnic tables and fire grills are provided. Pit toilets are available. There is no drinking water and garbage must be packed out. Leashed pets are permitted.

Reservations, fees: Reservations are not accepted. Sites are $20 per night, plus a $25 national park entrance fee per vehicle. Open year-round, weather permitting.

Directions: From Port Angeles, drive west on U.S. 101 to the junction with Highway 112. Bear right on Highway 112 and drive to Hoko-Ozette Road. Turn left and drive 21 miles to the ranger station. The camp parking lot is across from the ranger station on the northwest corner of Lake Ozette.

Contact: Olympic National Park, 360/565-3130, www.nps.gov/olym.

4 BEAR CREEK MOTEL AND RV PARK

Scenic rating: 7

on Bear Creek

Map 1.1, page 75

This quiet little spot is set where Bear Creek empties into the Sol Duc River. It's private and developed, with a choice of sunny or shaded sites in a wooded setting. There are many recreation options in the area, including fishing, hunting, and nature and hiking trails leading to the ocean. Sol Duc Hot Springs is 25 miles

north and well worth the trip. A restaurant next to the camp serves family-style meals.

Campsites, facilities: There are 12 sites for RVs of any length (full hookups); all sites are pull-through. There is also an area for tent camping and a motel on the premises. Picnic tables and fire rings are provided. Restrooms with flush toilets and showers, drinking water, a dump station, a café, and firewood are available. Boat-launching facilities are located within 0.5 mile. Some facilities are wheelchair accessible. Leashed pets are permitted.

Reservations, fees: Reservations are not accepted. RV sites are $25 per night, tent sites are $15 per night. Some credit cards are accepted. Open year-round.

Directions: From Aberdeen, drive north on U.S. 101 to Forks. Continue past Forks for 15 miles to Milepost 205 (just past Sappho) to the park on the right at 205860 Highway 101 West.

Contact: Bear Creek Motel and RV Park, Milepost 206, Beaver, 360/327-3660, www.hungrybearcafemotel.com.

5 BEAR CREEK

Scenic rating: 8

on the Sol Duc River

Map 1.1, page 75   **BEST (**

Fishing for salmon and hiking along the Sol Duc River make this a good launch point for recreation. There are also good opportunities for wildlife-viewing and photography, including a wheelchair-accessible viewing platform overlooking the Sol Duc River. This camp is also popular in the fall with hunters.

Campsites, facilities: There are 16 sites for tents. Vault toilets and fire pits are available. There is no drinking water and garbage must be packed out. Some facilities are wheelchair accessible. Leashed pets are permitted.

Reservations, fees: Reservations are not accepted. There is no fee for camping, but a Discover Pass is required. Open year-round.

Directions: From Olympia on I-5, take Exit 104

and drive north on U.S. 101 to the Aberdeen/ Highway 8 exit. Turn west on Highway 8 and drive 36 miles to Aberdeen. Continue through Aberdeen four miles to U.S. 101 and turn north and drive to Forks. Continue past Forks for 15 miles to Milepost 206 (two miles past Sappho) to the campground on the right.

Contact: Department of Natural Resources, Olympic Region, 360/374-6131, www.dnr. wa.gov.

6 KLAHOWYA

Scenic rating: 9

on the Sol Duc River in Olympic National Forest

Map 1.1, page 75

Klahowya features great views of Lake Crescent and Mount Olympus. It's a good choice if you don't want to venture far from U.S. 101 yet want to retain the feel of being in Olympic National Forest. Set along the Sol Duc River, this 32-acre camp is pretty and wooded, with hiking trails in the area. A favorite, Kloshe Nanitch Trail, is across the river and leads up to a lookout on Snider Ridge overlooking Sol Duc Valley. Pioneer's Path Trail, an easy, wheelchair-accessible, 0.3-mile loop with interpretive signs starts in the camp. Fishing for salmon and steelhead, in season, can be good about 0.25 mile downstream from camp; always check regulations. This camp gets medium use, but can fill up on weekends.

Campsites, facilities: There are 55 sites for tents or RVs up to 30 feet long and two hike-in tent sites requiring a 500-foot walk. Picnic tables and fire grills are provided. Drinking water, garbage bins, and vault and flush toilets are available. An amphitheater with summer interpretive programs is also available. A boat ramp is nearby. Some facilities are wheelchair accessible. Leashed pets are permitted.

Reservations, fees: Reservations are not accepted. Sites are $17 per night, $5 per night per additional vehicle. Open May-late October, weather permitting.

Directions: From U.S. 101 in Port Angeles, drive west for about 33 miles (10 miles west of Lake Crescent) to the campground on the right side of the road, close to Milepost 212. (Coming from the other direction on U.S. 101, drive eight miles east of Sappho to the campground.)

Contact: Olympic National Forest, Pacific Ranger District, 360/374-6522, www.fs.usda. gov.

7 LITTLETON HORSE CAMP

Scenic rating: 8

on Littleton Creek near Mount Muller Trailhead in Olympic National Forest

Map 1.1, page 75

This new campground allows equestrian campers to explore more than 25 miles of trails including Mount Muller, Olympic Discovery, and Snider Ridge Trails. The trail from camp heads through some lush vine maple tunnel trails and continues along panoramic ridge tops. Some sites are adjacent to stock corrals.

Campsites, facilities: There are six sites for tents or RVs and stock trailers, and five walk-in tent sites. Picnic tables and fire grills are provided. Vault toilets and garbage bins are available. There is no drinking water, but stock water is available May-October. Some facilities are wheelchair accessible. Leashed pets are permitted.

Reservations, fees: Reservations are not accepted. Sites are $10 per night, $5 per night per additional vehicle. Open year-round, weather permitting.

Directions: Littleton Horse Camp is located approximately 24 miles east of Forks and 31 miles west of Port Angeles. From U.S. 101, follow Forest Road 3071 (near Milepost 216) to the campground.

Contact: Olympic National Forest, Pacific Ranger District, 360/374-6522, www.fs.usda. gov.

8 LYRE RIVER

Scenic rating: 7

on the Lyre River

Map 1.2, page 76

This prime spot is one of the rare free campgrounds on the Olympic Peninsula. Although quite primitive, it does offer drinking water and an even more precious commodity in these parts: privacy. The camp is set along the Lyre River, about 0.5 mile from where it enters the Strait of Juan de Fuca. A popular camp for anglers, Lyre River offers good salmon fishing during fish migrations; always check fishing regulations. A wheelchair-accessible fishing pier is available.

Campsites, facilities: There are 11 primitive sites for tents only. Picnic tables, fire grills, and tent pads are provided. Vault toilets and drinking water are available. Garbage must be packed out. A roofed group shelter is available. Some facilities are wheelchair accessible. Leashed pets are permitted.

Reservations, fees: Reservations are not accepted. There is no fee for camping, but a Discover Pass is required. Open year-round, with limited services in winter.

Directions: From U.S. 101 in Port Angeles, drive north five miles to a fork with Highway 112. Turn right (west) on Highway 112 and drive about 15 miles to Milepost 46. Look to the right for a paved road between Mileposts 46 and 47, then turn right (north) and drive 0.4 mile to the camp entrance road on the left.

Contact: Department of Natural Resources, Olympic Region, 360/374-6131, www.dnr. wa.gov.

9 CRESCENT BEACH RV PARK

Scenic rating: 6

in Port Angeles on the Strait of Juan de Fuca

Map 1.2, page 76

Set on a half-mile stretch of sandy beach, this campground makes a perfect weekend spot. Popular activities include swimming, fishing, surfing, sea kayaking, and beachcombing. It borders Salt Creek Recreation Area, with direct access available. Numerous attractions and recreation options are available in Port Angeles.

Campsites, facilities: There are 41 sites with full or partial hookups (30 and 50 amps) for tents or RVs of any length, two cabins, and a grassy area for tent camping. Picnic tables and fire rings are provided. Restrooms with flush toilets and coin showers, coin laundry, firewood, Wi-Fi, recreation field, and horseshoe pits are available. Some facilities are wheelchair accessible, including a boardwalk that allows beach access. Leashed pets are permitted.

Reservations, fees: Reservations are accepted. RV sites are $46 per night, tent sites are $41 per night, $8 per person per night for more than two people, $5 per extra vehicle (one-time fee per stay) unless towed, and $8 per night per pet. Cabins are $175-195 per night. Weekly, monthly, and family rates are available. Credit cards are accepted. Open year-round.

Directions: From U.S. 101 in Port Angeles, drive north five miles to a fork with Highway 112. Turn right (west) on Highway 112 and drive 10 miles to Camp Hayden Road (between Mileposts 53 and 54). Turn right on Camp Hayden Road and drive four miles to the park on the left, on the beach.

Contact: Crescent Beach RV Park, 2860 Crescent Beach Road, Port Angeles, 360/928-3344, www.olypen.com/crescent.

10 SALT CREEK RECREATION AREA

🚶 🏊 🛶 🎣 🐴 🛶 ♿ 🚐 ⛺

Scenic rating: 8

west of Port Angeles near the Strait of Juan de Fuca

Map 1.2, page 76

The former site of Camp Hayden, a World War II-era facility, Salt Creek Recreation Area is a great spot for gorgeous ocean views, fishing, and hiking near Striped Peak, which overlooks the campground. Only a small beach area is available because of the rugged coastline, but there is an exceptionally good spot for tidepool viewing on the park's west side. The park covers 196 acres and overlooks the Strait of Juan de Fuca. It is known for its Tongue Point Marine Life Sanctuary. Recreation options include nearby hiking trails, swimming, fishing, horseshoes, and field sports. It's a good layover spot if you're planning to take the ferry out of Port Angeles to Victoria, British Columbia. The camp fills up quickly most summer weekends.

Campsites, facilities: There are 92 sites, some with partial hookups (30 and 50 amps), for tents or RVs of any length. Some sites are pull-through. Picnic tables and fire rings are provided. Restroom with flush toilets and coin showers, dump station, firewood, a playground, and a reservable covered picnic shelter are available. A camp host is on-site. Some facilities are wheelchair accessible. Leashed pets are permitted.

Reservations, fees: Reservations are accepted online or in person ($10 reservation fee). RV sites are $27-30 per night, tent sites are $22-25 per night, $5 per extra vehicle per night. Credit cards are not accepted. Open year-round.

Directions: From U.S. 101 in Port Angeles, drive north five miles to a fork with Highway 112. Turn right (west) on Highway 112 and drive 13 miles to Camp Hayden Road. Turn right (north) near Mile Marker 54 and drive 3.5 miles to the park entrance on the left. Note that the gate closes at 10pm.

Contact: Salt Creek Recreation Area, Clallam County, 3506 Camp Hayden Road, Port Angeles, 360/928-3441, www.clallam.net.

11 AL'S RV PARK

🚶 🚲 🏊 🛶 🚐 🐴 ♿ 🚐 ⛺

Scenic rating: 8

near Port Angeles

Map 1.2, page 76

This campground is a good choice for RV owners. The campground is set in the country at about 1,000 feet elevation yet is centrally located and not far from the Strait of Juan de Fuca. Nearby recreation options include an 18-hole golf course and a full-service marina. Olympic National Park and the Victoria ferry are a short drive away.

Campsites, facilities: There are 34 sites with full hookups (20, 30, and 50 amps) for RVs up to 40 feet long and a grassy area for tents. Picnic tables are provided. No open fires are allowed. Restrooms with flush toilets and showers, drinking water, cable TV, modem access, and a coin laundry are available. A store, café, propane gas, and ice are located within 0.5 mile. Boat docks and launching facilities are located within two miles. Some facilities are wheelchair accessible. Leashed pets are permitted.

Reservations, fees: Reservations are not accepted. Sites are $26-29 per night, $3 per person per night for more than two people. Weekly and monthly rates available. Credit cards are not accepted. Open year-round.

Directions: From Port Angeles, take U.S. 101 east for two miles to North Brook Avenue. Turn left (north) on North Brook Avenue, then left (almost immediately) on Lees Creek Road, and drive 0.5 mile to the park on the right.

Contact: Al's RV Park, 3506 Camp Hayden Road, 360/457-9844.

12 KOA PORT ANGELES-SEQUIM

🏃 🚴 🏊 🦌 ⛹ ♿ 🚐 ⛺

Scenic rating: 5

near Port Angeles

Map 1.2, page 76

This is a private, developed camp covering 13 acres in a country setting. A pleasant park, it features the typical KOA offerings, including a pool, recreation hall, and playground. Horseshoe pits and a sports field are also available. Hayrides are available in summer. Nearby recreation options include miniature golf, an 18-hole golf course, marked hiking trails, and tennis courts, and nearby side trips include Victoria, Butchart Gardens, and whale-watching tours.

Campsites, facilities: There are 82 sites with full and partial hookups (20, 30, and 50 amps) for tents or RVs of any length, 19 sites for tents, 12 cabins, and one lodge. Some sites are pull-through. Picnic tables and fire pits are provided. Restrooms with flush toilets and showers, drinking water, cable TV, Wi-Fi, propane gas, firewood, dump station, convenience store, coin laundry, ice, a playground, miniature golf, organized activities, bicycle rentals, a game room, and a seasonal heated swimming pool and spa are available. A café is located within two miles. Some facilities are wheelchair accessible. Leashed pets are permitted.

Reservations, fees: Reservations are accepted at 800/562-7558. Sites are $24-81 per night, $6 per person per night for more than two people (ages five and older), and $5 per extra vehicle per night. Some credit cards are accepted. Open March-October.

Directions: In Port Angeles, go east on U.S. 101 for seven miles to O'Brien Road. Turn right on O'Brien Road and drive half a block to the campground on the right.

Contact: KOA Port Angeles-Sequim, 360/457-5916, www.koa.com.

13 DUNGENESS RECREATION AREA

🏃 🛶 🦌 ⛹ 🚵 ♿ 🚐 ⛺

Scenic rating: 5

between Port Angeles and Sequim near the Strait of Juan de Fuca

Map 1.2, page 76

This 216-acre park overlooks the Strait of Juan de Fuca and is set near the Dungeness National Wildlife Refuge. Quite popular, it fills up on summer weekends. A highlight, the refuge sits on a seven-mile spit with a historic lighthouse at its end. Bird-watchers often spot bald eagles in the wildlife refuge. There is a one-mile bluff trail, and equestrian trails are available. A 100-acre upland hunting area is open during season. Nearby recreation options include marked hiking trails, fishing, and golfing. The toll ferry at Port Angeles can take you to Victoria, British Columbia.

Campsites, facilities: There are 64 sites, including five pull-through sites, for tents or RVs of any length (no hookups), and eight hike-in/bike-in sites, and one group site. Picnic tables and fire grills are provided. Restrooms with flush toilets and coin showers, drinking water, firewood, dump station, a playground, and a picnic area are available. A camp host is on-site. Some facilities are wheelchair accessible. Leashed pets are permitted.

Reservations, fees: Reservations are accepted only by downloading a reservation form at www.clallam.net/CountyParks. Sites are $22 per night, $5 per extra vehicle per night. Call for group camp rates. Discount for Clallam County residents. Open year-round; entrance gates close at dusk.

Directions: From Sequim, drive north on U.S. 101 for four miles to Kitchen-Dick Road. Turn right (north) on Kitchen-Dick Road and drive three miles to the park on the left.

Contact: Dungeness Recreation Area, Clallam County, 554 Voice of America West, Sequim, 360/683-5847, www.clallam.net.

14 SEQUIM WEST INN & RV PARK

🏊 🚐 🐕 ♿ 🚙 ⛺

Scenic rating: 5

in Sequim near the Dungeness River

Map 1.2, page 76

This two-acre camp is near the Dungeness River and within 10 miles of Dungeness National Wildlife Refuge. It's located in town and is a pleasant spot with full facilities and an urban setting. An 18-hole golf course and a full-service marina at Sequim Bay are close by.

Campsites, facilities: There are 27 pull-through sites for tents or RVs of any length (30 and 50 amp full hookups), 17 cabins, and 21 motel rooms. Picnic tables are provided. No open fires are allowed. Restrooms with flush toilets and showers, drinking water, cable TV, coin laundry, a pay phone, and ice are available. Propane gas, gasoline, a store, and a café are located within one mile. Some facilities are wheelchair accessible. Leashed pets are permitted.

Reservations, fees: Reservations are accepted. Sites are $33-42 per night, $2 per person per night for more than two adults. Weekly and monthly rates available. Some credit cards are accepted. Open year-round.

Directions: From Sequim and U.S. 101, take the Washington Street exit and drive west on Washington Street for 2.7 miles to the park on the left.

Contact: Sequim West Inn & RV Park, 740 W. Washington, Sequim, 360/683-4144 or 800/528-4527, http://sequimwestinn.com.

15 RAINBOW'S END RV PARK

🚴 🏊 🚐 🐕 🚙 ⛺

Scenic rating: 6

near Sequim

Map 1.2, page 76

This park, located just west of Sequim, is pretty and clean. It features a pond (no fishing), a creek running through the campground, and beautiful views of the Olympic Mountains. There is a special landscaped area available for reunions, weddings, and other gatherings. Nearby recreation opportunities include an 18-hole golf course, marked bike trails, a full-service marina, and tennis courts.

Campsites, facilities: There are 39 sites with full hookups (30 and 50 amps), including some pull-through sites, for RVs of any length. Ten tent sites are open in summer only. Picnic tables are provided at all sites; fire pits are provided at tent sites. Restrooms with flush toilets and showers, drinking water, dump station, cable TV, Wi-Fi, propane gas, firewood, coin laundry, a dog park, and a clubhouse are available. A store, café, and ice are located within one mile. Leashed pets are permitted.

Reservations, fees: Reservations are accepted. Sites are $32-40 per night, $2 per person per night for more than two people, $2 per extra vehicle per night. Weekly and monthly rates are available. Some credit cards are accepted. Open year-round.

Directions: From Sequim, drive west on U.S. 101 for one mile past the River Road exit to the park on the right (along the highway).

Contact: Rainbow's End RV Park, 261831 Hwy. 101, Sequim, 360/683-3863, www.rainbowsendrvpark.com.

16 JOHN WAYNE'S WATERFRONT RESORT

🏊 🚐 🐕 🚙 ⛺

Scenic rating: 5

on Sequim Bay

Map 1.2, page 76

This is Sequim Bay headquarters for salmon anglers. The camp is set in a wooded, hilly area, close to many activity centers and with an 18-hole golf course nearby.

Campsites, facilities: There are 42 sites with full hookups (30 amps) for tents or RVs of any length (30 sites are pull-through) and nine cabins. Picnic tables are provided. Restrooms with flush toilets and showers, drinking water, cable

TV, community fire rings, Wi-Fi, store, firewood, clubhouse, volleyball, badminton, horseshoe pits, tetherball, walking trails, and coin laundry are available. Boat docks and launching facilities are located across the street from the resort. Leashed pets are permitted.

Reservations, fees: Reservations are accepted. RV sites are $33-45 per night, tent sites are $28-35 per night, $3 per each additional person, $3 per pet per night. Some credit cards are accepted. Open year-round.

Directions: In Sequim, drive north 2.5 miles on U.S. 101 to Whitefeather Way (located between Mileposts 267 and 268). Turn right (north) on Whitefeather Way and drive 0.5 mile to West Sequim Bay Road. Turn left (west) and drive one block to the resort on the left.

Contact: John Wayne's Waterfront Resort, 2634 West Sequim Bay Road, Sequim, 360/681-3853, www.johnwaynewaterfrontresort.com.

17 SEQUIM BAY STATE PARK

Scenic rating: 8

on Sequim Bay

Map 1.2, page 76

Sequim translates to "quiet waters," which is an appropriate description of this area. Set in the heart of Washington's rain shadow, a region with far less rainfall than the surrounding areas, Sequim averages only 17 inches of rainfall a year. The 92-acre park features 4,909 feet of saltwater shoreline; two sandbars shield the park from the Strait of Juan de Fuca's rough waters. There is one mile of hiking trails.

Campsites, facilities: There are 49 sites for tents or RVs (no hookups), 16 sites with full hookups (30 amps) for RVs up to 40 feet long, three primitive tent sites near the water, and one tent-only group site for up to 40 people (available mid-May-mid-September). Picnic tables and fire grills are provided. Restrooms with flush toilets and coin showers, drinking water, a dump station, a picnic area with kitchen shelters, an amphitheater, athletic fields, a basketball court, tennis courts, horseshoe pits, playground, and interpretive center are available. Boat docks, launching facilities, and boat mooring are also available. Some facilities are wheelchair accessible. Leashed pets are permitted.

Reservations, fees: Reservations are accepted at 888/226-7688 or https://washington.goingtocamp.com ($8-10 reservation fee). Sites are $25-45 per night, $12 per night for hike-in/bike-in sites, $10 per extra vehicle per night, and the group site is $81.69 per night. Boat launch fee is $7 ($5 for boat dumping); boat moorage is $5 per foot with a $60 minimum. Some credit cards are accepted. Open year-round.

Directions: From Olympia on I-5, turn north on U.S. 101 and drive 100 miles (near Sequim) to the park entrance on the right (along the highway). The park is located 3.5 miles southeast of the town of Sequim.

Contact: Sequim Bay State Park, 360/683-4235, http://parks.state.wa.us.

18 FAIRHOLME

Scenic rating: 9

on Lake Crescent in Olympic National Park

Map 1.2, page 76

This camp is set on the shore of Lake Crescent, a pretty lake situated within the boundary of Olympic National Park, at an elevation of 580 feet. The campsites lie along the western end of the lake, in a cove with a boat ramp. Located less than one mile off U.S. 101, Fairholme gets heavy use during tourist months; some highway noise is audible at some sites. A naturalist program is often available in the summer. Waterskiing is permitted at Lake Crescent, but personal watercraft are prohibited.

Campsites, facilities: There are 88 sites for tents or RVs up to 21 feet long. Picnic tables and fire grills are provided. A dump station, restrooms with flush toilets (summer season), and drinking water are available. A store and café are located within one mile. Boat-launching facilities and rentals are nearby on Lake Crescent. Some facilities are wheelchair accessible. Leashed pets are permitted.

Reservations, fees: Reservations are not accepted. Sites are $20 per night, plus a $25 per vehicle national park entrance fee. Open May-October, weather permitting.

Directions: From Port Angeles, drive west on U.S. 101 for about 26 miles and continue along Lake Crescent to North Shore Road. Turn right and drive 0.5 mile to the camp on North Shore Road on the right.

Contact: Olympic National Park, 360/565-3130, www.nps.gov/olym.

19 LOG CABIN RESORT

Scenic rating: 10

on Lake Crescent in Olympic National Park

Map 1.2, page 76

Log Cabin Resort is one of my wife's favorite spots. This pretty camp along the shore of Lake Crescent is a good spot for boaters, as it features many sites near the water with excellent views. Fishing and swimming are two options at this family-oriented resort. It is home to a strain of Beardslee trout. Note the fishing is catch-and-release. Waterskiing is permitted, but no personal watercraft are allowed. A marked hiking trail traces the lake's 22-mile shoreline. This camp is extremely popular in the summer months; you may need to make reservations 3-12 months in advance.

Campsites, facilities: There are 38 sites with full hookups (20 and 30 amps) for RVs of any length, four sites for tents, 28 cabins, and one group site for 20 people. Picnic tables and fire barrels are provided. A dump station, restrooms with flush toilets and coin showers, a store, café, gift shop, coin laundry, firewood, ice, and a recreation field are available. Boat docks, launching facilities, and boat rentals are available. Some facilities are wheelchair accessible. Leashed pets are permitted.

Reservations, fees: Reservations are accepted at 888/717-0733. RV sites are $46 per night, tent sites are $25-33 per night, the group site is $59 per night, $5 per person per night for more than two people, $2 per extra vehicle per night, $15 per pet per night. Some credit cards are accepted. Open mid-May-mid-September.

Directions: In Port Angeles, drive 18 miles north on U.S. 101 to East Beach Road. Turn right and drive three miles (along Lake Crescent) to the camp on the left.

Contact: Log Cabin Resort, 888/896-3818, www.olympicnationalparks.com.

20 HEART O' THE HILLS

Scenic rating: 9

in Olympic National Park

Map 1.2, page 76

Heart O' the Hills is nestled on the northern edge of Olympic National Park at an elevation of 1,807 feet. You can drive into the park on Hurricane Ridge Road and take one of numerous hiking trails. Little Lake Dawn is less than 0.5 mile to the west, but note that most of the property around this lake is privately owned. Naturalist programs are available in summer months.

Campsites, facilities: There are 105 sites for tents or RVs up to 21 feet long. Picnic tables and fire pits are provided. Restrooms with flush toilets, drinking water, and garbage bins are available. Some facilities are wheelchair accessible. Leashed pets are permitted.

Reservations, fees: Reservations are not accepted. Sites are $20 per night, plus a $25 national park entrance fee per vehicle. Open year-round, weather permitting.

Directions: From U.S. 101 in Port Angeles at Hurricane Ridge Road, turn left and drive five miles to the camp on the left. (Access roads can be impassable in severe weather.)

Contact: Olympic National Park, 360/565-3130, www.nps.gov/olym.

21 FORT WORDEN STATE PARK

Scenic rating: 9

in Port Townsend

Map 1.3, page 77

This park is set on the northeastern tip of the Olympic Peninsula, at the northern end of Port Townsend, on a high bluff with views of Puget Sound. Highlights here include great lookouts and two miles of beach trails over the Strait of Juan de Fuca as it feeds into Puget Sound. The park covers 433 acres at historic Fort Worden (construction began in 1897 and was decommissioned in 1953) and includes buildings from the turn of the 20th century. It has 11,020 feet of saltwater shoreline. Recreation options include 11 miles of hiking trails and 8 miles of biking trails, including 2.6 miles of wheelchair-accessible trails. The Coast Artillery Museum, Rothschild House, Commanding Officers Quarters, and the Marine Science Center and Natural History Museum are open during the summer season. A ferry at Port Townsend will take you across the strait to Whidbey Island. Special note on reservations: This is an extremely popular park and campground and reservations are required online up to five months in advance or in person up to 11 months in advance.

Campsites, facilities: There are 50 sites with full hookups and 30 sites with partial hookups (30 and 50 amps) for tents or RVs up to 75 feet, including some pull-through sites. Picnic tables and fire grills are provided. Restrooms with flush toilets and coin showers, drinking water, coin laundry, a store, dump station, and firewood are available. A seasonal restaurant, conference facilities, a sheltered amphitheater, athletic fields, and interpretive activities are available nearby. Boat docks, buoys, floats, and launching facilities are also nearby, as are several golf courses. Some facilities are wheelchair accessible. Leashed pets are permitted.

Reservations, fees: Reservations are accepted at 888/226-7688 or https://washington. goingtocamp.com ($8-10 reservation fee). Sites are $36-42 per night, $10 per extra vehicle per night. Open year-round, with limited services in winter.

Directions: From Port Townsend, take Highway 20 north through town to Kearney Street. Turn left on Kearney Street and drive to the first stop sign, at Blaine Street. Turn right on Blaine Street and drive to the next stop sign, on Cherry Street. Turn left at Cherry Street and drive 1.75 miles to the park entrance at the end of the road.

Contact: Fort Worden State Park, 360/344-4400, http://parks.state.wa.us.

22 POINT HUDSON MARINA & RV PARK

Scenic rating: 5

in Port Townsend

Map 1.3, page 77

Point Hudson RV Park is located on the site of an old Coast Guard station near the beach in Port Townsend. This public facility is owned by the Port of Port Townsend. The park features ocean views and 2,000 feet of beach frontage. Known for its Victorian architecture, Port Townsend is called Washington's Victorian seaport. Fishing and boating are popular here, and nearby recreation opportunities include an 18-hole municipal golf course, a full-service marina, Fort Townsend State Park, Fort Flagler State Park, and Fort Worden State Park.

Campsites, facilities: There are 60 sites with full hookups (30 amps) for RVs of any length. Some sites are pull-through. Picnic tables are provided at some sites. No fires are allowed. Restrooms with flush toilets and coin showers, drinking water, cable TV, Wi-Fi, three restaurants, and coin laundry are available. A 100-plus-slip marina is on-site. Some facilities are wheelchair accessible. Leashed pets are permitted.

Reservations, fees: Reservations are accepted ($10 reservation fee). Sites are $30-56 per night,

$5 per extra vehicle per night. Some credit cards are accepted. Open year-round.

Directions: From Port Townsend on Highway 20, take the Water Street exit. Turn left (north) and continue (the road becomes Sims Way and then Water Street) to the end of Water Street at the marina. Turn left for registration.

Contact: Point Hudson Marina & RV Park, 360/385-2828, www.portofpt.com.

23 FORT TOWNSEND STATE PARK

🚶 🏊 🐴 🎣 ♿ 🚐 ⛺

Scenic rating: 10

near Quilcene

Map 1.3, page 77

This 414-acre park features a thickly wooded landscape, nearly 4,000 feet of saltwater shoreline on Port Townsend Bay, and 6.5 miles of hiking trails. Built in 1856, the historic fort is one of the oldest remaining in the state. The scenic campground has access to a good clamming beach (check regulations), and visitors can take two different short, self-guided walking tours. Note that the nearest boat ramps are at Port Townsend, Fort Flagler, and Hadlock. Mooring buoys are located just offshore of the park on the west side of Port Townsend Bay.

Campsites, facilities: There are 40 sites for tents or RVs up to 40 feet long, one hike-in/bike-in site, and one group site for up to 80 people. Picnic tables and fire grills are provided. Restrooms with flush toilets and coin showers, drinking water, a playground, ballfields, boat buoys, firewood, a dump station, and a picnic area with a kitchen shelter are available. Some facilities are wheelchair accessible. Leashed pets are permitted.

Reservations, fees: Reservations are accepted at https://washington.goingtocamp.com or 888/226-7688 ($8-10 reservation fee). Sites are $25-45 per night, $10 per extra vehicle per night; hike-in/bike-in sites are $12 per night. Call 360/385-3595 to reserve the group camp ($25 reservation fee); rates vary seasonally and

according to group size. Open mid-April-mid-October, weather permitting.

Directions: From Port Townsend, drive south on Highway 20 for two miles to Old Fort Townsend Road. Turn left and drive 0.5 mile to the park entrance road.

Contact: Fort Townsend State Park, 360/344-4431 or 360/385-3595, http://parks.state.wa.us.

24 FORT FLAGLER STATE PARK

🚶 🚴 🏊 🎣 🐴 ♿ 🚐 ⛺

Scenic rating: 10

near Port Townsend

Map 1.3, page 77   **BEST (**

Historic Fort Flagler is a pretty and unique state park, set on Marrowstone Island east of Port Townsend. The camp overlooks Puget Sound and offers 19,100 feet of gorgeous saltwater shore. The park's 784 acres include five miles of trails for hiking and biking, an interpretive trail, and a military museum featuring gun batteries that are open in the summer. The RV sites are situated right on the beach, with views of the Olympic and Cascade Mountains. Anglers like this spot for year-round rockfish and salmon fishing, and crabbing and clamming are good in season (check regulations). Fort Flagler, under construction on some level from 1897 until its closure in 1953, offers summer tours. There is a youth hostel in the park.

Campsites, facilities: There are 47 sites for tents, 55 sites with full hookups (30 amps) for RVs up to 50 feet long, 59 standard sites, two hike-in/bike-in sites, four vacation homes, a group tent site for up to 40 people, and a group site for tents or RVs of any length for up to 100 people. Picnic tables and fire grills are provided. Restrooms with flush toilets and coin showers, drinking water, interpretive activities, a dump station, playground, picnic shelters that can be reserved, a camp store, boat buoys, moorage dock, and a launch are available. Some facilities are wheelchair accessible. Leashed pets are permitted.

Reservations, fees: Reservations are accepted May-September at 888/226-7688 or https://washington.goingtocamp.com ($8-10 reservation fee). Sites are $20-45 per night, $10 per extra vehicle per night, $12 per night for hike-in/bike-in sites. The group sites are $140.42-280.83 per night with a minimum of 26 people. The vacation homes are $121-134.31 per night for 4-8 people and are available year-round. A watercraft launch permit is $7 per day. Some credit cards are accepted. Open year-round, weather permitting.

Directions: From Port Townsend at Highway 20, drive to Highway 19 (airport cutoff) and make a slight left turn on Highway 19. Drive 3.5 miles to the traffic light at Ness Corner Road and turn left. Drive about one mile on Ness Corner Road to Oak Bay Road/Highway 116. Continue one mile on Highway 116 and turn left at Flagler Road to stay on Highway 116. Remain on Flagler Road and drive about 6.5 miles to the end of the road and the park and campground.

Contact: Fort Flagler State Park, 360/385-1259, http://parks.state.wa.us.

25 KINNEY POINT STATE PARK

Scenic rating: 10

on Marrowstone Island

Map 1.3, page 77

Kinney Point is located on the south end of Marrowstone Island, part of Washington's Cascade Marine Trail. You'll need a non-motorized boat to reach the campsites at this 76-acre park; once you do, 683 feet of shoreline await.

Campsites, facilities: There are three primitive sites for tents. A vault toilet and kayak rack are available. There is no drinking water and all garbage must be packed out. Leashed pets are permitted.

Reservations, fees: Reservations are not accepted. Sites are $12 per night. Open year-round.

Directions: From Fort Flagler or Mystery Bay State Parks, head south down Marrowstone Island to Kinney Point.

Contact: Kinney Point State Park, 360/902-8844, http://parks.state.wa.us.

26 MORA

Scenic rating: 8

in Olympic National Park

Map 1.4, page 78

At an elevation of 50 feet, this is a good out-of-the-way choice near the Pacific Ocean and the Olympic Coast Marine Sanctuary. The Quillayute River feeds into the ocean near the camp, and upstream lies the Bogachiel, a prime steelhead river in winter months. A naturalist program is available during the summer. This camp includes eight sites that require short walks, and several of them are stellar.

Campsites, facilities: There are 94 sites for tents or RVs up to 35 feet long and one walk-in tent site. Picnic tables and fire pits are provided. Restrooms with flush toilets, drinking water, garbage bins, and a dump station ($10 fee) are available. Some facilities are wheelchair accessible. Leashed pets are permitted.

Reservations, fees: Reservations are not accepted. Sites are $20 per night, plus a $25 national park entrance fee per vehicle. Open year-round.

Directions: From Aberdeen, drive north on U.S. 101 for 108 miles to Forks. Continue past Forks for two miles to La Push Road/Highway 110. Turn left (west) and drive 12 miles to the campground on the left (well marked along the route).

Contact: Olympic National Park, 360/565-3130, www.nps.gov/olym.

27 QUILEUTE OCEANSIDE RESORT

🏃 🛶 🚐 🐕 ♿ 🚗 ⛺

Scenic rating: 8

near Forks

Map 1.4, page 78

This park is set along the Pacific Ocean and the coastal Dungeness National Wildlife Refuge. Operated by the Quileute Nation, it has some of the few ocean sites available in the area and offers such recreation options as fishing, surfing, beachcombing, boating, whale-watching, and sunbathing.

Campsites, facilities: There are 66 sites for RVs of any length (30 and 50 amp full hookups), six sites for tents, and 20 beach campsites. Cabins are also available. Picnic tables and fire rings are provided. Restrooms with flush toilets and coin showers, and a coin laundry are available. Gasoline, propane gas, and a convenience store with a deli and ice are nearby. Boat docks, a marina, and launching facilities are located within one mile. Some facilities are wheelchair accessible. Leashed pets are permitted.

Reservations, fees: Reservations are accepted. Tent sites are $15-20 per night, RV sites are $27-40 per night, $5 additional vehicle per night, $25 per pet per night. Cabins are $69-299 per night. Some credit cards are accepted. Open year-round.

Directions: From the town of Forks, drive north on U.S. 101 for 2.5 miles to La Push Road/Highway 110. Turn left (west) and drive 13 miles on La Push Road, which becomes Ocean Front Drive. Turn left onto Ocean Front Drive. The campground will be on the right.

Contact: Quileute Oceanside Resort, 330 Ocean Front Drive, La Push, 800/487-1267, www.quileuteoceanside.com.

28 THREE RIVERS RESORT

🏃 🛶 🐕 🚗 ⛺

Scenic rating: 8

near Forks on the Quillayute River

Map 1.4, page 78

Three Rivers Resort is a small, private camp set at the junction of the Quillayute, Sol Duc, and Bogachiel Rivers. Situated above this confluence, about six miles upstream from the ocean, this pretty spot features wooded, spacious sites. Hiking and fishing are popular here, and there is a fishing guide service. Salmon and steelhead migrate upstream, best on the Sol Duc and Bogachiel Rivers; anglers should check regulations. The coastal Dungeness National Wildlife Refuge and the Pacific Ocean, which often offer good whale-watching in the spring, are a short drive to the west. Hoh Rain Forest, a worthwhile side trip, is about 45 minutes away.

Campsites, facilities: There are 11 sites for tents, nine sites with partial hookups for RVs, two sites with full hookups (30 and 50 amps) for tents or RVs of any length, six rental cabins, and one vacation home. Picnic tables and fire pits are provided. Restrooms with flush toilets and coin showers, a convenience store, gas station, a café, coin laundry, firewood, and ice are available. Leashed pets are permitted.

Reservations, fees: Reservations are accepted. Tent sites are $22 per night, $7 per second tent per night; RV sites are $27-30 per night, $5 per pet per night. Some credit cards are accepted. Open year-round.

Directions: From Aberdeen, drive north on U.S. 101 for 108 miles to Forks. Continue past Forks for two miles to La Push Road/Highway 110. Turn left (west) and drive eight miles to the resort on the right.

Contact: Three Rivers Resort, 7765 LaPush Road, Forks, 360/374-5300, www.threeriversresortandguideservice.com.

29 KLAHANIE

Scenic rating: 8

on the North Fork Klahanie River

Map 1.4, page 78

This camp is likely off the radar of many travelers, so it is worth checking out. Sites nestle amid large, old-growth spruce and lots of ferns. It is quite pretty, set along a riparian zone on the South Fork Calawah River, and features a hiking trail that hugs the river for 0.25 mile and a second trail that follows the river for about one mile, starting at the east end of the campground.

Campsites, facilities: There are 15 sites for tents or RVs up to 21 feet. Picnic tables and fire grills are provided. Vault toilets are available. There is no drinking water and garbage must be packed out. Leashed pets are permitted.

Reservations, fees: Reservations are not accepted. Sites are $10 per night. Open May-Labor Day.

Directions: From Aberdeen, drive north on U.S. 101 to Forks. Continue past Forks for one mile to Forest Road 29. Turn right (east) and drive five miles to the campground on the right.

Contact: Olympic National Forest, Pacific Ranger District, 360/374-6522, www.fs.usda.gov.

30 BOGACHIEL STATE PARK

Scenic rating: 6

on the Bogachiel River

Map 1.4, page 78

A good base camp for salmon or steelhead fishing trips, this 123-acre park is set on the Bogachiel River, with marked hiking trails in the area. It can be noisy at times because a logging mill is located directly across the river from the campground. Also note that there is highway noise, and you can see the highway from some campsites. A one-mile hiking trail is

nearby, and opportunities for wildlife-viewing are outstanding in the park. Hunting is popular in the adjacent national forest. This region is heavily forested, with lush vegetation fed by an average of 140-160 inches of rain each year. This park was established in 1931.

Campsites, facilities: There are 26 sites for tents or RVs (no hookups), six sites with partial hookups (30 amps) for RVs up to 40 feet, two hike-in/bike-in sites, and one group tent site for 16-20 people. Picnic tables and fire grills are provided. Restrooms with flush toilets and coin showers, drinking water, dump station, and a picnic area are available. A primitive boat ramp is nearby. Some facilities are wheelchair accessible. Leashed pets are permitted.

Reservations, fees: Reservations are accepted mid-May to mid-September. Sites are $25-40 per night, the hike-in/bike-in site is $12 per night, $10 per extra vehicle per night. Call for group rates. Open year-round, with some sites closed in winter.

Directions: From Olympia on I-5, take Exit 104 and drive north on U.S. 101 to the Aberdeen/Highway 8 exit. Turn west on Highway 8 and drive 36 miles to Aberdeen. Continue through Aberdeen four miles to U.S. 101. Turn north on U.S. 101 and drive 102 miles to the park (six miles south of Forks) on the left side of the road.

Contact: Bogachiel State Park, 360/374-6356, http://parks.state.wa.us.

31 COTTONWOOD

Scenic rating: 8

on the Hoh River

Map 1.4, page 78

This primitive camp is set along the Hoh River, providing an alternative to Hoh Oxbow, Willoughby Creek, and Minnie Peterson Campgrounds. Like Hoh Oxbow, Cottonwood offers the bonus of a boat launch. Its distance from the highway makes it quieter here. The camp is popular for anglers and hunters (in season).

Campsites, facilities: There are eight sites for tents or RVs up to 30 feet long, including a group site for up to 10 people, and three sites for tents only. Picnic tables, fire grills, and tent pads are provided. Vault toilets, a boat launch, and drinking water are available. Garbage must be packed out. Some facilities are wheelchair accessible. Leashed pets are permitted.

Reservations, fees: Reservations are not accepted. There is no fee for camping, but a Discover Pass is required. Open year-round.

Directions: From Olympia on I-5, take Exit 104 and drive north on U.S. 101 to the Aberdeen/Highway 8 exit. Turn west on Highway 8 and drive 36 miles to Aberdeen. Continue through Aberdeen four miles to U.S. 101. Turn north on U.S. 101 and drive 92 miles to Oil City Road between Mileposts 177 and 178. Turn left (west) on Oil City Road and drive 2.3 miles. Turn left on Road H4060 (gravel) and drive one mile to the camp at the end of the road.

Contact: Department of Natural Resources, Olympic Region, 360/374-6131, www.dnr.wa.gov.

32 HOH OXBOW

Scenic rating: 7

on the Hoh River

Map 1.4, page 78

This is the most popular of the five camps on the Hoh River. It's primitive and close to the highway, and the price is right. The adjacent boat launch makes this the camp of choice for anglers, best in fall and winter for salmon and steelhead; check regulations. It is also a popular hunters' camp in the fall. One downer: There is some highway noise within range of the campsites. You can't see the traffic, but you can hear it, which can be irritating for those who want perfect quiet.

Campsites, facilities: There are eight sites for tents or RVs up to 25 feet. Picnic tables, fire grills, and tent pads are provided. Vault toilets, a hand boat launch, and drinking water are available. Garbage must be packed out. Some facilities are wheelchair accessible. Leashed pets are permitted.

Reservations, fees: Reservations are not accepted. There is no fee for camping, but a Discover Pass is required. Open year-round.

Directions: From Aberdeen, drive north on U.S. 101 for 90 miles to the campground (15 miles south of Forks). Exit between Mileposts 176 and 177 and look for the campground on the right, next to the river. Note: The road in is narrow and not advised for RVs or trailers.

Contact: Department of Natural Resources, Olympic Region, 360/374-6131, www.dnr.wa.gov.

33 WILLOUGHBY CREEK

Scenic rating: 9

in Hoh Clearwater State Forest

Map 1.4, page 78

This little-known camp along Willoughby Creek and the Hoh River is tiny and rustic, with good fishing nearby for steelhead and salmon during peak migrations in season. The area gets heavy rainfall. Other campground options in the vicinity include Hoh Oxbow, Cottonwood, and Minnie Peterson.

Campsites, facilities: There are three sites for self-contained RVs up to 16 feet. Picnic tables and fire grills are provided. There are no toilets and drinking water is not available. Garbage must be packed out. Leashed pets are permitted.

Reservations, fees: Reservations are not accepted. There is no fee for camping, but a Discover Pass is required. Open year-round.

Directions: From Olympia on I-5, take Exit 104 and drive north on U.S. 101 to the Aberdeen/Highway 8 exit. Turn west on Highway 8 and drive 36 miles to Aberdeen. Continue through Aberdeen four miles to U.S. 101. Turn north on U.S. 101 and drive about 90 miles. Exit between

Mileposts 178 and 179. At Hoh Rain Forest Road/Upper Hoh Valley Road, turn east and drive 3.5 miles to the campground on the right. **Contact:** Department of Natural Resources, Olympic Region, 360/374-6131, www.dnr. wa.gov.

34 MINNIE PETERSON
🏃‍♂️ 🛶 🐴 ♿ 🚐 ⛺

Scenic rating: 9

on the Hoh River

Map 1.4, page 78

If location is everything, then it's why this campground has become popular. Minnie Peterson is set on the Hoh River on the edge of the Hoh Rain Forest. It's quite pretty, forested with Sitka spruce and western hemlock, and offers nice riverside sites. Bring your rain gear.

Campsites, facilities: There are eight sites for tents or RVs up to 30 feet long. Picnic tables, fire grills, and tent pads are provided. Vault toilets are available. There is no drinking water and garbage must be packed out. Some facilities are wheelchair accessible. Leashed pets are permitted.

Reservations, fees: Reservations are not accepted. There is no fee for camping, but a Discover Pass is required. Open year-round.

Directions: From Olympia on I-5, take Exit 104 and drive north on U.S. 101 to the Aberdeen/ Highway 8 exit. Turn west on Highway 8 and drive 36 miles to Aberdeen. Continue through Aberdeen four miles to U.S. 101. Turn north on U.S. 101 and drive about 90 miles. Exit between Mileposts 178 and 179. At Hoh Rain Forest Road/Upper Hoh Valley Road, turn east and drive 4.5 miles to the campground on the left. **Contact:** Department of Natural Resources, Olympic Region, 360/374-6131, www.dnr. wa.gov.

35 UPPER CLEARWATER
🏃‍♂️ 🛶 🚐 🚣 🐴 ⛺

Scenic rating: 8

on the Clearwater River

Map 1.4, page 78

This is one of the three primitive camps set along the Clearwater River. Upper Clearwater is a great camp: It's very pretty, is unused by most tourists, and has a boat ramp. Campsites sit amid a forest of western hemlock, red alder, and big-leaf maple.

Campsites, facilities: There are nine sites for tents only. Picnic tables, fire grills, and tent pads are provided. Vault toilets and a covered shelter are available. There is no drinking water and garbage must be packed out. There are un-improved boat-launching facilities for small crafts, such as river dories, rafts, canoes, and kayaks. Leashed pets are permitted.

Reservations, fees: Reservations are not accepted. There is no fee for camping. Open year-round.

Directions: From Olympia on I-5, take Exit 104 and drive north on U.S. 101 to the Aberdeen/ Highway 8 exit. Turn west on Highway 8 and drive 36 miles to Aberdeen. Continue through Aberdeen four miles to U.S. 101. Turn north on U.S. 101 and drive about 60 miles to Milepost 147. Turn north on Clearwater Mainline Road and drive about 13 miles to C-3000 Road (a gravel one-lane road). Turn right and drive 3.3 miles to the camp entrance on the right. **Contact:** Department of Natural Resources, Olympic Region, 360/374-6131, www.dnr. wa.gov.

36 YAHOO LAKE
🏃‍♂️ 🚐 🐴 🚐 ⛺

Scenic rating: 10

on Yahoo Lake in Hoh Clearwater State Forest

Map 1.4, page 78

Yahoo Lake is the most primitive and remote campground in the Olympic region. The lake-side campground is set at an elevation of 2,400 feet and is a lovely secret known only to a rugged few.

Campsites, facilities: There are four sites for tents and RVs. Picnic tables, fire grills, and tent pads are provided. There are toilets, but no drinking water, and garbage must be packed out. Leashed pets are permitted.

Reservations, fees: Reservations are not accepted. There is no fee for camping, but a Discover Pass is required. Open year-round.

Directions: From Olympia on I-5, take Exit 104 and drive north on U.S. 101 to the Aberdeen/Highway 8 exit. Turn west on Highway 8 and drive 36 miles to Aberdeen. Continue through Aberdeen four miles to U.S. 101. Turn north on U.S. 101 and drive about 60 miles to Milepost 147. Turn north on Clearwater Mainline Road and drive about 13 miles to C-3000 Road (a gravel one-lane road). Turn right and drive 0.8 mile to C-3100 Road. Turn right on C-3100 Road (paved one-lane, then gravel one-lane). Continue 6.1 miles to trailhead. This road is not recommended for motor-home travel.

Contact: Department of Natural Resources, Olympic Region, Jefferson County, 360/374-6131, www.dnr.wa.gov.

37 KALALOCH

Scenic rating: 10

in Olympic National Park

Map 1.4, page 78   BEST

This camp, located on a bluff above the beach, offers some wonderful oceanview sites—which explains its popularity. It can fill quickly. Like other camps set on the coast of the Olympic Peninsula, heavy rain in winter and spring is common, and it's often foggy in the summer. A naturalist program is offered in the summer months. There are several good hiking trails in the area; check out the visitors center for maps and information.

Campsites, facilities: There are 170 sites for tents or RVs up to 35 feet long. A group tent site can accommodate up to 30 people (drinking

water and pit toilets are provided). Picnic tables and fire grills are provided. Restrooms with flush toilets, drinking water, garbage bins, food lockers, fish-cleaning stations, and a dump station are available. A store and a restaurant are located within one mile. Some facilities are wheelchair accessible. Leashed pets are permitted in the campground.

Reservations, fees: Reservations are accepted June 20-September 3 at 877/444-6777 or www.recreation.gov ($10 reservation fee). Sites are $22 per night, plus a $25 national park entrance fee per vehicle. The group site is $2 per person per night, plus a $20 reservation fee. Open year-round.

Directions: From Aberdeen, drive north on U.S. 101 for 83 miles to the campground on the left. It is located near the mouth of the Kalaloch River five miles north of the U.S. 101 bridge over the Queets River.

Contact: Olympic National Park, 360/565-3130, www.nps.gov/olym.

38 COPPERMINE BOTTOM

Scenic rating: 9

on the Clearwater River

Map 1.4, page 78   BEST

Few tourists ever visit this primitive, hidden campground set on the Clearwater River, a tributary of the Queets River, which runs to the ocean. The river dory-launching facility is a bonus and makes this a perfect camp for anglers and river runners who want to avoid the usual U.S. 101 crowds. Salmon fishing is popular here during the migratory journey of the anadromous fish.

Campsites, facilities: There are 10 sites for tents or RVs up to 30 feet long and one group site for up to 10 people. Picnic tables, fire grills, and tent pads are provided. Vault toilets, a group shelter, and a hand boat launch are available. There is no drinking water and garbage must be packed out. Leashed pets are permitted.

Reservations, fees: Reservations are not accepted. There is no fee for camping, but a Discover Pass is required. Open year-round.

Directions: From Olympia on I-5, take Exit 104 and drive north on U.S. 101 to the Aberdeen/Highway 8 exit. Turn west on Highway 8 and drive 36 miles to Aberdeen. Continue through Aberdeen four miles to U.S. 101. Turn north on U.S. 101 and drive about 60 miles to Milepost 147. Turn north on Clearwater Mainline Road and drive about 14 miles to C-3000 Road. Turn right (east) on C-3000 Road (a gravel one-lane road) and drive two miles to C-1010 Road. Turn right on C-1010 Road and drive one mile. The camp is on the left.

Contact: Department of Natural Resources, Olympic Region, 360/374-6131, www.dnr.wa.gov.

39 SOUTH BEACH

Scenic rating: 6

in Olympic National Park

Map 1.4, page 78

Little South Beach Campground is located in an open field with little shade or privacy, but the payoff is that it is just a stone's throw from the ocean.

Campsites, facilities: There are 50 sites for tents or RVs up to 21 feet long. Picnic tables and fire grills are provided. Drinking water and non-accessible restrooms with flush toilets are available during summer. In winter, only pit toilets are available, and there is no drinking water. Leashed pets are permitted in the campground.

Reservations, fees: Reservations are not accepted. Sites are $15 per night, plus a $25 national park entrance fee per vehicle. Open late May-mid-September.

Directions: From Aberdeen, drive north on U.S. 101 for 65 miles to the campground.

Contact: Olympic National Park, 360/565-3130, www.nps.gov/olym.

40 PACIFIC BEACH STATE PARK

Scenic rating: 10

near Pacific Beach

Map 1.4, page 78   **BEST (**

This is the only state park campground in Washington where you can see the ocean from your campsite. Set on just nine acres, within the town of Pacific Beach, it boasts 2,300 feet of beachfront. This spot is great for long beach walks, although it can be windy, especially in the spring and early summer. Because of those winds, this is a great place for kite-flying. Clamming (for razor clams) is permitted only in season. Note that rangers advise against swimming or body surfing because of strong riptides. Vehicle traffic is allowed seasonally on the uppermost portions of the beach, but ATVs are not allowed in the park, on the beach, or on sand dunes. This camp is popular and often fills up quickly.

Campsites, facilities: There are 22 sites for tents, 42 sites with partial hookups (30 amps) for RVs up to 60 feet long, and two yurts. Picnic tables are provided. No fires are permitted, except on the beach; charcoal and propane barbecues are allowed in campsites. Restrooms with flush toilets and coin showers, drinking water, a dump station, and a picnic area are available. Some facilities are wheelchair accessible. Leashed pets are permitted.

Reservations, fees: Reservations are accepted at 888/226-7688 or https://washington.goingtocamp.com ($8-10 reservation fee). Sites are $20-45 per night, hike-in/bike-in sites are $12 per night, $10 per extra vehicle per night, and yurts are $50-74 per night. Some credit cards are accepted. Open year-round.

Directions: From Hoquiam, drive north on Highway 109 for 37 miles to Pacific Beach and Main Street. Turn left on Main Street and drive 0.5 mile to 2nd Street. Turn left on 2nd Street and continue to the park entrance.

Contact: Pacific Beach State Park, 360/276-4297, http://parks.state.wa.us.

41 TIDELANDS RESORT

🏊 ⛴ 🚣 🐕 👨‍👩‍👧 🚐 ⛰

Scenic rating: 7

near Copalis Beach

Map 1.4, page 78

This flat, wooded resort covers 47 acres and provides beach access and a great ocean view. It's primarily an RV park, and the sites are pleasant. Ten sites are set on sand dunes, while the rest are in a wooded area. In the spring, azaleas and wildflowers abound. Horseshoe pits and a sports field offer recreation possibilities. Though it's more remote than at the other area campgrounds, clamming is an option in season. Various festivals are held in the area from spring through fall.

Campsites, facilities: There are 25 sites for tents or RVs (no hookups), 35 sites with full or partial hookups (20 and 30 amps) for tents or RVs of any length, and four cabins. Some sites are pull-through. Picnic tables and fire pits are provided. Restrooms with flush toilets and coin showers, drinking water, firewood, cable TV, and a play area are available. A casino and horseback riding are within five miles. A golf course is within six miles. Leashed pets are permitted.

Reservations, fees: Reservations are accepted. RV sites start at $30 per night, tent sites are $25 per night. Cabins are $119-189 per night (two-night minimum); extra tents or vehicles are $10 per night. Some credit cards are accepted. Open year-round.

Directions: From Hoquiam, drive west on State Route 109 for about 20 miles to the resort on the left. It is located between Mileposts 20 and 21, about one mile south of Copalis Beach.

Contact: Tidelands Resort, 2991 State Route 109 North, 360/289-8963, www.tidelandsresort.com.

42 OCEAN MIST RESORT

⛴ 🏊 🐕 👨‍👩‍👧 ♿ 🚐 ⛰

Scenic rating: 9

on Conners Creek near Ocean City

Map 1.4, page 78

Always call to determine whether space is available before planning a stay here. This is a membership resort RV campground, and members always come first. If space is available, they will rent sites to the public. Surf fishing is popular in the nearby Pacific Ocean, while the Copalis River offers salmon fishing and canoeing opportunities. It's about a one-block walk to the beach. There's a golf course within five miles.

Campsites, facilities: There are 94 sites with full hookups (30 amps) for RVs up to 45 feet, a grassy area for tents, three cabins, and one yurt. Picnic tables are provided. Restrooms with flush toilets and showers, drinking water, cable TV, Wi-Fi, dump station, two community fire pits, a spa, clubhouse, two playgrounds, ball courts, horseshoe pits, and coin laundry are available. A grocery store is within one mile in Ocean City. Some facilities are wheelchair accessible. Leashed pets are permitted.

Reservations, fees: Reservations are accepted in the summer. RV sites are $40-42 per night, tent sites are $10 per night. Call for cabin and yurt rates. Some credit cards are accepted. Open year-round.

Directions: From Hoquiam, drive west on State Route 109 for 19 miles to the resort on the left (one mile north of Ocean City).

Contact: Ocean Mist Resort, 2781 State Route 109, Ocean City, 360/289-3656, www.kmresorts.com.

43 OCEAN CITY STATE PARK

🏊 🐕 ♿ 🚐 ⛰

Scenic rating: 9

near Hoquiam

Map 1.4, page 78   BEST (

This 170-acre oceanfront camp, an excellent example of coastal wetlands and dune succession, features ocean beach, dunes, and dense thickets of pine surrounding freshwater marshes. The Ocean Shores Interpretive Center is located on the south end of Ocean Shores near the marina (open summer season only). This area is part of the Pacific Flyway, and the migratory route for gray whales and other marine mammals lies just offshore. Spring wildflowers are excellent and include lupine, buttercups, and wild strawberry. This is also a good area for surfing and kite-flying; spring is typically windy. Beachcombing, clamming, and fishing are possibilities at this park. An 18-hole golf course is nearby.

Campsites, facilities: There are 149 sites for tents or self-contained RVs (no hookups), 29 sites with full hookups (30 amps) for RVs up to 50 feet long; some sites are pull-through. There are also three hike-in/bike-in sites and one group camp for tents only that can accommodate 20-30 people. A second group camp for 20-40 people and two RVs (with hookups) is also available. Picnic tables and fire rings are provided. Restrooms with flush toilets and coin showers, drinking water, dump station, sheltered picnic area, and firewood are available. A ballfield and amphitheater are available nearby. A camp host is on-site. Some facilities are wheelchair accessible. Leashed pets are permitted.

Reservations, fees: Reservations are accepted at 888/226-7688 or https://washington.goingtocamp.com ($8-10 reservation fee). Sites are $20-45 per night, hike-in/bike-in sites are $12 per night, $10 per extra vehicle per night, and group sites are $88-114 per night. Some credit cards are accepted. Open year-round.

Directions: From Hoquiam, drive northwest on State Route 109 for 16 miles to State Route 115. Turn left and drive 1.2 miles south to the park on the right (1.5 miles north of Ocean Shores).

Contact: Ocean City State Park, 360/289-3553, http://parks.state.wa.us.

44 SOL DUC

Scenic rating: 10
on the Sol Duc River in Olympic National Park

Map 1.5, page 79

This site is a nice hideaway, with nearby Sol Duc Hot Springs a highlight. The problem is that this camp is very popular. It fills up quickly on weekends, and a fee is charged to use the hot springs, which have been fully developed since the early 1900s. The camp is set at 1,680 feet along the Sol Duc River.

Campsites, facilities: There are 82 sites for tents or RVs up to 35 feet long. There is also one group site for 9-24 people and up to eight head of stock (there are pit toilets, but no drinking water). Cabins and a lodge are available; call for details. Picnic tables and fire pits are provided. Restrooms with flush toilets and drinking water are available in the summer season; there is no water in the winter season, but pit toilets are available. A dump station is available nearby, and a store and café are within one mile. Some facilities are wheelchair accessible. Leashed pets are permitted.

Reservations, fees: Reservations are accepted for the RV and tent sites at 877/444-6777 ($10 reservation fee) or www.recreation.gov ($9 reservation fee). Sites are $21-43 per night, plus a $25 national park entrance fee per vehicle. Call for group rates. Open May-late October, with limited facilities in winter.

Directions: From Port Angeles, continue on U.S. 101 for 27 miles, just past Lake Crescent. Turn left at the Sol Duc turnoff and drive 12 miles to the camp.

Contact: Sol Duc Hot Springs Resort Campground, 866/476-5382; Olympic National Park, 360/565-3130, www.nps.gov/olym.

45 DEER PARK
🚶 🐕 ⛺

Scenic rating: 9

near Blue Mountain in Olympic National Park

Map 1.5, page 79

This camp is set in the Olympic Peninsula's high country at an elevation of 5,400 feet, just below 6,000-foot Blue Mountain. There are numerous trails in the area, including a major trailhead into the backcountry of Olympic National Park and the Buckhorn Wilderness.

Campsites, facilities: There are 14 sites for tents only. Picnic tables and fire grills are provided. Pit toilets are available. There is no drinking water. At times, garbage must be packed out. Leashed pets are permitted.

Reservations, fees: Reservations are not accepted. Sites are $15 per night, plus a $25 national park entrance fee. Open mid-June-late September.

Directions: From Port Angeles, drive east on U.S. 101 for about five miles to Deer Park Road. Turn right (south) and drive 18 miles to the campground at the end of the road. Note that the last six miles are gravel, steep and narrow, closed to RVs and trailers, and often closed to all vehicles in winter.

Contact: Olympic National Park, 360/565-3132, ww.nps.gov/olym.

46 DUNGENESS FORKS
🚶 🛶 🐕 ⛺

Scenic rating: 7

on the Dungeness and Gray Wolf Rivers in Olympic National Forest

Map 1.5, page 79

This pretty, wooded spot is nestled at the confluence of the Dungeness and Gray Wolf Rivers at an elevation of 1,000 feet. It offers seclusion, yet easy access from the highway. The campsites are set in the forest. If you want quiet, you'll often find it here. The Upper Dungeness Trailhead, located about seven miles south of camp, provides access to Buckhorn Wilderness and Olympic National Park. The trailhead for Gray Wolf Trail is four miles from camp, but note that portions of this trail are sometimes closed due to slides; check with rangers before embarking on a long trip. The Gray Wolf River is closed to fishing year-round to protect salmon. Fishing is permitted on the Dungeness River. Check regulations.

Campsites, facilities: There are 10 sites for tents only. Picnic tables and fire rings are provided. Vault toilets are available. There is no drinking water, and garbage must be packed out. Leashed pets are permitted.

Reservations, fees: Reservations are not accepted. Sites are $14 per night, $5 per extra vehicle per night. Open May-September, weather permitting.

Directions: From Olympia on I-5, turn north on U.S. 101 and drive approximately 100 miles to Palo Alto Road, located 1.5 miles north of Sequim Bay State Park and 3 miles southeast of Sequim. Turn left (south) on Palo Alto Road and drive about seven miles to Forest Road 2880. Turn right (west) and drive one mile (after crossing Dungeness River Bridge) to the campground on the right. Obtaining a U.S. Forest Service map is advised. Trailers and RVs are not recommended because of the steep, narrow, and unpaved access road.

Contact: Olympic National Forest, Hood Canal Ranger District, Quilcene Office, 360/765-2200, www.fs.fed.us.

47 HOH
🚶 🛶 🐕 ♿ 🚐 ⛺

Scenic rating: 10

in Olympic National Park

Map 1.5, page 79

This camp at a trailhead leading into the interior of Olympic National Park is located in the beautiful heart of a temperate, old-growth rainforest. Hoh Oxbow, Cottonwood, Willoughby Creek, and Minnie Peterson Campgrounds are nearby, set downstream on the Hoh River, outside national park boundaries. In the summer, there are naturalist programs, and a visitors center is nearby. This is one of the most popular camps in the park. The elevation is 578 feet.

Campsites, facilities: There are 88 sites for tents or RVs up to 21 feet long. Picnic tables and fire grills are provided. Restrooms with flush toilets and drinking water are available. Some facilities are wheelchair accessible. Leashed pets are permitted.

Reservations, fees: Reservations are not accepted. Sites are $20 per night, plus a $25 national park entrance fee per vehicle. Open year-round.

Directions: From Aberdeen, drive north on U.S. 101 for about 90 miles to Milepost 176. Turn east on Hoh River Road and drive 19 miles to the campground on the right (near the end of the road).

Contact: Olympic National Park, 360/565-3130, www.nps.gov/olym.

48 SOUTH FORK HOH
🏃 🏊 🎣 🐕 ♿ 🚐 ⛺

Scenic rating: 10
in Hoh Clearwater State Forest

Map 1.5, page 79

This rarely used, beautiful camp set along the cascading South Fork of the Hoh River is way out there. It's tiny and primitive but offers a guarantee of peace and quiet, something many U.S. 101 cruisers would cheerfully give a limb for after a few days of fighting crowds. The South Fork Trailhead in Olympic National Park is two miles away. When conditions are right, fishing for steelhead can be excellent (check regulations).

Campsites, facilities: There are seven sites for tents or RVs up to 30 feet. Picnic tables, fire grills, and tent pads are provided. Vault toilets are available. There is no drinking water and garbage must be packed out. Some facilities are wheelchair accessible. Leashed pets are permitted.

Reservations, fees: Reservations are not accepted. There is no fee for camping, but a Discover Pass is required. Open year-round.

Directions: From Olympia on I-5, take Exit 104 and drive north on U.S. 101 to the Aberdeen/Highway 8 exit. Turn west on Highway 8 and drive 36 miles to Aberdeen. Continue through Aberdeen four miles to U.S. 101. Turn north on U.S. 101 and drive about 94 miles. Exit at Milepost 176. At Hoh Mainline Road turn east and drive 6.5 miles. Turn left on Road H1000 and drive 7.5 miles to the campground on the right. Obtaining a Department of Natural Resources (DNR) map is advised.

Contact: Department of Natural Resources, Olympic Region, 360/374-6131, www.dnr.wa.gov.

49 DOSEWALLIPS WALK-IN
🏃 🚲 🐕 ⛺

Scenic rating: 7
on the Dosewallips River in Olympic National Park

Map 1.5, page 79

This road is closed to vehicles due to a road washout at Milepost 10. You can still get to the campground on foot or mountain bike, but it requires a 5.5-mile hike or bike ride. Set on the Dosewallips River at an elevation of 1,500 feet, the camp provides a major trailhead into the backcountry of Olympic National Park. The trail follows the Dosewallips River over Anderson Pass, proceeds along the Quinault River, and ultimately reaches Quinault Lake. Other hiking trails are available nearby. Dosewallips is a more remote option to Collins.

Campsites, facilities: There are 30 sites for tents only. Picnic tables and fire grills are provided. Pit toilets are available. There is no drinking water. Leashed pets are permitted.

Reservations, fees: Reservations are not accepted. There is no entrance fee and no fee for camping. Open mid-May-late September, weather permitting.

Directions: From Olympia on I-5, drive north on U.S. 101 for 60 miles to a signed turnoff near Brinnon (located about one mile north of Dosewallips State Park) for Forest Road 2610 (County Road 2500). Turn left (west) and drive 15 miles along the Dosewallips River to the washout. Note that the access road is not paved and is not recommended for RVs or trailers.

Contact: Olympic National Park, 360/565-3132, www.nps.gov/olym.

50 COLLINS

Scenic rating: 7

on the Duckabush River in Olympic National Forest

Map 1.5, page 79

Most vacationers cruising U.S. 101 don't have a clue about this quiet spot set on a great launch point for adventure, yet it's only five or six miles from the highway. This four-acre camp is located on the Duckabush River at 200 feet elevation. It has small, shaded sites, river access nearby (currents can be swift in high-water years), and plenty of fishing and hiking; check fishing regulations. Just one mile from camp is Duckabush Trail, which connects to trails in Olympic National Park. Murhut Falls Trail starts about three miles from the campground, providing access to a 0.8-mile trail to the falls. It's a 1.5-mile drive to Dosewallips State Park and a 30- to 35-minute drive to Olympic National Park.

Campsites, facilities: There are six sites for tents and 10 sites for RVs up to 21 feet long. Picnic tables and fire rings are provided. Vault toilets are available. There is no drinking water and garbage must be packed out. Leashed pets are permitted.

Reservations, fees: Reservations are not accepted. Sites are $14 per night, $5 per each additional vehicle. Open May-September, weather permitting.

Directions: From Olympia on I-5, drive north on U.S. 101 for 59 miles to Forest Road 2510 (near Duckabush). Turn left on Forest Road 2510 and drive six miles west to the camp on the left.

Contact: Olympic National Forest, Hood Canal Ranger District, Quilcene Office, 360/765-2200, www.fs.fed.us.

51 QUEETS WALK-IN

Scenic rating: 9

on the Queets River in Olympic National Park

Map 1.5, page 79

This primitive camp on the shore of the Queets River is a gem if you don't mind bringing your own water (or purifying river water). A trailhead leads into the interior of Olympic National Park. The elevation is 290 feet.

Campsites, facilities: There are 20 primitive sites for tents only. Picnic tables and fire pits are provided. Pit toilets are available. There is no drinking water and garbage must be packed out. Leashed pets are permitted.

Reservations, fees: Reservations are not accepted. Sites are $15 per night, plus a $25 national park entrance fee. Open year-round.

Directions: From Aberdeen, drive north on U.S. 101 for 38 miles to Lake Quinault, and continue for 19 miles to a signed turnoff for the campground at Forest Road 21. Turn right (northeast) on Forest Road 21 (an unpaved road) and drive 14 miles (along the Queets River) to the campground at the end of the road; not recommended for RVs or trailers.

Contact: Olympic National Park, 360/565-3130, www.nps.gov/olym.

52 GRAVES CREEK

Scenic rating: 6

near the Quinault River in Olympic National Park

Map 1.5, page 79

A road washout now requires a hike of 4.5 miles to reach this spot. This camp is located at an elevation of 540 feet and is a short distance from a trailhead leading into the backcountry of Olympic National Park. The East Fork Quinault River is nearby, and there are lakes in the area.

Campsites, facilities: There are 30 sites for tents only. Picnic tables and fire pits are provided. Pit toilets are available, but there is no drinking water. Leashed pets are permitted.

Reservations, fees: Reservations are not accepted. Sites are $20 per night, plus a $25 national park entrance fee. Open year-round.

Directions: From Aberdeen, drive north on U.S. 101 for 38 miles to the Lake Quinault turnoff and South Shore Road. Turn east on South Shore Road and drive 15 miles to the road washout. Park and hike 4.5 miles to the campground. The Graves Creek Ranger Station is located nearby.

Contact: Olympic National Park, 360/565-3130, www.nps.gov/olym.

53 LENA LAKE HIKE-IN

Scenic rating: 8

near the Hamma Hamma River in Olympic National Forest

Map 1.5, page 79   **BEST (**

Lena Lake is one of the most popular lakes on the Olympic Peninsula. Though it is comparatively crowded in the summer, you can usually get a site. The 55-acre lake is nestled along the Hamma Hamma drainage, between rugged peaks and adjacent to the Brothers Wilderness. It takes a three-mile hike-in from the trailhead at Lena Creek to reach this camp. This adventure is suitable for the entire family—an outstanding way to turn youngsters on to backpacking. (They may get a chuckle out of the "open-air" toilet or "potty with a view.") It's a lovely setting, too, with a pleasantly mild climate in summer. The lake is good for swimming and fishing for rainbow trout. The elevation is 1,800 feet.

Campsites, facilities: There are 29 primitive,

hike-in sites for tents only. A compost toilet and fire rings are available. There is no drinking water and garbage must be packed out. Leashed pets are permitted.

Reservations, fees: Reservations are not accepted. There is no fee for camping, but there is a $5 fee per day to park at the trailhead. Open May-September, weather permitting.

Directions: From Olympia on I-5, turn north on U.S. 101 and drive about 37 miles to Hoodsport. Continue north on U.S. 101 for 14 miles to Forest Road 25. Turn left (west) on Forest Road 25 and drive eight miles to the Lena Creek Camp and the trailhead. Hike 3.2 miles north to Lena Lake. Campsites are scattered around the lake.

Contact: Olympic National Forest, Hood Canal Ranger District, 360/877-5254, www.fs.fed.us.

54 LENA CREEK

Scenic rating: 7

on the Hamma Hamma River in Olympic National Forest

Map 1.5, page 79

This seven-acre camp, set amid both conifers and hardwoods, is located where Lena Creek empties into the Hamma Hamma River. A popular trailhead camp, Lena Creek features a three-mile trail from camp to Lena Lake, with four additional miles to Upper Lena Lake. A map of Olympic National Forest details the trail and road system. The camp is rustic with some improvements.

Campsites, facilities: There are 13 sites for tents or RVs to 21 feet. Picnic tables and fire rings are provided. Vault toilets are available. Drinking water is not available and garbage must be packed out. Leashed pets are permitted.

Reservations, fees: Reservations are not accepted. Sites are $14 per night, $5 per extra vehicle per night. Open mid-May-September.

Directions: From Olympia on I-5, turn

north on U.S. 101 and drive about 37 miles to Hoodsport. Continue north on U.S. 101 for 14 miles to Forest Road 25. Turn left (west) on Forest Road 25 and drive eight miles to the camp on the left.

Contact: Olympic National Forest, Hood Canal Ranger District, Quilcene Office, 360/765-2200, www.fs.fed.us.

55 HAMMA HAMMA

Scenic rating: 7

on the Hamma Hamma River in Olympic National Forest

Map 1.5, page 79

This camp is set on the Hamma Hamma River at an elevation of 600 feet. It's small and primitive, but it can be preferable to some of the developed camps on the U.S. 101 circuit. The Civilian Conservation Corps is memorialized in a wheelchair-accessible interpretive trail that begins in the campground and leads 0.25 mile along the river. The sites are set among conifers and hardwoods.

Campsites, facilities: There are 15 sites for tents or RVs up to 21 feet long. An eight-person cabin (with a flush toilet) is also available. Picnic tables and fire rings are provided. Vault toilets are available. There is no drinking water and garbage must be packed out. Some facilities are wheelchair accessible. Leashed pets are permitted.

Reservations, fees: Reservations are accepted for the cabin only at 877/444-6777 ($10 reservation fee) or www.recreation.gov ($9 reservation fee). Sites are $14 per night, $5 per night per additional vehicle. The cabin is $40-60 per night. The campsites are open May-September, weather permitting; the cabin is available year-round.

Directions: From Olympia on I-5, turn north on U.S. 101 and drive 37 miles to Hoodsport. Continue on U.S. 101 for 14 miles north to Forest Road 25. Turn left on Forest Road 25

and drive seven miles to the camp on the left side of the road.

Contact: Olympic National Forest, Hood Canal Ranger District, Quilcene Office, 360/765-2200, www.fs.fed.us.

56 WILLABY

Scenic rating: 8

on Lake Quinault in Olympic National Forest

Map 1.5, page 79

This pretty, 14-acre wooded camp is set on the shore of Lake Quinault, which covers about six square miles. Part of the Quinault Indian Reservation, the camp is adjacent to where Willaby Creek empties into the lake. The campsites vary—some are open with lake views, while others are more private with no view. The forest floor is covered with wall-to-wall greenery, with exceptional moss growth, and the tree cover consists of Douglas fir, western red cedar, western hemlock, and big-leaf maple. Quinault Rain Forest Nature Trail and the Quinault National Recreation Trail System are nearby. The elevation is 200 feet.

Campsites, facilities: There are 32 sites for tents or RVs up to 16 feet long and two walk-in sites for tents only. Picnic tables and fire pits are provided. Drinking water, garbage bins, and restrooms with flush toilets are available. Launching facilities and rentals are available at nearby Lake Quinault. Some facilities are wheelchair accessible. Leashed pets are permitted.

Reservations, fees: Reservations are accepted at 877/444-6777 ($10 reservation fee) or www. recreation.gov ($9 reservation fee). Sites are $25 per night, $7 per extra vehicle per night. Open year-round, weather permitting

Directions: From Aberdeen, drive north on U.S. 101 for 42 miles to the Lake Quinault-South Shore turnoff. Turn right (northeast) on South Shore Road and drive 1.5 miles to the camp on the southern shore of the lake.

Contact: Olympic National Forest, Pacific

Ranger District, Quinault Office, 360/288-2525, www.fs.fed.us; Quinault Reservation, 360/276-8215.

57 FALLS CREEK
🥾 ≈ 🏕 ♿ 🚐 ⛺

Scenic rating: 8
on Lake Quinault in Olympic National Forest

Map 1.5, page 79

This scenic, wooded three-acre camp is set where Falls Creek empties into Quinault Lake. A canopy of lush big-leaf maple hangs over the campground, which features both drive-in and walk-in sites; the latter require about a 125-yard walk. Quinault Rain Forest Nature Trail and the Quinault National Recreation Trail System are nearby. The camp is located adjacent to the Quinault Ranger Station and historic Lake Quinault Lodge at an elevation of 200 feet.

Campsites, facilities: There are 10 walk-in sites for tents only and 21 sites for tents or RVs up to 16 feet long. Picnic tables and fire pits are provided. Drinking water and restrooms with flush toilets are available. A camp host has firewood for sale nearby. A picnic area, boat launching facilities, and boat rentals are available at Lake Quinault. Some facilities are wheelchair accessible. Two leashed pets are permitted per site.

Reservations, fees: Reservations are accepted at 877/444-6777 ($10 reservation fee) or www.recreation.gov ($9 reservation fee). Sites are $25 per night, $7 per extra vehicle per night. Open Memorial Day weekend-Labor Day weekend.

Directions: From Aberdeen, drive north on U.S. 101 for 42 miles to the Lake Quinault-South Shore turnoff. Turn right (northeast) on South Shore Road and drive 2.5 miles to the camp on the southeast shore of Lake Quinault. Make a very sharp left turn into the campground.

Contact: Olympic National Forest, Pacific

58 GATTON CREEK WALK-IN
🥾 ≈ 🏕 ♿ 🚐 ⛺

Scenic rating: 9
on Lake Quinault in Olympic National Forest

Map 1.5, page 79

This five-acre wooded camp is set on the shore of Lake Quinault (elevation 200 feet), where Gatton Creek empties into it. Lake Quinault covers about six square miles and is part of the Quinault Indian Nation, which has jurisdiction here. The camp features great views across the lake to the forested slopes of Olympic National Park. Reaching the campsites requires about a 100-yard walk from the parking area. About nine miles of loop trails are accessible here; Quinault Rain Forest Nature Trail and the Quinault National Recreation Trail System are nearby.

Campsites, facilities: There are 15 walk-in sites for tents and 10 overflow sites for RVs up to 24 feet long. Picnic tables and fire pits are provided at the tent sites. Vault toilets, firewood, and a picnic area are available. Some facilities are wheelchair accessible. Leashed pets are permitted.

Reservations, fees: Reservations are not accepted. Sites are $20 per night. Open late May-early October, weather permitting.

Directions: From Aberdeen, drive north on U.S. 101 for 42 miles to the Lake Quinault-South Shore turnoff. Turn right (northeast) on South Shore Road and drive three miles to the camp on the southeast shore of Lake Quinault.

Contact: Olympic National Forest, Pacific Ranger District, Quinault Office, 360/288-2525, www.fs.fed.us; Quinault Reservation, 360/276-8215; Quinault Lodge, 360/288-2910.

59 CAMPBELL TREE GROVE

🥾 🛶 🐕 ♿ 🚐 ⛺

Scenic rating: 8

on the Humptulips River in Olympic National Forest

Map 1.5, page 79   **BEST (**

This 14-acre camp is set amid dense, old-growth forest featuring stands of both conifers and hardwoods, with licorice ferns growing on the trunks and branches of the big-leaf maples. The camp is a favorite for hikers, with trailheads nearby that provide access to the Colonel Bob Wilderness. One of the best, the 3,400-foot climb to the Colonel Bob Summit provides an 8.5-mile round-trip accessible from the Pete's Creek Trailhead, which is located a couple of miles south of camp on Forest Road 2204. Note that much of this summit hike is a great butt-kicker. The West Fork of the Humptulips River runs near the camp, and Humptulips Trail provides access. Fishing is an option here as well; check state regulations.

Campsites, facilities: There are eight tent sites and three sites for RVs up to 16 feet long. Picnic tables and fire grills are provided. Vault toilets and garbage bins are available. There is no drinking water. Some facilities are wheelchair accessible. Leashed pets are permitted.

Reservations, fees: Reservations are not accepted. There is no fee for camping. Open May-October, weather permitting.

Directions: From Aberdeen, drive north on U.S. 101 for 22 miles to Humptulips and continue for another five miles to Forest Road 22 (Donkey Creek Road). Turn right and drive eight miles to Forest Road 2204. Turn left (north) and drive nine miles to the campground.

Contact: Olympic National Forest, Pacific Ranger District, Quinault Office, 360/288-2525, www.fs.fed.us.

60 STAIRCASE

🥾 🛶 🐕 ♿ 🚐 ⛺

Scenic rating: 9

on the North Fork of the Skokomish River in Olympic National Park

Map 1.5, page 79

This camp is located near the Staircase Rapids of the North Fork of the Skokomish River, about one mile from where it empties into Lake Cushman. The elevation is 765 feet. A major trailhead at the camp leads to the backcountry of Olympic National Park, and other trails are nearby. Hiking trails along the river can be accessed nearby. Stock facilities are also available nearby. Note that Staircase Road is closed in winter.

Campsites, facilities: There are 47 sites for tents or RVs up to 35 feet. Picnic tables and fire pits are provided. Restrooms with flush toilets and drinking water are available during the summer season. In winter, only pit toilets are available. Some facilities are wheelchair accessible. Leashed pets are permitted in camp.

Reservations, fees: Reservations are not accepted. Sites are $20 per night, plus a $25 national park entrance fee per vehicle. Open year-round, with limited winter services.

Directions: From Olympia on I-5, take U.S. 101 and drive north about 37 miles to the town of Hoodsport and Lake Cushman Road (County Road 119). Turn left (west) and drive 17 miles to the camp at the end of the road (set about one mile above the inlet of Lake Cushman). The last several miles of the road are unpaved.

Contact: Olympic National Park, 360/565-3130, www.nps.gov/olym.

61 COHO

🥾 🛶 🚐 🐕 🚐 ⛺

Scenic rating: 10

on Wynoochee Lake in Olympic National Forest

Map 1.5, page 79   **BEST (**

This eight-acre camp sits on the shore of Wynoochee Lake, which is 4.4 miles long and covers 1,140 acres. The camp is set at an elevation of 900 feet. The fishing season opens June 1 and closes October 31. Powerboats, waterskiing, and personal watercraft are permitted. Points of interest include Working Forest Nature Trail, Wynoochee Dam Viewpoint and exhibits, and 16-mile Wynoochee Lake Shore Trail, which circles the lake. This is one of the most idyllic drive-to settings you could hope to find.

Campsites, facilities: There are 46 sites for tents or RVs up to 36 feet long, 10 walk-in sites for tents only, three yurts, and two group sites for 16 people each. Picnic tables are provided. Drinking water and flush toilets are available. A dump station is nearby. Boat docks and launching facilities are available at Wynoochee Lake. Leashed pets are permitted.

Reservations, fees: Reservations are accepted at 877/444-6777 ($10 reservation fee) or www.recreation.gov ($9 reservation fee). Sites are $20-25 per night, $5 per extra vehicle per night; the group site is $45 per night and yurts are $70 per night. Open May-November, weather permitting.

Directions: From Olympia on I-5, take Exit 104 and drive north on U.S. 101 to the Aberdeen/Highway 8 exit. Turn west on Highway 8 and drive 36 miles (it becomes U.S. 12 at Elma) to Montesano. Continue two miles on U.S. 12 to Wynoochee Valley Road. Turn right (north) on Wynoochee Valley Road and drive 12 miles to Forest Road 22. Continue north on Forest Road 22 (a gravel road) for 23 miles to Wynoochee Lake. Just south of the lake, bear left and drive on Forest Road 2294 (which runs along the lake's northwest shore) for one mile to the camp on the west shore of Wynoochee Lake. Obtaining a U.S. Forest Service map is helpful.

Contact: Olympic National Forest, Hood Canal Ranger District, Quilcene Office, 360/765-2200, www.fs.fed.us.

62 BROWN CREEK

Scenic rating: 9

on Brown Creek in Olympic National Forest

Map 1.5, page 79

Brown Creek is little known among out-of-town visitors. While this camp is accessible to two-wheel-drive vehicles, the access road connects to a network of primitive, backcountry forest roads. It is situated within the vast Olympic National Forest, which offers many opportunities for outdoor recreation. Wheelchair-accessible Brown Creek Nature Trail begins at the hand pump and makes a one-mile loop around the camp, featuring views of an active beaver pond. Obtain a U.S. Forest Service map to expand your trip.

Campsites, facilities: There are 12 sites for tents or RVs up to 20 feet long and eight sites for tents only. Picnic tables and fire rings are provided. Drinking water (summer only) and vault toilets are available. Garbage must be packed out. Some facilities are wheelchair accessible. Leashed pets are permitted.

Reservations, fees: Reservations are not accepted. Sites are $14 per night, $5 per extra vehicle per night. Open year-round, weather permitting.

Directions: From Olympia on I-5, take Exit 104 for U.S. 101/Highway 8. Drive north on U.S. 101 for 31 miles (about six miles past Shelton) to Skokomish Valley Road. Turn left (west) and drive 5.3 miles to Forest Road 23. Turn right on Forest Road 23 and drive nine miles to Forest Road 2353. Turn right on Forest Road 2353 and drive one mile to the South Fork Skokomish River Bridge. Cross the bridge, then turn right sharply onto Forest Road 2340 and drive 0.25 mile to the camp. Obtaining a U.S. Forest Service map is advisable.

Contact: Olympic National Forest, Hood Canal Ranger District, Quilcene Office, 360/765-2200, www.fs.fed.us.

63 LEBAR HORSE CAMP

🏕 🛶 🐴 🚗 ⛺

Scenic rating: 9

in Olympic National Forest

Map 1.5, page 79

This camp is exclusively for people with horses or pack animals, such as mules, mollies, llamas, and goats. The camp provides access to Lower South Fork Skokomish Trail, a 10.9 mile trip (one-way). The camp features beautiful old-growth forest, with western hemlock and Douglas fir.

Campsites, facilities: There are 13 sites for tents or RVs up to 28 feet long for the exclusive use of campers with pack animals. Picnic tables, fire grills, hitching posts, and high lines are provided. Vault toilets are available. There is no drinking water, and garbage must be packed out. A day-use area with a picnic shelter is available nearby. Leashed pets are permitted.

Reservations, fees: Reservations are not accepted. Sites are $14 per night (8 people max.), $5 per extra vehicle per night. Open May-September, weather permitting.

Directions: From Olympia on I-5, take Exit 104 for U.S. 101/Highway 8. Drive north on U.S. 101 for 31 miles (about six miles past Shelton) to Skokomish Valley Road. Turn left (west) and drive 5.3 miles to Forest Road 23. Turn right on Forest Road 23 and drive nine miles to Forest Road 2353. Turn right on Forest Road 2353 and drive one mile to the South Fork Skokomish River Bridge. Cross the bridge, turn left sharply to remain on Forest Road 2353, and drive 0.5 mile to the camp. Obtaining a U.S. Forest Service map is advisable.

Contact: Olympic National Forest, Hood Canal Ranger District, Quilcene Office, 360/765-2200, www.fs.fed.us.

64 BIG CREEK

🏕 🛶 🚐 🐴 🚗 ⛺

Scenic rating: 7

near Lake Cushman in Olympic National Forest

Map 1.5, page 79

Big Creek is an alternative to Staircase Camp on the North Fork of the Skokomish River and Camp Cushman and Recreation Park, both of which get heavier use. The sites here are large and well spaced for privacy over 30 acres, primarily of second-growth forest. Big Creek runs adjacent to the campground. A four-mile loop trail extends from camp and connects to Mount Eleanor Trail. A bonus: Two walk-in sites are located along the creek.

Campsites, facilities: There are 23 sites for tents or RVs up to 30 feet long. Picnic tables and fire grills are provided. Drinking water, vault toilets, and a sheltered picnic area are available. A boat dock and ramp are located at nearby Lake Cushman. Garbage must be packed out. Leashed pets are permitted.

Reservations, fees: Reservations are not accepted. Sites are $20 per night, $5 per extra vehicle per night. Open May-September, weather permitting.

Directions: From Olympia on I-5, take Exit 104 for U.S. 101/Highway 8. Drive north on U.S. 101 for 37 miles to Hoodsport and Lake Cushman Road (Highway 119). Turn left on Lake Cushman Road and drive nine miles (two miles north of Camp Cushman) to the T intersection with Forest Road 24. Turn left and the campground is on the right.

Contact: Olympic National Forest, Hood Canal Ranger District, Quilcene Office, 360/765-2200, www.fs.fed.us; visitors center, 360/877-2021.

65 SKOKOMISH PARK AT LAKE CUSHMAN

Scenic rating: 10

on Lake Cushman near Hoodsport

Map 1.5, page 79   BEST (

Set in the foothills of the Olympic Mountains on the shore of Lake Cushman, this 500-acre park features a 10-mile-long blue-water mountain lake, eight miles of park shoreline, forested hillsides, and awesome views of snowcapped peaks. Beach access and good trout fishing are other highlights. The park has eight miles of hiking trails. Windsurfing, waterskiing, and swimming are all popular here. A nine-hole golf course is nearby.

Campsites, facilities: There are 60 sites for tents, 34 sites with full hookups (20 and 30 amps) for RVs up to 30 feet long, two hike-in/bike-in sites, and one group camp for up to 80 people. Picnic tables and fire grills are provided. Restrooms with flush toilets and coin showers, drinking water, a camp store, picnic area, amphitheater, horseshoe pits, badminton, volleyball court, ice, and firewood are available. A restaurant is within five miles. Boat docks and launching facilities are also available. Some facilities are wheelchair accessible. Leashed pets are permitted.

Reservations, fees: Reservations are recommended ($7 reservation fee). RV sites start at $34 per night, tent sites start at $28 per night, hike-in/bike-in sites start at $23 per night, $10 per extra vehicle per night. The group camp starts at $179 per night. Some credit cards are accepted. Open year-round, weather permitting.

Directions: From Olympia on I-5, take the U.S. 101 exit and drive north 37 miles to Hoodsport and Highway 119 (Lake Cushman Road). Turn left (west) on Lake Cushman Road and drive 7.5 miles to the park on the left.

Contact: Skokomish Park at Lake Cushman, 7211 N. Lake Cushman Rd., Hoodsport, 360/877-5760, www.skokomishpark.com.

66 LAKE CUSHMAN RESORT

Scenic rating: 10

on Lake Cushman near Hoodsport

Map 1.5, page 79

This campground on Lake Cushman has full facilities for water sports, including boat launching and rentals. Waterskiing and fishing are popular. Lake Cushman Dam makes a good side trip. Trails in the Olympic National Forest and at Staircase in Olympic National Park are nearby.

Campsites, facilities: There are 50 sites for tents or RVs up to 22 feet long (no hookups), 21 sites with partial hookups (20 amps) for RVs up to 40 feet long, and 12 cabins. Double and triple tent sites are also available. Picnic tables and fire rings are provided. Drinking water, flush and portable toilets, firewood, a convenience store, boat docks and launching facilities, mooring, and boat rentals are available. Groups can be accommodated. Some facilities are wheelchair accessible. Leashed pets are permitted.

Reservations, fees: Reservations are recommended. RV sites are $34-40 per night, tent sites are $34-75 per night, $5 per each additional person per night, $6 per each additional vehicle, $10 per pet per stay, and mooring is $10-15 per day. Off-season rates available October 1-April 30. Some credit cards are accepted. Open mid-April-mid-October; cabins are open year-round.

Directions: From Olympia on I-5, take the U.S. 101 exit and drive north 37 miles to Hoodsport and Highway 119/Lake Cushman Road. Turn left (west) on Lake Cushman Road and drive 4.5 miles to the resort on the left.

Contact: Lake Cushman Resort, 4621 N. Lake Cushman Rd., Hoodsport, 360/877-9630 or 800/588-9630, www.lakecushman.com.

67 REST-A-WHILE RV PARK

Scenic rating: 5

on Hood Canal north of Hoodsport

Map 1.5, page 79

This seven-acre park, located at sea level on Hood Canal, offers waterfront sites and a private beach for clamming and oyster gathering, not to mention plenty of opportunities to fish, boat, and scuba dive. It's an alternative to Potlatch State Park and Glen-Ayr RV Park.

Campsites, facilities: There are 92 sites for tents or RVs up to 45 feet (30 and 50 amps); some sites are pull-through. Cabin and cottage rentals are also available. Picnic tables and fire rings are provided at some sites. Restrooms with flush toilets and showers, drinking water, cable TV, Wi-Fi, propane gas, firewood, a clubhouse, restaurant, coin laundry, and ice are available. A café is within walking distance. Boat and kayak rentals and a private beach for clamming and oyster gathering (in season) are also available. Some facilities are wheelchair accessible. Leashed pets are permitted.

Reservations, fees: Reservations are accepted. RV sites are $40-45 per night. Some credit cards are accepted. Open year-round.

Directions: From Olympia on I-5, take Exit 104 for U.S. 101/Highway 8. Drive north on U.S. 101 for 37 miles to Hoodsport. Continue 2.5 miles north on U.S. 101 to the park located at Milepost 329.

Contact: Rest-A-While RV Park, 27001 N. US Hwy. 101, Hoodsport, 360/877-9474 or 866/637-9474, www.restawhile.com.

68 GLEN-AYR RV PARK & MOTEL

Scenic rating: 5

on Hood Canal near Hoodsport

Map 1.5, page 79

This fully developed, nine-acre park is located at sea level on Hood Canal, where there are opportunities to fish and scuba dive. Salmon fishing is especially excellent. Swimming and boating round out the options. The park also has a spa, moorage, horseshoe pits, recreation field, and a motel.

Campsites, facilities: There are 36 sites with full hookups (30 and 50 amps) for RVs of any length, 14 motel rooms, a townhouse, two suites with kitchens, and one furnished cabin for up to six adults (no pets). Some sites are pull-through. Picnic tables are provided. No open fires are allowed. Restrooms with flush toilets and showers, drinking water, cable TV, Wi-Fi, propane gas, ice, a spa, recreation hall, barbecue, gazebo (with interior dining), seasonal organized activities, and coin laundry are available. A store and café are within one mile. A boat dock is located across the street from the park, with moorage for guests. Leashed pets are permitted in certain sites.

Reservations, fees: Reservations are accepted. Sites are $29-60 per night, $5 per person per night for more than two people, $5 per extra vehicle per night. Some credit cards are accepted. Open year-round.

Directions: From Olympia on I-5, take Exit 104 for U.S. 101/Highway 8. Drive north on U.S. 101 for 37 miles to Hoodsport. Continue one mile north on U.S. 101 to the park on the left.

Contact: Glen-Ayr RV Park & Motel, 25381 N. U.S. 101, Hoodsport, 360/877-9522 or 866/877-9522, www.glenayr.com.

69 POTLATCH STATE PARK

Scenic rating: 8

on Hood Canal

Map 1.5, page 79

This 125-acre state park features good shellfish harvesting in season. The park has 5,700 feet of shoreline on Hood Canal with 0.2 mile for hiking and biking. The shoreline and water bring people here for the good kayaking, windsurfing, scuba diving, clamming, and fishing. The park is named for the potlatch, a Skyhomish gift-giving ceremony. There are four major rivers, the Skokomish, Hamma Hamma, Duckabush, and Dosewallips, within a 30-mile radius of the park. The park receives an annual rainfall of 64 inches.

Campsites, facilities: There are 35 sites with full or partial hookups (30 and 50 amps) for RVs up to 60 feet long, 38 sites for tents, and two hike-in/bike-in sites. Picnic tables and fire grills are provided. Restrooms with flush toilets and coin showers, drinking water, a dump station, firewood, an amphitheater, a picnic area, and seasonal interpretive programs are available. Five mooring buoys are located at the park, and a boat launch and dock are available nearby. Groceries, gas, and propane are available three miles away. Some facilities are wheelchair accessible. Leashed pets are permitted.

Reservations, fees: Reservations are accepted in summer at 888/226-7688 or https://washington.goingtocamp.com. Sites are $20-45 per night, $12 per night for hike-in/bike-in sites, $10 per extra vehicle per night, $12 buoy fee per night. Open year-round.

Directions: From Olympia on I-5, take Exit 104 for U.S. 101/Highway 8. Drive north on U.S. 101 for 22 miles to Shelton. Continue north on U.S. 101 for 12 miles to the park on the right (located along the shoreline of Annas Bay on Hood Canal).

Contact: Potlatch State Park, 360/877-5361, http://parks.state.wa.us.

70 SCHAFER STATE PARK

🏃 🏊 🛶 🚣 🐴 ♿ 🚐 ⛺

Scenic rating: 8

on the Satsop River

Map 1.5, page 79

This unique destination boasts many interesting features, including buildings constructed from native stone. A heavily wooded, rural camp, Schafer State Park covers 119 acres along the East Fork of the Satsop River. The river is known for fishing and rafting. Fish for sea-run cutthroat in summer, salmon in fall, and steelhead in late winter. There are good canoeing and kayaking spots, some with Class II and III rapids, along the Middle and West Forks of the Satsop. Three miles of hiking trails are also available. At one time, this park was the Schafer Logging Company Park and was used by employees and their families. The park features outdoor exhibits, summer lectures, and a host of year-round events.

Campsites, facilities: There are 27 sites for tents and RVs up to 40 feet long, nine sites with water and electricity, four walk-in tent sites, one primitive site, one ADA site, and two group sites for up to 50 and 100 people respectively. Picnic tables and fire grills are provided. A restroom with flush toilets, coin showers, drinking water, picnic shelters that can be reserved, a dump station, and horseshoe pits are available. Some facilities are wheelchair accessible. Leashed pets are permitted.

Reservations, fees: Reservations are accepted for summer at 888/226-7688 or https://washington.goingtocamp.com. Sites are $20-45 per night, $10 per extra vehicle per night, hike-in/bike-in sites are $12 per night, and the group sites are $69.89-209.67 per night. Open late April-early October, weather permitting.

Directions: From Olympia on I-5, take Exit 104 to U.S. 101. Drive west on U.S. 101 for six miles to Highway 8. Turn west on Highway 8 and drive to Elma (Highway 8 becomes Highway 12). Continue west on Highway 12 for five miles to the Brady exit/West Satsop Road (four miles east of Montesano). Turn right (north) on West Satsop Road and drive eight miles to Schafer Park Road. Turn right and drive two miles to the park.

Contact: Schafer State Park, 360/482-3852, http://parks.state.wa.us.

71 LAKE SYLVIA STATE PARK

🚶‍♀️🏊‍♂️🚣‍♂️🛶🎣🐎🚵‍♂️♿🚗⛺

Scenic rating: 8

on Lake Sylvia

Map 1.5, page 79   **BEST (**

This 252-acre state park on the shore of Lake Sylvia features nearly three miles of freshwater shoreline. The park is located in a former logging camp in a wooded area set midway between Olympia and the Pacific Ocean. Expect plenty of rustic charm, with displays of old logging gear, a giant ball carved out of wood from a single log, and some monstrous stumps. The lake is good for fishing and ideal for canoes, prams, or small boats with oars or electric motors; no gas motors are permitted. Five miles of hiking trails and a 0.5-mile wheelchair-accessible trail meander through the park. Additional recreation options include trout fishing and swimming.

Campsites, facilities: There are 31 tent sites, four sites with partial hookups for RVs up to 30 feet long, two hike-in/bike-in sites, and one group site for tents only that can accommodate up to 50 people and five vehicles. Picnic tables and fire grills are provided. Restrooms with flush toilets and coin showers, drinking water, a dump station, boat launch, picnic area, a kitchen shelter that can be reserved, firewood, and a playground are available. A coin laundry and grocery store are located within two miles. Some facilities are wheelchair accessible. Leashed pets are permitted.

Reservations, fees: Reservations are accepted for individual sites and are required for the group site (Apr.-Sept.) at 888/226-7688 or https://washington.goingtocamp.com ($8-10 reservation fee). Sites are $20-45 per night, $10 per extra vehicle per night, hike-in/bike-in sites are $12 per night, and the group site is $71-171 per night (20-person min., 50-person max.). Open early April-mid-October, weather permitting.

Directions: From Olympia on I-5, take Exit 104 to U.S. 101. Drive west on U.S. 101 for six miles to Highway 8. Turn west on Highway 8 (it becomes Highway 12) and drive 26 miles to Montesano and West Pioneer Street (the only stoplight in town). Turn left on West Pioneer Street and drive three blocks to 3rd Street. Turn right and drive two miles to the park entrance (route is well signed).

Contact: Lake Sylvia State Park, 360/249-3621, http://parks.state.wa.us.

72 TRAVEL INN RESORT

🚶‍♀️🚴‍♂️🏊‍♂️🚣‍♂️🐎🚵‍♂️♿🚗⛺

Scenic rating: 7

on Lake Sylvia near Elma

Map 1.5, page 79

This is a membership campground, which means sites for RV travelers are available only if there is extra space. It can be difficult to get a spot May-September, but the park opens up significantly in the off-season. There are five major rivers or lakes within 15 minutes of this camp (Satsop, Chehalis, Wynoochee, Black River, and Lake Sylvia). Nearby Lake Sylvia State Park provides multiple marked hiking trails. Additional recreation options include trout fishing, swimming, and golf (three miles away).

Campsites, facilities: There are 134 sites with full or partial hookups (30 and 50 amps) for RVs of any length and three tent sites. Picnic tables are provided. Restrooms with flush toilets and showers, drinking water, coin laundry, two community fire pits, a gazebo, a seasonal heated swimming pool, playground, basketball, volleyball, badminton, shuffleboard, game room, cable TV, Wi-Fi and modem access, seasonal organized activities, and a clubhouse are available. A grocery store, gas station, propane, and restaurant are available within one mile. Some facilities are wheelchair accessible. Leashed pets are permitted.

Reservations, fees: Reservations are accepted May-September. Sites are $40-42 per night. No credit cards are accepted. Open year-round.

Directions: From Olympia on I-5, take Exit 104 to U.S. 101. Drive west on U.S. 101 for six miles to Highway 8. Turn west on Highway 8 and drive to Elma (Highway 8 becomes Highway 12). Take the first Elma exit and drive to the stop sign and Highway 12/East Main Street. Turn right and drive about 200 yards to the end of the highway and a stop sign. Turn right and drive another 200 yards to the resort on the right.

Contact: Travel Inn Resort, 801 East Main, Elma, 360/482-3877 or 800/871-2888, www.kmresorts.com.

73 KITSAP MEMORIAL STATE PARK

Scenic rating: 10

on Hood Canal

Map 1.6, page 80   **BEST (**

Kitsap Memorial State Park is a beautiful spot for campers along Hood Canal. The park covers only 58 acres but features sweeping views of Puget Sound and 1,797 feet of shoreline. The park has 1.5 miles of hiking trails and two open grassy fields for family play. Note that the nearest boat launch is four miles away, north on State Route 3 at Salisbury County Park. An 18-hole golf course and swimming, fishing, and hiking at nearby Anderson Lake Recreation Area are among the activities available. A short drive north will take you to historic Old Fort Townsend, which makes an excellent day trip.

Campsites, facilities: There are 21 sites for tents or RVs up to 30 feet long, 18 sites with partial hookups (30 amps) for RVs, three hike-in/bike-in sites, a group camp for 20-56 people, and four cabins. Picnic tables and fire grills are provided. Restrooms with flush toilets and showers, drinking water, a dump station, sheltered picnic area, firewood, a playground, ballfields, and a community meeting hall are available. Two gas stations with mini-marts are located just outside the park. Two boat buoys are available. Some facilities are wheelchair accessible. Leashed pets are permitted.

Reservations, fees: Reservations are not accepted for individual campsites, but are required for the group camp at 888/226-7688 or https://washington.goingtocamp.com ($8-10 reservation fee). Sites are $20-45 per night, hike-in/bike-in sites are $12 per night, $10 per extra vehicle per night. The group camp is $151 per night and the cabins are $45-69 per night. Open year-round.

Directions: From Tacoma on I-5, turn north on Highway 16 and drive 44 miles (Highway 16 turns into Highway 3). Continue north on Highway 3 and drive six miles to Park Street. Turn left and drive 200 yards to the park entrance on the right (it's well-marked). The park is located four miles south of the Hood Canal Bridge.

Contact: Kitsap Memorial State Park, 360/779-3205, http://parks.state.wa.us.

74 COVE RV PARK

Scenic rating: 5

near Dabob Bay near Brinnon

Map 1.6, page 80

This five-acre private camp enjoys a rural setting close to the shore of Dabob Bay (said to be home of the world's largest clam pile), yet it is fully developed. Campsites are graveled and grassy with a few trees. A walking trail skirts Marple Creek and scuba diving is popular in this area. Dosewallips State Park is a short drive away and a possible side trip.

Campsites, facilities: There are 24 sites with full hookups (30 and 50 amps) for RVs up to 40 feet. Picnic tables and fire rings are provided. Restrooms with flush toilets and coin showers, drinking water, cable TV, Wi-Fi, propane gas, a convenience store, bait and tackle, coin laundry, barbecue area, horseshoe pits, and ice are available. Boat docks and launching facilities are on Hood Canal 2.2 miles from the park. Leashed pets are permitted.

Reservations, fees: Reservations are accepted. Sites are $35 per night. Some credit cards are accepted. Open April 1-October 31.

Directions: From Olympia on I-5, drive north on U.S. 101 for about 60 miles to Brinnon (located about one mile north of Dosewallips State Park). Continue three miles north on U.S. 101 to the park on the right (before Milepost 303).

Contact: Cove RV Park, 303075 N. U.S. 101, Brinnon, 360/796-4723, www.coverv.com.

75 SEAL ROCK

Scenic rating: 9

on Dabob Bay in Olympic National Forest

Map 1.6, page 80

Seal Rock is a 30-acre camp set along the shore near the mouth of Dabob Bay. This is one of the few national forest campgrounds anywhere located on saltwater. It brings with it the opportunity to harvest oysters and clams in season, and it is an outstanding jumping-off point for scuba diving. Most campsites are set along the waterfront, spaced among trees. Carry-in boats, such as kayaks and canoes, can be launched from the north landing. The Native American Nature Trail and Marine Biology Nature Trail begin at the day-use area. These are short walks, each less than 0.5 mile. This camp is extremely popular in the summer, often filling up quickly.

Campsites, facilities: There are 41 sites for tents or RVs up to 21 feet long. Picnic tables and fire rings are provided. Restrooms with flush toilets, drinking water, garbage bins, and a picnic area are available. A camp host is on-site in summer. Boat docks and launching facilities are nearby on Hood Canal and in Dabob Bay. Some facilities, including viewing areas and trails, are wheelchair accessible. Leashed pets are permitted.

Reservations, fees: Reservations are not accepted. Sites are $18 per night, $5 per each additional vehicle. Open May-September, weather permitting.

Directions: From Olympia on I-5, drive north on U.S. 101 for about 60 miles to Brinnon (located about one mile north of Dosewallips State Park). Continue two miles north on U.S. 101 to Seal Rock and the camp on the right.

Contact: Olympic National Forest, Hood Canal Ranger District, Quilcene Office, 360/765-2200, www.fs.fed.us.

76 DOSEWALLIPS STATE PARK

Scenic rating: 8

on Dosewallips Creek

Map 1.6, page 80

This 1,039-acre park is set on the shore of Hood Canal at the mouth of the Dosewallips River. Most sites are grassy and are located in scenic and rustic settings. The campsite is popular because it's set right off a major highway; reservations or early arrival is advised. The park features 5,500 feet of saltwater shoreline on Hood Canal and 5,400 feet of shoreline on both sides of the Dosewallips River. Check regulations for fishing and clamming, which fluctuate according to time, season, and supply. There is no formal swimming area on the river, though it is a popular park activity. Please note that the river can be swift and may not be suitable for younger children. Mushrooming is available in season. The park often hosts an annual "Shrimp Fest" in April. Access is not affected by the nearby slide area.

Campsites, facilities: There are 75 sites for tents, 48 utility sites for RVs up to 60 feet (no hookups), three platform tent sites, 12 cabins, and two group sites for 20-80 people. Picnic tables and fire rings are provided. Restrooms with flush toilets and coin showers, drinking water, a dump station, a sheltered picnic area, interpretive activities, and a summer Junior Ranger Program are available. A wildlife-viewing platform, horseshoe pits, saltwater boat-launching facilities, and overnight mooring sites are available within the park. A store and café are available nearby. Some facilities are wheelchair accessible. Leashed pets are permitted.

Reservations, fees: Reservations are accepted at 888/226-7688 or https://washington.goingto-camp.com ($8-10 reservation fee). Sites are $20-45 per night, $10 per extra vehicle per night; hike-in/bike-in sites are $14 per night, platform tent rentals are $44-65 per night, group sites are $154-225 per night, cabins are $50-76 per night. Some credit cards are accepted. Open year-round with limited sites in winter.

Directions: From Olympia on I-5, drive north on U.S. 101 for about 60 miles (one mile south of Brinnon) to the state park entrance on the left.

Contact: Dosewallips State Park, 360/796-4415, http://parks.state.wa.us.

77 SCENIC BEACH STATE PARK

🚶 🏊 🚣 🐕 👫 ♿ 🚐 ⛺

Scenic rating: 10

on Hood Canal

Map 1.6, page 80

Scenic Beach is an exceptionally beautiful state park with beach access and superb views of the Olympic Mountains. The 88-acre campground accesses 1,500 feet of saltwater beachfront on Hood Canal. The park is also known for its wild rhododendrons in spring. Wheelchair-accessible paths lead to a country garden, gazebo, rustic bridge, and large trees. Many species of birds and wildlife can often be seen here. This camp is also close to Green Mountain Forest, where there is extensive hiking. A boat ramp is 0.5 mile east of the park. A nice touch here is that park staff will check out volleyballs and horseshoes during the summer.

Campsites, facilities: There are 52 sites for tents or RVs up to 60 feet (18 sites are pull-through) and a group camp for 20-40 people. Picnic tables and fire grills are provided. Restrooms with flush toilets and coin showers, drinking water, and a dump station are available. A sheltered picnic area, playground, horseshoe pits, and volleyball fields are nearby. A boat ramp, dock, and moorage are available

within one mile. Some facilities are wheelchair accessible. Leashed pets are permitted.

Reservations, fees: Reservations are accepted at 888/226-7688 or https://washington.goingto-camp.com ($8-10 reservation fee). Sites are $20-45 per night, $10 per extra vehicle per night. Call for group rates. Open year-round, weather permitting.

Directions: From the junction at Highway 16 and Highway 3 in Bremerton, turn north on Highway 3 and drive about nine miles and take the first Silverdale exit (Newberry Hill Road). Turn left and drive approximately three miles to the end of the road. Turn right on Seabeck Highway and drive six miles to Scenic Beach Road. Turn right and drive one mile to the park.

Contact: Scenic Beach State Park, 360/830-5079, http://parks.state.wa.us.

78 FAY BAINBRIDGE PARK

🚶 🏊 🚐 🐕 👫 ♿ 🚐 ⛺

Scenic rating: 10

on Bainbridge Island

Map 1.6, page 80   **BEST (**

This former state park is now run by the local parks and recreation district. Set on the edge of Puget Sound, it still offers beauty and great recreation. The park covers just 17 acres but features 1,420 feet of saltwater shoreline on the northeast corner of the island. You can hike several miles along the beach at low tide; the water temperature is typically about 55°F in summer. The primitive walk-in sites are heavily wooded, and the developed sites have great views of the sound. On clear days, campers can enjoy views of Mount Rainier and Mount Baker to the east, and at night the park provides beautiful vistas of the lights of Seattle. Clamming, diving, picnicking, beachcombing, and kite-flying are popular here. In the winter months, there is excellent salmon fishing just offshore of the park.

Campsites, facilities: There are 26 sites for RVs up to 40 feet long; seven sites have water only; 19 sites have water and electricity. There are also 14 sites for tents only, three hike-in/bike-in sites (one night max.), two cabins, and one group site for up to 16 people. Picnic tables and fire grills are provided. Restrooms with flush toilets and coin showers, drinking water, sheltered picnic areas, firewood, horseshoes, and playground are available. Mooring buoys are available nearby. A store and café are located within three miles. Some facilities are wheelchair accessible. Leashed pets are permitted.

Reservations, fees: Reservations are accepted online ($3 reservation fee). RV sites are $30-40 per night, tent sites are $20 per night, the cabins are $95 per night, and the group site is $65 per night; $10 per extra vehicle per night, hike-in/bike-in sites are $7 per person per night. Two-night minimum for weekend. Open year-round, weather permitting.

Directions: From Tacoma at I-5, turn north on Highway 16 and drive 30 miles to Bremerton to the junction with Highway 3. Turn north on Highway 3 and drive 18 miles to Highway 305. Turn south on Highway 305 and drive over the bridge to Bainbridge Island and continue three miles to Day Road. Turn left and drive 1.5 miles to Sunrise Drive. Turn left and drive two miles to the park on the right.

Note: From Seattle, this camp can be more easily accessed by taking the Bainbridge Island ferry and then Highway 305 north to Day Road at the northeast end of the island. From there, follow the directions above.

Contact: Bainbridge Island, 206/842-2306, www.biparks.org.

79 GREEN MOUNTAIN HORSE CAMP

🚶 🚴 🏇 ♿ ⛺ 🚐

Scenic rating: 7

in Green Mountain State Forest

Map 1.6, page 80

This is a prime spot. Operated by the Department of Natural Resources, the campground is located in Green Mountain State Forest. The Backcountry Horsemen of Washington hosts the camp, which features facilities for horses. Hand-pumped stock water is available, a plus for such a primitive site. Note that if the gate is closed, a four-mile hike is required to reach the sites.

Campsites, facilities: There are 12 sites for tents or RVs up to 25 feet. Picnic tables and fire grills are provided. Vault toilets, a group shelter, and horse corrals are available. There is no drinking water, and garbage must be packed out. Some facilities are wheelchair accessible. Leashed pets are permitted.

Reservations, fees: Reservations are not accepted. There is no fee for camping, but a Discover Pass is required. A gate limits vehicular access to the camp; walk-in access is available when the gate is closed. A free map and brochure are available. Open Memorial Day-Labor Day, with seasonal vehicle access.

Directions: From Tacoma on I-5, turn north on Highway 16 and drive 30 miles to Bremerton and the junction with Highway 3. Turn north on Highway 3 and drive to Newberry Hill Road. Turn left onto Seabeck Highway and drive two miles to Holly Road. Turn right on Holly Road and drive 2.2 miles to Tahuya Lake Road. Turn left and drive one mile to Green Mountain Road and the Department of Natural Resources parking lot and trailhead. If the gate is closed, it is a four-mile hike to the campground.

Contact: Department of Natural Resources, South Puget Sound Region, 360/825-1631, www.dnr.wa.gov.

80 ILLAHEE STATE PARK

🚶 🏊 � 🏇 🎣 ♿ 🚐 ⛺

Scenic rating: 9

near Bremerton

Map 1.6, page 80

This 75-acre park, named for a Native American word for earth or country, features the last stand of old-growth forest in Kitsap County, including one of the largest yew trees in America. The park also features 1,785 feet of saltwater frontage. The campsites are located in a pretty, forested area, and some are grassy. The shoreline is fairly rocky, set on the shore of Port Orchard Bay, although there is a small sandy area for sunbathers. Clamming is popular here. A fishing pier is available for anglers. Note that large vessels can be difficult to launch at the ramp here.

Campsites, facilities: There are 23 sites for tents or RVs up to 40 feet long (no hookups), two sites for tents or RVs up to 35 feet long (50 amp full hookups), and five hike-in/bike-in sites. Picnic tables and fire grills are provided. Restrooms with flush toilets and coin showers, drinking water, firewood, dump station, and a pier are available. Boat docks, launching facilities, five mooring buoys, and 356 feet of moorage float space are also available. A sheltered picnic area, horseshoes, volleyball, a field, and a playground are nearby. A coin laundry and ice are located within one mile. Some facilities are wheelchair accessible. Leashed pets are permitted.

Reservations, fees: Reservations are accepted May 15-September 15 at 888/226-7688 or https://washington.goingtocamp.com ($8-10 reservation fee). Sites are $20-45 per night, hike-in/bike-in sites are $12 per night, $10 per extra vehicle per night. A watercraft launching permit is $7; a trailer dumping permit is $5. Open year-round.

Directions: On Highway 3, drive to Bremerton and the East Bremerton exit. Drive east for 7.5 miles to Sylvan Way. Turn left and drive 1.5 miles to the park entrance road.

Contact: Illahee State Park, 360/478-6460, http://parks.state.wa.us.

81 MANCHESTER STATE PARK

🏃 🛶 🐾 ♿ 🚐 ⛺

Scenic rating: 9

near Port Orchard

Map 1.6, page 80

Manchester State Park is set on the edge of Port Orchard, providing excellent lookouts across Puget Sound. The park covers 111 acres, with 3,400 feet of saltwater shoreline on Rich Passage in Puget Sound. The landscape is filled with fir maple, hemlock, cedar, alder, and ash, which are very pretty in the fall. There are approximately 2.5 miles of hiking trails, including an interpretive trail. Group and day-use reservations are available. Note that the beach is closed to shellfish harvesting. In the early 1900s, this park site was used as a U.S. Coast Guard defense installation. A gun battery remains from the park's early days, along with two other buildings that are on the register of National Historical Monuments.

Campsites, facilities: There are 35 sites for tents, 15 sites with partial hookups (30 amps) for tents or RVs up to 60 feet long, three hike-in/bike-in sites, and one group site with hookups (30 amps) for tents or RVs that can accommodate up to 130 people. Picnic tables and fire grills are provided. Restrooms with flush toilets and coin showers, drinking water, dump station, firewood, sheltered picnic area, volleyball field, and horseshoe pit are available. Some facilities are wheelchair accessible. Leashed pets are permitted.

Reservations, fees: Reservations are accepted for individual sites (mid-May-mid-Sept.) and the group site at 888/226-7688 or https://washington.goingtocamp.com ($8-10 reservation fee). Sites are $20-45 per night, hike-in/bike-in sites are $12 per night, $10 per extra vehicle per night. The group site is $140.04 per night. Some credit cards are accepted. Open year-round, with limited winter facilities.

Directions: From Tacoma on I-5, turn north on Highway 16 and drive to the Port Orford/Sedgwick Road exit and Highway 160. Turn right (east) and drive one mile to Long Lake Road. Turn left and drive six miles to Milehill. Turn right on Milehill and drive about one mile to Colchester Road. Turn left on Colchester Road and drive through Manchester, continuing for two miles to the park.

Note: Directions to this park are flawed on most website maps and in other books. Use the directions above, and when nearing the camp, note that the route is signed.

Contact: Manchester State Park, 360/871-4065, http://parks.state.wa.us.

82 BLAKE ISLAND MARINE STATE PARK

Scenic rating: 10

near Seattle

Map 1.6, page 80

Blake Island offers a boat-in camp on a small island in the middle of the massive Seattle metropolitan area. At night, it can seem almost surreal. The park covers 476 acres and features magnificent views of the Seattle skyline and Olympic Mountains. It boasts five miles of saltwater shoreline, a 0.75-mile nature trail, and 15.5 miles of hiking and biking trails. Good bottom fishing is available off the reef. The tidelands make up an underwater park. Blake Island was an ancestral camping ground of the Suquamish tribe, and according to legend, the renowned Chief Seattle was born here. Native American-style dinners and dancing are available at Tillicum Village, a concession on the island. A bonus: primitive sites on the west side of the island available only by canoe or kayak.

Campsites, facilities: There are 44 boat-in sites, three canoe/kayak sites, and one group camp for up to 100 people. Picnic tables and fire grills are provided (only charcoal and gas grills are permitted). Drinking water, restrooms with flush toilets and coin showers, firewood, 1,500 feet of mooring with 24 mooring buoys, and two picnic shelters with a fire pit are available. There are also interpretive activities, horseshoe

pits, volleyball, and a field. Garbage must be packed out. A store and snack bar are available nearby. Some facilities are wheelchair accessible. Leashed pets are permitted.

Reservations, fees: Reservations are not accepted for individual sites, but are required for the group camp at 888/226-7688 or https://washington.goingtocamp.com ($8-10 reservation fee). Sites are $12-35 per night, and the group camp is $71-281 per night (20-person minimum). Buoys are $15 per night. Open year-round.

Directions: Blake Island is located eight miles west of Seattle, between Vashon and Bainbridge Islands. It is best reached by launching from Bremerton, Port Orchard, or Manchester. From Manchester, it is a two-mile cruise east to the island. Then trace the shore around to the buoy floats. There are four main camping areas located between Vashon Island and Bainbridge Island. The park can also be reached by tour boat through Argosy Cruises, 206/623-1445 or 206/622-8687.

Contact: Blake Island Marine State Park, 360/731-8330, http://parks.state.wa.us.

83 BELFAIR STATE PARK

Scenic rating: 8

on Hood Canal

Map 1.6, page 80

Belfair State Park is situated along the southern edge of Hood Canal, spanning 65 acres with 3,720 feet of saltwater shoreline. This park is known for its saltwater tidal flats, wetlands, and wind-blown beach grasses. Beach walking and swimming are good. The camp is set primarily amid conifer forest and marshlands on Hood Canal with nearby streams, tideland, and wetlands. A gravel-rimmed pool that is separate from Hood Canal creates a unique swimming area; water level is determined by the tides. Note that the DNR Tahuya Multiple-Use Area is nearby with trails for motorcycles, mountain biking, hiking, horseback riding, and off-road vehicles. Big Mission Creek and Little Mission Creek, both located in the park, are habitat for chum salmon during spawning season in fall.

Campsites, facilities: There are 116 sites for tents, 37 sites with full hookups (30 amps) for RVs up to 60 feet, and three hike-in/bike-in sites. There are also four cabins and one canoe/kayak site. Picnic tables and fire grills are provided. Restrooms with flush toilets and coin showers, drinking water, firewood, a bathhouse, dump station, swimming lagoon, playground, badminton, volleyball court, and horseshoe pits are available. A store and restaurant are located nearby. Some facilities are wheelchair accessible. Leashed pets are permitted.

Reservations, fees: Reservations are accepted at 888/226-7688 or https://washington.goingtocamp.com ($8-10 reservation fee). Sites are $20-45 per night, $10 per extra vehicle per night, hike-in/bike-in sites are $12 per night, and the water trail site is $12 per night. Some credit cards are accepted. Open year-round.

Directions: From Tacoma on I-5, drive to the Highway 16 West exit. Take Highway 16 northwest and drive about 27 miles toward Bremerton and Belfair (after the Port Orchard exits, note that the highway merges into three lanes). Get in the left lane for the Belfair/State Route 3 South exit. Take that exit and turn left at the traffic signal. Take State Route 3 eight miles south to Belfair to State Route 300 (at the signal just after the Safeway). Turn right and drive three miles to the park entrance.

Contact: Belfair State Park, 360/275-0668, http://parks.state.wa.us.

84 TWANOH STATE PARK
🏃 ➰ 🛶 🚤 🐴 🚶 ♿ 🎣 ⛰

Scenic rating: 8

near Union

Map 1.6, page 80

This state park is set on the shore of Hood Canal at one of the warmest saltwater bodies in Puget Sound—and likely the warmest saltwater beach in the state. Twanoh, from a Native American word meaning gathering place, covers 182 acres, with 3,167 feet of saltwater shoreline. Swimming and oyster, clam, and crab harvesting are popular here. Winter smelting is also popular; check regulations. In late fall, the chum salmon can be seen heading up the small creek; fishing for them is prohibited. Most of the park buildings are made of brick, stone, and round logs, built by the Civilian Conservation Corps in the 1930s. You'll also see extensive evidence of logging from the 1890s. Amenities include a tennis court, horseshoe pits, and a concession stand.

Campsites, facilities: There are 25 sites for tents or RVs (no hookups), 22 sites with full hookups (30 and 50 amps) for RVs up to 35 feet long, and one canoe/kayak site. Picnic tables and fire grills are provided. Restrooms with flush toilets and coin showers and drinking water are available. A seasonal snack bar, sheltered picnic area, firewood, boat ramp, boat dock, moorage buoys, marine pump-out station, wading pool, horseshoes, badminton, and volleyball are available nearby. Some facilities are wheelchair accessible. Leashed pets are permitted.

Reservations, fees: Reservations are accepted only for the group site at 888/226-7688 or https://washington.goingtocamp.com. Sites are $25-35 per night, $10 per extra vehicle per night. Open April-October, weather permitting.

Directions: From Bremerton, take Highway 3 southwest to Belfair and Highway 106. Turn right (west) and drive eight miles to the park. If driving from U.S. 101, turn east on Highway 106 and drive 12 miles to the park.

Contact: Twanoh State Park, 360/275-2222, http://parks.state.wa.us.

85 JARRELL COVE STATE PARK

🏃 🚴 🛶 🎣 ⚓ 🐕 ♿ ⛺

Scenic rating: 8

on Harstine Island

Map 1.6, page 80

Most visitors to this park arrive by boat. Campsites are near the docks, set on a rolling, grassy area. The park covers just 43 acres but boasts 3,500 feet of saltwater shoreline on the northeast end of Harstine Island in South Puget Sound. The park's dense forest presses nearly to the water's edge at high tides—a beautiful setting. At low tides, tideland mud flats are unveiled. The beach is rocky and muddy—not exactly Hawaii. Hiking and biking are limited to just one mile of trail.

Campsites, facilities: There are 22 sites for tents, one canoe/kayak site, and a walk-in group camp with a kitchen shelter that accommodates up to 45 people. Picnic tables and fire grills are provided. Restrooms with flush toilets and coin showers and drinking water are available. Boat docks, a marine pump-out station, and 14 mooring buoys are available. A picnic area and a horseshoe pit are nearby. Some facilities are wheelchair accessible. Leashed pets are permitted.

Reservations, fees: Reservations are accepted and are required for the group camp at 888/226-7688 or https://washington.goingtocamp.com ($8-10 reservation fee). Sites are $12-35 per night, $10 per extra vehicle per night, and the group site is $70-139 per night (20-person minimum). Buoys are $15 per night, docking fees are $0.70 per foot ($15 minimum). Open year-round.

Directions: From Olympia on I-5, turn north on U.S. 101 and drive 22 miles to Shelton and Highway 3. Turn north on Highway 3 and drive about eight miles to Pickering Road. Turn right and drive to the Harstine Bridge. Cross the bridge and continue to North Island Drive. Turn left and drive four miles to Wingert Road. Turn left and drive 0.25 mile to the park on the left.

Contact: Jarrell Cove State Park, 360/426-9226, http://parks.state.wa.us.

86 JARRELL'S COVE MARINA

🏃 🚴 🛶 🎣 🐕 ♿ 🚐

Scenic rating: 6

near Shelton

Map 1.6, page 80

The marina and nearby Puget Sound are the big draws here. This small camp features 1,000 feet of shoreline and 0.5 mile of public beach. Clamming is available in season.

Campsites, facilities: There are three sites with partial hookups for RVs up to 40 feet long. Picnic tables and barbecues are provided. Restrooms with flush toilets and coin showers, drinking water, propane gas, a dump station, a seasonal convenience store, bait and tackle, coin laundry, gasoline, marine fuel, boat docks, and moorage are available. Some facilities are wheelchair accessible. Leashed pets are permitted.

Reservations, fees: Reservations are accepted. Sites are $35 per night. Some credit cards are accepted. Open Memorial Day-Labor Day.

Directions: From Olympia on I-5, turn north on U.S. 101 and drive 22 miles to Shelton and Highway 3. Turn north on Highway 3 and drive about eight miles to Pickering Road. Turn right and drive to the Harstine Bridge. Cross the bridge and continue to North Island Drive. Turn left on North Island Drive and drive 2.8 miles to Haskell Hill Road. Turn left (west) on Haskell Hill Road and drive one mile to the marina.

Contact: Jarrell's Cove Marina, 220 E. Wilson Rd., Shelton, 360/426-8823 or 800/362-8823.

87 JOEMMA BEACH STATE PARK

Scenic rating: 8

on Puget Sound

Map 1.6, page 80

This beautiful camp set along the shore of the peninsula provides an alternative to nearby Penrose Point State Park. It covers 106 acres and features 3,000 feet of saltwater frontage on the southeast Kitsap Peninsula. This area is often excellent for boating, fishing, and crabbing. It is a forested park with the bonus of boat-in campsites. Hiking is limited to a trail less than a mile long.

Campsites, facilities: There are 19 sites for tents, two hike-in/bike-in sites, and two canoe/kayak sites. Picnic tables and fire grills are provided. Vault toilets, drinking water, boat-launching facilities, a dock and mooring buoys, and a picnic shelter that can be reserved are available. A grocery store is approximately five miles away. Some facilities are wheelchair accessible. Leashed pets are permitted.

Reservations, fees: Reservations are not accepted. Sites are $20-35 per night, hike-in/bike-in and boat-in sites are $12 per night, $10 per extra vehicle per night. Moorage is $0.70 per foot with a $15 per night minimum. Open mid-March-October.

Directions: From Tacoma, drive north on Highway 16 for about 10 miles to Highway 302/Purdy exit. At the light turn left onto Highway 302, which changes into Key Peninsula Highway. Stay on Key Peninsula Highway and drive about 15 miles to Whiteman Road. Turn right on Whiteman Road and drive four miles to Bay Road. Turn right and drive one mile to the park entrance (stay on the asphalt road when entering the park).

Contact: Joemma Beach State Park, 253/884-1944, http://parks.state.wa.us.

88 PENROSE POINT STATE PARK

Scenic rating: 8

on Puget Sound

Map 1.6, page 80

This park on Carr Inlet on Puget Sound, overlooking Lake Bay, has a remote feel, but it's actually not far from Tacoma. The park covers 162 acres, with two miles of saltwater frontage on Mayo Cove and Carr Inlet. The camp has impressive stands of fir and cedar nearby, along with ferns and rhododendrons. The park has 2.5 miles of trails for biking and hiking. Bay Lake is a popular fishing lake for trout and is located one mile away; a boat launch is available there. Penrose is known for its excellent fishing, crabbing, clamming, and oysters. The nearest boat launch to Puget Sound is located three miles away in the town of Home.

Campsites, facilities: There are 82 sites for tents or RVs up to 35 feet (no hookups), one water trail boat-in site, and a group camp for tents or RVs for 20-50 people. Picnic tables and fire grills are provided. Restrooms with flush toilets and coin showers, drinking water, a dump station, firewood, horseshoe pits, sheltered picnic areas, an interpretive trail, and a beach are available. Boat docks, a marine pump-out station, and mooring buoys are nearby. Some facilities are wheelchair accessible. Leashed pets are permitted.

Reservations, fees: Reservations are accepted May 15-September 15 and are required year-round for the group site at 888/226-7688 or https://washington.goingtocamp.com ($8-10 reservation fee). Sites are $20-37 per night, $10 per extra vehicle per night, primitive sites and boat-in sites are $12 per night; call for group rates. Boat mooring is $0.70 per foot with a $15 minimum. Some credit cards are accepted. Open year-round.

Directions: From Tacoma, drive north on Highway 16 for about 10 miles to the Highway 302/Purdy exit. At the light turn left onto Highway 302, which changes into Key

Peninsula Highway. Stay on Key Peninsula Highway and drive south nine miles through the towns of Key Center and Home to Cornwall Road KPS (second road after crossing the Home Bridge). Drive 1.25 miles more to 158 Avenue KPS. Turn left and continue on 158 Avenue KPS to the park entrance.

Contact: Penrose Point State Park, 253/884-2514, http://parks.state.wa.us.

89 GIG HARBOR RV RESORT

Scenic rating: 7

near Tacoma

Map 1.6, page 80

This is a popular layover spot for folks heading up to Bremerton. Just a short jaunt off the highway, it's pleasant, clean, and friendly. An 18-hole golf course, full-service marina, and tennis courts are located nearby. Look for the great view of Mount Rainier from the end of the harbor.

Campsites, facilities: There are 93 sites, most with full or partial hookups (20, 30 and 50 amps), including some long-term rentals, for tents or RVs of any length and one cabin. Some sites are pull-through. Restrooms with flush toilets and showers, drinking water, cable TV, Wi-Fi, propane gas, a dump station, a clubroom, coin laundry, playground, horseshoe pits, sports field, and a seasonal heated swimming pool are available. Some facilities are wheelchair accessible. Leashed pets are permitted.

Reservations, fees: Reservations are accepted. Tent sites are $31.50 per night, RV sites are $35-45 per night, $4-5 per each additional person per night, $4 per each additional vehicle per night, $2 per pet per day. The cabin is $54 per night. Some credit cards are accepted. Open year-round.

Directions: From Tacoma, drive northwest on Highway 16 for 12 miles to the Burnham Drive NW exit. Take that exit and enter the roundabout to the first right and Burnham Drive

NW. Turn right on Burnham Drive NW and drive 1.25 miles to the resort on the left.

Contact: Gig Harbor RV Resort, 9515 Burnham Dr. NW, Gig Harbor, 253/858-8138 or 800/526-8311, www.gigharborvresort.com.

90 AMERICAN SUNSET RV AND TENT RESORT

Scenic rating: 8

near Westport Harbor

Map 1.7, page 81

If location is everything, then this RV camp, set on a peninsula, is a big winner. It covers 32 acres and is 10 blocks from the ocean; hiking and biking trails are nearby. The park is divided into two areas: one for campers, another for long-term rentals. Nearby are Westhaven and Westport Light State Parks, popular with hikers, rockhounds, scuba divers, and surf anglers. Fishing and crabbing off the docks are also options; you can also swim, but not off the docks. Monthly rentals are available in summer.

Campsites, facilities: There are 118 sites with full hookups (20, 30, and 50 amps) for RVs up to 45 feet long, 34 sites for tents, one lighthouse unit, one beach house, one cabana, and one rental mobile home. Some sites are pull-through. Picnic tables and fire rings are provided. Restrooms with flush toilets and showers, drinking water, satellite TV, Wi-Fi, coin laundry, a convenience store, propane, a seasonal heated swimming pool, horseshoe pits, a playground, and a fish-cleaning station are available. A marina is located three blocks away. Leashed pets are permitted.

Reservations, fees: Reservations are accepted by phone. RV Sites are $43 per night, tent sites are $25 per night. Some discounts are available. Some credit cards are accepted. Open year-round.

Directions: From Aberdeen, drive south on State Route 105 for 22 miles to Westport and Montesano Street (the first exit in Westport).

Turn right (northeast) on Montesano Street and drive three miles to the resort on the left.

Contact: American Sunset RV and Tent Resort, 360/268-0207 or 800/569-2267, www.americansunsetrv.com.

91 TOTEM RV PARK

Scenic rating: 8

in Westport

Map 1.7, page 81

This 3.2-acre park is set 300 yards from the ocean and features an expanse of sand dunes between the park and the ocean. It has large, grassy sites close to Westhaven State Park, which offers day-use facilities. The owner is a fishing guide and can provide detailed fishing information. The salmon fishing within 10 miles of this park is often excellent in summer. Marked biking trails and a full-service marina are within five miles of the park.

Campsites, facilities: There are 80 sites with full or partial hookups (30 and 50 amps) for tents or RVs of any length. Some sites are pull-through. Restrooms with flush toilets and coin showers, drinking water, cable TV, Wi-Fi, a dump station, coin laundry, and ice are available. A pavilion, barbecue facilities with kitchen, and a fish-cleaning station are also available. Boat docks, launching facilities, and fishing charters are nearby. Propane gas, a store, and café are within 0.5 mile. Some facilities are wheelchair accessible. Leashed pets are permitted.

Reservations, fees: Reservations are accepted. Sites are $35-40 per night. Some credit cards are accepted. Open year-round.

Directions: From Aberdeen, drive south on State Route 105 for 20 miles to the turnoff for Westport. Turn right (north) on the State Route 105 spur and drive 4.3 miles to the docks and Nyhus Street. Turn left on Nyhus Street and drive two blocks to the park on the left.

Contact: Totem RV Park, 360/268-0025 or 888/TOTEM-RV (888/868-3678).

92 HOLAND CENTER

Scenic rating: 6

in Westport

Map 1.7, page 81

This pleasant, 18-acre RV park is one of several in the immediate area. The sites are graveled or grassy, with ample space and pine trees in between. There is no beach access from the park, but full recreational facilities are available nearby. About half of the sites are long-term rentals.

Campsites, facilities: There are 85 sites with full hookups for RVs up to 35 feet long. Some picnic tables are provided. No open fires are allowed. Restrooms with flush toilets and coin showers, cable TV, coin laundry, and storage sheds are available. Propane gas, a store, café, and ice are located within one mile. Boat docks and launching facilities are nearby. Leashed pets are permitted.

Reservations, fees: Reservations are accepted. Sites are $35 per night. Credit cards are accepted. Open year-round.

Directions: From Aberdeen, drive south on State Route 105 for 22 miles to Westport. Continue on State Route 105 to a Y intersection. Bear right on Montesano Street and drive approximately two miles to Wilson Street. The park is on the left.

Contact: Holand Center, State Route 105 and Wilson Street, 360/268-9582.

93 PACIFIC MOTEL
AND RV PARK

Scenic rating: 5

near Twin Harbors

Map 1.7, page 81

This five-acre park has shaded sites in a wooded setting. It's near Twin Harbors and Westport Light State Park, a day-use park nearby. Both parks have beach access. A full-service marina is located within two miles. About 25 percent of the sites are occupied with long-term rentals.

Campsites, facilities: There are 80 sites with full hookups (20, 30, and 50 amps) for RVs of any length, including 25 pull-through sites, and 12 sites for tents. Picnic tables and fire pits are provided. Restrooms with flush toilets and coin showers, drinking water, propane gas, a dump station, fish-cleaning station, recreation hall with a kitchen, cable TV, Wi-Fi, coin laundry, and a seasonal heated swimming pool are available. A store, café, and ice are located within one mile. Boat-launching and boat docks are nearby in a full-service marina. Leashed pets are permitted.

Reservations, fees: Reservations are accepted. RV sites are $38 per night, tent sites are $24 per night, $2 per person per night for more than two people. Some credit cards are accepted. Open year-round.

Directions: From Aberdeen, drive south on State Route 105 for approximately 21 miles to Westport. Go past the first Westport exit to a stop sign. Turn right onto the State Route 105 spur (becomes Forrest Street in Westport) and drive 1.8 miles to the park on the right.

Contact: Pacific Motel and RV Park, 360/268-9325, www.pacificmotelandrv.com.

94 TWIN HARBORS STATE PARK

Scenic rating: 8

near Westport

Map 1.7, page 81

The park covers 222 acres and is located four miles south of Westport. It was a military training ground in the 1930s. The campsites are close together and often crammed to capacity in the summer. Highlights include beach access and marked hiking trails, including Shifting Sands Nature Trail. The most popular recreation activities are surf fishing, surfing, beachcombing, and kite-flying. Fishing boats can be chartered nearby in Westport.

Campsites, facilities: There are 115 tent sites, 42 sites for RVs up to 35 feet long (30 amp full hookups), four hike-in/bike-in sites, five cabins, two yurts, and one group site for up to 60 people (no electricity). Picnic tables and fire grills are provided. Restrooms with flush toilets and coin showers, drinking water, a dump station, a picnic area with a kitchen shelter, and horseshoe pits are available. A store, café, and ice are available within one mile. Some facilities are wheelchair accessible. Leashed pets are permitted.

Reservations, fees: Reservations are accepted for individual sites and are required for the group site at 888/226-7688 or https://washington.goingtocamp.com ($8-10 reservation fee). Sites are $20-42 per night, $10 per extra vehicle per night, and hike-in/bike-in sites are $12 per night. Group rates vary according to size (20-person minimum, 60-person maximum, 10 vehicle limit). Some credit cards are accepted. Open year-round.

Directions: From Aberdeen, drive south on State Route 105 for 17 miles to the park entrance on the left (4 miles south of Westport).

Contact: Twin Harbors State Park, 360/268-9717, http://parks.state.wa.us.

95 PORTER CREEK

Scenic rating: 7

on Porter Creek in Capitol State Forest

Map 1.7, page 81

This primitive, rustic campground is set in the Capitol State Forest along the shore of Porter Creek and is managed by the Department of Natural Resources. The camp serves as a launch point for motorcycle and ATV trips. Within three miles, you can access trails that lead to a network of 87 miles of off-road vehicle trails and 84 miles of trails for non-motorized use—mountain biking is popular here.

Campsites, facilities: There are 16 sites for tents or RVs up to 16 feet (no hookups). Picnic tables and fire grills are provided. There is no drinking water and garbage must be packed out. Vault toilets are available. All-terrain vehicles are permitted. Some facilities are wheelchair accessible. Leashed pets are permitted.

Reservations, fees: Reservations are not accepted. There is no fee for camping, but a Discover Pass is required. Open May-November, weather permitting.

Directions: On I-5, drive to Exit 88 (10 miles north of Chehalis) and U.S. 12. Turn west on U.S. 12 and drive 21 miles to Porter and Porter Creek Road. Turn right (northeast) on Porter Creek Road and drive 3.4 miles (last half mile is gravel) to a junction. Continue straight on B-Line Road for 0.6 mile to the campground on the left.

Contact: Department of Natural Resources, Pacific Cascade Region North, 360/577-2025, www.dnr.wa.gov.

96 MIDDLE WADDELL

🚶‍♂️ 🚵 🐴 ♿ 🚐 ⛺

Scenic rating: 7
on Waddell Creek in Capitol State Forest

Map 1.7, page 81

This wooded campground is nestled along Waddell Creek in Capitol State Forest. The trails in the immediate vicinity are used primarily for all-terrain vehicles (ATVs), making for some noise. There is an extensive network of ATV trails in the area. Mountain bikers tend to prefer Fall Creek Camp.

Campsites, facilities: There are 24 sites for tents or RVs of any length. Picnic tables and fire grills are provided. Vault toilets are available. There is no drinking water and garbage must be packed out. Some facilities are wheelchair accessible. Leashed pets are permitted.

Reservations, fees: Reservations are not accepted. There is no fee for camping, but a Discover Pass is required. Open May-November, weather permitting.

Directions: From Olympia on I-5, drive south for about 10 miles to Exit 95 and Highway 121. Turn west on Highway 121 and drive four

miles to Littlerock. Continue west for one mile to Waddell Creek Road. Turn right and drive three miles and look for the campground entrance road on the left.

Contact: Department of Natural Resources, Pacific Cascade Region North, 360/577-2025, www.dnr.wa.gov.

97 FALL CREEK

🚶‍♂️ 🚵 🐴 ♿ ⛺ 🚐

Scenic rating: 7
on Fall Creek in Capitol State Forest

Map 1.7, page 81

With good access to an 84-mile network of trails for non-motorized use, this camp is something of a mountain-biking headquarters. Although ATVs are allowed in the campground, they are not allowed on the adjacent trails. This wooded camp also provides horse facilities.

Campsites, facilities: There are eight sites for tents or RVs up to 45 feet (no hookups). Picnic tables and fire grills are provided. There is no drinking water and garbage must be packed out. Vault toilets, a corral, a hitching post, a watering trough, and a horse-loading ramp are available. A day-use staging area is also available. Some facilities are wheelchair accessible. Leashed pets are permitted.

Reservations, fees: Reservations are not accepted. There is no fee for camping, but a Discover Pass is required. Open May-November, weather permitting.

Directions: From Olympia, take I-5 to exit 95 onto Maytown Road SW and turn west. (If coming from I-5 South, you will cross under I-5.) Drive west on Maytown Road SW to Littlerock, where the road becomes 128th Avenue SW. Continue on 128th Avenue SW until it ends at Waddell Creek Road SW. Turn right (northwest) on Waddell Creek Road SW and drive two miles to the Triangle. Turn left. The road will become Sherman Valley Road SW. Drive one mile on Sherman Valley Road SW; the pavement ends and it becomes the

"C-Line" road and enters the Capitol State Forest. Drive four miles and turn left at the second turnoff to the left, Road C-6000, signed Fall Creek Campground. Drive three miles to the campground on the right, just beyond a small bridge.

Contact: Department of Natural Resources, Pacific Cascade Region North, 360/577-2025, www.dnr.wa.gov.

98 MARGARET MCKENNY HORSE CAMP

Scenic rating: 7

in Capitol State Forest

Map 1.7, page 81

With trails linked to an extensive network of trails for non-motorized use only, this camp is used primarily as a trailhead for horseback riders and mountain bikers. Most of the campsites are well away from the stream.

Campsites, facilities: There are 24 sites for tents or RVs up to 45 feet. Picnic tables, fire pits, and grills are provided. Vault toilets, a campfire circle, and a horse-loading ramp are available. There is no drinking water and garbage must be packed out. A campground host is on-site in summer. Some facilities are wheelchair accessible. Leashed pets are permitted.

Reservations, fees: Reservations are not accepted. There is no fee for camping, but a Discover Pass is required. Open May-November, weather permitting.

Directions: From Olympia on I-5, drive south for about 10 miles to Exit 95 and Highway 121. Turn west on Highway 121 and drive four miles to Littlerock. Continue west for one mile to Waddell Creek Road. Turn right and drive 2.5 miles and look for the campground entrance road on the left.

Contact: Department of Natural Resources,

Pacific Cascade Region North, 360/577-2025, www.dnr.wa.gov.

99 GRAYLAND BEACH STATE PARK

Scenic rating: 8

near Grayland

Map 1.7, page 81

This state park features 412 acres and almost 7,500 feet of beach frontage. All the campsites are within easy walking distance of the ocean. The campsites are relatively spacious for a state park, but they are not especially private. This park is popular with out-of-towners, especially during summer. Recreation options include fishing, beachcombing, and kite-flying. The best spot for surfing is five miles north at Westhaven State Park.

Campsites, facilities: There are 55 sites with full hookups (30 and 50 amps) and 38 sites with partial hookups for tents and RVs up to 60 feet long, four tent sites, four hike-in/bike-in sites, and 16 yurts. Picnic tables and fire grills are provided. Drinking water and restrooms with flush toilets and coin showers, an amphitheater, and a dump station are available. Some facilities are wheelchair accessible. Leashed pets are permitted.

Reservations, fees: Reservations are accepted at 888/226-7688 or https://washington.goingto-camp.com ($8-10 reservation fee). Sites are $12-45 per night, $10 per extra vehicle per night, hike-in/bike-in sites are $12 per night, and yurts are $59-89 per night. Some credit cards are accepted. Open year-round.

Directions: From Aberdeen, drive south on State Route 105 for 22 miles to the park entrance. The park is just south of the town of Grayland on the right (west).

Contact: Grayland Beach State Park, 360/267-4301, http://parks.state.wa.us.

100 BAY CENTER/ WILLAPA BAY KOA

🚶 🚵 🛶 🚤 🐎 ♿ 🚐 ⛺

Scenic rating: 7

on Willapa Bay

Map 1.7, page 81

This KOA is 200 yards from Willapa Bay, within walking distance of a beach that seems to stretch to infinity. A trail leads to the beach and from here you can walk for miles in either direction. The beach sand is mixed with agates, driftwood, and seaweed. Dungeness crabs, clams, and oysters all live near shore. Another bonus is that herds of Roosevelt elk roam the nearby woods. Believe it or not, there are also black bears, although they are seldom seen here. The park covers five acres, and the campsites are graveled and shaded.

Campsites, facilities: There are 42 sites with full or partial hookups (20, 30, and 50 amps) for RVs of any length, 23 sites for tents, four cabins, and two yurts. Some sites are pull-through. Picnic tables and fire rings are provided. Restrooms with flush toilets and showers, drinking water, propane gas, dump station, cable TV, Wi-Fi, a recreation hall, camp store, firewood, coin laundry, and ice are available. A café, boat docks, and launching facilities are nearby. Some facilities are wheelchair accessible. Leashed pets are permitted, with certain restrictions.

Reservations, fees: Reservations are accepted at 800/562-7810. Sites are $48-80 per night, $5 per person per night for more than two people, $4 per extra vehicle per night. Some credit cards are accepted. Open mid-March-December 1.

Directions: From Nemah on U.S. 101, drive north for five miles to the Bay Center/Dike exit (located between Mileposts 42 and 43, 16 miles south of Raymond). Turn left (west) and drive three miles to the campground.

Contact: Bay Center/Willapa Bay KOA, 360/875-6344, www.koa.com.

101 RAINBOW FALLS STATE PARK

🚶 🚵 🏊 🛶 🚤 🐎 �#🏕 ♿ 🚐 ⛺

Scenic rating: 8

on the Chehalis River Bay

Map 1.7, page 81

This 139-acre park is set on the Chehalis River and boasts 3,400 feet of freshwater shoreline. The camp features stands of old-growth cedar and fir and is named after a few small cascades with drops of about 10 feet. The park has 10 miles of hiking trails, including an interpretive trail, seven miles of bike trails, and seven miles of horse trails. A pool at the base of Rainbow Falls is excellent for swimming. Another attraction, a small fuchsia garden, has more than 40 varieties. There are also several log structures built by the Civilian Conservation Corps in 1935.

Campsites, facilities: There are 40 sites for tents or RVs up to 32 feet (no hookups), eight sites with partial hookups (30 and 50 amps) for tents or RVs up to 60 feet long, three hike-in/bike-in sites, two equestrian sites with hitching points and stock water, and one group site for up to 60 people. Picnic tables and fire rings are provided. Restrooms with flush toilets and coin showers, drinking water, a dump station, firewood, a picnic area, interpretive activities, a playground, horseshoe pits, and a softball field are available. Some facilities are wheelchair accessible. Leashed pets are permitted.

Reservations, fees: Reservations are accepted only for the group site at 360/291-3767. Sites are $20-45 per night, $10 per extra vehicle per night, and hike-in/bike-in sites are $12 per night. Open year-round.

Directions: From Chehalis on I-5, take Exit 77 to drive west 11.7 miles on Highway 6 to milepost 40. Drive 0.4 mile past the marker to River Road. Turn right (west) on River Road and drive 2.7 miles to the Bailey Bridge. Turn right to cross the bridge and immediately turn left onto Leudinghaus Road. Drive 2.2 miles west on Leudinghaus Road to the park entrance on

the left. Once inside the park, the campground is on the right.
Contact: Rainbow Falls State Park, 360/291-3767, http://parks.state.wa.us.

102 OCEAN PARK RESORT

Scenic rating: 5

on Willapa Bay

Map 1.7, page 81

This wooded, 10-acre campground is located 0.5 mile from Willapa Bay. With grassy, shaded sites, it caters primarily to RVs. Fishing, crabbing, and clamming are popular in season. Ocean Park has several festivals during the summer season. During these festivals, this resort fills up. To the north, Leadbetter Point State Park provides a side-trip option.

Campsites, facilities: There are 70 sites with full hookups for RVs of any length, 13 sites for tents, and a two-bedroom mobile home. Some sites are pull-through. Picnic tables are provided. Fire pits are provided at tent sites. Restrooms with flush toilets and coin showers, drinking water, propane gas, a recreation hall, coin laundry, Wi-Fi, playground, firewood, and a basketball hoop are available. A store and café are available within one mile. Boat docks and launching facilities are located nearby on Willapa Bay. Some facilities are wheelchair accessible. Leashed pets are permitted, with certain restrictions.

Reservations, fees: Sites are $31-38 per night, plus $3 per person per night for more than two people. Some credit cards are accepted. Open year-round.

Directions: From Kelso/Longview on I-5, turn west on Highway 4 and drive 63 miles to U.S. 101. Turn south on U.S. 101 and drive 13 miles to the junction with Highway 103. Turn right (north) on Highway 103 and drive 11 miles to the town of Ocean Park and 259th Street. Turn right (east) on 259th Street and drive two blocks to the resort at the end of the road.

Contact: Ocean Park Resort, 360/665-4585 or 800/835-4634, www.opresort.com.

103 WESTGATE CABINS & RV PARK

Scenic rating: 9

near Long Beach

Map 1.7, page 81

Highlights at this pretty and clean four-acre camp include beach access, oceanfront sites (about one-fourth have ocean views), and all the amenities. There are 28 miles of beach that can be driven on. Additional facilities within five miles of the park include an 18-hole golf course.

Campsites, facilities: There are 39 sites with full hookups (30 amps) for RVs up to 50 feet long and six cabins. Some sites are pull-through. Picnic tables are provided. Restrooms with flush toilets and showers, drinking water, cable TV, Wi-Fi, coin laundry, gas station, a recreation hall with kitchen, a fish-cleaning station, and ice are available. A store and café are available about four miles away. Boat docks and launching facilities are located nearby on Willapa Bay. Leashed pets are permitted, but not in cabins.

Reservations, fees: Reservations are accepted. Sites are $38 per night, plus $2 per person per night for more than two people. The cabins are $70-90 per night. Some credit cards are accepted. Open year-round.

Directions: From Kelso/Longview on I-5, turn west on Highway 4 and drive 63 miles to U.S. 101. Turn left (south) on U.S. 101 and drive 13 miles to the junction with Highway 103. Turn right (north) on Highway 103 and drive nine miles to the park on the left (located at the south edge of the town of Ocean Park).

Contact: Westgate Cabins & RV Park, 360/665-4211, www.vacationwestgate.com.

104 ANDERSEN'S RV PARK ON THE OCEAN

🚴 🛶 🚐 🦌 ⛵ ♿ 🚌

Scenic rating: 7

near Long Beach

Map 1.7, page 81

Timing is everything here. When the dates are announced for the local festivals, reservations start pouring in and the sites at this park can be booked a year in advance. Located near the city limits of Long Beach, this five-acre camp features a path through the dunes that will get you to the beach in a flash. It is set in a flat, sandy area with gravel sites. Recreation options include beach bonfires, beachcombing, surf fishing, and clamming (seasonal). Additional facilities found within five miles of the park include marked dune trails, a nine-hole golf course, a riding stable, and tennis courts. The park is big-rig friendly.

Campsites, facilities: There are 60 sites for RVs of any length (20, 30, and 50 amp full hookups) and two cottages. Picnic tables and fire pits are provided. Restrooms with flush toilets and showers, drinking water, cable TV, Wi-Fi, a dump station, coin laundry, ice, propane, fax machine, group facilities, a horseshoe pit, and a playground are available. A store and café are available within two miles. Some facilities are wheelchair accessible. Leashed pets are permitted.

Reservations, fees: Reservations are recommended. Sites are $50-70 per night, plus $2 per person per night for more than two people. The cottages start at $150 per night. Some credit cards are accepted. Open year-round.

Directions: From Kelso/Longview on I-5, turn west on Highway 4 and drive 63 miles to U.S. 101. Turn left (south) on U.S. 101 and drive 13 miles to the junction with Highway 103. Turn right (north) on Highway 103 and drive five miles to the park on the left.

Contact: Andersen's RV Park on the Ocean, 360/642-2231 or 800/645-6795, www.andersensrv.com.

105 OCEANIC RV PARK

🚴 🛶 🚐 🦌 🚌

Scenic rating: 3

in Long Beach

Map 1.7, page 81

This two-acre park is located in the heart of downtown, within walking distance of restaurants and stores. It is also within five miles of an 18-hole golf course, marked bike trails, and a full-service marina.

Campsites, facilities: There are 20 pull-through sites with full hookups (30 and 50 amps) for RVs of any length. No open fires are allowed. Restrooms with flush toilets and showers, Wi-Fi, coin laundry, a restaurant, and propane gas are available. A store and ice are located within one mile. Boat docks, launching facilities, and boat rentals are nearby. Leashed pets are permitted.

Reservations, fees: Reservations are accepted. Sites are $35 per night, plus $5 per person per night for more than two people. Open year-round.

Directions: From Kelso/Longview on I-5, turn west on Highway 4 and drive 63 miles to U.S. 101. Turn left (south) on U.S. 101 and drive 13 miles to the junction with Highway 103. Turn right (north) on Highway 103 and drive two miles to Long Beach. Continue to the park at the south junction of Pacific Highway (Highway 103) and 5th Avenue on the right.

Contact: Oceanic RV Park, 360/642-3836.

106 MERMAID INN AND RV PARK

🚴 🛶 🚐 🦌 🚌

Scenic rating: 3

near Long Beach

Map 1.7, page 81

Situated along the highway, this three-acre park is within four blocks of the beach. It is also within five miles of several nine-hole golf courses, a full-service marina, and a riding stable.

Campsites, facilities: There are 11 sites with full hookups (20 and 30 amps) for RVs up to 40 feet and 10 motel rooms. Picnic tables are provided. Restrooms with flush toilets and showers, drinking water, cable TV, Wi-Fi, a picnic area with barbecue, a fish-cleaning station, and coin laundry are available. Propane gas, a gas station, store, restaurant, and ice are located within one mile. Leashed pets are permitted, with certain restrictions.

Reservations, fees: Reservations are accepted. Sites are $35-65 per night, plus $1.50 per person per night for more than two people. Some credit cards are accepted. Open year-round.

Directions: From Kelso/Longview on I-5, turn west on Highway 4 and drive 63 miles to U.S. 101. Turn left (south) on U.S. 101 and drive 13 miles to the junction with Highway 103. Turn right (north) on Highway 103 and drive three miles to the park on the right.

Contact: Mermaid Inn and RV Park, 360/642-2600, www.mermaidinnatlongbeachwa.com.

107 DRIFTWOOD RV PARK

Scenic rating: 2

near Long Beach

Map 1.7, page 81

This two-acre park features grassy, shaded sites and beach access close by. A fenced pet area is a bonus. Additional facilities within five miles of the park include a nine-hole golf course and a full-service marina.

Campsites, facilities: There are 56 sites with full hookups (30 amps) for RVs of any length. Many sites are pull-through. Picnic tables are provided and portable fire pits can be rented. Restrooms with flush toilets and showers, drinking water, coin laundry, cable TV, Wi-Fi, group facilities, and a fenced pet area are available. Propane gas, a gas station, store, and restaurant are available within one mile. Some facilities are wheelchair accessible. Leashed pets are permitted, with certain restrictions.

Reservations, fees: Reservations are accepted. Sites are $34-48 per night, plus $3 per person per night for more than two people. Some credit cards are accepted. Open year-round.

Directions: From Kelso/Longview on I-5, turn west on Highway 4 and drive 63 miles to U.S. 101. Turn left (south) on U.S. 101 and drive 13 miles to the junction with Highway 103. Turn right (north) on Highway 103 and drive 2.25 miles to the park on the right, at 14th Street North and Pacific Avenue.

Contact: Driftwood RV Park, 360/642-2711 or 888/567-1902, www.driftwoodrvpark.net.

108 SAND CASTLE RV PARK

Scenic rating: 3

in Long Beach

Map 1.7, page 81

This park is set across the highway from the ocean. Although not particularly scenic, it is clean and does provide nearby beach access. The park covers two acres, has grassy areas, and is one of several in the immediate area. Additional facilities found within five miles of the park include a nine-hole golf course, marked bike trails, a full-service marina, and two riding stables.

Campsites, facilities: There are 38 sites with full hookups (30 and 50 amps) for RVs of any length and an area for tent camping. Some sites are pull-through. Picnic tables are provided. Restrooms with flush toilets and coin showers, drinking water, cable TV, Wi-Fi, a snack bar, ice, coin laundry, and a fish-cleaning station are available. Propane gas, a gas station, a store, and a café are available within one mile. Boat docks, launching facilities, and rentals are within five miles. Leashed pets are permitted.

Reservations, fees: Reservations are accepted. RV sites are $29-34 per night, tent sites are $20 per night, $2 per person per night for more than two people, $5 per extra vehicle per night. Some credit cards are accepted. Open year-round.

Directions: From Kelso/Longview on I-5, turn west on Highway 4 and drive 63 miles to U.S. 101. Turn left (south) on U.S. 101 and drive 13 miles to the junction with Highway 103. Turn right (north) on Highway 103 and drive two miles to the park on the right.

Contact: Sand Castle RV Park, 360/642-2174, www.sandcastlerv.com.

109 PACIFIC HOLIDAY RESORT

🎣 🛶 🎇 🐾 🚴 🚻 🚐 ⛰️

Scenic rating: 5

near Long Beach

Map 1.7, page 81

This is a membership-only resort RV campground, and members always come first. If space is available, they will accept reservations from non-members. One of the finest razor clam and surf fishing beaches in the world is just outside your door on the beautiful Long Beach Peninsula. Excellent deep-sea fishing at Ilwaco is just eight miles away. Oysters and Dungeness crabs abound at Willapa Bay, just five miles away, and lake and stream fishing are just minutes from this campground. There's also a golf course a long drive (and a short putt) away.

Campsites, facilities: There are 119 sites with full hookups for RVs up to 45 feet, 10 sites for tents, and three studio cabins; some sites are pull-through. Picnic tables are provided. Restrooms with flush toilets and showers, drinking water, cable TV, swimming pool, game room, playground, and a coin laundry are available. Some facilities are wheelchair accessible. Leashed pets are permitted.

Reservations, fees: Reservations are required. Sites are $28-42 per night. Call for cabin rates. Some credit cards are accepted. Open year-round.

Directions: From Kelso/Longview on I-5, turn west on Highway 4 and drive 63 miles to U.S.

101. Turn left (south) on U.S. 101 and drive 13 miles to the junction with Highway 103. Turn right (north) on Highway 103. The resort will be on the left.

Contact: Pacific Holiday Resort, 12109 Pacific Way, Long Beach, 360/642-2770, www.sunriseresorts.com.

110 WESTERN LAKES

🎇 🥾 🛶 🎣 🐾 🚻 ♿ ⛰️

Scenic rating: 9

near Naselle

Map 1.7, page 81

You want quiet and solitude? You found it. This tiny, primitive jewel of a campground sits near two lakes—Snag Lake and Western Lake (the lower lake)—in a wooded area near Western Lakes, just outside of Naselle. Snag Lake, the area's feature, provides fishing for rainbow trout, brook trout, and cutthroat trout. No gas motors are permitted, so it is ideal for float tubes, prams, rowboats, or canoes (with electric motors permitted). There are some good hiking trails nearby, including a route that connects the two lakes. The lake and campground offer good views of Radar Ridge. It's a prime camp for travelers heading to the coast who want a day or two of privacy before they hit the crowds.

Campsites, facilities: There are four walk-in sites for tents. Picnic tables and fire grills are provided. Vault toilets are available. There is no drinking water, and garbage must be packed out. Some facilities are wheelchair accessible. Leashed pets are permitted.

Reservations, fees: Reservations are not accepted. There is no fee for camping, but a Discover Pass is required. Open year-round.

Directions: From Kelso/Longview on I-5, turn west on Highway 4 and drive 60 miles (near Naselle) to Milepost 3 and C-Line Road. Turn right (north) and head uphill on C-Line Road (two-lane gravel road), take the left fork at Naselle Youth Camp entrance, and drive 2.9 miles to C-2600 (gravel one-lane road). Turn left on Road C-2600 and drive 0.9 mile (after 0.4

mile it becomes C-Line Road) to C-2650. Turn right and drive 0.3 mile to the campground on the right at Western Lake.

Contact: Department of Natural Resources, Pacific Cascade Region North, 360/577-2025, www.dnr.wa.gov.

111 SNAG LAKE

Scenic rating: 9
near Naselle

Map 1.7, page 81

This is a classic little DNR camp on small Snag Lake—the kind of place time forgot. Any other clichés? No, seriously, time did forget this place. Very few people know about this spot and it can get you away from the crowds. Tiny Snag Lake is perfect for canoeing, fishing, wildlife-watching, or just kicking back. Gold Lake is nearby, as are several other small lakes.

Campsites, facilities: There are five walk-in sites for tents only. Picnic tables and fire grills are provided. Vault toilets are available. There is no drinking water and garbage must be packed out. Leashed pets are permitted.

Reservations, fees: Reservations are not accepted. There is no fee for camping. Open year-round.

Directions: From Kelso/Longview on I-5, turn west on Highway 4 and drive 60 miles (near Naselle) to Milepost 3 and C-Line Road. Turn right (north) and head uphill on C-Line Road (two-lane gravel road). Take the left fork at Naselle Youth Camp entrance, and drive 2.9 miles to C-2600 (gravel one-lane road). Turn left on Road C-2600 and drive 0.6 mile to C-2650. Turn right and drive 0.2 mile to the campground.

Contact: Department of Natural Resources, Pacific Cascade Region North, 360/577-2025, www.dnr.wa.gov.

112 SOU'WESTER LODGE

Scenic rating: 7
in Seaview on the Long Beach Peninsula

Map 1.7, page 81

This one-of-a-kind place features a lodge that dates back to 1892, vintage trailers available for rent, and cottages. Various cultural events are held at the park throughout the year, including fireside evenings with theater and chamber music. The park covers three acres, provides beach access, and is one of the few sites in the immediate area that provides spots for tent camping. This park often attracts creative people such as musicians and artists, and some arrive for vacations in organized groups. It is definitely not for Howie and Ethel from Iowa. Fishing is a recreation option. The area features the Lewis and Clark Interpretive Center, a lighthouse, museums, fine dining, bicycle and boat rentals, bicycle and hiking trails, and bird sanctuaries. Additional facilities found within five miles of the park include an 18-hole golf course, a full-service marina, and a riding stable. The lodge was originally built for U.S. Senator Henry Winslow Corbett.

A side note: Tch-Tch stands for "trailers, classic, hodge-podge." Like I said, the place is unique—and management has a great sense of humor.

Campsites, facilities: There are 28 sites with full hookups (20 and 30 amps) for RVs of any length, 13 sites for tents, a historic lodge, four cottages, and 12 1950s-style trailers in vintage condition. Some RV sites are pull-through. Picnic tables are provided at some sites. Restrooms with flush toilets and showers, drinking water, Wi-Fi, a classic VHS library, picnic area with pavilion, and community fire pits and grills are available. Propane gas, dump station, a store, gas station, café, and ice are located within one mile. Boat-launching facilities are nearby. Some facilities are wheelchair accessible. Leashed pets are permitted.

Reservations, fees: Reservations are accepted. Sites are $25-40 per night, trailers are

$83-192 per night, and cabins are $123-133 per night. Some credit cards are accepted. Open year-round.

Directions: From Kelso/Longview on I-5, turn west on Highway 4 and drive 63 miles to U.S. 101. Turn left (south) on U.S. 101 and drive 13 miles to the junction with Highway 103 (flashing light). Turn left to stay on U.S. 101 and drive one block to Seaview Beach Access Road (38th Place). Turn right and drive toward the ocean. Look for the campground on the left.

Contact: Sou'Wester Lodge, 360/642-2542, www.souwesterlodge.com.

113 CAUFFMAN WILDWOOD CAMPGROUND & RV PARK

Scenic rating: 5

in Long Beach

Map 1.7, page 81

Cauffman Wildwood is situated on Washington's tradition-steeped southwestern coast—the Long Beach Peninsula. Surrounded by the Pacific Ocean, the Columbia River, and Willapa Bay, this is a favorite vacation destination and a refuge for migrating birds and those seeking solitude by the ocean.

Campsites, facilities: There are 30 grassy sites with full hookups (20 and 30 amps) for RVs up to 60 feet, 25 wooded sites for tents, and seven group sites for up to 10 tents. Picnic tables and fire pits are provided. Restrooms with flush toilets and coin showers, drinking water, Wi-Fi, a small lake with fish, children's activities, and firewood are available. Leashed pets are permitted.

Reservations, fees: Reservations are accepted. RV sites are $35 per night, tent sites are $25 per night, $5 per each additional person per night, children age 16 and under are free. Call for group rates. Some credit cards are accepted. Open April-October.

Directions: From Kelso on I-5, turn west on Highway 4 and drive 60 miles to Highway 401. Turn left (south) on U.S. 101 South and drive 15 miles to Peninsula Road/Sandridge Road. The campground will be on the left.

Contact: Wildwood Campground & RV Park, 5411 Sandridge Road, Long Beach, 360/642-2131, www.wildwoodcampsites.com.

114 ILWACO KOA

Scenic rating: 5

near Fort Canby State Park

Map 1.7, page 81

This 17-acre camp is about nine miles from the beach and includes a secluded area for tents. You'll find a boardwalk nearby, as well as the Lewis and Clark Museum, lighthouses, an amusement park, and fishing from a jetty or charter boats. The Washington State International Kite Festival is held in Long Beach the third week of August. The World Kite Museum and Hall of Fame, also in Long Beach, is open year-round. Additional facilities found within five miles of the campground include a maritime museum, hiking trails, and a nine-hole golf course. In my experience, attempts to phone this park were thwarted by a busy signal for weeks.

Campsites, facilities: There are 17 sites with full hookups and 20 sites with partial hookups for RVs of any length, a tent area for up to 40 tents, three group sites for up to 24 people each, and five cabins. All RV sites are pull-through. Picnic tables and fire rings are provided. Restrooms with flush toilets and showers, drinking water, cable TV, propane gas, a dump station, recreation hall, a camp store, coin laundry, ice, horseshoe pits, volleyball net, and a playground are available. Some facilities are wheelchair accessible. Leashed pets are permitted.

Reservations, fees: Reservations are accepted at 800/562-3258. RV sites are $44-55 per night, tent sites are $33 per night, $5 per person per night for more than two people. Cabins are $77 per night and the group site is $150 per night. Some credit cards are accepted. Open mid-May-mid-September.

Directions: From Kelso/Longview on I-5, turn west on Highway 4 and drive 63 miles to U.S. 101. Turn left (south) on U.S. 101 and drive 13 miles to the junction with Highway 103. The campground is located at the junction.

Contact: Ilwaco KOA, 360/642-3292, www. koa.com.

115 CAPE DISAPPOINTMENT STATE PARK

Scenic rating: 10

near Ilwaco

Map 1.7, page 81

This park covers 1,882 acres on the Long Beach Peninsula and is fronted by the Pacific Ocean. There is access to 27 miles of ocean beach and two lighthouses. The park contains old-growth forest, lakes, both freshwater and salt-water marshes, streams, and tidelands. It is the choice spot in the area for tent campers. There are two places to camp: a general camping area and the Lake O'Neil area, which offers sites right on the water. Highlights at the park include hiking trails and opportunities for surf, jetty, and ocean fishing. An interpretive center highlights the Lewis and Clark expedition as well as maritime and military history. North Head Lighthouse is open for touring. Colbert House Museum is open during the summer.

Campsites, facilities: There are 137 sites for tents or RVs up to 45 feet (no hookups), 60 sites with full hookups (20 and 30 amps) and 18 sites with partial hookups (water and electricity) for RVs up to 45 feet, five primitive hike-in/bike-in sites, three cabins, and 14 yurts. Picnic tables and fire grills are provided. Restrooms with flush toilets and coin showers, drinking water, a dump station, boat ramp, dock (135 feet), a picnic area, interpretive activities, a horseshoe pit, athletic fields, a small store, and firewood are available. Some facilities are wheelchair accessible. Leashed pets are permitted.

Reservations, fees: Reservations are accepted at 888/226-7688 or https://washington.going-tocamp.com ($8-10 reservation fee). Sites are $20-45 per night, primitive tent sites are $12 per night, and cabins and yurts are $59-69 per night. Some credit cards are accepted. Open year-round.

Directions: From the junction of Highway 4 and Highway 103 (a flashing light, south of Nemah), turn west on Highway 103 (toward Ilwaco) and drive two miles to Ilwaco and Highway 100. Turn right and drive three miles to the park entrance on the right.

Contact: Cape Disappointment State Park, 360/642-3078, http://parks.state.wa.us.

116 MAUCH'S SUNDOWN RV PARK

Scenic rating: 5

in Chinook near Fort Columbia State Park

Map 1.7, page 81

The park covers four acres, has riverside access, and is in a wooded, hilly setting with grassy sites. About 50 percent of the sites are rented monthly, usually throughout the summer. Nearby fishing from shore is available.

Campsites, facilities: There are 45 sites with full or partial hookups (30 amps) for tents or RVs of any length; some sites are pull-through. Picnic tables are provided. No open fires are allowed. Restrooms with flush toilets and coin showers, drinking water, a dump station, and a coin laundry are available. A café is located within three miles. Boat docks and launching facilities are nearby on the Columbia River. Small pets are permitted.

Reservations, fees: Reservations are accepted. Sites are $15-30 per night, plus $2 per person per night for more than two people. Some credit cards are accepted. Open year-round.

Directions: From Kelso/Longview on I-5, turn west on Highway 4 and drive 60 miles to Highway 401. Turn left (south) on Highway 401 and drive to U.S. 101. Take U.S. 101 to the right and continue for 0.5 mile (do not go over the bridge) to the park on the right.

Contact: Mauch's Sundown RV Park, 158 U.S. 101, 360/777-8713.

117 VISTA PARK

Scenic rating: 7

near the Columbia River

Map 1.7, page 81

This public camp covers 70 acres and features a half mile of sandy beach and a Lewis and Clark interpretive site. A short hiking trail is nearby. The camp also has nearby access to the Columbia River, where recreational options include fishing, swimming, and boating. Additional facilities found within five miles of the park include a full-service marina and tennis courts. In Skamokawa, the River Life Interpretive Center stays open year-round.

Campsites, facilities: There are 15 sites with full hookups and 24 sites with partial hookups for RVs of any length, 16 sites for tents or RVs of any length (no hookups), and five yurts. Group camping is also available. Picnic tables and fire pits are provided. Restrooms with flush toilets and coin showers, drinking water, a dump station, ice, firewood, tennis courts, basketball courts, a group picnic shelter, geocaching, and two playgrounds are available. A café is located within walking distance. Boat docks, launching facilities, and kayak rentals are nearby. Some facilities are wheelchair accessible. Leashed pets are permitted, with some restrictions.

Reservations, fees: Reservations are accepted. RV sites are $23-30 per night, tent sites are $18 per night, and yurts are $47-55 per night, $5 per night for each additional vehicle. Some credit cards are accepted. Open year-round.

Directions: From Kelso/Longview on I-5, turn west on Highway 4 and drive 35 miles to Skamokawa. Continue west on Highway 4 for 0.5 mile to the park on the left.

Contact: Vista Park, Port of Wahkiakum No. 2, 360/795-8605, www.vistapark.wordpress.com.

SEATTLE AND THE PUGET SOUND

Seattle offers a wide array of recreation, with a pre-eminent scope of parks and campgrounds: Many state parks are home to gorgeous water-view campsites; well-furnished RV parks offer a layover respite; and hidden lakes, such as Cascade Lake on Orcas Island, will surprise you with their beauty. But—you need a boat to do it right. A powerboat, sailboat, or kayak offers near-unlimited access to Puget Sound and the linked inlets, bays, and canals—not to mention boat-in campsites. And with some 25 boat-in campsites available, often along calm, sheltered waters, there is no better place to sea kayak.

One of my favorite views anywhere is from the top of Mount Constitution on Orcas Island. On a clear day, you can look out over an infinity of sun-swept charm—and you'll know this is why you came.

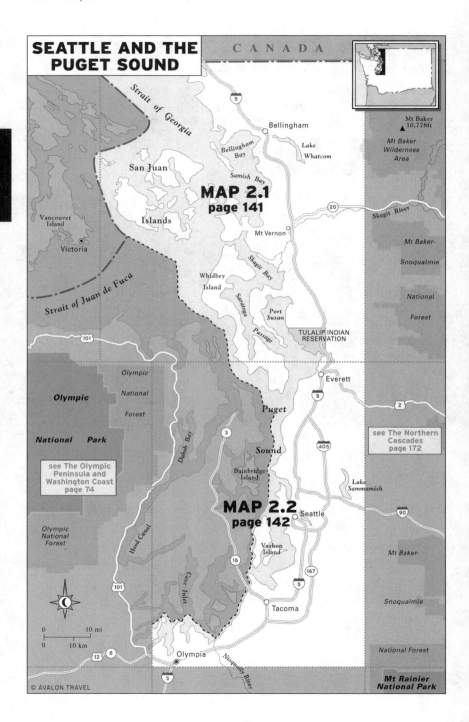

Map 2.1

Sites 1-46
Pages 143-164

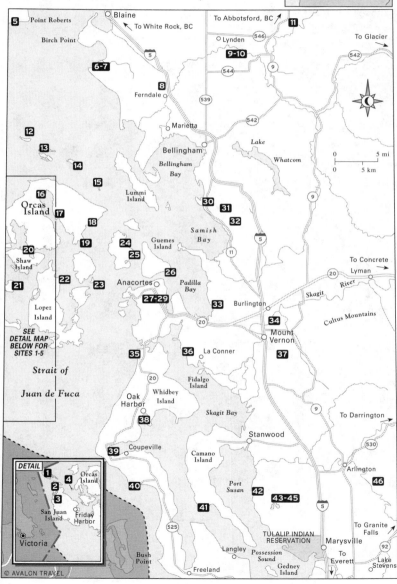

Map 2.2

Sites 47-57
Pages 165-169

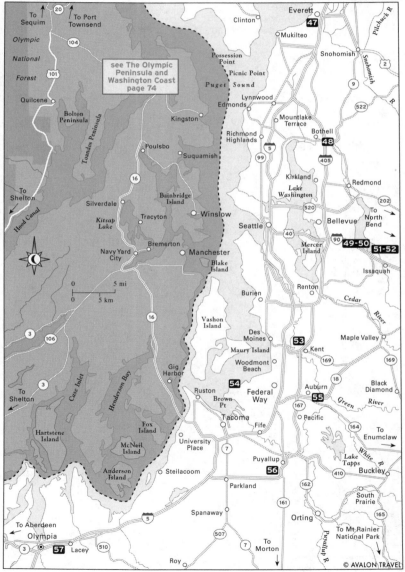

◻1 STUART ISLAND MARINE STATE PARK BOAT-IN

Scenic rating: 9

northwest of San Juan Island

Map 2.1, page 141

For most campers, this is really stalking the unknown. Stuart Island is a remote little spot on the edge of Canadian waters that covers 433 acres and has excellent harbors for mooring. It's the westernmost of the marine parks, making it a jumping-off point for Sucia Island, Orcas Island, and San Juan Island parks. There is good fishing at nearby Reid and Provost Harbors. On holiday weekends, it usually fills up; on summer weekends, it is typically about 70 percent filled; and on weekdays, it is about half filled. That makes it the second-busiest park in the area, receiving about 70,000 visitors per year.

Campsites, facilities: There are 18 primitive boat-in campsites, including four reserved for non-motorized boaters only. Picnic tables and fire rings are provided. Drinking water (summer season only) and pit and composting toilets are available. Garbage must be packed out. There are 20 buoys, and floats are available for overnight moorage for boats up to 45 feet. Leashed pets are permitted.

Reservations, fees: Reservations are not accepted. Sites are $12 per night, moorage is $0.70 per foot per boat with a $15 minimum. Open year-round, with limited facilities in winter.

Directions: The park is on the north side of Stuart Island and is accessible only by boat. Stuart Island is located northwest of San Juan Island.

Contact: Stuart Island Marine State Park, 360/378-2044, http://parks.state.wa.us.

◻2 POSEY ISLAND STATE PARK BOAT-IN

Scenic rating: 9

near Roche Harbor

Map 2.1, page 141

This is a beautiful little spot you'll want all to yourself. It's difficult to get here, however, as you must arrive by non-motorized boat—kayak, canoe, or pelican sailboat. The best way to reach the camp is by sea kayak, paddling in from San Juan Island out of Roche Harbor. There are no docks or mooring buoys. Situated on a one-acre island, this is not only one of the smallest designated campgrounds in Washington, but also one of the most idyllic and beautiful to reach by small boat, with lots of wildflowers in spring, including chocolate lilies. In an attempt to keep it from being loved to death, no more than 16 people are permitted on the island at one time. There's not much here, and that's exactly why it is so well loved. Everything becomes simplified, so it feels as if you have the entire world to yourself. And on Posey Island, you do.

Campsites, facilities: There are two primitive boat-in campsites for a maximum of 16 people at any time. Picnic tables and fire rings are provided. A composting toilet is available. There is no drinking water. Garbage must be packed out.

Reservations, fees: Reservations are accepted mid-May-September at 360/378-2044 or https://washington.goingtocamp.com ($8-10 reservation fee). Sites are $12 per night. Open year-round.

Directions: This little island is located just north of Roche Harbor (on San Juan Island) and is accessible only by small boat. From Roche Harbor, head northwest and cruise about one mile from the outlet to reach Posey Island.

Contact: San Juan Marine Area, South, 360/378-2044, http://parks.state.wa.us.

3 LAKEDALE RESORT AT THREE LAKES

🚴 🏊 🛶 🎣 🐾 🚐 ⛺

Scenic rating: 7

on San Juan Island

Map 2.1, page 141

This is a nice spot on 82 acres for visitors who want the solitude of an island camp, yet all the amenities of a privately run campground. Fishing, swimming, and boating are available at the three Lakedale lakes. A sand volleyball court, a half-court basketball area, and a grassy sports field are also on-site. Roche Harbor and Wescott Bay are nearby to the north, and Friday Harbor and its restaurants are nearby to the south.

Campsites, facilities: There are 64 sites for tents and seven sites with partial hookups for tents or RVs up to 40 feet long. There are also six group tent sites for up to 20-40 people each, six log cabins, one longhouse, and 10 luxury lodge rooms. Picnic tables and fire rings are provided. Restrooms with flush toilets and coin showers, drinking water, and firewood are available. A convenience store and ice are available. Boat docks, a swimming beach, and boat and fishing gear rentals are available on-site. Leashed pets are permitted in campgrounds and log cabins.

Reservations, fees: Reservations are accepted at 800/617-2267 ($8-10 reservation fee). RV sites are $64 per night, tent sites are $45-57 per night, hike-in/bike-in sites are $35 per night, group sites are $200 per night, cabins are $179-279 per night with a fee of $35 per pet. Discounts are offered off-season. Some credit cards are accepted. Open Memorial Day-September for camping; cabins and lodge rooms are available year-round.

Directions: From Burlington and Highway 20, turn west on Highway 20 and drive 12 miles to the Highway 20 North spur, following signs to the San Juan Islands Ferry Terminal in Anacortes. Take the ferry to Friday Harbor on San Juan Island. From the ferry landing at Friday Harbor, drive two blocks on Spring Street to 2nd Street. Turn right (northwest) on 2nd Street and drive 0.5 mile to Tucker Avenue (it becomes Roche Harbor Road). Continue 4.5 miles to the resort on the left.

Contact: Lakedale Resort at Three Lakes, 360/378-2350, www.lakedale.com; Washington State Ferries, 800/843-3779, www.wsdot. wa.gov/ferries.

4 JONES ISLAND MARINE STATE PARK BOAT-IN

🚶 🛶 🎣 🐾 ⛺

Scenic rating: 9

near Orcas Island

Map 2.1, page 141

This small island may seem like a hidden spot, but it is an easy boat ride out of Doe Harbor at Orcas Island. It gets about the second-heaviest use of all the island campgrounds in the region. The campground is near the beach, so you don't have to carry your gear very far. The area offers good fishing and scuba diving. A note of caution: Raccoons have become pests, and campers are advised to keep food well contained. Rangers here make a special request that campers not feed the raccoons, deer, or other wildlife. Sunsets often provide breathtaking beauty from this island. In addition, it is set amid a national wildlife and migratory bird refuge. Another plus is that two big lawn areas are ideal for family and group camping. Note that the docks are in place April-mid-October.

Campsites, facilities: There are 24 primitive boat-in campsites (two sites are for non-motorized boaters only) and a group site for up to 65 people. Picnic tables and fire rings are provided. Drinking water (May-September only) and composting toilets are available. Garbage must be packed out. Boat buoys and floats are available for overnight moorage for boats up to 45 feet. Leashed pets are permitted.

Reservations, fees: Reservations are not accepted for single sites, but are required for the group site ($25 nonrefundable reservation fee). Sites are $12 per night; moorage is $0.70

per foot per boat with a $15 minimum. Call for group rates. Open year-round, with limited facilities in winter; docks are removed October-March.

Directions: The campground is on tiny Jones Island, located between Orcas Island and San Juan Island. This camp is accessible only by boat. Look for the boat buoys just offshore from the campsites.

Contact: Jones Island Marine State Park, 360/378-2044, http://parks.state.wa.us.

5 LIGHTHOUSE MARINE PARK

Scenic rating: 6

on Point Roberts

Map 2.1, page 141

This park is located on Point Roberts—so remote you must drive through Canada and then return south into the United States to reach it. The park features a boardwalk, a boat launch, and a sandy beach. Wildlife-watching and hiking are favorite activities here because of the beautiful views.

Campsites, facilities: There are 30 sites for tents and RVs. Group camping is also available. Picnic tables and fire pits are provided. Drinking water and restrooms with flush toilets and coin showers are available. A kitchen shelter is available for rent. A grocery store, a cafe, and a coin laundry are located within one mile. Leashed pets are permitted.

Reservations, fees: Reservations are accepted and recommended ($13 reservation fee). Sites are $18-25 per night, the group sites are $110-130 per night. Boat launch is $10 per day. Some credit cards are accepted. Open April-October.

Directions: From Bellingham, take I-5 north through Blaine and the border customs into Canada to Highway 99 North. Continue northwest on Highway BC 99N for 18 miles to BC 17. Turn left (west) and drive six miles to the town of Tsawwassen and 56th Street. Turn left on 56th Street and drive to the Point Roberts

border crossing. Drive straight on Tyee Drive, past the marina, to Lighthouse Marine Park on the left.

Contact: Lighthouse Marine Park, Whatcom County Parks and Recreation, 360/945-4911, www.co.whatcom.wa.us/parks.

6 BIRCH BAY STATE PARK

Scenic rating: 8

on Birch Bay

Map 2.1, page 141 **BEST**

Birch Bay State Park covers 194 acres and features nearly two miles of beach as well as great views of the Canadian coast range and some of the San Juan Islands. For water lovers, it has the best of both worlds, with 8,255 feet of saltwater shoreline and 14,923 feet of freshwater shoreline on Terrell Creek. More than 100 different species of birds, many of which migrate on the Pacific Flyway, can be seen here. Terrell Creek Marsh Interpretive Trail extends 0.5 mile through a forest of black birch trees, Douglas fir, and western hemlock and one of the few remaining saltwater/freshwater estuaries in northern Puget Sound. Bald eagles and great blue herons feed along the banks of Terrell Creek. Several 18-hole golf courses are located nearby. The campground is divided into two loops; hookups for RVs are in the North Loop.

Campsites, facilities: There are 147 sites for tents or self-contained RVs, 20 sites with full or partial hookups (30 amps) for RVs up to 60 feet long, one primitive group site for tents and RVs that can accommodate up to 40 people, and two group camps with five sites each. Picnic tables and fire grills are provided. Restrooms with flush toilets and coin showers and a dump station are available. A boat ramp (for boats less than 16 feet only), sheltered and unsheltered picnic areas, an amphitheater, basketball court, interpretive activities, and a camp host are available. A store, restaurant, coin laundry, and ice are located within one mile. Some

facilities are wheelchair accessible. Leashed pets are permitted.

Reservations, fees: Reservations are accepted and are required for groups at 888/226-7688 or https://washington.goingtocamp.com ($8-10 reservation fee). Sites are $25-45 per night, $10 per extra vehicle per night. Call for group rates. Some credit cards are accepted. Open year-round.

Directions: From Bellingham, drive north on I-5 to Exit 266. At Exit 266 take Grandview west and continue seven miles to Jackson Road. Turn right on Jackson Road and drive one mile to Helweg Road. Turn left and drive 0.25 mile to the reservation office.

Contact: Birch Bay State Park, 360/371-2800, http://parks.state.wa.us.

7 BEACHSIDE RV PARK

Scenic rating: 8

on Birch Bay

Map 2.1, page 141

This pretty park is surrounded by evergreens and bay views. Hiking, fishing, mountain biking, and nearby golf are also options. Note that most sites are filled with monthly renters.

Campsites, facilities: There are 72 pull-through sites with full hookups (30 and 50 amps) for RVs and five tent sites. Picnic tables are provided. Restrooms with flush toilets and showers, drinking water, a group fire pit, Wi-Fi, a library, lounge, DVD/video exchange, horseshoe pit, barbecue area, and coin laundry are available. A boat launch, grocery store, and restaurant are located within one mile. Leashed pets are permitted with certain restrictions.

Reservations, fees: Reservations are recommended. Sites are $25-35 per night for up to four people and two vehicles; $2 per person per night for more than four people. Weekly and monthly rates are available. Some credit cards are accepted. Open year-round.

Directions: From Bellingham, drive north on I-5 to Exit 270. Turn west on Birch Bay-Lynden Road and drive five miles to Birch Bay Drive. Turn left and drive one mile to the park on the left.

Contact: Beachside RV Park, 360/371-5962 or 800/596-9586, www.beachsidervpark.com.

8 THE CEDARS RV RESORT

Scenic rating: 5

in Ferndale

Map 2.1, page 141

This resort provides more direct access from I-5 than nearby Windmill Inn or KOA Lynden, and you can usually get a site here. It's a nice, clean park covering 22 acres with spacious sites and trees. Horseshoe pits, a game room, and a recreation field provide possible activities for campers. Several golf courses are nearby.

Campsites, facilities: There are 167 sites with full or partial hookups (20, 30, and 50 amps), including pull-through sites, for tents or RVs of any length and a grassy area for dispersed tent camping. Picnic tables and fire pits are provided. Restrooms with flush toilets and showers, drinking water, cable TV, Wi-Fi, two dump stations, coin laundry, a playground, horseshoe pits, badminton, volleyball, recreation room, a seasonal heated pool, convenience store, and ice are available. Leashed pets are permitted.

Reservations, fees: Reservations are accepted ($6 reservation fee for non-members). RV sites are $40-55 per night, tent sites are $31-36 per night, $3 per pet per night, additional fee for more than four people. Some credit cards are accepted. Open year-round.

Directions: From Bellingham on I-5, drive north to Ferndale and Exit 263. Take Exit 263 and turn right (north) on Portal Way. Drive less than one mile to the resort on the left.

Contact: The Cedars RV Resort, 360/384-2622, www.holidaytrailsresorts.com/thecedars.

9 WINDMILL INN

Scenic rating: 7

near the Nooksack River

Map 2.1, page 141

This nice little spot, only 15 minutes from Puget Sound, is set near the Nooksack River and Wiser Lake. As the last stop before the U.S./Canada border, the camp serves primarily as a layover for people heading north. The quiet and pretty setting abounds with trees and flowers. Area attractions include Mount Baker, the quaint little shops of Lynden, and the nearby Birch Bay area, which offers many recreation options.

Campsites, facilities: There are eight sites for RVs of any length and 15 motel rooms. Picnic tables are provided. Restrooms with flush toilets and coin showers, drinking water, cable TV, and a park are available. A store, propane gas, a café, coin laundry, and ice are available within one mile. Boat-launching facilities are located within 1.5 miles.

Reservations, fees: Reservations are not accepted. Sites are $18-30 per night. Some credit cards are accepted. Open year-round.

Directions: In Bellingham on I-5, take Exit 256 for Highway 539 (called Meridian Street in Bellingham). Turn north on Highway 539 and drive 10 miles to Lynden. The RV park is on the right side of the road as you enter Lynden.

Contact: Windmill Inn, 360/354-3424.

10 KOA LYNDEN/ BELLINGHAM

Scenic rating: 9

in Lynden

Map 2.1, page 141   **BEST (**

Lynden is a quaint Dutch town with a windmill and the Pioneer Museum. The park features green lawns, flowers, and trees surrounding a miniature golf course and three fishing ponds, where you can fish for trout. This KOA stars as a unique layover spot for vacationers heading north to Canada via Highway 539 and Highway 546. Nearby recreational options include several golf courses. Bellingham, a historic waterfront town with good restaurants and Victorian mansions, is also close by.

Campsites, facilities: There are 30 sites for tents or RVs (no hookups), 107 sites with full or partial hookups (30 and 50 amps) for RVs up to 60 feet, and 15 cabins. Some sites are pull-through. Picnic tables are provided and most sites have fire pits. Restrooms with flush toilets and showers, drinking water, Wi-Fi, propane gas, a dump station, firewood, a recreation hall, convenience store, café (summer season only), espresso bar, ice cream parlor, coin laundry, ice, a playground, miniature golf, horseshoe pits, volleyball, and a seasonal heated swimming pool are available. Fishing tackle and boat rentals are available. Leashed pets are permitted.

Reservations, fees: Reservations are accepted at 800/562-4779. RV sites start at $42 per night, tent sites start at $35 per night, cabins start at $71 per night, $5 per person per night for more than two people. Some credit cards are accepted. Open year-round.

Directions: From I-5 at Bellingham, take Exit 256 to Highway 539. Turn north and drive 12 miles to Highway 546. Turn east on Badger Road and drive three miles to Line Road. Turn right on Line Road and drive 0.5 mile to the campground on the right.

Contact: KOA Lynden/Bellingham, 360/354-4772, www.koa.com.

11 SUMAS RV PARK

Scenic rating: 5

in Sumas

Map 2.1, page 141

Located near the U.S./Canada border, this campground is a layover spot to spend American dollars before heading into British Columbia and making the conversion. The camp is set in the grassy flatlands; it has graveled sites and a few trees. Nearby recreation options include an 18-hole golf course.

Campsites, facilities: There is a grassy area for tents and 50 sites with full or partial hookups (20, 30, and 50 amps) for tents or RVs of any length. Some sites are pull-through. Picnic tables are provided at some sites; fire rings are provided at most sites. Restrooms with flush toilets and coin showers, drinking water, modem access, a dump station, and coin laundry are available. A store, ice, café, rodeo grounds, and a ballpark are located within one mile. Leashed pets are permitted.

Reservations, fees: Reservations are accepted. RV sites are $30 per night, tent sites are $20-30 per night, $4 per person per night for more than two people. Some credit cards are accepted. Open year-round.

Directions: From I-5 at Bellingham, take Exit 256 to Highway 539. Turn north on Highway 539 and drive 12 miles to Highway 546. Turn right (east) on Highway 546 (Badger Road) and drive 14 miles (the road becomes Highway 9) to Sumas and look for Cherry Street. Turn right (south) at Cherry Street (the road becomes Easterbrook Road) and drive two blocks to the park on the left.

Contact: Sumas RV Park, 9600 Easterbrook Rd., 360/988-8875, http://sumasrvpark.com.

12 PATOS ISLAND MARINE STATE PARK BOAT-IN

Scenic rating: 9

near Sucia Island

Map 2.1, page 141

If you're going to get stranded on an island, this is not a bad choice, provided you like your companion. There are good hiking trails and excellent fishing and clam-digging opportunities here. Covering approximately 200 acres, it's primitive and used by few. Patos Lighthouse is a favorite attraction on this island. It also features great views of the Canadian islands, and sunsets are often drop-dead beautiful.

Campsites, facilities: There are seven primitive boat-in campsites. Picnic tables and fire rings are provided. Vault and pit toilets are available. There is no drinking water and garbage must be packed out. Two boat buoys are available for overnight moorage. Leashed pets are permitted.

Reservations, fees: Reservations are not accepted. Sites are $12 per night, buoys are $15 per night. Open year-round, with limited facilities in winter.

Directions: The park is located on the west side of Patos Island, which is 2.5 miles northwest of Sucia Island and five miles northwest of Orcas Island. It's accessible only by boat and is the northernmost of the coastal islands.

Contact: Patos Island Marine State Park, 360/376-2073, http://parks.state.wa.us.

13 SUCIA ISLAND MARINE STATE PARK BOAT-IN

Scenic rating: 9

near Orcas Island

Map 2.1, page 141

Here's a classic spot with rocky outcrops for lookout points and good beach and fishing areas. Sucia Island covers 562 acres and provides opportunities for hiking, clamming, crabbing, kayaking, and scuba diving. Although primitive, the campground is beautiful and well worth the trip, making it the busiest park in the chain of San Juan Islands. It also has the most moorage. This camp is full during summer, often even on weekdays.

Campsites, facilities: There are 60 primitive boat-in campsites and three group sites for up to 50 people each. Picnic tables and fire rings are provided. Drinking water (May-September), composting toilets, four picnic shelters, and two docks are available. Garbage must be packed out. Boat buoys and floats are available for overnight moorage, and you can anchor without a fee in all bays and coves. Some

facilities are wheelchair accessible. Leashed pets are permitted.

Reservations, fees: Reservations are not accepted for individual sites, but are required for the group sites at 360/376-2073. Sites are $12 per night, buoys are $15 per night. Call for group rates. Open year-round, with limited facilities in winter.

Directions: The park is located on the north side of Sucia Island (2.5 miles north of Orcas Island). It's accessible only by boat.

Contact: Sucia Island Marine State Park, 360/376-2073, http://parks.state.wa.us.

14 MATIA ISLAND MARINE STATE PARK BOAT-IN

🏃‍♂️ 🏊 🎣 🚤 🏕️

Scenic rating: 9

near Orcas Island

Map 2.1, page 141

Campsites here are located just a short walk from the docking facilities (available April-October), a big plus since many of the other island campgrounds don't have docks. Otherwise the camp is primitive, so it gets lighter use than the other campgrounds set on islands in the area. A one-mile loop trail from the campground leads through an old-growth cedar forest. Other highlights include good fishing and beachcombing. Scuba diving is also popular. This island is a U.S. Fish and Wildlife refuge.

Campsites, facilities: There are six primitive boat-in campsites. Composting toilets are available. Fires are not permitted. There is no drinking water, and garbage must be packed out. There is a boat dock, and buoys and floats are available for overnight moorage. Note that docks are in place April-October, weather permitting.

Reservations, fees: Reservations are not accepted. Sites are $12 per night, moorage is $0.70 per foot per boat ($15 minimum), and buoys are

$15 per night. Open year-round, with limited facilities in winter.

Directions: The campground is located on the northeast side of Matia Island, which is 2.5 miles northeast of Orcas Island (between Clark Island to the southeast, Sucia Island to the northwest, and Orcas Island to the south). It's accessible only by boat.

Contact: Matia Island Marine State Park, 360/376-2073, http://parks.state.wa.us.

15 CLARK ISLAND MARINE STATE PARK BOAT-IN

🏃‍♂️ 🏊 🎣 🚤 🏕️ 🏕️

Scenic rating: 9

northeast of Orcas Island

Map 2.1, page 141

Clark Island State Park offers beautiful beaches with opportunities for scuba diving, beachcombing, and sunbathing. It is a short boat trip from nearby Orcas Island. You can pretend you're on a deserted Caribbean island. Well, almost. From the campground, there are excellent views of the other nearby islands.

Campsites, facilities: There are 15 primitive boat-in campsites and a group site for up to 12 people. Picnic tables and fire rings are provided. Two vault toilets and one composting toilet is available. There is no drinking water and garbage must be packed out. Boat buoys for overnight moorage are available for boats up to 45 feet long. Leashed pets are permitted.

Reservations, fees: Reservations are accepted for the group site at 360/376-2073 ($25 reservation fee). Sites are $12 per night, buoys are $15 per night. Open year-round, with limited facilities in winter.

Directions: The campground is on tiny Clark Island, located northeast of Orcas Island. It's accessible only by boat. Look for the moorage floats set just offshore from the campsites.

Contact: Clark Island Marine State Park, 360/376-2073, http://parks.state.wa.us.

16 WEST BEACH RESORT FERRY-IN

🚶 🚲 🏊 🛶 🛥 🎣 🐕 👨‍👧 🚐 ⛺

Scenic rating: 9

on Orcas Island

Map 2.1, page 141   **BEST (**

Right on the beach, this resort offers salmon fishing, boating, swimming, and an apple orchard. Some sites have ocean views and rent by the week in July and August. An excellent alternative to Moran State Park, which is often full, it offers the same recreation opportunities. There is excellent fishing, crabbing, and scuba diving at the resort, and fishing charters and guided kayak tours are available. The beaches at Orcas Island are prime spots for whale-watching and beautiful views, especially at sunrise and sunset.

Campsites, facilities: There are 12 sites for tents or RVs of any length (20 and 30 amp full hookups), 15 sites for tents, and one overflow area for tents. There are also nine tent cabins. Picnic tables and fire pits are provided. Restrooms with flush toilets and coin showers (March-October only), a convenience store, café, playground, coin laundry, ice, Wi-Fi, fish-cleaning station, and firewood are available. A spa is available for a fee. Also on-site are a boat ramp, dock, full-service marina, rentals, moorage, and dry storage. A dump station is nearby. Leashed pets are permitted.

Reservations, fees: Reservations are accepted at 877/937-8224. RV sites are $33-49 per night for up to three people, tent sites are $20-45 per night, $7 per night for each additional person (maximum of six), $7 per extra vehicle per night, $7 per pet per night. Tent cabins are $99-179 per night, $12 per each additional vehicle, $12 per pet per night. Some credit cards are accepted. Open year-round.

Directions: From Burlington and I-5, take exit 230 (San Juan Islands) for Highway 20. Turn west on Highway 20 and drive 12 miles to the Highway 20 North spur, following signs to the San Juan Islands Ferry Terminal in Anacortes. Take the ferry to Orcas Island. From the ferry landing, turn left and drive nine miles on Horseshoe Highway/Orcas Road to the entrance of Eastsound. Continue 0.25 mile to Enchanted Forest Road. Turn left and drive 2.4 miles to the end of Enchanted Forest Road and the resort.

Contact: West Beach Resort, 360/376-2240, www.westbeachresort.com; Washington State Ferries, 206/464-6400 or 888/808-7977 (Washington only).

17 MORAN STATE PARK FERRY-IN

🚶 🚲 🛶 🚣 🐕 ♿ 🚐 ⛺

Scenic rating: 10

on Orcas Island

Map 2.1, page 141   **BEST (**

This state park is drop-dead beautiful. It covers 5,252 acres, with surprise lakes, hiking trails, and the best mountaintop views anywhere in the chain of islands. There are actually four separate campgrounds plus a primitive area. You can drive to the summit of Mount Constitution, which tops out at 2,409 feet, then climb up the steps to a stone observation tower (built in 1936 by the Civilian Conservation Corps). The tower provides sensational 360-degree views of Vancouver, Mount Baker, the San Juan Islands, the Cascade Mountains, and several cities on the distant shores of mainland America and Canada. No RVs are allowed on the winding road to the top. There are five freshwater lakes (no gas-motor boats permitted) with fishing for rainbow trout, cutthroat trout, and kokanee salmon, 33 miles of hiking trails, 11 miles of biking trails, and six miles of horse trails. The landscape features old-growth forest, primarily lodgepole pine, and several small waterfalls. Nearby recreation options include a nine-hole golf course.

Campsites, facilities: There are 151 sites for tents or RVs up to 45 feet (no hookups), including some pull-through sites, 15 primitive hike-in/bike-in tent sites, and a group site for up to 56 people. Picnic tables and fire grills are provided. Restrooms with flush toilets and coin showers, drinking water, a dump station, a picnic area with log kitchen shelter, firewood, and a snack bar are available. Boat docks, limited fishing supplies, launching facilities, and boat rentals are located at the concession stand in the park. Some facilities are wheelchair accessible. Leashed pets are permitted.

Reservations, fees: Reservations are accepted at 888/226-7688 or https://washington.goingtocamp.com ($8-10 reservation fee). Sites are $25-35 per night, bike-in/hike-in sites are $12 per night, and $10 per extra vehicle per night. Call for group rates. Note that some campers consider the ferry-crossing fee for RVs very high; call ahead for prices. Some credit cards are accepted. Open year-round.

Directions: From Seattle on I-5, drive north to Burlington and Highway 20. Turn west on Highway 20 and drive 12 miles to the Highway 20 North spur, following signs to the San Juan Islands Ferry Terminal in Anacortes. Take the ferry to Orcas Island. From the ferry landing, turn left on Horseshoe Highway/Orcas Road and drive 13 miles to Moran State Park (well marked). Stop at the campground registration booth for directions to your site.

Contact: Moran State Park, 360/376-2326, http://parks.state.wa.us; Washington State Ferries, 206/464-6400 or 888/808-7977 (Washington state only).

Moran State Park, also on this island, is a more developed alternative with many recreation options.

Campsites, facilities: There are nine primitive hike-in sites for tents only and one boat-in site. Picnic tables and fire grills are provided. Vault toilets are available. There is no drinking water, and garbage must be packed out. Three mooring buoys are available. Open year-round, with limited facilities in winter. Leashed pets are permitted.

Reservations, fees: Reservations are not accepted. Sites are $12-35 per night, buoys are $15 per night. Open year-round.

Directions: From Seattle on I-5, drive north to Burlington and Highway 20. Turn west on Highway 20 and drive 12 miles to the Highway 20 North spur, following signs to the San Juan Islands Ferry Terminal in Anacortes. Take the ferry to Orcas Island, then drive on the Horseshoe Highway past Moran State Park and continue to the town of Olga and Doe Bay Road. Drive east on Doe Bay Road for 0.5 mile to Obstruction Pass Road. Turn right and drive 0.7 mile to Trailhead Road. Bear right and drive straight for less than a mile to the parking area. Hike 0.5 mile to the campground.

Contact: Obstruction Pass State Park, 360/376-2326, http://parks.state.wa.us; Washington State Ferries, 206/464-6400 or 888/808-7977 (Washington state only).

18 OBSTRUCTION PASS STATE PARK HIKE-IN

Scenic rating: 8

on Orcas Island

Map 2.1, page 141

It takes a ferryboat ride, a tricky drive, and a 0.5-mile walk to reach this campground, but that helps set it apart from others. Your journey will take you to a unique, primitive spot set in a forested area with good hiking near the shore of Orcas Island. The irony is that Obstruction Pass is so unusual that it is often heavily used.

19 DOE ISLAND MARINE STATE PARK BOAT-IN

Scenic rating: 9

near Orcas Island

Map 2.1, page 141   **BEST (**

Doe Island State Park is a tiny, primitive park that receives little use. It has a rocky shoreline, which makes an ideal fish habitat, and the scuba diving and fishing are exceptional. Docking is available April-mid-October; please note that the mooring buoys located just offshore are privately owned.

Campsites, facilities: There are five primitive boat-in campsites. Picnic tables and fire rings are provided. A vault toilet is available. There is no drinking water and garbage must be packed out. Leashed pets are permitted.

Reservations, fees: Reservations are not accepted. Sites are $12 per night, moorage is $0.70 per foot per boat ($15 minimum), and buoys are $15 per night. Open year-round, with limited facilities in winter.

Directions: This small, secluded island is just off the southeastern shore of Orcas Island off Doe Bay. It's accessible only by boat.

Contact: Doe Island Marine State Park, 360/376-2073, http://parks.state.wa.us.

20 BLIND ISLAND STATE PARK BOAT-IN
🏊 🛥 ⚓ 🐕 ⛺

Scenic rating: 9

near Shaw Island

Map 2.1, page 141

This island has few trees and is known for its rocky shoreline. It's dangerous and ill advised to try beaching cruiser-style boats. Only non-motorized boats are permitted, and skilled kayakers will not have difficulty landing unless the water is rough. Blind Island State Park is a designated natural area and is committed to conserving a natural environment in a minimally developed state. This is not a place for large groups to throw big barbecues, but rather a quiet place for campers to enjoy the natural environment.

Campsites, facilities: There are four primitive boat-in campsites. Picnic tables and fire rings are provided. A composting toilet is available. There is no drinking water and garbage must be packed out. Boat buoys are available for overnight moorage. Leashed pets are permitted.

Reservations, fees: Reservations are not accepted. Sites are $12 per night, buoys are $15

per night. Open year-round, with limited facilities in winter.

Directions: The campground is located just west of the Shaw Island ferry landing on little Blind Island in Blind Bay. The nearest boat ramps are at Obstruction Pass on Orcas Island or Odlin County Park on Lopez Island.

Contact: Blind Island State Park, 360/378-2044, http://parks.state.wa.us.

21 TURN ISLAND MARINE STATE PARK BOAT-IN
🏃 🛥 ⚓ 🐕 ⛺

Scenic rating: 10

near Friday Harbor

Map 2.1, page 141   **BEST (**

This spot is gorgeous, and while this is one of about 30 campgrounds in the area that can be reached only by boat, note that Turn Island State Park has no docks, only mooring buoys. This tiny island is just off San Juan Island's eastern side. Quiet, primitive, and beautiful, this spot offers good trails for tromping around and year-round angling for rockfish. There are pretty beaches for shell collectors. The island is within the San Juan Islands National Wildlife Refuge.

Campsites, facilities: There are 12 primitive boat-in campsites. Picnic tables are provided. Fires are not permitted. Composting toilets are available. There is no drinking water and garbage must be packed out. Three buoys are available for overnight moorage. Leashed pets are permitted.

Reservations, fees: Reservations are not accepted. Sites are $12 per night, buoys are $12 per night. Open year-round, with limited facilities in winter.

Directions: Turn Island is located off the northeast tip of San Juan Island (in the San Juan Channel). It is accessible only by boat.

Contact: Turn Island Marine State Park, 360/378-2044, http://parks.state.wa.us.

22 SPENCER SPIT STATE PARK FERRY-IN

🛶 🚤 🏕 🦌 ♿ 🚐 ⛺

Scenic rating: 9

on Lopez Island

Map 2.1, page 141

Spencer Spit State Park offers one of the few island campgrounds accessible to cars via ferry. It also features walk-in sites for privacy, which require anywhere from a 50-foot to a 200-yard walk to the tent sites. A sand spit extends far into the water and provides a lagoon and good access to prime clamming areas. The park covers 200 acres. Picnicking, beachcombing, and sunbathing are some pleasant activities for campers looking for relaxation.

Campsites, facilities: There are 37 sites for tents or self-contained RVs up to 20 feet long (no hookups), seven primitive walk-in sites for tents only, seven hike-in/bike-in sites, three marine trail sites, and three group sites for up to 50 people each. Picnic tables and fire grills are provided. Restrooms with flush toilets, drinking water, a picnic area, three kitchen shelters, and a dump station are available; 12 mooring buoys are available on the Cascadia Marine Trail. Boat docks and a launch are within two miles, and showers are approximately three miles away. Some facilities are wheelchair accessible. Leashed pets are permitted.

Reservations, fees: Reservations are accepted at 888/226-7688 or https://washington.goingtocamp.com ($8-10 reservation fee, $25 fee for groups). Sites are $25 per night, primitive and marine trail sites are $12 per night, $10 per extra vehicle per night, and $15 per night for mooring buoys. Call for group rates. Open year-round, with limited winter facilities.

Directions: From Seattle on I-5, drive north to Burlington and Highway 20. Turn west on Highway 20 and drive 12 miles to the Highway 20 North spur, following signs to the San Juan Islands Ferry Terminal in Anacortes. Take the ferry to Lopez Island. The park is within four miles of the ferry terminal.

Contact: Spencer Spit State Park, 360/468-2251, http://parks.state.wa.us; Washington State Ferries, 206/464-6400 or 888/808-7977 (Washington state only).

23 JAMES ISLAND MARINE STATE PARK BOAT-IN

🥾 🏊 🛶 🚤 🏕 ⛺

Scenic rating: 9

near Decatur Island

Map 2.1, page 141

Small, hidden James Island provides good opportunities for hiking, fishing, and scuba diving. The 113-acre island is quiet and primitive, with lots of trees and a pretty beach for walking or sunbathing.

Campsites, facilities: There are 13 primitive boat-in campsites; three are designated sites for non-motorized boaters. Picnic tables and fire rings are provided. Composting and pit toilets are available. There is no drinking water and garbage must be packed out. Boat floats and four buoys are available for moorage off the east side of the island. A moorage dock on the west side of the island is open April-mid-October. Leashed pets are permitted.

Reservations, fees: Reservations are not accepted. Sites are $12 per night, moorage is $0.70 per foot per boat for boats up to 45 feet ($15 minimum), and buoys are $15 per night. Open year-round, with limited facilities in winter.

Directions: This island is east of Decatur Island in Rosario Strait and is only accessible by boat. The campground is on the east side of the island.

Contact: James Island Marine State Park, 360/378-2073, http://parks.state.wa.us.

24 PELICAN BEACH BOAT-IN

🥾 🏊 🚤 🛶 🏕 ⛺

Scenic rating: 9

on Cypress Island

Map 2.1, page 141

This forested island campground offers a group

shelter, beach access, and hiking trails. It is located in the Cypress Island Natural Resource Conservation Area. The 1.2-mile trail to Eagle Cliff is a must, although it is closed February-mid-July to protect endangered species. Like Cypress Head, this scenic camp is set on the oceanfront in a well-treed area. Pelican Beach has become even more popular than Cypress Head, not only with individual kayakers, but also with commercial operations that work as outfitters who organize trips for small groups of kayakers. The rangers ask that you practice low-impact camping here.

Campsites, facilities: There are several primitive boat-in campsites. Pit toilets and a group picnic shelter are available. There is no drinking water, and garbage must be packed out. Six mooring buoys are available nearby. Leashed pets are permitted but are not allowed at the lake or on the Eagle Cliff trails.

Reservations, fees: Reservations are not accepted. There is no fee for camping, but a Discover Pass is required. Open year-round.

Directions: This camp is set on the east shore of Cypress Island and is accessible only by boat. Cypress Island can be accessed by boat from Anacortes. Cruise west through Guemes Channel to Bellingham Channel (located between Cypress Island and Guemes Island). Turn north in Bellingham Channel and cruise to the campground on the southeast side of Cypress Island, just north of Cypress Head.

Contact: Department of Natural Resources, Northwest Region, 360/856-3500, www.dnr.wa.gov.

25 CYPRESS HEAD BOAT-IN

Scenic rating: 9

on Cypress Island

Map 2.1, page 141

An alternative to Pelican Beach, this primitive but pretty camp is situated right on Puget Sound in a forested setting of primarily Douglas fir and madrone. This camp is popular and often gets heavy use from kayakers. A trail provides access to Cypress Island Natural Resource Conservation Area. The rangers ask that you practice low-impact camping.

Campsites, facilities: There are seven primitive boat-in campsites. Picnic tables and fire grills are provided. Vault toilets are available. There is no drinking water, and garbage must be packed out. Four mooring buoys are available nearby. Leashed pets are permitted.

Reservations, fees: Reservations are not accepted. There is no fee for camping, but a Discover Pass is required. Open year-round.

Directions: This camp is set on the east shore of Cypress Island and is accessible only by boat. Cypress Island can be accessed by boat from Anacortes. Cruise west through Guemes Channel to Bellingham Channel (located between Cypress Island and Guemes Island). Turn north in Bellingham Channel and cruise to the campground on the southeast side of Cypress Island (just north of Deepwater Bay, just south of Pelican Beach Campground).

Contact: Department of Natural Resources, Northwest Region, 360/856-3500, www.dnr.wa.gov.

26 SADDLEBAG ISLAND MARINE STATE PARK BOAT-IN

Scenic rating: 9

near Guemes Island

Map 2.1, page 141

Saddlebag Island State Park is a good cruise from Anacortes. The island is quiet and primitive, with a nice beach near the campground for beachcombing and fine crabbing in the bay. Wildflowers are in bloom April-June. This island receives moderate use.

Campsites, facilities: There are five primitive boat-in campsites; one site is for non-motorized boaters only. Picnic tables and fire rings are provided. A composting toilet is available. There is no drinking water or mooring buoys, and garbage must be packed out. Leashed pets are permitted.

Reservations, fees: Reservations are not accepted. Sites are $12 per night. Open year-round, with limited facilities in winter.

Directions: From Seattle on I-5, drive north to Burlington and Highway 20. Turn west on Highway 20 and drive 12 miles to the Highway 20 North spur, following signs to the San Juan Islands Ferry Terminal in Anacortes. Launch your boat and cruise northeast around the southeast tip of Guemes Island. As you approach, Hat Island will be to your right, Huckleberry Island to your left, and Saddlebag Island straight ahead in Padilla Bay. Continue to Saddlebag Island. The camp is accessible only by boat.

Contact: Saddlebag Island Marine State Park, 360/376-2073, http://parks.state.wa.us.

27 PIONEER TRAILS RV RESORT & CAMPGROUND

🚶 🏊 🛶 🐕 🚴 🚐

Scenic rating: 9

near Anacortes on Fidalgo Island

Map 2.1, page 141

This site offers resort camping in the beautiful San Juan Islands. Tall trees, breathtaking views, cascading waterfalls, and country hospitality can all be found here. Side trips include nearby Deception Pass State Park (eight minutes away) and ferries to Victoria (British Columbia), Friday Harbor, Orcas Island, and other nearby islands (it is imperative to arrive early at the ferry terminal). Nearby recreation activities include horseshoes, an 18-hole golf course, relaxing spas, and lake fishing. Those familiar with this park may remember the group of old covered wagons that were here; they're gone now.

Campsites, facilities: There are 150 sites with full hookups (30, 50, and 100 amps), including some pull-through sites, for RVs of any length and five cabins. Picnic tables and fire rings are provided. Restrooms with flush toilets and showers, drinking water, a dump station, cable

TV, Wi-Fi, a pay phone, and coin laundry are available. A recreation hall, playground, horseshoe pits, and a basketball court are available nearby. Leashed pets are permitted with certain restrictions.

Reservations, fees: Reservations are recommended. Sites are $42-55 per night, cabins start at $55 per night, $5 per extra vehicle per night, $2-3 per night per each additional person. A three-night minimum is required on holidays. Debit cards, cash, and checks are accepted. Open year-round.

Directions: From Burlington and I-5, take Exit 230 for Highway 20 West. Drive west and cross over the Padilla Bridge onto Fidalgo Island. Watch for the Highway 20 sign and turn left at Mile Post 48. Go up the hill and take the first road on the right (Miller Road). Drive 0.25 mile and look for the park on the right side of the road.

Contact: Pioneer Trails RV Resort & Campground, 360/293-5355 or 888/777-5355, www.pioneertrails.com.

28 WASHINGTON PARK

🚶 🚴 🛻 🐕 🚴 ♿ 🚐 ⛰

Scenic rating: 6

in Anacortes

Map 2.1, page 141

This 220-acre city park is set in the woods on a peninsula at the west end of Fidalgo Island. It features many hiking trails. A 2.2-mile paved loop route for vehicles, hikers, and bicyclists stretches around the perimeter of the park. The Washington State Ferry terminals are located 0.5 mile away, providing access to the San Juan Islands. This is a popular camp, and it's a good idea to arrive early to claim your spot.

Campsites, facilities: There are 68 sites, including 46 with partial hookups, for tents or RVs up to 35 feet, a dispersed area for hike-in/bike-in camping, and one group tent site for up to 30 people. Some sites are pull-through. Restrooms with flush toilets and coin showers, drinking water, a playground, recreation field, dump station, a picnic area that can be reserved, and a boat launch are available. Some facilities are wheelchair accessible. Leashed pets are permitted.

Reservations, fees: Reservations are accepted online; 29 sites are first-come, first-served. Sites are $17-26 per night, the group site is $98 per night, boat launch is $7-9 per day. The group picnic area is $46-66 per day. Open year-round.

Directions: From Burlington and I-5, turn west on Highway 20 and drive to Anacortes and Commercial Avenue. Turn right on Commercial Avenue and drive approximately 0.5 mile to 12th Street. Turn left and drive about three miles (west of the ferry landing the road changes names several times) to Sunset Avenue. Turn left on Sunset Avenue. The park entrance and campground are on the left.

Contact: Washington Park, City of Anacortes, 360/293-1927 or 360/293-1918, www.cityofanacortes.org.

29 FIDALGO BAY RESORT
🏊 🛶 🚤 🛖 🚐

Scenic rating: 4
near Anacortes on Fidalgo Bay

Map 2.1, page 141

This 40-acre park is five minutes from Anacortes and right on Fidalgo Bay, providing easy access to boating, fishing, and swimming. More than one mile of beach is available. A golf course is available two miles away. A number of sites are filled with monthly renters. This resort is owned by the Samish Indian Nation.

Campsites, facilities: There are 139 sites with full hookups (20, 30, and 50 amps) for RVs of any length; many sites are pull-through. There are also eight cabins. Picnic tables and fire pits are provided at most sites. Restrooms with flush toilets and showers, drinking water, cable TV, Wi-Fi, a clubhouse, a large fire pit, a small boat launch, a convenience store, video rentals, propane, and a coin laundry are available. Leashed pets are permitted.

Reservations, fees: Reservations are

recommended at 800/727-5478. Sites are $34-68 per night, $5 per person per night for more than two people, $5 per night per extra vehicle, $2 per night per pet. Call for cabin rates. Some credit cards are accepted. Open year-round.

Directions: From Burlington and Highway 20, turn west on Highway 20 and drive about 14 miles to Fidalgo Bay Road. Turn right on Fidalgo Bay Road and drive one mile to the resort on the right.

Contact: Fidalgo Bay Resort, 360/293-5353, www.fidalgobay.com.

30 LARRABEE STATE PARK
🚶 🚲 🛶 🚂 🐎 ♿ 🚐 ⛺

Scenic rating: 9
on Samish Bay

Map 2.1, page 141   **BEST (**

Larrabee State Park—the first state park established in Washington—sits on Samish Bay in Puget Sound and boasts 8,100 feet of saltwater shoreline. The park's 2,748 acres include two freshwater lakes, coves, and tidelands, as well as 15 miles of hiking trails and 13 miles of mountain-biking trails. A setting of conifers and thick forests mixes with waterways, streams, and marsh before concluding at a beautiful stretch of coastline, a prime spot for sunsets and wildlife-viewing. Fishing is available on Fragrance Lake and Lost Lake, which are hike-in lakes. Chuckanut Mountain is nearby. A relatively short drive south will take you to Anacortes, where you can catch a ferry to islands in the San Juan chain.

Campsites, facilities: There are 51 sites for tents, 26 sites for tents or RVs up to 60 feet (30 amp full hookups), eight primitive tent sites, and a group site for up to 40 people. Picnic tables and fire grills are provided. Restrooms with flush toilets and coin showers, drinking water, a dump station, a picnic area with electricity and two covered shelters, amphitheater, and firewood are available. Boat-launching facilities are available nearby. Some facilities are wheelchair accessible. Leashed pets are permitted.

Reservations, fees: Reservations are accepted at 888/226-7688 or https://washington.going-tocamp.com ($7-9 reservation fee). Tent sites are $25-40 per night, primitive tent sites are $12 per night, sites with hookups are $35-45 per night, $10 per extra vehicle per night. Call for group rates. Some credit cards are accepted. Open year-round with limited winter facilities.

Directions: From Bellingham on I-5, take Exit 250 to Fairhaven Parkway. Turn right on Fairhaven Parkway. Drive less than a mile to State Route 11/Chuckanut Drive (second stoplight). Turn left (stay left at the next stoplight) and drive six miles to the park entrance on the right.

Contact: Larrabee State Park, 360/676-2093, http://parks.state.wa.us.

31 LIZARD LAKE HIKE-IN
🏃 ⛱ 🍴 🐴 ⛺

Scenic rating: 6

near Bellingham

Map 2.1, page 141

Lizard Lake is located just 0.2 mile north by trail from Lily Lake, but this hike-in/equestrian camp is even smaller and more isolated. It's set in a pretty, forested area. This is a prime area for hiking, and hikers and horse packers alike use the nearby trails. Fishing is an option at Lily Lake.

Campsites, facilities: There are three primitive hike-in sites for tents only. Tent pads and fire grills are provided. There are no toilets or drinking water; practice backcountry sanitation methods. Garbage must be packed out. Leashed pets are permitted.

Reservations, fees: Reservations are not accepted. There is no fee for camping, but a Discover Pass is required. Open year-round.

Directions: From Bellingham on I-5, drive south to Exit 240 to Samish Lake Road and drive 0.5 mile north to Barrel Springs Road.

Turn left and drive one mile to Road B-1000. Turn right and drive 1.5 miles to the Blanchard Hill Trailhead. Hike 3.2 miles, bear left, and continue 0.75 mile (just past Lily Lake) to the campground. A map is advisable and available at www.dnr.wa.gov.

Contact: Department of Natural Resources, Northwest Region, 360/856-3500, www.dnr.wa.gov.

32 LILY LAKE HIKE-IN
🏃 ⛱ 🍴 🐴 ⛺

Scenic rating: 6

near Bellingham

Map 2.1, page 141

This tiny, remote hike-in campground is one of those camps that few people ever go to or even know about. Set on little Lily Lake, it's completely secluded and primitive; you'll have to pack in everything you need and pack out everything that's left. Recreation options include fishing and hiking; hikers and horse packers alike use the nearby trails. Nearby Lizard Lake provides an even smaller camp.

Campsites, facilities: There are six primitive hike-in sites for tents only. Tent pads and fire rings are provided. There are no toilets or drinking water. Garbage must be packed out. Leashed pets are permitted.

Reservations, fees: Reservations are not accepted. There is no fee for camping, but a Discover Pass is required. Open year-round.

Directions: From Bellingham on I-5, drive south to Exit 240. On Samish Lake Road drive 0.5 mile north to Barrel Springs Road. Turn left and drive one mile to Road B-1000. Turn right and drive 1.5 miles to the Blanchard Hill Trailhead. Hike 3.2 miles, bear left, and continue 0.5 mile to the campground. A map is advisable and available at www.dnr.wa.gov.

Contact: Department of Natural Resources, Northwest Region, 360/856-3500, www.dnr.wa.gov.

33 BAY VIEW STATE PARK
🏊 🎣 ⛴ 🦌 🏕 ♿ 🚐 ⛰

Scenic rating: 10
on Padilla Bay

Map 2.1, page 141   **BEST (**

This campground set on Padilla Bay has a large, grassy area for kids, making it a good choice for families. Bordering 11,000 acres of Padilla Bay and the National Estuarine Sanctuary, this 25-acre park boasts 1,285 feet of saltwater shoreline. From the park, you can enjoy views of the San Juan Islands fronting Padilla Bay. On a clear day, you can see the Olympic Mountains to the west and Mount Rainier to the south. Kayakers should note that Padilla Bay becomes a large mud flat during low tides. Windsurfing is becoming popular, but tracking tides and wind is required. The Breazeale Padilla Bay Interpretive Center is located 0.5 mile north of the park. For a nice day trip, take the ferry at Anacortes to Lopez Island (there are several campgrounds there as well).

Campsites, facilities: There are 46 sites for tents or self-contained RVs, 29 sites with full hookups for RVs up to 60 feet long, one group tent site for 20-64 people, and six cabins. Picnic tables and fire rings are provided. Restrooms with flush toilets and coin showers, drinking water, firewood, a dump station, and a picnic area with a beach shelter are available. Horseshoes, volleyball, interpretive activities, windsurfing, waterskiing, swimming, and boating are available. A store and coin laundry are eight miles away in Burlington. Some facilities are wheelchair accessible. Leashed pets are permitted.

Reservations, fees: Reservations are accepted for individual sites and are required for groups at 888/226-7688 or https://washington.goingto-camp.com ($7-9 reservation fee). Sites are $25-45 per night, $10 per extra vehicle per night. Cabins are $45-79 per night with a $15 pet fee. Call for group site fees. Some credit cards are accepted. Open year-round, but some campsites are closed in winter.

Directions: From Seattle on I-5, drive north to Burlington and Exit 230 for Highway 20. Turn west on Highway 20 and drive seven miles west (toward Anacortes) to Bay View-Edison Road. Turn right (north) on Bay View-Edison Road and drive four miles to the park on the right.

Contact: Bay View State Park, 360/757-0227, http://parks.state.wa.us.

34 BURLINGTON/ ANACORTES KOA
🏊 🎣 🦌 🏕 🚐 ⛰

Scenic rating: 5
in Burlington

Map 2.1, page 141

This is a fine KOA campground, complete with all the amenities. The sites are spacious and comfortable. Possible side trips include tours of the Boeing plant in Everett, about 30 miles away, Victoria, Vancouver Island, and the San Juan Islands.

Campsites, facilities: There are 120 sites, most with full or partial hookups, for tents or RVs of any length and 11 cabins. Some sites are pull-through. Restrooms with flush toilets and showers, drinking water, a dump station, cable TV, Wi-Fi, a coin laundry, limited groceries, ice, propane gas, firewood, and a barbecue area are available. There is also an indoor heated pool, spa, recreation hall, game room, playground, nine-hole miniature golf, bicycle rentals, horseshoe pits, and a sports field. Leashed pets are permitted.

Reservations, fees: Reservations are recommended in summer at 800/562-9154. Sites are $50-67 per night, cabins are $85-150 per night. Some credit cards are accepted. Open year-round.

Directions: From Burlington, take I-5 north to Exit 236/Bow Hill Road. Turn right on Bow Hill Road and drive to Old Highway 99 North Road. Turn right and drive a short distance south to N. Green Road. The campground is on the left.

Contact: Burlington/Anacortes KOA, 360/724-5511, www.koa.com.

35 DECEPTION PASS STATE PARK

🏃 🚵 🏊 🛶 🚁 🐎 ♿ 🚐 ⛺

Scenic rating: 10

on Whidbey Island

Map 2.1, page 141

This state park is located at beautiful Deception Pass on the west side of Whidbey Island. It features 4,134 acres with almost 15 miles of saltwater shoreline and six miles of freshwater shoreline on three lakes. The landscape ranges from old-growth forest to sand dunes. This diverse habitat has attracted 174 species of birds. An observation deck overlooks the Cranberry Lake wetlands. The park also features spectacular views of shoreline, mountains, and islands, often with dramatic sunsets. At one spot, rugged cliffs drop to the turbulent waters of Deception Pass. Recreation options include fishing at Pass Lake, a freshwater lake within the park. Fly-fishing for trout is a unique bonus for anglers. Note that each lake has different regulations for boating. Scuba diving is also popular. The park provides 38 miles of hiking trails, 1.2 miles of wheelchair-accessible trails, and three miles of biking trails. There are several historic Civilian Conservation Corps buildings throughout the park. One thing to consider: You may occasionally see (and hear) U.S. Navy jets from nearby Whidbey Island Air Station flying near the campground for several hours at a time.

Campsites, facilities: There are 167 sites for tents or self-contained RVs up to 60 feet (no hookups), 143 sites with partial hookups (30 amps) for RVs up to 50 feet long, five hiker/biker tent sites, cabins, and a group site for up to 50 people. Some sites are pull-through. Picnic tables and fire rings are provided. Restrooms with flush toilets and coin showers, drinking water, and a dump station are available. A concession stand, park store, firewood, horseshoe pit, an amphitheater, interpretive activities, sheltered picnic areas, a boat launch, boat rentals, and mooring buoys are available. Some facilities are wheelchair accessible. Leashed pets are permitted.

Reservations, fees: Reservations are accepted at 888/226-7688 or https://washington.goingtocamp.com ($7-9 reservation fee). Sites without hookups are $20-30 per night, sites with hookups are $30-40 per night, hiker/biker sites are $12 per night, the group site is $150 per night, cabins are $45-95 per night, $10 per extra vehicle per night. Some credit cards are accepted. Open year-round, with limited winter services.

Directions: From Seattle on I-5, drive north to Burlington and Exit 230/Highway 20. Take that exit and drive west on Highway 20 for 12 miles to Highway 20 South. Turn south on Highway 20 South and drive six miles (across the bridge at Deception Pass) to the park entrance (three miles south of the bridge) on the right.

Contact: Deception Pass State Park, 360/675-3767, http://parks.state.wa.us.

36 HOPE ISLAND MASON STATE PARK BOAT-IN

🚁 🛶 ⛺

Scenic rating: 8

in Skagit Bay

Map 2.1, page 141

Here's your chance to have an island all to yourself. This camp on the north side of Hope Island is lightly used and is a primitive alternative to the more developed drive-to sites nearby. Located between Squaxin Island and Steamboat Island, it features a 106-acre county park in Puget Sound and a landscape of old-growth forests and saltwater marshes. The park has a 1.5-mile beach, the top spot. The catch? You must have a boat to reach it. Solitude is your reward. A little-known option, a single campsite for kayakers is on the northeast tip of Skagit Island. It's largely a secret, and with no mooring buoy, likely to remain that way. Note that there are two Hope Islands in this region; this island was named by Commander Charles Wilkes, who was charting Puget Sound.

Campsites, facilities: There are eight

primitive boat-in campsites. Fires are not permitted. Vault toilets and five mooring buoys are available. There is no drinking water and garbage must be packed out.

Reservations, fees: Reservations are not accepted. Sites are $12 per night, buoys are $15 per night. Open year-round, with limited facilities in winter.

Directions: Hope Island is in Skagit Bay, directly between the Swinomish Reservation on Fidalgo Island to the east and Whidbey Island to the west. After launching from the harbor at Cornet on Whidbey Island, cruise east out of Cornet Bay and turn south (Skagit Island will be on your left). Continue one mile to Hope Island. The boating access is on the north side of the island. It's accessible only by private boat.

Contact: Hope Island Mason State Park, 360/463-1861, http://parks.state.wa.us.

37 RIVERBEND RV PARK

Scenic rating: 5

on the Skagit River

Map 2.1, page 141

Riverbend RV Park is a pleasant layover spot for I-5 travelers. While not particularly scenic, it is clean and spacious. Access to the Skagit River here is a high point, with fishing for salmon, trout, and Dolly Varden in season; check regulations. Nearby recreational options include a casino and an 18-hole golf course. Note that about half of the sites are filled with monthly renters.

Campsites, facilities: There are 90 sites with full hookups (30 and 50 amps) for RVs of any length and 25 sites for tents. Most sites are pull-through. Picnic tables are provided at RV sites and fire pits are at some tent sites. Restrooms with flush toilets and coin showers, drinking water, a dump station, coin laundry, a playground, and horseshoe pits are available. A store, café, and ice are located within 0.25 mile. Leashed pets are permitted with certain restrictions.

Reservations, fees: Reservations are accepted. RV sites are $36 per night, tent sites are $22 per night. Some credit cards are accepted. Open year-round.

Directions: From Seattle on I-5, drive north to Mount Vernon and the College Way exit. Take the College Way exit and drive one block west to Freeway Drive. Turn right (north) and drive 0.25 mile to Stewart Road. Turn left and drive a short distance to the park entrance on the right.

Contact: Riverbend RV Park, 360/428-4044.

38 STAYSAIL RV PARK

Scenic rating: 4

in Oak Harbor on Whidbey Island

Map 2.1, page 141

This popular city park fills quickly on summer weekends. With graveled sites, it is geared toward RVers but is also suitable for tent campers. Fishing, swimming, boating, and sunbathing are all options in the vicinity. Several miles of paved trails run along the waterfront. A full-service marina is nearby. Within a few miles are an 18-hole golf course and tennis courts. Fort Ebey and Fort Casey State Parks are both a short drive away and make excellent side trips.

Campsites, facilities: There are 56 sites with full hookups for RVs of any length and 30 sites for tents. Picnic tables are provided. No campfires are allowed. Restrooms with flush toilets and coin showers, drinking water, and a dump station are available. A playground, picnic shelter, ballfields, volleyball, basketball, and tennis courts, and horseshoe pits are also available. Propane gas, a store, café, coin laundry, and ice are available within one mile. Boat-launching facilities, swimming, a lagoon, wading pools, a day-use area, and walking trails are at Oak Harbor. Some facilities are wheelchair accessible. Leashed pets are permitted.

Reservations, fees: Reservations are not accepted. Sites are $12-20 per night. Open year-round.

Directions: From Burlington and I-5, turn

west on Highway 20 and drive 28 miles to the intersection of Highway 20 and Pioneer Way in the town of Oak Harbor on Whidbey Island. Drive straight through the intersection onto Beeksma Drive and continue about one block to the park on the left.

Contact: Staysail RV Park, City of Oak Harbor, 360/279-4530, www.oakharbor.org.

39 FORT EBEY STATE PARK

🚶 🚴 🏊 ⛵ 🏕️ ♿ 🚐 ⛺

Scenic rating: 9

on Whidbey Island

Map 2.1, page 141

This park is situated on the west side of Whidbey Island at Point Partridge. It covers 649 acres and has access to a rocky beach that is good for exploring. There are also up to 28 miles of trails for hiking and biking. Fort Ebey is the site of a historic World War II bunker, where concrete platforms mark the locations of the historic gun batteries. Other options here include fishing and wildlife viewing. There is limited fishing available for smallmouth bass at Lake Pondilla, which is only about 100 yards away from the campground and a good place to see bald eagles. The saltwater shore access provides a good spot for surfing and paragliding.

Campsites, facilities: There are 39 sites with no hookups and 11 sites with hookups for tents or self-contained RVs up to 60 feet long. There is also one boat-in site and one group site for up to 60 people. Picnic tables and fire grills are provided. Restrooms with flush toilets and coin showers, drinking water, firewood, amphitheater, and picnic area are available. Some facilities are wheelchair accessible. Leashed pets are permitted.

Reservations, fees: Reservations are accepted May-September at 888/226-7688 or https://washington.goingtocamp.com ($7-9 reservation fee). Sites are $25-45 per night, the boat-in site is $12 per night, $10 per extra vehicle per night. Call for group rates. Some credit cards are accepted. Open year-round.

Directions: From Burlington and I-5, turn west on Highway 20 and drive 23 miles (Whidbey Island) to Libbey Road (eight miles past Oak Harbor). Turn right and drive 1.5 miles to Hill Valley Drive. Turn left and enter the park.

Contact: Fort Ebey State Park, 360/678-4636, http://parks.state.wa.us.

40 FORT CASEY STATE PARK

🚶 🏊 ⛵ 🚤 🏕️ ♿ 🚐 ⛺

Scenic rating: 10

on Whidbey Island

Map 2.1, page 141

Fort Casey State Park offers more than 10,000 feet of shoreline on Puget Sound at Admiralty Inlet; fishing is often good in this area, in season. The park's 998 acres include a lighthouse, Keystone Spit, and 1.8 miles of hiking trails. As part of Ebey's Landing National Historic Reserve, there is a coast artillery post featuring two historic guns on display. The lighthouse and interpretive center are open seasonally. Remote-control glider flying is allowed in a designated area, and there is a parade field perfect for kite-flying. The underwater park, another highlight, attracts divers. You can also take a ferry from here to Port Townsend on the Olympic Peninsula.

Campsites, facilities: There are 22 sites for tents and 13 sites with partial hookups for tents or self-contained RVs up to 40 feet. Picnic tables and fire grills are provided. Restrooms with flush toilets and coin showers, drinking water, a seasonal interpretive center, a picnic area, firewood, and an amphitheater are available. Boat-launching facilities are located in the park. Some facilities are wheelchair accessible. Leashed pets are permitted.

Reservations, fees: Reservations are accepted May-September at 888/226-7688 or https://washington.goingtocamp.com ($7-9 reservation fee). Sites are $25-45 per night, $10 per extra vehicle per night. Open year-round.

Directions: From Burlington and I-5, turn

west on Highway 20 and drive 35 miles to Coupeville. Continue south on Highway 20 (adjacent to Whidbey Island Naval Air Station) and then turn right (still Highway 20, passing Crockett Lake and the Camp Casey barracks) to the park entrance.

Contact: Fort Casey State Park, 360/678-4519, http://parks.state.wa.us.

41 CAMANO ISLAND STATE PARK

Scenic rating: 10

on Camano Island

Map 2.1, page 141   BEST (

This park features panoramic views of Puget Sound, the Olympic Mountains, and Mount Rainier. Set on the southwest point of Camano Island, near Lowell Point and Elger Bay along the Saratoga Passage, this wooded camp offers quiet and private campsites. The park covers 244 acres and features 6,700 feet of rocky shoreline and beach, three miles of hiking trails, and just one mile of bike trails. Good inshore angling for rockfish is available year-round, and salmon fishing is also good in season. A diving area with kelp is available. There is also a self-guided nature trail.

Campsites, facilities: There are 88 sites for tents or self-contained RVs up to 40 feet, two hiker/biker sites, one group site for up to 100 people, and five cabins. Picnic tables and fire grills are provided. Restrooms with flush toilets and coin showers, drinking water, a dump station, firewood, a playground, a sheltered picnic area with a kitchen, summer interpretive programs, an amphitheater, and a large grassy play area in the day-use area are available. Boat-launching facilities are located in the park. An 18-hole golf course is nearby. Some facilities are wheelchair accessible. Leashed pets are permitted.

Reservations, fees: Reservations are not accepted for individual sites, but are required for the cabins and the group site at 360/387-1550.

Sites are $25-45 per night, $10 per extra vehicle per night. Cabins are $55-76 per night. The group site is $99 per night for 1-25 people, $171 per night for 26-50 people, $244 per night for 51-75 people, and $316 per night for 76-100 people. Open year-round.

Directions: From Seattle on I-5, drive north (17 miles north of Everett) to Exit 212. Take Exit 212 to Highway 532. Drive west on Highway 532 to Stanwood and continue three miles (to Camano Island) to a fork. Bear left at the fork and continue south for six miles on East Camano Drive, bearing to the right where the road becomes Elger Bay Road, to Mountain View Road. Turn right and drive two miles (climbs a steep hill) and continue to Lowell Point Road. Turn left and continue to the park entrance road. (The park is 14 miles southwest of Stanwood).

Contact: Camano Island State Park, 360/387-3031, http://parks.state.wa.us.

42 KAYAK POINT COUNTY PARK

Scenic rating: 5

near Tulalip Indian Reservation on Puget Sound

Map 2.1, page 141

This camp usually fills on summer weekends. Set on the shore of Puget Sound, this large, wooded county park covers 670 acres on Port Susan. It provides good windsurfing and whale-watching as well as hiking; there's an 18-hole golf course nearby. Good for crabbing and fishing, a pier is also available.

Campsites, facilities: There are 30 sites with partial hookups, including some pull-through sites, for tents or RVs up to 32 feet and 10 yurts with heat and electricity for up to five people. Picnic tables and fire rings are provided. Restrooms with flush toilets and showers, drinking water, firewood, a picnic area with covered shelter, and a 300-foot fishing pier are available. Launching facilities are located in the park. Some facilities are wheelchair accessible. Leashed pets are permitted.

Reservations, fees: Reservations are accepted online. Sites are $28-40 per night, $10 per each additional vehicle per night, and yurts are $65-85 per night. Some credit cards are accepted. Open year-round.

Directions: From Everett and I-5, drive 5 miles north to Exit 199 (Tulalip) at Marysville. Take Exit 199, bear left on Tulalip Road, and drive west for 13 miles (road name changes to Marine Drive) through the Tulalip Indian Reservation to the park entrance road on the left (marked for Kayak Point).

Contact: Kayak Point County Park, Snohomish County, 360/652-7992, https://snohomishcountywa.gov.

43 WENBERG COUNTY PARK

Scenic rating: 8

on Lake Goodwin

Map 2.1, page 141

Wenberg County Park is set along the east shore of Lake Goodwin, where the trout fishing can be great. The park covers 45 acres with 1,140 feet of shoreline frontage on the lake. Powerboats are allowed, and a seasonal concession stand provides food. Hiking is limited to a 0.5-mile trail. This is a popular weekend spot for Seattle-area residents.

Management of Wenberg Park was transferred from the state to Snohomish County, and with that came several significant changes. The reservation protocol is different, of course, and no alcohol is permitted.

Campsites, facilities: There are 70 sites with full or partial hookups for tents and RVs up to 40 feet long. Some sites are pull-through. Picnic tables and fire grills are provided. Restrooms with flush toilets and coin showers, drinking water, a dump station, two sheltered picnic areas, concession stand, firewood, swimming beach with bathhouse, and a playground are available. Boat-launching facilities and docks

are located on Lake Goodwin. Some facilities are wheelchair accessible. Leashed pets are permitted.

Reservations, fees: Reservations are accepted at 425/388-6600 or online. Sites are $40 per night, $10 per extra vehicle per night. Some credit cards are accepted. Open year-round.

Directions: From Everett on I-5, drive north to Exit 206. Take Exit 206/Smokey Point, turn west, and drive 2.4 miles to Highway 531. Bear right on Highway 531 and drive 2.7 miles to East Lake Goodwin Road. Turn left and drive 1.6 miles to the park entrance on the right.

Contact: Wenberg County Park, 360/652-7417, https://snohomishcountywa.gov.

44 CEDAR GROVE SHORES RV PARK

Scenic rating: 5

on Lake Goodwin

Map 2.1, page 141

This wooded resort is set on the shore of Lake Goodwin near Wenberg County Park. The camp is a busy place in summer, with highlights including trout fishing, waterskiing, and swimming. A security gate is closed at night. Tent campers should try Lake Goodwin Resort. An 18-hole golf course is nearby.

Campsites, facilities: There are 48 sites with full hookups (30 and 50 amps) for RVs of any length. Some sites are pull-through. Restrooms with flush toilets and coin showers, drinking water, coin laundry, a dump station, modem access, propane gas, ice, a clubhouse, a recreation room, horseshoe pits, and firewood are available. A store and café are located within one mile. Boat docks and launching facilities are nearby on Lake Goodwin. Some facilities are wheelchair accessible. Leashed pets are permitted.

Reservations, fees: Reservations are accepted. Sites are $40-47 per night, $5 per adult per night for more than two people, $1 fee per pet. Some credit cards are accepted. Open year-round.

Directions: From Everett on I-5, drive north for 10 miles to Exit 206. Take Exit 206/Smokey Point and drive west for 2.2 miles to Lakewood Road. Turn right and drive 3.2 miles to Westlake Goodwin Road. Turn left (the park is marked) and drive 0.75 mile to the resort on the left.

Contact: Cedar Grove Shores RV Park, 360/652-7083 or 866/342-4981, www.cg-srvpark.com.

45 LAKE GOODWIN RESORT

🏊 🎣 🚐 🚵 🚍 ⛺

Scenic rating: 5

on Lake Goodwin

Map 2.1, page 141

This private campground is set on Lake Goodwin, which is known for good trout fishing. Motorboats are permitted on the lake, and an 18-hole golf course is located nearby. Other activities include swimming in the lake, horseshoe pits, shuffleboard, and a recreation field.

Campsites, facilities: There are 85 sites with full or partial hookups (30 and 50 amps) for RVs of any length, 11 sites for tents, and four cabins. Some sites are pull-through. Picnic tables and fire grills are provided. Restrooms with flush toilets and coin showers, drinking water, propane gas, a convenience store with recreation equipment, coin laundry, ice, Wi-Fi, a playground, and firewood are available. Boat moorage and a fishing pier are located nearby on Lake Goodwin.

Reservations, fees: Reservations are accepted at 800/242-8169. RV sites are $40-58 per night, tent sites are $26 per night, $2-5 per each additional person. Cabins are $75-98 per night, $10 per each additional person per night. Some credit cards are accepted. Open year-round.

Directions: From Everett on I-5, drive north for 10 miles to Exit 206. Take Exit 206/Smokey Point, turn west, and drive two miles to Highway 531/Lakewood Road. Bear right on

Highway 531 and drive 3.5 miles to the resort on the left.

Contact: Lake Goodwin Resort, 360/652-8169, www.lakegoodwinresort.com.

46 RIVER MEADOWS PARK WALK-IN

🚶 🚲 🏊 🛶 🚣 🎣 🏕 ♿ ⛺

Scenic rating: 6

on the Stillaguamish River

Map 2.1, page 141

This Snohomish County park has 150 acres of open meadows and forests along the banks of the Stillaguamish River. The campground gets light to average use. This area of the river is popular for non-motorized boating such as canoeing, kayaking, and inner tubing. Hiking trails meander through the park, and other activities include cycling, bird-watching, and fishing for steelhead in season. The Festival of the River is held in August. Native Americans once occupied the property, and ancient Olcott artifacts have been found here.

Campsites, facilities: There are 14 walk-in sites for tents only and six yurts. Picnic tables and fire pits are provided at the tent sites. Flush toilets, drinking water, reservable picnic shelters, and a swimming beach are available. Some facilities are wheelchair accessible. Leashed pets are permitted.

Reservations, fees: Reservations are accepted online. Sites are $28-40 per night, yurts are $65-85 per night. Some credit cards are accepted. Open year-round.

Directions: From Seattle, drive north on I-5 to Exit 203 and the junction with Highway 530. Turn east on Highway 530 and drive approximately 3.5 miles to the town of Arlington and Highway 9. Turn left (north) and drive a short distance to Highway 530. Turn right (east) on Highway 530 and drive approximately one mile to Arlington Heights Road. Turn right (south) and drive two miles to Jordan Road. Bear right and drive approximately three miles to the park entrance on the right.

Contact: River Meadows Park, 360/435-3441, https://snohomishcountywa.gov.

47 LAKESIDE RV PARK

Scenic rating: 6

in Everett

Map 2.2, page 142

With 75-100 of the 150 RV spaces dedicated to permanent rentals, this camp can be a crap-shoot for vacationers in summer; the remaining spaces get filled nightly with vacationers all summer. The park is landscaped with annuals, roses, other perennials, and shrubs, which provide privacy and gardens for each site. There's a pond stocked with trout year-round, providing fishing for a fee.

Campsites, facilities: There are 150 sites, some pull-through, with full hookups (20, 30, and 50 amps) for RVs of any length. Restrooms with flush toilets and showers, drinking water, cable TV, coin laundry, propane gas, a play-ground, off-leash dog area, horseshoe pits, modem access, and pay phones are available. Some facilities are wheelchair accessible. Leashed pets are permitted.

Reservations, fees: Reservations are recommended at 800/468-7275. RV sites are $52 per night. Some credit cards are accepted. Open year-round.

Directions: From Everett on I-5, drive north to Exit 186. Take Exit 186 and turn west on 128th Street. Drive about two miles to Old Highway 99. Turn left and drive 0.25 mile to the park on the left.

Contact: Lakeside RV Park, 425/347-2970 or 800/468-7275.

48 LAKE PLEASANT RV PARK

Scenic rating: 6

on Lake Pleasant

Map 2.2, page 142

A large, developed camp geared primarily toward RVers, this park is set on Lake Pleasant. The setting is pretty, with lakeside sites and plenty of trees. Just off the highway, it's a popular camp, so expect lots of company, especially in summer. This is a good spot for a little trout fishing. The lake is not suitable for swimming. Note that half of the sites are monthly rentals. All sites are paved.

Campsites, facilities: There are 184 sites with full hookups (30 and 50 amps) for RVs up to 45 feet long; half of these sites are available for overnight use. Some sites are pull-through. Picnic tables are provided. No campfires are allowed. Restrooms with flush toilets and showers, drinking water, cable TV, modem and Wi-Fi access, a dump station, coin laundry, a playground, and propane gas are available. Some facilities are wheelchair accessible. Leashed pets are permitted with certain restrictions.

Reservations, fees: Reservations are recommended. Sites are $44 per night. Visa and MasterCard are accepted. Open year-round.

Directions: From the junction of I-5 and I-405 (just south of Seattle), take I-405 and drive to Exit 26. Take that exit to the Bothell/Everett Highway over the freeway and drive south for about one mile; look for the park on the left side.

Contact: Lake Pleasant RV Park, 425/487-1785 or 800/742-0386.

49 TRAILER INNS RV PARK/BELLEVUE

🚶 🚴 🏊 🐕 👫 🚐

Scenic rating: 5

near Lake Sammamish State Park

Map 2.2, page 142

This park features all the amenities for RV travelers. Lake Sammamish State Park is about two miles away. Nearby recreation options include an 18-hole golf course, hiking trails, marked bike trails, and tennis courts.

Campsites, facilities: There are 103 sites with full hookups (30 and 50 amps) for RVs up to 45 feet long. Some sites are pull-through and about half of the sites are permanently rented. Picnic tables are provided. Restrooms with flush toilets and showers, drinking water, propane gas, cable TV, modem and Wi-Fi access, a recreation hall, an indoor swimming pool, spa, sauna, a coin laundry, ice, picnic area, and a playground are available. A store and a cafe are available within one mile. Leashed pets are permitted.

Reservations, fees: Reservations are accepted at 800/659-4684. Sites are $30-60 per night for two people, two children, and two pets. Weekly rates are available. Some credit cards are accepted. Open year-round.

Directions: At the junction of I-405 and I-90 south of Seattle, turn east on I-90 and drive 1.5 miles to Exit 11A. Take Exit 11A (a two-avenue exit) and stay in the right lane for 150th Avenue SE. After the lanes split, stay in the left lane and drive to the intersection of 150th Avenue SE and 37th. Continue straight through the light and look for the park entrance at the fifth driveway on the right (about one mile from I-90).

Contact: Trailer Inns RV Park and Recreation Center, 425/747-9181 or 800/659-4684, www.trailerinnsrv.com.

50 VASA PARK RESORT

🚶 🚴 🏊 🚐 🏕 🏃 🚐 ⛺

Scenic rating: 5

on Lake Sammamish

Map 2.2, page 142

I was giving a seminar in Bellevue one evening when a distraught-looking couple walked in and pleaded, "Where can we camp tonight?" I answered, "Just look in the book," and they ended up staying at this camp. It was the easiest sale I ever made. This is the most rustic of the parks in the immediate Seattle area. The resort is on the western shore of Lake Sammamish, and the state park is at the south end of the lake. Lake activities include fishing for smallmouth bass, waterskiing, and personal watercraft riding. There is a two-week maximum stay during the summer. An 18-hole golf course, hiking trails, and marked bike trails are close by. The park is within easy driving distance of Seattle.

Campsites, facilities: There are 16 sites for tents or RVs of any length (partial hookups) and six sites with full hookups for RVs of any length. Picnic tables are provided. Restrooms with flush toilets and coin showers, drinking water, a dump station, coin laundry, a playground, and a boat-launching facility are available. Propane gas, firewood, a store, and a café are located within one mile. Leashed pets are permitted.

Reservations, fees: Reservations are accepted. Sites are $32-40 per night, $4.50 per adult per night for more than two people, $2.50 per child. Some credit cards are accepted. Open mid-May-mid-October.

Directions: From Bellevue, drive east on I-90 to Exit 13. Take Exit 13 to West Lake Sammamish Parkway SE and drive north for one mile; the resort is on the right. Note: Larger rigs should pull into the parking lot on the left.

Contact: Vasa Park Resort, 425/746-3260, www.vasaparkresort.com.

51 ISSAQUAH VILLAGE RV PARK

Scenic rating: 7

in Issaquah

Map 2.2, page 142

Although Issaquah Village RV Park doesn't allow tents, it's set in a beautiful environment ringed by the Cascade Mountains, making it a scenic choice in the area. Lake Sammamish State Park is just a few miles north. Most of the sites are asphalt, and 20 percent are long-term rentals.

Campsites, facilities: There are 56 sites, including two pull-through sites, with full hookups (30 and 50 amps) for RVs of any length. Picnic tables are provided. Restrooms with flush toilets and showers, drinking water, cable TV, Wi-Fi, a dump station (fee), pay phone, coin laundry, picnic areas, playground, and propane gas are available. Some facilities are wheelchair accessible. Leashed pets are permitted.

Reservations, fees: Reservations are recommended. Sites are $50-54 per night. Some credit cards are accepted. Open year-round.

Directions: From Seattle on I-405 (preferred) or I-5, drive to the junction of I-90. Take I-90 east and drive 17 miles to Exit 17 (Front Street). Drive under the freeway and turn right at 229th Avenue SE. Turn right on SE 66th Street (about 50 feet from the first right turn). Proceed on 66th, as it turns into 1st Avenue and brings you to the park entrance.

Contact: Issaquah Village RV Park, 425/392-9233 or 800/258-9233, www.ivrvpark.com.

52 BLUE SKY RV PARK

Scenic rating: 5

near Lake Sammamish State Park in Issaquah

Map 2.2, page 142

Blue Sky RV Park is situated in an urban setting just outside of Seattle. It provides a good off-the-beaten-path alternative to the more crowded metro area, yet it is still only a short drive from the main attractions in the city. Nearby Lake Sammamish State Park provides more rustic recreation opportunities, including hiking and fishing. All sites are paved and level, and about half of the sites are filled with monthly renters.

Campsites, facilities: There are 51 sites with full hookups for RVs of any length. Some sites are pull-through. Picnic tables are provided at some sites. Restrooms with flush toilets and showers, drinking water, cable TV, coin laundry, and a covered picnic pavilion with barbecue are available. Some facilities are wheelchair accessible. Leashed pets are permitted.

Reservations, fees: Reservations are accepted. Sites are $45 per night, $5 per person per night for more than two people. Open year-round.

Directions: From I-5 in Seattle, drive east on I-90 for 22 miles to Exit 22 (Preston/Fall City exit). Turn right at the stop sign, then turn left onto 302nd Avenue SE. Proceed 0.5 mile to the campground entrance at the end of the road.

Contact: Blue Sky RV Park, 9002 302nd Ave. SE, Issaquah, 425/222-7910, www.blueskypreston.com.

53 SEATTLE/TACOMA KOA

Scenic rating: 5

in Kent on the Green River

Map 2.2, page 142

This is a popular urban campground, not far from the highway yet in a pleasant setting. The sites are spacious, and many are pull-throughs that accommodate large RVs. A public golf course is located nearby. During the summer, take a tour of Seattle from the campground. The tour highlights include the Space Needle, Pike Place Market, Pioneer Square, Woodland Park Zoo, Seattle Aquarium, Boeing Museum of Flight, Safeco Field, and Puget Sound.

Campsites, facilities: There are 147 sites with full or partial hookups (30 and 50 amps) for

RVs up to 55 feet long and 14 sites for tents. Restrooms with flush toilets and showers, drinking water, a dump station, coin laundry, Wi-Fi, limited groceries, firewood, propane gas, ice, RV supplies, free movies, and a seasonal pancake breakfast are available. A large playground, a seasonal heated swimming pool, three-wheel fun-cycle rentals, and a recreation room are also available. Cable TV is provided at some sites. Some facilities are wheelchair accessible. Leashed pets are permitted with certain restrictions.

Reservations, fees: Reservations are recommended at 800/562-1892. Sites are $48-55 per night, $4-5 per person per night for more than two people, $1.50 per pet per night. Some credit cards are accepted. Open year-round.

Directions: From Seattle, drive south on I-5 for 10 miles to Exit 152 for 188th Street/Orillia Road. Drive east on Orillia Road for three miles (the road becomes 212th Street) to the campground on the right.

Contact: Seattle/Tacoma KOA, 253/872-8652, www.koa.com.

54 DASH POINT STATE PARK

🏃 🚵 🏊 🛶 🛥 🎣 🐕 ♿ 🚐 ⛺

Scenic rating: 8

near Federal Way

Map 2.2, page 142

This urban state park set on Puget Sound features unobstructed water views. The park covers 398 acres, with 3,300 feet of saltwater shoreline and 11 miles of trails for hiking. Fishing, windsurfing, swimming, boating, and mountain biking are all popular. Tacoma offers a variety of activities and attractions, including the Tacoma Art Museum (with a children's gallery); the Washington State Historical Society Museum; the Seymour Botanical Conservatory at Wrights Park; Point Defiance Park, Zoo, and Aquarium; the Western Washington Forest Industries Museum; and the Fort Lewis Military Museum.

Campsites, facilities: There are 114 tent sites, 27 sites with partial hookups for RVs up to 40 feet, and a group site for up to 96 people. Cabins are also available. Picnic tables and fire grills are provided. Restrooms with flush toilets and coin showers, drinking water, an amphitheater, two sheltered picnic areas, a dump station, and firewood are available. Some facilities are wheelchair accessible. Leashed pets are permitted.

Reservations, fees: Reservations are accepted for individual sites and required for the group site at 888/226-7688 or https://washington. goingtocamp.com ($7-9 reservation fee). Sites are $25-45 per night, $10 per extra vehicle per night. Cabins are $65-80 per night. Call for group rates. Open year-round.

Directions: On I-5 in Tacoma, drive to Exit 143/320th Street. Take that exit and turn west on 320th Street and drive four miles to 47th Street (a T intersection). Turn right on 47th Street and drive to Highway 509 (another T intersection). Turn left on Highway 509/Dash Point Road and drive one mile to the park. Note: The camping area is on the south side of the road; the day-use area is on the north side of the road.

Contact: Dash Point State Park, 253/661-4955, http://parks.state.wa.us.

55 GAME FARM WILDERNESS PARK CAMP

🏃 🛶 🐕 ♿ 🚐 ⛺

Scenic rating: 6

on the Stuck River in Auburn

Map 2.2, page 142

The Game Farm Wilderness Park is just minutes from downtown Auburn and centrally located to Mount Rainier, Seattle, and the Cascade Mountains. The campground is located along the scenic Stuck River and is adjacent to an 18-hole disc golf course.

Campsites, facilities: There are 18 sites with partial hookups for tents or RVs of any length, with a maximum of five people per site. Picnic tables and fire grills are provided. Restrooms with flush toilets, drinking water (available March-November), a picnic shelter, and a dump station are available. Some facilities are wheelchair accessible. Leashed pets are permitted.

Reservations, fees: Reservations are accepted at 253/931-3043. Sites are $25 per night, with a discount for Auburn residents. Some credit cards are accepted. Open April-mid-October, with a one-week maximum stay limit.

Directions: On I-5 (north of Tacoma), drive to Exit 142 and Highway 18. Turn east on Highway 18˚and drive to the Auburn/Enumclaw exit. Take that exit and drive to the light at Auburn Way. Turn left on Auburn Way South and drive one mile to Howard Road. Exit to the right on Howard Road and drive 0.2 mile to the stop sign at R Street. Turn right on R Street and drive 1.5 miles to Stuck River Drive SE (just over the river). Turn left and drive 0.25 mile upriver to the park on the left at 2401 Stuck River Drive.

Contact: City of Auburn Parks and Recreation Department, 253/931-3043, www.auburnwa.gov.

56 MAJESTIC MOBILE MANOR RV PARK
🏃 🚴 🏊 🛶 🎣 🐕 🚐

Scenic rating: 7
on the Puyallup River near Tacoma

Map 2.2, page 142

This clean, pretty park along the Puyallup River and with views of Mount Rainier caters to RVers. (Note that at least half of the sites are filled with monthly renters.) Recreation options within 10 miles include an 18-hole golf course, a full-service marina, and tennis courts. Tacoma offers a variety of activities and attractions, including the Tacoma Art Museum (with a children's gallery); the Washington State Historical Society Museum; the Seymour Botanical Conservatory at Wrights Park; Point Defiance Park, Zoo, and Aquarium; the Western Washington Forest Industries Museum; and the Fort Lewis Military Museum.

Campsites, facilities: There are 88 sites with full hookups for RVs up to 75 feet. Restrooms with flush toilets and showers, drinking water, cable TV, Wi-Fi access, propane gas, a dump station, a recreation hall, a convenience store, coin laundry, ice, and a seasonal heated swimming pool are available. Leashed pets are permitted.

Reservations, fees: Reservations are accepted. Sites are $55 per night, $2 per person per night for more than two people. Open year-round.

Directions: From the north end of Tacoma on I-5, take Exit 135 to Highway 167. Drive east on Highway 167 (River Road) for four miles to the park on the right.

Contact: Majestic Mobile Manor RV Park, 253/845-3144 or 800/348-3144, www.majesticrvpark.com.

57 OLYMPIA CAMPGROUND
🏃 🚴 🏊 🐕 🎣 🚐 ⛰

Scenic rating: 7
near Olympia

Map 2.2, page 142

This campground in a natural, wooded setting has all the comforts. Nearby recreation options include an 18-hole golf course, hiking trails, marked bike trails, and tennis courts.

Campsites, facilities: There are 95 sites with full or partial hookups (20 and 30 amps) for tents or RVs of any length and two cabins. Some sites are pull-through. Picnic tables are provided and fire rings are at some sites. Restrooms with flush toilets and showers, drinking water, modem and Wi-Fi access, propane gas, a dump station, recreation hall, convenience store, coin laundry, ice, a playground, seasonal heated swimming pool, gas station, and firewood are available. A café is located within two miles. Leashed pets are permitted.

Reservations, fees: Reservations are accepted. RV sites are $38 per night, tent sites are $25 per night, cabins are $50 per night, $4-10 per person per night for more than two people. Some credit cards are accepted. Open year-round.

Directions: From Olympia on I-5, take Exit 101 to Tumwater Boulevard. Turn left and drive 0.25 mile to Center Street. Turn right and drive one mile to 83rd Avenue (Center ends at 83rd). Turn right and drive an eighth of a mile to the park on the left. Turn in at the Texaco station entrance (the campground is behind the store).

Contact: Olympia Campground, 360/352-2551, www.olympiacampground.com.

THE NORTHERN CASCADES

Mount Baker is the centerpiece in a forested landscape with hundreds of lakes, rivers, and hidden campgrounds. The only limit here is weather. The Northern Cascades are deluged with snowfall in winter and Mount Baker often receives a foot per day for weeks. Although that shortens the recreation season to just a few months in summer, it also has another effect. With so many destinations available for such a short time, many remain largely undiscovered. First-time campers should start with the state parks, which offer beautiful, easy-to-reach settings. Many roadside camps provide choice layover spots for vacationing travelers. Seasoned campers can search for lesser-known camps in the national forests. Many beautiful spots are set alongside lakes and streams, often with trailheads into nearby wilderness that feature abundant wildlife, good fishing, and great hiking.

THE NORTHERN CASCADES

C A N A D A

Skagit Valley Provincial Park

Manning Provincial Park

Cathedral Provincial Park

Mt Baker Wilderness Area

Ross Lake

Okanogan

Saddle Pk 8,345ft ▲

North Cascades

National

Mt Baker 10,775ft ▲

Forest

Baker Lake

Methow River

Chewuch River

Lake Shannon

20

River

National Park

MAP 3.2 page 174

see Northeastern Washington page 238

Skagit

MAP 3.1 page 173

Lake Chelan NRA

20

Mt Baker-Snoqualmie National Forest

C a s c a d e   R a n g e

Suiattle River

Sauk River

Lake

Chelan

Glacier Pk 10,541ft ▲

Wenatchee

National

Forest

Pateros

Monroe

2

Skykomish

River

Wenatchee

Stormy Mtn 7,198ft ▲

97

2

Winton

River

2

MAP 3.3 page 175

Cashmere Mtn 8,501ft ▲

MAP 3.4 page 176

90

Snoqualmie Pass 3,022ft

Wenatchee

28

Columbia

97

0   20 mi

0   20 km

Quincy

281

River

90

Mt Baker-Snoqualmie

National Forest

Ellensburg

Mt Rainier National Park

Gifford Pinchot National Forest

see Southeastern Washington page 354

Mt Rainier 14,411ft ▲

see The Columbia River Gorge and Mount Rainier page 300

82

© AVALON TRAVEL

Map 3.1

Sites 1-37
Pages 177-193

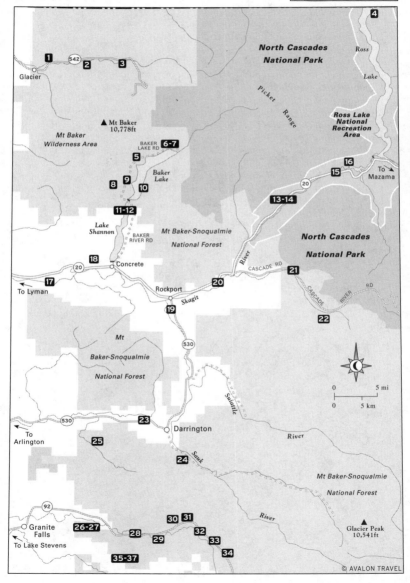

North Cascades
National Park

Ross
Lake

Picket Range

Glacier

Mt Baker
10,778ft

Mt Baker
Wilderness Area

BAKER LAKE RD

Baker
Lake

Ross Lake
National
Recreation
Area

To Mazama

Lake
Shannon

BAKER
RIVER RD

Mt Baker-Snoqualmie
National Forest

North Cascades
National Park

Concrete

To Lyman

Rockport

Skagit

CASCADE RD

CASCADE RIVER RD

Mt
Baker-Snoqualmie
National Forest

To
Arlington

Darrington

Sauk

Suiattle

River

0   5 mi
0   5 km

Granite Falls

To Lake Stevens

Mt Baker-Snoqualmie
National Forest

Glacier Peak
10,541ft

River

© AVALON TRAVEL

Map 3.2

Sites 38-65
Pages 193-206

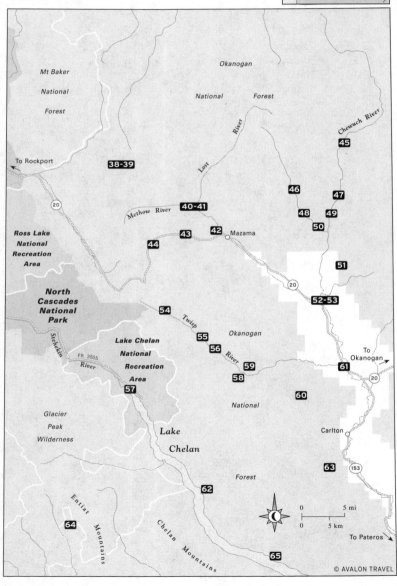

Map **3.3**

Sites 66-88
Pages 206-217

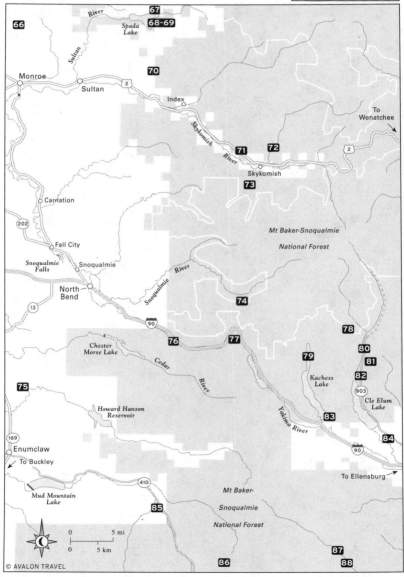

Map **3.4**

Sites 89-130
Pages 217-235

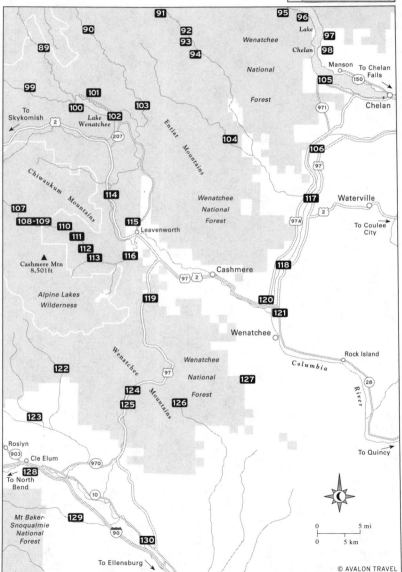

© AVALON TRAVEL

1 DOUGLAS FIR
🏃🏊🎣♿🚐⛺

Scenic rating: 10

on the Nooksack River in Mount
Baker-Snoqualmie National Forest

Map 3.1, page 173

Set along the Nooksack River, this camp features river views from some campsites. It is a beautiful camp, surrounded by old-growth Douglas fir, silver fir, and western hemlock. Trout fishing is available on the river, and there are hiking trails in the area.

Campsites, facilities: There are 30 sites for tents or RVs up to 55 feet long. Picnic tables and fire grills are provided. Drinking water, vault toilets, and a picnic shelter are available. A store, café, coin laundry, and ice are located within five miles at Glacier. Some facilities are wheelchair accessible. Leashed pets are permitted.

Reservations, fees: Reservations are accepted at 877/444-6777 ($10 reservation fee) or www.recreation.gov ($9 reservation fee). Sites are $18-20 per night, $9 per night per additional vehicle. Open May-September, weather permitting.

Directions: From Bellingham on I-5, take the Highway 542 exit and drive 33 miles to Glacier. Continue two miles northeast on Highway 542 to the campground on the left.

Contact: Mount Baker-Snoqualmie National Forest, Mount Baker Ranger District, 360/856-5700, www.fs.usda.gov or www.hoodoo.com.

2 EXCELSIOR GROUP CAMP
🏃🎣⛺

Scenic rating: 6

near the Nooksack River in Mount
Baker-Snoqualmie National Forest

Map 3.1, page 173

This campground is set near the Nooksack River less than one mile from Nooksack Falls and 1.5 miles from the site of the Excelsior Mine. The Excelsior Pass Trailhead is about five minutes away. There are numerous hiking trails available within a 30-minute drive in the Mount Baker Wilderness.

Campsites, facilities: There are two group tent sites for up to 50 and 75 people each. Picnic tables and fire grills are provided. Vault toilets, garbage bins, and drinking water are available. Leashed pets are permitted.

Reservations, fees: Reservations are accepted at 877/444-6777 ($10 reservation fee) or www.recreation.gov ($9 reservation fee). Sites are $125 per night. Open May-late September, weather permitting.

Directions: From Bellingham on I-5, take the Highway 542 exit and drive 37.5 miles (6.5 miles east of Glacier) to the camp on the right. Note: RVs and trailers are not recommended for this road.

Contact: Mount Baker-Snoqualmie National Forest, Mount Baker Ranger District, 360/856-5700, www.fs.usda.gov.

3 SILVER FIR
🏃🎣❄🎣♿🚐⛺

Scenic rating: 9

on the North Fork of the Nooksack River in
Mount Baker-Snoqualmie National Forest

Map 3.1, page 173　　　　**BEST (**

This campground is set on the North Fork of the Nooksack River. It is within 30 minutes of the Heather Meadows area, which provides some of the best hiking trails in the entire region. In addition, a one-mile round-trip to Artist Ridge promises views of Mount Baker and Mount Shuksan. The first part of the trail to the first viewpoint is wheelchair accessible. Fishing is available nearby, and in the winter the area offers cross-country skiing. You're strongly advised to obtain a U.S. Forest Service map in order to take maximum advantage of the recreational opportunities in the area.

Campsites, facilities: There are 20 sites for tents or RVs of any length including a few double sites. Picnic tables and barbecue grills are provided. Drinking water, vault toilets, garbage bins, and a group picnic shelter are available. Some facilities are wheelchair accessible. Leashed pets are permitted.

Reservations, fees: Reservations are accepted at 877/444-6777 ($10 reservation fee) or www.recreation.gov ($9 reservation fee). Sites are $16-30 per night, $8 per night per additional vehicle. Open May-early September, weather permitting.

Directions: From I-5 at Bellingham, turn east on Highway 542 and drive 33 miles to Glacier. Continue east on Highway 542 for 12.5 miles to the campground on the right.

Contact: Mount Baker-Snoqualmie National Forest, Mount Baker Ranger District, 360/856-5700, www.fs.usda.gov or www.hoodoo.com.

4 HOZOMEEN

Scenic rating: 9

on Ross Lake in Ross Lake National Recreation Area

Map 3.1, page 173

Hozomeen Campground, at 1,600 feet elevation, is just inside the U.S./Canada border at the northeast end of Ross Lake. It takes quite an effort to get here, which tends to weed out all but the most stalwart campers. This is good news for those few, for they will find a quiet, uncrowded camp in a beautiful setting. No firewood gathering is permitted here.

Campsites, facilities: There are 75 sites for tents or RVs of any length (but getting there requires traveling over 39 miles of rough road). Picnic tables and fire grills are provided. Pit toilets and drinking water are available. Garbage must be packed out. A boat launch on nearby Ross Lake is available. Some facilities are wheelchair accessible. Leashed pets are permitted.

Reservations, fees: There is no entrance fee for North Cascades National Park. Reservations are not accepted. There is no fee for camping. Open mid-June-September.

Directions: This campground is accessible only through Canada. From the town of Hope, British Columbia, turn south on Silver-Skagit Road; it is a narrow dirt/gravel road, which is often rough. Drive south for 39 miles to the campground at the north end of Ross Lake.

Contact: North Cascades National Park, 360/856-5700, www.nps.gov/noca.

5 PARK CREEK

Scenic rating: 6

near Baker Lake in Mount Baker-Snoqualmie National Forest

Map 3.1, page 173

This pretty camp is set at an elevation of 800 feet on Park Creek amid a heavily wooded area comprising old-growth Douglas fir and western hemlock. Park Creek is a feeder stream to nearby Baker Lake. The camp is primitive and small but gets its fair share of use.

Campsites, facilities: There are 12 sites for tents or RVs up to 36 feet long. Picnic tables and fire grills are provided. Vault toilets are available, but there is no drinking water. Boat docks, launching facilities, and rentals are nearby on Baker Lake. Leashed pets are permitted.

Reservations, fees: Reservations are accepted at 877/444-6777 ($10 reservation fee) or www.recreation.gov ($9 reservation fee). Sites are $12 per night, $6 per night per additional vehicle. Open mid-May-early September, weather permitting.

Directions: From I-5 at Burlington, turn east on Highway 20 and drive approximately 24 miles to Milepost 82 and Baker Lake Highway (Forest Road 11). Turn north on Baker Lake Highway and drive about 19.5 miles to Forest Road 1144. Turn left (northwest) and drive about 200 yards to the campground on the left. Obtaining a U.S. Forest Service map is helpful.

Contact: Mount Baker-Snoqualmie National Forest, Mount Baker Ranger District, 360/856-5700, www.fs.usda.gov.

6 SHANNON CREEK

Scenic rating: 9

near Baker Lake in Mount Baker-Snoqualmie National Forest

Map 3.1, page 173

This pretty camp is set at an elevation of 909 feet at the north end of Baker Lake.

Campsites, facilities: There are 19 sites, including two double sites, for tents or RVs up to 36 feet long. Picnic tables and fire grills are provided. Drinking water, garbage bins, firewood, a picnic shelter, and vault toilets are available. A boat launch is available, and docks and rentals are nearby on Baker Lake. Some facilities are wheelchair accessible. Leashed pets are permitted.

Reservations, fees: Reservations are accepted at 877/444-6777 ($10 reservation fee) or www.recreation.gov ($9 reservation fee). Sites are $14-16 per night, $26 per night for the double sites, and $7 per night per additional vehicle. Open mid-May-mid-September, weather permitting.

Directions: From I-5 at Burlington, turn east on Highway 20 and drive approximately 24 miles to Milepost 82 and Baker Lake Highway (Forest Road 11). Turn north on Baker Lake Highway and drive. Obtaining a U.S. Forest Service map is helpful.

Contact: Mount Baker-Snoqualmie National Forest, Mount Baker Ranger District, 360/856-5700, www.fs.usda.gov.

7 SWIFT CREEK

Scenic rating: 9

near Baker Lake in Mount Baker-Snoqualmie National Forest

Map 3.1, page 173

Formerly the private Baker Lake Resort, newly christened Swift Creek Campground resides in mixed-conifer forest on the edge of picturesque Baker Lake. The camp is in a prime location for hiking, boating, and fishing, as well as skiing and snowshoeing in winter months. There is a small beach on-site and an impressive view of Mount Baker's 10,781-foot snowcapped peaks.

Campsites, facilities: There are 20 single sites, two double sites, and two group sites for tents or RVs up to 40 feet long. Picnic tables and fire grills are provided. Drinking water, garbage bins, firewood, and vault toilets are available. A paved boat ramp (suitable for large boats) and a 20-slip dock are on-site. Boat rentals are available nearby. Some facilities are wheelchair accessible. Leashed pets are permitted.

Reservations, fees: Reservations are accepted at 877/444-6777 ($10 reservation fee) or www.recreation.gov ($9 reservation fee). Single sites are $18 per night, double sites are $34 per night, the group site is $75 per night, $9 per night per additional vehicle. Open mid-May-mid-September, weather permitting.

Directions: Swift Creek Campground is three miles south of Shannon Creek (see listing in this chapter) on the same road. From I-5 at Mount Vernon, take Exit 230 and head east on Highway 20/North Cascades Highway for 18 miles. Pass Sedro-Woolley and take Baker Lake Highway to Baker Lake. Swift Creek Campground is about halfway up the lake on the right side, just past Milepost 20. Obtaining a U.S. Forest Service map is helpful.

GPS Coordinates: 48.72889, -121.65722

Contact: Mount Baker-Snoqualmie National Forest, Mount Baker Ranger District, 360/856-5700, www.fs.usda.gov or www.hoodoo.com.

8 BOULDER CREEK

Scenic rating: 8

near Baker Lake in Mount Baker-Snoqualmie National Forest

Map 3.1, page 173

This camp provides an alternative to Horseshoe Cove. It is set on Boulder Creek about one mile from the shore of Baker Lake. Fishing is fair here for rainbow trout, but typically far better at Baker Lake. A boat launch is located at Panorama Point, about 15 minutes away. Wild berries can be found in the area in season. The campground offers prime views of Mount Baker.

Campsites, facilities: There are eight sites for tents or RVs up to 22 feet long and one group site for up to 25 people. Picnic tables and fire grills are provided. Vault toilets are available, but there is no drinking water. Boat docks and launching facilities are nearby on Baker Lake. Leashed pets are permitted.

Reservations, fees: Reservations are required for the group site and are available for some family sites at 877/444-6777 ($10 reservation fee) or www.recreation.gov ($9 reservation fee). Family sites are $14 per night, $7 per night per additional vehicle; the group site is $40 per night. Open mid-May-early September, weather permitting.

Directions: From I-5 at Burlington, turn east on Highway 20 and drive approximately 24 miles to Milepost 82 and Baker Lake Highway (Forest Road 11). Turn north on Baker Lake Highway and drive 17.4 miles to the campground on the right.

Contact: Mount Baker-Snoqualmie National Forest, Mount Baker Ranger District, 360/856-5700, www.fs.usda.gov or www.hoodoo.com.

9 PANORAMA POINT

Scenic rating: 10

on Baker Lake in Mount Baker-Snoqualmie National Forest

Map 3.1, page 173   BEST (

With incredible scenic views of Mount Baker, Mount Shuk, Baker Lake, and Anderson Mountain, this camp is true to its name. Panorama Point is a well-maintained campground on the northwest shore of Baker Lake. The reservoir is one of the better fishing lakes in the area, often with good prospects for rainbow trout. Powerboating and waterskiing are permitted. Hiking trails are nearby.

Campsites, facilities: There are 16 sites for tents or RVs up to 45 feet long and a few multi-sites. Picnic tables are provided. Drinking water, vault toilets, firewood, and garbage bins are available. A convenience store and ice are located within one mile. A boat ramp is adjacent to the camp. Boat docks and rentals are nearby. Some facilities are wheelchair accessible. Leashed pets are permitted.

Reservations, fees: Reservations are accepted at 877/444-6777 ($10 reservation fee) or www.recreation.gov ($9 reservation fee). Sites are $16-30 per night, $8 per night per additional vehicle. Open mid-May-mid-September, weather permitting.

Directions: From I-5 at Burlington, turn east on Highway 20 and drive approximately 24 miles to Milepost 82 and Baker Lake Highway (Forest Road 11). Turn north on Baker Lake Highway and drive 18.7 miles to the campground entrance on the right on the shore of Baker Lake.

Contact: Mount Baker-Snoqualmie National Forest, Mount Baker Ranger District, 360/856-5700, www.fs.usda.gov or www.hoodoo.com.

10 MAPLE GROVE

Scenic rating: 9

on Baker Lake in Mount Baker-Snoqualmie National Forest

Map 3.1, page 173   BEST (

Looking for a quiet spot on the edge of a popular lake? Here it is. This rustic campground on the shore of Baker Lake is hike-in or boat-in only. Many camps on this lake fill on summer weekends, and boating activity, including fishing, powerboating, and waterskiing, is high. Privacy and great mountain views are your reward for the extra effort, and it's all free.

Campsites, facilities: There are five primitive tent sites that are accessible only by boat or on foot. Picnic tables and fire grills are provided. Vault toilets are available. There is no drinking water. Boat-launching facilities and a dock are located nearby on Baker Lake. Leashed pets are permitted.

Reservations, fees: Reservations are not accepted. A Northwest Forest Pass ($5 daily fee or $30 annual fee per parked vehicle) is required when parking at the trailhead. Open year-round.

Directions: From I-5 at Burlington, turn east on Highway 20 and drive approximately 24 miles to Milepost 82 and Baker Lake Highway (Forest Road 11). Turn left (north) on Baker Lake Highway and drive 13.3 miles to Forest Road 1106. Turn right (east) on Forest Road 1106 and drive across Baker Dam to Forest Road 1107. Turn left and drive 0.5 mile to the parking area and the trailhead on the left. Or take Trail 610/Baker Lake Trail (located on the east side of the lake, 0.5 mile north of the dam) and walk four miles to camp. Obtaining a U.S. Forest Service map is recommended.

To reach the camp by boat, launch at one of the campgrounds on the west side of the lake (Horseshoe Cove is the closest).

Contact: Mount Baker-Snoqualmie National Forest, Mount Baker Ranger District, 360/856-5700, www.fs.usda.gov.

11 HORSESHOE COVE/GROUP

🥾 🚣 🏊 🚤 🎣 🐕 ♿ 🚐 ⛺

Scenic rating: 9

on Baker Lake in Mount Baker-Snoqualmie National Forest

Map 3.1, page 173

This camp is set along 5,000-acre Baker Lake. Anglers will often find good fishing for rainbow trout and kokanee salmon. Other highlights include swimming access from the campground and a boat ramp. Some hiking trails can be found nearby. The Baker Lake Basin has many trails, and the Mount Baker National Recreation Area is located within 30 minutes.

Campsites, facilities: There are 35 single and two multi-sites for tents or RVs up to 40 feet long and three group sites for up to 25 people each. Picnic tables and fire grills are provided. Drinking water, flush toilets, garbage bins, and firewood are available. A boat ramp and swimming beach are adjacent to camp. Canoes, kayaks, and paddleboats are available for rent; check with the camp host. Some facilities are wheelchair accessible. Leashed pets are permitted.

Reservations, fees: Reservations are accepted at 877/444-6777 ($10 reservation fee) or www.recreation.gov ($9 reservation fee). Single sites are $18 per night, multi-sites are $34 per night, group sites are $75 per night, $9 per night per each additional vehicle. Open May-September, weather permitting.

Directions: From I-5 at Burlington, turn east on Highway 20 and drive approximately 24 miles to Milepost 82 and the Baker Lake Highway (Forest Road 11). Turn north on Baker Lake Highway and drive about 14.8 miles to Forest Road 1118. Turn right (east) on Forest Road 1118 and drive two miles to the campground. A U.S. Forest Service map is recommended.

Contact: Mount Baker-Snoqualmie National Forest, Mount Baker Ranger District, 360/856-5700, www.fs.usda.gov or www.hoodoo.com.

12 BAYVIEW CAMPGROUND

🥾 🚣 🏊 🚤 🐕 🚐 ⛺

Scenic rating: 9

on Baker Lake in Mount Baker-Snoqualmie National Forest

Map 3.1, page 173

This campground sits adjacent to Baker Lake, which covers 5,000 acres and offers fishing for rainbow trout and kokanee salmon. Sites are set in a second-growth forest with brush understory providing some privacy between you and your neighbor. Many sites are close to the water. A group site is located away from the main campground. There is a nice quiet little cove that is usually boat free and is a great place to float and relax. A hiking trail connects Bayview and Horseshoe Cove Campgrounds.

Campsites, facilities: There are 24 sites for tents or RVs up to 30 feet and one group site for up to 50 people. Picnic tables and fire grills are provided. Vault toilets, garbage bins, and firewood are available. Hand-pumped drinking water may be available. A boat ramp is located nearby near Horseshoe Cove Camp. Leashed pets are permitted.

Reservations, fees: Reservations are accepted at 877/444-6777 ($10 reservation fee) or www.recreation.gov ($9 reservation fee). Sites are $16 per night, $8 per each additional vehicle. The group site is $75 per night. Some credit cards are accepted. Open mid-May–mid-September, weather permitting.

Directions: From I-5 at Burlington, turn east on Highway 20 and drive approximately 24 miles to Milepost 82 and the Baker Lake Highway (Forest Road 11). Turn north on Baker Lake Highway and drive about 14.8 miles to Forest Road 1118. Turn right (east) on Forest Road 1118 and drive 1.75 miles to Forest Road 1118.011. Turn left and drive 0.75 mile to the campground. A U.S. Forest Service map is recommended.

Contact: Mount Baker-Snoqualmie National Forest, Mount Baker Ranger District, 360/856-5700 www.fs.usda.gov or www.hoodoo.com.

13 GOODELL CREEK
🚤 🏕 ♿ 🚐 ⛺

Scenic rating: 7
on Goodell Creek and the Skagit River in Ross Lake National Recreation Area

Map 3.1, page 173

Goodell Creek Campground is an alternative to nearby, larger Newhalem Creek Campground. This one is set at 500 feet elevation, where Goodell Creek pours into the Skagit River in the Ross Lake National Recreation Area. It's a popular put-in camp for raft trips downriver; that makes the group sites popular here. No firewood gathering is permitted.

Campsites, facilities: There are 21 sites for tents or RVs up to 22 feet long and three group sites (one at Upper Goodell and two at Lower Goodell) for up to 50 people each for tents or RVs up to 30 feet long. Picnic tables and fire rings are provided. Drinking water is available in the family sites, but not in the group sites. Pit toilets, garbage bins, and a picnic shelter are available. A dump station is across the road at Newhalem Creek campground. Some facilities are wheelchair accessible. Leashed pets are permitted.

Reservations, fees: Reservations are required for group sites only at 877/444-6777 or www.recreation.gov ($9 reservation fee). Sites are $16 per night, group sites are $25 per night. There is no entrance fee for North Cascades National Park. Family sites are open year-round, but there are no services (and no fees) in the winter; group sites are open Memorial Day weekend–September.

Directions: On I-5, drive to Exit 230/Highway 20 at Burlington. Turn east on Highway 20 and drive 46 miles to Marblemount. Continue east on Highway 20 for 13 miles to the campground entrance. RVs and buses are not allowed on the road to Upper Goodell Campground.

Contact: North Cascades National Park, 360/856-5700, www.nps.gov/noca.

14 NEWHALEM CREEK
🚶 🏕 ♿ 🚐 ⛺

Scenic rating: 7
near the Skagit River in Ross Lake National Recreation Area

Map 3.1, page 173

This spot is set along the Skagit River west of Newhalem at 500 feet elevation. Good hiking possibilities abound in the immediate area, and naturalist programs are available. Be sure to visit the North Cascades Visitor Center at the top of the hill from the campground. No firewood gathering is permitted here. If this camp is full, try Goodell Creek Campground, located just one mile west on Highway 20.

Campsites, facilities: There are 54 sites for tents or RVs of any length, and two group sites for tents or RVs up to 45 feet long for up to 30 people each. Picnic tables and fire grills are provided. Restrooms with flush toilets, drinking water, and a dump station are available. The group camp has a covered pavilion. Some facilities are wheelchair accessible. Leashed pets are permitted.

Reservations, fees: Reservations are accepted for family sites and are required for group camps at 877/444-6677 or www.recreation.gov ($9 reservation fee). Family sites are $16 per night; group sites are $32-40 per night. There is no entrance fee for North Cascades National Park. Open mid-May-mid-September.

Directions: On I-5, drive to Exit 230/Highway 20 at Burlington. Turn east on Highway 20 and drive 46 miles to Marblemount. Continue 14 miles east on Highway 20 to the camp.

Contact: North Cascades National Park, 360/856-5700, www.nps.gov/noca/.

15 GORGE LAKE

Scenic rating: 9

on Gorge Lake on the Skagit River in Ross Lake National Recreation Area

Map 3.1, page 173

This small camp is set near the north shore of Gorge Lake, with lake views from many sites, and close to Colonial Creek and Goodell Creek. There is some tree cover. Gorge Lake is very narrow and has trout fishing (check regulations). The camp is not well known and gets low use. One problem here is that the lake level can fluctuate (but not as much as Ross Lake), leaving the camps high and dry. No firewood gathering is permitted. There are two other lakes nearby on the Skagit River—Diablo Lake and Ross Lake. The elevation is 900 feet.

Campsites, facilities: There are six sites for tents or RVs up to 22 feet long. Picnic tables and fire grills are provided. Vault toilets are available. There is no drinking water, and garbage

must be packed out. A boat ramp is nearby. Leashed pets are permitted.

Reservations, fees: Reservations are not accepted. There is no fee for camping. There is no entrance fee for North Cascades National Park. Open year-round.

Directions: From I-5 near Burlington, take exit 230 for Highway 20. Turn east on Highway 20 and drive 46 miles to Marblemount. Continue east on Highway 20 for another 20 miles to the junction with Diablo Road. Bear left and drive 0.6 mile to the campground on the right.

Contact: North Cascades National Park, 360/856-5700, www.nps.gov/noca.

16 COLONIAL CREEK

Scenic rating: 7

on Diablo Lake in Ross Lake National Recreation Area

Map 3.1, page 173

Colonial Creek Campground sits at an elevation of 1,200 feet along the shore of Diablo Lake in the Ross Lake National Recreation Area. The five-mile-long lake offers many hiking and fishing opportunities. A naturalist program and guided walks are available during the summer months. No firewood gathering is permitted at this campsite.

Campsites, facilities: There are 142 campsites for tents or RVs up to 45 feet long, including a few walk-in tent sites. Picnic tables and fire grills are provided. Restrooms with flush toilets, drinking water, garbage bins, a dump station, three boat docks, and a boat ramp are available. Some facilities are wheelchair accessible, including a fishing pier. Leashed pets are permitted.

Reservations, fees: Reservations are accepted for South Loop sites at 877/444-6677 ($10 reservation fee) or www.recreation.gov ($9 reservation fee). Sites are $16 per night. There is no entrance fee for North Cascades National Park. Open mid-May-mid-October; 18 lakefront sites are open through the winter (no services provided).

Directions: From I-5 at Burlington, take Exit 230 and drive east to Highway 20. Turn east on Highway 20 and drive 46 miles to Marblemount. Continue east on Highway 20 for 24 miles to the campground entrance.

Contact: North Cascades National Park, 360/856-5700, www.nps.gov.noca.

17 RASAR STATE PARK

Scenic rating: 8

on the Skagit River

Map 3.1, page 173

This park borders North Cascade National Park and is also near 10,778-foot Mount Baker and the Baker River watershed. Fishing the 4,000 feet of shoreline and hiking are the attractions here, as is bird-watching.

Campsites, facilities: There are 20 sites with partial hookups (30 amps) and 18 sites with no hookups for tents or RVs up to 40 feet, three primitive hike-in/bike-in sites, eight walk-in sites, two four-person Adirondack shelters, three cabins, and three group sites for 20-80 people. Picnic tables and fire grills are provided. Restrooms with flush toilets and coin showers, drinking water, dump station, a kitchen shelter, an amphitheater, playground, and park store are available. Firewood gathering is prohibited, but firewood is available for sale. Some facilities are wheelchair accessible. Leashed pets are permitted.

Reservations, fees: Reservations are accepted and are required for the group site at 888/226-7688 or https://washington.tocamp.com ($8-10 reservation fee). Sites are $12-35 per night, $10 per extra vehicle per night, and cabins are $59-93 per night. Call for group rates. Open year-round.

Directions: From I-5 at Burlington, take Exit 232 (Cook Road) and drive six miles (to a traffic light) to Highway 20 in Sedro-Woolley. Turn left (east) on Highway 20 and drive 15 miles to Lusk Road. Turn right on Lusk Road and drive 0.75 mile to Cape Horn Road. Turn left on Cape Horn Road and drive one mile to the park entrance.

Contact: Rasar State Park, 360/826-3942, http://parks.state.wa.us.

18 CREEKSIDE CAMPING

Scenic rating: 6

near the Skagit River

Map 3.1, page 173

This pretty, wooded campground is centrally located to nearby recreational opportunities at Baker Lake and the Skagit River. Trout fishing is good here, and tackle is available nearby. Horseshoe pits and a recreation hall are also available. About half of the sites are filled with monthly renters.

Campsites, facilities: There are 29 sites with full or partial hookups (20 and 30 amp) for tents, trailers, or RVs up to 40 feet long. Picnic tables and fire rings are provided. Restrooms with flush toilets and showers, drinking water, a dump station, coin laundry, games and videos, and horseshoe pits are available. A café is located within one mile. Leashed pets are permitted.

Reservations, fees: Reservations are recommended. RV sites are $36 per night, tent sites are $24 per night. Open year-round.

Directions: From Seattle, drive north on I-5 to Exit 232 (Cook Road). Take the exit up and over the highway to the flashing light and Highway 20. Turn left on Cook Road/Highway 20 and drive four miles to the light at Highway 20. Turn left at Highway 20 and drive 17 miles to Baker Lake Highway, between Mileposts 182 and 183. Turn left on Baker Lake Highway and drive 0.25 mile to the camp on the right.

Contact: Creekside Camping, 39602 Baker Lake Highway, Concrete, 360/826-3566.

19 HOWARD MILLER STEELHEAD PARK

Scenic rating: 5

on the Skagit River

Map 3.1, page 173

This Skagit County park provides grassy sites and access to the Skagit River. The river is designated a Wild and Scenic River. The steelhead fishing is often good in season. Campsites at this spot are sunny and spacious. Groups can be accommodated. A bald eagle sanctuary is located at the east end of the park. November-January is the best time to see bald eagles here. This camp is most popular in July, August, and September, when the weather is best, but also attracts visitors in early winter who arrive primarily for bald eagle-watching.

Campsites, facilities: There are 56 sites with full or partial hookups for tents or RVs of any length, 10 walk-in tent sites, two cabins, and two Adirondack shelters. Picnic tables and fire pits are provided. Restrooms with flush toilets and coin showers, drinking water, a dump station, a clubhouse, picnic shelter, playground, interpretive center, and horseshoe pits are available. A store and ice are located within one mile. Boat-launching facilities are located in the park. Some facilities are wheelchair accessible. Leashed pets are permitted.

Reservations, fees: Reservations are recommended ($7 reservation fee). RV sites are $30 per night, tent sites are $16 per night, cabins are $60-70 per night ($20 pet fee), Adirondack shelters are $30 per night, $5 per extra vehicle per night. Winter rates are available. Some credit cards are accepted. Open year-round.

Directions: On I-5, drive to Exit 230/Highway 20 at Burlington. Turn east on Highway 20 and drive 44 miles to Rockport and Rockport-Darrington Road (Highway 530). Turn right (south) and drive three blocks to the camp on the right.

Contact: Howard Miller Steelhead Park, 360/853-8808; Skagit County Parks, 360/336-9414, www.skagitcounty.net/parksandrecreation.

20 GLACIER PEAK RESORT AND WINERY

Scenic rating: 9

on the Skagit River

Map 3.1, page 173

This beautiful camp is nestled in the trees along the Skagit River. The resort covers 125 acres, including 1.5 miles of river frontage. A restaurant called The Eatery has received awards for its pecan pie and is also known for its homestyle meals. Fishing, river walks, and nearby hiking trails among the glaciers and waterfalls can be accessed close to the campground. There are also three hydroelectric plants nearby that offer tours. Recreational facilities include horseshoes and a sports field for volleyball, croquet, and badminton. This resort is popular July-September, when reservations are often required to get a spot.

Campsites, facilities: There are 48 sites for tents or RVs of any length (full hookups), 40 cabins, seven theme cabins, five chalets, and six mobile homes. Some sites are pull-through. Restrooms with flush toilets and coin showers, drinking water, Wi-Fi, a pay phone, coin laundry, horseshoe pits, a restaurant, bunny-hole golf, and a sports field for volleyball, croquet, and badminton are available. Some facilities are wheelchair accessible. Leashed pets are permitted.

Reservations, fees: Reservations are recommended. RV sites are $29 per night, tent sites are $19 per night, cabins are $129-209 per night ($30 pet deposit). Some credit cards are accepted. Open year-round.

Directions: From Burlington, drive east on Highway 20 for 44 miles to Rockport. Continue east on Highway 20 for six miles to the resort on the left (between Mileposts 103 and 104).

Contact: Glacier Peak Resort and Winery, 360/873-2250, www.northcascades.com.

21 MARBLE CREEK

Scenic rating: 7

on Marble Creek in Mount Baker-Snoqualmie National Forest

Map 3.1, page 173

This primitive campground is set on Marble Creek amid old-growth Douglas fir and western hemlock. Fishing for rainbow trout is possible here. A trailhead to Hidden Lake just inside the boundary of North Cascades National Park can be found about five miles from camp at the end of Forest Road 1540.

Campsites, facilities: There are 23 sites for tents or RVs up to 40 feet long, including a few multi-sites. Picnic tables and fire grills are provided. Vault toilets, garbage bins, and firewood are available. There is no drinking water. Some facilities are wheelchair accessible. Leashed pets are permitted.

Reservations, fees: Reservations are accepted at 877/444-6777 ($10 reservation fee) or www. recreation.gov ($9 reservation fee). Sites are $14 per night, multi-sites are $20 per night, $7 per night per additional vehicle. Open mid-May-mid-September, weather permitting.

Directions: From I-5 in Burlington, take Exit 230/Highway 20. Turn east on Highway 20 and drive 46 miles to Marblemount and Forest Road 15 (Cascade River Road). Cross the bridge, turn east on Cascade River Road, and drive eight miles to Forest Road 1530. Turn right (south) on Forest Road 1530 and drive to the campground. Obtaining a U.S. Forest Service map is advised.

Contact: Mount Baker-Snoqualmie National Forest, Mount Baker Ranger District, 360/856-5700, www.fs.usda.gov or www.hoodoo.com.

22 MINERAL PARK: EAST AND WEST

Scenic rating: 7

in Mount Baker-Snoqualmie National Forest

Map 3.1, page 173

This campground is just six miles from Cascade Pass along a narrow, bumpy gravel road and is best suited for tents and small trailers. Campsites are near the Cascade River at the convergence of the North and South Forks.

Campsites, facilities: There are 24 sites, including two double sites, for tents or RVs up to 32 feet long. Picnic tables and fire grills are provided. Vault toilets, firewood, and garbage bins are available, but there is no drinking water. Leashed pets are permitted.

Reservations, fees: Reservations are accepted at 877/444-6777 ($10 reservation fee) or www. recreation.gov ($9 reservation fee). Sites are $12 per night, $6 per night per additional vehicle, and double sites are $22 per night. Open mid-May-mid-September, weather permitting.

Directions: From I-5 in Burlington, take Exit 230/Highway 20. Turn east on Highway 20 and drive 46 miles to Marblemount and Forest Road 15 (Cascade River Road). Cross the bridge over the Skagit River, turn east on Cascade River Road, and drive 16 miles to the campground. Obtaining a U.S. Forest Service map is advised.

Contact: Mount Baker-Snoqualmie National Forest, Mount Baker Ranger District, 360/856-5700, www.fs.usda.gov or www.hoodoo.com.

23 SQUIRE CREEK COUNTY PARK

Scenic rating: 7

on Squire Creek

Map 3.1, page 173

This pretty park is set amid old-growth forest, primarily Douglas fir and cedar, along Squire Creek. A family-oriented park, it often fills on summer weekends. The park covers 53 acres and features several nearby trailheads. A trail from the park provides a 4.5-mile loop that heads toward White Horse Mountain. Other trailheads are located within five miles in nearby Mount Baker-Snoqualmie National Forest, about three miles from the boundaries of the Boulder River Wilderness. No alcohol is permitted in this park.

Campsites, facilities: There are 33 sites for tents or RVs up to 40 feet long (no hookups). Picnic tables and fire rings are provided. Restrooms with flush toilets, coin showers, drinking water, firewood, and picnic shelters that can be reserved are available. A store is located three miles east in Darrington. Some facilities are wheelchair accessible. Leashed pets are permitted.

Reservations, fees: Reservations are accepted. Sites are $22-40 per night, $10 per night per additional vehicle. Open year-round, with limited winter services.

Directions: From Seattle, drive north on I-5 to Exit 208 and the junction with Highway 530. Turn east on Highway 530 and drive 26 miles to the park on the left. The park is at Milepost 45.2, approximately three miles west of the town of Darrington.

Contact: Squire Creek County Park, 360/435-3441, https://snohomishcountywa.gov.

24 CLEAR CREEK

Scenic rating: 8

on Clear Creek and the Sauk River in Mount Baker-Snoqualmie National Forest

Map 3.1, page 173

This nice, secluded spot is set in old-growth fir on the water, but it doesn't get heavy use. It's located at the confluence of Clear Creek and the Sauk River, a designated Wild and Scenic River. Fishing is available for rainbow trout, Dolly Varden trout, whitefish, and steelhead in season. A trail from camp leads about one mile up to Frog Pond.

Campsites, facilities: There are 13 sites for

tents or RVs up to 40 feet long. Picnic tables and fire grills are provided. Vault toilets, garbage bins, and firewood are available. There is no drinking water. A store, café, coin laundry, and ice are located within four miles. Some facilities are wheelchair accessible. Leashed pets are permitted.

Reservations, fees: Reservations are accepted at 877/444-6777 ($10 reservation fee) or www.recreation.gov ($9 reservation fee). Sites are $14 per night, $7 per extra vehicle per night. Open late May-mid-September, weather permitting.

Directions: From Seattle, drive north on I-5 to Exit 208 and the junction with Highway 530. Turn east on Highway 530 and drive 32 miles to Darrington and Forest Road 20 (Mountain Loop Highway). Turn right (south) on Forest Road 20 and drive 3.3 miles to the campground entrance on the left.

Contact: Mount Baker-Snoqualmie National Forest, Darrington Ranger District, 360/436-1155, www.fs.usda.gov or www.hoodoo.com.

25 RIVER MEADOWS COUNTY PARK

Scenic rating: 5

on the Stillaguamish River near Arlington

Map 3.1, page 173

This 150-acre camp on the shore of the Stillaguamish River offers a wide variety of activities. There are miles of trails for hiking, a mile of river for fishing or swimming, open meadows for seasonal activities ranging from kite-flying and kickball to snowshoeing and cross-country skiing. There's even geocaching.

Campsites, facilities: There are 14 sites for tents or RVs of any length (no hookups), three of which are walk-in sites for tents only. Six yurts are also available. Picnic tables and fire rings are provided. Restrooms with flush toilets, drinking water, firewood, and three reservable picnic shelters are available. A store is located five miles away in Arlington. Some

facilities are wheelchair accessible. Leashed pets are permitted.

Reservations, fees: Reservations are accepted. Sites are $22-28 per night, $10 per night per additional vehicle, and yurts are $45-85 per night. Open year-round, with limited winter services.

Directions: From Seattle, drive north on I-5 for 42 miles to Exit 208 and the junction with Highway 530. Turn east on Highway 530 and drive five miles to Arlington Heights Road. Turn right on Arlington Heights Road and drive 1.5 miles to Jordan Road. Take a sharp right onto Jordan Road and drive about two miles to the park on the right.

Contact: River Meadows County Park, 20416 Jordan Road, Arlington, 360/435-3441, https://snohomishcountywa.gov.

26 TURLO

Scenic rating: 8
in Mount Baker-Snoqualmie National Forest

Map 3.1, page 173

The westernmost camp on this stretch of Highway 92, Turlo is set at 900 feet elevation along the South Fork of the Stillaguamish River. A U.S. Forest Service Public Information Center is nearby. Riverside campsites are available, and the fishing can be good here. A few hiking trails can be found in the area.

Campsites, facilities: There are 18 sites for tents or RVs up to 40 feet long. Picnic tables and fire rings are provided. Vault toilets, drinking water, garbage bins, and firewood are available. A camp host is on-site. A store, café, and ice are located one mile away. Some facilities are wheelchair accessible. Leashed pets are permitted.

Reservations, fees: Reservations are accepted at 877/444-6777 ($10 reservation fee) or www.recreation.gov ($9 reservation fee). Sites are $16 per night, $8 per extra vehicle per night. Open year-round, weather permitting.

Directions: From I-5 and Everett, turn east on

U.S. 2 and drive five miles to Highway 9. Turn north and drive four miles to Highway 92. Turn east on Highway 92 and drive approximately 15 miles to the town of Granite Falls. Continue another 11 miles east on Highway 92 to the campground entrance on the right.

Contact: Mount Baker-Snoqualmie National Forest, Darrington Ranger District, 360/436-1155 www.fs.usda.gov or www.hoodoo.com.

27 VERLOT

Scenic rating: 9
in Mount Baker-Snoqualmie National Forest

Map 3.1, page 173

This pretty campground is set along the South Fork of the Stillaguamish River. Some campsites provide river views. The camp is a short distance from the Lake Twenty-Two Research Natural Area and Maid of the Woods Trail. Fishing is another recreation option.

Campsites, facilities: There are 24 single and two multi-sites for tents or RVs up to 40 feet long. Picnic tables and fire rings are provided. Restrooms with flush toilets, drinking water, garbage bins, firewood, and a visitors center are available. A store, café, and ice are located within one mile. Some facilities are wheelchair accessible. Leashed pets are permitted.

Reservations, fees: Reservations are accepted at 877/444-6777 ($10 reservation fee) or www.recreation.gov ($9 reservation fee). Sites are $18 per night, $24-30 for multi-sites, and $9 per extra vehicle per night. Open year-round, weather permitting.

Directions: From I-5 and Everett, turn east on U.S. 2 and drive five miles to Highway 9. Turn north and drive four miles to Highway 92. Turn east on Highway 92 and drive approximately 15 miles to the town of Granite Falls, and continue another 11.6 miles east on Highway 92 to the campground entrance on the right.

Contact: Mount Baker-Snoqualmie National Forest, Darrington Ranger District, 360/436-1155, www.fs.usda.gov or www.hoodoo.com.

28 GOLD BASIN

🚶 🚴 🏊 🛶 🐕 ♿ 🚐 ⛺

Scenic rating: 9

in Mount Baker-Snoqualmie National Forest

Map 3.1, page 173

Note: Closed since 2016, the Forest Service plans to reopen this campground in 2018. Call to confirm status before planning a trip.

This is the largest campground in Mount Baker-Snoqualmie National Forest; since it's loaded with facilities, it's a favorite with RVers. Set at an elevation of 1,100 feet along the South Fork of the Stillaguamish River, the campground features riverside sites, easy access, and a wheelchair-accessible interpretive trail. This area once provided good fishing, but a slide upstream put clay silt into the water, and it has hurt the fishing. Rafting and hiking are options.

Campsites, facilities: There are 80 sites without hook-ups for tents or RVs up to 45 feet long, 10 tent-only sites, and one group site for up to 75 people. Picnic tables and fire rings are provided. Drinking water, restrooms with flush toilets and coin showers, firewood, and garbage bins are available. A camp host is on-site. A store, café, and ice are located within 2.5 miles. Some facilities are wheelchair accessible. Leashed pets are permitted.

Reservations, fees: Reservations are accepted at 877/444-6777 ($10 reservation fee) or www.recreation.gov ($9 reservation fee). Sites are $22-35 per night, $10 per extra vehicle per night. The group site is $100-125 per night. Open mid-May-September, weather permitting.

Directions: From I-5 and Everett, turn east on U.S. 2 and drive five miles to Highway 9. Turn north and drive four miles to Highway 92. Turn east on Highway 92 and drive about 15 miles to the town of Granite Falls and Mountain Loop Highway. Continue east on Mountain Loop Highway for 13.5 miles to the campground entrance on the left.

Contact: Mount Baker-Snoqualmie National Forest, Darrington Ranger District, 360/436-1155, www.fs.usda.gov or www.hoodoo.com.

29 ESSWINE GROUP CAMP

🚶 🚴 🛶 🐕 🚐 ⛺

Scenic rating: 6

in Mount Baker-Snoqualmie National Forest

Map 3.1, page 173

This small, quiet camp is a great place for a restful group getaway. Even though the elevation is only 1,600 feet, it still has a beautiful view. The only drawback? No drinking water. Fishing access is available nearby. The Boulder River Wilderness is located to the north; see a U.S. Forest Service map for trailhead locations.

Campsites, facilities: There is one group site for tents or RVs up to 35 feet long for up to 25 people. Picnic tables and fire pits are provided. Vault toilets, garbage bins, and firewood are available, but there is no drinking water. A store, café, and ice are located within seven miles. Leashed pets are permitted.

Reservations, fees: Reservations are accepted at 877/444-6777 ($10 reservation fee) or www.recreation.gov ($9 reservation fee). The site is $75 per night. Open mid-May-September, weather permitting.

Directions: From I-5 and Everett, turn east on U.S. 2 and drive five miles to Highway 9. Turn north and drive four miles to Highway 92. Turn east on Highway 92 and drive about 15 miles to the town of Granite Falls and Mountain Loop Highway. Continue northeast on Mountain Loop Highway for 16 miles to the campground entrance on the left.

Contact: Mount Baker-Snoqualmie National Forest, Darrington Ranger District, 360/436-1155, www.fs.usda.gov or www.hoodoo.com.

30 BOARDMAN CREEK GROUP CAMP

🏃 🛶 🐕 ♿ 🚐 ⛺

Scenic rating: 7

in Mount Baker-Snoqualmie National Forest

Map 3.1, page 173

Boardman is located at the far end of the Mountain Loop Road, about eight miles east of the Verlot Public Service Center on the Stillaguamish River. River access highlights this pretty camp, converted from a single-site into a group campground. The fishing near here can be excellent for rainbow trout, Dolly Varden, whitefish, and steelhead in season. The camp road parallels Mountain Loop Highway. Forest roads in the area will take you to several backcountry lakes, including Boardman Lake, Lake Evan, and Ashland Lakes. Get a U.S. Forest Service map, set up your camp, and go for it.

Insider's tip: When not reserved by groups, Boardman is available for individuals on a first-come, first-served basis; check with the Gold Basin host.

Campsites, facilities: There is one group camp for up to 35 people and RVs of any length. Picnic tables and fire pits are provided. Vault toilets, garbage bins, and firewood are available. There is no drinking water. A camp host is available Memorial Day-Labor Day. Some facilities are wheelchair accessible. Leashed pets are permitted.

Reservations, fees: Reservations are accepted at 877/444-6777 ($10 reservation fee) or www.recreation.gov ($9 reservation fee). The site is $60 per night. Open late May-early September, weather permitting.

Directions: From I-5 and Everett, turn east on U.S. 2 and drive five miles to Highway 9. Turn north and drive four miles to Highway 92. Turn east on Highway 92 and drive about 15 miles to the town of Granite Falls and Mountain Loop Highway. Continue northeast on Mountain Loop Highway for 16.5 miles to the campground entrance on the left.

Contact: Mount Baker-Snoqualmie National Forest, Darrington Ranger District, 360/436-1155, www.fs.usda.gov or www.hoodoo.com.

31 BEDAL

🏃 🛶 🐕 ♿ 🚐 ⛺

Scenic rating: 9

in Mount Baker-Snoqualmie National Forest

Map 3.1, page 173

A bit primitive, this campground is set at the confluence of the North and South Forks of the Sauk River. It offers shaded sites, river views, and good fishing. North Fork Falls is about one mile up the North Fork from camp and worth the trip.

Campsites, facilities: There are 21 single sites and one double site for tents or RVs up to 21 feet long. Picnic tables and fire grills are provided. Vault toilets, garbage bins, firewood, and a picnic shelter are available. There is no drinking water. A U.S. Forest Service district office is located 19 miles from the campground, in Darrington. Some facilities are wheelchair accessible. Leashed pets are permitted.

Reservations, fees: Reservations are accepted at 877/444-6777 ($10 reservation fee) or www.recreation.gov ($9 reservation fee). Single sites are $14 per night, the double is $26 per night, $7 per extra vehicle per night. Open May-early September, weather permitting.

Directions: From Seattle, drive north on I-5 to Exit 208 and the junction with Highway 530. Turn east on Highway 530 and drive 32 miles to Darrington and Forest Road 20 (Mountain Loop Highway). Turn right (south) on Forest Road 20 and drive 19 miles to the campground on the right. Obtaining a U.S. Forest Service map is advised.

Contact: Mount Baker-Snoqualmie National Forest, Darrington Ranger District, 360/436-1155, www.fs.usda.gov or www.hoodoo.com.

32 RED BRIDGE

Scenic rating: 9

in Mount Baker-Snoqualmie National Forest

Map 3.1, page 173

Red Bridge is a classic spot, one of several in the vicinity, and a good base camp for a back-packing expedition. The campground is set at 1,300 feet elevation on the South Fork of the Stillaguamish River near Mallardy Creek. It has pretty, riverside sites with old-growth fir. Swimming, tubing, and canoeing are not recommended in this particular part of the river; the water surface can be deceptive and there are powerful undercurrents, so please use extreme caution. A trailhead two miles east of camp leads to Granite Pass in the Boulder River Wilderness.

Campsites, facilities: There are 15 sites for tents or RVs up to 40 feet long including a few multi-sites. Picnic tables and fire grills are provided. There is no drinking water, but vault toilets, garbage bins, and firewood are available. Some facilities are wheelchair accessible. Leashed pets are permitted.

Reservations, fees: Reservations are accepted at 877/444-6777 ($10 reservation fee) or www.recreation.gov ($9 reservation fee). Single sites are $14 per night, multi-sites are $26 per night, $7 per extra vehicle per night. Open mid-May-mid-September, weather permitting.

Directions: From I-5 and Everett, turn east on U.S. 2 and drive five miles to Highway 9. Turn north and drive four miles to Highway 92. Turn east on Highway 92 and drive about 15 miles to the town of Granite Falls and Mountain Loop Highway. Continue northeast on Mountain Loop Highway for 18 miles to the campground entrance on the right.

Contact: Mount Baker-Snoqualmie National Forest, Darrington Ranger District, 360/436-1155, www.fs.usda.gov or www.hoodoo.com.

33 TULALIP MILL GROUP CAMP

Scenic rating: 7

in Mount Baker-Snoqualmie National Forest

Map 3.1, page 173

This campground is set along the South Fork of the Stillaguamish River, close to several other camps: Turlo, Verlot, Gold Basin, Esswine, Boardman Creek, Coal Creek, and Red Bridge. A trailhead about one mile east of camp leads north into the Boulder River Wilderness. Numerous creeks and streams crisscross this area, providing good fishing prospects.

Campsites, facilities: There is one group camp for tents or RVs up to 22 feet long for up to 60 people. Picnic tables and fire grills are provided. Vault toilets and garbage bins are available. There is no drinking water. Some facilities are wheelchair accessible. Leashed pets are permitted.

Reservations, fees: Reservations are accepted at 877/444-6777 ($10 reservation fee) or www.recreation.gov ($9 reservation fee). Note that for online reservations, this camp is mistakenly called Tulalip and not Tulalip Mill. The site is $85 per night. Open mid-May-September, weather permitting.

Directions: From I-5 and Everett, turn east on U.S. 2 and drive five miles to Highway 9. Turn north and drive four miles to Highway 92. Turn east on Highway 92 and drive about 15 miles to the town of Granite Falls and Mountain Loop Highway. Continue east on Mountain Loop Highway for 18.5 miles to the campground entrance on the right.

Contact: Mount Baker-Snoqualmie National Forest, Darrington Ranger District, 360/436-1155, www.fs.usda.gov or www.hoodoo.com.

34 COAL CREEK GROUP CAMP

Scenic rating: 8

in Mount Baker-Snoqualmie National Forest

Map 3.1, page 173

A U.S. Forest Service map will unlock the beautiful country around this campground set along the South Fork of the Stillaguamish River. Fishing access is available for rainbow trout, Dolly Varden, whitefish, and steelhead in season. Nearby forest roads lead to Coal Lake and a trailhead that takes you to other backcountry lakes.

Campsites, facilities: There is one group site for tents or RVs up to 30 feet long for up to 25 people. Picnic tables and fire grills are provided. Vault toilets, garbage bins, and firewood are available. There is no drinking water. Leashed pets are permitted.

Reservations, fees: Reservations are accepted at 877/444-6777 ($10 reservation fee) or www. recreation.gov ($9 reservation fee). The site is $75 per night. Open mid-May–late September, weather permitting.

Directions: From I-5 and Everett, turn east on U.S. 2 and drive five miles to Highway 9. Turn north and drive four miles to Highway 92. Turn east on Highway 92 and drive about 15 miles to the town of Granite Falls and Mountain Loop Highway. Continue northeast on Mountain Loop Highway for 23.5 miles to the campground entrance on the left.

Contact: Mount Baker-Snoqualmie National Forest, Darrington Ranger District, 360/436-1155, www.fs.usda.gov or www.hoodoo.com.

35 BEAVER PLANT LAKE HIKE-IN

Scenic rating: 8

on Beaver Plant Lake

Map 3.1, page 173   **BEST (**

This campground is on Beaver Plant Lake, one of four campgrounds detailed in the area (the others are Upper Ashland Lake, Lower Ashland Lake, and Twin Falls Lake camps). Excellent hiking trails are a highlight of the region. This trail system is within the Morning Star Natural Resources Conservation Area, and much of the trail system is on raised boardwalks. One hiking trail connects to all four lakes. From this trail, you can also access Bald Mountain Trail, which then leads to Cutthroat Trail. It's a nine-mile hike from Beaver Plant Lake to Cutthroat Lake. The Department of Natural Resources (DNR) pleads: "Please stay on the trails."

Campsites, facilities: There are five tent sites. Fire grills are provided. There is no drinking water and garbage must be packed out. Leashed pets are permitted.

Reservations, fees: Reservations are not accepted. There is no fee for camping, but a Discover Pass is required. Open year-round, weather permitting.

Directions: From I-5 and Everett, turn east on U.S. 2 and drive five miles to Highway 9. Turn north and drive four miles to Highway 92. Turn east on Highway 92 and drive about 15 miles to the town of Granite Falls and Mountain Loop Highway. Continue east on Mountain Loop Highway for 15 miles to Forest Road 4020. Turn right (south) on Forest Road 4020 and drive 2.5 miles to Forest Road 4021. Turn right on Forest Road 4021 and drive two miles to the Ashland Lakes Trailhead. From the trailhead, hike 2.1 miles to the campground.

Contact: Department of Natural Resources, Northwest Region, 360/856-3500, www.dnr. wa.gov.

36 UPPER ASHLAND LAKE HIKE-IN

Scenic rating: 9

near Upper Ashland Lake

Map 3.1, page 173

Reaching this primitive and beautiful camp requires a 2.5-mile hike that's well worth the effort. The site is little known, so you can expect quiet and privacy. Several good hiking trails can be found near camp; the rangers ask that you stay on the trails. A map available from the Department of Natural Resources is helpful.

Campsites, facilities: There are four tent sites. Fire grills are provided. There is no drinking water and garbage must be packed out. Leashed pets are permitted.

Reservations, fees: Reservations are not accepted. There is no fee for camping, but a Discover Pass is required. Open mid-June-October, weather permitting.

Directions: From I-5 and Everett, turn east on U.S. 2 and drive five miles to Highway 9. Turn north and drive four miles to Highway 92. Turn east on Highway 92 and drive about 15 miles to the town of Granite Falls and Mountain Loop Highway. Turn north on Mountain Loop Highway and drive 15 miles to Forest Road 4020. Turn right (south) on Forest Road 4020 and drive 2.5 miles to Forest Road 4021. Turn right on Forest Road 4021 and drive 2 miles to the Ashland Lakes Trailhead. From the trailhead, hike 2.5 miles to the campground.

Contact: Department of Natural Resources, Northwest Region, 360/856-3500, www.dnr.wa.gov.

37 LOWER ASHLAND LAKE HIKE-IN
🏃 ⛵ 🐕 ⛺

Scenic rating: 8
on Lower Ashland Lake

Map 3.1, page 173

This campground on Lower Ashland Lake, set adjacent to Upper Ashland Lake, can be reached by hiking in three miles. The camp is within the Morning Star Basin Natural Resources Conservation Area and there is a trail system that connects the four campgrounds and lakes in the area. DNR pleads: "Please stay on the trails."

Campsites, facilities: There are five tent sites.

Fire rings are provided. There is no drinking water and garbage must be packed out. Leashed pets are permitted.

Reservations, fees: Reservations are not accepted. There is no fee for camping, but a Discover Pass is required. Open mid-June-October, weather permitting.

Directions: From I-5 and Everett, turn east on U.S. 2 and drive five miles to Highway 9. Turn north and drive four miles to Highway 92. Turn east on Highway 92 and drive about 15 miles to the town of Granite Falls and Mountain Loop Highway. Turn north on Mountain Loop Highway and drive 15 miles to Forest Road 4020. Turn right (south) on Forest Road 4020 and drive 2.5 miles to Forest Road 4021 (high-clearance vehicles only on Road 4021). Turn right on Forest Road 4021 and drive two miles to the Ashland Lakes Trailhead. From the trailhead, hike three miles to the campground.

Contact: Department of Natural Resources, Northwest Region, 360/856-3500, www.dnr.wa.gov.

38 HARTS PASS WALK-IN
🏃 🏠 ♿ ⛺

Scenic rating: 10
in Okanogan-Wenatchee National Forest

Map 3.2, page 174   **BEST** ◖

At 6,198 feet elevation, Harts Pass is one of the highest drive-through mountain passes in Washington. It features great panoramic views of Mount Gardner, Silver Star, Tower, Golden Horn, Mount Azurite, Ballard, Crater Mountain, Mount Baker (on a clear day), Jack Mountain, the Pickets Range, Pasayten Peak, and Mount Robinson. This pretty little campground is near the Pasayten Wilderness, which offers 500 miles of trails leading to alpine meadows and glacier-fed lakes and streams, and along ridges to spectacular mountain heights. The Pacific Crest Trail passes near the camp and offers a great view of the northern Cascade Range. No trailers are permitted on the access road.

Campsites, facilities: There are five walk-in tent sites requiring a 50-foot walk. No RVs or trailers are allowed. Picnic tables and fire grills are provided. Vault toilets are available, but there is no drinking water. Garbage must be packed out. Some facilities are wheelchair accessible. Leashed pets are permitted.

Reservations, fees: Reservations are not accepted. Sites are $8 per night, $5 per each additional vehicle per night. Open mid-July-late September, weather permitting.

Directions: From Burlington, drive east on Highway 20 for 120 miles to Mazama Road. Turn left on Mazama Road and drive 0.25 mile to County Road 9140. Turn left and drive northwest for seven miles to Lost River, where the pavement ends and the road soon becomes Forest Road 5400. Continue on Forest Road 5400 for 12.5 miles northwest to the campground (across from a guard station). Note: Forest Road 5400 is a narrow, curving road with steep slide cliffs that is closed to trailers. Drive slowly and yield to trucks.

Contact: Okanogan-Wenatchee National Forest, Methow Valley Ranger District, 509/996-4003, www.fs.usda.gov; Methow Valley Visitor Center, 509/996-4000.

39 MEADOWS

Scenic rating: 9

near the Pacific Crest Trail in
Okanogan-Wenatchee National Forest

Map 3.2, page 174

Set adjacent to the Pacific Crest Trail, this campground is about one mile from Harts Pass and offers the same opportunities. With its plentiful spruce and subalpine fir, the camp is beautiful in summer; springtime brings an array of wildflowers. No trailers are permitted on the access road.

Campsites, facilities: There are 14 tent sites. Picnic tables and fire grills are provided. Vault toilets are available. There is no drinking water, and garbage must be packed out. Some facilities

are wheelchair accessible. Leashed pets are permitted.

Reservations, fees: Reservations are not accepted. Sites are $8 per night, $5 per each additional vehicle per night. Open mid-July-September, weather permitting.

Directions: From Burlington, drive east on Highway 20 for 120 miles to Mazama Road. Turn left on Mazama Road and drive 0.25 mile to County Road 9140. Turn left and drive northwest for seven miles to Lost River, where the pavement ends and the road soon becomes Forest Road 5400. Continue on Forest Road 5400 for 12.5 miles to Forest Road 5400-500. Turn left (south) and drive one mile to the campground. Note: Forest Road 5400 is a narrow, curving road with steep slide cliffs that is closed to trailers. Drive slowly and yield to trucks.

Contact: Okanogan-Wenatchee National Forest, Methow Valley Ranger District, 509/996-4003, www.fs.usda.gov; Methow Valley Visitor Center, 509/996-4000.

40 BALLARD

Scenic rating: 6

in Okanogan-Wenatchee National Forest

Map 3,2, page 174

Ballard is set at an elevation of 2,521 feet, about 0.5 mile from River Bend. Numerous hiking trails can be found in the area, as well as access to West Fork Methow and Lost River Monument Creek Trails. It is also possible to hike west and eventually hook up with the Pacific Crest Trail. Possible side trips include Winthrop to the south, which boasts a historical museum, a state fish hatchery, and Pearrygin Lake State Park. Livestock are not permitted in the campground, but a hitching rail and stock truck dock are available at the Robinson Creek Trailhead near the campground, where there are several primitive sites.

Campsites, facilities: There are seven sites for tents or RVs up to 28 feet long. Picnic tables and fire grills are provided. Vault toilets are available, but there is no drinking water. Garbage must be packed out. Some facilities are wheelchair accessible. Leashed pets are permitted. No livestock are permitted in camp.

Reservations, fees: Reservations are not accepted. Sites are $8 per night, $5 per each additional vehicle per night. Open late May-October, weather permitting.

Directions: From Burlington, drive east on Highway 20 for 120 miles to Mazama Road. Turn left on Mazama Road and drive 0.25 mile to County Road 9140. Turn left and drive northwest for seven miles to Lost River, where the pavement ends and the road soon becomes Forest Road 5400. Continue northwest on Forest Road 5400 for two miles to the campground on the left.

Contact: Okanogan-Wenatchee National Forest, Methow Valley Ranger District, 509/996-4003, www.fs.usda.gov; Methow Valley Visitor Center, 509/996-4000.

41 RIVER BEND

Scenic rating: 6

in Okanogan-Wenatchee National Forest

Map 3.2, page 174

This campground is located along the Methow River at 2,600 feet elevation, about two miles from the boundary of the Pasayten Wilderness. Several trails near the camp provide access to the wilderness, and another trail follows the Methow River west for about eight miles before hooking up with the Pacific Crest Trail near Azurite Peak.

Campsites, facilities: There are five sites for tents, trailers, or RVs up to 30 feet long. Picnic tables and fire grills are provided. Vault toilets are available. There is no drinking water, and garbage must be packed out. Leashed pets are permitted.

Reservations, fees: Reservations are not accepted. Sites are $8 per night, $5 per each

additional vehicle per night. Open late May-late October, weather permitting.

Directions: From Burlington, drive east on Highway 20 for 120 miles to Mazama Road. Turn left on Mazama Road and drive 0.25 mile to County Road 9140. Turn left and drive northwest for seven miles to Lost River, where the pavement ends and the road soon becomes Forest Road 5400. Continue northwest on Forest Road 5400 for two miles to Forest Road 5400-600. Continue straight on Forest Road 5400-600 and drive 0.5 mile to the campground on the left.

Contact: Okanogan-Wenatchee National Forest, Methow Valley Ranger District, 509/996-4003, www.fs.usda.gov; Methow Valley Visitor Center, 509/996-4000.

42 EARLY WINTERS

Scenic rating: 6

in Okanogan-Wenatchee National Forest

Map 3.2, page 174

Located on each side of the highway, this campground has an unusual configuration. The confluence of Early Winters Creek and the Methow River mark the site of this campground. The elevation is 2,160 feet. You'll find great views of Goat Wall here. Campsites are flat, and the open landscape, set in a sparse lodgepole pine and fir forest, provides an arid feel to the area. Several hiking trails can be found within five miles, including one that leads south to Cedar Creek Falls. Other possible side trips include Goat Wall to the north and the town of Winthrop to the south, which boasts a historical museum, a state fish hatchery, and Pearrygin Lake State Park.

Campsites, facilities: There are 12 sites for tents or RVs up to 24 feet long. Picnic tables and fire grills are provided. Drinking water, vault toilets, and garbage bins are available. There is a small store and snack bar in Mazama, about two miles away. Some facilities are wheelchair accessible. Leashed pets are permitted.

Reservations, fees: Reservations are not accepted. Sites are $8 per night for one vehicle, $5 per each additional vehicle per night. Open mid-May-October, weather permitting.

Directions: From Burlington, drive east on Highway 20 for 116 miles to the campground (if you reach County Road 1163 near Mazama, you have gone two miles too far).

Contact: Okanogan-Wenatchee National Forest, Methow Valley Ranger District, 509/996-4003, www.fs.usda.gov; Methow Valley Visitor Center, 509/996-4000.

43 KLIPCHUCK

Scenic rating: 7

in Okanogan-Wenatchee National Forest

Map 3.2, page 174

This camp is located at an elevation of 3,000 feet along Early Winters Creek. The camp area is set amid majestic trees, primarily Douglas fir and subalpine firs. Klipchuck provides hiking aplenty, but note that rattlesnakes are occasionally seen in this area. A short loop trail from the camp leads about five miles up and over Delancy Ridge to Driveway Butte and down to the creek, although the trail is somewhat overgrown. Another trail starts nearby on Forest Road 200 (Sandy Butte-Cedar Creek Road) and goes two miles up Cedar Creek to lovely Cedar Creek Falls. Still another option from the campground is a four-mile trail along Early Winters Creek. This region is best visited in the spring and fall, with summer hot and dry.

Campsites, facilities: There are 46 sites for tents or RVs up to 34 feet long. Sites can be combined to accommodate groups. Picnic tables and fire grills are provided. Drinking water, vault toilets, and garbage bins are available. Some facilities are wheelchair accessible. Leashed pets are permitted.

Reservations, fees: Reservations are not accepted. Sites are $12 per night for one vehicle, $5 per each additional vehicle per night. Open late May-late September, weather permitting.

Directions: From Burlington, drive east on Highway 20 for 115 miles to Forest Road 300. (If you reach the Methow River Valley, you have gone four miles past the turnoff.) Turn left (marked) and drive northwest one mile to the camp at the end of the road. The camp is 19 miles northwest of Winthrop.

Contact: Okanogan-Wenatchee National Forest, Methow Valley Ranger District, 509/996-4003, www.fs.usda.gov; Methow Valley Visitor Center, 509/996-4000.

44 LONE FIR

Scenic rating: 9

in Okanogan-Wenatchee National Forest

Map 3.2, page 174

Lone Fir is set at 3,640 feet elevation along the banks of Early Winters Creek. A loop trail through the campground woods is wheelchair accessible for 0.4 mile. The area has had some timber operations in the past, but there are no nearby clear-cuts. To the west, Washington Pass Overlook offers a spectacular view. Anglers can fish in the creek, and many hiking and biking trails crisscross the area, including the trailhead for Cutthroat Lake. Other possible side trips include Goat Wall to the north and the town of Winthrop to the south, which boasts a historical museum, a state fish hatchery, and Pearrygin Lake State Park.

Campsites, facilities: There are 27 sites for tents or RVs up to 36 feet long. Picnic tables and fire grills are provided. Drinking water, vault toilets, and garbage bins are available. Some facilities are wheelchair accessible. Leashed pets are permitted.

Reservations, fees: Reservations are not accepted. Sites are $12 per night for one vehicle, $5 per each additional vehicle per night. Open late June-September, weather permitting.

Directions: From Burlington, drive east on Highway 20 for 107 miles to the campground (11 miles west of Mazama) on the right.

Contact: Okanogan-Wenatchee National

Forest, Methow Valley Ranger District, 509/996-4003, www.fs.usda.gov; Methow Valley Visitor Center, 509/996-4000.

45 CAMP FOUR

🚶 🚵 ⛵ 🎣 🐎 ♿ 🚐 ⛺

Scenic rating: 6
in Okanogan-Wenatchee National Forest

Map 3.2, page 174

Camp Four is the smallest and most primitive of the three camps along the Chewuch River (the others are Chewuch and Falls Creek). It is set at an elevation of 2,400 feet. Trailers are not recommended. There are three trailheads five miles north of camp: two at Lake Creek and another at Andrews Creek. They all have corrals, hitching rails, truck docks, and water for stock at the trailheads, but no livestock are permitted in the campground itself. Trails leading into the Pasayten Wilderness leave from both locations.

Campsites, facilities: There are three tent sites and two sites for tents or RVs up to 16 feet long. Fire grills and picnic tables are provided. Vault toilets are available, but there is no drinking water. Garbage must be packed out. Some facilities are wheelchair accessible. Leashed pets are permitted, but no livestock are permitted in camp.

Reservations, fees: Reservations are not accepted. Sites are $8 per night for one vehicle, $5 per each additional vehicle per night. Open late May-October, weather permitting.

Directions: From Burlington, drive east on Highway 20 for 134 miles to Winthrop and County Road 1213/West Chewuch Road. Turn north on County Road 1213/West Chewuch Road and drive 6.5 miles (where it merges with Forest Road 51). Continue north on Forest Road 51 for 11 miles to the campground on the right.

Contact: Okanogan-Wenatchee National Forest, Methow Valley Ranger District, 509/996-4003, www.fs.usda.gov; Methow Valley Visitor Center, 509/996-4000.

46 HONEYMOON

🚶 🐎 ♿ 🚐 ⛺

Scenic rating: 8
in Okanogan-Wenatchee National Forest

Map 3.2, page 174

This small camp is set along Eightmile Creek at an elevation of 3,280 feet. If you continue north seven miles to the end of Forest Road 5130, you'll reach a trailhead that provides access to the Pasayten Wilderness. Why is it named Honeymoon? Well, it seems that a forest ranger and his bride chose this quiet and secluded spot along the creek to spend their wedding night.

Campsites, facilities: There are five sites for tents or small RVs up to 18 feet long. Picnic tables and fire grills are provided. Vault toilets are available, but there is no drinking water. Garbage must be packed out. Some facilities are wheelchair accessible. Leashed pets are permitted.

Reservations, fees: Reservations are not accepted. Sites are $8 per night for one vehicle, $5 per each additional vehicle per night. Open late May-September, weather permitting.

Directions: From Burlington, drive east on Highway 20 for 134 miles to Winthrop and County Road 1213/West Chewuch Road. Turn north on County Road 1213/West Chewuch Road and drive 6.5 miles (where it merges with Forest Road 5130). Continue north on Forest Road 5130 for 10 miles to the campground on the right.

Contact: Okanogan-Wenatchee National Forest, Methow Valley Ranger District, 509/996-4003, www.fs.usda.gov; Methow Valley Visitor Center, 509/996-4000.

47 CHEWUCH

🚶 🚵 ⛵ 🎣 🐎 ♿ 🚐 ⛺

Scenic rating: 6
in Okanogan-Wenatchee National Forest

Map 3.2, page 174

Chewuch Camp is set along the Chewuch River at an elevation of 2,278 feet and is surrounded by ponderosa pines. It is a small camp where catch-and-release fishing is a highlight. There are also hiking and biking trails in the area. By traveling north, you can access trailheads that lead into the Pasayten Wilderness. This camp provides an alternative to the more developed nearby Falls Creek Campground.

Campsites, facilities: There are 16 sites for tents or RVs up to 35 feet long. Picnic tables and fire grills are provided. Drinking water, vault toilets, and garbage bins are available. Some facilities are wheelchair accessible. Leashed pets are permitted.

Reservations, fees: Reservations are not accepted. Sites are $12 per night for one vehicle, $5 per each additional vehicle per night. Open late May-November, weather permitting.

Directions: From Burlington, drive east on Highway 20 for 134 miles to Winthrop and County Road 1213/West Chewuch Road. Turn north on County Road 1213/West Chewuch Road and drive 6.5 miles (where it merges with Forest Road 51). Continue north on Forest Road 51 for seven miles to the campground on the right.

Contact: Okanogan-Wenatchee National Forest, Methow Valley Ranger District, 509/996-4003, www.fs.usda.gov; Methow Valley Visitor Center, 509/996-4000.

48 FLAT
Scenic rating: 6
in Okanogan-Wenatchee National Forest

Map 3.2, page 174

This campground is set along Eightmile Creek, two miles from where it empties into the Chewuch River. The elevation is 2,858 feet. Buck Lake is about three miles away. This is the closest of six camps to County Road 1213. Other options include Honeymoon, Nice, and Falls Creek.

Campsites, facilities: There are 12 sites for tents or RVs up to 36 feet long. Picnic tables and fire grills are provided. Vault toilets and

drinking water are available. Garbage must be packed out. Some facilities are wheelchair accessible. Leashed pets are permitted.

Reservations, fees: Reservations are not accepted. Sites are $8 per night for one vehicle, $5 per each additional vehicle per night. Open early May-November, weather permitting.

Directions: From Burlington, drive east on Highway 20 for 134 miles to Winthrop and County Road 1213 (West Chewuch Road). Turn north on West Chewuch Road and drive 6.5 miles (the road becomes Forest Road 51). Continue on Forest Road 51 and drive three miles to Forest Road 5130 (Eightmile Creek Road). Turn left (northwest) and drive two miles to the campground on the left.

Contact: Okanogan-Wenatchee National Forest, Methow Valley Ranger District, 509/996-4003, www.fs.usda.gov; Methow Valley Visitor Center, 509/996-4000.

49 FALLS CREEK
Scenic rating: 7
in Okanogan-Wenatchee National Forest

Map 3.2, page 174

About a 20-minute drive out of Winthrop, Falls Creek is a quiet and pretty campground located at the confluence of its namesake, Falls Creek, and the Chewuch River. The elevation is 2,100 feet. Highlights include fishing access and a 0.25-mile trail (wheelchair accessible) to a waterfall located across the road from the campground.

Campsites, facilities: There are seven sites for tents or RVs up to 18 feet long. Picnic tables and fire grills are provided. Vault toilets and drinking water are available. Garbage must be packed out. Some facilities are wheelchair accessible. Leashed pets are permitted.

Reservations, fees: Reservations are not accepted. Sites are $8 per night for one vehicle, $5 per each additional vehicle per night. Open May-late September, weather permitting.

Directions: From Burlington, drive east on

Highway 20 for 134 miles to Winthrop and County Road 1213 (West Chewuch Road). Turn north on West Chewuch Road and drive 6.5 miles (becomes Forest Road 51). Continue on Forest Road 51 and drive 5.2 miles to the campground on the right. Obtaining a U.S. Forest Service map is advised.

Contact: Okanogan-Wenatchee National Forest, Methow Valley Ranger District, 509/996-4003, www.fs.usda.gov; Methow Valley Visitor Center, 509/996-4000.

50 NICE

Scenic rating: 6
in Okanogan-Wenatchee National Forest

Map 3.2, page 174

Nice is situated along Eightmile Creek, about four miles from Buck Lake. Youngsters will enjoy exploring a nearby beaver pond. A trail leading into the Pasayten Wilderness can be found at the end of Forest Road 5130. Pearrygin Lake State Park is just a few miles to the south, near Winthrop. Note: There is no turnaround area for RVs.

Campsites, facilities: There are three sites for tents or RVs up to 35 feet. Picnic tables and fire grills are provided. Vault toilets are available, but there is no drinking water. Garbage must be packed out. Some facilities are wheelchair accessible. Leashed pets are permitted.

Reservations, fees: Reservations are not accepted. Sites are $8 per night for one vehicle, $5 per each additional vehicle per night. Open late May-late September, weather permitting.

Directions: From Burlington, drive east on Highway 20 for 134 miles to Winthrop and County Road 1213 (West Chewuch Road). Turn north on West Chewuch Road and drive 6.5 miles (the road becomes Forest Road 51). Continue on Forest Road 51 and drive three miles to Forest Road 5130 (Eightmile Creek Road). Turn left (northwest) and drive four miles to the campground on the left.

Contact: Okanogan-Wenatchee National Forest, Methow Valley Ranger District, 509/996-4003, www.fs.usda.gov; Methow Valley Visitor Center, 509/996-4000.

51 PEARRYGIN LAKE STATE PARK

Scenic rating: 8
on Pearrygin Lake

Map 3.2, page 174   **BEST(**

Pearrygin Lake is fed from underground springs and Pearrygin Creek, the lifeblood for this setting and the adjacent 1,185-acre state park. Located in the beautiful Methow Valley, it's ringed by the Northern Cascade Mountains. The park is known for its expansive green lawns, which lead to 11,000 feet of waterfront and sandy beaches. The camp is frequented by red-winged and yellow-headed blackbirds, as well as by marmots. Wildflower- and wildlife-viewing are excellent in the spring. The campground has access to a sandy beach and facilities for swimming, boating, waterskiing, fishing, and hiking. The sites are set close together and don't offer much privacy, but they are spacious and shaded, and a variety of recreation options make it worth the crunch.

Campsites, facilities: There are 76 tent sites, 50 sites with full hookups (15 and 30 amp), and 27 sites with partial hookups for tents or RVs up to 60 feet long. There are also two hike-in/bike-in sites, two cabins, a vacation house, and two group sites for up to 48 and 80 people each. Picnic tables and fire grills are provided. Restrooms with flush toilets and coin showers, drinking water, a dump station, firewood, Junior Ranger program, horseshoe pits, swimming beach, and volleyball court are available. A store, deli, and ice are located within one mile. Boat launching and dock facilities and boat rentals are available. Some facilities are wheelchair accessible. Leashed pets are permitted.

Reservations, fees: Reservations are accepted and are required for group camps, cabins, and the vacation house at 888/226-7688 or https://washington.goingtocamp.com ($8-10 reservation fee). Tent sites are $20-35 per night, RV sites with partial hookups are $25-40 per night, RV sites with full hookups are $30-45 per night, $10 per extra vehicle per night, hike-in/bike-in sites are $12 per night. Cabins are $69-79 per night. Call for rates for the group sites and the vacation house. Some credit cards are accepted. Open April-early November.

Directions: From Winthrop and Highway 20, drive north through town (road changes to East Chewuch Road). Continue 1.5 miles north from town to Bear Creek Road. Turn right and drive 1.5 miles to the end of the pavement and the park entrance on the right. Turn right, drive over the cattle guard, and continue 0.75 mile to the West Campground or 1.5 miles to the East Campground.

Contact: Pearrygin Lake State Park, 509/996-2370, http://parks.state.wa.us.

52 KOA WINTHROP

🚴 🏊 🛶 🚙 🐎 🎿 ♿ 🚐 ⛺

Scenic rating: 7

on the Methow River

Map 3.2, page 174

Here's another campground set along the Methow River, which offers opportunities for fishing, boating, swimming, and rafting. The park has a free shuttle into Winthrop, an interesting town with many restored, early-1900s buildings lining the main street. One such building, the Shafer Museum, displays an array of period items. If you would like to observe wildlife, take a short, two-mile drive southeast out of Winthrop on County Road 9129 on the east side of the Methow River. Turn east on County Road 1631 into Davis Lake and follow the signs to the Methow River Habitat Management Area Headquarters. Depending on the time of year, you may see mule deer, porcupines, bobcats, mountain lions, snowshoe hares, black bears, red squirrels, and many species of birds. If you're looking for something

tamer, other nearby recreation options include an 18-hole golf course and tennis courts.

Campsites, facilities: There are 60 sites with full or partial hookups and 15 sites with no hookups for RVs of any length plus 35 tent sites. Some sites are pull-through. There are also 20 one- and two-room cabins. Picnic tables and fire grills are provided. Restrooms with flush toilets and showers, drinking water, firewood, a dump station, recreation hall, high-speed modem and Wi-Fi access, bike and video rentals, a convenience store, coin laundry, ice, a playground, and a seasonal heated swimming pool are available. Propane gas and a café are located within one mile. There is a courtesy shuttle to and from Winthrop. Some facilities are wheelchair accessible. Leashed pets are permitted.

Reservations, fees: Reservations are accepted at 800/562-2158. RV sites with full hookups are $47-53 per night, RV sites with partial hookups are $42-47 per night, tent sites are $35-40 per night, cabins are $60-135 per night, $3-8 per person per night for more than two people. Some credit cards are accepted. Open mid-April-October.

Directions: From Winthrop, drive east on Highway 20 for one mile to the camp on the left. The camp is between Mileposts 194 and 195.

Contact: KOA Winthrop, 509/996-2258, www.koa.com.

53 BIG TWIN LAKE CAMPGROUND

🚶 🚴 🏊 🛶 🚤 🐎 🎿 ♿ 🚐 ⛺

Scenic rating: 5

on Big Twin Lake

Map 3.2, page 174

As you might figure from the name, this campground is set along the shore of Big Twin Lake. With its sweeping lawn and shade trees, the camp features views of the lake from all campsites. No gas motors are permitted on the lake. Fly-fishing is good for rainbow trout, with special regulations in effect: one-fish limit, single barbless hook, artificial lures only. This is an ideal lake for a float tube, rowboat with a casting platform, or a pram. A short drive out of Winthrop (County Road 9129) leads to the Methow River Habitat Management Area Headquarters. Depending on the time of year, you may see mule deer, porcupines, bobcats, mountain lions, snowshoe hares, black bears, red squirrels, and many species of birds. Other recreation options include an 18-hole golf course and tennis courts.

Campsites, facilities: There are 50 sites with full or partial hookups for RVs of any length, and 35 tent sites. Some sites are pull-through. Picnic tables and fire grills are provided. Restrooms with flush toilets and coin showers, drinking water, a dump station, firewood, ice, Wi-Fi, and a playground are available. Boat docks, launching facilities, and boat rentals are on Big Twin Lake. Some facilities are wheelchair accessible. Leashed pets are permitted.

Reservations, fees: Reservations are accepted. RV sites are $34 per night, tent sites are $25 per night, $7 per person per night for more than two people, $7 per extra vehicle per night. Monthly rates are available. Open mid-April-October.

Directions: From Winthrop, drive east on Highway 20 for three miles to Twin Lakes Road. Turn right (west) on Twin Lakes Road and drive two miles to the campground on the right.

Contact: Big Twin Lake Campground, 509/996-2650, www.methownet.com/bigtwin.

54 ROADS END

Scenic rating: 8

in Okanogan-Wenatchee National Forest

Map 3.2, page 174

This quiet trailhead camp is located at the end of Twisp River Road. Set at an elevation of 3,600 feet along the Twisp River, it features a major trailhead that provides fishing access and a chance to hike for mountain views and explore the Lake Chelan-Sawtooth Wilderness. The trail intersects with Copper Creek Trail and the Pacific Crest Trail about nine miles from the camp. A U.S. Forest Service map is essential. Note that this camp is closed in the off-season to protect bull trout, an endangered species.

Campsites, facilities: There are four sites for tents or small RVs up to 16 feet long. Picnic tables and fire grills are provided. Vault toilets are available. There is no drinking water, and garbage must be packed out. Some facilities are wheelchair accessible. Leashed pets are permitted.

Reservations, fees: Reservations are not accepted. Sites are $8 per night for one vehicle, $5 per each additional vehicle per night. Open late May-early September, weather permitting.

Directions: From Burlington, drive east on Highway 20 for 145 miles to Twisp and County Road 9114 (Twisp River Road). Turn west on County Road 9114 and drive 11 miles (becomes Forest Road 44, then eventually Forest Road 4440). Continue west for 13.5 miles to the campground. Obtaining a U.S. Forest Service map is advisable.

Contact: Okanogan-Wenatchee National Forest, Methow Valley Ranger District, 509/996-4003, www.fs.usda.gov; Methow Valley Visitor Center, 509/996-4000.

55 SOUTH CREEK

Scenic rating: 6

in Okanogan-Wenatchee National Forest

Map 3.2, page 174

Although small, quiet, and little known, South Creek Campground packs a wallop with good recreation options. It's set at the confluence of the Twisp River and South Creek at a major trailhead that accesses the Lake Chelan-Sawtooth Wilderness. The South Creek Trailhead provides a hike to Louis Lake. The elevation at the camp is 3,100 feet.

Campsites, facilities: There are four sites for

tents or RVs up to 24 feet long. Picnic tables and fire grills are provided. A vault toilet is available. There is no drinking water, and garbage must be packed out. Some facilities are wheelchair accessible. Leashed pets are permitted.

Reservations, fees: Reservations are not accepted. Sites are $8 per night for one vehicle, $5 per each additional vehicle per night. Open late May-September, weather permitting.

Directions: From Burlington, drive east on Highway 20 for 145 miles to Twisp and County Road 9114 (Twisp River Road). Turn right on County Road 9114 and drive 17.5 miles (becomes Forest Road 44). Continue west (becomes Forest Road 4440 and a dirt road) for 4.5 miles to the campground on the left.

Contact: Okanogan-Wenatchee National Forest, Methow Valley Ranger District, 509/996-4003, www.fs.usda.gov; Methow Valley Visitor Center, 509/996-4000.

56 POPLAR FLAT

Scenic rating: 7

in Okanogan-Wenatchee National Forest

Map 3.2, page 174

This campground is set at 2,900 feet elevation along the Twisp River. This area provides many wildlife-viewing opportunities for deer, black bears, and many species of birds. Several trails in the area, including Twisp River Trail, follow streams and some provide access to the Lake Chelan-Sawtooth Wilderness.

Campsites, facilities: There are 16 sites for tents or RVs up to 22 feet long including a group site for up to 12 people. Picnic tables and fire grills are provided. Drinking water, vault toilets, and garbage bins are available. A day-use picnic area with a shelter is nearby. Some facilities are wheelchair accessible. Leashed pets are permitted.

Reservations, fees: Reservations are not accepted. Sites are $12 per night for one vehicle, $5 per each additional vehicle per night. Open mid-May-September, weather permitting.

Directions: From Burlington, drive east on Highway 20 for 145 miles to Twisp and County Road 9114 (Twisp River Road). Turn west on County Road 9114 and drive 11 miles (becomes Forest Road 44 and then Forest Road 4440). Continue west for 9.5 miles to the campground on the left.

Contact: Okanogan-Wenatchee National Forest, Methow Valley Ranger District, 509/996-4003, www.fs.usda.gov; Methow Valley Visitor Center, 509/996-4000.

57 WEAVER POINT BOAT-IN

Scenic rating: 7

on Lake Chelan in North Cascades National Park

Map 3.2, page 174

The largest campground in the Stehekin area, this boat-in campground on Lake Chelan gets high use on summer weekends. The only direct access to Stehekin is by boat or an 8.5-mile hike to Stehekin Landing from the campground; a shuttle is also available for the first four miles. It's a fairly easy tromp, with no steep grades.

Campsites, facilities: There are 22 sites accessible only by boat, ferry, or floatplane. Picnic tables and fire grills are provided. Drinking water and vault toilets are available. Garbage must be packed out. Food storage lockers are available and must be used. One dock is available for boats.

Reservations, fees: Reservations are not accepted. There is no fee for camping. There is no entrance fee for North Cascades National Park. There is a $5 per day docking fee (or $40 annual pass). Open year-round, with limited facilities in winter.

Directions: From Wenatchee, drive on U.S. 97 for approximately 40 miles to Chelan and the ferry. Take the ferry and proceed to Weaver Point.

Contact: North Cascades National Park, 360/856-5700, www.nps.gov/noca; Lake

Chelan Boat Company, 509/682-4584, www.ladyofthelake.com.

58 TWISP RIVER HORSE CAMP

🚶🐎♿🚐⛰

Scenic rating: 7

in Okanogan-Wenatchee National Forest

Map 3.2, page 174

This camp is only for horses and their owners. It is set on the Twisp River at an elevation of 3,000 feet. The camp features nearby access to trails, including North Fork Twisp River Trail, which leads to Copper Pass, and South Fork Twisp River Trail, which leads to Lake Chelan National Recreation Area and Twisp Pass. South Creek Trail is also available and leads from the camp to Lake Chelan National Recreation Area.

Campsites, facilities: There are 12 sites for tents or RVs up to 30 feet long. Picnic tables and fire grills are provided. Vault toilets are available. There is no drinking water, and garbage must be packed out. For horses, a loading ramp, hitching rails, and feed stations are available. Some facilities are wheelchair accessible. Leashed pets are permitted.

Reservations, fees: Reservations are not accepted. A Northwest Forest Pass ($5 daily fee or $30 annual fee per parked vehicle) is required. Open May-September, weather permitting.

Directions: From Burlington, drive east on Highway 20 for 145 miles to Twisp and County Road 9114 (Twisp River Road). Turn west on County Road 9114 and drive 11 miles (becomes Forest Road 44). Continue west on Forest Road 44 for 3.5 miles to War Creek Campground on the left. Continue 250 yards to Forest Road 4430. Turn left (drive over the bridge) and drive approximately nine miles (the road becomes Forest Road 4435) to the campground on the right.

Contact: Okanogan-Wenatchee National Forest, Methow Valley Ranger District, 509/996-4003, www.fs.usda.gov; Methow Valley Visitor Center, 509/996-4000.

59 WAR CREEK

🚶🏊🐎♿🚐⛰

Scenic rating: 6

in Okanogan-Wenatchee National Forest

Map 3.2, page 174

This trailhead camp is set at 2,400 feet elevation and provides several routes into the Lake Chelan-Sawtooth Wilderness. War Creek Trail, Eagle Creek Trail, and Oval Creek Trail all offer wilderness access and trout fishing. Backpackers can extend this trip into Lake Chelan National Recreation Area, for a 15-mile trek that finishes at the shore of Lake Chelan and the National Park Service outpost. Rattlesnakes are occasionally spotted in this region in the summer.

Campsites, facilities: There are 10 sites for tents or RVs up to 22 feet long. Picnic tables and fire grills are provided. Vault toilets, hand-pumped drinking water, and firewood are available. Garbage must be packed out. Some facilities are wheelchair accessible. Leashed pets are permitted.

Reservations, fees: Reservations are not accepted. Sites are $8 per night for one vehicle, $5 per each additional vehicle per night. Open May-October, weather permitting.

Directions: From Burlington, drive east on Highway 20 for 145 miles to Twisp and County Road 9114 (Twisp River Road). Turn west on County Road 9114 and drive 11 miles (becomes Forest Road 44). Continue west on Forest Road 44 for 3.5 miles to the campground on the left.

Contact: Okanogan-Wenatchee National Forest, Methow Valley Ranger District, 509/996-4003, www.fs.usda.gov; Methow Valley Visitor Center, 509/996-4000.

60 BLACKPINE LAKE

Scenic rating: 7

on Blackpine Lake in Okanogan-Wenatchee National Forest

Map 3.2, page 174

This campground features great views of some local peaks. About one-third of the campsites have views; the rest are set in a forest of Douglas fir and ponderosa pine. This popular spot often fills up on summer weekends and occasionally even during the week. Fishing is available for stocked rainbow trout. Note that boating is permitted, but no gas motors are allowed, only electric motors. Less than 0.25 mile long, an interpretive trail leads around the north end of the lake.

Campsites, facilities: There are 23 sites for tents or RVs up to 30 feet long. Picnic tables and fire grills are provided. Drinking water, vault toilets, and garbage bins are available. A boat launch and two floating docks are available nearby. Some facilities are wheelchair accessible. Leashed pets are permitted.

Reservations, fees: Reservations are not accepted. Sites are $12 per night, $5 per each additional vehicle per night. Open May-September, weather permitting.

Directions: From Burlington, drive east on Highway 20 for 145 miles to Twisp and County Road 9114 (Twisp River Road). Turn west on County Road 9114 and drive 10 miles to County Road 1090. Turn left and drive over a bridge (becomes Forest Road 43) and continue eight miles to the campground on the right.

Contact: Okanogan-Wenatchee National Forest, Methow Valley Ranger District, 509/996-4003, www.fs.usda.gov; Methow Valley Visitor Center, 509/996-4000.

61 RIVERBEND RV PARK

Scenic rating: 6

on the Methow River

Map 3.2, page 174

The shore of the Methow River skirts this campground, and there is a nice separate area for tent campers set right along the river. Some of the RV sites are also riverfront. Trout fishing, river rafting, and swimming are popular here. The nearby Methow River Habitat Management Area Headquarters offers wildlife-viewing for mule deer, porcupines, bobcats, mountain lions, snowshoe hares, black bears, red squirrels, and many species of birds. Other recreation options include an 18-hole golf course and tennis courts.

Campsites, facilities: There are 69 sites with full hookups (20, 30, and 50 amps) for RVs of any length and 35 sites for tents. Some sites are pull-through. Picnic tables and fire pits are provided. Restrooms with flush toilets and coin showers, an RV dump station, firewood, a convenience store, coin laundry, ice, a playground, horseshoe pits, a basketball court, propane gas, Wi-Fi access, group picnic shelter, and RV storage are available. Groups can be accommodated. Leashed pets are permitted.

Reservations, fees: Reservations are recommended at 800/686-4498. RV sites start at $35 per night, tent sites start at $27 per night, $5-7 per person per night for more than two people, $5 per night per extra vehicle, and $5 per pet. Weekly and monthly rates are available. Some credit cards are accepted. Open year-round.

Directions: From Twisp, drive west on Highway 20 for two miles to the park on the right, between Mileposts 199 and 200.

Contact: Riverbend RV Park, 509/997-3500 or 800/686-4498, www.riverbendrv.com.

62 PRINCE CREEK

Scenic rating: 10

on Lake Chelan in Wenatchee National Forest

Map 3.2, page 174

This camp is set along the east shore of Lake Chelan at the mouth of Prince Creek, 18 miles south of Stehekin on Trail 1247. It's a busy camp on summer weekends. A trail from camp follows Prince Creek into the Lake Chelan-Sawtooth Wilderness and then connects to a network of other trails, all of which lead to various lakes and streams. Be prepared to protect food from bears; use bear-proof food hangs or the on-site bear box provided. The elevation is 1,100 feet.

Campsites, facilities: There are six tent sites accessible only by boat, ferry, or floatplane. Picnic tables and fire rings are provided. Vault toilets are available, but there is no drinking water. Garbage must be packed out. A floating dock can accommodate about three boats.

Reservations, fees: Reservations are not accepted. There is no fee for camping. There is a $5 per day docking fee (or $40 annual pass) when bringing a private boat. Open May-mid-November, weather permitting.

Directions: From Wenatchee, drive on U.S. 97-A about 40 miles to Chelan and the ferry. Take the ferry and proceed to Prince Creek, 35 miles from Chelan. Note that the ferry will not stop here if water level does not allow for safe landing, which sometimes occurs in the early spring.

Contact: Okanogan and Wenatchee National Forest, Chelan Ranger District, 509/682-4900, www.fs.usda.gov; Lake Chelan Boat Company, 509/682-4584, www.ladyofthelake.com.

63 FOGGY DEW

Scenic rating: 6

in Okanogan-Wenatchee National Forest

Map 3.2, page 174

This private, remote campground is set at the confluence of Foggy Dew Creek and the North Fork of Old Creek. The elevation is 2,400 feet. Several trails for hiking and horseback riding nearby provide access to various backcountry lakes and streams. To get to the trailheads, follow the forest roads near camp. Bicycles are allowed on Trails 417, 429, and 431. There is also access to a motorcycle-use area.

Campsites, facilities: There are 12 sites for tents or RVs up to 25 feet long. Picnic tables and fire grills are provided. Vault toilets are available. There is no drinking water, and garbage must be packed out. Some facilities are wheelchair accessible. Leashed pets are permitted.

Reservations, fees: Reservations are not accepted. Sites are $8 per night for one vehicle, $5 per each additional vehicle per night. Open late May-September, weather permitting.

Directions: From Burlington, drive east on Highway 20 for 145 miles to Twisp. Continue east on Highway 20 for three miles to Highway 153. Turn south on Highway 153 and drive 12 miles to County Road 1029 (Gold Creek Road). Turn right (south) and drive one mile to Forest Road 4340. Turn right (west) and drive four miles to the campground on the left.

Contact: Okanogan-Wenatchee National Forest, Methow Valley Ranger District, 509/996-4003, www.fs.usda.gov; Methow Valley Visitor Center, 509/996-4000.

64 PHELPS CREEK AND EQUESTRIAN

Scenic rating: 7

in Wenatchee National Forest

Map 3.2, page 174

These camps are set at an elevation of 2,800

feet at the confluence of Phelps Creek and the Chiwawa River. There's a key trailhead for backpackers and horseback riders nearby that provides access to the Glacier Peak Wilderness and Spider Meadows. Phelps Creek Trail is routed out to Spider Meadows, a five-mile hike one-way, and Buck Creek Trail extends into the Glacier Peak Wilderness. The Chiwawa River is closed to fishing to protect endangered species. A U.S. Forest Service map is advisable.

Campsites, facilities: There are seven sites for tents or RVs up to 30 feet long at Phelps Creek and six sites for tents or RVs up to 30 feet long at Phelps Creek Equestrian. Picnic tables and fire grills are provided. Vault toilets are available. There is no drinking water, but stock water is available at Trinity Trailhead. Garbage must be packed out. Horse facilities, including loading ramps and high lines, are nearby. Leashed pets are permitted.

Reservations, fees: Reservations are not accepted. Sites are $14 per night for one vehicle, $10 per each additional vehicle. Open mid-June-October, weather permitting.

Directions: From I-5 and Everett, turn east on U.S. 2 and drive 87 miles to State Route 207. Turn north on State Route 207 and drive four miles to Chiwawa Loop Road. Turn right (east) on Chiwawa Loop Road and drive 1.4 miles to Chiwawa River Road (Forest Road 6200). Bear left (north) and continue for 23.6 miles to the campground (the last 12 miles of road are gravel).

Contact: Okanogan-Wenatchee National Forest, Wenatchee River Ranger District, Lake Wenatchee Ranger Station, 509/548-2550, www.fs.usda.gov.

65 DEER POINT BOAT-IN

Scenic rating: 9
on Lake Chelan in Wenatchee National Forest

Map 3.2, page 174

Here's another little-known spot set along the remote east shore of Lake Chelan. It provides good protection from down-lake winds but is exposed to up-lake winds. Anglers at Lake Chelan often use this spot as their boat-in camp headquarters. Be prepared to protect food from bears; use bear-proof food hangs or use the bear box that is on-site.

Campsites, facilities: There are five tent sites accessible only by boat, ferry, or floatplane. Picnic tables and fire rings are provided. Vault toilets are available. There is no drinking water, and garbage must be packed out. A floating dock can accommodate about eight boats.

Reservations, fees: Reservations are not accepted. There is no fee for camping. There is a $5 per day dock-site fee (or $40 annual pass) when bringing a private boat. For ferry rates, which vary according to boat and age of passenger, phone 509/682-4584; typically rates are in the $35-60 range round-trip. Open May-October, weather permitting.

Directions: From Wenatchee, drive north on U.S. 97 approximately 40 miles to Chelan and the ferry. Take the ferry and proceed to Deer Point (the ferry does not schedule a stop at this campground but will usually stop here if you request it in advance).

Contact: Okanogan-Wenatchee National Forest, Chelan Ranger District, 509/682-4900, www.fs.usda.gov; Lake Chelan Boat Company, 509/682-4584, www.ladyofthelake.com.

66 FLOWING LAKE PARK

Scenic rating: 6
near Snohomish

Map 3.3, page 175

This campground has a little something for everyone, including swimming, powerboating, waterskiing, and good fishing on Flowing Lake. The campsites are in a wooded setting (that is, no lake view), and it is a 0.25-mile walk to the beach. A one-mile nature trail is nearby. Note the private homes on the lake; all visitors are asked to respect the privacy of the owners.

Campsites, facilities: There are 42 sites,

most with partial hookups, for tents or RVs up to 40 feet; some sites are pull-through. Four cabins and four hike-in sites for tents only are also available. Picnic tables and fire grills are provided. Restrooms with flush toilets and coin showers, drinking water, and firewood are available. A picnic shelter, a fishing dock, launching facilities, swimming beach, playground, and amphitheater are available nearby. Some facilities are wheelchair accessible. Leashed pets are permitted.

Reservations, fees: Reservations are accepted. Sites are $28-40 per night, $10 per night for a second vehicle, cabins are $55-65 per night, pets are $10 per night. Open year-round with limited winter facilities.

Directions: From I-5 and Everett, take the Snohomish-Wenatchee exit and turn east on U.S. 2; drive to Milepost 10 and look for 100th Street SE (Westwick Road). Turn left and drive two miles (becomes 171st Avenue SE) to 48th Street SE. Turn right and drive about 0.5 mile into the park at the end of the road.

Contact: Flowing Lake County Park, 360/568-2274; Snohomish County Parks, 425/388-6600, https://snohomishcountywa.gov.

67 CUTTHROAT LAKES HIKE-IN

🏃 🏊 ⛵ 🐕 ⛺

Scenic rating: 9

on Bald Mountain

Map 3.3, page 175

Reaching this spot is worth the effort. After hiking in 4.5 miles, you'll find beautiful lakeside camps, trout fishing, and hiking. The "lakes" are actually small ponds, but they're very pretty. No campfires are allowed; backpacking stoves are required for cooking. DNR pleads: "Please stay on the trails."

Campsites, facilities: There are five tent sites at this primitive, hike-in campground. Campfires are not allowed. There is no drinking water and garbage must be packed out. Leashed pets are permitted.

Reservations, fees: Reservations are not accepted. There is no fee for camping. Open mid-June-October, weather permitting.

Directions: From I-5 and Everett, turn east on U.S. 2 and drive five miles to Highway 9. Turn north and drive four miles to Highway 92. Turn east on Highway 92 and drive about 15 miles to the town of Granite Falls and Mountain Loop Highway. Continue northeast on Mountain Loop for 18 miles to Forest Road 4030 (at the bridge). Turn right (south) and drive for three miles to Forest Road 4032 (follow the Mallardy Ridge signs). Bear right and take Forest Road 4032 for one mile to the end, where the Bailey Trailhead begins. Hike 4.5 miles to Cutthroat Lakes.

Contact: Department of Natural Resources, Northwest Region, 360/856-3500, www.dnr.wa.gov.

68 LITTLE GREIDER LAKE HIKE-IN

🏃 🏊 ⛵ 🐕 ⛺

Scenic rating: 10

on Little Greider Lake

Map 3.3, page 175

This is prime country for hiking, backpacking, and trout fishing, and the rangers ask that you stay on trails and avoid walking through meadows and wetlands. The primitive, wooded campground is on Little Greider Lake. Similar to the Big Greider camp, pretty Little Greider gets more use. But hey, the truth is that in this area, Boulder Lake is the most desirable spot of all.

Campsites, facilities: There are six tent sites at this primitive, hike-in campground. Fire grills are provided. There is no drinking water and garbage must be packed out. Leashed pets are permitted.

Reservations, fees: Reservations are not accepted. There is no fee for camping. Open mid-June-October, weather permitting.

Directions: From I-5 and Everett, turn east on U.S. 2 and drive 24 miles to Sultan. Continue

0.5 mile east to Sultan Basin Road. Turn left (north) on Sultan Basin Road and drive 13.6 miles to Olney Pass, where all vehicles must register. Continue to a fork in the road and Road SLS 4000. Bear right on Road SLS 4000 and drive 6.5 miles. Note that the road to the Greider Lake Trailhead has been decommissioned. From the trailhead, the hike is now 4.5 miles to the campground.

Contact: Department of Natural Resources, Northwest Region, 360/856-3500, www.dnr. wa.gov.

69 BIG GREIDER LAKE HIKE-IN

Scenic rating: 10

on Big Greider Lake

Map 3.3, page 175

This primitive campground on Big Greider Lake is a hideaway in a gorgeous setting, set at the base of a large rock basin. Although campers are few, a lot of day hikers do make the three-mile tromp to the lake. DNR pleads: "Please stay on the trails." The landscape features subalpine terrain. Fishing is an option. This camp provides an alternative to Little Greider Lake Campground, adjacent to Little Greider Lake.

Campsites, facilities: There are three tent sites at this primitive, hike-in campground. Fire grills are provided. There is no drinking water and garbage must be packed out. Leashed pets are permitted.

Reservations, fees: Reservations are not accepted. There is no fee for camping. Open mid-June-October, weather permitting.

Directions: From I-5 and Everett, turn east on U.S. 2 and drive 24 miles to Sultan. Continue 0.5 mile east to Sultan Basin Road. Turn left (north) on Sultan Basin Road and drive 13.6 miles to Olney Pass, where all vehicles must register. Continue to a fork in the road and Road SLS 4000. Bear right on Road SLS 4000 and drive 6.5 miles. Note that the road to the Greider Lake Trailhead has been decommissioned. From the trailhead, the hike is now five miles to the campground.

Contact: Department of Natural Resources, Northwest Region, 360/856-3500, www.dnr. wa.gov.

70 WALLACE FALLS STATE PARK WALK-IN

Scenic rating: 8

near Gold Bar

Map 3.3, page 175   BEST (

This 4,735-acre park is extremely busy on summer days. The centerpiece is its namesake 265-foot waterfall, but there is also plenty of shoreline along the Wallace and Skykomish Rivers, as well as Wallace, Jay, and Shaw Lakes. (Note that cougars have been spotted near Wallace Falls.) The campground is located in a heavily treed area at the trailhead to the falls. The trail leads along the Wallace River and is a lovely hike. The park has 12 miles of hiking trails, including a 0.25-mile interpretive trail, and five miles of biking trails. Nearby recreation options include fishing for trout and steelhead (in season), swimming, rafting, kayaking, and canoeing at Big Eddy Park, five miles east. Rock climbing is possible at Index Town Wall, 12 miles east.

Campsites, facilities: There are two walk-in tent sites and five cabins. Picnic tables and fire grills are provided. Restrooms with coin showers and flush toilets, drinking water, firewood, and interpretive activities are available. A picnic area with kitchen shelters is available nearby. Some facilities are wheelchair accessible. Leashed pets are permitted.

Reservations, fees: Reservations are not accepted for campsites but are required for cabins at 888/226-7688 or https://washington.goingto-camp.com ($8-10 reservation fee). Sites are $20-35 per night, $10 per extra vehicle per night, cabins are $45-69 per night (with pets, $15). Open year-round.

Directions: From I-5 and Everett, turn east on U.S. 2 and drive 28 miles to the town of Gold Bar and look for the sign for Wallace Falls State Park. Turn left (northeast) at the sign and drive two miles to the park.

Contact: Wallace Falls State Park, 360/793-0420, http://parks.state.wa.us.

71 MONEY CREEK CAMPGROUND

Scenic rating: 5
in Mount Baker-Snoqualmie National Forest

Map 3.3, page 175

You have a little surprise waiting for you here. Trains go by regularly day and night, and the first time it happens while you're in deep sleep, you might just launch a hole right through the top of your tent. The Burlington Northern rail runs along the western boundary of the campground. By now you've got the picture: This can be a noisy camp. Money Creek Campground is on the Skykomish River, with hiking trails a few miles away. The best of these is Dorothy Lake Trail.

Campsites, facilities: There are 24 sites, including two double sites, for tents or RVs up to 40 feet long. Picnic tables and fire grills are provided. Vault toilets, drinking water, garbage bins, and firewood are available. A store, café, and ice are located 3.5 miles to the east. Some facilities are wheelchair accessible. Leashed pets are permitted.

Reservations, fees: Reservations are accepted at 877/444-6777 ($10 reservation fee) or www. recreation.gov ($9 reservation fee). Single sites are $16-18 per night, double sites are $32-40 per night, $9 per extra vehicle per night. Open mid-May-mid-September, weather permitting.

Directions: From I-5 and Everett, turn east on U.S. 2 and drive 46 miles to Old Cascade

Highway, 11 miles east of Index. Turn right (south) on Old Cascade Highway and drive across the bridge to the campground.

Contact: Mount Baker-Snoqualmie National Forest, Skykomish Ranger District, 360/677-2414, www.fs.usda.gov or www.hoodoo.com.

72 BECKLER RIVER

Scenic rating: 7
in Mount Baker-Snoqualmie National Forest

Map 3.3, page 175

Located on the Beckler River at an elevation of 900 feet, this camp has scenic riverside sites in second-growth timber, primarily Douglas fir, cedar, and big-leaf maple. Fishing at the campground is poor; it's better well up the river. The Skykomish Ranger Station, which sells maps, is just a couple of miles away.

Campsites, facilities: There are 27 sites, including two double sites, for tents or RVs up to 40 feet long. Picnic tables and fire grills are provided. Vault toilets, drinking water, and firewood are available. A camp host is on-site. A store, café, and ice are located within two miles. Some facilities are wheelchair accessible. Leashed pets are permitted.

Reservations, fees: Reservations are accepted at 877/444-6777 ($10 reservation fee) or www. recreation.gov ($9 reservation fee). Single sites are $16 per night, double sites are $30 per night, $8 per extra vehicle per night. Open late May-early September, weather permitting.

Directions: From I-5 and Everett, turn east on U.S. 2 and drive 49 miles to Skykomish. Continue east on U.S. 2 for 0.5 mile to Forest Road 65. Turn left (north) on Forest Road 65 and drive 1.6 miles to the camp on the left.

Contact: Mount Baker-Snoqualmie National Forest, Skykomish Ranger District, 360/677-2414, www.fs.usda.gov or hoodoo.com.

73 MILLER RIVER GROUP

Scenic rating: 8

in Mount Baker-Snoqualmie National Forest

Map 3.3, page 175

This campground is located along the Miller River, a short distance from the boundary of the Alpine Lakes Wilderness. If you continue another seven miles on Forest Road 6410, you'll get to a trailhead leading to Dorothy Lake, a 1.5-mile hike. This pretty lake is two miles long. The trail continues past the lake to many other backcountry lakes. Backpackers must limit their party to no more than 12 people per group. A U.S. Forest Service map is essential. The camp host at nearby Money Creek oversees this campground.

Campsites, facilities: There is one reservable group camp for up to 100 people, plus 18 single sites, for tents or RVs up to 30 feet long. Picnic tables and fire grills are provided. Vault toilets, drinking water, and a group picnic area are available. A store, café, and ice are within five miles. Some facilities are wheelchair accessible. Leashed pets are permitted.

Reservations, fees: Reservations are accepted at 877/444-6777 ($10 reservation fee) or www.recreation.gov ($9 reservation fee). Single sites are $14 per night plus $7 extra vehicle fee. Group sites are $75 per night for up to 30 people, $125 per night for 31-75 people, and $150 per night for 76-100 people. Open mid-May-mid-September, weather permitting.

Directions: From I-5 and Everett, turn east on U.S. 2 and drive 46 miles to Old Cascade Highway, 11 miles east of Index. Turn right (south) on Old Cascade Highway (across the bridge) and drive one mile to Forest Road 6410. Turn right (south) and drive two miles to the campground on the left.

Contact: Mount Baker-Snoqualmie National Forest, Skykomish Ranger District, 360/677-2414, www.fs.usda.gov or hoodoo.com.

74 MIDDLE FORK

Scenic rating: 8

in Mount Baker-Snoqualmie National Forest

Map 3.3, page 175

Set at an elevation of 1,600 feet, this is one of the newest and most remote campgrounds in the Mount Baker-Snoqualmie National Forest. Getting there is a challenge, but this spot is popular with locals who tough out the graveled, potholed road to swim and fish here.

Campsites, facilities: There are 39 sites for tents or RVs up to 45 feet, including a few doubles, and two group sites for up to 25 people. Picnic tables and fire grills are provided. Drinking water, vault toilets, a camp host, picnic shelter, and firewood are available. Some facilities are wheelchair accessible. Leashed pets are permitted.

Reservations, fees: Reservations are accepted at 877/444-6777 ($10 reservation fee) or www.recreation.gov ($9 reservation fee). Single sites are $14 per night, double sites are $26 per night, $7 extra vehicle fee. The group site is $40 per night. Open mid-May-early October, weather permitting.

Directions: In Seattle on I-5, turn east on I-90 and drive to North Bend and Exit 34. Take that exit and drive north on 468th Street for 0.6 mile to SE Middle Fork Road (Forest Service Road 56). Turn right and drive 12 miles to the campground (0.5 mile past the Middle Fork Trail trailhead). Obtaining a U.S. Forest Service map is advisable.

Contact: Mount Baker-Snoqualmie National Forest, Snoqualmie Ranger District, North Bend office, 425/888-1421, www.fs.usda.gov or hoodoo.com.

75 KANASKAT-PALMER STATE PARK
🏕 🛶 🏊 🐕 ♿ 🚐 ⛺

Scenic rating: 8
on the Green River

Map 3.3, page 175

This wooded campground offers private campsites near the Green River. The park covers 320 acres with two miles of river frontage; the river can be accessed from the day-use area but not from the campground. It is set on a small, low, forested plateau. In summer, the river is ideal for expert-level rafting and kayaking, and the park is used as a put-in spot for the rafting run down the Green River Gorge. This area has much mining history, and coal mining continues, as does cinnabar mining (the base ore for mercury). Nearby Flaming Geyser gets its name from a coal seam. In winter, the river attracts a run of steelhead and salmon. The park has three miles of hiking trails.

Campsites, facilities: There are 25 sites for tents, 19 pull-through sites with partial hookups (30 amps) for RVs up to 50 feet long, six yurts, and one group camp for up to 80 people, which includes two Adirondack shelters, a picnic shelter, and a community fire ring. Picnic tables are provided. Restrooms with flush toilets and showers, drinking water, a sheltered picnic area, horseshoe pits, and a dump station are available. A convenience store and deli are within two miles. Some facilities are wheelchair accessible. Leashed pets are permitted.

Reservations, fees: Reservations are accepted for individual sites in summer and are required for the group camp at 888/226-7688 or https://washington.goingtocamp.com ($8-10 reservation fee). Sites are $20-45 per night, $10 per extra vehicle per night, and yurts are $40-69 per night. Call for group rates. Some credit cards are accepted. Open year-round, weather permitting.

Directions: From Puyallup at the junction of Highway 167 and Highway 410, turn southeast on Highway 410 and drive 25 miles to Enumclaw and Porter Street/Highway 169.

Turn right and drive three miles to SE 400th Street. Turn right on SE 400th Street and drive one mile to SE 392nd Street. Veer right on SE 392nd Street and drive one mile to SE Vezie Cumberland Road. Turn left and drive three miles to Cumberland Kanaskat Road SE and continue 2.5 miles to the park.

Contact: Kanaskat-Palmer State Park, 360/886-0148, http://parks.state.wa.us.

76 TINKHAM
🏕 🛶 🎿 🐕 ♿ 🚐 ⛺

Scenic rating: 9
in Mount Baker-Snoqualmie National Forest

Map 3.3, page 175

This camp is often used as an overflow for Denny Creek. About half of the sites face the Snoqualmie River, making this a pretty spot. Fishing can be good (check regulations) and the creek provides hiking options. Wilderness trails for the Alpine Lakes Wilderness are located 5-10 miles away. The elevation is 1,600 feet.

Campsites, facilities: There are 47 sites for tents or RVs up to 40 feet long. Picnic tables and fire pits are provided. Drinking water, vault toilets, garbage bins, and firewood are available. A camp host is on-site. Some facilities are wheelchair accessible. Leashed pets are permitted.

Reservations, fees: Reservations are accepted at 877/444-6777 ($10 reservation fee) or www.recreation.gov ($9 reservation fee). Sites are $16-18 per night, $8 per extra vehicle per night. Open mid-May-mid-September, weather permitting.

Directions: In Seattle on I-5, turn east on I-90. Drive east on I-90 to Exit 42. Take that exit and turn right on Tinkham Road (Forest Road 55), and drive southeast 1.5 miles to the campground on the left. Obtaining a U.S. Forest Service map is advisable.

Contact: Mount Baker-Snoqualmie National Forest, Snoqualmie Ranger District, North Bend office, 425/888-1421, www.fs.usda.gov or hoodoo.com.

77 DENNY CREEK

🚶 🚴 🏊 🏕 ♿ 🚤 ⛺

Scenic rating: 9

in Mount Baker-Snoqualmie National Forest

Map 3.3, page 175   **BEST (**

This camp is set at 1,900 feet elevation along Denny Creek, which is pretty and offers nearby recreation access. The campground is secluded in an area of Douglas fir, hemlock, and cedar, with hiking trails available in addition to swimming opportunities. Denny Creek Trail starts from the campground and provides a 4.5-mile round-trip hike that features Keckwulee Falls and Denny Creek Waterslide. You can climb to Hemlock Pass and Melakwa Lake. There is access for backpackers into the Alpine Lakes Wilderness.

Campsites, facilities: There are 29 single sites, some with partial hookups (30 amps), and four double sites for tents or RVs up to 40 feet long; there is also one group site with partial hookups for up to 35 people. Picnic tables and fire grills are provided. Drinking water, flush toilets, and firewood are available. Some facilities are wheelchair accessible. Leashed pets are permitted.

Reservations, fees: Reservations are accepted at 877/444-6777 ($10 reservation fee) or www.recreation.gov ($9 reservation fee). Sites are $20-24 per night, double sites are $35 per night, $10 per extra vehicle per night. The group site is $85 per night. Open mid-May-mid-September, weather permitting.

Directions: In Seattle on I-5, turn east on I-90. Drive east on I-90 to Exit 47. Take that exit, cross the freeway, and at the T intersection turn right and drive 0.25 mile to Denny Creek Road (Forest Road 58). Turn left on Denny Creek Road and drive two miles to the campground on the left.

Contact: Mount Baker-Snoqualmie National Forest, Snoqualmie Ranger District, North Bend office, 425/888-1421, www.fs.usda.gov or hoodoo.com.

78 OWHI WALK-IN

🚶 🚴 🏊 🏕 🚤 🏊 🏕 ⛺

Scenic rating: 9

on Cooper Lake in Wenatchee National Forest

Map 3.3, page 175

This spot has everything you need for a drive-to wilderness experience. Well, everything but drinking water. It's located on the shore of Cooper Lake, near the boundary of the Alpine Lakes Wilderness. The campsites require a walk of 100-300 feet. Some sites have lake views, whereas others have lots of vegetation and provide privacy. The old-growth Douglas fir and western hemlock are highlights. A nearby trailhead provides access to several lakes in the wilderness and extends to the Pacific Crest Trail. Fishing, swimming, and canoeing are all popular at Cooper Lake. No motors, including electric motors, are permitted at the lake, making it ideal for canoes, float tubes, and prams. The campground is minimally developed. The elevation is 2,800 feet.

Campsites, facilities: There are 22 walk-in sites for tents only. Picnic tables and fire grills are provided. Vault toilets and garbage bins are available, but there is no drinking water. Primitive boat-launching facilities are nearby. Leashed pets are permitted.

Reservations, fees: Reservations are not accepted. Sites are $14 per night, $6 per night for an extra vehicle with a two-vehicle maximum. Open late May-early October, weather permitting.

Directions: In Seattle on I-5, turn east on I-90. Drive east on I-90 for 78 miles to Exit 80 (2 miles before Cle Elum). Turn north on Bullfrog Road and drive four miles to Highway 903. Turn left (north) on Highway 903 and drive 16 miles to Forest Road 46. Turn left (west) on Forest Road 46 and drive five miles to Forest Road 4616 (pavement ends). Turn right and drive less than 0.5 mile to the campground. Campsites are located 100-300 feet from the parking lot; camping is not allowed in the parking lot.

Contact: Okanogan-Wenatchee National

Forest, Cle Elum Ranger District, 509/852-1100, www.fs.usda.gov.

79 KACHESS & KACHESS GROUP

Scenic rating: 8
on Kachess Lake in Wenatchee National Forest

Map 3.3, page 175

This is the only campground on the shore of Kachess Lake, but note that the water level can drop significantly in summer during low-rain years. It is the most popular campground in the local area, often filling in July and August, especially on weekends. Recreation opportunities include waterskiing, fishing, hiking, and bicycling. A trail from camp heads north into the Alpine Lakes Wilderness. The elevation is 2,300 feet.

Campsites, facilities: There are 122 single sites and 30 double sites for tents or RVs up to 32 feet long. A group site for 20-50 people is also available. Picnic tables and fire grills are provided. Drinking water, flush and vault toilets, firewood, and a camp host are available. Some facilities are wheelchair accessible. Leashed pets are permitted, but are not allowed in swimming areas.

Reservations, fees: Reservations are accepted for family sites and required for the group site at 877/444-6777 ($10 reservation fee) or www. recreation.gov ($9 reservation fee). Sites are $21-42 per night, $8 per extra vehicle per night. The group site is $115 per night. Open late May-mid-September, weather permitting.

Directions: In Seattle on I-5, turn east on I-90. Drive east on I-90 for 59 miles to Exit 62. Take that exit to Forest Road 49 and turn northeast; drive 5.5 miles to the campground on the right at the end of the paved road.

Contact: Okanogan-Wenatchee National Forest, Cle Elum Ranger District, 509/852-1100, www.fs.usda.gov.

80 SALMON LA SAC

Scenic rating: 6
in Wenatchee National Forest

Map 3.3, page 175

This is a base camp for backpackers and day hikers and is also popular with kayakers. It's located along the Cle Elum River at 2,400 feet elevation, about 0.25 mile from a major trailhead, the Salmon La Sac Trailhead. Hikers can follow creeks heading off in several directions, including into the Alpine Lakes Wilderness. A campground host is available for information.

Campsites, facilities: There are 69 sites, including 12 double sites, for tents or RVs up to 21 feet long. Picnic tables and fire grills are provided. Drinking water and vault toilets are available. Some facilities are wheelchair accessible. Leashed pets are permitted.

Reservations, fees: Reservations are accepted at 877/444-6777 ($10 reservation fee) or www. recreation.gov ($9 reservation fee). Sites are $21-42 per night, $8 per extra vehicle per night (applies to the second vehicle at single sites; third and fourth vehicles at double sites). Open late May-mid-September, weather permitting.

Directions: In Seattle on I-5, turn east on I-90. Drive east on I-90 for 78 miles to Exit 80 (2 miles before Cle Elum). Take that exit, turn north on Bullfrog Road, and drive four miles to Highway 903. Continue north on Highway 903 for 17 miles to the campground on the left.

Contact: Okanogan-Wenatchee National Forest, Cle Elum Ranger District, 509/852-1100, www.fs.usda.gov.

81 RED MOUNTAIN

Scenic rating: 6
in Wenatchee National Forest

Map 3.3, page 175

This alternative to nearby Wish Poosh has two big differences: There is no drinking water, and it's not on Cle Elum Lake. The camp sits along the Cle Elum River one mile from the lake, just above where the river feeds into it. The elevation is 2,200 feet.

Campsites, facilities: There are 10 sites for tents and small RVs up to 20 feet long. Picnic tables and fire grills are provided. Vault toilets and garbage bins are available, but there is no drinking water. Leashed pets are permitted.

Reservations, fees: Reservations are not accepted. Sites are $14 per night, $6 per night for a second vehicle with a two-vehicle maximum. Open mid-May-late November, weather permitting.

Directions: In Seattle on I-5, turn east on I-90. Drive east on I-90 for 78 miles to Exit 80 (2 miles before Cle Elum). Take that exit and turn north on Bullfrog Road; drive four miles to Highway 903. Continue north on Highway 903 for 14 miles to the campground on the left.

Contact: Okanogan-Wenatchee National Forest, Cle Elum Ranger District, 509/852-1100, www.fs.usda.gov.

82 CLE ELUM RIVER & CLE ELUM GROUP
🚶 🚴 🛶 🛖 🚐 ⛺

Scenic rating: 6
in Wenatchee National Forest

Map 3.3, page 175

The gravel roads in the campground make this setting a bit more rustic than nearby Salmon La Sac. It serves as a valuable overflow campground for Salmon La Sac and is similar in setting and opportunities. The group site fills on most summer weekends. A nearby trailhead provides access into the Alpine Lakes Wilderness.

Campsites, facilities: There are 23 sites, including some pull-through, for tents or RVs up to 30 feet long and a group site for up to 100 people. Picnic tables and fire grills are provided. Drinking water, firewood, and vault toilets are available. Leashed pets are permitted.

Reservations, fees: Reservations are not accepted for family sites but are required for the group site at 877/444-6777 ($10 reservation fee) or www.recreation.gov ($9 reservation fee). Sites are $18-36 per night, $6 per extra vehicle per night (applies to a second vehicle at single sites; third and fourth vehicles for double sites). The group site is $115 per night. Open late May-mid-September, weather permitting.

Directions: In Seattle on I-5, turn east on I-90. Drive east on I-90 for 78 miles to Exit 80 (2 miles before Cle Elum). Take that exit, turn north on Bullfrog Road, and drive four miles to Highway 903. Continue north on Highway 903 for 13 miles to the campground on the left.

Contact: Okanogan-Wenatchee National Forest, Cle Elum Ranger District, 509/852-1100, www.fs.usda.gov.

83 LAKE EASTON STATE PARK
🚶 🚴 🛶 🎣 🛶 🎿 🐾 🔭 ♿ 🚐 ⛺

Scenic rating: 8
on Lake Easton

Map 3.3, page 175

This campground offers many recreational opportunities. For starters, it's set along the shore of Lake Easton on the Yakima River in the Cascade foothills. The landscape features old-growth forest, dense vegetation, and freshwater marshes, and the park covers 516 acres of the best of it. Two miles of trails for hiking and biking are available. The park provides opportunities for both summer and winter recreation, including swimming, fishing, boating, cross-country skiing, and snowmobiling. Note that high-speed boating is not recommended because Lake Easton is a shallow reservoir with stumps often hidden just below the water surface; the boat speed limit is 10 mph (10-horsepower motor limit). Nearby recreation options include an 18-hole golf course and hiking trails. Kachess Lake and Keechelus Lake are just a short drive away.

Campsites, facilities: There are 137 sites, including 45 sites with hookups (30 amps), for tents or RVs up to 60 feet, two primitive walk-in tent sites, and one group walk-in site for tents only that accommodates up to 50 people. Picnic tables and fire grills are provided. Restrooms with flush toilets and showers, drinking water, a dump station, an amphitheater, a playground, basketball, horseshoe pits, Junior Ranger program, movie nights, and a swimming beach are available. A store, café, and ice are located within one mile. Boat-launching facilities, dock, and floats are located on Lake Easton. Some facilities are wheelchair accessible. Leashed pets are permitted.

Reservations, fees: Reservations are accepted and are required for the group site at 888/226-7688 or https://washington.goingtocamp.com ($8-10 reservation fee). RV sites are $25-45 per night, walk-in tent sites are $12 per night, $10 per extra vehicle per night. Call for group rates. Some credit cards are accepted. Open May-mid-October, with limited winter facilities.

Directions: From Seattle, drive east on I-90 for 68 miles to Exit 70. Take that exit to Lake Easton Road. Turn right and drive 1.5 miles to Lake Easton State Park Road. Turn right and enter the park.

Contact: Lake Easton State Park, 509/656-2586, http://parks.state.wa.us.

84 CAYUSE HORSE CAMP

🥾 🚲 🛶 🐴 🚐 ⛺

Scenic rating: 6

in Wenatchee National Forest

Map 3.3, page 175

Cayuse is for horse campers only. It's located along the Cle Elum River at major trailheads for horses and hikers and marked trails for bikers. Horses must be kept in corrals that share common borders. Hikers can follow creeks heading off in several directions, including into the Alpine Lakes Wilderness. The elevation is 2,400 feet.

Campsites, facilities: There are 11 single sites and three double sites for tents or RVs up to 35 feet long. Picnic tables and fire pits are provided. Drinking water, vault toilets, and a camp

host are available. Stock facilities include corrals, troughs, and hitching posts. Bring your own stock feed. Leashed pets are permitted.

Reservations, fees: Reservations are accepted at 877/444-6777 ($10 reservation fee) or www.recreation.gov ($9 reservation fee). Sites are $21-42 per night, $8 per night for each additional vehicle (applies to second vehicle at single sites; third or fourth vehicle at double sites). Open mid-May-mid-September, weather permitting.

Directions: In Seattle on I-5, turn east on I-90. Drive east on I-90 for 78 miles to Exit 80 (2 miles before Cle Elum). Take that exit and turn north on Bullfrog Road; drive four miles to Highway 903. Continue north on Highway 903 for 17 miles to the campground on the right.

Contact: Okanogan-Wenatchee National Forest, Cle Elum Ranger District, 509/852-1100, www.fs.usda.gov.

85 DALLES

🥾 🛶 🐴 ♿ 🚐 ⛺

Scenic rating: 10

in Mount Baker-Snoqualmie National Forest

Map 3.3, page 175

This campground is set at the confluence of Minnehaha Creek and the White River. Aptly, its name means "rapids." A nature trail is nearby, and the White River entrance to Mount Rainier National Park is about 14 miles south on Highway 410. The camp sits amid a grove of old-growth trees; a particular point of interest is a huge old Douglas fir that is 9.5 feet in diameter and more than 235 feet tall. This is one of the prettiest camps in the area. It gets moderate use in summer.

Campsites, facilities: There are 46 sites for tents or RVs up to 40 feet long. Picnic tables and fire grills are provided. Vault toilets, drinking water, and firewood are available. A camp host is on-site. There is a large shaded picnic area for day use. Some facilities are wheelchair accessible. Leashed pets are permitted.

Reservations, fees: Reservations are accepted at 877/444-6777 ($10 reservation fee) or www.recreation.gov ($9 reservation fee). Sites are $18-20 per night, $9 per extra vehicle per night. Open mid-May-late September, weather permitting.

Directions: From Enumclaw, drive east on Highway 410 for 25.5 miles to the campground (3 miles inside the forest boundary) on the right.

Contact: Mount Baker-Snoqualmie National Forest, White River Ranger District, 360/825-6585, www.fs.usda.gov or hoodoo.com.

86 CORRAL PASS

Scenic rating: 10
in Mount Baker-Snoqualmie National Forest

Map 3.3, page 175

This is the most remote of the campgrounds in the area. Set at an elevation of 5,600 feet, it's primitive, quiet, and an ideal base camp for a hiking trip. Groups of horse packers heading into the adjacent Norse Peak Wilderness frequent the camp. The best trip is the two-mile backpack up to Hidden Lake and then along a river canyon for four miles to Echo Lake. Several trails nearby lead to backcountry fishing lakes and streams. In late summer and fall, visitors can find wild berries in the area.

Campsites, facilities: There are 20 tent sites. Picnic tables and fire grills are provided. Vault toilets, garbage bins, hitch rails, and a horse-loading ramp are available. There is no drinking water. Downed firewood can be gathered. Leashed pets are permitted.

Reservations, fees: Reservations are not accepted. There is no fee for camping, but a Northwest Forest Pass ($5 daily fee or $30 annual pass per parked vehicle) is required. Open June-late September, weather permitting.

Directions: From Enumclaw, drive east on Highway 410 for 31.6 miles to Forest Road 7174 (near Silver Springs Camp). Turn left (east) and drive seven miles to the camp on the right.

This curvy dirt road is not suitable for RVs or trailers.

Contact: Mount Baker-Snoqualmie National Forest, White River Ranger District, 360/825-6585, www.fs.usda.gov.

87 CROW CREEK

Scenic rating: 5
in Wenatchee National Forest

Map 3.3, page 175

Set at an elevation of 2,900 feet, this campground on the Little Naches River is popular with off-road bikers and four-wheel-drive enthusiasts and is similar to Kaner Flat, except that there is no drinking water. A trail heading out from the camp leads into the backcountry and then forks in several directions. One route leads to the American River, another follows West Quartz Creek, and another goes along Fife's Ridge into the Norse Peak Wilderness (where no motorized vehicles are permitted). There is good seasonal hunting and fishing in this area.

Campsites, facilities: There are 15 sites for tents or RVs up to 30 feet long. Picnic tables and fire grills are provided. Vault toilets and garbage bins are available. There is no drinking water. Downed firewood may be gathered. Leashed pets are permitted.

Reservations, fees: Reservations are not accepted. Sites are $10 per night, $5 per extra vehicle per night. Open May-October, weather permitting.

Directions: From Yakima, drive northwest on U.S. 12 for 18 miles to Highway 410. Bear northwest on Highway 410 and drive 24.5 miles to Little Naches Road/Forest Road 1900. Turn northeast and drive 2.5 miles to Forest Road 1902. Turn left (west) and drive 0.5 mile to the campground on the right.

Contact: Okanogan-Wenatchee National Forest, Naches Ranger District, 509/653-1400, www.fs.usda.gov.

88 KANER FLAT

🏃 ⛵ 🎣 ♿ 🚙 ⛺

Scenic rating: 7

in Wenatchee National Forest

Map 3.3, page 175

This campground is set near the Little Naches River, at an elevation of 2,678 feet. It is located at the site of a wagon-train camp on the Old Naches Trail, a route used in the 1800s by wagon trains, Native Americans, and the U.S. Cavalry on their way to westside markets. The narrow-clearance Naches Trail is now used by motorcyclists and four-wheel-drive enthusiasts. Kaner Flat is popular among that crowd, and it is larger and more group-friendly than nearby Crow Creek Campground.

Campsites, facilities: There are 43 single sites and six double sites for tents or RVs up to 30 feet and one group site for up to 60 people. Picnic tables and fire grills are provided. Restrooms with flush toilets, drinking water, and vault toilets are available. Some facilities are wheelchair accessible. Leashed pets are permitted.

Reservations, fees: Reservations are accepted at 877/444-6777 ($10 reservation fee) or www.recreation.gov ($9 reservation fee). Sites are $12-17 per night, the group site is $60 per night, $5 per night for each additional vehicle. Open mid-May-late November, weather permitting.

Directions: From Yakima, drive northwest on U.S. 12 for 18 miles to Highway 410. Bear northwest on Highway 410 and drive 24.5 miles to Little Naches Road/Forest Road 1900. Turn northeast and drive 2.5 miles to the campground on the right.

Contact: Okanogan-Wenatchee National Forest, Naches Ranger District, 509/653-1400, www.fs.usda.gov.

89 NAPEEQUA CROSSING

🏃 🚲 ⛵ 🎣 🚙 ⛺

Scenic rating: 8

in Wenatchee National Forest

Map 3.4, page 176   **BEST (**

A trail across the road from this camp on the White River heads east for about 3.5 miles to Twin Lakes in the Glacier Peak Wilderness. It's definitely worth the hike, with scenic views and wildlife observation as your reward. But note that Twin Lakes is closed to fishing. Sightings of ospreys, bald eagles, and golden eagles can brighten the trip. This is also an excellent spot for fall colors.

Campsites, facilities: There are five sites for tents or RVs up to 30 feet long. Picnic tables and fire grills are provided. Vault toilets are available, but you are advised to bring your own toilet paper. There is no drinking water, and garbage must be packed out. Leashed pets are permitted.

Reservations, fees: Reservations are not accepted. There is no fee for camping. Open year-round, weather and snow level permitting.

Directions: From Leavenworth, drive west on U.S. 2 for 14 miles to Coles Corner and State Route 207. Turn north and drive 10 miles to Forest Road 6400 (White River Road). Turn right and drive 5.9 miles to the campground on the left.

Contact: Okanogan-Wenatchee National Forest, Wenatchee River Ranger District, 509/548-2550, www.fs.usda.gov.

90 CHIWAWA HORSE CAMP

🏃 🚲 ⛵ 🎣 ♿ 🚙 ⛺

Scenic rating: 8

in Wenatchee National Forest

Map 3.4, page 176

This camp is not designated solely for horse campers, as many horse camps are. Rather, it's for all users, but it features many facilities for horseback riding. It is seldom full but is popular among equestrians. Two short trails specifically designed for physically challenged visitors lead around the campground, covering about a mile. A trailhead at the camp also provides access to a network of backcountry trails. The elevation is 2,500 feet.

Campsites, facilities: There are 21 sites for tents or RVs up to 45 feet long. Some sites are pull-through. Picnic tables and fire grills are provided. Drinking water and vault toilets are available. Garbage must be packed out. Horse facilities include mounting ramps, high lines, water troughs, and a loading ramp. Some facilities are wheelchair accessible. Leashed pets are permitted.

Reservations, fees: Reservations are not accepted. Sites are $14 per night, $10 per each additional vehicle per night. Open May-October, weather permitting.

Directions: From I-5 and Everett, turn east on U.S. 2 and drive 87 miles to State Route 207. Turn right on State Route 207 and drive 4.3 miles to Chiwawa Loop Road. Turn right and drive 1.2 miles to Chiwawa River Road/Forest Road 6200. Turn left and drive 14.8 miles to the campground on the right. Note: The last five miles are gravel.

Contact: Okanogan-Wenatchee National Forest, Wenatchee River Ranger District, 509/548-2550, www.fs.usda.gov.

91 COTTONWOOD

Scenic rating: 8

in Wenatchee National Forest

Map 3.4, page 176

Cottonwood Camp is set along the Entiat River, adjacent to a major trailhead leading into the Glacier Peak Wilderness. Note that dirt bikes are allowed on four miles of trail, Entiat River Trail to Myrtle Lake, but no motorcycles or mountain bikes are allowed inside the boundary of the Glacier Peak Wilderness; violators will be prosecuted by backcountry rangers. In other words, cool your jets. Let backpackers have some peace and quiet. A bonus near the camp is good berry picking in season. Trout fishing is another alternative. The camp is set at an elevation of 3,100 feet.

Campsites, facilities: There are 25 sites for tents or RVs up to 20 feet long. Picnic tables and fire grills are provided. Drinking water, vault toilets, and garbage bins are available. Some facilities are wheelchair accessible. Leashed pets are permitted.

Reservations, fees: Reservations are not accepted. Sites are $10 per night, $8 extra vehicle fee. Open June-mid-October, weather permitting.

Directions: From I-5 and Everett, turn east on U.S. 2 and drive 120 miles to U.S. 2/U.S. 97. Bear right on U.S. 2/U.S. 97 and drive one mile to Euclid Avenue/U.S. 97. Take that ramp and drive 18 miles on U.S. 97/U.S. 97-A to Entiat River Road. Turn left (northwest) and drive 37 miles to the campground.

Contact: Okanogan-Wenatchee National Forest, Entiat Ranger District, 509/784-4700, www.fs.usda.gov.

92 SILVER FALLS

Scenic rating: 10

in Wenatchee National Forest

Map 3.4, page 176　　　　**BEST (**

This campground is set in an enchanted spot at the confluence of Silver Creek and the Entiat River. A trail from camp leads 0.5 mile to the base of beautiful Silver Falls. This trail continues in a loop for another mile past the falls, parallel to the river. Fishing is available above Entiat Falls, located two to three miles upriver from Silver Falls. The elevation at the camp is 2,400 feet.

Campsites, facilities: There are 30 sites for tents or RVs up to 30 feet long, plus one group site for up to 40 people and 60 vehicles. Picnic tables and fire grills are provided. Drinking water, vault toilets, and garbage bins are available. A camp host is available in summer. Some

facilities are wheelchair accessible. Leashed pets are permitted.

Reservations, fees: Reservations are accepted for the group site at 877/444-6777 ($10 reservation fee) or www.recreation.gov ($9 reservation fee). Sites are $12 per night, $10 per night per additional vehicle; the group site is $60 per night. Open mid-May-mid-October, weather permitting.

Directions: From I-5 and Everett, turn east on U.S. 2 and drive 120 miles to U.S. 2/U.S. 97. Bear right on U.S. 2/U.S. 97 and drive one mile to Euclid Avenue/U.S. 97. Take that ramp and drive 18 miles on U.S. 97/U.S. 97-A to Entiat River Road. Turn left (northwest) and drive 29 miles to the campground on the left.

Contact: Okanogan-Wenatchee National Forest, Entiat Ranger District, 509/784-4700, www.fs.usda.gov.

93 LAKE CREEK

Scenic rating: 7
in Wenatchee National Forest

Map 3.4, page 176

This camp is located at the confluence of Lake Creek and the Entiat River, at a trail crossroads. It ties in to the Mad Lake trail system, where all-purpose trails are available for hiking, horseback riding, and mountain biking. Another trail ties in to a loop system that features the Devils Backbone to Ramona Park. These also link to a network of trails in the Lake Creek Basin in the Chelan Mountains, and several others head south and west into the Entiat Mountains. Fishing is available on the Entiat River, but not in the vicinity of Entiat Falls. Check fishing regulations. Note that there is another Lake Creek Camp in the Lake Wenatchee and Leavenworth Ranger District.

Campsites, facilities: There are 18 single sites and one double site for tents or RVs up to 25 feet long. Picnic tables and fire grills are provided. Drinking water and vault toilets are available. Some facilities are wheelchair accessible. Leashed pets are permitted.

Reservations, fees: Reservations are not accepted. Sites are $10 per night, $8 per night per additional vehicle. Pay fees in person at the Entiat Ranger Station. Open May-mid-October, weather permitting.

Directions: From I-5 and Everett, turn east on U.S. 2 and drive 120 miles to U.S. 2/U.S. 97. Bear right on U.S. 2/U.S. 97 and drive one mile to Euclid Avenue/U.S. 97. Take that ramp and drive 18 miles on U.S. 97/U.S. 97-A to Entiat River Road. Turn left (northwest) and drive 27 miles to the campground on the left.

Contact: Okanogan-Wenatchee National Forest, Entiat Ranger District, 2108 Entiat Way, 509/784-4700, www.fs.usda.gov.

94 FOX CREEK

Scenic rating: 7
in Wenatchee National Forest

Map 3.4, page 176

This camp is located along the Entiat River near Fox Creek. Fishing is prohibited in the vicinity of Entiat Falls, so make sure you understand the regulations. This camp features several campsites that are closer to the river than those at nearby Lake Creek, making it the more popular campground of the two. The elevation is 2,100 feet.

Campsites, facilities: There are 16 sites for tents or RVs up to 28 feet. Picnic tables and fire grills are provided. Drinking water, vault toilets, and garbage bins are available. Some facilities are wheelchair accessible. Leashed pets are permitted.

Reservations, fees: Reservations are not accepted. Sites are $10 per night, $8 per night per additional vehicle. Open May-mid-October, weather permitting.

Directions: From I-5 and Everett, turn east on U.S. 2 and drive 120 miles to U.S. 2/U.S. 97. Bear right on U.S. 2/U.S. 97 and drive one mile to Euclid Avenue/U.S. 97. Take that ramp and drive 18 miles on U.S. 97/U.S. 97-A to Entiat River Road. Turn left (northwest) and drive 26 miles to the campground.

Contact: Okanogan-Wenatchee National Forest, Entiat Ranger District, 509/784-4700, www.fs.usda.gov.

95 SNOWBERRY BOWL

Scenic rating: 7

in Wenatchee National Forest

Map 3.4, page 176

Snowberry Bowl is set less than four miles from Twenty-Five Mile Creek State Park and Lake Chelan. Sites are nestled amid a forest of Douglas fir and ponderosa pine, which provide privacy screening. The elevation is 2,000 feet.

Campsites, facilities: There are seven sites for tents or RVs up to 40 feet long and two double sites for up to 15 people each. Picnic tables, fire rings, and tent pads on sand are provided. Drinking water, vault toilets, and garbage bins are available. Some facilities are wheelchair accessible. Leashed pets are permitted.

Reservations, fees: Reservations are not accepted. Single sites are $10 per night, double sites are $20 per night, $8 per night per additional vehicle. Open year-round, with limited winter facilities.

Directions: From Chelan, drive south on U.S. 97-A for three miles to South Lakeshore Road. Turn right and drive 13.5 miles (passing the state park) to Shady Pass Road. Turn left and drive 2.5 miles to a Y intersection with Slide Ridge Road. Bear left and drive 0.5 mile to the campground on the right.

Contact: Okanogan-Wenatchee National Forest, Chelan Ranger District, 509/682-4900, www.fs.usda.gov.

96 TWENTY-FIVE MILE CREEK STATE PARK

Scenic rating: 8

near Lake Chelan

Map 3.4, page 176   **BEST (**

This campground is located on Twenty-Five Mile Creek near where it empties into Lake Chelan. A 235-acre marine camping park, it sits on the forested south shore of Lake Chelan between the mountains and the lake, surrounded by spectacular scenery, featuring a rocky terrain with forested areas. Known for its boat access, this park can serve as your launching point for exploring the up-lake wilderness portions of Lake Chelan. Fishing access for trout and salmon is close by, and fishing supplies, a dock, a modern marina, and boat moorage are available. There is also a small wading area for kids. Forest Road 5900, which heads west from the park, accesses several trailheads leading into the U.S. Forest Service lands of the Chelan Mountains.

Campsites, facilities: There are 46 sites for tents, 21 sites with full or partial hookups (30 amps) for RVs up to 30 feet, and a group site for up to 50 people. Picnic tables and fire grills are provided. Restrooms with flush toilets, coin showers, and drinking water are available. A dump station, firewood, a boat dock, fishing pier, marina, boat ramp, boat moorage, a picnic area, gasoline, and a seasonal camp store are available at the park. Some facilities are wheelchair accessible. Leashed pets are permitted.

Reservations, fees: Reservations are accepted at 888/226-7688 or https://washington.goingtocamp.com ($8-10 reservation fee). Sites are $20-45 per night, $10 per night per extra vehicle. Call for group rates. Some credit cards are accepted. Open late March-October, weather permitting.

Directions: From Chelan, drive south on U.S. 97-A for three miles to South Lakeshore Road. Turn right and drive 15 miles to the park on the right.

Contact: Twenty-Five Mile Creek State Park,

509/687-3610, http://parks.state.wa.us; Lake Chelan Boat Company, 888/682-4584, www. ladyofthelake.com.

97 MITCHELL CREEK BOAT-IN

Scenic rating: 8

on Lake Chelan in Wenatchee National Forest

Map 3.4, page 176

This is one of 13 national forest campgrounds set on Lake Chelan. It can be reached by private boat, floatplane, or ferry. Though the ferry does not make a scheduled stop, it's possible to arrange a drop-off at the campsite with advance notice.

Campsites, facilities: There are seven tent sites accessible only by boat, ferry, or floatplane. Picnic tables and fire rings are provided. Vault toilets and a group shelter are available, but there is no drinking water. Garbage must be packed out. An on-site floating dock has a 17-boat capacity.

Reservations, fees: Reservations are not accepted. There is no fee for camping. There is a $5 per day dock-site fee if bringing a private boat. Open May-late October, weather permitting.

Directions: From Wenatchee, drive north on U.S. 97-A for 40 miles to the town of Chelan. Take your boat to the campground, 15 miles from Chelan.

Contact: Okanogan-Wenatchee National Forest, Chelan Ranger District, 509/682-4900, www.fs.usda.gov.

98 KAMEI RESORT

Scenic rating: 6

on Lake Wapato

Map 3.4, page 176

This resort is on Lake Wapato, about two miles from Lake Chelan. Note that this is a seasonal lake that closes in early September. No open fires are allowed. If you have an extra day, take the ferry ride on Lake Chelan.

Campsites, facilities: There are 55 sites with partial hookups (30 and 50 amps) for tents or RVs of any length. Three rental trailers are also available. Picnic tables are provided. Restrooms with flush toilets and showers, drinking water, and ice are available. Boat docks, launching facilities, and rentals are nearby. Some facilities are wheelchair accessible. Leashed pets are permitted.

Reservations, fees: Reservations are accepted beginning in January each year. Sites are $30 per night, rental trailers are $55-80 per night ($5 pet fee). Specify camp site when reserving. Open late April-Labor Day.

Directions: From Chelan, drive west on Highway 150 for seven miles to Wapato Lake Road. Turn right (north) on Wapato Lake Road and drive four miles to the resort on the right.

Contact: Kamei Resort, 509/687-3690, www. golakechelan.net.

99 SODA SPRINGS-LITTLE WENATCHEE RIVER

Scenic rating: 7

in Wenatchee National Forest

Map 3.4, page 176

Set along Little Wenatchee River Road, this campground is a small, quiet, closer-to-civilization alternative to Tumwater. But note that it lacks both drinking water and a trailer turnaround. It's off the beaten path in a pleasant wooded area, at an elevation of 2,000 feet. A small, cold soda spring is located next to the campground. There are some excellent hiking trails nearby.

Campsites, facilities: There are five sites for tents only. Picnic tables and fire grills are provided. Vault toilets are available, but there is no drinking water. Garbage must be packed out. Leashed pets are permitted.

Reservations, fees: Reservations are not

accepted. There is no fee for camping. Open May-late October, weather permitting.

Directions: From I-5 and Everett, turn east on U.S. 2 and drive 87 miles to State Route 207. Turn north on State Route 207 and drive 11 miles to Forest Road 6500. Turn left (west) on Forest Road 6500 and drive seven miles to the campground on the left.

Contact: Okanogan-Wenatchee National Forest, Wenatchee River Ranger District, Wenatchee River Ranger Station, 509/548-2550, www.fs.usda.gov.

100 GLACIER VIEW

Scenic rating: 9

on Lake Wenatchee in Wenatchee National Forest

Map 3.4, page 176

This popular campground is set on the southwestern shore of Lake Wenatchee, near the head of the lake. It's a happening spot for boating, swimming, fishing, and windsurfing, and it fills up on summer weekends. Fishing is average. There are also some good hiking trails in the area and a golf course within a 10-minute drive. The camp sits at an elevation of 1,900 feet. Insider's note: The walk-in sites are set on the lake's shore, requiring a walk of about 100 feet.

Campsites, facilities: There are 23 sites for tents or small RVs 15 feet or less. Picnic tables and fire grills are provided. Drinking water, vault toilets, and garbage bins are available. A primitive boat launch for small boats is available. Some facilities are wheelchair accessible. Leashed pets are permitted.

Reservations, fees: Reservations are not accepted. Sites are $18 per night, $10 per night per extra vehicle, $7 boat launch fee. Open May-mid-October, weather permitting.

Directions: From Leavenworth, drive west on U.S. 2 for 14 miles to State Route 207. Turn right on State Route 207 North and drive 3.5 miles to Cedar Brae Road. Turn left (west) on Cedar

Brae Road and drive 0.3 mile to a campground sign. Turn left at the sign and drive 3.4 miles to Forest Road 6607, a gravel road. Continue on Forest Road 6607 to the campground at the end of the road.

Contact: Okanogan-Wenatchee National Forest, Wenatchee River Ranger District, Lake Wenatchee Ranger Station, 509/548-2550, www.fs.usda.gov.

101 LAKE WENATCHEE STATE PARK

Scenic rating: 8

on Lake Wenatchee

Map 3.4, page 176   **BEST (**

Lake Wenatchee is the centerpiece for a 489-acre park with two miles of waterfront. Glaciers and the Wenatchee River feed Lake Wenatchee, and the river, which bisects the park, helps make it a natural wildlife area. Thanks to a nice location and pull-through sites that are spaced just right, you can expect plenty of company at this campground. The secluded campsites are set at the southeast end of Lake Wenatchee, which offers plenty of recreation opportunities, with a boat ramp nearby. A swimming beach is available at the north shore. There are eight miles of hiking trails, seven miles of bike trails, five miles of horse trails, and a 1.1-mile interpretive snowshoe trail in winter. Horse rentals are available nearby. In winter, there are 11 miles of multi-use trails and 23 miles of groomed cross-country skiing trails. Note: Bears are active in the park, so all food must be stored in bear-proof facilities.

Campsites, facilities: In the South Camp, there are 100 sites for tents or RVs up to 40 feet (no hookups) and one group tent site for 20-80 people. In the North Camp, there are 55 sites for tents or RVs of any length (no hookups) and 42 sites with partial hookups (30 and 50 amps) for RVs of any length; some sites are pull-through. Picnic tables and fire grills are provided. Restrooms with flush toilets and showers, drinking water, a dump station, a store, ice, firewood, two picnic shelters, amphitheater, volleyball, a restaurant, a playground, and guided horseback rides are available. Boat docks, launching facilities, rentals, and golf are nearby. Some facilities are wheelchair accessible. Leashed pets are permitted.

Reservations, fees: Reservations are accepted and required for the group camp at 888/226-7688 or https://washington.goingtocamp.com ($8-10 reservation fee). Sites are $20-45 per night, $10 per extra vehicle per night. Call for group rates. Open year-round, with limited winter facilities.

Directions: From Leavenworth, drive west on U.S. 2 for 15 miles to State Route 207 at Coles Corner. Turn right (north) and drive 3.5 miles to Cedar Brae Road. Turn left on Cedar Brae Road and drive 2.5 miles to the south park entrance. For the north park entrance, continue past Cedar Brae Road for one mile.

Contact: Lake Wenatchee State Park, 509/763-3101, http://parks.state.wa.us.

102 NASON CREEK

Scenic rating: 7

near Lake Wenatchee in Wenatchee National Forest

Map 3.4, page 176

This campground is located on Nason Creek near Lake Wenatchee, bordering Lake Wenatchee State Park. Recreation activities include swimming and waterskiing. Boat rentals, horseback riding, and golfing are available nearby.

Campsites, facilities: There are 73 sites, including a few double sites, for tents or RVs of any length. Some sites are pull-through. Picnic tables and fire grills are provided. Drinking water, restrooms with flush toilets and showers, and garbage bins are available. Boat-launching facilities are nearby. Some facilities are wheelchair accessible.

Reservations, fees: Reservations are accepted

at 877/444-6777 ($10 reservation fee) or www.recreation.gov ($9 reservation fee). Sites are $23 per night, $14 per night per extra vehicle. Open mid-May-mid-October, weather permitting.

Directions: From I-5 and Everett, turn east on U.S. 2 and drive 87 miles to State Route 207, 1 mile west of Winton. Turn right on State Route 207 and drive 3.5 miles to Cedar Brae Road. Turn left (west) and drive 100 yards to the campground.

Contact: Okanogan-Wenatchee National Forest, Wenatchee River Ranger District, Lake Wenatchee Ranger Station, 509/548-2550, www.fs.usda.gov.

103 GOOSE CREEK

Scenic rating: 7

on Goose Creek in Wenatchee National Forest

Map 3.4, page 176

With trails for dirt bikes available directly from the camp, Goose Creek is used primarily by motorcycle riders. A main trail links to the Entiat off-road vehicle trail system, so this camp gets high use during the summer. The camp is set near a small creek.

Campsites, facilities: There are 26 single sites and three double sites for tents or RVs of any length. Picnic tables and fire rings are provided. Drinking water, vault toilets, and garbage bins are available. Some facilities are wheelchair accessible. Leashed pets are permitted.

Reservations, fees: Reservations are not accepted. Sites are $14-28 per night, $10 per each additional vehicle per night. Open mid-May-late October, weather permitting.

Directions: From I-5 and Everett, turn east on U.S. 2 and drive 87 miles to State Route 207, 1 mile west of Winton. Turn north on State Route 207 and drive 4.3 miles to Chiwawa Loop Road. Turn right and drive 1.5 miles to Chiwawa River Road/Forest Road 6200. Turn left and drive three miles to Forest Road 6100. Turn right and drive 0.6 mile to the camp on the right.

Contact: Okanogan-Wenatchee National Forest, Wenatchee River Ranger District, Lake Wenatchee Ranger Station, 509/548-2550, www.fs.usda.gov.

104 PINE FLATS

Scenic rating: 5

in Wenatchee National Forest

Map 3.4, page 176

This camp has ready access to the Mad River off-road vehicle (ORV) area and is popular with bikers and ORV enthusiasts. The area boasts more than 100 miles of trails, which are ideal for quads and dirt bikes. It ties into many loop trails. The elevation is 1,600 feet.

Campsites, facilities: There are six sites for tents only and one group site for tents only that accommodates 20-50 people and 20 vehicles. Picnic tables and fire grills are provided. Drinking water and pit and flush toilets are available. Garbage must be packed out.

Reservations, fees: Reservations are not accepted for individual sites but are required for the group site at 877/444-6777 ($9 reservation fee) or www.recreation.gov ($10 reservation fee). Sites are $8 per night per vehicle, $6 per night per additional vehicle; the group site is $60 per night. Open late May-October, weather permitting.

Directions: From Wenatchee, drive north on U.S. 2/U.S. 97 for 1.5 miles to U.S. 97/U.S. 97-A. Drive north 14 miles on U.S. 97/U.S. 97-A to Entiat River Road. Turn left (northwest) at Entiat River Road and drive 10 miles to Mad River Road/Forest Service Road 5700. Turn left at Mad River Road/Forest Service Road 5700 and drive just over one mile to the campground.

Contact: Okanogan and Wenatchee National Forest, Entiat Ranger District, 509/784-4700, www.fs.usda.gov.

105 LAKE CHELAN STATE PARK

Scenic rating: 10

on Lake Chelan

Map 3.4, page 176   **BEST (**

This park is the recreation headquarters for Lake Chelan. It provides boat docks and concession stands on the shore of the 50-mile lake. The park covers 127 acres, featuring 6,000 feet of shoreline on the forested south shore. Water sports include fishing, swimming, scuba diving, and waterskiing. Summers tend to be hot and dry, but expansive lawns looking out on the lake provide a fresh feel, especially in the early evenings. A daily ferry service provides access to the roadless community at the head of the lake. The word "chelan" is a Chelan Indian word and translates to both "lake" and "blue water." Nearby attractions include the Holden Mine site and Holden Village and hiking in Glacier Peak Wilderness.

Campsites, facilities: There are 109 sites for tents, 18 sites with full hookups and 17 sites with partial hookups (30 and 50 amps) for RVs up to 30 feet. Picnic tables and fire grills are provided. Restrooms with flush toilets and coin showers, drinking water, firewood, a picnic area with a kitchen shelter, a dump station, store, restaurant, ice, playground, horseshoe pits, ball field, beach area, boat dock, and launching facilities and moorage are available. Some facilities are wheelchair accessible. Leashed pets are permitted.

Reservations, fees: Reservations are accepted at 888/226-7688 or https://washington.goingtocamp.com ($8-10 reservation fee). RV sites are $25-45 per night, tent sites are $20-35 per night, $10 per extra vehicle per night. Some credit cards are accepted. Open year-round, weather permitting.

Directions: From Wenatchee, drive north on U.S. 97-A for nine miles to State Route 971 (Navarre Coulee Road). Turn left (north) and drive seven miles to the end of the highway at South Lakeshore Road. Turn right, then immediately look for the park entrance to the left.

Contact: Lake Chelan State Park, 509/687-3710, http://parks.state.wa.us.

106 DAROGA STATE PARK

Scenic rating: 5

on the Columbia River

Map 3.4, page 176

This 90-acre state park is set along 1.5 miles of shoreline on the Columbia River. It sits on the elevated edge of the desert scablands. This camp fills up quickly on summer weekends. Desert Canyon Golf Course is two miles away. Fishing, along with walking and biking trails, are available out of the camp.

Campsites, facilities: There are 28 sites with partial hookups (30 amps) for tents or RVs up to 32 feet long, 17 walk-in or boat-in sites (requiring a 0.25-mile trip) for tents only, and two group sites for up to 150 people each. Some sites are pull-through. Picnic tables and fire pits are provided. Restrooms with flush (near RV sites) and vault (near walk-in sites) toilets, coin showers, drinking water, a dump station, firewood, a swimming beach, boat-launching facilities and docks, a playground, baseball field, basketball courts, softball and soccer fields, and a picnic area with a kitchen shelter are available. Some facilities are wheelchair accessible. Leashed pets are permitted.

Reservations, fees: Reservations are accepted at 888/226-7688 or https://washington.goingto-camp.com ($8-10 reservation fee). Sites are $12-40 per night, $10 per extra vehicle per night. Call for group rates. Open mid-March-mid-October, weather permitting.

Directions: From East Wenatchee, drive north on U.S. 97 (east side of the Columbia River) for 18 miles to the camp. For boat-in camps, launch boats from the ramp at the park and go 0.25 mile.

Contact: Daroga State Park, 509/664-6380; state park information, 360/902-8844, http://parks.state.wa.us.

107 BLACKPINE HORSE CAMP

Scenic rating: 8

in Wenatchee National Forest

Map 3.4, page 176

Blackpine Horse Camp is used primarily by horse campers for horse pack trips. It is set on Black Pine Creek near Icicle Creek at a major trailhead leading into the Alpine Lakes Wilderness. It's one of seven rustic camps on the creek, with the distinction of being the only one with facilities for horses. The elevation is 3,000 feet.

Campsites, facilities: There are 10 sites for tents or RVs up to 60 feet long. Picnic tables and fire grills are provided. Solar pumped drinking water, vault toilets, and garbage bins are available. Horse facilities, including a hitching rail and loading ramp, are also available. Leashed pets are permitted.

Reservations, fees: Reservations are not accepted. Sites are $16 per night, $10 per night per extra vehicle. Open mid-May-late October, weather permitting.

Directions: From I-5 and Everett, turn east on U.S. 2 and drive 103 miles to Leavenworth and County Road 7600 (Icicle Creek Road). Turn south and drive 19.2 miles to the campground on the left. Note: Because of road washout, access may change in the future.

Contact: Okanogan-Wenatchee National Forest, Wenatchee River Ranger District, 509/548-2550, www.fs.usda.gov.

108 ROCK ISLAND

Scenic rating: 8

in Wenatchee National Forest

Map 3.4, page 176

Rock Island is one of several campgrounds in the immediate area along Icicle Creek and is located about one mile from the trailhead that takes hikers into the Alpine Lakes Wilderness. This is a pretty spot with good fishing access. The elevation is 2,900 feet.

Campsites, facilities: There are 20 single sites and two double sites for tents or RVs up to 22 feet long. Picnic tables and fire grills are provided. Drinking water, vault toilets, and garbage bins are available. Some facilities are wheelchair accessible. Leashed pets are permitted.

Reservations, fees: Reservations are not accepted. Sites are $18-36 per night, $10 per each additional vehicle per night. Open May-late October, weather permitting.

Directions: From I-5 and Everett, turn east on U.S. 2 and drive 103 miles to Leavenworth and County Road 7600/Icicle Creek Road. Turn right (south) and drive 17.7 miles to the campground.

Contact: Okanogan-Wenatchee National Forest, Wenatchee River Ranger District, 509/548-2550, www.fs.usda.gov.

109 CHATTER CREEK

Scenic rating: 8

in Wenatchee National Forest

Map 3.4, page 176

Note: At time pf publication, the campground was closed due to fire damage. Check with the ranger station for updates.

Icicle and Chatter Creeks are the backdrop for this creekside campground. The elevation is 2,800 feet. Trails lead out in several directions from the camp into the Alpine Lakes Wilderness.

Campsites, facilities: There are 12 sites for tents or RVs up to 22 feet long and one group site for up to 45 people and 12 vehicles. Picnic tables and fire grills are provided. Drinking water, vault toilets, garbage bins, firewood, and a picnic shelter with fireplace are available. Some facilities are wheelchair accessible. Leashed pets are permitted.

Reservations, fees: Reservations are not accepted. Sites are $18 per night, $10 per night per extra vehicle; the group site is $100 per night with no extra vehicle fee. Some credit cards are accepted. Open April-late October, weather permitting.

Directions: From I-5 and Everett, turn east on U.S. 2 and drive 103 miles to Leavenworth and County Road 7600/Icicle Creek Road. Turn right (south) and drive 16.1 miles to the campground on the right.

Contact: Okanogan-Wenatchee National Forest, Wenatchee River Ranger District, 509/548-2550, www.fs.usda.gov.

110 IDA CREEK

Scenic rating: 8

in Wenatchee National Forest

Map 3.4, page 176

This campground is one of several small, quiet camps along Icicle and Ida Creeks. Recreation options are similar to Chatter Creek and Rock Island Campgrounds, with hiking and fishing among them.

Campsites, facilities: There are 10 sites for tents or RVs up to 30 feet long. Picnic tables and fire grills are provided. Drinking water, vault toilets, and garbage bins are available. Some facilities are wheelchair accessible. Leashed pets are permitted.

Reservations, fees: Reservations are not accepted. Sites are $19 per night, $12 per night per extra vehicle. Open May-late October, weather permitting.

Directions: From I-5 and Everett, turn east on U.S. 2 and drive 103 miles to Leavenworth and County Road 7600/Icicle Creek Road. Turn right (south) and drive 14.2 miles to the campground on the left.

Contact: Okanogan-Wenatchee National Forest, Wenatchee River Ranger District, 509/548-2550, www.fs.usda.gov.

111 JOHNNY CREEK

Scenic rating: 8

in Wenatchee National Forest

Map 3.4, page 176

Johnny Creek Campground is split into two parts, which sit on both sides of the road along Icicle and Johnny Creeks. It is fairly popular. Upper Johnny has a forest setting, whereas Lower Johnny is set alongside the creek, with adjacent forest. Nearby recreation opportunities include trail access into the Alpine Lakes Wilderness, horseback riding, and a golf course. The elevation is 2,300 feet.

Campsites, facilities: There are 56 single sites and nine double sites for tents or RVs up to 50 feet long. Picnic tables and fire grills are provided. Drinking water, vault toilets, and garbage bins are available. Some facilities are wheelchair accessible. Leashed pets are permitted.

Reservations, fees: Reservations are not accepted. Single sites are $22 per night, double sites are $38-44 per night, $12-14 per each additional vehicle per night. Open May-late October, weather permitting.

Directions: From I-5 and Everett, turn east on U.S. 2 and drive 103 miles to Leavenworth and County Road 7600/Icicle Creek Road. Turn right (south) and drive 12.4 miles to the campground (with camps on each side of the road).

Contact: Okanogan-Wenatchee National Forest, Wenatchee River Ranger District, 509/548-2550, www.fs.usda.gov.

112 BRIDGE CREEK

Scenic rating: 8

in Wenatchee National Forest

Map 3.4, page 176

This camp is a small, quiet spot along Icicle and Bridge Creeks. The elevation is 1,800 feet. About two miles south of the camp at Eightmile Creek, a trail accesses the Alpine Lakes Wilderness. Horseback-riding opportunities are within four miles, and golf is within five miles.

Campsites, facilities: There are six sites for tents or small RVs up to 19 feet long and one group site for up to 70 people. Picnic tables and fire grills are provided. Drinking water, vault toilets, garbage bins, and firewood are available. The group site does not have drinking water. Leashed pets are permitted.

Reservations, fees: Reservations are required for the group site at 877/444-6777 ($10 reservation fee) or www.recreation.gov ($9 reservation fee). Sites are $19 per night, $12 per night per extra vehicle. The group site is $100 per night. Open mid-April-late October, weather permitting.

Directions: From I-5 and Everett, turn east on U.S. 2 and drive 103 miles to Leavenworth and County Road 7600/Icicle Creek Road. Turn right (south) and drive 9.4 miles to the campground on the left.

Contact: Okanogan-Wenatchee National Forest, Wenatchee River Ranger District, 509/548-2550, www.fs.usda.gov.

113 EIGHTMILE

Scenic rating: 8

in Wenatchee National Forest

Map 3.4, page 176

Trailheads are located within two miles of this campground along Icicle and Eightmile Creeks, providing access to fishing, as well as a backpacking route into the Alpine Lakes

Wilderness. Horseback-riding opportunities are within four miles, and golf is within five miles. The elevation is 1,800 feet.

Campsites, facilities: There are 41 single sites and four double sites for tents or RVs up to 50 feet long. There is also one group site for up to 70 people and 25 vehicles. Picnic tables and fire grills are provided. Drinking water, vault toilets, and garbage bins are available. Some facilities are wheelchair accessible. Leashed pets are permitted.

Reservations, fees: Reservations are accepted for some sites and are required for the group site at 877/444-6777 ($10 reservation fee) or www.recreation.gov ($9 reservation fee). Single sites are $22 per night, double sites are $44 per night, $14 per night per extra vehicle; the group site is $100 per night. Open mid-April-late October.

Directions: From I-5 and Everett, turn east on U.S. 2 and drive 103 miles to Leavenworth and County Road 7600/Icicle Creek Road. Turn right (south) and drive eight miles to the campground on the left.

Contact: Okanogan-Wenatchee National Forest, Wenatchee River Ranger District, 509/548-2550, www.fs.usda.gov.

114 TUMWATER

Scenic rating: 7

in Wenatchee National Forest

Map 3.4, page 176

Note: At time of publication, the campground remained closed due to flood and fire damage. Contact the ranger station for updates.

This large, popular camp provides a little bit of both worlds. It provides a good layover spot for campers cruising U.S. 2, but it also features two nearby forest roads, each less than a mile long, which end at trailheads that provide access to the Alpine Lakes Wilderness. The camp is on the Wenatchee River in Tumwater Canyon. This section of river is closed to fishing. The elevation is 2,050 feet.

Campsites, facilities: There are 84 single sites and two double sites for tents or RVs up to 50 feet long; there is also one electric group site for tents or RVs up to 25 feet long that can accommodate up to 70 people and 40 vehicles. Picnic tables and fire grills are provided. Drinking water, restrooms with flush toilets, firewood, picnic shelter with fireplace, playground, horseshoes, and basketball court are available. Some facilities are wheelchair accessible. Leashed pets are permitted.

Reservations, fees: Reservations are required for the group site at 877/444-6777 ($10 reservation fee) or www.recreation.gov ($9 reservation fee). Single sites are $23 per night, double sites are $46 per night, $7-14 per each additional vehicle per night; the group site is $100 per night. Open May-mid-October, weather permitting.

Directions: From I-5 and Everett, turn east on U.S. 2 and drive 99 miles to the campground (10 miles west of Leavenworth).

Contact: Okanogan-Wenatchee National Forest, Wenatchee River Ranger District, 509/548-2550, www.fs.usda.gov.

115 LEAVENWORTH/ PINE VILLAGE KOA

Scenic rating: 8

near the Wenatchee River

Map 3.4, page 176   **BEST (**

This lovely resort on 30 acres is near the Bavarian-themed village of Leavenworth, to which the park provides a free shuttle in the summer. The spectacularly scenic area is surrounded by the Cascade Mountains and set among ponderosa pines. The camp has access to the Wenatchee River, not to mention many luxurious extras, including a spa and a heated pool. The park allows campfires and has firewood available. Nearby recreation options include an 18-hole golf course, horseback riding, white-water rafting, and hiking trails. Make a point to spend a day in Leavenworth if possible; it offers authentic German food and architecture, along with music and art shows in the summer.

Campsites, facilities: There are 60 sites with full hookups and 60 sites with partial hookups (30 and 50 amps) for RVs up to 65 feet long, 40 tent sites, 20 cabins, two cottages, and 15 lodges. Some sites are pull-through. Picnic tables are provided, and fire grills are available at some sites. Restrooms with flush toilets and showers, drinking water, dump stations, Wi-Fi access, bicycle rentals, firewood, a recreation hall, cable TV, a convenience store, propane, coin laundry, ice, a playground, horseshoe pits, volleyball, a spa and sauna, a seasonal heated swimming pool, snack bar and espresso stand, doggie run, and a beach area are available. A café is located within one mile. Some facilities are wheelchair accessible. Leashed pets are permitted.

Reservations, fees: Reservations are accepted at 800/562-5709. RV sites are $50-111 per night, tent sites are $25-46 per night, $5 per extra vehicle per night, and $5 per person per night for more than two people. Some credit cards are accepted. Open year round.

Directions: From I-5 and Everett, turn east on U.S. 2 and drive 103 miles to Leavenworth. Continue east on U.S. 2 for 0.25 mile to River Bend Drive. Turn left (north) and drive 0.5 mile to the campground on the right.

Contact: Leavenworth/Pine Village KOA, 509/548-7709, www.koa.com.

116 ICICLE RIVER RV RESORT

Scenic rating: 9

on Icicle River

Map 3.4, page 176

This pretty, wooded spot is set along the Icicle River, where fishing and swimming are available. The 50-acre resort is clean and scenic. An 18-hole golf course and hiking trails are nearby.

Campsites, facilities: There are 108 sites with full or partial (30 and 50 amps) hookups for RVs of any length, six rustic cabins, and two full-service cabins. Picnic tables and fire pits (at most sites) are provided. Restrooms with flush toilets and showers, drinking water, coin laundry, cable TV, Wi-Fi access, a spa, firewood, and propane gas are available. Horseshoe pits and two pavilions are available nearby. Leashed pets are permitted only in the campground.

Reservations, fees: Reservations are accepted. Sites are $37-45 per night, $5 per extra vehicle per night, $3-5 per person per night for more than two adults. Cabins are $45-100 per night. Some credit cards are accepted. Open April-mid-October, weather permitting.

Directions: From I-5 and Everett, turn east on U.S. 2 and drive 103 miles to Leavenworth and County Road 7600/Icicle Road. Turn right (south) and drive three miles to the resort on the left.

Contact: Icicle River RV Resort, 509/548-5420, www.icicleriverrv.com.

117 ENTIAT CITY PARK

Scenic rating: 8

on the Columbia River

Map 3.4, page 176

If you're hurting for a spot for the night, you can usually find a campsite here. The campground is on Lake Entiat, which is a dammed portion of the Columbia River. Access to nearby launching facilities makes this a good camping spot for boaters. Waterskiing and personal watercraft are allowed. A dirt trail leads from the lake to the town of Entiat.

Campsites, facilities: There are 25 tent sites and 31 sites with partial hookups for RVs of any length. Picnic tables and barbecue stands are provided. Restrooms with flush toilets and coin showers, drinking water, a dump station, and a playground are available. Boat docks and launching facilities are nearby. A store, café, propane, and coin laundry are available within 1.5 miles. Some facilities are wheelchair accessible. No open fires, dogs, or alcohol are permitted.

Reservations, fees: Reservations are available at 800/736-8428 ($5 reservation fee). RV sites are $20-40 per night, tent sites are $15-30 per night, $2 per each additional person for more than four people, $2 per extra vehicle per night. Group rates are available. Open year-round.

Directions: From Wenatchee, drive north on U.S. 97-A for 16 miles to Entiat; the park entrance is on the right (Shearson Street is adjacent on the left). Turn right and drive a short distance to the park along the shore of Lake Entiat.

Contact: Entiat City Park, 800/736-8428; City Hall, 509/784-1500, www.entiat.org.

118 LINCOLN ROCK STATE PARK

Scenic rating: 5

on Lake Entiat

Map 3.4, page 176

Lincoln Rock State Park is an 80-acre park set along the shore of Lake Entiat, created by the Rocky Reach Dam on the Columbia River. The park features lawns and shade trees amid an arid landscape. There are two miles of paved, flat trails suitable for both hiking and biking. Water sports include swimming, boating, and waterskiing. Beavers are occasionally visible in the Columbia River. Oh, yeah, and the name? Look for a basalt outcropping in the shape of the former president's famous profile and you'll see why.

Campsites, facilities: There are 69 sites with partial or full hookups (30 amps) for RVs up to 65 feet long, 27 sites for tents or self-contained RVs up to 60 feet long, and 12 cabins. Picnic tables and fire grills are provided. Restrooms with flush toilets and coin showers, drinking water, dump station, playground, athletic fields, horseshoe pits, swimming beach, amphitheater, interpretive center, three picnic shelters, and firewood are available. Boat docks, moorage,

and launching facilities are located on Lake Entiat. Some facilities are wheelchair accessible. Leashed pets are permitted.

Reservations, fees: Reservations are accepted at 888/226-7688 or https://washington.goingtocamp.com ($8-10 reservation fee). Sites are $20-45 per night, $10 per extra vehicle per night; cabins are $45-125 per night. Some credit cards are accepted. Open March-mid-October, weather permitting.

Directions: From East Wenatchee, drive northeast on U.S. 2 for seven miles to the park on the left.

Contact: Lincoln Rock State Park, 509/884-8702; state park information, 360/902-8844, http://parks.state.wa.us.

119 BLU-SHASTIN RV PARK

Scenic rating: 6

near Peshastin

Map 3.4, page 176

This 13-acre park is set in a mountainous area near Peshastin Creek. Gold panning in the river is a popular activity here; during the gold rush, the Peshastin was the best-producing river in the state—and it still is. The camp has sites on the riverbank and plenty of shade trees. A heated pool, recreation field, and horseshoe pits provide possible activities in the park. Hiking trails and marked bike trails are nearby. Rafting, tubing, and golfing are nearby and are popular in the summer. Snowmobiling is an option during the winter.

Campsites, facilities: There are 86 sites for tents or RVs of any length (20 and 30 amp full hookups); four sites are pull-through. Picnic tables and fire rings are provided. Restrooms with flush toilets and showers, drinking water, Wi-Fi, cable TV, a recreation hall, firewood, coin laundry, ice, a playground, horseshoes, badminton, volleyball, and a seasonal heated swimming pool are available. Propane gas, a store, and a café are located within seven miles. Leashed pets are permitted.

Reservations, fees: Reservations are recommended at 888/548-4184. RV sites are $33 per night, tent sites are $28 per night. Some credit cards are accepted. Open year-round, weather permitting.

Directions: From Leavenworth, drive east on U.S. 2 for five miles to U.S. 97. Turn right (south) on U.S. 97 and drive seven miles to the park on the right.

Contact: Blu-Shastin RV Park, 888/548-4184, www.blushastin.com.

120 WENATCHEE RIVER COUNTY PARK

Scenic rating: 5

in Monitor

Map 3.4, page 176

This camp is situated between Highway 2 and the Wenatchee River. Though not the greatest setting, with some highway noise, it is convenient for RV campers. You can usually get a tree-covered site in the campground, despite it being a small park. The adjacent river is fast moving and provides white-water rafting in season, with a put-in spot at the park.

Campsites, facilities: There are 43 sites with full hookups, four sites with partial hookups, and two sites with no hookups for RVs of any length. Several sites are pull-through. Picnic tables and fire pits are provided. Drinking water, restrooms with flush toilets and coin showers, a recreation room, propane, coin laundry, dump station, sand volleyball court, playground, ping-pong table, horseshoe pit, golfing cage, basketball hoop, media and bicycle lending library, and Wi-Fi are available. A convenience store and a restaurant are within 0.5 mile. Some facilities are wheelchair accessible. Leashed pets are permitted (limit of two pets).

Reservations, fees: Reservations are available at 509/667-7503. Sites are $28-38 per night, $5 per night per person for more than four people, and $5 per extra vehicle per night. Two-night

minimum. Some credit cards are accepted. Open April 1-October 31.

Directions: From Wenatchee and U.S. 2, take the State Route 285/N. Wenatchee exit, keeping left to merge onto State Route 285/N. Wenatchee Avenue. Drive 2.5 miles to N. Miller. Turn south and drive a short distance to Washington Street. Turn left and drive 0.5 mile to Orondo Avenue. Turn left and drive a short distance to the park entrance on the left.

Contact: Wenatchee River County Park, 509/667-7503, www.wenatcheeriverpark.org.

121 WENATCHEE CONFLUENCE STATE PARK

Scenic rating: 10

in Wenatchee

Map 3.4, page 176

This 197-acre state park is set at the confluence of the Wenatchee and Columbia Rivers. The park features expansive lawns shaded by deciduous trees and fronted by the two rivers. Wenatchee Confluence has something of a dual personality: The north portion of the park is urban and recreational, while the southern section is a designated natural wetland area. There are 10.5 miles of paved trail for hiking, biking, and in-line skating. A pedestrian bridge crosses the Wenatchee River. An interpretive hiking trail is available in the Horan Natural Area. Other recreation possibilities include fishing, swimming, boating, and waterskiing. Sports enthusiasts will find playing fields as well as tennis and basketball courts. Daroga State Park and Lake Chelan to the north offer side-trip possibilities.

Campsites, facilities: There are 51 sites with full hookups (30 amps) for RVs up to 65 feet, eight tent sites, and a group tent site for 50-300 people. Picnic tables and fire grills are provided. Restrooms with flush toilets and coin showers, drinking water, a boat launch, dump station, swimming beach, playground, horseshoe pits, a picnic shelter that can be reserved, and athletic fields are available. Some facilities are wheelchair accessible. Leashed pets are permitted.

Reservations, fees: Reservations are accepted April-September at 888/226-7688 or https://washington.goingtocamp.com ($8-10 reservation fee). Sites are $20-45 per night, $10 per extra vehicle per night. Call for group rates. Some credit cards are accepted. Open year-round.

Directions: From Wenatchee and U.S. 2, take the Easy Street exit and drive south to Penny Road. Turn left and drive a short distance to Chester Kimm Street. Turn right and drive to a T intersection and Old Station Road. Turn left on Old Station Road and drive past the railroad tracks to the park on the right. The park is 1.3 miles from U.S. 2.

Contact: Wenatchee Confluence State Park, 509/664-6373, http://parks.state.wa.us.

122 BEVERLY

Scenic rating: 8

in Wenatchee National Forest

Map 3.4, page 176

This primitive campground is set on the North Fork of the Teanaway River, a scenic area of the river. It is primarily a hiker's camp, with several trails leading up nearby creeks and into the Alpine Lakes Wilderness. Self-issued permits (available at the trailhead) are required for wilderness hiking. The elevation is 3,100 feet.

Campsites, facilities: There are four single sites and six double sites for tents or RVs up to 21 feet long. Picnic tables and fire grills are provided. Vault toilets are available, but there is no drinking water. Garbage must be packed out. Leashed pets are permitted.

Reservations, fees: Reservations are not accepted. Sites are $8 per night per vehicle. Open June-mid-November, weather permitting.

Directions: In Seattle on I-5, turn east on I-90. Drive east on I-90 for 78 miles to Cle Elum and

Exit 85. Take Exit 85 to Highway 970. Turn east on Highway 970 and drive seven miles to Teanaway Road (Highway 970). Turn left (north) on Teanaway Road and drive 13 miles to the end of the paved road. Bear right (north) on Forest Road 9737 and drive four miles to the campground on the left.

Contact: Okanogan-Wenatchee National Forest, Cle Elum Ranger District, 509/852-1100, www.fs.usda.gov.

123 INDIAN CAMP

Scenic rating: 6

on the Middle Fork of the Teanaway River

Map 3.4, page 176

At time of publication, Indian Camp was closed due to the 2017 Jolly Mountain Fire. Call for updates.

This campground along the Middle Fork of the Teanaway River is located in a primitive setting with sunny, open sites along the water. Fishing for brook trout is best here when the season first opens in June. Quiet and solitude are highlights of this little-used camp. It's an easy drive from here to trailheads accessing the Mount Stuart Range. Be sure to bring your own drinking water. This is a popular snowmobile area in winter.

Campsites, facilities: There are 11 sites for tents or RVs up to 35 feet long. Picnic tables and fire grills are provided. Pit toilets are available, but there is no drinking water. Garbage must be packed out. Some saddle-stock facilities are available, including hitching posts. Some facilities are wheelchair accessible. Leashed pets are permitted.

Reservations, fees: Reservations are not accepted. There is no fee for camping, but a Discover Pass is required. Open year-round, weather and snow level permitting.

Directions: From Seattle, drive east on I-90 for 80 miles to Cle Elum and Exit 85 and Highway 970. Turn east on Highway 970 and drive 6.9 miles to Teanaway Road. Turn left on Teanaway Road and drive 7.3 miles to West Fork Teanaway Road. Turn left and drive 0.6 mile to Middle Fork Teanaway Road. Turn right and drive 3.9 miles to the campground on the left.

Contact: Department of Natural Resources, Southeast Region, 509/925-8510, www.dnr.wa.gov.

124 SWAUK

Scenic rating: 6

in Wenatchee National Forest

Map 3.4, page 176

Some decent hiking trails can be found at this campground along Swauk Creek. A short loop trail, about one mile round-trip, is the most popular. Fishing is marginal, and there is some highway noise from U.S. 97. The elevation is 3,200 feet. Three miles east of the camp on Forest Road 9716 is Swauk Forest Discovery Trail. This three-mile interpretive trail explains some of the effects of logging and U.S. Forest Service management of the forest habitat.

Campsites, facilities: There are 21 sites, including two double sites, for tents or RVs up to 25 feet long. Fire grills and picnic tables are provided. Flush and vault toilets and firewood are available. There is no drinking water. Leashed pets are permitted.

Reservations, fees: Reservations are not accepted. Sites are $18 per night, double sites are $36 per night, $6 per extra vehicle per night (applies to third and fourth vehicle at double sites). Open late May–early September, weather permitting.

Directions: In Seattle on I-5, turn east on I-90. Drive east on I-90 for 80 miles to Cle Elum and Exit 85. Take Exit 85 to Highway 970. Turn east on Highway 970 and drive 20 miles north on Highway 970/U.S. 97 to the campground on the right (near Swauk Pass).

Contact: Okanogan-Wenatchee National Forest, Cle Elum Ranger District, 509/852-1100, www.fs.usda.gov.

125 MINERAL SPRINGS

Scenic rating: 6

in Wenatchee National Forest

Map 3.4, page 176

This campground is at the confluence of Medicine and Swauk Creeks. Note that this camp is set along a highway, so there is some highway noise. Fishing, berry picking, and hunting are good in season in this area. It is at an elevation of 2,800 feet. Most use the camp as a one-night layover spot.

Campsites, facilities: There are six sites for tents or RVs up to 21 feet long and one group site for 20-50 people. Picnic tables and fire rings are provided. Drinking water, vault toilets, and a camp host are available. Leashed pets are permitted. A restaurant is nearby.

Reservations, fees: Reservations are required for the group site at 877/444-6777 ($10 reservation fee) or www.recreation.gov ($9 reservation fee). Sites are $16 per night, $7 per extra vehicle per night. The group site is $85 per night. Open mid-May–mid-September, weather permitting.

Directions: From Seattle, drive east on I-90 for 80 miles to Cle Elum and Exit 85 and Highway 970. Turn east on Highway 970 and drive 17 miles to the campground on the left.

Contact: Okanogan-Wenatchee National Forest, Cle Elum Ranger District, 509/852-1100, www.fs.usda.gov.

126 KEN WILCOX HORSE CAMP

Scenic rating: 8

in Wenatchee National Forest

Map 3.4, page 176

This camp near Haney Meadows has been adopted by a local equestrian association that helps maintain the horse trails; it is also the launch point for an extensive trail system. The last couple miles of road are pretty rough though, suitable only for high-clearance vehicles or pickups. The elevation is 5,500 feet.

Campsites, facilities: There are 25 sites for tents or RVs up to 30 feet long. Picnic tables and fire pits are provided. Vault toilets are available. There is no drinking water, although stock water is available. Garbage must be packed out. Stock facilities include hitching equipment, such as rails and rings for suspending a high line.

Reservations, fees: Reservations are not accepted. There is no fee for camping, but a Northwest Forest Pass ($5 daily fee or $30 annual fee per parked vehicle) is required. Open early July-mid-October, weather permitting (the access road is not plowed).

Directions: In Seattle on I-5, turn east on I-90. Drive east on I-90 for 80 miles to Cle Elum and Exit 85. Take Exit 85 to Highway 970. Turn east on Highway 970 and drive 24 miles to the summit of Blewett (Swauk) Pass and Forest Road 9716. Turn right on Forest Road 9716 (gravel) and drive about four miles to Forest Road 9712. Turn left on Forest Road 9712 and drive about five miles to the camp on the left.

Contact: Okanogan-Wenatchee National Forest, Cle Elum Ranger District, 509/852-1100, www.fs.usda.gov.

127 SQUILCHUCK STATE PARK

Scenic rating: 7
southwest of Wenatchee

Map 3.4, page 176

This 288-acre park (Squilchuck is Chinook for "muddy water") sits at an elevation of 4,000 feet in a fir and pine forest. Recreation opportunities include 10 miles of hiking and biking trails; in winter, this park sees sledding, snowshoeing, and cross-country skiing.

Campsites, facilities: There is one group site for tents or RVs up to 30 feet long (no hookups) that can accommodate 20-150 people. Picnic tables and fire rings are provided. A restroom with flush toilets and coin showers, drinking water, and a lodge with kitchen are available. Some facilities are wheelchair accessible. Leashed pets are permitted.

Reservations, fees: Reservations are required at 509/664-6373 ($25 reservation fee). The group site is $150 per night for 20-50 people, $209 per night for 51-100 people, and $278 per night for 101-150 people. Open May-mid-September, with limited winter facilities.

Directions: From U.S. 2 in Wenatchee, drive south on Wenatchee Avenue to Squilchuck Road and follow the signs for about eight miles to the park.

Contact: Squilchuck State Park, 509/664-6373, http://parks.state.wa.us.

128 TRAILER CORRAL RV PARK

Scenic rating: 7
in Cle Elum

Map 3.4, page 176

This wooded campground about one mile from the Yakima River offers a choice of grassy or graveled sites. Nearby recreation options include an 18-hole golf course, marked hiking trails, and tennis courts.

Campsites, facilities: There are 23 sites with partial hookups for RVs of any length, three tent sites, and six cabins. Picnic tables and cable TV are provided, and fire rings are available on request. Restrooms with flush toilets and showers, firewood, and coin laundry are available. A store is located within one mile. Boat-launching facilities are nearby. Leashed pets are permitted.

Reservations, fees: Reservations are accepted. RV sites are $25 per night, tent sites are $20 per night, $2 per person per night for more than two people. Open year-round.

Directions: From Seattle, drive east on I-90 for 80 miles to Cle Elum and Exit 85 and Highway 970. Turn east on Highway 970 and drive 1.5 miles to the park on the left.

Contact: Trailer Corral RV Park, 2781 Hwy. 970, 509/674-2433.

129 ICEWATER CREEK

Scenic rating: 7

in Wenatchee National Forest

Map 3.4, page 176

Icewater Creek Camp is most popular with off-road motorcyclists because there are two ORV trails leading from the camp, both of which network with an extensive system of off-road riding trails. The best route extends along the South Fork Taneum River area. The campground sports small trees and open sites. Fishing is fair, primarily for six- to eight-inch cutthroat trout.

Campsites, facilities: There are 14 sites for tents or RVs up to 26 feet long, including three double sites. Picnic tables and fire rings are provided. Firewood is available. There is no drinking water. Leashed pets are permitted.

Reservations, fees: Reservations are not accepted. Single sites are $18 per night, double sites are $36 per night, $6 per night for each additional vehicle. Open May-late September, weather permitting.

Directions: From Seattle, take I-5 east on I-90. Drive east on I-90 for 80 miles to Cle Elum. Continue east for 9.3 miles to Exit 93/Elks Height Road. Take that exit and drive to the stop sign at Elks Height Road. Turn left and drive 0.3 mile to Taneum Road. Turn right on Taneum Road and drive 3.4 miles to East Taneum Road. Turn right on East Taneum Road and drive 0.1 mile to West Taneum Road. Turn right on West Taneum Road and drive 8.4 miles to the campground on the left.

Contact: Okanogan-Wenatchee National Forest, Cle Elum Ranger District, 509/852-1100, www.fs.usda.gov.

130 ELLENSBURG KOA

Scenic rating: 8

in Ellensburg

Map 3.4, page 176   **BEST (**

This KOA is one of the few campgrounds in a 25-mile radius. Exceptionally clean and scenic, it offers well-maintained, shaded campsites along the Yakima River. Rafting and fly-fishing on the nearby Yakima River are popular. Other nearby recreation options include a nine-hole golf course and tennis courts. The Kittitas County Historical Museum is in town at 3rd and Pine Streets.

Campsites, facilities: There are 95 sites with full or partial hookups (30 and 50 amps) for RVs up to 40 feet, 37 sites for tents, and four cabins. Some sites are pull-through. Picnic tables and fire rings are provided. Restrooms with flush toilets and showers, cable TV, a dump station, propane, Wi-Fi, firewood, bicycle rentals, convenience store, coin laundry, ice, a playground, video rentals, a horseshoe pit, volleyball, a seasonal wading pool, and a seasonal heated swimming pool are available. A café is located within one mile. Extra parking is available for horse trailers, vans, and boats. Some facilities are wheelchair accessible. Leashed pets are permitted.

Reservations, fees: Reservations are accepted at 800/562-7616. RV sites are $37-41 per night, tent sites are $22-38 per night, cabins are $70-90 per night, $5 per person per night for more than two people, and $3 per extra vehicle per night. Some credit cards are accepted. Open mid-February-mid-November.

Directions: From Seattle, drive east on I-90 for 106 miles to Exit 106 (near Ellensburg). Take that exit and continue less than a mile to Thorp Highway. Turn right at Thorp Highway and drive a short distance to the KOA entrance (well marked).

Contact: Ellensburg KOA, 32 S. Thorp Hwy., Ellensburg, 509/925-9319, www.koa.com.

NORTHEASTERN WASHINGTON

© RANDAL KETCHEM/123RF

A lot of people call this area "God's country," and once you've camped here you'll understand why. The vast number of lakes, streams, and forests provide unlimited adventure. National forests like Colville, Kaniksu, and Wenatchee are ideal for mountain hideaways. You'll find remote ridges and valleys with conifers, along with many small streams and lakes. The Pacific Northwest's largest river system—including the Columbia River, Franklin D. Roosevelt Lake, and the Spokane River—carves waterways and features campsites with boating and facilities. You could spend a lifetime here—days hiking and fishing, and nights camping out under the stars. And that's exactly what some people do, like my friend Rich Landers, the outdoors writer for the *Spokane Spokesman-Review*. My favorite destinations are the dozens of lesser-known camps, often along small lakeshores, that provide good fishing and hiking. This is a wilderness to enjoy.

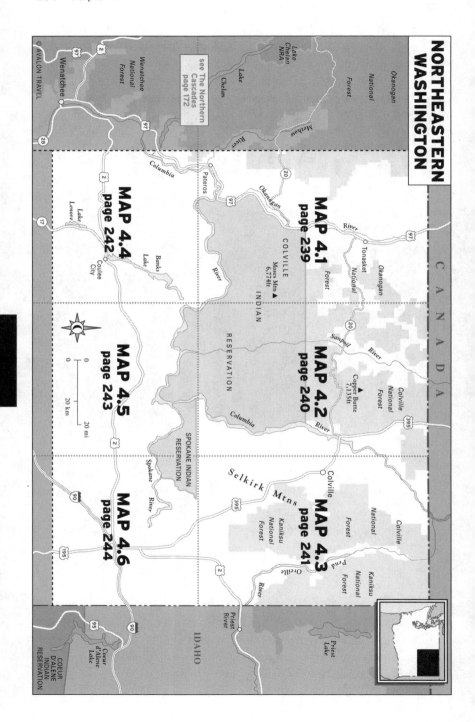

NORTHEASTERN WASHINGTON

see The Northern
Cascades
page 172

MAP 4.1
page 239

MAP 4.2
page 240

MAP 4.3
page 241

MAP 4.4
page 242

MAP 4.5
page 243

MAP 4.6
page 244

© AVALON TRAVEL

CANADA

IDAHO

Map 4.1

Sites 1-32
Pages 245-258

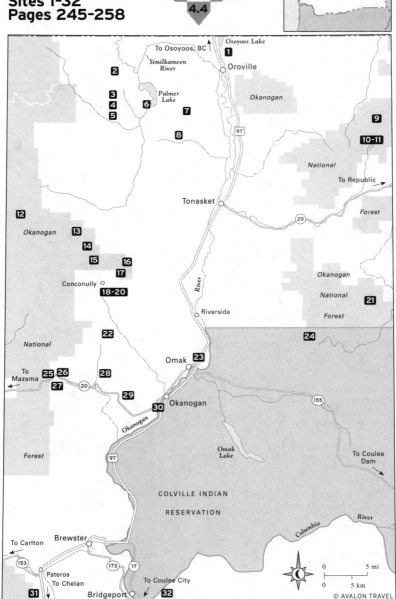

Map 4.2

Sites 33-59
Pages 259-270

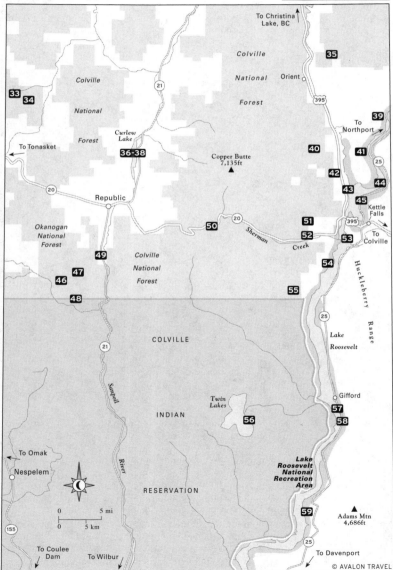

© AVALON TRAVEL

Map 4.3

Sites 60-91
Pages 271-285

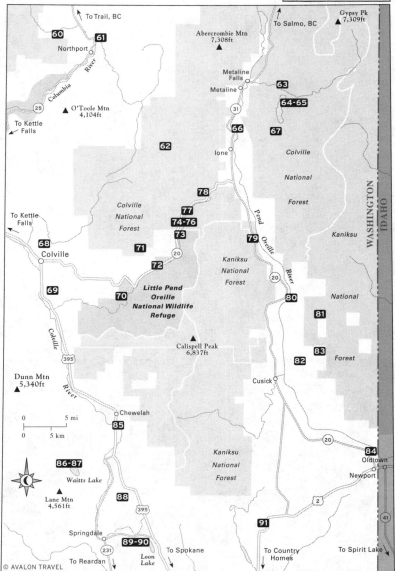

© AVALON TRAVEL

Map 4.4

**Sites 92-100
Pages 286-290**

4.1
4.5

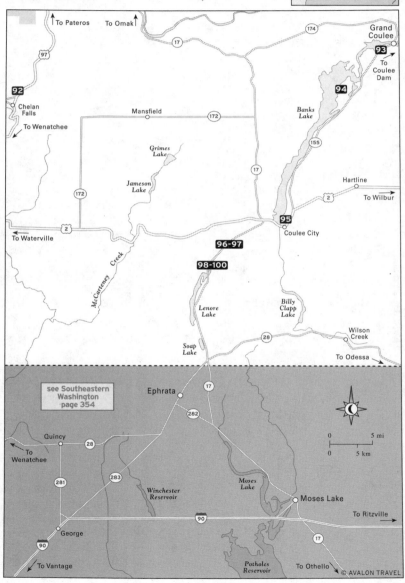

To Pateros
To Omak
174
Grand Coulee
97
93
To Coulee Dam
92
Chelan Falls
94
Mansfield
172
Banks Lake
To Wenatchee
155
Grimes Lake
17
Hartline
Jameson Lake
2
To Wilbur
172
To Waterville
2
95
Coulee City
McCartney Creek
96-97
98-100
Billy Clapp Lake
Lenore Lake
Wilson Creek
28
Soap Lake
To Odessa

see Southeastern Washington page 354

Ephrata
17
282
Quincy
28
To Wenatchee
281
283
Winchester Reservoir
Moses Lake
Moses Lake
George
90
To Ritzville
90
17
To Vantage
Potholes Reservoir
To Othello

0   5 mi
0   5 km

© AVALON TRAVEL

Map 4.5
Sites 101-108
Pages 290-293

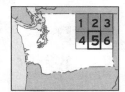

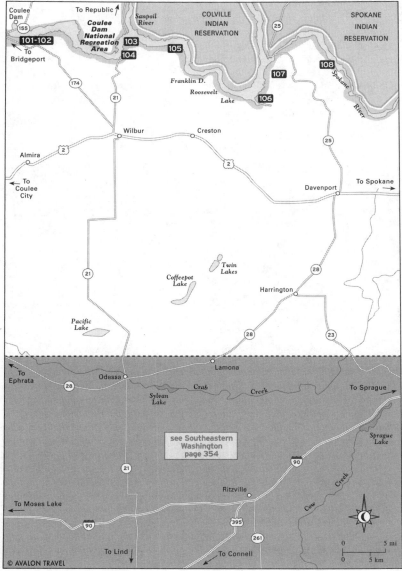

© AVALON TRAVEL

Map 4.6

Sites 109-117
Pages 294-298

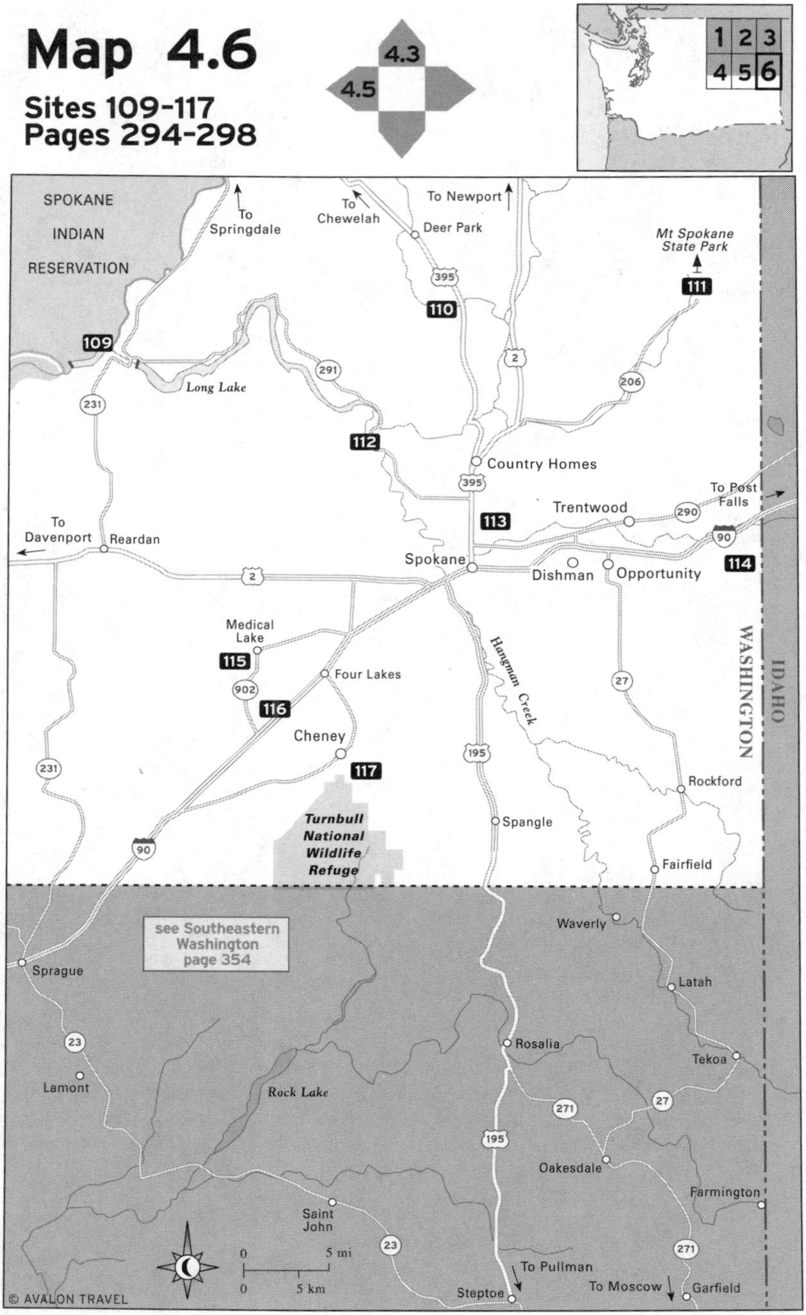

4.3

4.5

| 1 | 2 | 3 |
| 4 | 5 | 6 |

SPOKANE INDIAN RESERVATION

To Springdale

To Chewelah

To Newport

Deer Park

Mt Spokane State Park

111

395

110

2

206

109

231

Long Lake

291

112

395

Country Homes

113

Trentwood

290

To Post Falls

90

To Davenport

Reardan

2

Spokane

Dishman

Opportunity

114

WASHINGTON

IDAHO

Medical Lake

115

902

116

Four Lakes

Cheney

Hangman Creek

27

231

117

90

Turnbull National Wildlife Refuge

195

Spangle

Rockford

Fairfield

see Southeastern Washington page 354

Waverly

Sprague

Latah

23

Rosalia

Tekoa

Lamont

Rock Lake

271

27

195

Oakesdale

Farmington

Saint John

23

To Pullman

271

Steptoe

To Moscow

Garfield

0   5 mi
0   5 km

© AVALON TRAVEL

1 OSOYOOS LAKE VETERANS MEMORIAL PARK

🏊 🛶 � ❄️ 🐕 ♿ 🚐 ⛺

Scenic rating: 9

on Osoyoos Lake

Map 4.1, page 239

The park is set along the shore of Osoyoos Lake, a 14-mile-long lake created from the Okanogan River, located south of the Canadian Rockies. The park covers 47 acres and provides a base of operations for a fishing vacation. The lake has rainbow trout, kokanee salmon, smallmouth bass, crappie, and perch. Fishing gear and concessions are available. Water sports are also popular in the summer, and in winter, this is an ideal location for ice-skating, ice fishing, and snow play. Expansive lawns lead down to the sandy shore of the lake, which is a winter nesting area for geese. A nine-hole golf course is nearby. A historical note: Many years ago, the area was the site of the annual *okanogan* (rendezvous) of the Salish Indians from what are now Washington and British Columbia. They would gather and share supplies of fish and game for the year.

Campsites, facilities: There are 61 sites for tents or RVs up to 32 feet long (no hookups), 18 sites with full or partial hookups, and six primitive walk-in sites for tents only. Picnic tables and fire grills are provided. Restrooms with flush toilets and coin showers, dump station, a store, café, firewood, horseshoes, and volleyball are available. A coin laundry and ice machine are located within one mile. Boat-launching and dock facilities are nearby. Some facilities are wheelchair-accessible. Leashed pets are permitted.

Reservations, fees: Reservations are accepted online at https://orovillepark.goingtocamp.com ($8 reservation fee). Sites are $16-33 per night, $10 per each additional vehicle per night. Some credit cards are accepted. Open April-October, weather permitting.

Directions: From Oroville, just south of the Canadian border, drive north on U.S. 97 for one mile to the park entrance on the right.

Contact: Osoyoos Lake Veterans Memorial Park, 509/476-3321, http://www.oroville-wa.com.

2 CHOPAKA LAKE

🏊 🛶 🚐 🐕 ♿ 🚐 ⛺

Scenic rating: 8

on Chopaka Lake

Map 4.1, page 239   **BEST (**

This campground provides a classic setting for the expert angler. It's nestled along the western shore of Chopaka Lake, which is extremely popular with trout anglers. No motorboats are permitted on the lake. That makes it a winner for fly fishers (barbless hooks required) using float tubes.

Campsites, facilities: There are 16 sites for tents or RVs up to 20 feet long. Picnic tables and fire grills are provided. Vault toilets, drinking water, a fishing platform, and primitive boat-launching facilities are available. Garbage must be packed out. Some facilities are wheelchair accessible. Leashed pets are permitted.

Reservations, fees: Reservations are not accepted. There is no fee for camping, but a Discover Pass is required. Open year-round, weather permitting; drive-in access is usually passable mid-April-mid-November.

Directions: From Wenatchee, drive north on U.S. 97 for 120 miles to Tonasket and Forest Street. Turn left and drive 0.2 mile (crossing the Okanogan River) to Highway 7. Turn right (north) on Highway 7 (Loomis-Oroville Highway) and drive five miles. At the fork, continue on Loomis-Oroville Highway for about 12 miles to Toats Coulee Road, 2.1 miles north of Loomis. Turn left and drive 5.5 miles to Toats Coulee Campground. Continue 2.1 miles to Nine Mile Road. Turn right and drive approximately 3.5 miles to Chopaka Road. Turn right and drive 3.5 miles to Chopaka Lake Road. Turn left and drive one mile to the camp on the left.

Contact: Department of Natural Resources,

Northeast Division, 509/684-7474, www.dnr.wa.gov.

3 COLD SPRINGS

Scenic rating: 8

near Cold Creek

Map 4.1, page 239

It's quite a drive to get here, but you'll be happy you made the effort to reach this pretty forested camp. Campsites are located near a small stream amid a forest of lodgepole pine, western larch, and several species of fir, including Douglas fir. Trails for horseback riding, hiking, and snowmobiling run through the area. Because the camp is little known and remote, it's advisable to obtain a map of the area from the Department of Natural Resources.

Campsites, facilities: There are nine campsites for tents or RVs up to 20 feet long. Picnic tables, fire grills, and tent pads are provided. Vault toilets and drinking water are available. Garbage must be packed out. Some facilities are wheelchair accessible. Leashed pets are permitted.

Reservations, fees: Reservations are not accepted. There is no fee for camping, but a Discover Pass is required. Open year-round.

Directions: From Wenatchee, drive north on U.S. 97 for 120 miles to Tonasket and Forest Street. Turn left and drive 0.2 mile (crossing the Okanogan River) to Highway 7. Turn right (north) on Highway 7 (Loomis-Oroville Highway) and drive five miles. At the fork, continue on Loomis-Oroville Highway for about 12 miles to Toats Coulee Road, 2.1 miles north of Loomis. Turn left and drive 5.5 miles to the Toats Coulee camp. Continue on the main road for 2.1 miles to Nine Mile Road. Turn right and drive approximately 5.5 miles to the camp on the left.

Contact: Department of Natural Resources, Northeast Region, 509/684-7474, www.dnr.wa.gov.

4 NORTH FORK NINE MILE

Scenic rating: 6

on the North Fork of Toats Coulee Creek

Map 4.1, page 239

Deer and black bears frequent this campground situated in the forest along the North Fork of Toats Coulee Creek and Nine Mile Creek. This camp is popular in the fall with hunters. Trout fishing is fair at Toats Coulee Creek; check regulations. It's advisable to obtain a map from the Department of Natural Resources that details the area.

Campsites, facilities: There are 11 sites for tents or RVs up to 20 feet long. Picnic tables and fire grills are provided. Vault toilets and drinking water are available. Garbage must be packed out. Some facilities are wheelchair accessible. Leashed pets are permitted.

Reservations, fees: Reservations are not accepted. There is no fee for camping, but a Discover Pass is required. Open year-round, weather permitting.

Directions: From Wenatchee, drive north on U.S. 97 for 120 miles to Tonasket and Forest Street. Turn left and drive 0.2 mile (crossing the Okanogan River) to Highway 7. Turn right (north) on Highway 7 (Loomis-Oroville Highway) and drive five miles. At the fork, continue on Loomis-Oroville Highway for about 12 miles to Toats Coulee Road, 2.1 miles north of Loomis. Turn left and drive 5.5 miles to the Toats Coulee camp. Continue 2.3 miles to the campground, 0.2 mile past Nine Mile Road.

Contact: Department of Natural Resources, Northeast Region, 509/684-7474, www.dnr.wa.gov.

5 TOATS COULEE

Scenic rating: 6

on Toats Coulee Creek

Map 4.1, page 239

Toats Coulee consists of two primitive

campsites set a short distance apart. The camp is set in a wooded spot along Toats Coulee Creek. Trout fishing is available; check regulations. The best hiking is located 10 miles northwest in the Pasayten Wilderness (to reach this trailhead, continue driving up the campground road). These camps are popular in the fall with hunters. In the winter, a road for snowmobile use follows the South Fork of Toats Coulee Creek, swinging south and then heading east along Cecil Creek.

Campsites, facilities: There are nine single sites and two double sites for tents or RVs up to 20 feet long. Picnic tables and fire grills are provided. Vault toilets are available. There is no drinking water and garbage must be packed out. Some facilities are wheelchair accessible. Leashed pets are permitted.

Reservations, fees: Reservations are not accepted. There is no fee for camping, but a Discover Pass is required. Open year-round.

Directions: From Wenatchee, drive north on U.S. 97 for 120 miles to Tonasket and Forest Street. Turn left and drive 0.2 mile (crossing the Okanogan River) to Highway 7. Turn right (north) on Highway 7 (Loomis-Oroville Highway) and drive five miles. At the fork, continue on Loomis-Oroville Highway for about 12 miles to Toats Coulee Road, 2.1 miles north of Loomis. Turn left and drive 5.5 miles to the camp on the left.

Contact: Department of Natural Resources, Northeast Region, 509/684-7474, www.dnr. wa.gov.

6 PALMER LAKE

Scenic rating: 9

on Palmer Lake

Map 4.1, page 239   **BEST (**

This shorefront camp is the only one at Palmer Lake. The campsites are set close to the lake's very scenic shore. It fills up during the summer, even on weekdays, frequently with visitors from Canada. Fishing is often good for kokanee

salmon and rainbow trout. Powerboating and waterskiing are permitted. There are numerous migration routes in the region; the Sinlahekin Valley to the south of Palmer Lake is part of the winter range for deer. Endangered bighorn sheep, cougars, bald and golden eagles, black bears, and grouse are among the wildlife that can be spotted.

Campsites, facilities: There are eight sites for tents or RVs up to 20 feet long. Picnic tables and fire grills are provided. Vault toilets are available. There is no drinking water and garbage must be packed out. A primitive boat launch is located at the opposite end of the lake; four-wheel drive is required. Some facilities are wheelchair accessible. Leashed pets are permitted.

Reservations, fees: Reservations are not accepted. There is no fee for camping, but a Discover Pass is required. Open year-round, weather permitting.

Directions: From Wenatchee, drive north on U.S. 97 for 120 miles to Tonasket and Forest Street. Turn left and drive 0.2 mile, crossing the Okanogan River, to Highway 7. Turn right (north) on Highway 7 (Loomis-Oroville Highway) and drive 18.5 miles, 8.5 miles past Loomis. Stay to the right and drive to the camp at the north end of the lake.

Contact: Department of Natural Resources, Northeast Region, 509/684-7474, www.dnr. wa.gov.

7 SUN COVE RESORT

Scenic rating: 9

on Wannacut Lake near Oroville

Map 4.1, page 239

This beautiful resort is surrounded by trees and hills and set along the shore of Wannacut Lake, a spring-fed lake that doesn't get much traffic. The lake is approximately three miles long and 2.5 miles wide. An 8-mph speed limit is enforced for boats. Fishing, swimming, boating, and hiking are all summertime options. The park provides full facilities, including a heated pool, playground, and recreation hall.

Campsites, facilities: There are 27 sites for RVs of any length, including 19 sites with full hookups, 10 sites for tents, two cottages, and 10 motel units with kitchens. Picnic tables are provided. No wood fires are allowed. Restrooms with flush toilets and coin showers, a dump station, recreation hall, general store, restaurant, coin laundry, ice, fishing supplies and fishing licenses, a playground, horseshoe pits, and a seasonal heated swimming pool are available. Boat docks, launching facilities, and rentals are also available. Some facilities are wheelchair accessible. Leashed pets are permitted in the campground.

Reservations, fees: Reservations are accepted. Sites are $33 per night, $5 per person for more than four people. Some credit cards are accepted. Open late April-mid-October.

Directions: From Oroville, just south of the Canadian border, drive west on Ellemehan Mountain Road for about six miles to Wannacut Lake Road. Turn left (south) and drive five miles to the resort at the end of the road.

Contact: Sun Cove Resort, 93 E. Wannacut Lane, Oroville, 509/476-2223, www.thesuncoveresort.com.

8 SPECTACLE LAKE RESORT

Scenic rating: 7

on Spectacle Lake

Map 4.1, page 239

This pleasant resort on the shore of long, narrow Spectacle Lake has grassy, shaded sites. Space is usually available here, although reservations are accepted. Recreation options include boating, fishing, swimming, waterskiing, watercraft, and hunting (in season).

Campsites, facilities: There are 34 sites for tents or RVs of any length (20 and 30 amp full hookups) and 16 motel rooms with kitchenettes. Picnic tables and fire pits are provided.

Restrooms with flush toilets and showers, propane gas, a dump station, a convenience store, coin laundry, ice, a playground, volleyball, horseshoes, recreation hall, exercise room, and seasonal heated swimming pool are available. Boat docks, launching facilities, and rentals are also nearby. Some facilities are wheelchair accessible. Leashed pets are permitted.

Reservations, fees: Reservations are accepted. Sites are $35 per night, $3-5 per each additional person. Some credit cards are accepted. Open mid-April-late October.

Directions: In Tonasket on U.S. 97, turn west (left if arriving from the south), cross the bridge, and continue to Highway 7. Turn right on Highway 7 and drive about 12 miles to Holmes Road. Turn left (south) on Holmes Road and drive 0.5 mile to McCammon Road. Turn right (west) and drive one block to the resort at the end of the road.

Contact: Spectacle Lake Resort, 10 McCammon Rd., Tonasket, 509/223-3433, www.spectaclelakeresort.com.

9 LOST LAKE

Scenic rating: 7

on Lost Lake in Okanogan National Forest

Map 4.1, page 239

This camp is set on the shore of Lost Lake at an elevation of 3,800 feet. As a launch point for fishing, swimming, hiking, hunting, and horseback riding, it keeps visitors happy. No gas motors are permitted on the lake. The lake is similar to Beth and Beaver Lakes, but rounder. The Big Tree Botanical Area is about one mile away. Note that the group site is often booked one year in advance.

Campsites, facilities: There are 19 sites for tents or RVs up to 31 feet long, including six double sites. There is also one group site for up to 100 people. Picnic tables and fire rings are provided. Drinking water, vault toilets, and garbage bins are available. Boat-launching facilities and swimming platforms, a ball field, and horseshoe pits are nearby. Some facilities are wheelchair accessible. Leashed pets are permitted.

Reservations, fees: Reservations are not available for single and double sites but are required for the group site at 877/444-6777 ($10 reservation fee) or www.recreation.gov ($9 reservation fee). Sites are $12-24 per night, $5 per night per additional vehicle; group sites are $40 per night for 1-25 people, $60 per night for 26-50 people, and $80 per night for 51-100 people. Open May-mid-October, weather permitting.

Directions: From East Wenatchee, drive north on U.S. 97 for 120 miles to Tonasket and Highway 20. Turn east on Highway 20 and drive 20 miles to Bonaparte Lake Road (County Road 4953). Turn left (north) and drive six miles to Forest Road 32. Turn right (north) and drive four miles to Forest Road 33. Bear left (northwest) and drive five miles to a four-way intersection. Turn left on Forest Road 33-050 and drive 0.3 mile to the campground on the right.

Contact: Okanogan-Wenatchee National Forest, Tonasket Ranger District, 509/486-2186, www.fs.usda.gov.

10 BONAPARTE LAKE

Scenic rating: 7

on Bonaparte Lake in Okanogan National Forest

Map 4.1, page 239

This campground is located on the southern shore of Bonaparte Lake at an elevation of 3,600 feet. The lake is stocked with rainbow trout, brook trout, and mackinaw trout. A 10-mph speed limit keeps the lake quiet, ideal for fishing. Several trails nearby provide access to Mount Bonaparte Lookout.

Campsites, facilities: There are 25 single sites and three double sites for tents or RVs of any length, one bike-in/hike-in site (requiring a walk of less than 100 feet), and one group site

for up to 100 people. Picnic tables and fire grills are provided. Drinking water, vault toilets, and garbage bins are available. A store, café, gas, and ice are available within one mile. Boat docks and launching facilities are also available. Some facilities are wheelchair accessible. Leashed pets are permitted.

Reservations, fees: Reservations are not accepted. Sites are $12-24 per night, hike-in/bike-in sites are $8 per night, the group site is $100 per night, $5 per night per additional vehicle. Open mid-May-mid-October, weather permitting.

Directions: From East Wenatchee, drive north on U.S. 97 for 120 miles to Tonasket and Highway 20. Turn east on Highway 20 and drive 20 miles to Bonaparte Lake Road (County Road 4953). Turn left (north) and drive six miles to Bonaparte Lake and Forest Road 32 and the campground on the left.

Contact: Okanogan-Wenatchee National Forest, Tonasket Ranger District, 509/486-2186, www.fs.usda.gov.

11 BONAPARTE LAKE RESORT

Scenic rating: 6

on Bonaparte Lake

Map 4.1, page 239

Fishing is popular at this resort, set on the southeast shore of Bonaparte Lake. A 10-mph speed limit keeps the lake quiet, ideal for fishing. Other recreational activities include hiking and hunting in the nearby U.S. Forest Service lands and snowmobiling, cross-country skiing, and ice fishing in the winter. Poker tournaments are held occasionally.

Campsites, facilities: There are 30 sites with full hookups (20 and 30 amps) for RVs of any length, 13 sites for tents, and 10 cabins. Some sites are pull-through. Picnic tables and fire rings are provided. Restrooms with flush toilets and showers, propane, a dump station, firewood, a recreation hall, convenience store, restaurant, coin laundry, ice, boat docks, launching facilities, and boat rentals are available. Some facilities are wheelchair accessible. Leashed pets are permitted.

Reservations, fees: Reservations are accepted. Sites are $18-28 per night. Some credit cards are accepted. Open year-round, with limited winter facilities.

Directions: From East Wenatchee, drive north on U.S. 97 for 20 miles to Tonasket and Highway 20. Turn east on Highway 20 and drive 20 miles to Bonaparte Lake Road (County Road 4953). Turn left (north) and drive six miles to Bonaparte Lake and the resort on the left.

Contact: Bonaparte Lake Resort, 615 Bonaparte Lake Rd., Tonasket, 509/486-2828, www.bonapartelakeresort.com.

12 TIFFANY SPRINGS

Scenic rating: 7
near Tiffany Lake in Okanogan National Forest

Map 4.1, page 239

Set at an elevation of 6,800 feet, this camp is less than a mile hike from Tiffany Lake. Tiffany Mountain rises 8,200 feet in the distance. The lake provides fishing for rainbow trout and brook trout. There are also some good hiking trails in the area. The Tiffany Mountain area provides a network of 26 miles of hiking trails, accessed from either here at Tiffany Springs or at Tiffany Lake. The area is still recovering from a 2006 wildfire, so it's fairly open with some scattered, burnt trees.

Campsites, facilities: There are six sites for tents or small RVs up to 16 feet long. Picnic tables and fire grills are provided. Vault toilets are available. There is no drinking water, and garbage must be packed out. Some facilities are wheelchair accessible. Leashed pets are permitted.

Reservations, fees: Reservations are not accepted. There is no fee for camping. Open June-mid-October, weather permitting.

Directions: From East Wenatchee, drive

north on U.S. 97 for 88 miles to Okanogan and County Road 9229. Turn north and drive 17.5 miles northwest to Conconully and County Road 2017. Turn left on County Road 2017 and drive two miles (road becomes Forest Road 42) to Forest Road 37. Turn right (northwest) on Forest Road 37 and drive 21 miles to Forest Road 39. Turn right (northeast) on Forest Road 39 and proceed eight miles to the campground on the left.

Contact: Okanogan-Wenatchee National Forest, Tonasket Ranger District, 509/486-2186, www.fs.usda.gov.

13 SALMON MEADOWS

Scenic rating: 6
in Okanogan National Forest

Map 4.1, page 239

This camp is located along Salmon Creek at an elevation of 4,500 feet. Come in the spring for a spectacular wildflower display in an adjacent meadow. The camp features a forest setting, mainly Douglas fir, spruce, and some western larch. Trails from the campground are routed out to Angel Pass, two miles one-way, for views of the Tiffany area.

Campsites, facilities: There are eight single sites and one double site for tents or small RVs up to 16 feet long. Picnic tables and fire grills are provided. Vault toilets and a horse corral are available. There is no drinking water. A gazebo is available at the day-use area. Garbage must be packed out. Leashed pets are permitted.

Reservations, fees: Reservations are not accepted. Sites are $8 per night, $5 per night per additional vehicle. Open mid-May-mid-October, weather permitting.

Directions: From East Wenatchee, drive north on U.S. 97 for 88 miles to Okanogan and County Road 9229. Turn left (north) on County Road 9229 and drive 17.5 miles to Conconully and County Road 2361. Continue northwest on County Road 2361 and drive four miles (becomes Forest Road 38) to Kerr Campground.

Continue past Kerr for 4.5 miles to the campground on the right.

Contact: Okanogan-Wenatchee National Forest, Tonasket Ranger District, 509/486-2186, www.fs.usda.gov.

14 KERR

Scenic rating: 6
in Okanogan National Forest

Map 4.1, page 239

This camp sits at an elevation of 3,100 feet along Salmon Creek, about four miles north of Conconully Reservoir, and is one of many campgrounds near the lake. Fishing prospects are marginal for trout here. There are numerous recreation options available at Conconully Reservoir, including far better fishing.

Campsites, facilities: There are 12 sites for tents or RVs up to 30 feet long. Picnic tables and fire grills are provided. Vault toilets are available. There is no drinking water and garbage must be packed out. Some facilities are wheelchair accessible. Leashed pets are permitted.

Reservations, fees: Reservations are not accepted. Sites are $8-16 per night, $5 per night per additional vehicle. Open mid-May-mid-October, weather permitting.

Directions: From East Wenatchee, drive north on U.S. 97 for 88 miles to Okanogan and County Road 9229. Turn left (north) on County Road 9229 and drive 17.5 miles to Conconully and County Road 2361. Continue northwest on County Road 2361 and drive four miles (becomes Forest Road 38) to the campground on the left.

Contact: Okanogan-Wenatchee National Forest, Tonasket Ranger District, 509/486-2186, www.fs.usda.gov.

15 ORIOLE

Scenic rating: 6
in Okanogan National Forest

Map 4.1, page 239

This camp is located at 2,900 feet elevation along Salmon Creek and offers a creek view from some of the campsites. This forest setting features well-spaced campsites among western larch and lodgepole pine. This is a primitive camp, similar to Kerr and Salmon Meadows, which are also set on Salmon Creek.

Campsites, facilities: There are seven single sites and three double sites for tents or small trailers. Picnic tables and fire grills are provided. Drinking water, vault toilets, and garbage bins are available. Some facilities are wheelchair accessible. Leashed pets are permitted.

Reservations, fees: Reservations are not accepted. Sites are $8-16 per night, $5 per night per additional vehicle. Open mid-May-October, weather permitting.

Directions: From East Wenatchee, drive north on U.S. 97 for 88 miles to Okanogan and County Road 9229. Turn left (north) on County Road 9229 and drive 17.5 miles to Conconully and County Road 2361. Continue northwest on County Road 2361 and drive 2.5 miles to Forest Road 025. Turn left and drive 0.5 mile (crossing the creek) to the campground on the left.

Contact: Okanogan-Wenatchee National Forest, Tonasket Ranger District, 509/486-2186, www.fs.usda.gov.

16 SUGARLOAF

Scenic rating: 6
on Sugarloaf Lake in Okanogan National Forest

Map 4.1, page 239

Sugarloaf Lake is a small lake, about 20 acres, and this small camp is set near its shore. It provides fishing for rainbow trout, but the lake level often drops substantially during summer, so this camp gets little use in late summer and early fall. Conconully State Park and Information Center are nearby.

Campsites, facilities: There are four tent sites. Picnic tables and fire rings are provided. Hand-pumped drinking water and vault toilets are available. Garbage must be packed out. Boat-launching facilities are available nearby. No boats with gas motors are permitted. Leashed pets are permitted.

Reservations, fees: Reservations are not accepted. Sites are $8 per night, $5 per night per additional vehicle. Open mid-May-mid-October, weather permitting.

Directions: From East Wenatchee, drive north on U.S. 97 for 88 miles to Okanogan and County Road 9229. Turn north and drive about 17.5 miles northwest to Conconully and County Road 4015. Turn right (northwest) on County Road 4015 and drive 4.5 miles to the campground on the left.

Contact: Okanogan-Wenatchee National Forest, Tonasket Ranger District, 509/486-2186, www.fs.usda.gov.

17 KOZY KABINS AND RV PARK

Scenic rating: 7

in Conconully

Map 4.1, page 239

This quiet and private park in Conconully has a small creek running through it and plenty of greenery. A full-service marina is located close by. There is hunting in season, and snowmobiling is an option in the winter. If you continue northeast of town on County Road 4015, the road will get a bit narrow for a while but will widen again when you enter the Sinlahekin Habitat Management Area, which is managed by the Department of Fish and Wildlife. There are some primitive campsites in this valley, especially along the shores of the lakes in the area.

Campsites, facilities: There are 15 sites with full hookups (30 amps) for RVs up to 40 feet long, six tent sites, and seven cabins. Picnic tables are provided. Restrooms with flush toilets and coin showers, a community fire pit, and firewood are available. Propane gas, general store, café, coin laundry, and ice are located within one block. Boat docks, launching facilities, and boat rentals are nearby. Leashed pets are permitted.

Reservations, fees: Reservations are accepted at 888/502-2246. Sites are $26 per night. Some credit cards are accepted. Open year-round.

Directions: From U.S. 97 in Okanogan, turn north (left if arriving from the south) on Pine Street/Conconully Highway and drive 17.5 miles northwest to Conconully and Broadway Street. Turn right (east) and drive one block to A Avenue. The park is at the junction of A Avenue and Broadway Street.

Contact: Kozy Kabins and RV Park, 111 Broadway St., Conconully, 509/826-6780.

18 CONCONULLY STATE PARK

Scenic rating: 9

in Conconully

Map 4.1, page 239   BEST (

Conconully State Park, which dates to 1910, is set along Conconully Reservoir and covers 81 acres, with 5,400 feet of shoreline. Anglers will be happy here, with opportunities for trout, bass, and kokanee salmon. A boat launch, beach access, swimming, and fishing provide all sorts of water sports possibilities. A 0.5-mile nature trail is available. A side-trip option is Sinlahekin habitat management area, which is accessible via County Road 4015. This route heads northeast along the shore of Conconully Reservoir on the other side of U.S. 97. The road is narrow at first, but it becomes wider as it enters the Habitat Management Area.

Campsites, facilities: There are 39 sites with no hookups and 20 sites with partial hookups for tents or RVs up to 75 feet. There are also five cabins. Picnic tables and fire grills are provided. Restrooms with flush toilets and coin showers, a dump station, firewood, and a playground are available. A store, café, coin laundry, and ice are located within one mile. Boat-launching and dock facilities are nearby. A sheltered picnic area, horseshoe pits, baseball field, and interpretive activities are available nearby. Some facilities are wheelchair accessible. Leashed pets are permitted.

Reservations, fees: Reservations are accepted for some sites at 888/226-7588 or https://washington.goingtocamp.com ($8-10 reservation fee); the remaining sites are first-come, first-served. Sites are $20-40 per night, $10 per extra vehicle per night. The cabins are $40-74 per night, pets are $15 per night. Open year-round.

Directions: On U.S. 97 at Omak, take the North Omak exit. At the base of the hill, turn right and drive two miles until you reach Conconully Road. Turn right and drive 15 miles north to the park entrance.

Contact: Conconully State Park, 509/826-7408, http://parks.state.wa.us.

19 LIAR'S COVE RESORT

🚶🚴🏊🛶🎣🏕🐕♿🚐🏕

Scenic rating: 6

south of Conconully

Map 4.1, page 239

Roomy sites for RVs can be found at this camp on the shore of Conconully Reservoir. Tents are allowed, too. Fishing, swimming, boating, and hiking opportunities are located nearby.

Campsites, facilities: There are 35 sites for tents or RVs of any length (30 and 50 amp full hookups), two cabins, one mobile home, and three motel rooms. Picnic tables and fire pits are provided. Restrooms with flush toilets and coin showers, cable TV, Wi-Fi, ice, swimming beach, boat docks, launching facilities, and boat and water toy rentals are available. Propane gas, a dump station, store, and café are within one mile. Some facilities are wheelchair accessible. Leashed pets are permitted.

Reservations, fees: Reservations are accepted. RV sites are $32-35 per night, tent sites are $20-25 per night, pets are $5 per night. Some credit cards are accepted. Open April-October.

Directions: From U.S. 97 in Okanogan, turn north (left if arriving from the south) on Pine Street/Conconully Highway and drive 16.5 miles northwest to Conconully and look for the park on the left.

Contact: Liar's Cove Resort, 509/826-1288 or 800/830-1288, www.liarscoveresort.com.

20 SHADY PINES RESORT

🚶🚴🏊🛶🎣🏕🐕♿🚐🏕

Scenic rating: 6

on Conconully Reservoir

Map 4.1, page 239

This camp is set on the western shore of Conconully Reservoir. It is near Conconully State Park and provides an option if the state park campground is full—a common occurrence in summer. But note that on summer weekends, this camp often fills as well. The nearby Sinlahekin Habitat Management Area, which is managed by the Department of Fish and Wildlife, offers a possible side trip.

Campsites, facilities: There are 21 sites with full hookups (20, 30, and 50 amps) for RVs up to 40 feet, two tent sites, and six cabins. Some sites are pull-through. Picnic tables and fire rings are provided. Restrooms with flush toilets and coin showers, ice, firewood, gift and tackle shop, fish-cleaning station, coin laundry, boat-launching facilities, and boat rentals are available. Propane gas, a dump station, store, café, and coin laundry are located within one mile. Some facilities are wheelchair accessible. Leashed pets are permitted.

Reservations, fees: Reservations are accepted at 800/552-2287. RV sites are $31-33 per night, tent sites are $21 per night, $7 per night per extra vehicle. Weekly rates are available. Some credit cards are accepted. Open mid-April-late October.

Directions: From U.S. 97 in Okanogan, turn north (left if arriving from the south) on Pine Street/Conconully Highway and drive 16.5 miles northwest to Conconully and Broadway Street. Turn left (west) and drive one mile. The park is on the west shore of the lake.

Contact: Shady Pines Resort, 509/826-2287, www.shadypinesresort.com.

21 LYMAN LAKE

Scenic rating: 5

on Lyman Lake in Okanogan National Forest

Map 4.1, page 239

Little known and little used, this campground along the shore of Lyman Lake is an idyllic spot for those wanting solitude and quiet. The lake is quite small, just five acres at most, but fishing for stocked rainbow trout is an option.

Campsites, facilities: There are four sites for tents or RVs up to 30 feet long. Picnic tables and fire grills are provided. Vault toilets are available. There is no drinking water, and garbage must be packed out. Leashed pets are permitted.

Reservations, fees: Reservations are not accepted. There is no fee for camping. Open mid-May-mid-October, weather permitting.

Directions: From East Wenatchee, drive north on U.S. 97 for 120 miles to Tonasket and Highway 20. Turn east on Highway 20 and drive 12.5 miles to County Road 9455. Turn right (southeast) on County Road 9455 and drive 13 miles to County Road 3785. Turn right (south) on County Road 3785 and drive 2.5 miles to the campground entrance on the right.

Contact: Okanogan-Wenatchee National Forest, Tonasket Ranger District, 509/486-2186, www.fs.usda.gov.

22 ROCK LAKES

Scenic rating: 8

on Rock Lake

Map 4.1, page 239   **BEST (**

This camp is set in a forested area along the shore of Rock Lake. Fishing for rainbow trout and brook trout is a plus at Rock Lake. A downer is that access for launching even car-top boats is difficult, requiring a 0.25-mile hike. That makes it a better bet for float tubes. Note that the best fishing is early in the season and that the lake level often drops because of irrigation use. Some roads in the area are used by hikers and bikers. A good bet is to combine a trip here with nearby Leader Lake. Highway 20 east of I-5 is a designated scenic route.

Campsites, facilities: There are eight sites for tents or RVs up to 20 feet long. Picnic tables and fire pits are provided. Vault toilets are available. There is no drinking water, and garbage must be packed out. Leashed pets are permitted.

Reservations, fees: Reservations are not accepted. There is no fee for camping, but a Discover Pass is required. Open year-round.

Directions: From East Wenatchee, drive north on U.S. 97 for 88 miles to Okanogan and Highway 20. Turn west and drive 10 miles to Loup Loup Canyon Road. Turn left on Loup Loup Canyon Road and drive 4.8 miles to Rock Lakes Road. Turn left on Rock Lakes Road and drive 5.8 miles to the campground entrance. Turn left and drive 0.25 mile to the campground.

Contact: Department of Natural Resources, Northeast Region, 509/684-7474, www.dnr.wa.gov.

23 CARL PRECHT MEMORIAL RV PARK

🏃 🏊 🚣 🛶 🐴 🚶 ♿ 🚐 ⛺

Scenic rating: 6

in Omak

Map 4.1, page 239

East Side Park is in the town of Omak, along the shore of the Okanogan River. Home to the Omak Stampede and World Famous Suicide Race, it covers about 76 acres and features the Carl Precht RV Park, with campsites positioned on concrete pads surrounded by grass. Trout fishing is often good here, and there is a boat ramp near the campground. Nearby recreation options include an 18-hole golf course, a swimming pool, and a sports field.

Campsites, facilities: There are 68 sites with full hookups (20 and 30 amps) for RVs of any length and five tent sites. Some sites are pull-through. Picnic tables are provided. Restrooms with flush toilets and coin showers (seasonal), a dump station, a picnic area, Wi-Fi, a seasonal heated swimming pool, a playground, tennis and basketball courts, baseball and soccer fields, horseshoe pits, a skateboarding park, and a fitness trail are available. A store, café, gasoline, and ice are located within one mile. Some facilities are wheelchair accessible. Leashed pets are permitted.

Reservations, fees: Reservations are not accepted. RV sites are $25 per night, tent sites are $15 per night. Winter rates are available. Open year-round, weather permitting.

Directions: From U.S. 97 in Omak, turn west (left, if coming from the south) on Highway 155 and drive 0.3 mile to the campground on the left.

Contact: City of Omak, 509/826-1170, www.omakcity.com.

24 CRAWFISH LAKE

🏊 🚣 🏠 🐴 ♿ 🚐 ⛺

Scenic rating: 8

on Crawfish Lake in Okanogan National Forest

Map 4.1, page 239

This pretty, remote, and primitive camp is set at 4,500 feet elevation along the shore of Crawfish Lake. Crawdads were once abundant here, but overfishing has depleted their numbers. Swimming and fishing for trout are more popular.

Campsites, facilities: There are 15 single sites and four double sites for tents or RVs up to 30 feet long. Picnic tables and fire grills are provided. Vault toilets are available. There is no drinking water, and garbage must be packed out. Boat-launching facilities are located on the lake. Some facilities are wheelchair accessible. Leashed pets are permitted.

Reservations, fees: Reservations are not accepted. There is no fee for camping. Open mid-May-mid-October, weather permitting.

Directions: From East Wenatchee, drive north on U.S. 97 for 102 miles to Riverside and County Road 9320. Turn right (east) on County Road 9320 and drive 20 miles (becomes Forest Road 30) to Forest Road 30-100. Turn right and drive 0.5 mile to the campground on the right.

Contact: Okanogan-Wenatchee National Forest, Tonasket Ranger District, 509/486-2186, www.fs.usda.gov.

25 LOUP LOUP

🏃 🚴 ❄ 🐴 ♿ 🚐 ⛺

Scenic rating: 6

near Loup Loup Ski Area in Okanogan National Forest

Map 4.1, page 239

This camp provides a good setup for large groups of up to 100 people. It is located next to the Loup Loup Ski Area at 4,200 feet elevation. The camp features a setting of western larch trees, along with good access to biking and hiking trails as well as the ski area.

Campsites, facilities: There are 25 sites for tents or RVs up to 36 feet long. Picnic tables and fire rings are provided. Drinking water, vault toilets, and garbage bins are available. Some facilities are wheelchair accessible. Leashed pets are permitted.

Reservations, fees: Reservations are not accepted. Sites are $12 per night, $5 extra vehicle fee with two-vehicle maximum. Open May-mid-October, weather permitting.

Directions: From East Wenatchee, drive north on U.S. 97 for 88 miles to Okanogan and Highway 20. Turn west and drive 21 miles to Forest Road 42. Turn right (north) on Forest Road 42 and drive one mile to the campground on the left.

Contact: Okanogan-Wenatchee National Forest, Methow Valley Ranger District, 509/996-4003, www.fs.usda.gov; Methow Valley Visitor Center, 509/996-4000.

26 SPORTSMAN CAMP

Scenic rating: 6
in Lower Loomis State Forest

Map 4.1, page 239

In season, this is a popular camp with hunters, who may bring horses; although there are no livestock facilities, horses are allowed in the camp. The landscape is shady and grassy with a small stream. Some roads in the area can be used by hikers and bikers. Highway 20 east of I-5 is a designated scenic route.

Campsites, facilities: There are four sites for tents or RVs up to 20 feet long and a small, dispersed area for tents. Picnic tables and fire pits are provided. Vault toilets are available, but there is no drinking water. Garbage must be packed out. A gazebo shelter with a fire pit is also available. Some facilities are wheelchair accessible. Leashed pets are permitted.

Reservations, fees: Reservations are not accepted. There is no fee for camping, but a

Discover Pass is required. Open year-round, weather permitting.

Directions: From East Wenatchee, drive north on U.S. 97 for 88 miles to Okanogan and Highway 20. Turn west and drive 15 miles to Sweat Creek Road. Turn right on Sweat Creek Road and drive one mile to the campground on the right.

Contact: Department of Natural Resources, Northeast Region, 509/684-7474, www.dnr.wa.gov.

27 JR

Scenic rating: 7
in Okanogan National Forest

Map 4.1, page 239

This camp is located along Frazier Creek near the Loup Loup summit and ski area at an elevation of 3,900 feet. Recreation possibilities in the surrounding area include fishing, hunting, cross-country skiing, snowmobiling, hiking, and bicycling. This is a small layover for travelers looking for a spot on Highway 20.

Campsites, facilities: There are six sites for tents or RVs up to 16 feet long. Picnic tables and fire rings are provided. Vault toilets are available. There is no drinking water, and garbage must be packed out. Leashed pets are permitted.

Reservations, fees: Reservations are not accepted. Sites are $8 per night, $5 extra vehicle fee. Open late May-mid-October, weather permitting.

Directions: From East Wenatchee, drive north on U.S. 97 for 88 miles to Okanogan and Highway 20. Turn west and drive 22 miles to the campground on the right.

Contact: Okanogan-Wenatchee National Forest, Methow Valley Ranger District, 509/996-4003, www.fs.usda.gov; Methow Valley Visitor Center, 509/996-4000.

28 ROCK CREEK

Scenic rating: 6

on Rock Creek and Loup Loup Creek

Map 4.1, page 239

This wooded campground is situated at the confluence of Rock and Loup Loup Creeks. The camp is used primarily in the fall as a base camp for hunters and occasionally during the summer, mostly on weekends. It's advisable to obtain a map detailing the area from the Department of Natural Resources.

Campsites, facilities: There are five sites for tents or RVs up to 20 feet long. Picnic tables and fire pits are provided. Vault toilets, drinking water, and a picnic area are available. Some facilities are wheelchair accessible. Leashed pets are permitted.

Reservations, fees: Reservations are not accepted. There is no fee for camping, but a Discover Pass is required. Open year-round.

Directions: From East Wenatchee, drive north on U.S. 97 for 88 miles to Okanogan and Highway 20. Turn west and drive 10 miles to Loup Loup Canyon Road. Turn left on Loup Loup Canyon Road and drive 3.9 miles to the camp on the left.

Contact: Department of Natural Resources, Northeast Region, 509/684-7474, www.dnr. wa.gov.

29 LEADER LAKE

Scenic rating: 7

on Leader Lake

Map 4.1, page 239

This primitive but pretty camp is set along the shore of Leader Lake. It is just far enough off the beaten path to get missed by many travelers. The camp has forest cover. The boat ramp is a bonus, and trout fishing can be good in season. Note that the water level often drops in summer because of irrigation use.

Campsites, facilities: There are 16 sites for tents or RVs up to 30 feet long. Picnic tables and fire pits are provided. Vault toilets are available. There is no drinking water, and garbage must be packed out. Boat-launching facilities are nearby. Some facilities are wheelchair accessible. Leashed pets are permitted.

Reservations, fees: Reservations are not accepted. There is no fee for camping, but a Discover Pass is required. Open year-round.

Directions: From East Wenatchee, drive north on U.S. 97 for 88 miles to Okanogan and Highway 20. Turn west and drive eight miles to Leader Lake Road. Turn left and drive 0.4 mile to the campground.

Contact: Department of Natural Resources, Northeast Region, 509/684-7474, www.dnr. wa.gov.

30 AMERICAN LEGION PARK

Scenic rating: 6

in Okanogan

Map 4.1, page 239

This city park is located along the shore of the Okanogan River in an urban setting. The sites are graveled and sunny. Anglers may want to try their hand at the excellent bass fishing here. There is a historical museum at the park. A local farmers market is held on summer weekends.

Campsites, facilities: There are 35 sites for tents or RVs of any length (no hookups); all sites are pull-through. Picnic tables are provided. Restrooms with flush toilets, coin showers, and drinking water are available. A boat ramp is nearby. A store, café, coin laundry, gasoline, and ice are located within one mile. Some facilities are wheelchair accessible. Leashed pets are permitted.

Reservations, fees: Reservations are not accepted. Sites are $5-10 per night. Open April-October, weather permitting.

Directions: From East Wenatchee, drive north on U.S. 97 for 88 miles to Okanogan and Highway 215. Turn left (north) on Highway

215/2nd Avenue and drive about three miles to the campground on the right.

Contact: Okanogan City Hall, 509/422-3600, www.okanagoncity.com.

31 ALTA LAKE STATE PARK

❀ 🏕 ⛵ 🚤 🛶 🏇 ♿ 🚐 ⛰

Scenic rating: 8

on Alta Lake

Map 4.1, page 239

This state park is nestled among the pines along the shore of Alta Lake. The park covers 186 acres, and the lake is two miles long and 0.25-mile wide. Alta Lake brightens a region where the mountains and pines meet the desert and features good trout fishing in summer, along with a boat launch and a 0.5-mile-long swimming beach. Windsurfing is often excellent on windy afternoons. Because of many hidden rocks just under the lake surface, waterskiing can be dangerous. An 18-hole golf course and a riding stable are close by, and a nice one-mile hiking trail leads up to a scenic lookout. Lake Chelan is about 30 minutes away. Note that the park retains evidence of damage from the 2014 Carlton Complex Fire.

Campsites, facilities: There are 91 developed tent sites, 32 sites with partial hookups for RVs up to 38 feet long, and two group sites for 15-85 people. Picnic tables and fire grills (campfires are not allowed after July 1) are provided. Restrooms with flush toilets and coin showers, firewood, a dump station, a small camp store, and ice are available. A sheltered picnic area and boat-launching facilities are nearby. Some facilities are wheelchair accessible. Leashed pets are permitted.

Reservations, fees: Reservations are accepted at 888/226-7688 or https://washington.goingtocamp.com ($8-10 reservation fee). Sites are $20-40 per night, $10 per extra vehicle per night. The group site is $116-165 per night with a minimum of 15 people. Open April-October, weather permitting.

Directions: From East Wenatchee, drive north on U.S. 97 for 64 miles to Highway 153 (just south of Pateros). Turn left (northwest) on Highway 153 and drive two miles to Alta Lake Road. Turn left (southwest) and drive two miles to the park.

Contact: Alta Lake State Park, 509/923-2473; state park information, 360/902-8844, http://parks.state.wa.us.

32 BRIDGEPORT STATE PARK

🏕 ⛵ 🚤 🏇 ♿ 🚐 ⛰

Scenic rating: 8

on Rufus Woods Lake

Map 4.1, page 239

Bridgeport State Park is located along the shore of Rufus Woods Lake, a reservoir on the Columbia River above Chief Joseph Dam. It's a big place, covering 748 acres, including 7,500 feet of shoreline and 18 acres of lawn, with some shade amid the desert landscape. Highlights include beach access, a boat launch, and the aptly named "haystacks," unusual volcanic formations. Fishing is best by boat because shore fishing requires a Colville Tribe fishing license (for sale at the Bridgeport Hardware Store), in addition to a state fishing license. The lake has plenty of rainbow trout and walleye. Windsurfing in the afternoon wind and waterskiing are popular at the lake. Nearby recreation options include a nine-hole golf course.

Campsites, facilities: There are 14 sites for tents or RVs (no hookups), 20 sites with partial hookups for RVs up to 45 feet long, and one group site for 20-75 people. Picnic tables and fire grills are provided. Restrooms with flush toilets and coin showers, a picnic area, and a dump station are available. A store, café, and ice are located within two miles. Boat docks and launching facilities are nearby on both the upper and lower portions of the reservoir. Interpretive programs are available in summer. Some facilities are wheelchair accessible. Leashed pets are permitted.

Reservations, fees: Reservations are accepted at 888/226-7688 or www.washingotn.

goingtocamp.com ($8-10 reservation fee). Sites are $20-40 per night, $10 per night per additional vehicle. Call for group rates. Open year-round.

Directions: From East Wenatchee, drive north on U.S. 97 for 71 miles to Highway 17. Turn south on Highway 17 and drive eight miles southeast to the park entrance on the left.

Contact: Bridgeport State Park, 509/686-7231, http://parks.state.wa.us.

33 BETH LAKE
🏃🏊🚣🚗🏡♿🚐⛺

Scenic rating: 7
on Beth Lake in Okanogan National Forest

Map 4.2, page 240

This campground is set between Beth Lake and Beaver Lake, both small, narrow lakes stocked with rainbow trout and brook trout. A 1.9-mile-long hiking trail (one-way) connects the two lakes. Other side trips in the area include Lost Lake, Bonaparte Lake, and several hiking trails, one of which leads up to the Mount Bonaparte Lookout. The elevation is 2,800 feet.

Campsites, facilities: There are 13 sites for tents or RVs up to 35 feet long, plus one double site. Picnic tables and fire rings are provided. Drinking water, vault toilets, and garbage bins are available. Boat-launching facilities are available nearby. Some facilities are wheelchair accessible. Leashed pets are permitted.

Reservations, fees: Reservations are not accepted. Single sites are $8 per night, double sites are $12 per night, $5 per night per additional vehicle. Open mid-May-mid-October, weather permitting.

Directions: From East Wenatchee, drive north on U.S. 97 for 120 miles to Tonasket and Highway 20. Turn east on Highway 20 and drive 20 miles to Bonaparte Lake Road (County Road 4953). Turn left (north) and drive six miles to Bonaparte Lake and Forest Road 32. Continue (north) on Forest Road 32 and drive six miles to County Road 9480. Turn left (northwest) and drive one mile to the campground on the left.

Contact: Okanogan-Wenatchee National Forest, Tonasket Ranger District, 509/486-2186, www.fs.usda.gov.

34 BEAVER LAKE
🏃🏊🚣🚗🏡🚐⛺

Scenic rating: 7
on Beaver Lake in Okanogan National Forest

Map 4.2, page 240

This camp calls the southeastern shore of long, narrow Beaver Lake home. Situated at 2,700 feet elevation, it is one of several lakes in this area. Beth Lake is nearby and accessible with an hour-long hike. Both Beaver and Beth Lakes are stocked with trout. (The Department of Fish and Wildlife has proposed treating the lake to remove certain species of fish that are negatively impacting the trout population.) In addition to fishing, swimming, hunting, and hiking are all possibilities here.

Campsites, facilities: There are nine single and two multiple sites for tents or RVs up to 21 feet long. Picnic tables are provided. Drinking water, vault toilets, and garbage bins are available. Boat-launching facilities are located within 100 yards of the campground. No boats with gas engines are permitted; electric motors are allowed. Leashed pets are permitted.

Reservations, fees: Reservations are not accepted. Sites are $8-16 per night, plus $5 per additional vehicle per night. Open mid-May-mid-October, weather permitting.

Directions: From East Wenatchee, drive north on U.S. 97 for 120 miles to Tonasket and Highway 20. Turn east on Highway 20 and drive 20 miles to Bonaparte Lake Road (County Road 4953). Turn left (north) and drive six miles to Bonaparte Lake and Forest Road 32. Continue (north) on Forest Road 32 and drive six miles to the campground on the left.

Contact: Okanogan-Wenatchee National Forest, Tonasket Ranger District, 509/486-2186, www.fs.usda.gov.

35 PIERRE LAKE

Scenic rating: 8

on Pierre Lake in Colville National Forest

Map 4.2, page 240

At just 105 acres, Pierre Lake is a quiet jewel of a camp near the Canadian border and only a short drive from U.S. 395. It is popular and usually fills on summer weekends. The camp is set on the west shore of the lake where there is fishing for rainbow trout, cutthroat trout, brook trout, crappie, bass, and catfish. While there is no speed limit, the lake is too small for big, fast boats.

Campsites, facilities: There are 15 sites for tents or small RVs. Picnic tables and fire grills are provided. Drinking water and vault toilets are available. Garbage must be packed out. Boat docks and launching facilities are available on-site. A convenience store and ice are located within seven miles. Some facilities are wheelchair accessible. Leashed pets are permitted.

Reservations, fees: Reservations are not accepted. Sites are $6 per night. Open mid-April–mid-October, weather permitting.

Directions: From Spokane, drive north on U.S. 395 for 74 miles to Colville. Continue north on U.S. 395 for about 25 miles to Barstow and Pierre Lake Road (County Road 4013). Turn right (north) on Pierre Lake Road and drive nine miles to the campground on the west side of Pierre Lake.

Contact: Colville National Forest, Three Rivers Ranger District, 509/738-7700, www.fs.usda.gov.

36 CURLEW LAKE STATE PARK

Scenic rating: 8

on Curlew Lake

Map 4.2, page 240   **BEST (**

Boredom is banned at this park, set on the eastern shore of Curlew Lake. The park covers 87 acres and the lake is 5.5 miles long. Fishing is often good for trout and largemouth bass at the lake, and there are additional lakes and streams in the region. There is also beach access, swimming, waterskiing, and two miles of hiking and biking trails. The park is also used as a base for bicycle touring, with mountain biking available on a fairly steep trail that provides a view of the valley. There is an active osprey nest, and nearby recreation options include a nine-hole golf course. The park borders an airfield and is located in the heart of a historic gold-mining district.

Campsites, facilities: There are 18 sites with full hookups and seven sites with partial hookups (30 amps) for RVs up to 35-40 feet and 57 sites for tents. Some sites are pull-through. Picnic tables and fire rings are provided. Restrooms with flush toilets and coin showers, a dump station, drinking water, firewood, ice, and boat-launching and dock facilities are available. Boat fuel is available at the marina on the north side of the lake. Some facilities are wheelchair accessible. Leashed pets are permitted.

Reservations, fees: Reservations are accepted for some sites at 888/226-7688 or https://washington.goingtocamp.com ($8-10 reservation fee); the remaining sites are first-come, first-served. Sites are $20-45 per night, $10 per extra vehicle per night. Open April-October, weather permitting.

Directions: From Spokane on I-90, turn north on U.S. 395 and drive 87 miles to Kettle Falls and Highway 20. Turn west on Highway 20 and continue 34 miles to Highway 21 (2 miles east of Republic). Turn right (north) and drive six miles to the park entrance on the left.

Contact: Curlew Lake State Park, 509/775-3592, http://parks.state.wa.us.

37 TIFFANYS RESORT

Scenic rating: 7

on Curlew Lake

Map 4.2, page 240

Tiffanys Resort is located in a pretty, wooded setting along the western shore of Curlew Lake. This 6.5-mile-long lake is good for waterskiing. Fishing can be good for rainbow trout and largemouth bass. Most of the sites are fairly spacious. This is a smaller, more private alternative to Black Beach Resort.

Campsites, facilities: There are 15 sites for tents or RVs up to 40 feet (30 and 50 amp full hookups), four sites for tents, and 19 cabins. Picnic tables are provided, and fire pits are available on request. Restrooms with flush toilets and showers, firewood, a convenience store, coin laundry, ice, Wi-Fi, basketball hoop, volleyball, horseshoes, a playground, and a swimming beach are available. Boat docks, launching facilities, fish-cleaning stations, and rentals are available. Leashed pets are permitted.

Reservations, fees: Reservations are accepted. Sites are $25-35 per night, $3-5 per night per additional person. Some credit cards are accepted. Open April-late October.

Directions: From Colville, drive west on Highway 20 for 36 miles into the town of Republic and Klondike Road. Turn right on Klondike Road and drive 10.2 miles (Klondike Road will turn into West Curlew Lake Road) to Tiffany Road. Turn right and drive 0.5 mile to the resort at the end of the road.

Contact: Tiffanys Resort, 509/775-3152, www.tiffanysresort.com.

38 BLACK BEACH RESORT

Scenic rating: 7

on Curlew Lake

Map 4.2, page 240

Here's another resort along Curlew Lake. This one is much larger than Tiffanys Resort, with beautiful waterfront sites and full facilities. Waterskiing, personal watercraft, swimming, and fishing are all options. Fossil digging near the town of Republic is also popular.

Campsites, facilities: There are 86 sites for tents or RVs of any length (20 and 30 amp full hookups), nine sites for tents or RVs of any length (no hookups), and 12 lodging units. Some sites are pull-through. Picnic tables are provided, and fire pits are available at some sites. Restrooms with flush toilets and coin showers, dump station, convenience store, coin laundry, Wi-Fi, firewood, ice, volleyball, basketball hoop, horseshoes, and a playground are available. Boat docks, launching facilities, a fish-cleaning station, and boat rentals are located at the resort. Some facilities are wheelchair accessible. Leashed pets are permitted.

Reservations, fees: Reservations are accepted. RV sites are $29-36 per night, tent sites are $27 per night, $4 per person per night for more than four people, $5 pet fee. Weekly and monthly rates are available. Some credit cards are accepted. Campground open April-October; four cabins are available in winter.

Directions: From Colville, drive west on Highway 20 for approximately 36 miles to the town of Republic and Klondike Road. Turn right on Klondike Road (will become West Curlew Lake Road) and drive 7.5 miles to Black Beach Road. Turn right and drive 0.75 mile to the resort.

Contact: Black Beach Resort, 509/775-3989, www.blackbeachresort.com.

39 NORTH GORGE

Scenic rating: 7

on Franklin Roosevelt Lake in Lake Roosevelt National Recreation Area

Map 4.2, page 240

This is the first and northernmost of many campgrounds I discovered along the west shore of 130-mile-long Franklin Roosevelt Lake, which was formed by damming the Columbia

River at Coulee. Recreation options include waterskiing and swimming, plus fishing for walleye, trout, bass, and sunfish. During the winter, the lake level lowers; for a unique trip, walk along the lake's barren edge. Note that this campground provides full facilities May 1-September 30, then limited facilities in the off-season. Lake Roosevelt National Recreation Area offers recreation options such as free ranger programs, guided canoe trips, historical tours, campfire talks, and guided hikes. Watch for bald eagles in winter. Side-trip options include visiting the Colville Tribal Museum and touring the Grand Coulee Dam Visitor Center.

Campsites, facilities: There are 12 sites for tents or RVs up to 26 feet long. Picnic tables and fire grills are provided. Drinking water, vault toilets, boat docks, and launching facilities are available. Note that if the lake level drops below an elevation of 1,272 feet, there is no drinking water. Leashed pets are permitted.

Reservations, fees: Reservations are not accepted. Sites are $18 per night, $9 per night off-season. Open year-round, with limited winter access.

Directions: From Spokane on I-90, drive north on U.S. 395 for 84 miles to the town of Kettle Falls and Highway 25. Turn right (north) on Highway 25 and drive 20 miles to the campground entrance.

Contact: Lake Roosevelt National Recreation Area, 509/754-7800, www.nps.gov/laro.

40 DAVIS LAKE

Scenic rating: 8
on Davis Lake in Colville National Forest

Map 4.2, page 240

This tiny campground is set at 4,600 feet elevation at Little Davis Lake. It is a scenic spot, and the fishing for cutthroat trout is often good. Only small boats are permitted on the small, shallow lake, which covers just 17 acres. No gas motors are permitted, but the lake can be ideal for float tubes, canoes, and prams with electric motors or oars. A one-mile trail loops the lake.

Campsites, facilities: There are four sites for tents or RVs up to 16 feet long. Picnic tables and fire grills are provided. Vault toilets are available. There is no drinking water, and garbage must be packed out. A primitive boat ramp is available nearby. Leashed pets are permitted.

Reservations, fees: Reservations are not accepted. There is no fee for camping. Open mid-May-October, weather permitting.

Directions: From Spokane, drive north on U.S. 395 for 84 miles to Kettle Falls. Continue north on U.S. 395 for nine miles to Deadman Creek Road. Turn west on Deadman Creek Road and drive about three miles to County Road 465 (Jack Knife cutoff). Turn right and drive 2.5 miles. Bear right and drive about 0.5 mile to County Road 480. Turn left and drive about three miles to County Road 080. Turn right and drive about three miles to Davis Lake. Note: The access road is very rough; high-clearance vehicles are recommended.

Contact: Colville National Forest, Three Rivers Ranger District, 509/738-7700, www.fs.usda.gov.

41 SNAG COVE

Scenic rating: 8
on Franklin Roosevelt Lake in Lake Roosevelt National Recreation Area

Map 4.2, page 240

Snag Cove has a setting similar to North Gorge Campground. It is set amid ponderosa pines along the west shore of Franklin Roosevelt Lake. This small camp has just nine sites, but the nearby boat launch makes it a find.

Campsites, facilities: There are nine sites for tents or RVs up to 35 feet long. Picnic tables and fire grills are provided. Vault toilets are available. When the lake level drops (to elevation 1,265 feet), there is no drinking water. Boat-launching facilities and docks are nearby. Some

facilities are wheelchair accessible. Leashed pets are permitted.

Reservations, fees: Reservations are not accepted. Sites are $9-18 per night, $8 boat-launch fee (good for seven days). Open year-round, weather permitting.

Directions: From Spokane, turn north on U.S. 395 and drive 84 miles to the town of Kettle Falls. Continue north on U.S. 395 (crossing the Columbia River) for seven miles to the Hedlund Bridge turnoff. Turn right, cross Hedlund Bridge, and drive 7.5 miles to the campground on the right.

Contact: Lake Roosevelt National Recreation Area, 509/754-7800, www.nps.gov/laro.

42 KETTLE RIVER

Scenic rating: 7

on Franklin Roosevelt Lake in Lake Roosevelt National Recreation Area

Map 4.2, page 240

Kettle River Campground is set along the long, narrow Kettle River Arm of Franklin Roosevelt Lake; it features campsites amid ponderosa pines. The nearest boat launch is located at Napoleon Bridge.

Campsites, facilities: There are 13 sites for tents or RVs up to 40 feet long. Picnic tables and fire grills are provided. Vault toilets are available. When the lake level drops below an elevation of 1,272 feet, there is no drinking water. Boat docks are nearby. Some facilities are wheelchair accessible. Leashed pets are permitted.

Reservations, fees: Reservations are not accepted. Sites are $9-18 per night. Open year-round, weather permitting.

Directions: From Spokane, turn north on U.S. 395 and drive 84 miles to the town of Kettle Falls. Continue north on U.S. 395 (crossing the Columbia River) for seven miles to the campground on the right.

Contact: Lake Roosevelt National Recreation Area, 509/754-7800, www.nps.gov/laro.

43 KAMLOOPS ISLAND

Scenic rating: 10

on Franklin Roosevelt Lake in Lake Roosevelt National Recreation Area

Map 4.2, page 240   **BEST (**

This is one of the more primitive campgrounds located along Franklin Roosevelt Lake. Located at Kamloops Island, an optimum area for waterskiing and fishing, it features unbelievably beautiful views of water and mountains. It is located near the mouth of the Kettle River Arm of the lake. While the scenic beauty merits a 10, note that the nearest boat launch is way across the lake at Kettle Falls and that if the lake level drops below an elevation of 1,272 feet, there is no drinking water.

Campsites, facilities: There are 17 sites for tents or RVs to 40 feet long. Picnic tables and fire grills are provided. Vault toilets are available. When the lake level drops, there is no drinking water. Boat docks are nearby. Leashed pets are permitted.

Reservations, fees: Reservations are not accepted. Sites are $9-18 per night. Open year-round, weather permitting.

Directions: From Spokane, turn north on U.S. 395 and drive 84 miles to the town of Kettle Falls. Continue north on U.S. 395 (crossing the Columbia River) for seven miles to the Hedlund Bridge turnoff. Turn right, cross Hedlund Bridge, and drive to the campground on the left.

Contact: Lake Roosevelt National Recreation Area, 509/754-7800, www.nps.gov/laro.

44 EVANS

Scenic rating: 9

on Franklin Roosevelt Lake in Lake Roosevelt National Recreation Area

Map 4.2, page 240

This campground is another in a series set along the shore of Franklin Roosevelt Lake.

This one sits along the eastern shoreline, just south of the town of Evans. Fishing, swimming, and waterskiing are among the activities here. Lake Roosevelt National Recreation Area offers recreation options such as free ranger programs, guided canoe trips, historical tours, campfire talks, and guided hikes. Watch for bald eagles in winter. Side-trip options include visiting the Colville Tribal Museum and touring the Grand Coulee Dam Visitor Center.

Campsites, facilities: There are 43 sites for tents or RVs up to 55 feet long and one group site for tents or RVs up to 55 feet long that accommodates up to 25 people. Picnic tables and fire pits are provided. Drinking water (seasonal) and flush toilets are available. A boat dock, launch facilities, a dump station, playground, swimming beach, camp host, and a picnic area are available nearby. Some facilities are wheelchair accessible. Leashed pets are permitted.

Reservations, fees: Reservations are not accepted for individual sites but are required for the group site at 877/444-6777 or www.recreation.gov ($10 reservation fee). Sites are $9-18 per night, the group site is $55 per night, $8 boat-launch fee (good for seven days). Open year-round, with limited facilities in the winter.

Directions: From Spokane on I-90, drive north on U.S. 395 for 84 miles to the town of Kettle Falls and Highway 25. Turn right (north) on Highway 25 and drive eight miles to the campground entrance on the left.

Contact: Lake Roosevelt National Recreation Area, 509/754-7800 or 509/754-7889, www.nps.gov/laro.

45 MARCUS ISLAND

Scenic rating: 8

on Franklin Roosevelt Lake in Lake Roosevelt National Recreation Area

Map 4.2, page 240

Located south of Evans camp on the eastern shore of Franklin Roosevelt Lake, this campground is quite similar to that camp. Waterskiing, fishing, and swimming are the primary recreation options. Lake Roosevelt National Recreation Area offers numerous recreation options, such as free programs conducted by rangers that include guided canoe trips, historical tours, campfire talks, and guided hikes. This lake is known as a prime location to view bald eagles, especially in winter. Side-trip options include visiting the Colville Tribal Museum in the town of Coulee Dam and touring the Grand Coulee Dam Visitor Center. Almost one mile long and twice as high as Niagara Falls, the dam is one of the largest concrete structures ever built; it is open for self-guided tours.

Campsites, facilities: There are 27 sites for tents or RVs up to 40 feet long. Picnic tables and fire grills are provided. Drinking water, vault toilets, and a picnic area are available. A boat launch and dock are available nearby. Note that if the lake level drops below an elevation of 1,265 feet, there is no drinking water. Leashed pets are permitted.

Reservations, fees: Reservations are not accepted. Sites are $9-18 per night, $8 boat-launch fee (good for seven days). Open year-round, weather permitting.

Directions: From Spokane on I-90, drive north on U.S. 395 for 84 miles to the town of Kettle Falls and Highway 25. Turn right (north) on Highway 25 and drive four miles to the campground entrance on the left.

Contact: Lake Roosevelt National Recreation Area, 509/754-7800, www.nps.gov/laro.

46 SWAN LAKE

Scenic rating: 8

on Swan Lake in Colville National Forest

Map 4.2, page 240

Scenic views greet visitors on the drive to Swan Lake and at the campground as well. The camp is set on the shore of Swan Lake, at an elevation of 3,700 feet. Swan Lake Trail, a beautiful hiking trail, circles the lake. Fishing for rainbow trout is an option. Swimming, boating (gas motors prohibited), mountain biking, and hiking are some of the possibilities here. This is a good out-of-the-way spot for RV cruisers seeking a rustic setting. It commonly fills on summer weekends.

Campsites, facilities: There are 21 sites, including six double sites, for tents or RVs of any length, four walk-in sites for tents only, and a group site for 20-50 people. Picnic tables and fire grills are provided. Drinking water, vault toilets, and garbage bins are available. A picnic shelter with barbecue, a boat dock, and launching facilities are available nearby. Gas motors are prohibited on the lake. Some facilities are wheelchair accessible. Leashed pets are permitted.

Reservations, fees: Reservations are not accepted for individual sites, but are required for the group site at 877/444-6777 ($10 reservation fee) or www.recreation.gov ($9 reservation fee). Sites are $10 per night, $2 per each additional vehicle. The group site is $35 per night. Open May-November, weather permitting.

Directions: From Spokane on I-90, turn north on U.S. 395 and drive 87 miles to Highway 20. Turn west on Highway 20 and drive 36 miles to the town of Republic and Highway 21. Turn south on Highway 21 and drive seven miles to Forest Road 53 (Scatter Creek Road). Turn right (southwest) on Forest Road 53 and drive eight miles to the campground at the end of the road.

Contact: Colville National Forest, Republic Ranger District, 509/775-3305, www.fs.usda.gov.

47 FERRY LAKE

🚶🚴🏊🛶💧🏕️🐕🚐⛺

Scenic rating: 7
on Ferry Lake in Colville National Forest

Map 4.2, page 240

Ferry Lake is one of three fishing lakes within a four-square-mile area; the others are Swan Lake and Long Lake. Swimming, boating (gas motors prohibited), mountain biking, and hiking are some of the possibilities here. The lake is regularly stocked with rainbow trout. Campsites are quiet and well-shaded.

Campsites, facilities: There are nine sites for tents or RVs up to 20 feet long. Fire grills and picnic tables are provided. Vault toilets and garbage bins are available. No drinking water is available. Launching facilities are nearby. Leashed pets are permitted.

Reservations, fees: Reservations are not accepted. Sites are $6 per night, $2 per extra vehicle per night. Open May-October, weather permitting.

Directions: From Spokane on I-90, turn north on U.S. 395 and drive 87 miles to Highway 20. Turn west on Highway 20 and drive 36 miles to the town of Republic and Highway 21. Turn south on Highway 21 and drive seven miles to Forest Road 53 (Scatter Creek Road). Turn right (southwest) on Forest Road 53 and drive about seven miles to Forest Road 5330. Turn right (north) on Forest Road 5330 and drive one mile to Forest Road 100. Turn right and drive one mile to the campground on the left.

Contact: Colville National Forest, Republic Ranger District, 509/775-3305, www.fs.usda.gov.

48 LONG LAKE

🚶🚴🏊🛶💧🏕️🐕🚐⛺

Scenic rating: 9
on Long Lake in Colville National Forest

Map 4.2, page 240   **BEST (**

Long Lake is the third and smallest of the three lakes in this area; the others are Swan Lake and Ferry Lake. Expert anglers can have a quality experience here fly-fishing for cutthroat trout. No gas motors are allowed on the lake, and fishing is restricted (fly-fishing only), but it's ideal for a float tube or a pram. The lake is set adjacent to little Fish Lake, and a 0.5-mile trail runs between the two. The drive on Highway 21 south of Republic is particularly beautiful, with views of the Sanpoil River.

Campsites, facilities: There are 12 sites for tents or RVs up to 30 feet long. Picnic tables and fire grills are provided. Drinking water, vault toilets, and garbage bins are available. Primitive launching facilities are nearby. Leashed pets are permitted.

Reservations, fees: Reservations are not accepted. Sites are $8 per night, $2 per extra vehicle per night. Open May-October, weather permitting.

Directions: From Spokane on I-90, turn north on U.S. 395 and drive 87 miles to Highway 20. Turn west on Highway 20 and drive 36 miles to the town of Republic and Highway 21. Turn south on Highway 21 and drive seven miles to Forest Road 53 (Scatter Creek Road). Turn right (southwest) on Forest Road 53 and drive seven miles to Forest Road 400. Turn left (south) and drive 1.5 miles to the camp on the right.

Contact: Colville National Forest, Republic Ranger District, 509/775-3305, www.fs.usda. gov.

49 TEN MILE

Scenic rating: 7

in Colville National Forest

Map 4.2, page 240

This spot is secluded and primitive. Located about nine miles from Swan Lake, Ferry Lake, and Long Lake, this campground along the Sanpoil River is a good choice for a multi-day trip visiting each of the lakes. The Sanpoil River provides fishing for rainbow trout, and a hiking trail leads west from camp for about 2.5 miles.

Campsites, facilities: There are eight sites for tents or RVs up to 21 feet long. Picnic tables and fire rings are provided. Vault toilets and garbage bins are available. There is no drinking water. Leashed pets are permitted.

Reservations, fees: Reservations are not accepted. Sites are $6 per night, $2 per extra vehicle per night; fees are charged Memorial Day-Labor Day weekends. Open mid-May-mid-October, weather permitting.

Directions: From Spokane on I-90, turn north on U.S. 395 and drive 87 miles to Highway 20. Turn west on Highway 20 and drive 36 miles to Republic and Highway 21. Turn south on Highway 21 and drive 10 miles to the campground entrance on the left.

Contact: Colville National Forest, Republic Ranger District, 509/775-3305, www.fs.usda. gov.

50 SHERMAN OVERLOOK

Scenic rating: 6

at Sherman Pass in Colville National Forest

Map 4.2, page 240

Sherman Pass Scenic Byway (Highway 20) runs through here, so the camp has some road noise. This roadside campground is located near Sherman Pass (5,575 feet elevation), one of the few high-elevation mountain passes open year-round in Washington. Several nearby trails provide access to various peaks and vistas in the area. One of the best is the Kettle Crest National Recreation Trail, with the trailhead located one mile from camp. This trail extends for 45 miles, generally running north to south, and provides spectacular views of the Cascades on clear days. No other campgrounds are in the immediate vicinity.

Campsites, facilities: There are 10 sites for tents or small RVs. Picnic tables and fire grills are provided. Vault toilets are available. There is no drinking water and garbage must be packed out. Some facilities are wheelchair accessible. Leashed pets are permitted.

Reservations, fees: Reservations are not accepted. Sites are $6 per night. Open June-mid-September, weather permitting.

Directions: From Spokane on I-90, turn north on U.S. 395 and drive 87 miles to Highway 20. Turn west on Highway 20 and drive 19.5 miles to the campground on the right.

Contact: Colville National Forest, Three Rivers Ranger District, 509/738-7700, www. fs.usda.gov.

51 TROUT LAKE

Scenic rating: 8

on Trout Lake in Colville National Forest

Map 4.2, page 240

Trout Lake is a little lake, just eight acres, at an elevation of 3,100 feet. It provides fishing for rainbow trout, with prospects similar to that of Davis Lake. No gas motors are permitted, but electric motors are allowed on small boats. Nearby, five-mile-long Hoodoo Canyon Trail, accessible for hiking or biking, offers spectacular views; stock animals are prohibited.

Campsites, facilities: There are five sites for tents only. Picnic tables and fire pits are provided. Vault toilets are available. There is no drinking water, and garbage must be packed out. A very small boat ramp is available nearby. Some facilities are wheelchair accessible. Leashed pets are permitted.

Reservations, fees: Reservations are not accepted. There is no fee for camping. Open late May-September, weather permitting.

Directions: From Spokane, turn north on U.S. 395 and drive 87 miles to Colville and Highway 20. Turn west on Highway 20 and drive 15 miles (crossing the Columbia River) to Trout Lake Road (Forest Road 020). Turn right on Trout Lake Road and drive five miles to the campground at the end of the road.

Contact: Colville National Forest, Three Rivers Ranger District, 509/738-7700, www.fs.usda.gov.

52 CANYON CREEK

Scenic rating: 7

near the East Portal Historical Site in Colville National Forest

Map 4.2, page 240

This campground is located 0.4 mile from the highway, just far enough to keep it from road noise. It's a popular spot among campers looking for a layover, with the bonus of trout fishing in the nearby creek. Canyon Creek lies within hiking distance of the East Portal Historical Site. The camp is set in a pretty area not far from the Columbia River, which offers a myriad of recreation options. The Bangs Mountain Auto Tour, a scenic route with mountain vistas, is a good side trip.

Campsites, facilities: There are 12 sites for tents or RVs up to 30 feet long. Picnic tables and fire grills are provided. Vault toilets are available. There is no drinking water, and garbage must be packed out. Some facilities are wheelchair accessible. Leashed pets are permitted.

Reservations, fees: Reservations are not accepted. Sites are $6 per night. Open late April-early October, weather permitting.

Directions: From Spokane, drive north on U.S. 395 for 87 miles to Highway 20. Turn west on Highway 20 and drive 18 miles (crossing the Columbia River) to Forest Road 136. Turn left (south) and drive for 0.3 mile to the campground on the left.

Contact: Colville National Forest, Three Rivers, Ranger District, 509/738-7700, www.fs.usda.gov.

53 KETTLE FALLS

Scenic rating: 8

on Franklin Roosevelt Lake in Lake Roosevelt National Recreation Area

Map 4.2, page 240

Kettle Falls campground is located along the eastern shore of Roosevelt Lake, about two miles south of the highway bridge near West Kettle Falls. The camp only fills occasionally. In the summer, rangers offer evening campfire programs. Waterskiing, swimming, and fishing are all options. Local side trips include St. Paul's Mission in Kettle Falls, which was built in 1846 and is one of the oldest churches in Washington.

Campsites, facilities: There are 76 sites for tents or RVs of any length; some sites are pull-through. There are also two group sites for up to 50 and 75 people. Picnic tables and fire grills are provided. Restrooms with flush toilets, drinking water, a dump station, firewood, a small marina (late May-early September) with a store, swimming beach, softball fields, amphitheater, picnic shelter, camp host, and a playground are available. A store is located within one mile. Boat docks, fuel, fish-cleaning stations, and launching facilities are available. Some facilities are wheelchair accessible. Leashed pets are permitted.

Reservations, fees: Reservations are accepted and are required for group sites at 877/444-6777 or www.recreation.gov ($10 reservation fee). Sites are $9-18 per night, the group site is $55 per night ($25 reservation fee), $8 boat-launch fee (good for seven days). Some credit cards are accepted. Open year-round, with limited winter facilities.

Directions: From Spokane, drive north on U.S. 395 for 84 miles to the town of Kettle Falls. Continue on U.S. 395 for three miles to Kettle Park Road. Turn left and drive two miles to the campground on the right.

Contact: Lake Roosevelt National Recreation Area, 509/754-7800 or 509/754-7889, www.nps.gov/laro.

54 HAAG COVE

Scenic rating: 8

on Franklin Roosevelt Lake in Lake Roosevelt National Recreation Area

Map 4.2, page 240   **BEST (**

This campground is tucked away in a cove along the western shore of Franklin Roosevelt Lake (Columbia River), about two miles south of Highway 20. A good side trip is to the Sherman Creek Habitat Management Area, located just north of camp. It's rugged and steep, but a good place to see and photograph wildlife, including bald eagles, golden eagles, and 200 other species of birds, along with the occasional black bear, cougar, and moose. Note that no boat launch is available at this camp,

but boat ramps are available at Kettle Falls and French Rock. Also note that no drinking water is available if the lake level drops below an elevation of 1,275 feet.

Campsites, facilities: There are 16 sites for tents or RVs up to 35 feet. Picnic tables and fire grills are provided. Drinking water and vault toilets are available. Boat docks are available nearby. Some facilities are wheelchair accessible. Leashed pets are permitted.

Reservations, fees: Reservations are not accepted. Sites are $9-18 per night. Open year-round, weather permitting, with limited winter access.

Directions: From Spokane, drive north on U.S. 395 for 84 miles to the town of Kettle Falls and Highway 20. Continue on Highway 20 and drive 7.5 miles to Kettle Falls Road. Turn left (south) and drive two miles to the campground on the right.

Contact: Lake Roosevelt National Recreation Area, 509/754-7800, www.nps.gov/laro.

55 LAKE ELLEN EAST & LAKE ELLEN WEST

Scenic rating: 7

on Lake Ellen in Colville National Forest

Map 4.2, page 240

This 82-acre lake is a favorite for power boating (with no speed limit) and fishing for rainbow trout, which are a good size and plentiful early in the season. There are two small camps available here. The boat launch is located at the west end of the lake. It is located about three miles west of the Columbia River and the Lake Roosevelt National Recreation Area.

Campsites, facilities: There are 11 sites at Lake Ellen East and five sites at Lake Ellen West for tents or RVs up to 18 feet long. Picnic tables and fire grills are provided. Vault toilets are available. There is no drinking water, and garbage must be packed out. Boat docks are available nearby. Some facilities are wheelchair accessible. Leashed pets are permitted.

Reservations, fees: Reservations are not accepted. Sites are $6 per night. Open mid-April-October, weather permitting.

Directions: From Spokane, drive north on U.S. 395 for 87 miles to Colville and Highway 20. Turn west on Highway 20 and drive 14 miles (crossing the Columbia River) to County Road 3. Turn left and drive south for 4.5 miles to County Road 412. Turn right on County Road 412 and drive five miles to the Lake Ellen East Campground or continue another 0.7 mile to Lake Ellen West Campground.

Contact: Colville National Forest, Three Rivers Ranger District, 509/738-7700, www. fs.usda.gov.

56 RAINBOW BEACH RESORT

Scenic rating: 8

on Twin Lakes Reservoir

Map 4.2, page 240

This quality resort is set along the shore of Twin Lakes Reservoir in the Colville Indian Reservation. Busy in summer, the camp fills up virtually every day in July and August. Nearby recreation options include hiking trails, marked bike trails, a full-service marina, and tennis courts.

Campsites, facilities: There are nine sites with full hookups for RVs of any length, including five pull-through sites, seven sites for tents, and 26 cabins. Picnic tables and fire pits are provided (at tent sites). Restrooms with flush toilets and coin showers, drinking water, propane gas, gasoline, firewood, a recreation hall, a convenience store, coin laundry, ice, a roped swimming area, boat rentals, docks and launching facilities, a playground, volleyball, and horseshoe pits are available. Leashed pets are permitted.

Reservations, fees: Reservations are accepted. Sites are $25-30 per night, cabins are $60-216 per night, $15 per pet per stay. Some credit cards are accepted. Campsites are

available April-October; cabins are available year-round.

Directions: From Spokane, drive north on U.S. 395 for 84 miles to the town of Kettle Falls and Highway 20. Turn west on Highway 20 and drive five miles to the turnoff for Inchelium Highway. Turn left (south) and drive about 20 miles to Inchelium and Bridge Creek-Twin Lakes County Road. Turn right (west) and drive two miles to Stranger Creek Road. Turn left and drive 0.25 mile to the resort on the right.

Contact: Rainbow Beach Resort, 509/722-5901.

57 CLOVERLEAF

Scenic rating: 8

on Franklin Roosevelt Lake in Lake Roosevelt National Recreation Area

Map 4.2, page 240

Cloverleaf is a small and primitive camp located on the east shore of Roosevelt Lake, just south of the town of Gifford. In this particular area of Roosevelt Lake, waterskiing and other high-speed boating are not advised because of submerged hazards, but fishing is fine. The tree cover in the area consists primarily of ponderosa pine. Lake Roosevelt National Recreation Area offers recreation options such as free ranger programs, guided canoe trips, historical tours, campfire talks, and guided hikes. Watch for bald eagles in winter. Side-trip options include visiting the Colville Tribal Museum and touring the Grand Coulee Dam Visitor Center. Note that no drinking water is available if the lake level drops below 1,282 feet elevation. Gifford Campground to the south provides an alternative when this camp is full.

Campsites, facilities: There are nine sites for tents only. Picnic tables and fire grills are provided. Drinking water and vault toilets are available. A dock and a picnic area are nearby. Leashed pets are permitted.

Reservations, fees: Reservations are not accepted. Sites are $9-18 per night, $8 boat-launch fee (good for seven days). Open April-October.

Directions: From Spokane on I-90, drive west for four miles to U.S. 2. Turn west on U.S. 2 and drive 34 miles to Highway 25. Turn right (north) on Highway 25 and drive 61 miles to Davenport and the campground (located about two miles south of Gifford).

Contact: Lake Roosevelt National Recreation Area, 509/754-7800, www.nps.gov/laro.

58 GIFFORD

Scenic rating: 7

on Franklin Roosevelt Lake in Lake Roosevelt National Recreation Area

Map 4.2, page 240

Fishing and waterskiing are two of the draws at this camp on the eastern shore of Franklin Roosevelt Lake (Columbia River). The nearby boat ramp is a big plus.

Campsites, facilities: There are 42 sites for tents or RVs up to 55 feet long and one group site for tents or RVs up to 20 feet long that can accommodate up to 50 people and 15 vehicles. Picnic tables and fire grills are provided. Drinking water (seasonal) and flush and vault toilets are available. A camp host is on-site. Boat docks and launching facilities, a dump station, playground, and a picnic area are nearby. Some facilities are wheelchair accessible. Leashed pets are permitted.

Reservations, fees: Reservations are not accepted for individual sites but are required for the group site at 877/444-6777 or www.recreation.gov ($10 reservation fee). Sites are $9-18 per night, the group site is $55 per night, $8 boat-launch fee (good for seven days). Open year-round, with limited winter facilities.

Directions: From Spokane on I-90, drive west for four miles to U.S. 2. Turn west on U.S. 2 and drive 34 miles to Davenport and Highway 25. Turn right (north) on Highway 25 and drive 60 miles to the campground (located about three miles south of Cloverleaf) on the left.

Contact: Lake Roosevelt National Recreation

Area, 509/754-7800, 509/754-7889, or 509/738-2300, www.nps.gov/laro.

59 HUNTERS

Scenic rating: 8

on Franklin Roosevelt Lake in Lake Roosevelt National Recreation Area

Map 4.2, page 240

This campground, on a shoreline point along Franklin Roosevelt Lake (Columbia River), offers good swimming, fishing, and waterskiing. It is located on the east shore of the lake, adjacent to the mouth of Hunters Creek and near the town of Hunters. Note: No drinking water is available if the lake level drops below an elevation of 1,245 feet.

Campsites, facilities: There are 39 sites for tents or RVs up to 55 feet long and three group sites for tents or RVs up to 26 feet long that can accommodate up to 25 people each. Picnic tables and fire grills are provided. Drinking water, restrooms with flush toilets, vault toilets, a dump station, playground, and a picnic area are available. A camp host is on-site. A store and ice are available within one mile. Boat docks and launching facilities are nearby. Leashed pets are permitted.

Reservations, fees: Reservations are not accepted for individual sites but are required for group sites at 877/444-6777 or www.recreation.gov ($10 reservation fee). Sites are $9-18 per night, $8 boat-launch fee (good for seven days), and the group site is $55 per night. Open year-round, with limited winter facilities.

Directions: From Spokane on I-90, drive west for four miles to U.S. 2. Turn west on U.S. 2 and drive 34 miles to Davenport and Highway 25. Turn north on Highway 25 and drive 47 miles to Hunters and the campground access road on the left (west) side of the road (well marked). Turn left at the access road and drive two miles to the campground at the end of the road.

Contact: Lake Roosevelt National Recreation

Area, 509/754-7800 or 509/754-7889, www.nps.gov/laro.

60 SHEEP CREEK

🏃 🚴 🛶 🐾 ♿ � 🔺

Scenic rating: 8

near the Columbia River and the Canadian border

Map 4.3, page 241

This campground is in a forested area along Sheep Creek, about four miles from the Columbia River and close to the Canadian border. Although a primitive camp, it has drinking water and is a "locals' spot" on the Fourth of July weekend. A wheelchair-accessible fishing platform and trail are available. Sheep Creek provides opportunities for trout fishing. Huckleberry picking is good in August.

Campsites, facilities: There are 11 sites for tents or RVs up to 30 feet long. Picnic tables and fire grills are provided. Vault toilets, drinking water, and a group picnic shelter with barbecues are available. Garbage must be packed out. Restaurants and stores are located within five miles. Some facilities are wheelchair accessible. Leashed pets are permitted.

Reservations, fees: Reservations are not accepted. There is no fee for camping, but a Discover Pass is required. Open mid-April-November, weather permitting.

Directions: From Spokane, drive north on U.S. 395 for 87 miles to Kettle Falls and Highway 25. Turn north on Highway 25 and drive 33 miles to Northport. Continue north on Highway 25 for 0.75 mile to Sheep Creek Road (across the Columbia River Bridge). Turn left on Sheep Creek Road and drive 4.3 miles (on a gravel road) to the campground entrance on the right.

Contact: Department of Natural Resources, Northeast Region, 509/684-7474, www.dnr.wa.gov.

61 UPPER COLUMBIA RV PARK AND CAMPGROUND

🏃 🛶 🐾 🎣 🚐 🔺

Scenic rating: 5

near Colville on the Columbia River

Map 4.3, page 241

This rustic resort is set on a peaceful stretch of the upper Columbia River amid forests and wildflowers. Campsites are grassy, and the natural greenery provides privacy. Summertime recreation options include berry picking, bird- and wildlife-watching, fishing, hiking, and gold panning.

Campsites, facilities: There are 22 sites for tents or RVs up to 60 feet, all with full hookups (20, 30, or 50 amps), and two cabins. Some sites are pull-through. Picnic tables and fire pits are provided. Restrooms with flush toilets and coin showers, a dump station, convenience store, and a playground are available. Gasoline and a boat launch are within five miles. Leashed pets are permitted in the campground.

Reservations, fees: Reservations are accepted. Tent sites are $25 per night, RV sites are $30-35 per night, $2 per night per extra person, and cabins are $59-69 per night. Weekly and monthly rates are available. Some credit cards are accepted. Open year-round, with higher rates November-March.

Directions: From Spokane, drive north on Highway 395 for about 70 miles to Colville. Take the Williams Lake exit and drive 18 miles to Highway 25. Turn right and drive to the Waneta customs sign. Turn right on Northport Waneta Road and drive five miles to the campground entrance.

Contact: Upper Columbia RV Park and Campground, 4706 Northport Waneta Rd., Colville, 509/732-4367, www.campingfriend.com.

62 BIG MEADOW LAKE

Scenic rating: 8

on Big Meadow Lake in Colville National Forest

Map 4.3, page 241   **BEST (**

Big Meadow Lake is set at 3,400 feet elevation and has 71 surface acres. The camp, located in a scenic area, is quiet, remote, and relatively unknown, and the lake provides trout fishing. The U.S. Forest Service has built a wildlife-viewing platform, where ospreys, ducks, geese, and occasionally even moose, elk, and cougars may be spotted.

Campsites, facilities: There are 17 sites for tents or RVs up to 32 feet long and a historic cabin nearby. Fire grills and picnic tables are provided. Vault toilets are available. There is no drinking water, and garbage must be packed out. A boat launch, restrooms, and a wheelchair-accessible nature trail and fishing pier are available nearby. Some facilities are wheelchair accessible. Leashed pets are permitted.

Reservations, fees: Reservations are not accepted. There is no fee for camping. Open May-November, weather permitting.

Directions: From Spokane, drive north on U.S. 395 for 87 miles to Colville and Highway 20. Turn east on Highway 20 and drive one mile to Colville-Aladdin Northpoint Road (County Road 9435). Turn north and drive 20 miles to Meadow Creek Road. Turn right (east) and drive six miles to the campground on the right. Note: The surface of the access road changes dramatically depending on the season.

Contact: Colville National Forest, Three Rivers Ranger District, Colville Office, 509/684-7000, www.fs.usda.gov.

63 MILL POND

Scenic rating: 6

near Sullivan Lake in Colville National Forest

Map 4.3, page 241

Note: At time of publication, Mill Pond was closed pending repairs to the dam. The campground may open for the 2019 summer season. Call for updates.

Mill Pond Campground, located along the shore of a small reservoir just north of Sullivan Lake, offers a good base camp for backpackers. Note that boat size is limited to crafts that can be carried and hand launched; about a 50-foot walk from the parking area to the lake is necessary. A 1.5-mile hiking trail (no bikes) circles Mill Pond and ties into a historical and wheelchair-accessible interpretive trail (located at the opposite end of the lake). For more ambitious hikes, nearby Hall Mountain Trail and Elk Creek Trail provide beautiful valley and mountain views. Nearby Sullivan Lake is well known for giant, but elusive, brown trout; it produced the state record. There are also rainbow trout in the lake.

Campsites, facilities: There are 10 sites for tents or small RVs. Picnic tables and fire grills are provided. Drinking water, vault toilets, and garbage service are available. Boats can be hand launched after a 50-foot walk; no gas motors are permitted. Supplies are available in Metaline Falls. Some facilities are wheelchair accessible. Leashed pets are permitted.

Reservations, fees: Reservations are not accepted. Sites are $18 per night, $9 per each additional vehicle per night. Open late May-early September, weather permitting.

Directions: From Spokane, drive north on U.S. 395 for six miles to U.S. 2. Turn northeast on U.S. 2 and drive 30 miles to the Metaline turn-off and Highway 211 North. Turn northwest on Highway 211 and drive 15 miles to Usk and Highway 20. Turn left (northwest) and drive 31 miles to Tiger and Highway 31. Continue (north) on Highway 31 and drive three miles to the sign marking the Sullivan Lake Ranger Station. Turn right on Sullivan Lake Road/County Road 9345 and drive a short distance, cross the bridge over the Pend Oreille River, and continue 13 miles to the campground on the left.

Contact: Scenic Canyons Recreational Services, 435/245-6521, www.sceniccanyons.

com; Colville National Forest, Sullivan Lake Ranger District, 509/446-7500, www.fs.usda. gov.

64 EAST SULLIVAN

Scenic rating: 7

on Sullivan Lake in Colville National Forest

Map 4.3, page 241

East Sullivan Campground is the largest on Sullivan Lake and by far the most popular. It fills up in summer. The camp is located on the lake's north shore. Some come here to try to catch giant brown trout or smaller, more plentiful rainbow trout. The boating and hiking are also good. The beautiful Salmo-Priest Wilderness is located just three miles to the east. It gets light use, which means quiet, private trails. This is a prime place to view wildlife, so carry binoculars while hiking for a chance to spot the rare woodland caribou and Rocky Mountain bighorn sheep. A nearby grass airstrip provides an opportunity for fly-in camping, but pilots should note that there are chuckholes present and holes from lots of ground squirrels. Only planes suited for primitive landing conditions should be flown in; check the Federal Aviation Administration (FAA) guide to airports.

Campsites, facilities: There are 38 sites, including six double sites, for tents or RVs up to 55 feet long and one group site for up to 40 people; some sites are pull-through. Picnic tables and fire grills are provided. Drinking water and vault toilets are available. A boat dock, launching facilities, a picnic area, swimming area and floating platform, camp host, and dump station are nearby. Some facilities are wheelchair accessible. Leashed pets are permitted.

Reservations, fees: Reservations are accepted for individual sites and are required for the group site at 877/444-6777 ($10 reservation fee) or www.recreation.gov ($9 reservation fee). Sites are $18-36 per night, $9 per night extra vehicle fee, and the group site is $67

per night. Open mid-May-September, weather permitting.

Directions: From Spokane, drive north on U.S. 395 for six miles to U.S. 2. Turn northeast on U.S. 2 and drive 30 miles to the Metaline turn-off and Highway 211 North. Turn northwest on Highway 211 and drive 15 miles to Usk and Highway 20. Turn left (northwest) and drive 31 miles to Tiger and Highway 31. Continue (north) on Highway 31 and drive three miles to the sign marking the Sullivan Lake Ranger Station. Turn right on Sullivan Lake Road/County Road 9345 and drive a short distance, cross the bridge over the Pend Oreille River, and continue 12 miles to the campground on the left.

Contact: Colville National Forest, Sullivan Lake Ranger District, 509/446-7500 or 801/226-3564, www.fs.usda.gov.

65 WEST SULLIVAN

Scenic rating: 7

on Sullivan Lake in Colville National Forest

Map 4.3, page 241

If East Sullivan is full, this small campground set along the northwestern shore of Sullivan Lake can fit the bill. This is a popular destination for boating, fishing for trout, swimming, sailing, waterskiing, and hiking. Beautiful Salmo-Priest Wilderness, three miles to the east, provides quiet, private trails. Wildlife-viewing is prime here; carry binoculars to spot caribou and bighorn sheep.

Campsites, facilities: There are 10 sites for tents or RVs up to 30 feet long. Picnic tables and fire grills are provided. Drinking water and vault toilets, a picnic shelter, a developed swimming beach, and a floating swim platform are available. A camp host is on-site. A dump station is within one mile. Some facilities are wheelchair accessible. Leashed pets are permitted.

Reservations, fees: Reservations are accepted at 877/444-6777 ($10 reservation fee) or www.recreation.gov ($9 reservation fee). Mid-May mid-September, sites are $18 per night, $9 per each additional vehicle. Mid-September-October, sites are $8 per night with limited services. Open mid-May-October 31, weather permitting.

Directions: From Spokane, drive north on U.S. 395 for six miles to U.S. 2. Turn northeast on U.S. 2 and drive 30 miles to the Metaline turn-off and Highway 211 North. Turn northwest on Highway 211 and drive 15 miles to Usk and Highway 20. Turn left (northwest) and drive 31 miles to Tiger and Highway 31. Continue (north) on Highway 31 and drive three miles to the sign marking the Sullivan Lake Ranger Station. Turn right on Sullivan Lake Road/County Road 9345 and drive a short distance, cross the bridge over the Pend Oreille River, and continue 12 miles to the campground on the left (set at the foot of Sullivan Lake, just across the road from the Sullivan Lake Ranger Station).

Contact: Colville National Forest, Sullivan Lake Ranger District, 509/446-7500, www.fs.usda.gov.

66 EDGEWATER

Scenic rating: 6

in Colville National Forest

Map 4.3, page 241

Edgewater Camp is set on the shore of the Pend Oreille River about two miles downstream from the Box Canyon Dam. Although not far out of Ione, the camp has a primitive feel to it. Fishing for largemouth bass, rainbow trout, and brown trout is popular here, though suckers and squawfish present somewhat of a problem.

Campsites, facilities: There are 19 single sites and one double site for tents or RVs up to 72 feet long. Picnic tables and fire grills are provided. Drinking water is available until Labor Day. Vault toilets, garbage bins, and firewood are

available. A boat launch and a picnic area are available nearby. Leashed pets are permitted.

Reservations, fees: Reservations are accepted at 877/444-6777 ($10 reservation fee) or www.recreation.gov ($9 reservation fee). Sites are $18-36 per night, $9 per extra vehicle per night. Open mid-May-early September, weather permitting.

Directions: From Spokane, drive north on U.S. 395 for six miles to U.S. 2. Turn northeast on U.S. 2 and drive 30 miles to the Metaline turn-off and Highway 211 North. Turn northwest on Highway 211 and drive 15 miles to Usk and Highway 20. Turn left (northwest) and drive 31 miles to Tiger and Highway 31. Continue on Highway 31 and drive 15 miles to the town of Metaline Falls (Highway 31 is known as Lehigh Avenue in town); continue 2.5 miles to Sullivan Lake Road (County Road 9345). Turn right (east) on Sullivan Lake Road and drive 0.25 mile to County Road 3669. Turn left (north) on County Road 3669 and drive two miles to the campground entrance road on the left. Turn left and drive 0.25 mile to the campground.

Contact: Colville National Forest, Sullivan Lake Ranger District, 509/446-7500, www.fs.usda.gov.

67 NOISY CREEK & NOISY CREEK GROUP

Scenic rating: 7

on Sullivan Lake in Colville National Forest

Map 4.3, page 241

This campground is situated on the southeast end of Sullivan Lake, adjacent to where Noisy Creek pours into Sullivan Lake. Note that the lake level can be drawn down for irrigation, leaving this camp well above the lake. Noisy Creek Trail near camp heads east along Noisy Creek and then north up to Hall Mountain (elevation 6,323 feet), a distance of 5.3 miles; this is bighorn sheep country. The Lakeshore Trailhead is located at the nearby day-use area. Waterskiing is allowed on the 3.5-mile-long lake, and the boat ramp near the camp provides a good launch point.

Campsites, facilities: There are 19 sites for tents or RVs up to 45 feet long and one group camp for up to 50 people. If the group camp is not reserved, it is available as an overflow area. Picnic tables and fire grills are provided. Drinking water and flush toilets are available. A camp host is on-site. Boat-launching facilities and a picnic area are nearby. Some facilities are wheelchair accessible. Leashed pets are permitted.

Reservations, fees: Reservations are accepted for individual sites and required for the group camp at 877/444-6777 ($10 reservation fee) or www.recreation.gov ($9 reservation fee). Sites are $18 per night, $9 per night extra vehicle fee, and the group site is $67 per night. Open May-September, weather permitting.

Directions: From Spokane, drive north on U.S. 395 for six miles to U.S. 2. Turn northeast on U.S. 2 and drive 30 miles to the Metaline turn-off and Highway 211 North. Turn northwest on Highway 211 and drive 15 miles to Usk and Highway 20. Turn left (northwest) and drive 31 miles to Tiger and Highway 31. Continue (north) on Highway 31 and drive three miles to the sign marking the Sullivan Lake Ranger Station. Turn right on Sullivan Lake Road/County Road 9345 and drive a short distance, cross the bridge over the Pend Oreille River, and continue nine miles to the campground on the right (on the south end of Sullivan Lake).

Contact: Colville National Forest, Sullivan Lake Ranger District, 509/446-7500, www.fs.usda.gov.

68 DOUGLAS FALLS

on Mill Creek

Scenic rating: 8

Map 4.3, page 241   BEST (

This campground is just outside of Colville in a wooded area along Mill Creek. A 0.2-mile walk from the campground takes you to a beautiful overlook of Douglas Falls. Another unique highlight is a cabled free-span bridge. And best of all, this camp is free!

Campsites, facilities: There are 12 sites for tents or RVs up to 30 feet long. Picnic tables and fire grills are provided. Vault toilets, drinking water, and a group picnic shelter are available. Garbage must be packed out. A camp host is on-site. A baseball field is nearby. Some facilities are wheelchair accessible. Leashed pets are permitted.

Reservations, fees: Reservations are not accepted. There is no fee for camping, but a Discover Pass is required. Open Memorial Day weekend-November, weather permitting.

Directions: From Spokane, drive north on U.S. 395 for 87 miles to Colville and Highway 20. Turn east on Highway 20 and drive 1.1 miles to Aladdin Road. Turn left (north) and drive two miles to Douglas Falls Road. Turn left and drive three miles to the campground on the left.

Contact: Department of Natural Resources, Northeast Region, 509/684-7474, www.dnr.wa.gov.

69 ROCKY LAKE

near Colville

Scenic rating: 6

Map 4.3, page 241

The campground is set on Rocky Lake, a shallow, weedy pond lined with a lot of rocks. This camp is good for overnight camping, but nearby Douglas Falls is better for a long-term stay. Fishing for rainbow trout is an option. If you backtrack about 10 miles on Rocky Lake Road, you'll see the entrance signs for the Little Pend Oreille Wildlife Refuge, a premium area for hiking, fishing, hunting, and wildlife photography.

Campsites, facilities: There are seven sites for tents or RVs up to 20 feet long. Picnic tables and fire grills are provided. Vault toilets, drinking water, and a boat launch are available. Garbage must be packed out. Some facilities are wheelchair accessible. Leashed pets are permitted.

Reservations, fees: Reservations are not accepted. There is no fee for camping, but a Discover Pass is required. Sites are available from the opening day of fishing season to June 1; other times, the camp is open only for day-use. Call ahead to confirm.

Directions: From Spokane, drive north on U.S. 395 for 87 miles to Colville and Highway 20. Turn east on Highway 20 and drive six miles to Artman-Gibson Road. Turn right on Artman-Gibson Road and drive 3.2 miles to a one-lane gravel road. Turn right on the gravel road (un-named) and drive about 0.5 mile. Bear left and continue another two miles to the campground.

Contact: Department of Natural Resources, Northeast Region, 509/684-7474, www.dnr.wa.gov.

70 STARVATION LAKE
🎣 🚤 🐕 ♿ 🚐 ⛺

Scenic rating: 8

near Colville

Map 4.3, page 241

Starvation Lake is only 15 feet deep and has a weed problem, so it's OK for trout fishing but not for swimming. It is possible to drown here if you get your feet tangled in the weeds. Ospreys and bald eagles frequent the area. It's advisable to obtain a detailed map of the area. The camp is used extensively by locals during the early fishing season (end of April-early June) but is not crowded thereafter, when the fishing becomes catch-and-release; check regulations. Boats must not exceed 16 feet.

Campsites, facilities: There are eight sites for tents or RVs up to 30 feet long. Some sites are pull-through. Picnic tables and fire grills are provided. Vault toilets, drinking water, primitive boat launch, and a fishing dock are available. A camp host is on-site. Garbage must be packed out. Some facilities are wheelchair accessible. Leashed pets are permitted.

Reservations, fees: Reservations are not accepted. There is no fee for camping, but a Discover Pass is required. Open mid-April-November, weather permitting.

Directions: From Spokane, drive north on U.S. 395 for 74 miles to Colville and Highway 20. Turn east on Highway 20 and drive 10.5 miles to a gravel road (sign says Starvation Lake). Turn right on the gravel road and drive 0.3 mile to the intersection. Turn left and drive 0.5 mile to the campground on the right.

Contact: Department of Natural Resources, Northeast Region, 509/684-7474, www.dnr.wa.gov.

71 LITTLE TWIN LAKES
🎣 🚤 🐕 🚐 ⛺

Scenic rating: 6

in Colville National Forest

Map 4.3, page 241

Sites at this pretty, wooded campground on the shore of Little Twin Lakes have lake views and are free. Fishing is best here for cutthroat trout. Nearby Lake Roosevelt National Recreation Area offers recreation options, and side-trip ideas include Colville Tribal Museum and Grand Coulee Dam Visitor Center.

Campsites, facilities: There are seven sites for tents or RVs up to 16 feet long. Fire grills and picnic tables are provided. There is no drinking water. Vault toilets and firewood are available. Garbage must be packed out. Boat docks and launching facilities are located nearby. Leashed pets are permitted.

Reservations, fees: Reservations are not accepted. There is no fee for camping. Open May-early September, weather permitting.

Directions: From Spokane, drive north on U.S. 395 for 87 miles to Colville and Highway 20. Turn east on Highway 20 and drive 12.5 miles to County Road 4915. Turn left (northeast) and drive 1.5 miles to Forest Road 4939. Turn right (north) and drive 4.5 miles to the campground on the right.

Contact: Colville National Forest, Three

Rivers Ranger District, Colville Office, 509/684-7000, www.fs.usda.gov.

72 FLODELLE CREEK

🚶‍♂️ 🚲 ⛵ 🎣 🐕 ♿ 🚐 ⛺

Scenic rating: 8

near Colville

Map 4.3, page 241

This campground is set where hiking, hunting, and fishing are quite good. It's advisable to obtain a detailed map of the area. Off-road vehicle trails are available at this camp and at nearby Sherry Creek camp, and they are often in use, so don't count on a particularly quiet camping experience. This spot can provide good fishing, best for brook trout. Wildlife includes black bears, moose, mosquitoes, and black gnats, the latter occasionally so prevalent that they are considered wildlife. Be prepared.

Campsites, facilities: There are eight sites for tents or RVs up to 30 feet long. Picnic tables and fire grills are provided. Vault toilets and drinking water are available. Garbage must be packed out. Some facilities are wheelchair accessible. Leashed pets are permitted.

Reservations, fees: Reservations are not accepted. There is no fee for camping, but a Discover Pass is required. Open May-November, weather permitting.

Directions: From Spokane, drive north on U.S. 395 for 87 miles to Colville and Highway 20. Turn east on Highway 20 and drive 19.4 miles to an unnamed two-lane gravel road on the right. Turn right on that road and drive 0.25 mile to the campground entrance road on the left.

Contact: Department of Natural Resources, Northeast Region, 509/684-7474, www.dnr.wa.gov.

73 SHERRY CREEK

🚶‍♂️ 🚲 ⛵ 🎣 🐕 🚐 ⛺

Scenic rating: 6

near Sherry Lake

Map 4.3, page 241

This camp is set near the off-road vehicle (ORV) trail network of the Pend Oreille Lake system. It is located on Sherry Creek, about three miles from Sherry Lake, and is basically a fishing camp, with lots of brook trout and a few rainbow trout. It's advisable to obtain a detailed map of the area. Biking and hiking on the ORV trails is an option. The 78-mile network of ORV trails can be accessed from this campground. This area has good numbers of black bears and even some moose, and because it is set next to a wetland, there can be tons of mosquitoes in summer. Snowmobiling and cross-country skiing are popular in the winter.

Campsites, facilities: There are eight sites for tents or RVs up to 50 feet long, including three group sites for 12-16 people each. Some sites are pull-through. Picnic tables and fire pits are provided. Vault toilets, drinking water, and a ramp for unloading OHVs are available. Garbage must be packed out. Leashed pets are permitted.

Reservations, fees: Reservations are not accepted. There is no fee for camping, but a Discover Pass is required. Open May-November, weather permitting.

Directions: From Spokane, drive north on U.S. 395 for 74 miles to Colville and Highway 20. Turn east on Highway 20 and drive 23.8 miles to a gravel road. Turn right and drive approximately 0.5 mile to the campground.

Contact: Department of Natural Resources, Northeast Region, 509/684-7474, www.dnr.wa.gov.

74 LAKE GILLETTE

🧍🚴🏊⛵🛥️🐴♿🚐🏕️

Scenic rating: 8

on Lake Gillette in Colville National Forest

Map 4.3, page 241

This pretty and popular camp is situated right on the shore of Lake Gillette. Like neighboring Gillette Campground, it fills up quickly in the summer. The camp is popular with off-road vehicle (OHV) users, primarily motorcyclists. An OHV system can't be accessed directly from the campground, but is close. Note that OHV riding in and out of camp is prohibited. Fishing at Lake Gillette is best for cutthroat trout.

Campsites, facilities: There are eight single sites and six double sites for tents or RVs up to 50 feet long. Fire grills and picnic tables are provided. Drinking water, vault toilets, bear-proof garbage bins, firewood, and an amphitheater are available. A camp host is on-site. A store, ice, gas, and a café are located within one mile. Boat docks, launching facilities, and rentals are nearby. Some facilities are wheelchair accessible. Leashed pets are permitted.

Reservations, fees: Reservations are not accepted. Single sites are $18 per night, double sites are $36 per night, $9 per extra vehicle per night. Open mid-May-early September, weather permitting.

Directions: From Spokane, drive north on U.S. 395 for 74 miles to Colville and Highway 20. Turn east on Highway 20 and drive 20 miles to County Road 4987 (Lake Gillette Road). Turn right (east) on Lake Gillette Road and drive 0.5 mile to the campground on the left.

Contact: Colville National Forest, Three Rivers Ranger District, Colville Office, 509/684-7000, www.fs.usda.gov.

75 GILLETTE

🧍🚴🏊⛵🛥️❄️🐴♿🚐🏕️

Scenic rating: 7

near Lake Gillette in Colville National Forest

Map 4.3, page 241

This beautiful and extremely popular campground, located just south of Beaver Lodge Resort and Lake Thomas, is near Lake Gillette, one in a chain of four lakes. There are a few hiking and biking trails in the area. In winter, downhill and cross-country skiing is available.

Campsites, facilities: There are 30 sites for tents or RVs up to 55 feet long. Picnic tables and fire grills are provided. Drinking water, vault toilets, restrooms with flush toilets, and bear-proof garbage bins are available. A camp host is on-site. A store and ice are located within one mile. Boat docks, launching facilities, and rentals are nearby. Some facilities are wheelchair accessible. Leashed pets are permitted.

Reservations, fees: Reservations are not accepted. Sites are $18-36 per night, $9 per extra vehicle per night. Open late May-early September, weather permitting.

Directions: From Spokane, drive north on U.S. 395 for 74 miles to Colville and Highway 20. Turn east on Highway 20 and drive 20 miles to County Road 4987 (Lake Gillette Road). Turn right (east) on Lake Gillette Road and drive 0.5 mile to the campground on the right.

Contact: Colville National Forest, Three Rivers Ranger District, Colville Office, 509/684-7000, www.fs.usda.gov.

76 BEAVER LODGE RESORT

🧍🚴🏊⛵🛥️❄️🐴🏄♿🚐🏕️

Scenic rating: 9

on Lake Thomas

Map 4.3, page 241

This developed camp is set along the shore of Lake Gillette, one in a chain of four lakes. A highlight in this area: the numerous opportunities for off-road vehicles (OHVs) provided by a network of OHV trails. In addition, hiking trails and marked bike trails are close to the camp. In winter, downhill and cross-country skiing are available.

Campsites, facilities: There are 14 sites with full or partial hookups (30 amps) for tents or RVs up to 34 feet long, 24 sites for tents or RVs up to 40 feet (no hookups), and 10 cabins. Picnic tables and fire pits are provided. Restrooms with flush toilets and coin showers, drinking water, gasoline, propane gas, firewood, a convenience store, café, ice, boat rentals, and a playground are available. A dump station is located within one mile. Boat docks and launching facilities are nearby. Some facilities are wheelchair accessible. Leashed pets are permitted.

Reservations, fees: Reservations are accepted. Sites are $18-35 per night, cabins are $60-109, $5 per extra vehicle per night. Some credit cards are accepted. Open year-round.

Directions: From Spokane, drive north on U.S. 395/Division Street for 74 miles to Colville and Highway 20. Turn east on Highway 20 and drive 25 miles to the resort on the right.

Contact: Beaver Lodge Resort, 509/684-5657, www.beaverlodgeresort.org.

77 LAKE THOMAS

Scenic rating: 6
on Lake Thomas in Colville National Forest

Map 4.3, page 241

This camp on the shore of Lake Thomas offers a less crowded alternative to the campgrounds at Lake Gillette. The lake provides fishing for cutthroat trout. Other nearby options include Lake Gillette and Beaver Lodge Resort, with trails, boating, and winter sports.

Campsites, facilities: There are 16 sites for tents or RVs up to 16 feet long. Picnic tables and fire grills are provided. Drinking water, vault toilets, and bear-proof garbage bins are available. A camp host is on-site. Boat docks, launching facilities, and rentals are nearby.

Some facilities are wheelchair accessible. Leashed pets are permitted.

Reservations, fees: Reservations are not accepted. Sites are $18-36 per night, $9 per extra vehicle per night. Open late May-early September, weather permitting; the boat ramp remains open until snow closure.

Directions: From Spokane, drive north on U.S. 395 for 74 miles to Colville and Highway 20. Turn east on Highway 20 and drive 20 miles to County Road 4987 (Lake Gillette Road). Turn right (east) on Lake Gillette Road and drive one mile to the campground on the left.

Contact: Colville National Forest, Three Rivers Ranger District, 509/684-7000, www.fs.usda.gov.

78 LAKE LEO

Scenic rating: 6
on Lake Leo in Colville National Forest

Map 4.3, page 241

Lake Leo is the northernmost and quietest camp on the chain of lakes in the immediate vicinity. This lake provides fishing for cutthroat trout. Frater and Nile Lakes, both fairly small, are located one mile north. In winter, a Nordic ski trail starts adjacent to the camp. Fishing and boating are two recreation options here.

Campsites, facilities: There are eight sites for tents or RVs up to 30 feet long. Picnic tables and fire grills are provided. Drinking water, vault toilets, and bear-proof garbage bins are available. A boat ramp and launching facilities are nearby. Some facilities are wheelchair accessible. Leashed pets are permitted.

Reservations, fees: Reservations are not accepted. Sites are $18 per night, $9 per extra vehicle per night. Open mid-April-September, with reduced services and fees after Labor Day weekend; the boat ramp remains open until snow closure.

Directions: From Spokane on I-90, drive north on U.S. 395 for 74 miles to Colville and Highway 20. Turn east on Highway 20 and drive 23 miles to the campground entrance on the right.

Contact: Colville National Forest, Three Rivers Ranger District, 509/684-7000, www. fs.usda.gov.

79 BLUESLIDE RESORT

🧗 🚴 🏊 🛶 🏄 🐕 🏕️ 🚐 ⛰️

Scenic rating: 7

in Cusick

Map 4.3, page 241

This resort is situated along the western shore of the Pend Oreille River. It offers a headquarters for anglers and vacationers. Four or five bass tournaments are held each spring during May and June, and the river is stocked with both rainbow trout and bass. The resort offers full facilities for anglers, including tackle and a marina. The park is lovely, with grassy, shaded sites, and is located along the waterfowl migratory path. Lots of groups camp here in the summer. Recreation options include bicycling nearby. All-terrain vehicle (ATV) trails here can take you all the way to Canada.

Campsites, facilities: There are 49 sites with full or partial hookups (20, 30, and 50 amps) for tents or RVs of any length and five cabins. Picnic tables and fire pits are provided. Restrooms with flush toilets and showers, drinking water, a meeting hall, a community fire pit, several sports fields, a convenience store, propane, coin laundry, ice, firewood, a playground, basketball, tetherball, volleyball, horseshoe pits, a seasonal heated swimming pool, boat docks, and launching facilities are available. Leashed pets are permitted.

Reservations, fees: Reservations are accepted. Sites are $25-50 per night. Cabins are $95-250 per night. Some credit cards are accepted. Open mid-May-mid-October.

Directions: From Spokane, drive north on Division Street for six miles to U.S. 2. Turn north on U.S. 2 and drive 26 miles northeast to Highway 211. Turn left and drive 18 miles

to Highway 20. Turn left and drive 22 miles to the park (located on the right at Milepost 400).

Contact: Blueslide Resort, 509/445-1327, www. blueslideresort.com.

80 PANHANDLE

🧗 🏊 🛶 🏄 🐕 ♿ 🚐 ⛰️

Scenic rating: 9

in Colville National Forest

Map 4.3, page 241

Among tall trees and with views of the river, this is a scenic spot to set up camp along the eastern shore of the Pend Oreille River. This camp is located in an area of mature trees and makes a good base for a fishing or waterskiing trip. Fishing for largemouth and smallmouth bass is popular, with an annual bass tournament held every summer in the area. A network of hiking trails can be accessed by taking forest roads to the east.

Campsites, facilities: There are 13 sites for tents or RVs up to 33 feet long. Picnic tables and fire grills are provided. Drinking water, vault toilets, bear-proof garbage bins, and firewood are available. A camp host is on-site. A small boat launch is nearby. Some facilities are wheelchair accessible. Leashed pets are permitted.

Reservations, fees: Reservations are accepted at 877/444-6777 ($10 reservation fee) or www. recreation.gov ($9 reservation fee). Sites are $18 per night, $9 extra vehicle fee. Open late May-early September, weather permitting; the boat ramp remains open until snow closure.

Directions: From Spokane, drive north on U.S. 395/Division Street for six miles to U.S. 2. Turn north on U.S. 2 and drive 30 miles to the Metaline turnoff and Highway 211 North. Take Highway 211 North and drive 15 miles to the junction of Highway 20. Cross Highway 20, driving through the town of Usk. Continue across the Pend Oreille River to Le Clerc Road. Turn left and drive 15 miles north on Le Clerc Road to the campground on the left.

Contact: Colville National Forest, Newport

Ranger District, 509/447-7300, www.fs.usda. gov.

81 BROWNS LAKE

🏃 🏊 🛶 ⛟ 🎣 🐴 ♿ 🚐 ⛺

Scenic rating: 8

on Browns Lake in Colville National Forest

Map 4.3, page 241

This campground is set along the shore of Browns Lake, with lakeside sites bordering old-growth hemlock and cedar. No motorized boats are permitted on the lake, and only fly-fishing is allowed, so it can be ideal for float tubes, canoes, and prams. A 1.25-mile hiking trail leaves the campground and ties into a wheelchair-accessible interpretive trail with beautiful views along the way. At the end of the trail sits a fishing-viewing platform in Browns Creek, which feeds into the lake. South Skookum Lake is about five miles away.

Campsites, facilities: There are 18 sites for tents or RVs up to 28 feet long. Picnic tables and fire grills are provided. Vault toilets are available. There is no drinking water. A primitive boat launch is available for small boats, such as canoes, rowboats, and inflatables. Some facilities are wheelchair accessible. Leashed pets are permitted.

Reservations, fees: Reservations are not accepted. Sites are $16 per night, $8 per each additional vehicle per night. Open May-end of October, weather permitting.

Directions: From Spokane, drive north on U.S. 395/Division Street for six miles to U.S. 2. Turn north on U.S. 2 and drive 30 miles to the Metaline turnoff and Highway 211 North. Turn northwest on Highway 211 and drive 15 miles to Usk and Highway 20. Drive north on Highway 20 a short distance to County Road 3389. Turn right (east) on Kings Lake-Boswell Road (County Road 3389) and drive (over the Pend Oreille River) five miles to a fork with

Forest Road 5030. Turn left and drive three miles to the campground at the end of the road.

Contact: Colville National Forest, Newport Ranger District, 509/447-7300, www.fs.usda. gov.

82 SKOOKUM CREEK

🏃 🚴 🏊 🛶 ⛟ 🎣 🐴 ♿ 🚐 ⛺

Scenic rating: 5

near the Pend Oreille River

Map 4.3, page 241

Skookum Creek Campground is set in a wooded area along Skookum Creek, about 1.5 miles from where it empties into the Pend Oreille River. It's a good canoeing spot, has drinking water, and gets little attention. And you can't beat the price of admission—free.

Campsites, facilities: There are 10 sites for tents or RVs up to 30 feet long. Picnic tables and fire grills are provided. Drinking water and vault toilets are available. Garbage must be packed out. A group picnic shelter with a barbecue is available nearby. Some facilities are wheelchair accessible. Leashed pets are permitted.

Reservations, fees: Reservations are not accepted. There is no fee for camping, but a Discover Pass is required. Open mid-April-October, weather permitting.

Directions: From Spokane, drive north on U.S. 395 for six miles to U.S. 2. Turn north on U.S. 2 and drive 41 miles to Newport and Highway 20. Turn west on Highway 20 and drive 16 miles northwest to the town of Usk. Continue east across the bridge for 0.9 mile to Le Clerc Road. Turn right on Le Clerc Road and drive 2.2 miles to a one-lane gravel road. Turn left and drive a short distance to another gravel road. Turn left and drive 0.25 mile to the campground.

Contact: Department of Natural Resources, Northeast Region, 509/684-7474, www.dnr. wa.gov.

83 SOUTH SKOOKUM LAKE

🧍🏊🚣🛶🐕♿🏊⛺

Scenic rating: 7

on South Skookum Lake in Colville National Forest

Map 4.3, page 241

This camp is situated on the western shore of South Skookum Lake, at the foot of Kings Mountain (elevation 4,383 feet). This is a good fishing lake, stocked with cutthroat trout, and is popular with families. A 1.3-mile hiking trail circles the water. South Baldy, a staffed fire lookout, is nearby and is a nice day-hike destination.

Campsites, facilities: There are 25 sites for tents or RVs up to 30 feet long. Picnic tables and fire rings are provided. Drinking water, garbage bins, and vault toilets are available. A camp host is on-site. A boat ramp for small boats and several docks, including a wheelchair-accessible fishing dock, are available nearby. Some facilities are wheelchair accessible. Leashed pets are permitted.

Reservations, fees: Reservations are not accepted. Sites are $18 per night, $9 per extra vehicle per night. Open late May-September, weather permitting.

Directions: From Spokane, drive north on U.S. 395/Division Street for six miles to U.S. 2. Turn north on U.S. 2 and drive 30 miles to the Metaline turnoff and Highway 211. Turn northwest on Highway 211 and drive 15 miles to Usk and Highway 20. Drive north on Highway 20 a short distance to Kings Lake-Boswell Road (County Road 3389). Turn right (east) on Kings Lake-Boswell Road and drive eight miles (over the Pend Oreille River) to the campground entrance road on the right. Turn right and drive 0.25 mile to the campground.

Contact: Colville National Forest, Newport Ranger District, 509/447-7300, www.fs.usda.gov.

84 PIONEER PARK

🧍🏊🚣🛶🐕♿🏊⛺

Scenic rating: 8

in Colville National Forest

Map 4.3, page 241

Pioneer Park Campground is set along the shore of Box Canyon Reservoir on the Pend Oreille River near Newport. The launch and adjoining parking area are suitable for larger boats. Waterskiing and water sports are popular here. There is a wheelchair-accessible interpretive trail with a boardwalk and beautiful views of the river. Signs along the way explain the history of the Kalispel tribe.

Campsites, facilities: There are 17 sites for tents or RVs up to 33 feet long. Picnic tables and fire rings are provided. Drinking water, vault toilets, bear-proof garbage bins, firewood, and a sheltered picnic area are available. A camp host is on-site. Boat docks, launching facilities, and rentals are nearby. Some facilities are wheelchair accessible. Leashed pets are permitted.

Reservations, fees: Reservations are accepted at 877/444-6777 ($10 reservation fee) or www.recreation.gov ($9 reservation fee). Sites are $18 per night, $9 extra vehicle fee. Open early May-early September, weather permitting.

Directions: From Spokane, drive north on U.S. 395 for six miles to U.S. 2. Turn north on U.S. 2 and drive 41 miles to Newport. Turn west on Highway 20 and drive 16 miles northwest to the town of Usk. Continue across the Pend Oreille River to Le Clerc Road (County Road 9305). Turn left on Le Clerc Road and drive two miles to the campground on the left.

Contact: Colville National Forest, Newport Ranger District, 509/447-7300, www.fs.usda.gov.

85 THE 49ER MOTEL & RV PARK

🏃 🚴 🏊 ✹ 🐕 🚐 ⛺

Scenic rating: 6

near Chewelah

Map 4.3, page 241

This region is the heart of mining country. The park has grassy sites and is located next to a motel in a mountainous setting. Nearby recreation options include a 27-hole golf course, hiking trails, and marked bike trails. This park is a good deal for RV cruisers—a rustic setting right in town. In winter, note that the 49 Degrees North Ski & Snowboard Park is located 12 miles to the east.

Campsites, facilities: There are 26 sites for tents or RVs up to 36 feet long (20 and 30 amp full hookups) and 13 motel rooms. Most sites are pull-through. Picnic tables are provided. Restrooms with flush toilets and showers, drinking water, a dump station, cable TV, and phone hookups are available. Propane gas, gasoline, a store, café, ice, and coin laundry are within one mile. Leashed pets are permitted.

Reservations, fees: Reservations are accepted. RV sites are $25-30 per night, tent sites are $11 per person per night, $5 per pet. Weekly and monthly rates are available. Some credit cards are accepted. Open year-round.

Directions: From Spokane, drive north on U.S. 395 for 44 miles to Chewelah; the park is on the right (on U.S. 395 at the south edge of town).

Contact: The 49er Motel & RV Park, 509/935-8613.

86 WINONA BEACH RESORT

🏊 🚣 🛥 🐕 🎣 ♿ 🚐 ⛺

Scenic rating: 9

on Waitts Lake

Map 4.3, page 241

This beautiful and comfortable resort on the shore of Waitts Lake has spacious sites and friendly folks. The park fills up in July and August, and during this time cabins are available for rent (by the week, not the night). In the spring, fishing for brown trout and rainbow trout can be quite good. The trout head to deeper water in the summer, and bluegill and perch are easier to catch then. Waterskiing is also popular.

Campsites, facilities: There are 54 sites with full hookups (30 amps), including 20 lakeside sites, and three sites with partial hookups (electricity and water) for tents or RVs up to 40 feet long, seven sites for tents, and eight cabins. Picnic tables and fire rings are provided. Restrooms with flush toilets and coin showers, drinking water, a dump station, firewood, a snack bar, general store, playground, volleyball, horseshoe pits, basketball, a swimming beach, an antiques store, and ice are available. Boat docks, launching facilities, and boat rentals are on-site. Some facilities are wheelchair accessible. Leashed pets are permitted.

Reservations, fees: Reservations are accepted. RV sites are $39-45 per night, tent sites are $32 per night, $4 per each additional person for more than four people, $5 per pet per night. Weekly and monthly rates are available. Some credit cards are accepted. Open April-September.

Directions: From Spokane, drive north on U.S. 395 for 42 miles to the Valley-Waitts Lake exit. Turn left (west) at that exit and drive one mile to Highway 231. Turn right (north) on Highway 231 and drive 1.5 miles to the town of Valley and Valley-Waitts Lake Road. Turn left and drive three miles to Winona Beach Road. Turn left and drive 0.25 mile to the resort at the end of the road.

Contact: Winona Beach Resort, 509/937-2231, www.winonabeach.net.

87 SILVER BEACH RESORT

🏃 🏊 🚣 🚐 🐕 🎣 ♿ 🚐

Scenic rating: 6

on Waitts Lake

Map 4.3, page 241

Silver Beach Resort offers grassy sites on the

shore of Waitts Lake, where fishing and water-skiing are popular. In the spring, fishing for brown trout and rainbow trout can be quite good.

Campsites, facilities: There are 51 sites for RVs up to 36 feet long (30 amp full hookups), including two pull-through sites, and six cabins. Picnic tables are provided and fire pits can be rented. Restrooms with flush toilets and coin showers, drinking water, Wi-Fi, propane gas, a dump station, convenience store, restaurant, coin laundry, ice, firewood, a playground, boat docks, launching facilities, and boat rentals are available. Some facilities are wheelchair accessible. Leashed pets are permitted.

Reservations, fees: Reservations are accepted. Sites are $36 per night, $4 per person per night for more than two people, $4 per pet per night. Cabins are $95-130 per night. Weekly rates are available. Some credit cards are accepted. Open mid-April-mid-September.

Directions: From Spokane, drive north on U.S. 395 for 42 miles to the Valley-Waitts Lake exit. Turn left (west) at that exit and drive six miles to Waitts Lake and the resort on the left-hand side near the shore of the lake.

Contact: Silver Beach Resort, 509/937-2811, www.silverbeachresort.net.

88 JUMP OFF JOE LAKE RESORT

🏊 ⛵ 🚤 🎣 ♿ 🚐 ⛰️

Scenic rating: 7

on Jump Off Joe Lake

Map 4.3, page 241

Located on the edge of Jump Off Joe Lake, this wooded campground offers lake views and easy boating access. Recreational activities include boating, fishing, and swimming. Spokane and Grand Coulee Dam are both within a short drive and provide excellent side-trip options. Within 10 miles to the north are an 18-hole golf course and casino.

Campsites, facilities: There are 20 sites for tents, 20 sites for tents or RVs of any length

(30 amp full hookups), and five cabins. Picnic tables and fire rings are provided. Restrooms with flush toilets and coin showers, drinking water, horseshoe pits, recreation field, a swimming beach, a convenience store, and a picnic area are available. The resort also rents boats and has a boat ramp and dock. Some facilities are wheelchair accessible. Leashed pets are permitted.

Reservations, fees: Reservations are accepted. Sites are $25-27 per night, $5 per night per extra person, $5 per pet per night. Some credit cards are accepted. Open April-October.

Directions: From Spokane, drive north on U.S. 395 for about 40 miles (three miles south of the town of Valley) to the Jump Off Joe Road exit (Milepost 198). Take that exit, turn west, and drive 1.2 miles to the resort on the right.

Contact: Jump Off Joe Lake Resort, 509/937-2133.

89 SHORE ACRES RESORT

🏊 ⛵ 🚤 🎣 🏕️ 🚐

Scenic rating: 8

on Loon Lake

Map 4.3, page 241   **BEST (**

Located along the shore of Loon Lake at 2,400 feet elevation, this family-oriented campground has a long expanse of beach and offers an alternative to Granite Point Park across the lake. Some sites have lake views. Loon Lake is approximately four miles long, and waterskiing, wakeboarding, and personal watercraft are allowed. Fishing is best for mackinaw trout in spring (downriggers suggested) as well as kokanee salmon and rainbow trout. Warm weather brings perch, sunfish, and bass out of their hiding places.

Campsites, facilities: There are 25 sites for RVs up to 40 feet (full hookups) and 11 cabins. Picnic tables are provided. Restrooms with flush toilets and showers, drinking water, a dump station, cable TV, a general store, restaurant, tackle, firewood, ice, community fire pits, a playground, a swimming area, boat docks, personal watercraft and boat rentals, moorage, and launching facilities are available. Some facilities are wheelchair accessible. Leashed pets are permitted with certain restrictions.

Reservations, fees: Reservations are accepted. Sites are $40 per night, $6.50 per night per extra person, $10 per night per each additional vehicle, $10 per pet per night. Cabins are $115-140 per night. Weekly and monthly rates are available. Some credit cards are accepted. Open mid-April-September.

Directions: From Spokane, drive north on U.S. 395 for 30 miles to Highway 292. Turn left (west) on Highway 292 and drive two miles to Shore Acres Road. Turn left and drive another two miles to the resort.

Contact: Shore Acres Resort, 509/233-2474, www.shoreacresresort.com.

90 GRANITE POINT PARK

Scenic rating: 8

on Loon Lake

Map 4.3, page 241

This camp is located on the shore of Loon Lake, a clear, clean, spring-fed lake that covers 1,200 acres and features a sandy beach and swimming area. The RV park features grass sites—no concrete. In the spring, mackinaw trout range 4-30 pounds and can be taken by deepwater trolling (downriggers suggested). Easier to catch are kokanee salmon and rainbow trout in the 12- to 14-inch class. A sprinkling of perch, sunfish, and bass come out of their hiding places when the weather heats up. Waterskiing and windsurfing are popular in summer months, and personal watercraft are allowed.

Campsites, facilities: There are 10 sites with full or partial hookups (30 amps) for RVs up to 40 feet and 21 cottages with kitchens. Some spots are filled with long-term renters. Picnic tables are provided. Restrooms with flush toilets and showers, drinking water, a recreation hall, convenience store, café, coin laundry, ice, a playground, basketball and volleyball courts,

horseshoe pits, three swimming areas with a 0.75-mile beach, two swimming docks, boat docks, boat rentals, and launching facilities are available. Propane gas is located within one mile.

Reservations, fees: Reservations are accepted. Sites are $35-38 per night. Cabins are $86-184 per night. Weekly and monthly rates are available. Open May-September.

Directions: From Spokane, drive north on U.S. 395/Division Street for 26 miles (8 miles past the town of Deer Park) to the park on the left.

Contact: Granite Point Park, 509/233-2100, www.granitepointpark.com.

91 PEND OREILLE COUNTY PARK

Scenic rating: 6

near Newport

Map 4.3, page 241

This 440-acre park is wooded and features eight miles of trails throughout for hikers, bicyclists, and equestrians. There is some road noise from U.S. 2, but it's not intolerable. Pend Oreille is the only campground around, and it's not a bad choice if you're looking for a layover spot. It's a good alternative to the often-crowded Mount Spokane State Park. Nearby activities include fishing and hunting.

Campsites, facilities: There are 17 sites for tents and RVs up to 18 feet (no hookups). An equestrian group camp is planned for the area. Picnic tables and fire pits are provided. Drinking water, vault toilets, firewood, and a picnic area are available. A camp host is on-site. Some facilities are wheelchair accessible. Leashed pets are permitted.

Reservations, fees: Reservations are not accepted. Sites are $10 per night. Open late May-early September, weather permitting.

Directions: From Spokane, drive north on U.S. 395/Division Street for six miles to U.S. 2. Turn north on U.S. 2 and drive 31 miles to the county park entrance on the left (west side). Or from Newport: Drive east on U.S 2 for 15 miles (past County Road 211) to the park entrance on the right.

Contact: Pend Oreille County, Department of Public Works, 509/447-4821, www.pendoreilleco.org.

92 LAKESHORE RV PARK AND MARINA

Scenic rating: 7

on Lake Chelan

Map 4.4, page 242

This municipal park and marina on Lake Chelan is a popular family camp, with fishing, swimming, boating, waterskiing, personal watercraft, and hiking among the available activities. City amenities are within walking distance. The camp fills up in the summer, including on weekdays in July and August. This RV park covers 22 acres, featuring a large marina and a 15-acre day-use area. An 18-hole championship golf course and putting green, lighted tennis courts, a water-slide park, bowling alley, and a visitors center are nearby. A casino is six miles west of Chelan. A trip worth taking, the ferry ride goes to several landings on the lake; the ferry terminal is 0.5 mile from the park.

Campsites, facilities: There are 165 sites for tents or RVs up to 40 feet long (30 and 50 amp full hookups). Some sites are pull-through. Picnic tables are provided. Restrooms with flush toilets and coin showers, Wi-Fi, cable TV, a dump station, a covered picnic area, playground, putting course, Rally Alley, snack bar, swimming beaches, tennis courts, volleyball, and basketball are available. A store, café, coin laundry, ice, and propane gas are available within one mile. A marina with boat docks, paddleboard and watercraft rentals, and launching facilities are on-site. Some facilities are wheelchair accessible. Leashed pets are permitted, except during some holiday periods.

Reservations, fees: Reservations are accepted at 509/682-8023 ($5 reservation fee). RV sites are $32-65 per night, $5 per person per night for more than four people, $10 per night per additional vehicle; tent sites are $41 per night. Monthly rates are available November 1-April 30. Some credit cards are accepted. Open year-round.

Directions: From Wenatchee, drive north on U.S. 97-A for 38 miles to Chelan (after crossing the Dan Gordon Bridge, the road name changes to Saunders Street). Continue for 0.1 mile to Johnson Street. Turn left and drive 0.2 mile (becomes Highway 150/Manson Highway) to the campground on the left.

Contact: City of Chelan, Lakeshore RV Park and Marina, 509/682-8023, www.chelancityparks.com.

93 COULEE PLAYLAND RESORT

Scenic rating: 7

on Banks Lake in Electric City near the Grand Coulee Dam

Map 4.4, page 242

This park on North Banks Lake, south of the Grand Coulee Dam, is pretty and well treed, with spacious sites for both tents and RVs. The Grand Coulee Laser Light Show (seasonal) is just three miles away and is well worth a visit. Boating, fishing for many species, waterskiing, and personal watercraft are all popular. In addition, hiking trails, marked bike trails, a full-service marina, and tennis courts are close by.

Campsites, facilities: There are 65 sites with full hookups (20, 30, and 50 amps) for tents or RVs of any length, a grassy area for tents, and one yurt. Some sites are pull-through. Picnic tables and fire grills are provided. Restrooms with flush toilets and coin showers, a dump station, Wi-Fi, a general store, coin laundry, firewood, ice, a playground, boat docks, launching facilities, boat rentals, gas, and a bait and tackle shop are available. Propane gas and a café are located within one mile. Some

facilities are wheelchair accessible. Leashed pets are permitted.

Reservations, fees: Reservations are accepted. Sites are $38-45 per night, $6 per extra person per night. The yurt is $99 per night. Some credit cards are accepted. Open year-round, with limited winter facilities.

Directions: From the junction of Highway 17 and U.S. 2 (north of Ephrata), drive east on U.S. 2 for five miles to Highway 155. Turn left (north) and drive 26 miles to Grand Coulee and Electric City. The resort is just off the highway on the left.

Contact: Coulee Playland Resort, 509/633-2671, www.couleeplayland.com.

94 STEAMBOAT ROCK STATE PARK

Scenic rating: 10

on Banks Lake

Map 4.4, page 242

Steamboat Rock State Park is surrounded by desert. The park covers 5,043 acres and features nine miles of shoreline along Banks Lake, a reservoir created by the Grand Coulee Dam. A column of basaltic rock, with a surface area of 600 acres, rises 800 feet above the lake. Two campground areas and a large day-use area are set on green lawns sheltered by tall poplars. The park has 13 miles of hiking and biking trails, as well as 10 miles of horse trails. There is also a swimming beach. Fishing and waterskiing are popular; so is rock climbing. A hiking trail leads to Northrup Lake. Horse trails are also available in nearby Northrup Canyon. The one downer is mosquitoes, which are very prevalent in early summer. During the winter, the park is used by snowmobilers, cross-country skiers, and ice anglers.

Campsites, facilities: There are 136 sites with full hookups (50 amps) for RVs up to 50 feet, 26 sites for tents or RVs up to 30 feet (no hookups), 80 primitive sites (including five equestrian sites), and 12 primitive boat-in sites. Picnic

tables and fire grills are provided. Restrooms with flush toilets and coin showers, a dump station, firewood, a café, a playground, and volleyball are available. Vault toilets are available at the primitive sites. Boat-launching facilities, docks, moorage, and a marine dump station are nearby. Some facilities are wheelchair accessible. Leashed pets are permitted.

Reservations, fees: Reservations are accepted for some sites April-October at 888/226-7688 or https://washington.goingtocamp.com ($8-10 reservation fee). Sites are $20-45 per night, primitive sites are $12 per night (first-come, first-served), $10 per extra vehicle per night. Some credit cards are accepted. Open year-round, with limited winter facilities.

Directions: From East Wenatchee, drive north on U.S. 2 for 70 miles to Highway 155 (5 miles east of Coulee City). Turn north and drive 16 miles to the park on the left.

Contact: Steamboat Rock State Park, 509/633-1304, http://parks.state.wa.us.

95 COULEE CITY PARK

Scenic rating: 6

on Banks Lake

Map 4.4, page 242

Coulee City Park is a well-maintained park located in shade trees on the southern shore of 30-mile-long Banks Lake. You can see the highway from the park, and there is some highway noise. Campsites are usually available. The busiest time of the year is Memorial Day weekend because of the local rodeo. Boating, fishing, waterskiing, and riding personal watercraft are popular. A one-mile walking trail leads from the campground and meanders along the eastern shore of the lake. An 18-hole golf course is close by.

Campsites, facilities: There is a large grassy area for tents and 55 sites for tents or RVs of any length (30 and 50 amp full hookups). Some sites are pull-through. Picnic tables and fire rings are provided. Restrooms with flush toilets and showers, group fire pits, a dump station, swimming beach, and a playground are available. Propane gas, gasoline, firewood, a store, restaurant, coin laundry, and ice are located within one mile. Boat docks and launching facilities are on-site. Some facilities are wheelchair accessible. Leashed pets are permitted.

Reservations, fees: Reservations are not accepted. RV sites are $30 per night, tent sites are $15 per night, $10 per extra vehicle per night. Open April-late October, weather permitting.

Directions: From Coulee City, drive east on U.S. 2 for 0.5 mile to the park on the left. The park is within the city limits.

Contact: Coulee City Park, 509/632-5331, www.couleecity.com.

96 SUN LAKES-DRY FALLS STATE PARK

Scenic rating: 10

on Park Lake

Map 4.4, page 242	BEST (

Sun Lakes State Park is situated on the shore of Park Lake, which is used primarily by anglers, boaters, and water-skiers. This 4,027-acre park features 12 miles of shoreline and nine lakes. A trail at the north end of Lake Lenore (a 15-minute drive) leads to the Lake Lenore Caves. Dry Falls, a former waterfall, lies near the foot of the park. The cascades are history, however; only a barren 3.5-mile-wide, 400-foot climb awaits. A seasonal interpretive center is at Dry Falls. Nearby recreation possibilities include a nine-hole golf course and miniature golf.

Campsites, facilities: There are 152 sites for tents or RVs (no hookups) and 39 sites for RVs up to 65 feet (30 and 50 amp full hookups), and one group camp for up to 75 people. Picnic tables and fire pits are provided. Restrooms with flush toilets and coin showers, a dump station, snack bar, coin laundry, ice, horseshoe pits, playground, drinking water, and firewood are available. A store is located within one mile. Boat docks, launching facilities, moorage,

and boat rentals are nearby. Some facilities are wheelchair accessible. Leashed pets are permitted.

Reservations, fees: Reservations are accepted April-September at 888/226-7688 or https://washington.goingtocamp.com ($8-10 reservation fee). Sites are $20-40 per night. Call for group rates. Some credit cards are accepted. Open year-round, with limited services in winter.

Directions: From Ephrata, drive northeast on Highway 28 to Soap Lake and Highway 17. Turn left (north) on Highway 17 and drive 17 miles to the park on the right.

Contact: Sun Lakes-Dry Falls State Park, 509/632-5583, http://parks.state.wa.us; Dry Falls Interpretive Center, 509/632-5214.

97 SUN LAKES PARK RESORT

Scenic rating: 6

in Sun Lakes State Park

Map 4.4, page 242

Run by the concessionaire that operates within Sun Lakes State Park, this camp offers full facilities and is a slightly more developed alternative to the state park's campground.

Campsites, facilities: There are 152 sites for tents or RVs of any length with full hookups (20, 30, and 50 amps) and 69 cabins. Some sites are pull-through. Picnic tables are provided. Campers may use their own barbecue; all fires must be off the ground and self-contained. Restrooms with flush toilets and coin showers, propane gas, dump station, convenience store and gift shop, firewood, snack bar, coin laundry, ice, a playground, boat rentals, a seasonal heated swimming pool, miniature golf, and a nine-hole golf course are available. Boat docks and launching facilities are nearby. Some facilities are wheelchair accessible. Leashed pets are permitted.

Reservations, fees: Reservations are accepted. Sites are $43-49 per night, $10 per extra vehicle per night. Open mid-April-mid-October, weather permitting.

Directions: From Ephrata, drive northeast on Highway 28 to Soap Lake and Highway 17. Turn left (north) on Highway 17 and drive 17 miles to Sun Lakes State Park on the right. Enter the park and drive to the resort (well-marked).

Contact: Sun Lakes Park Resort, 509/632-5291, www.sunlakesparkresort.com.

98 BLUE LAKE RESORT

🚲 ⛴ 🛶 🎣 🐎 ♿ 🎿 🚐 ⛺

Scenic rating: 6

on Blue Lake

Map 4.4, page 242

Blue Lake Resort is set in a desertlike area along the shore of Blue Lake between Sun Lakes State Park and Lake Lenore Caves State Park. Both parks make excellent side trips. Activities at Blue Lake include trout fishing, swimming, boating, waterskiing, and riding personal watercraft. Tackle and boat rentals are available at the resort. Blue Lake is one of the most popular opening day lakes in Washington and is regularly planted with rainbow, brown, and tiger trout fingerlings.

Campsites, facilities: There are 80 sites with full or partial hookups, including six pull-through sites, for RVs of any length, 30 tent sites, and 10 cabins. Picnic tables and fire pits are provided. Restrooms with flush toilets and showers, a dump station, firewood, Wi-Fi, a store, propane, ice, tackle, RV and boat storage, a roped swimming area, volleyball, a playground, horseshoe pits, badminton, and a marina with boat docks, launching facilities, fish-cleaning station, boat fuel, and boat rentals are available. Some facilities are wheelchair accessible. Leashed pets are permitted.

Reservations, fees: Reservations are accepted at 509/632-5364 or www.bluelakeresortwashington.com. Sites are $25 per night, $5 per person per night for more than four people, $5 per night for additional vehicle, $10 per pet per night. Some credit cards are accepted. Open April-September.

Directions: From the junction of I-90 and Highway 17 (just south of Moses Lake), drive north on Highway 17 for 36 miles to the resort on the right. The resort is 15 miles south of Coulee City.

Contact: Blue Lake Resort, 509/632-5364 or 509/632-5388, www.bluelakeresortwashington.com.

99 LAURENT'S SUN VILLAGE RESORT

🚶 🚲 ⛴ 🛶 🎣 🐎 🎿 🚐 ⛺

Scenic rating: 6

on Blue Lake in Coulee City

Map 4.4, page 242

Like Blue Lake Resort, this campground is situated along the shore of Blue Lake. The hot desert setting is perfect for swimming and fishing. Late July and early August are the busiest times of the year here. Nearby recreation possibilities include a nine-hole golf course and miniature golf.

Campsites, facilities: There are 95 sites, most with full hookups, for RVs of any length, four tent sites, and five cabins. Some sites are pull-through. Picnic tables are provided. Restrooms with flush toilets and coin showers, group fire pits, propane gas, dump station, coin laundry, a store, café, bait and tackle, ice, firewood, a playground, boat docks, launching facilities, and boat rentals are available. Leashed pets are permitted.

Reservations, fees: Reservations are accepted by phone. Sites are $30 per night, cabins are $65-115 per night, $3-7 per person per night for more than four people, $4 per night for each additional vehicle, $5-7 per night per pet. Two- to three-night minimum. Weekly rates are available. Some credit cards are accepted. Open late April-late September.

Directions: From the junction of I-90 and Highway 17 (just south of Moses Lake), drive north on Highway 17 for 36 miles to Blue Lake and Park Lake Road. Turn right (east) on Park Lake Road (the south entrance) and drive 0.5 mile to the resort on the right.

Contact: Laurent's Sun Village Resort, 509/632-5664, www.laurentsresort.com.

100 COULEE LODGE RESORT

Scenic rating: 8

on Blue Lake

Map 4.4, page 242

This camp is set at Blue Lake, which often provides outstanding fishing for a mix of stocked rainbow trout and brown trout in early spring. Blue Lake offers plenty of summertime recreation options, including a swimming beach. Nearby recreation possibilities include a nine-hole golf course and miniature golf.

Campsites, facilities: There are 18 sites for tents or RVs up to 35 feet long (30 amp full hookups), 14 sites for tents only. Six cabins and eight mobile homes are also available. Some sites are pull-through. Picnic tables and fire pits are provided. Restrooms with flush toilets and coin showers, propane gas, convenience store, firewood, coin laundry, boat docks, boat and personal watercraft rentals, launching facilities, and ice are available. A café is located within five miles. Leashed pets are permitted.

Reservations, fees: Reservations are accepted. Sites are $30 per night, $5 per each additional person per night, $5 per extra vehicle per night, and $5 per pet per night. Cabins are $89-119 per night, mobile homes are $109-129 per night. Some credit cards are accepted. Open mid-April-September.

Directions: From the junction of I-90 and Highway 17 (just south of Moses Lake), drive north on Highway 17 for 39 miles to the north end of Blue Lake.

Contact: Coulee Lodge Resort, 509/632-5565, www.couleelodgeresort.com.

101 SPRING CANYON

Scenic rating: 6

on Franklin Roosevelt Lake in Lake Roosevelt National Recreation Area

Map 4.5, page 243   BEST (

This large, developed campground is a popular vacation destination. Fishing for bass, walleye, trout, and sunfish is popular at Franklin Roosevelt Lake, as is waterskiing. The campground is not far from Grand Coulee Dam. Lake Roosevelt National Recreation Area offers numerous activity options, such as free programs conducted by rangers that include guided canoe trips, historical tours, campfire talks, and guided hikes. This lake is known as a prime location to view bald eagles, especially in winter. Side-trip options include visiting the Colville Tribal Museum in the town of Coulee Dam and touring the Grand Coulee Dam Visitor Center. Almost one mile long and twice as high as Niagara Falls, the dam is one of the largest concrete structures ever built. It is open for self-guided tours.

Campsites, facilities: There are 87 sites for tents or RVs (no hookups) up to 55 feet and two group sites for tents or RVs up to 26 feet that accommodate up to 25 people. Picnic tables and fire grills are provided. Drinking water (seasonal), restrooms with flush toilets, a dump station, picnic area, swimming beach, playground, and amphitheater are available. A camp host is on-site. Boat docks, launching facilities, marine dump station, and fish-cleaning station are nearby. Some facilities are wheelchair accessible. Leashed pets are permitted.

Reservations, fees: Reservations are accepted and are required for the group sites at 877/444-6777 or www.recreation.gov ($10 reservation fee). Sites are $9-18 per night, $8 boat-launch fee (good for seven days). Call for group rates. Open year-round, weather permitting.

Directions: From the junction of I-90 and Highway 17 (just south of Moses Lake), drive north on Highway 17 for 45 miles to U.S. 2. Turn east on U.S. 2 and drive five miles to

Highway 155. Turn left (north) and drive 26 miles to Grand Coulee and Highway 174. Turn right (east) on Highway 174 and drive three miles to the campground entrance on the left.

Contact: Lake Roosevelt National Recreation Area, 509/754-7800, www.nps.gov/laro.

102 LAKEVIEW TERRACE MOBILE AND RV PARK

Scenic rating: 6

near Franklin Roosevelt Lake

Map 4.5, page 243

This pleasant resort is situated near Franklin Roosevelt Lake, which was created by Grand Coulee Dam. It provides a slightly less crowded alternative to the national park camps in the vicinity. A mobile home park is also on the property. Nearby Spring Canyon offers a full-service marina and various recreation options on the water.

Campsites, facilities: There are 20 pull-through sites with full hookups (30 and 50 amps) for RVs of any length and three sites for tents only. Restrooms with flush toilets and showers, a coin laundry, and a playground are available. Boat docks, launching facilities, and rentals are nearby. Some facilities are wheelchair accessible. Leashed pets are permitted.

Reservations, fees: Reservations are recommended. Sites are $35 per night. Credit cards are not accepted. Open year-round.

Directions: From Grand Coulee, drive east on Highway 174 for 3.5 miles to the park entrance on the left.

Contact: Lakeview Terrace Mobile and RV Park, 509/633-2169.

103 KELLER FERRY

Scenic rating: 7

on Franklin Roosevelt Lake in Lake Roosevelt National Recreation Area

Map 4.5, page 243

This camp is set along the shore of Franklin Roosevelt Lake, a large reservoir created by Grand Coulee Dam, which sits about 15 miles west of camp. Franklin Roosevelt Lake is known for its walleye fishing; although more than 30 species live in this lake, 90 percent of the fish caught are walleye. They average 1-4 pounds and always travel in schools. Trout and salmon often swim below the bluffs near Keller Ferry. Waterskiing, fishing, and swimming are all recreation options here.

Campsites, facilities: There are 55 sites for tents or RVs up to 25 feet long, a camping area for tents only, and two group sites for tents or RVs up to 16 feet long for up to 25 people each. Picnic tables and fire grills are provided. Drinking water (seasonal), restrooms with flush toilets, a dump station, ice, a picnic area, a swimming beach, a playground, boat docks, launching facilities, fuel, and fish-cleaning stations are available. Some facilities are wheelchair accessible. Leashed pets are permitted.

Reservations, fees: Reservations are accepted. Sites are $9-18 per night. Call for group rates. Open year-round, weather permitting.

Directions: From Spokane on U.S. 90, turn west on U.S. 2 and drive 71 miles to Wilbur and Highway 21. Turn north and drive 14 miles to the campground on the left.

Contact: Lake Roosevelt Adventures, 509/647-5755 or 800/816-2431, https://lakerooseveltadventures.com; Lake Roosevelt National Recreation Area, 509/754-7800 or 509/654-7889, www.nps.gov/laro.

104 RIVER RUE RV PARK

Scenic rating: 7

near the Columbia River

Map 4.5, page 243

This camp is located in high desert terrain yet is surrounded by lots of trees. You can fish, swim, water ski, or rent a houseboat at Lake Roosevelt, one mile away. Personal watercraft are allowed. Another nearby side trip is to the Grand Coulee Dam. A nine-hole golf course is available in Wilbur.

Campsites, facilities: There are 24 sites with full or partial hookups (20, 30, and 50 amps) for tents or RVs of any length and eight sites for tents or RVs of any length (no hookups). Some sites are pull-through. Picnic tables and fire rings are provided. Restrooms with flush toilets and showers, limited groceries, ice, a deli, RV supplies, fishing tackle, and propane gas are available. Recreational facilities include a playground and horseshoe pits. Some facilities are wheelchair accessible. Leashed pets are permitted.

Reservations, fees: Reservations are accepted. RV sites are $31.50 per night, tent sites are $21 per night, $3 per person per night for more than two people. Winter rates are available. Some credit cards are accepted. Open year-round, with limited services in winter.

Directions: On U.S. 2 at Wilbur, drive west on U.S. 2 for one mile to Highway 174. Turn right (north) on Highway 174 and drive 0.25 mile to Highway 21. Turn right (north) on Highway 21 and drive 13 miles to the park on the right.

Contact: River Rue RV Park, 509/647-2647, www.riverrue.com.

105 JONES BAY

Scenic rating: 6

on Franklin Roosevelt Lake in Lake Roosevelt National Recreation Area

Map 4.5, page 243

This small and primitive campground is set on Jones Bay on Franklin Roosevelt Lake. Well known by locals, it gets high use on summer weekends but is quiet most weekdays. The camp is located at the bottom of a canyon in a cove with ponderosa pines. Fishing for bass, walleye, trout, and sunfish is popular at Franklin Roosevelt Lake.

Campsites, facilities: There are nine sites for tents or RVs up to 30 feet long. Picnic tables and fire grills are provided. Vault toilets are available. There is no drinking water. A boat launch and dock are nearby. Leashed pets are permitted.

Reservations, fees: Reservations are not accepted. Sites are $9-18 per night, $8 boat-launch fee (good for seven days). Open year-round, weather permitting, with limited winter access.

Directions: From Spokane on U.S. 90, turn west on U.S. 2 and drive 71 miles to Wilbur and Highway 21. Turn right (north) on Highway 21 and drive seven miles to Jones Bay Road (a dirt road, marked). Turn right and drive eight miles to the campground entrance road on the right. A high-clearance vehicle is recommended.

Contact: Lake Roosevelt National Recreation Area, 509/754-7800, www.nps.gov/laro.

106 HAWK CREEK

Scenic rating: 8

on Franklin Roosevelt Lake in Lake Roosevelt National Recreation Area

Map 4.5, page 243

This pleasant camping spot is located along the shore of Roosevelt Lake (Columbia River), adjacent to the mouth of Hawk Creek. This is often a good fishing spot for walleye, trout, and bass. Note that there is no drinking water if the lake level drops below an elevation of 1,265 feet.

Campsites, facilities: There are 21 sites for tents or RVs up to 45 feet long. Picnic tables and fire grills are provided. Drinking water and vault toilets are available. Boat docks and launching facilities are nearby. Leashed pets are permitted.

Reservations, fees: Reservations are not accepted. Sites are $9-18 per night, $8 boat-launch fee (good for seven days). Open year-round, with limited winter facilities.

Directions: From Spokane on I-90, drive west for four miles to U.S. 2. Turn west on U.S. 2 and drive 34 miles to Davenport and Highway 25. Turn right (north) on Highway 25 and drive 23 miles to Miles-Creston Road. Turn left (northwest) and drive 10 miles to the campground at the mouth of Hawk Creek on the left.

Contact: Lake Roosevelt National Recreation Area, 509/754-7800, www.nps.gov/laro.

107 FORT SPOKANE

Scenic rating: 8

on Franklin Roosevelt Lake in Lake Roosevelt National Recreation Area

Map 4.5, page 243

Rangers offer evening campfire programs and guided daytime activities at this modern campground on the shore of Roosevelt Lake. This park also hosts living-history demonstrations. Fort Spokane is one of more than two dozen campgrounds on the 130-mile-long lake. A 190-mile scenic vehicle route encircles most of the lake.

Campsites, facilities: There are 67 sites for tents or RVs of any length, four sites for tents only, and two group sites for tents or RVs up to 26 feet long that can accommodate up to 30 people each. Picnic tables and fire grills are provided. Restrooms with flush toilets, drinking water (seasonal), a dump station, and a playground are available. A camp host is on-site. A picnic area, swimming beach, and visitors center are nearby. A store, gas station, and ice are located within one mile. Boat docks, launching facilities, and a marine dump station are nearby. Some facilities are wheelchair accessible. Leashed pets are permitted.

Reservations, fees: Reservations are not accepted for individual sites but are required for group sites at 877/444-6777 or www.recreation.gov ($10 reservation fee). Sites are $9-18 per night, $8 boat-launch fee (good for seven days). Call for group rates. Open year-round, with limited winter facilities.

Directions: From Spokane on I-90, drive west for four miles to U.S. 2. Turn west on U.S. 2 and drive 34 miles to Davenport and Highway 25. Turn right (north) on Highway 25 and drive 22 miles to the campground entrance on the right.

Contact: Lake Roosevelt National Recreation Area, 509/754-7800, 509/754-7889, or 509/633-3830, www.nps.gov/laro.

108 PORCUPINE BAY

Scenic rating: 8

on Franklin Roosevelt Lake in Lake Roosevelt National Recreation Area

Map 4.5, page 243

Note: At time of publication, this campground remained closed due to a landslide. Check the park service website for updates on repairs and re-opening.

This camp is extremely popular, and the sites are filled most of the summer. Its proximity to a nearby dock and launch makes it an especially good spot for campers with boats. A swimming beach is located adjacent to the campground.

Campsites, facilities: There are 31 sites for tents or RVs up to 50 feet long. Picnic tables and fire grills are provided. Drinking water, vault toilets, restrooms with flush toilets, dump station, picnic area, and playground are available. Boat docks and launching facilities are nearby. Some facilities are wheelchair accessible. Leashed pets are permitted.

Reservations, fees: Reservations are not accepted. Sites are $9-18 per night, $8 boat-launch fee (good for seven days). Open year-round, weather permitting, with limited winter access.

Directions: From Spokane on I-90, drive west for four miles to U.S. 2. Turn west on U.S. 2 and drive 34 miles to Davenport and Highway 25. Turn right (north) on Highway 25 and drive 19 miles to Porcupine Bay Road. Turn right (east) and drive 4.3 miles to the campground at the end of the road.

Contact: Lake Roosevelt National Recreation Area, 509/754-7800, www.nps.gov/laro.

109 LAKE SPOKANE CAMPGROUND

Scenic rating: 8

on the Spokane River

Map 4.6, page 244

This campground is located about 45 minutes from Spokane. The camp is set on a terrace above Lake Spokane (Spokane River), where fishing can be good for rainbow trout and the occasional brown trout. This area is also popular for power boating, waterskiing, and personal watercraft. Crowded in summer, it gets a lot of use from residents of the Spokane area. Note that this campground and lake were previously known as Long Lake.

Campsites, facilities: There are 11 sites for tents or RVs up to 30 feet long. Picnic tables and fire grills are provided. Drinking water, vault toilets, and garbage bins are available. A camp host is on-site. A boat launch, dock, swimming beach, and a day-use area are nearby. Some facilities are wheelchair accessible. Leashed pets are permitted.

Reservations, fees: Reservations are not accepted. There is no fee for camping, but a Discover Pass is required. Open May-September, weather permitting.

Directions: From Spokane on I-90, drive west for four miles to U.S. 2. Turn west on U.S. 2 and drive 21 miles to Reardan and Highway 231. Turn right (north) on Highway 231 and drive 14.2 miles to Highway 291. Turn right and drive 4.7 miles to the campground entrance on the right.

Contact: Department of Natural Resources, Northeast Region, 509/684-7474, www.dnr. wa.gov.

110 DRAGOON CREEK

Scenic rating: 5

near the Little Spokane River

Map 4.6, page 244

This spot is frequented by locals but is often missed by out-of-town vacationers. The camp is set along Dragoon Creek, a tributary to the Little Spokane River. Its campsites are situated in a forest of ponderosa pine and Douglas fir. Although fairly close to U.S. 395, it remains quiet and rustic.

Campsites, facilities: There are 22 sites for tents or RVs up to 30 feet long. Picnic tables and fire grills are provided. Vault toilets and drinking water are available. Garbage must be packed out. Some facilities are wheelchair accessible. Leashed pets are permitted.

Reservations, fees: Reservations are not accepted. There is no fee for camping, but a Discover Pass is required. Open May-September, weather permitting, with a camp host available.

Directions: From Spokane, drive north on U.S. 395 for 10.2 miles to North Dragoon Creek Road. Turn left on North Dragoon Creek Road and drive 0.4 mile to the campground entrance at the end of the road.

Contact: Department of Natural Resources, Northeast Region, 509/684-7474, www.dnr. wa.gov.

111 MOUNT SPOKANE STATE PARK

🏃 🚵 ❄️ 🏕️ 🚙 ⛺

Scenic rating: 8

on Mount Spokane

Map 4.6, page 244   **BEST (**

This state park provides one of the better short trips available out of Spokane. It is set on the slopes of Mount Spokane (5,883 feet), and little brother Mount Kit Carson (5,180 feet) sits alongside it. The park covers 13,919 acres in the Selkirk Mountains and features a stunning view from the top of Mount Spokane. The lookout takes in Washington, Idaho, Montana, and Canada. The park has 86 miles of hiking trails, occasionally routed into old-growth forest and amid granite outcroppings. The Mount Spokane Ski and Snowboard Park operates here in winter.

Campsites, facilities: There are eight sites for tents or RVs up to 30 feet (no hookups). The Quartz Mountain Lookout is also available to rent. Picnic tables and fire grills are provided. Restrooms with flush toilets, drinking water, and a picnic area with a kitchen shelter are available. Leashed pets are permitted.

Reservations, fees: Reservations are not accepted. Sites are $20-31 per night, $10 per extra vehicle per night; call for rates for the Lookout. Open July-September, weather permitting.

Directions: From Spokane, drive north on U.S. 395 for six miles to U.S. 2. Turn north on U.S. 2 and drive six miles to Highway 206. Turn right (northeast) on Highway 206 and drive 15 miles to the park.

Contact: Mount Spokane State Park, 509/238-4258, http://parks.state.wa.us; Quartz Mountain Lookout, 888/226-7688.

112 RIVERSIDE STATE PARK

🏃 🚵 🚤 🚐 ❄️ 🐎 ♿ 🚙 ⛺

Scenic rating: 8

in Nine Mile Falls near Spokane

Map 4.6, page 244

This 12,000-acre park is set along the Spokane and Little Spokane Rivers and features freshwater marshes in a beautiful setting. There are many recreation options, including fishing for bass, crappie, and perch, 55 miles of hiking and biking trails, and 25 miles of horseback riding trails, as well as riding stables in the park. The 40-mile Spokane River Centennial Trail can be accessed from the park. The park also has a 600-acre area for dirt bikes in summer and snowmobiles in winter. An 18-hole golf course is located nearby. A local point of interest is the unique Bowl and Pitcher rock formation in the Spokane River.

Campsites, facilities: There are four different camping areas. The Bowl and Pitcher campground has 16 sites for tents or RVs (no hookups) up to 45 feet, 16 sites with full or partial hookups for tents or RVs up to 45 feet, and two group tent sites for 40 and 60 people respectively (20-person minimum). The equestrian campground has 10 sites with corrals. Nine Mile Recreation Area (May-September) has three sites for tents only and 21 sites for RVs of any length (no hookups). The Lake Spokane Campground (May-September) has 11 primitive sites and four boat-in sites. Picnic tables and fire grills are provided. Restrooms with flush toilets and showers, drinking water, a picnic area with a kitchen shelter, dump station, interpretive center, camp store, firewood, and horse stable are available. A restaurant, gasoline, groceries, and ice are located within three miles. Boat-launching facilities, a dock, and boat rentals are located on-site. Some facilities are wheelchair accessible. Leashed pets are permitted.

Reservations, fees: Reservations are accepted for individual sites and required for group and equestrian sites at 888/226-7688 or https://washington.goingtocamp.com ($8-10 reservation fee). Sites are $12-45 per night, $10 per extra vehicle per night. Call for group rates. Open year-round, with limited number of sites available in winter.

Directions: In Spokane on I-90, take Exit 280/Maple Street North (cross the Maple Street Bridge), and drive north 1.1 miles to Maxwell Street. Turn left (west) and drive 1.9 miles, bearing left along the Spokane River to the park entrance. From the park entrance, continue for 1.5 miles on Aubrey L. White Parkway to the campground.

Alternate route for long RVs: In Spokane on I-90, take Exit 280/Maple Street North (cross the Maple Street Bridge), and drive north 4.5 miles to Francis Avenue. Turn left and drive three miles to Rifle Club Road. Turn left and drive to Aubrey L. White Parkway and the park entrance. From the entrance, continue 1.5 miles to the campground.

Contact: Riverside State Park, 509/465-5064, http://parks.state.wa.us.

113 TRAILER INNS RV PARK/SPOKANE

🚶 🐕 👨‍👩‍👧 🚐 ⛺

Scenic rating: 5

in Spokane

Map 4.6, page 244

This large RV park makes a good layover spot on the way to Idaho. It's as close to a hotel as an RV park can get. The pull-through sites are shaded. Nearby recreation options include an 18-hole golf course, a racquet club, and tennis courts. Note that when busy, many of the sites are taken by monthly campers.

Campsites, facilities: There are 93 sites for tents or RVs of any length (15, 30, and 50 amp full hookups); in summer, only about 10 sites are available for overnight campers. Some sites are pull-through. Picnic tables are provided. Restrooms with flush toilets and showers, drinking water, propane gas, cable TV, phone hookups, Wi-Fi and modem access, TV room, coin laundry, ice, a picnic area, and a playground are available. A dump station, store, and café are within one mile. Leashed pets are permitted.

Reservations, fees: Reservations are accepted at 800/659-4864. RV sites are $32-42 per night, tent sites are $26 per night, $5 per person per night for more than two people. Weekly rates are available. Some credit cards are accepted. Open year-round.

Directions: Note that your route will depend on the direction you're heading: In Spokane eastbound on I-90, take Exit 285 (Sprague Avenue/Eastern Road) to Eastern Road. Drive 0.1 mile on Eastern Road to 4th Avenue. Turn right (west) on 4th Avenue and drive two blocks to the park. In Spokane westbound on I-90, take Exit 284 (Havana Street). Drive one block south on Havana Street to 4th Avenue. Turn left (east) on 4th Avenue and drive one mile to the park.

Contact: Trailer Inns RV Park/Spokane, 509/535-1811, www.trailerinnsrv.com.

114 KOA SPOKANE

🚶 🚲 🏊 🚣 🎣 🐕 👨‍👩‍👧 ♿ 🚐 ⛺

Scenic rating: 5

on the Spokane River in Spokane Valley

Map 4.6, page 244

This KOA campground is located close to the shore of the Spokane River. Nearby you'll find the 37-mile Centennial Trail along the river, as well as an 18-hole golf course and tennis courts. Other options include touring the gardens of Manito Park or visiting Riverfront Park, which has an IMAX theater and aerial gondola rides over the Spokane River.

Campsites, facilities: There are 87 sites with full hookups (30 and 50 amps), 20 sites with partial hookups, and 27 sites with no hookups for tents or RVs of any length, plus seven cabins (four deluxe). Some sites are pull-through. Picnic tables are provided. No wood fires are allowed, but portable fire rings are available. Restrooms with flush toilets and showers, drinking water, cable TV, a dump station, playground, convenience store, coin laundry, ice, Wi-Fi, pet walk, volleyball, horseshoe pits, basketball, and a seasonal heated swimming pool are available. A café and gasoline are located within two miles. Some facilities are wheelchair accessible. Leashed pets are permitted.

Reservations, fees: Reservations are accepted at 800/562-3309. Sites are $33-73 per night, $3-4 per night per person for more than two people. Some credit cards are accepted. Open year-round.

Directions: From Spokane, drive east on I-90 for 13 miles to Barker/Exit 293. Take that exit to Barker Road. Turn north on Barker Road and drive 1.5 miles to the campground on the left.

Contact: KOA Spokane, 509/924-4722, www. koa.com.

115 WEST MEDICAL LAKE RESORT

🥾 🚲 🛶 🚤 ⚓ 🐕 ♿ ⛺

Scenic rating: 7

on West Medical Lake

Map 4.6, page 244

This resort functions primarily as a fish camp for anglers. There are actually two lakes: West Medical is the larger of the two and has better fishing, with boat rentals available; Medical Lake is just 0.25 mile wide and 0.5 mile long, and boating is restricted to rowboats, canoes, kayaks, and sailboats. The lakes got their names from the wondrous medicinal powers once attributed to their waters. This family-operated shorefront resort, one of several campgrounds on these lakes, is a popular spot for Spokane locals.

Campsites, facilities: There are 20 tent sites. Picnic tables are provided at all sites and fire pits are provided at tent sites. Restrooms with flush toilets and showers, drinking water, a café, bait, tackle, and ice are available. Boat and fishing docks, launching facilities, a fish-cleaning station, and boat and barge rentals are nearby. Some facilities are wheelchair

accessible. Leashed pets are permitted (limit two per site).

Reservations, fees: Reservations are accepted. Tent sites are $15 per night for two people, $5 per night for each additional person. Some credit cards are accepted. Open late April-September.

Directions: In Spokane on I-90, drive west to Exit 264 and Salnave Road. Take that exit and turn north on Salnave Road; drive six miles to Fancher Road. Turn right (west) and drive 200 yards. Bear left on Fancher Road and drive 200 yards to the resort.

Contact: West Medical Lake Resort, 509/299-3921.

116 SUN COVE FAMILY RV RESORT

🏊 🛶 🐕 ♿ 🚐 ⛺

Scenic rating: 7

on Clear Lake

Map 4.6, page 244

This resort at Clear Lake features a 300-foot dock with benches that can be used for fishing. If you figured that most people here are anglers, well, that is correct. Fishing can be good for rainbow trout, brown trout, largemouth bass, crappie, bullhead, and catfish. Most of the campsites are at least partially shaded. Summer weekends are often busy.

Campsites, facilities: There are 17 sites with full or partial hookups (30 and 50 amps) for RVs up to 40 feet and 10 sites for tents only. Picnic tables and fire pits are provided. Restrooms with flush toilets and coin showers, drinking water, a café, ice, bait and tackle, boat docks and launch, boat rentals, and moorage are available. Some facilities are wheelchair accessible. Leashed pets are permitted.

Reservations, fees: Reservations are accepted. RV sites with full or partial hookups are $35 per night, tent sites are $25 per night, $5 per person per night for more than four people. Some credit cards are accepted. Open mid-April-mid-October.

Directions: In Spokane on I-90, drive west to Exit 264 and Salnave Road. Take that exit and turn right (north) on Salnave Road; drive a short distance to Clear Lake Road. Turn right (north) on Clear Lake Road and drive three miles to the resort on the left (well signed).

Contact: Sun Cove Resort, 509/216-6776.

117 PONDEROSA FALLS

Scenic rating: 6

in Cheney

Map 4.6, page 244

Formerly Yogi Bear's Camp Resort, Ponderosa Falls is now a member of the KM Resorts family. The resort is located 10 minutes from downtown Spokane, yet provides a wooded, rural setting with towering ponderosa pines. Highlights include an 18-hole golf course nearby and several other courses within 20 minutes of the resort.

Campsites, facilities: There are 156 sites for tents or RVs up to 40 feet (30 and 50 amp full hookups), seven cabins, and five bungalows. Some sites are pull-through. Picnic tables are provided. No open fires are allowed. Restrooms with flush toilets and showers, drinking water, cable TV, Wi-Fi, a dump station, propane, coin laundry, an RV wash station, three playgrounds, a camp store, a heated indoor pool, spa, exercise room, game room, snack shack, dog walk, and sports facilities are available. Some facilities are wheelchair accessible. Leashed pets are permitted.

Reservations, fees: Reservations are accepted. Sites are $50 per night. Some credit cards are accepted. Open year-round.

Directions: In Spokane on I-90, drive west to Exit 272. Take that exit, turn east on Hayford Road (becomes Aero Road), and drive approximately two miles to Thomas Mallen Road. Turn right (south) on Thomas Mallen Road and drive 0.25 mile to the resort on the right.

Contact: Ponderosa Falls, 509/747-9415 or 800/494-7275, www.kmresorts.com.

THE COLUMBIA RIVER GORGE AND MOUNT RAINIER

© KAMCHATKA/123RF

Standing at the rim of Mount St. Helens volcano is like looking inside the bowels of the earth. Half-moon crater walls drop almost 2,100 feet down to a lava plug dome, one mile across and still building, where a wisp of smoke emerges from the center. At its edges, plumes of dust rise from continuous rock falls. The plug dome gives way to the blast zone where the mountain completely blew out its side, spreading across 230 square miles of devastation. It's largely a moonscape but for Spirit Lake on the northeast flank, where thousands of trees still float, log-jammed from the eruption in May 1980. Beyond this scene, the most famous spots are Mounts St. Helens, Rainier, and Adams; the latter are two of most beautiful mountains in the Cascade Range. St. Helens provides the most eye-popping views and most developed visitors centers, Rainier the most pristine wilderness, and Adams some of the best lakeside camps. All offer outstanding hiking and excellent campgrounds.

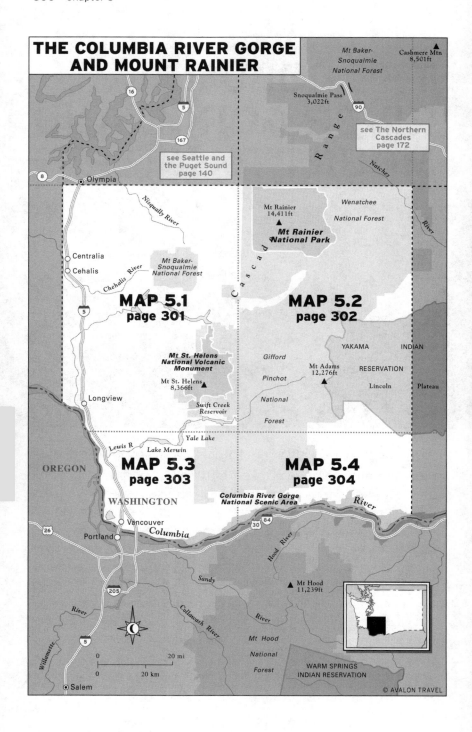

THE COLUMBIA RIVER GORGE AND MOUNT RAINIER

see Seattle and the Puget Sound page 140

see The Northern Cascades page 172

Mt Baker-Snoqualmie National Forest

Cashmere Mtn 8,501ft

Snoqualmie Pass 3,022ft

Cascade Range

Natches River

Olympia

Nisqually River

Mt Rainier 14,411ft
Mt Rainier National Park

Wenatchee National Forest

Centralia

Cehalis

Chehalis River

Mt Baker-Snoqualmie National Forest

MAP 5.1 page 301

MAP 5.2 page 302

YAKAMA INDIAN

RESERVATION

Lincoln Plateau

Mt St. Helens National Volcanic Monument

Mt St. Helens 8,366ft

Gifford

Pinchot

National

Forest

Mt Adams 12,276ft

Longview

Swift Creek Reservoir

Lewis R

Lake Merwin

Yale Lake

MAP 5.3 page 303

MAP 5.4 page 304

OREGON

WASHINGTON

Columbia River Gorge National Scenic Area

River

Vancouver

Columbia

Portland

Hood River

Sandy

River

Mt Hood 11,239ft

Collewash River

River

Mt Hood

National

Forest

WARM SPRINGS INDIAN RESERVATION

Willamette River

Salem

0   20 mi
0   20 km

© AVALON TRAVEL

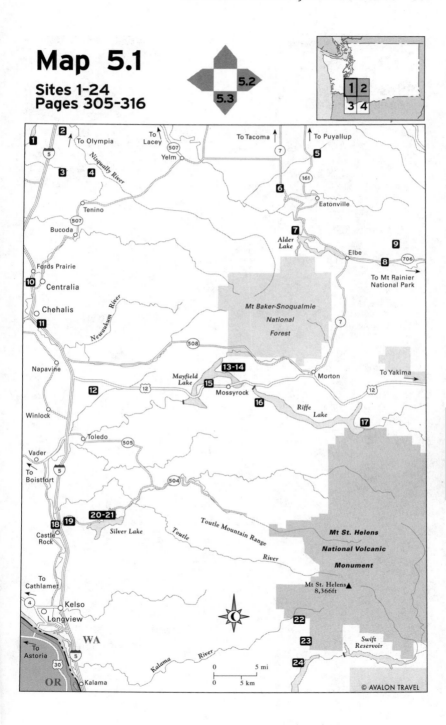

Map 5.1

Sites 1-24
Pages 305-316

Map 5.2

Sites 25-77
Pages 316-340

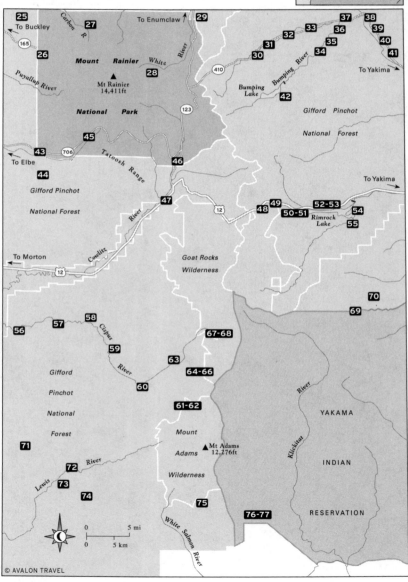

Map 5.3

**Sites 78-87
Pages 341-345**

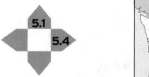

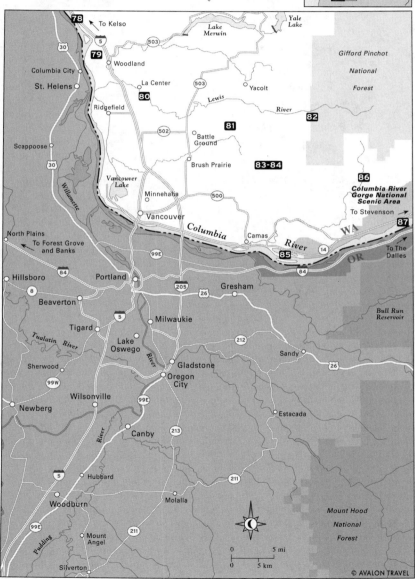

Map 5.4

Sites 88-101
Pages 345-352

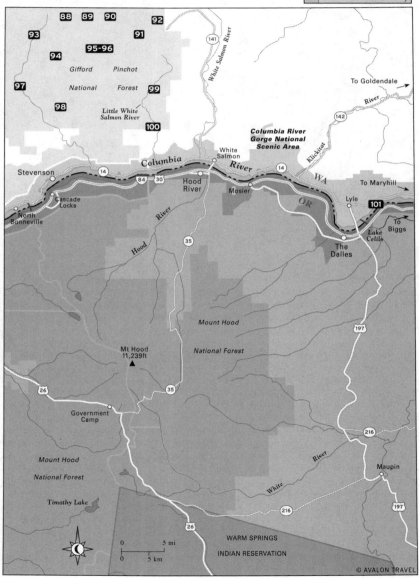

1 COLUMBUS PARK

Scenic rating: 8

on Black Lake

Map 5.1, page 301

This spot along the shore of Black Lake is pretty enough for special events, such as weddings and reunions. The campsites are wooded, and a stream (no fishing) runs through the campground. Black Lake is good for fishing, however. An 18-hole golf course is nearby.

Campsites, facilities: There are 30 sites for tents or RVs up to 40 feet (30 amp partial hookups) and one tent site. There are also 46 sites with full hookups that are usually rented by the month. Picnic tables are provided. Restrooms with flush toilets and showers, drinking water, a dump station, coin laundry, ice, firewood, propane, a playground, volleyball, horseshoe pits, boat docks, and launching facilities are available. A picnic area for special events is nearby. Propane gas and a store are located within one mile; there is a restaurant within three miles. Some facilities are wheelchair accessible. Leashed pets are permitted, but not on the swimming beach.

Reservations, fees: Reservations are accepted and are recommended during summer. RV sites are $30-37 per night, the tent site is $30 per night, overflow camping is $60 per night (two RV min.), $7 per each additional vehicle. Open year-round.

Directions: From I-5 in Olympia, take Exit 104, which merges onto U.S. 101. Drive northwest on U.S. 101 for 1.7 miles to Black Lake Boulevard. Turn left (south) on Black Lake Boulevard and drive 3.5 miles to the park on the left.

Contact: Columbus Park, 360/786-9460, www.columbuspark.net.

2 AMERICAN HERITAGE CAMPGROUND

Scenic rating: 6

near Olympia

Map 5.1, page 301

This spacious, wooded campground situated just 0.5 mile off the highway is close to many activities, including an 18-hole golf course, hiking trails, marked bike trails, and tennis courts. The park features novelty cycle rentals, free wagon rides, and free nightly movies during the summer season. It's pretty and exceptionally clean, making for a pleasant layover on your way up or down I-5. The park has a 5,000-square-foot pavilion for special events or groups.

Campsites, facilities: There are 72 sites with full or partial hookups (30 amps) for tents or RVs of any length, 23 sites for tents, and one cabin. Picnic tables and fire rings are provided. Restrooms with flush toilets and showers, drinking water, propane gas, dump station, group pavilion, seasonal recreation programs, a convenience store, coin laundry, ice, a playground, a seasonal heated swimming pool, and firewood are available. Leashed pets are permitted.

Reservations, fees: Reservations are accepted by phone. RV sites with full hookups are $40 per night, RV sites with partial hookups are $33 per night, tent sites are $25 per night, $4-10 per person per night for more than two people. The cabin is $50 per night. Some credit cards are accepted. Open year-round, with limited winter facilities.

Directions: From Olympia, drive five miles south on I-5 to Exit 99. Take that exit and drive 0.25 mile east to Kimmie Street. Turn right (south) on Kimmie Street and drive 0.25 mile to the end of the road to the campground on the left.

Contact: American Heritage Campground, 360/943-8778, www.americanheritagecampground.com.

3 MILLERSYLVANIA STATE PARK
🚶 🚴 🏊 🛶 🎣 🏕️ 🐕 ♿ 🚐 ⛺

Scenic rating: 8

on Deep Lake

Map 5.1, page 301

Millersylvania State Park is set on the shore of Deep Lake and features 3,300 feet of waterfront. The park has 8.6 miles of hiking trails amid an abundance of old-growth cedar and fir trees, of which 7.6 miles are open to bikes. Boating at Deep Lake is restricted to hand-launched boats, with a 5-mph speed limit. A fishing dock is available at the boat-launch area. Another highlight: a one-mile fitness trail. Look for the remains of a former railroad and skid trails dating from the 1800s, still present in the park.

Campsites, facilities: There are 120 developed tent sites, 48 sites with partial hookups (30 and 50 amps) for RVs up to 35 feet, and a group tent site for 20-40 people. Picnic tables and fire grills are provided. Restrooms with flush toilets and coin showers, drinking water, a dump station, firewood, boat docks and launching facilities, exercise trail, and amphitheater are available. A picnic area, boat rentals, summer interpretive activities, and horseshoe pits are nearby. A store, restaurant, and ice are located within one mile. Some facilities are wheelchair accessible. Leashed pets are permitted.

Reservations, fees: Reservations are accepted May-September at 888/226-7688 or https://washington.goingtocamp.com ($8-10 reservation fee). Sites are $20-45 per night, $10 per extra vehicle per night. Call for group rates. Some credit cards are accepted. Open year-round, with limited facilities mid-November-March.

Directions: From Olympia, drive south on I-5 for 10 miles to Exit 95 and Highway 121. Turn east on Maytown Road (Highway 121) and drive 2.7 miles to Tilley Road. Turn left (north) and drive 1.3 miles to the park.

Contact: Millersylvania State Park, 360/753-1519, http://parks.state.wa.us.

4 OFFUT LAKE RESORT
🏊 🛶 🚐 🏕️ 🚴 ♿ 🚐 ⛺

Scenic rating: 8

on Offut Lake

Map 5.1, page 301 **BEST (**

This wooded campground is set on Offut Lake, just enough off the beaten track to provide a bit of seclusion. Fishing, swimming, and boating are favorite activities here. Anglers will find everything they need, including tackle and boat rentals, at the resort. Boating is restricted to a 5-mph speed limit, and no gas motors are permitted on the lake. Several fishing derbies are held here every year.

Campsites, facilities: There are 31 sites with full hookups (30 and 50 amps) for RVs up to 40 feet, 25 sites for tents, and nine cabins. Picnic tables, fire rings, and cable TV are provided. Restrooms with flush toilets and coin showers, drinking water, Wi-Fi, a picnic shelter, dump station, firewood, a convenience store, bait and tackle, coin laundry, ice, a playground, basketball, and horseshoe pits are available. Boat rentals and docks are available; no gas motors are permitted. Some facilities are wheelchair accessible. Leashed pets are permitted.

Reservations, fees: Reservations are accepted. RV sites are $36-38 per night, tent sites are $30 per night, $10 per person per night for more than two adults and two children, $10 per extra vehicle per night, $10 moorage fee per night, $5 per pet per night. Some credit cards are accepted. Open year-round.

Directions: From Olympia, drive south on I-5 for seven miles to Exit 99. Take that exit and turn east on 93rd Avenue; drive four miles to Old Highway 99. Turn right (south) and drive four miles to Offut Lake Road. Turn left (east) and drive 1.5 miles to the resort.

Contact: Offut Lake Resort, 360/264-2438, www.offutlakeresort.com.

5 RAINBOW RV RESORT

Scenic rating: 8

on Tanwax Lake

Map 5.1, page 301

This wooded park along the shore of Tanwax Lake has spacious sites with views of mountains, forest, and lake. Highlights include good fishing for trout, perch, crappie, bass, bluegill, catfish, and bullhead. Powerboating and waterskiing are popular on hot summer weekends.

Campsites, facilities: There are about 60 sites with full hookups for tents or RVs up to 40 feet. Picnic tables are provided at most sites, and portable fire pits are available. Restrooms with flush toilets and coin showers, drinking water, propane gas, firewood, recreation hall, convenience store, coin laundry, a café, ice, cable TV, boat docks and launch, boat rentals, and boat moorage are available. Some facilities are wheelchair accessible. Leashed pets are permitted.

Reservations, fees: Reservations are accepted. RV sites are $30-34 per night, tent sites are $20 per night. Some credit cards are accepted. Open year-round.

Directions: From Tacoma, drive south on I-5 to Exit 127 and Highway 512. Turn east on Highway 512 and drive to Highway 161. Turn right (south) on Highway 161 and drive to Tanwax Drive. Turn left (east) on Tanwax Drive and continue 200 yards to the resort.

Contact: Rainbow RV Resort, 360/879-5115, www.rainbowrvresort.com.

6 HENLEY'S SILVER LAKE RESORT

Scenic rating: 8

on Silver Lake

Map 5.1, page 301   BEST (

Silver Lake is a 150-acre, spring-fed lake that can provide good trout fishing. This full-facility resort is set up as a family vacation destination. A rarity, this private campground caters both to tent campers and RVers. Silver Lake is beautiful and stocked with trout. Highlights include a 250-foot fishing dock and rental rowboats.

Campsites, facilities: There are 20 sites with full or partial hookups for RVs, a large area for dispersed tent camping, and six cabins. Picnic tables are provided and fire pits are available at most sites. Restrooms with flush toilets, drinking water, showers, snacks, bait and tackle, boat rentals, a boat ramp, and a dock are available. A grocery store, gasoline, and supplies are available within 3.5 miles. Some facilities are wheelchair accessible. Leashed pets are permitted except in the cabins.

Reservations, fees: Reservations are accepted. RV sites are $34 per night, tent sites are $30 per night, $8 per extra person per night, $6 per extra vehicle per night. Cabins are $95 per night, $10 per pet per night. Open year-round, weather permitting.

Directions: From Tacoma, drive south on I-5 for five miles to Exit 127 and Highway 512. Turn east on Highway 512 and drive two miles to Highway 7. Turn right (south) on Highway 7 and drive 19 miles (2 miles straight beyond the blinking light) to Silver Lake Road on the right (well marked). Turn right and drive 0.25 mile to the resort entrance on the left.

Contact: Henley's Silver Lake Resort, 360/832-3580, www.henleysilverlake.com.

7 ALDER LAKE PARK

Scenic rating: 6

on Alder Lake

Map 5.1, page 301

The 161-acre recreation area at Alder Lake features four camping areas and a group camp; one of the camps is located four miles east of the main park entrance. Alder Lake is a 3,065-acre lake (7.5 miles long) often with good fishing for kokanee salmon, rainbow trout, and cutthroat trout. Rocky Point features a sunny beach and is set near the mouth of feeder streams, often the best fishing spots on the lake. At the west end of the lake, anglers can catch catfish, perch, and crappie. The campsites have lots of trees and shrubbery. On clear, warm summer weekends, these camps can get crowded. The camps are always booked full for summer holiday weekends as soon as reservations are available in January. Another potential downer, the water level fluctuates here. Powerboating, waterskiing, and personal watercraft are allowed at this lake. Mount Rainier Scenic Railroad leaves from Elbe regularly and makes its way through the forests to Mineral Lake. It features open deck cars, live music, and restored passenger cars.

Campsites, facilities: There are four camping areas with 173 sites with full or partial hookups (30 and 50 amps) for tents or RVs up to 40 feet, 62 sites for tents, and one group area with 35 sites for tents or RVs (full hookups). Picnic tables and fire rings are provided. Restrooms with flush toilets and coin showers, drinking water, vault toilets, and a dump station are available. Boat docks and launching facilities are available nearby. A swimming beach, picnic area, playground, and fishing dock are also available nearby. Some facilities are wheelchair accessible. Leashed pets are permitted.

Reservations, fees: Reservations are accepted at 888/226-7688 or www.tacomapower.com ($8-10 reservation fee). Sites are $24-35 per night, $10 per extra vehicle per night. The group camp is $37 per site per night, with a five-site minimum ($15 reservation fee). Some credit cards are accepted. Open year-round, excluding December 20-January 1.

Directions: From Chehalis, drive south on I-5 for six miles to U.S. 12. Turn east and drive 31 miles to Morton and Highway 7. Turn north on Highway 7 and drive 17 miles to Elbe. Bear left on Highway 7 and drive to the park entrance road on the left (on the east shore of Alder Lake). Turn left and drive 0.2 mile to the park entrance gate.

Contact: Alder Lake Park, Tacoma Power, 360/569-2778, www.tacomapower.com.

8 SAHARA CREEK HORSE CAMP

Scenic rating: 6

near Elbe

Map 5.1, page 301

While this camp is called a "horse camp," it is actually a multiple-use camp open to campers without horses. This pretty camp is set near the foot of Mount Rainier and features multiple trailheads and a camp host on-site. Note that no motorized vehicles or mountain bikes are allowed on trails. In winter, miles of groomed cross-country ski trails are available in the area.

Campsites, facilities: There are 20 sites for tents or RVs up to 25 feet long. Picnic tables and fire pits are provided. Drinking water, stock water, a covered pavilion, vault toilets, high lines, a horse mounting ramp, and hitching posts are available. Garbage must be packed out. Some facilities are wheelchair accessible. Leashed pets are permitted.

Reservations, fees: Reservations are not accepted. There is no fee for camping, but a Discover Pass is required. Open year-round.

Directions: From Chehalis, drive south on I-5 for six miles to U.S. 12. Turn east and drive 31 miles to Morton and Highway 7. Turn north on Highway 7 and drive 17 miles to Elbe and Highway 706. Turn right (east) and drive five miles to the campground on the left.

Contact: Department of Natural Resources, South Puget Sound Region, 360/825-1631, www.dnr.wa.gov.

9 ELBE HILLS

Scenic rating: 6

near Elbe

Map 5.1, page 301

Elbe Hills is not an official, designated campground, but rather a trailhead with room for campsites for four-wheelers, equestrians, or hikers. The Department of Natural Resources manages this wooded campground and provides eight miles of trails for short-wheelbase four-wheel-drive vehicles. The area features a technical obstacle course. In some places, you must have a winch to make it through the course. In winter, groomed cross-country ski trails are available in the area. Note: The area is always gated, and arrangements for access must be made in advance.

Campsites, facilities: There are 20 primitive sites for tents or RVs up to 25 feet. Picnic tables and fire grills are provided. A vault toilet and a group shelter are available. There is no drinking water and garbage must be packed out. Leashed pets are permitted.

Reservations, fees: Reservations are required at 360/825-1631 (8am-4pm Mon.-Fri.). There is no fee for camping, but a Discover Pass is required. Open year-round, weather permitting.

Directions: From Chehalis, drive south on I-5 for six miles to U.S. 12. Turn east and drive 31 miles to Morton and Highway 7. Turn north on Highway 7 and drive 17 miles to Elbe and Highway 706. Turn right (east) and drive six miles to Stoner Road (a Department of Natural Resources access road). Turn left and drive 2.5 miles to The 9 Road. Bear right on The 9 Road and drive one mile; look for a spur road on the left. Turn left and drive about 100 yards to the four-wheel-drive trailhead.

Contact: Department of Natural Resources, South Puget Sound Region, 360/825-1631, www.dnr.wa.gov.

10 PEPPERTREE WEST MOTOR INN & RV PARK

Scenic rating: 5

in Centralia

Map 5.1, page 301

If you're driving I-5 and looking for a stopover, this spot offers an option for RVers. Surrounded by Chehalis Valley farmland, it's near an 18-hole golf course, hiking trails, and tennis courts.

Campsites, facilities: There are 42 sites with full or partial hookups (30 amps) for RVs up to 40 feet and 25 motel rooms. Most sites are pull-through. Restrooms with flush toilets and coin showers, drinking water, cable TV, a dump station, coin laundry, and ice are available. Boat-launching facilities are nearby. A store, propane, and a café are also nearby. Some facilities are wheelchair accessible. Leashed pets are permitted.

Reservations, fees: Reservations are accepted. RV sites are $25 per night. Some credit cards are accepted. Open year-round.

Directions: From Centralia on I-5, take Exit 81 to Melon Street. Turn west and then take the first right (Alder Street) to the park (located in the southeast corner of Centralia).

Contact: Peppertree West Motor Inn & RV Park, 360/736-1124.

11 STAN HEDWALL PARK

Scenic rating: 5

on the Newaukum River

Map 5.1, page 301

This park is set along the Newaukum River, and its proximity to I-5 makes it a good layover spot for vacation travelers. Recreational opportunities include fishing, hiking, and golf; an 18-hole course and hiking trails are nearby.

Campsites, facilities: There are 29 sites with partial hookups (30 and 50 amps) for RVs of any length. Picnic tables are provided. Restrooms with flush toilets and coin showers, drinking water, a dump station, cable TV, horseshoe pits, and a playground are available. Propane gas, a store, café, and coin laundry are located within one mile. Leashed pets are permitted.

Reservations, fees: Reservations are accepted. Sites are $20 per night. Open April-November, weather permitting.

Directions: From Chehalis on I-5, take Exit 76 to Rice Road. Turn south and drive 0.13 mile to the park.

Contact: Stan Hedwall Park, City of Chehalis, 360/748-0271, www.ci.chehalis.wa.us.

12 LEWIS AND CLARK STATE PARK

🏃 🏕 🐎 🎣 🚙 ⛺

Scenic rating: 8

near Chehalis

Map 5.1, page 301

The highlight of this state park is an immense old-growth forest that contains some good hiking trails and a 0.5-mile nature trail. This famous grove lost half of its old-growth trees along the highway when they were blown down in the legendary 1962 Columbus Day storm. This was a cataclysmic event for one of the last major stands of old-growth forest in the state. The park covers 616 acres and features primarily Douglas fir and red cedar, wetlands, and dense vegetation. There are eight miles of horse trails and five miles of hiking trails. June is Youth Fishing Month, when youngsters age 14 and younger can fish the creek. Jackson House tours, in which visitors can see a pioneer home built in 1845 north of the Columbia River, are available year-round by appointment.

Campsites, facilities: There are 25 sites for tents or self-contained RVs (no hookups), nine sites with full hookups (30 amps) for RVs up to 35 feet, five primitive equestrian sites, one hiker-biker site, and one group camp for up to 50 people. Picnic tables and fire grills are provided. Restrooms with flush toilets and coin showers, drinking water, a small store, firewood, a picnic area, an amphitheater, day-use area that can be reserved, playground, horseshoe pits, volleyball, badminton, and interpretive activities are available. Leashed pets are permitted.

Reservations, fees: Reservations are not accepted for family sites but are required for the bunkhouse at 360/902-8600 or 800/360-4240. Sites are $12-45 per night, $10 per extra vehicle per night. Call for group site rates. Open April-late September.

Directions: From Chehalis, drive south on I-5 six miles to Exit 68 and U.S. 12. Turn east on U.S. 12 for three miles to Jackson Highway. Turn right and drive three miles to the park entrance on the right.

Contact: Lewis and Clark State Park, 360/864-2643, http://parks.state.wa.us.

13 IKE KINSWA STATE PARK

🏃 🚲 🏕 🎣 🚤 🐎 🎣 ♿ 🚙 ⛺

Scenic rating: 8

on Mayfield Lake

Map 5.1, page 301

This state park is set alongside the north shore of Mayfield Lake. The park features 46,000 feet of shore, forested campsites, and 1.5 miles of hiking trails. Mayfield Lake is a treasure trove of recreational possibilities. Fishing is a year-round affair here, with trout and tiger muskie often good. Boating, waterskiing, swimming, and driftwood collecting are all popular. The park is named after a prominent member of the Cowlitz tribe. Two fish hatcheries are located nearby. A spectacular view of Mount St. Helens can be found at a vista point 11 miles east. This popular campground often fills on summer weekends. Be sure to reserve well in advance.

Campsites, facilities: There are 31 developed tent sites, 41 sites with full hookups (30 amps) and 31 sites with partial hookups for RVs up to 36 feet, and nine cabins. Picnic tables and fire grills are provided. Restrooms with flush toilets and coin showers, drinking water, a dump station, store, playground, picnic area, horseshoe pits, and firewood are available. Boat docks and launching facilities are nearby. Some facilities are wheelchair accessible. Leashed pets are permitted.

Reservations, fees: Reservations are accepted at 888/226-7688 or https://washington.goingto-camp.com ($8-10 reservation fee). RV sites are $30-45 per night, tent sites are $20-35 per night, $10 per extra vehicle per night. Cabins are $45-69 per night, $15 per pet per night. Some credit cards are accepted. Some camping sections are open year-round.

Directions: From Chehalis, drive south on I-5 for six miles to Exit 68 and U.S. 12. Turn east on U.S. 12 and drive 14 miles to Silver Creek Road (State Route 122). Turn left (north) and drive 1.9 miles to a Y intersection. Bear right on State Route 122/Harmony Road and drive 1.6 miles to the park entrance.

Contact: Ike Kinswa State Park, 360/983-3402; state park information, 360/902-8844, http://parks.state.wa.us.

14 HARMONY LAKESIDE RV PARK

Scenic rating: 6

on Mayfield Lake

Map 5.1, page 301

This park fills up on weekends in July, August, and September. It is set on Mayfield Lake, a 10-mile-long lake with numerous recreational activities, including fishing, boating, riding personal watercraft, and waterskiing. Some sites feature lake views. Nearby Ike Kinswa State Park is a side-trip option.

Campsites, facilities: There are 80 sites with full or partial hookups (30 and 50 amps) for RVs of any length; some sites are pull-through. Cabins are also available. Picnic tables and fire grills are provided. Restrooms with coin showers, drinking water, a dump station, ice, firewood, Wi-Fi, cable TV, coin laundry, boat docks, and launching facilities are available. Group facilities, including a banquet and meeting room, are also available. Leashed pets are permitted in the campsites.

Reservations, fees: Reservations are recommended. Sites are $41-56 per night, cabins are $65-150 per night, $5 per night for each additional person, $11 per night for each additional vehicle. Winter and monthly rates are available. Some credit cards are accepted. Open year-round.

Directions: From Chehalis, drive south on I-5 for six miles to Exit 68 and U.S. 12. Turn east on U.S. 12 and drive 21 miles to Mossyrock (Highway 122). Turn left (north) and drive 3.5 miles to the park on the left.

Contact: Harmony Lakeside RV Park, 360/983-3804, www.mayfieldlake.com.

15 MAYFIELD LAKE PARK

Scenic rating: 7

on Mayfield Lake

Map 5.1, page 301

Mayfield Lake is the centerpiece of this 50-acre park. Insider's tip: Campsites 42-54 are set along the lake's shoreline. The camp has a relaxing atmosphere and comfortable, wooded sites. Fishing is primarily for trout, bass, and silver salmon. Other recreational activities include waterskiing, swimming, and boating. For a great side trip, tour nearby Mount St. Helens.

Campsites, facilities: There are 54 sites with partial hookups for tents or RVs up to 45 feet and a group camp with 12 sites for tents or RVs up to 45 feet long. Picnic tables and fire rings are provided. Restrooms with flush toilets and coin showers, drinking water, boat launch, dump station, a day-use area with a picnic shelter that can be reserved, playground, horseshoe pits, and a volleyball court are available. Some facilities are wheelchair accessible. Leashed pets are permitted.

Reservations, fees: Reservations are accepted at 888/226-7688 or https://washington.goingtocamp.com ($8-10 reservation fee). Sites are $30-37 per night, $10 per extra vehicle per night. The group camp is $200 per night ($15 reservation fee). Open mid-April-mid-October; the group camp is open Memorial Day weekend-mid-October.

Directions: From Longview, drive north on I-5 to Exit 68 and U.S. 12. Turn east on U.S. 12 and drive approximately 17 miles to Beach Road. Turn left and drive 0.25 mile to the park entrance.

Contact: Mayfield Lake Park, Tacoma Power, 360/985-2364, www.tacomapower.com.

16 MOSSYROCK PARK

🏃🚴🏊🎣🚤🏕🐕🎠⛳♿🚐⛺

Scenic rating: 8

on Riffe Lake

Map 5.1, page 301　　　　**BEST (**

This park is located along the southwest shore of Riffe Lake. It is an extremely popular campground. For anglers, it provides the best of both worlds: a boat launch on Riffe Lake, which offers coho salmon, rainbow trout, and bass, and nearby Swofford Pond, a 240-acre pond stocked with rainbow trout, brown trout, bass, catfish, and bluegill. Swofford Pond is located south of Mossyrock on Swofford Road; no gas motors are permitted. This campground provides access to a 0.5-mile loop nature trail. Bald eagles and ospreys nest on the north side of the lake in the 14,000-acre Cowlitz Wildlife Area.

Campsites, facilities: There are 152 sites for tents or RVs of any length; half of the sites have partial hookups. There are also 12 walk-in sites, one group camp with 48 sites (25 with electric hookups) for tents or RVs of any length, and two primitive group camps of 12 sites (no hookups) for tents or RVs of any length. Picnic tables and fire rings are provided. Restrooms with flush toilets and coin showers, drinking water, a dump station, seasonal convenience store, seasonal snack bar, coin laundry, fish-cleaning stations, two boat launches, playground, picnic area that can be reserved, a swimming area, horseshoe pit, volleyball net, BMX track, camp host, and interpretive displays are available. Some facilities are wheelchair accessible. Leashed pets are permitted.

Reservations, fees: Reservations are accepted at 888/226-7688 or https://washington.goingtocamp.com ($8-10 reservation fee). Sites are $22-35 per night, $10 per extra vehicle per night. The primitive group camp is $200 per night. Some credit cards are accepted

in summer. Open year-round, excluding December 20-January 1.

Directions: From Chehalis, drive south on I-5 for six miles to Exit 68 and Highway 12 East. Take Highway 12 East and drive 21 miles to Williams Street (flashing yellow light). Turn right and drive several blocks in the town of Mossyrock to a T intersection with State Street. Turn left and drive 3.5 miles (becomes Mossyrock Road East, then Ajlune Road) to the park. Ajlune Road leads right into the park.

Contact: Mossyrock Park, Tacoma Power, 360/983-3900, www.mytpu.org.

17 TAIDNAPAM PARK

🏊🎣🚤🏕🐕🏄♿🚐⛺

Scenic rating: 8

on Riffe Lake

Map 5.1, page 301

This 50-acre park is located at the east end of Riffe Lake. Nestled in a cover of Douglas fir and maple, it is surrounded by thousands of acres of undeveloped greenbelt. Fishing is permitted year-round at the lake, with coho salmon, rainbow trout, and bass available. This camp was named after the Upper Cowlitz Indians, also known as Taidnapam.

Campsites, facilities: There are 96 sites with full hookups and 43 sites with partial hookups for tents or RVs of any length, as well as 24 walk-in tent sites and a group camp of 22 sites with full or partial hookups for tents or RVs of any length. There is also a primitive group camp with 12 sites. Picnic tables and fire rings are provided. Restrooms with flush toilets and coin showers, drinking water, dump station, a fishing bridge, fish-cleaning stations, two boat launches, picnic shelter, playground, swimming beach, horseshoe pit, volleyball net, and interpretive displays are available. Some facilities are wheelchair accessible. Leashed pets are permitted.

Reservations, fees: Reservations are accepted at 888/226-7688 or https://washington.goingtocamp.com ($8-10 reservation fee).

Sites are $22-37 per night, $10 per extra vehicle per night. The group camp is $730 per night; the primitive group camp is $200 per night. Some credit cards are accepted in summer season. Open year-round, excluding December 20-January 1.

Directions: From Chehalis, drive south on I-5 for six miles to Exit 68 and Highway 12 East. Take Highway 12 East and drive 37 miles (5 miles past Morton) to Kosmos Road. Turn right and drive 200 yards to No. 100 Champion Haul Road. Turn left and drive four miles to the park entrance on the right.

Contact: Taidnapam Park, Tacoma Power, 360/497-7707, www.mytpu.org.

18 PARADISE COVE RESORT & RV PARK

Scenic rating: 7

near the Toutle River

Map 5.1, page 301

This wooded park is situated about 400 yards from the Toutle River and 0.5 mile from the Cowlitz River. Take your pick: Seaquest State Park and Silver Lake to the east provide two excellent, activity-filled side-trip options. This is a major stopover for visits to Mount St. Helens.

Campsites, facilities: There are 60 sites with full and partial hookups for tents or RVs of any length (20, 30, and 50 amps) and a large dispersed tent camping area. Some sites are pull-through. Picnic tables are provided. Restrooms with flush toilets and showers, drinking water, and coin laundry are available. Some facilities are wheelchair accessible. Leashed pets are permitted.

Reservations, fees: Reservations are accepted. Sites are $15-30 per night. Some credit cards are accepted. Open year-round.

Directions: From Longview, drive 10 miles north on I-5 to Castle Rock and Exit 52. Take Exit 52 and turn right on the frontage road and drive a short distance to Burma Road. Turn left

and drive a short distance to the resort, just off the freeway (within view of the freeway).

Contact: Paradise Cove Resort & RV Park, 112 Burma Rd., 360/274-6785, http://paradisecove.faithweb.com.

19 LONGVIEW NORTH/ MOUNT ST. HELENS KOA

Scenic rating: 6

near Silver Lake

Map 5.1, page 301

This RV park is located just outside Castle Rock, only three miles from the Mount St. Helens Visitor Center. It is close to the highway. Fishing and boating are available nearby on Silver Lake. Note that some sites are filled with monthly renters.

Campsites, facilities: There are 90 sites with full or partial hookups (20 and 30 amps) for tents or RVs up to 45 feet long and 10 sites for tents. Picnic tables are provided. Restrooms with flush toilets and coin showers, drinking water, cable TV, modem access, coin laundry, propane gas, horseshoe pits, a meeting room, and dump station are available. A convenience store and gasoline are nearby. Some facilities are wheelchair accessible. Leashed pets are permitted.

Reservations, fees: Reservations are recommended in the summer. RV sites are $34-40 per night, tent sites are $26 per night, $3-5 per person per night for more than two people. Some credit cards are accepted. Open year-round.

Directions: From Longview, drive 10 miles north on I-5 to Castle Rock and Exit 49 and Highway 504. Take Exit 49 and drive east on Highway 504 for two miles to Tower Road. Turn left (well signed) and drive a short distance to a Y intersection and Schaffran Road. Bear right and drive approximately 300 yards to the park on the right

Contact: Longview North/Mount St. Helens KOA, 360/274-8522, www.koa.com.

20 SEAQUEST STATE PARK

Scenic rating: 6

near Silver Lake

Map 5.1, page 301

This camp fills nightly because it is set along the paved road to the awesome Johnston Ridge Observatory, the premier lookout of Mount St. Helens. This state park is adjacent to Silver Lake, one of western Washington's finest fishing lakes for bass and trout. But that's not all: The Mount St. Helens Visitor Center is located across the road from the park entrance. This heavily forested, 475-acre park features more than one mile of lake shoreline and seven miles of hiking trails. The park is popular for day use as well as camping. No hunting or fishing is allowed.

The irony of the place is that some out-of-towners on vacation think that this park is located on the ocean because of its name, Seaquest. The park has nothing to do with the ocean, of course; it is named after Alfred L. Seaquest, who donated the property to the state for parkland. One interesting fact: He stipulated in his will that if liquor were ever sold on the property that the land would be transferred to Willamette University.

Campsites, facilities: There are 55 developed tent sites, 33 sites with full or partial hookups (30 amps) for tents or RVs up to 50 feet, five yurts, and one group site for up to 25 people. Picnic tables and fire grills are provided. Restrooms with flush toilets and coin showers, drinking water, a picnic area, playground, horseshoe pits, dump station, firewood, and a volleyball court are available. Some facilities are wheelchair accessible. Leashed pets are permitted.

Reservations, fees: Reservations are accepted at 888/226-7688 or https://washington.goingto-camp.com ($8-10 reservation fee). Sites are $20-45 per night, $10 per extra vehicle per night, the yurts are $45-69 per night. Call for group rates. Some credit cards are accepted. Open year-round.

Directions: From Longview, drive 10 miles north on I-5 to Castle Rock and Exit 49 and Highway 504. Take Exit 49 and drive east on Highway 504 for 5.5 miles to the park.

Contact: Seaquest State Park, 360/274-8633, http://parks.state.wa.us.

21 SILVER LAKE MOTEL AND RESORT

Scenic rating: 8

on Silver Lake

Map 5.1, page 301   **BEST (**

This park is set near the shore of Silver Lake and features a view of Mount St. Helens. One of Washington's better lakes for largemouth bass and trout, Silver Lake also has perch, crappie, and bluegill. Powerboating, personal watercraft riding, and waterskiing are popular. This spot is considered a great anglers' camp. The sites are set along a horseshoe-shaped driveway on grassy sites. Access is quick to Mount St. Helens, nearby to the east.

Campsites, facilities: There are 19 sites with full or partial hookups (30 amps) for RVs of any length, seven sites for tents, five cabins, and six motel rooms. Picnic tables are provided. Restrooms with flush toilets and coin showers, drinking water, Wi-Fi, meeting room, a convenience store, bait and tackle, fish-cleaning station, ice, boat docks, boat rentals, launching facilities, and a playground are available. A dump station is within one mile, and a café is within four miles. Some facilities are wheelchair accessible. Leashed pets are permitted in the campground.

Reservations, fees: Reservations are accepted. RV sites are $25-30 per night, tent sites are $20-25 per night, $5 per extra vehicle per night. Some credit cards are accepted. Open mid-March-mid-November.

Directions: From Longview, drive 10 miles north on I-5 to Castle Rock and Exit 49 and Highway 504. Take Exit 49 and drive east on

Highway 504 for six miles to the resort on the right.

Contact: Silver Lake Motel and Resort, 360/274-6141, www.silverlake-resort.com.

22 KALAMA HORSE CAMP

🚶🏇♿🚗⛺

Scenic rating: 8

near Mount St. Helens

Map 5.1, page 301

The most popular horse camp in the area, Kalama Horse Camp receives the enthusiastic volunteer support of local equestrians. The camp fills on weekends partly because of a network of 53 miles of horse trails accessible from camp. It is located very near Mount St. Helens.

Campsites, facilities: There are 17 sites for tents or RVs up to 25 feet long and two double sites. Picnic tables and fire grills are provided. Vault toilets are available. There is no drinking water and garbage must be packed out. Horse facilities include 10- by 10-foot corrals, a staging and mounting assist area, stock water, a stock-loading ramp, hitching rails, and manure disposal bins. A 24- by 36-foot log cabin shelter with a picnic area with horseshoe pits is also available. Boat-launching facilities are located on Lake Merrill. Some facilities are wheelchair accessible. Leashed pets are permitted.

Reservations, fees: Reservations are not accepted. Sites are $8-12 per night, $16 per night for double sites, $5 per night per extra vehicle. Open April-mid-December, weather permitting.

Directions: From Woodland on I-5, take Exit 21 for Highway 503. Drive east on Highway 503 for 23 miles to the Highway 503 spur. Continue northeast on the Highway 503 spur to Forest Road 81 (at Yale Lake, one mile south of Cougar). Turn left on Forest Road 81 and drive about eight miles to the camp on the right.

Contact: Gifford Pinchot National Forest, Mount St. Helens National Volcanic Monument, 360/449-7800, www.fs.usda.gov.

23 MERRILL LAKE

🚶🚲🏕️🛶🚗🐕♿⛺

Scenic rating: 7

near Mount St. Helens

Map 5.1, page 301

Campers seeking a quiet setting will enjoy this site, which has a reputation as the top fly-fishing area of western Washington. Due to its popularity, there is a three-day stay limit. The campground is nestled in old-growth Douglas fir on the shore of Lake Merrill, very near Mount St. Helens. It's free and provides an alternative to the more developed parks in the area, especially those along the main access roads to viewing areas of the volcano. The lake provides fishing for brown trout and cutthroat trout but is restricted to fly-fishing only, with no gas motors permitted. These restrictions make it ideal for fly fishers with prams or float tubes.

Campsites, facilities: There are nine sites for tents only. Picnic tables, fire grills, and tent pads are provided. Vault toilets are available. There is no drinking water and garbage must be packed out. A campground host is on-site. Boat-launching facilities are located on Lake Merrill. Some facilities are wheelchair accessible. Leashed pets are permitted.

Reservations, fees: Reservations are not accepted. There is no fee for camping, but a Discover Pass is required. Open April 15-November, weather permitting.

Directions: From Woodland on I-5, take Exit 21 for Highway 503. Drive east on Highway 503 for 23 miles to the Highway 503 spur. Continue northeast on the Highway 503 spur to Forest Road 81 (at Yale Lake, one mile south of Cougar). Turn left on Forest Road 81 and drive 4.5 miles to the campground access road on the left.

Contact: Department of Natural Resources, Pacific Cascade Region South, 360/577-2025 or 360/274-4196, www.dnr.wa.gov; Pacific Cascade Region information, 360/274-2055.

24 LONE FIR RESORT

🏃 🚲 🏊 🛶 ⛵ 🐕 🚤 ♿ 🚐 ⛺

Scenic rating: 4

near Yale Lake

Map 5.1, page 301

This private campground is located near Yale Lake (the smallest of four lakes in the area) and, with grassy sites and plenty of shade trees, is designed primarily for RV use. Mount St. Helens provides a side-trip option. The trailhead for the summit climb is located nearby at Climber's Bivouac on the south flank of the volcano; a primitive campground with dispersed sites for hikers only is available there. Note: This trailhead is the only one available for the summit climb. Though infrequent, the trail to the summit can be closed because of volcanic activity at the plug dome.

Campsites, facilities: There are 27 sites with full hookups (30 and 50 amps) for RVs of any length, three tent sites, four cabins, and 12 motel rooms. Some sites are pull-through. Picnic tables are provided, and fire pits are available at some sites. Restrooms with flush toilets and coin showers, satellite TV, drinking water, coin laundry, clubhouse, playground, Wi-Fi, community fire pit, horseshoe pits, ice, a snack bar, snowshoe rentals, restaurant, and a seasonal heated swimming pool are available. Propane gas, a store, boat docks, and launching facilities are nearby. Some facilities are wheelchair accessible. Leashed pets are permitted.

Reservations, fees: Reservations are accepted. RV sites are $36 per night, tent sites are $26 per night for up to four people, $5 per night for each extra person. Some credit cards are accepted. Open year-round.

Directions: In Woodland on I-5, take Exit 21 for Highway 503. Drive east on Highway 503 for 29 miles to Cougar and the resort turnoff (marked, in town, with the park visible from the road) on the left.

Contact: Lone Fir Resort, 360/238-5210, www.lonefirresort.com.

25 EVANS CREEK

🏃 🚲 🐕 ⛺

Scenic rating: 7

in Mount Baker-Snoqualmie National Forest

Map 5.2, page 302

This primitive campground is located close to Evans Creek in an off-road vehicle area near the northwestern corner of Mount Rainier National Park. If you're looking for a quiet, secluded spot, this isn't it. The two nearby roads that lead into the park are secondary or gravel roads and provide access to several other primitive campgrounds and backcountry trails in the park. A national forest map details the back roads and hiking trails.

Campsites, facilities: There are 23 sites for tents or small trailers. Picnic tables and fire grills are provided. Drinking water and vault toilets are available. Garbage must be packed out. Downed wood can be gathered for campfires. Leashed pets are permitted.

Reservations, fees: Reservations are not accepted. There is no fee for camping, but a Northwest Forest Pass ($5 daily fee, $30 annual fee per vehicle) is required to park at the trailhead. Open year-round, weather permitting.

Directions: From Tacoma on I-5, turn east on Highway 167 and drive nine miles to Highway 410. Continue 11 miles east on Highway 410 to the town of Buckley and Highway 165. Turn south on Highway 165 and drive 11 miles to Forest Road 7920. Turn left and drive 1.5 miles to the campground on the right.

Contact: Mount Baker-Snoqualmie National Forest, White River Ranger District, 360/825-6585, www.fs.usda.gov.

26 MOWICH LAKE WALK-IN

🏃 🛶 🐕 ⛺

Scenic rating: 8

near the Carbon River in Mount Rainier National Park

Map 5.2, page 302

This walk-in camp features campsites set

adjacent to and above Mowich Lake, with a lake view from some of the sites. A 200-yard walk is required to reach the campsites. Some backpackers use the camp as a launch point for trips into the Mount Rainier Wilderness. The Wonderland Trail can be accessed at this campground. Fishing is poor for trout at Mowich Lake because it is not stocked and lacks a habitat for natural spawning.

Campsites, facilities: There are 10 walk-in sites for tents only. Picnic tables are provided at some sites. Vault toilets are available. There is no drinking water and garbage must be packed out. Campfires are not permitted; use a backpacking stove. Leashed pets are permitted in camp, but not on trails.

Reservations, fees: Reservations are not accepted. There is a $25 per vehicle park entrance fee. Open June-October, weather permitting.

Directions: From Tacoma on I-5, turn east on Highway 167 and drive nine miles to Highway 410. Continue 11 miles east on Highway 410 to the town of Buckley and Highway 165. Turn right (south) on Highway 165 and drive to a fork with Carbon River Park Road. Bear right and stay on Highway 165 for eight miles to the campground at the end of the road. Only high-clearance vehicles are recommended on this access road.

Contact: Mount Rainier National Park, 360/569-2211, www.nps.gov/mora.

27 IPSUT CREEK HIKE-IN

Scenic rating: 8

near the Carbon River in Mount Rainier National Park

Map 5.2, page 302

This hike-in campsite is only open to hikers with a backcountry camping permit; access requires a 5.5-mile hike in and a Wilderness Permit from Mount Rainier National Park. From the campground, the seven-mile (round-trip) Carbon Glacier Trail follows the Carbon River through the forest to the snout of the glacier; watch for falling rocks. In addition, the Carbon River Rain Forest Nature Trail begins at the Carbon River entrance to the park. This 0.3-mile loop trail explores the only inland rainforest at Mount Rainier National Park. Note that fishing is prohibited on Ipsut Creek above the campground at the water supply intake. The elevation is 2,300 feet.

Campsites, facilities: There are 29 sites for tents and two group camps for up to 25 and 30 people respectively. Picnic tables and fire rings are provided. Drinking water, vault toilets, and a small amphitheater are available.

Reservations, fees: Reservations are not accepted. There is no fee to camp, but a backcountry permit is required. There is $25 park entrance fee. Open midsummer to early fall, weather permitting.

Directions: From Puyallup, drive east on Highway 167 to Highway 410. Turn east on Highway 410 and drive 11 miles to the town of Buckley and Highway 165. Turn right (south) on Highway 165 and drive to a fork with Carbon River Park Road. Bear left and drive five miles to the campground on the left.

Contact: Mount Rainier National Park, 360/569-2211, www.nps.gov/mora.

28 WHITE RIVER

Scenic rating: 7

on the White River in Mount Rainier National Park

Map 5.2, page 302

This campground is set on the White River at 4,400 feet elevation. The Glacier Basin Trail, a seven-mile round-trip, starts at the campground and leads along the Emmons Moraine for a short distance before ascending above it. A view of the Emmons Glacier, the largest glacier in the continental United States, is possible by hiking the spur trail, the Emmons Moraine Trail. It is sometimes possible to spot mountain goats, as well as mountain climbers, on the surrounding mountain slopes. Note that another trail near camp leads a short distance (but vertically, for a rise of 2,200 feet) to the Sunrise Visitor Center. Local rangers recommend that trailers be left at the White River Campground and the 11-mile road trip to Sunrise be made by car. From there, you can take several trails that lead to backcountry lakes and glaciers.

Campsites, facilities: There are 112 sites for tents or RVs up to 27 feet. Picnic tables and fire grills are provided. Flush toilets and drinking water are available. A small amphitheater is nearby. Some facilities are wheelchair accessible. Leashed pets are permitted in camp, but not on trails or in the wilderness.

Reservations, fees: Reservations are not accepted. Sites are $20 per night, plus $25 per vehicle park entrance fee. Some credit cards are accepted. Open July–mid-September.

Directions: From Enumclaw, drive southeast on Highway 410 to the entrance of Mount Rainier National Park and White River Road. Turn right and drive seven miles to the campground on the left.

Contact: Mount Rainier National Park, 360/569-2211, www.nps.gov/mora.

29 SILVER SPRINGS

🏃 🛶 🏕 👨‍🦽 🚐 ⛺

Scenic rating: 9

in Mount Baker-Snoqualmie National Forest

Map 5.2, page 302

Silver Springs Campground along the White River on the northeastern border of Mount Rainier National Park offers a good alternative to the more crowded camps in the park. It's located in a beautiful section of large old-growth forest, primarily with Douglas fir, cedar, and hemlock that tower over the White River. Salmon can be seen heading upriver at certain times of year. Recreational options include kayaking, fishing, and hiking. A U.S. Forest Service information center is located one mile away from the campground entrance on Highway 410.

Campsites, facilities: There are 55 sites for

tents or RVs up to 40 feet long and two double sites. Picnic tables and fire grills are provided. Flush toilets, drinking water, and downed firewood for gathering are available. The group site has a picnic shelter. Some facilities are wheelchair accessible. Leashed pets are permitted.

Reservations, fees: Reservations are accepted at 877/444-6777 ($10 recreation fee) or www. recreation.gov ($9 reservation fee). Single sites are $20 per night, double sites are $32 per night, $10 per night extra vehicle fee. Open mid-May–late September, weather permitting.

Directions: From Enumclaw, drive east on Highway 410 for 31 miles (1 mile south of the turnoff for Corral Pass) to the campground entrance on the right.

Contact: Mount Baker-Snoqualmie National Forest, White River Ranger District, 360/825-6585, www.fs.fed.us or www.hoodoo.com.

30 LODGEPOLE

🏃 🛶 🏕 🏠 🐕 👨‍🦽 🚐 ⛺

Scenic rating: 6

on the American River in Wenatchee National Forest

Map 5.2, page 302

This campground is set at an elevation of 3,500 feet along the American River, just eight miles east of the boundary of Mount Rainier National Park. Winter activities in the park include cross-country skiing, snowshoeing, and inner-tube sledding down slopes. Fishing access is available nearby.

Campsites, facilities: There are 34 sites for tents or RVs up to 42 feet long. Call to confirm site availability for large RVs. Picnic tables and fire grills are provided. Drinking water, vault toilets, garbage service, and firewood are available. A camp host is on-site. Some facilities are wheelchair accessible. Leashed pets are permitted.

Reservations, fees: Reservations are accepted at 877/444-6777 ($10 reservation fee) or www.recreation.gov ($9 reservation fee). Sites are $18 per night, $9 per night for each additional vehicle. Open mid-May-mid-September, weather permitting.

Directions: From Yakima, drive northwest on U.S. 12 for 18 miles to Highway 410. Bear northwest on Highway 410 and drive 40.5 miles (8 miles east of the national park boundary) to the campground on the right.

Contact: Okanogan-Wenatchee National Forest, Naches Ranger District, 509/653-1401, www.fs.usda.gov or www.hoodoo.com.

31 PLEASANT VALLEY

Scenic rating: 7

in Wenatchee National Forest

Map 5.2, page 302

It's always strange how campgrounds get their names. Pleasant Valley? More like Camp Thatcher, as in Thatcher ants, which have infested the campground and can inflict painful bites on you and your pet. Even the Forest Service advises, "Camp at your own risk. No refunds." If you're still set on camping here, plan to stay off the ground and away from the anthills, or bring an RV. That said, the campground (elevation of 3,300 feet) does provide a good base camp for a hiking or fishing trip. A trail from the camp follows Kettle Creek up to the American Ridge and Kettle Lake in the William O. Douglas Wilderness. It joins another trail that follows the ridge and then drops down to Bumping Lake (a U.S. Forest Service map is essential). You can fish here for whitefish, steelhead, trout, and salmon in season; check regulations. In the winter, the area is popular with cross-country skiers.

Campsites, facilities: There are 17 sites for tents or RVs up to 32 feet long. Picnic tables and fire grills are provided. Drinking water, garbage service, vault toilets, and a picnic shelter are available. Downed firewood may be gathered. A camp host is on-site. Some facilities are wheelchair accessible. Leashed pets are permitted.

Reservations, fees: Reservations are accepted at 877/444-6777 ($10 reservation fee) or www.recreation.gov ($9 reservation fee). Sites are $16 per night, $8 per night for each additional vehicle. Open mid-May-mid-September, weather permitting.

Directions: From Yakima, drive northwest on U.S. 12 for 18 miles to Highway 410. Bear northwest on Highway 410 and drive 37 miles to the campground on the left.

Contact: Okanogan-Wenatchee National Forest, Naches Ranger District, 509/653-1401, www.fs.usda.gov or www.hoodoo.com.

32 HELLS CROSSING

Scenic rating: 7

in Wenatchee National Forest

Map 5.2, page 302

Hells Crossing Campground lies along the American River at an elevation of 3,250 feet. A steep trail from the camp leads up to Goat Peak and follows the American Ridge in the William O. Douglas Wilderness. Other trails join the ridgeline trail and connect with lakes and streams. Fishing here is for trout, steelhead, salmon, and whitefish in season; check regulations.

Campsites, facilities: There are 12 sites for tents or RVs up to 20 feet long and six sites for tents only. Picnic tables and fire grills are provided. Drinking water (at the west end of camp) and vault toilets are available. Downed firewood may be gathered. Leashed pets are permitted.

Reservations, fees: Reservations are accepted at 877/444-6777 ($10 reservation fee) or www.recreation.gov ($9 reservation fee). Sites are $14 per night, $7 per night for each additional vehicle. Open mid-May-mid-September, weather permitting.

Directions: From Yakima, drive northwest on U.S. 12 for 18 miles to Highway 410. Bear northwest on Highway 410 and drive 33.5 miles to the campground on the right.

Contact: Okanogan-Wenatchee National

Forest, Naches Ranger District, 509/653-1401, www.fs.usda.gov or www.hoodoo.com.

33 PINE NEEDLE GROUP CAMP

Scenic rating: 7

in Wenatchee National Forest

Map 5.2, page 302

This reservations-only group campground sits on the edge of the William O. Douglas Wilderness along the American River at an elevation of 3,000 feet. There are trails leading south into the backcountry at nearby camps; consult a U.S. Forest Service map. The camp is easy to reach, rustic, and beautiful. Fishing is available for whitefish, trout, steelhead, and salmon in season. For a side trip, visit Bumping Lake to the south, where recreation options include boating, fishing, and swimming.

Campsites, facilities: There is one group site for tents or RVs up to 30 feet long that can accommodate up to 60 people. Picnic tables and fire grills are provided. Vault toilets are available. There is no drinking water here, but it is available 2.5 miles west at Hells Crossing campground. Garbage must be packed out. Downed firewood may be gathered. Leashed pets are permitted.

Reservations, fees: Reservations are accepted at 877/444-6777 ($10 reservation fee) or www. recreation.gov ($9 reservation fee). The camp is $50 per night. Open mid-May–mid-November, weather permitting.

Directions: From Yakima, drive northwest on U.S. 12 for 18 miles to Highway 410. Bear northwest on Highway 410 and drive 30.5 miles to the campground on the left.

Contact: Okanogan-Wenatchee National Forest, Naches Ranger District, 509/653-1401, www.fs.usda.gov.

34 COUGAR FLAT

Scenic rating: 5

in Wenatchee National Forest

Map 5.2, page 302

Cougar Flat suffered heavy storm damage in 2013. At time of publication, it remained closed until repairs could be completed. Call to confirm availability.

One of several camps in the immediate vicinity, this spot along the Bumping River is close to good fishing; a trail from the camp follows the river and then heads up the tributaries. The elevation is 3,100 feet.

Campsites, facilities: There are eight sites for tents or RVs up to 40 feet long and four walk-in sites for tents only. Picnic tables and fire grills are provided. Drinking water, vault toilets, and garbage bins are available. Some facilities are wheelchair accessible. Leashed pets are permitted.

Reservations, fees: Reservations are accepted at 877/444-6777 ($10 reservation fee) or www. recreation.gov ($9 reservation fee). Sites are $16 per night, $8 per night for each additional vehicle. Open mid-May–mid-September, weather permitting.

Directions: From Yakima, drive northwest on U.S. 12 for 18 miles to Highway 410. Turn left (northwest) on Highway 410 and drive 28.5 miles to Forest Road 1800. Turn left (southwest) and drive six miles (along the Bumping River) to the campground on the left.

Contact: Okanogan-Wenatchee National Forest, Naches Ranger District, 509/653-1401, www.fs.usda.gov or www.hoodoo.com.

35 SODA SPRINGS

Scenic rating: 6

in Wenatchee National Forest

Map 5.2, page 302

Highlights at this camp along the Bumping River include natural mineral springs and a nature trail. The mineral spring is located next to a trail across the river from the campground, where the water bubbles up out of the ground. This cold-water spring is popular with some campers for soaking and drinking. Many campers use this camp for access to nearby Bumping Lake. Fishing access is available. A sheltered picnic area is provided.

Campsites, facilities: There are 26 sites for tents or RVs up to 30 feet long. Picnic tables and fire grills are provided. Drinking water, vault toilets, firewood, a picnic shelter with a fireplace, and garbage service are available. A camp host is on-site. Some facilities are wheelchair accessible. Leashed pets are permitted.

Reservations, fees: Reservations are accepted at 877/444-6777 ($10 reservation fee) or www.recreation.gov ($9 reservation fee). Sites are $18 per night, $9 per night for each additional vehicle. Open mid-May–mid-September, weather permitting.

Directions: From Yakima, drive northwest on U.S. 12 for 18 miles to Highway 410. Turn left (northwest) on Highway 410 and drive 28.5 miles to Forest Road 1800. Turn left (southwest) and drive five miles (along the Bumping River) to the campground on the left.

Contact: Okanogan-Wenatchee National Forest, Naches Ranger District, 509/653-1401, www.fs.usda.gov or www.hoodoo.com.

36 CEDAR SPRINGS

Scenic rating: 6

in Wenatchee National Forest

Map 5.2, page 302

The Bumping River runs alongside this camp, set at an elevation of 2,800 feet. Fishing here follows the seasons for trout, steelhead, and whitefish; check regulations. If you continue driving southwest for 11 miles on Forest Road 1800/Bumping River Road, you'll reach Bumping Lake, where recreation options abound.

Campsites, facilities: There are 15 sites for tents or RVs up to 22 feet long, including two double sites. Picnic tables and fire grills are provided. Drinking water and vault toilets are available. Leashed pets are permitted.

Reservations, fees: Reservations are accepted at 877/444-6777 ($10 reservation fee) or www.recreation.gov ($9 reservation fee). Single sites are $16 per night, $8 per night for each additional vehicle. Open mid-May–mid-September, weather permitting.

Directions: From Yakima, drive northwest on U.S. 12 for 18 miles to Highway 410. Bear northwest on Highway 410 and drive 28.5 miles to the campground access road (Forest Road 1800/Bumping River Road). Turn left (southwest) and drive 0.5 mile to the campground on the left.

Contact: Okanogan-Wenatchee National Forest, Naches Ranger District, 509/653-1401, www.fs.usda.gov or www.hoodoo.com.

37 INDIAN FLAT GROUP CAMP

Scenic rating: 7

in Wenatchee National Forest

Map 5.2, page 302

This reservations-only group campground is set along the American River at an elevation of 2,600 feet. Fishing access is available for trout, steelhead, and whitefish in season; check regulations. A trail starts just across the road from camp and leads into the backcountry, west along Fife's Ridge, and farther north to the West Quartz Creek drainage.

Campsites, facilities: There is one group site for tents or RVs up to 30 feet long, with a maximum capacity of 66 campers and 22 vehicles. Picnic tables and fire grills are provided. Drinking water, vault toilets, and firewood are available. Garbage must be packed out. Leashed pets are permitted.

Reservations, fees: Reservations are accepted at 877/444-6777 ($10 reservation fee) or www.recreation.gov ($9 reservation fee). The camp is $70 per night on weekdays and $100 per night on weekends. Open late May-mid-November, weather permitting.

Directions: From Yakima, drive northwest on U.S. 12 for 18 miles to Highway 410. Bear northwest on Highway 410 and drive 27 miles to the campground on the left.

Contact: Okanogan-Wenatchee National Forest, Naches Ranger District, 509/653-1401, www.fs.usda.gov.

38 LITTLE NACHES

Scenic rating: 5

in Wenatchee National Forest

Map 5.2, page 302

This campground on the Little Naches River near the American River is just 0.1 mile off the road and 24 miles from Mount Rainier. The easy access is a major attraction for highway cruisers, but the location also means you can sometimes hear highway noise, and at four sites, you can see highway vehicles. Trees act as a buffer between the highway and the campground at other sites. Fishing access is available from camp. The elevation is 2,562 feet.

Campsites, facilities: There are 17 sites for tents or RVs up to 49 feet long and one double site. Picnic tables and fire grills are provided. Drinking water, vault toilets, firewood, and garbage service are available. A camp host is on-site. Leashed pets are permitted.

Reservations, fees: Reservations are accepted at 877/444-6777 ($10 reservation fee) or www.recreation.gov ($9 reservation fee). Sites are $14-26 per night, $7 per night for each additional vehicle. Open mid-May-mid-September, weather permitting.

Directions: From Yakima, drive northwest on U.S. 12 for 18 miles to Highway 410. Bear northwest on Highway 410 and drive 25 miles to the campground access road (Forest Road 1900). Turn left and drive 100 yards to the campground on the left.

Contact: Okanogan-Wenatchee National Forest, Naches Ranger District, 509/653-1401, www.fs.usda.gov or www.hoodoo.com.

39 HALFWAY FLAT

Scenic rating: 7

in Wenatchee National Forest

Map 5.2, page 302

Fishing, hiking, and off-road vehicle (OHV) opportunities abound at this campground along the Naches River. A motorcycle trail leads from the campground into the backcountry adjacent to the William O. Douglas Wilderness; no motorized vehicles are permitted in the wilderness itself, however. Do not expect peace and quiet. This campground is something of a chameleon—sometimes primarily a family campground, but at other times dominated by OHV users.

Campsites, facilities: There are eight single sites and three double sites for tents or RVs up to 27 feet long and an area for dispersed tent or RV camping. Picnic tables and fire grills are provided. Drinking water, vault toilets, and garbage service are available. Some facilities are wheelchair accessible. Leashed pets are permitted.

Reservations, fees: Reservations are not accepted. Sites are $18 per night, dispersed campsites are $10 per night, $5 per night per additional vehicle. Open mid-May-mid-September, weather permitting.

Directions: From Yakima, drive northwest on U.S. 12 for 18 miles to Highway 410. Turn left (northwest) on Highway 410 and drive 17 miles to Forest Road 1704. Turn left and drive one mile to the campground.

Contact: Okanogan-Wenatchee National Forest, Naches Ranger District, 509/653-1401, www.fs.usda.gov.

40 SAWMILL FLAT

Scenic rating: 6

in Wenatchee National Forest

Map 5.2, page 302

This campground on the Naches River near Halfway Flat is used by motorcyclists more than any other types of campers. It offers fishing access and a hiking trail that leads west from Halfway Flat Campground for several miles into the backcountry. Fishing is primarily for trout in summer, whitefish in winter—check regulations. Another trailhead is located at Boulder Cave to the south.

Campsites, facilities: There are 24 sites for tents or RVs up to 38 feet long. Picnic tables and fire grills are provided. Drinking water, vault toilets, garbage bins, firewood, and an Adirondack group shelter are available. A camp host is on-site in summer. Downed firewood may be gathered. Some facilities are wheelchair accessible. Leashed pets are permitted.

Reservations, fees: Reservations are accepted at 877/444-6777 ($10 reservation fee) or www.recreation.gov ($9 reservation fee). Sites are $18 per night, $9 per night for each additional vehicle. Open mid-May-mid-September, weather permitting.

Directions: From Yakima, drive northwest on U.S. 12 for 18 miles to Highway 410. Bear northwest on Highway 410 and drive 23.5 miles to the campground on the left.

Contact: Okanogan-Wenatchee National Forest, Naches Ranger District, 509/653-1401, www.fs.usda.gov or www.hoodoo.com.

41 COTTONWOOD

Scenic rating: 7

in Wenatchee National Forest

Map 5.2, page 302

Pretty, shaded sites and river views are the main draw at this camp along the Naches River. The fishing is similar to that of the other camps in the area—primarily for trout in summer and whitefish in winter. The elevation here is 2,300 feet.

Campsites, facilities: There are 13 sites for tents or RVs up to 22 feet long and three sites for tents only. Picnic tables and fire grills are provided. Drinking water, vault toilets, and garbage service are available. A store, café, and ice are available nearby. Leashed pets are permitted.

Reservations, fees: Reservations are accepted at 877/444-6777 ($10 reservation fee) or www.recreation.gov ($9 reservation fee). Sites are $16 per night, $8 per night for each additional vehicle. Open mid-May-mid-September, weather permitting.

Directions: From Yakima, drive northwest on U.S. 12 for 18 miles to Highway 410. Turn left (northwest) on Highway 410 and drive 17.5 miles to the campground on the left.

Contact: Okanogan-Wenatchee National Forest, Naches Ranger District, 509/653-1401, www.fs.usda.gov or www.hoodoo.com.

42 BUMPING LAKE CAMPGROUND

Scenic rating: 7

in Wenatchee National Forest

Map 5.2, page 302

This popular campground is set at an elevation of 3,200 feet near Bumping Lake amid a forest of primarily lodgepole pine. One of the more developed camps in the area, Bumping comprises two campgrounds—an upper and a lower section—and both fill quickly on summer weekends. A variety of water activities are allowed on Bumping Lake, including waterskiing, fishing (for salmon and trout), and swimming; the nearby boat launch makes it a winner for campers with boats. A picnic area is adjacent to the boat facilities and several hiking trails lead into the William O. Douglas Wilderness surrounding the lake. Woods and water—this spot has them both.

Campsites, facilities: There are 56 sites for tents or RVs up to 40 feet long and one site for tents only. Picnic tables and fire grills are provided. Drinking water, vault toilets, a boat launch, and a dump station ($10 fee) are available. Some facilities are wheelchair accessible. Leashed pets are permitted.

Reservations, fees: Reservations are accepted at 877/444-6777 ($10 reservation fee) or www.recreation.gov ($9 reservation fee). Sites are $18-34 per night, $9-10 per night for each additional vehicle. Open June-mid-September, weather permitting.

Directions: From Yakima, drive northwest on U.S. 12 for 18 miles to Highway 410. Turn left (northwest) on Highway 410 and drive 28.5 miles to Forest Road 1800. Turn left (southwest) and drive 11 miles (along the Bumping River); look for the campground entrance road on the right.

Contact: Okanogan-Wenatchee National Forest, Naches Ranger District, 509/653-1401, www.fs.usda.gov or www.hoodoo.com.

43 MOUNTHAVEN RESORT

🚶 ❄ 🐕 🚣 ⛺ 🚐

Scenic rating: 6
near Mount Rainier National Park

Map 5.2, page 302

This campground is located within 0.5 mile of the Nisqually (southwestern) entrance to Mount Rainier National Park. In turn, it can provide a launching point for your vacation. One option: Enter the park at the Nisqually entrance, then drive on Nisqually Paradise Road for about five miles to Longmire Museum; general park information and exhibits about the plants and geology of the area are available. If you then continue into the park for 10 more miles, you'll arrive at the Jackson Visitor Center in Paradise, which has more exhibits and an observation deck. This road is the only one into the park that's open year-round. Winter activities in the park include cross-country skiing, snowshoeing, and inner-tube sledding

down slopes. A creek runs through this wooded camp.

Campsites, facilities: There are 16 sites with full hookups (20 and 30 amps) for RVs of any length, one site for tents only, and nine furnished cabins. Picnic tables and fire grills are provided. A restroom with a toilet and shower, drinking water, coin laundry, pay phone, firewood, and a playground are available. A restaurant and a store are within one mile. Leashed pets are permitted.

Reservations, fees: Reservations are accepted. RV sites are $47 per night for up to four people, $3 per night for each additional person, $3 per pet per night. The tent site is $30 per night. Some credit cards are accepted. Open year-round.

Directions: From Chehalis, drive south on I-5 for 10 miles to U.S. 12. Turn east and drive 31 miles to Morton and Highway 7. Turn left (north) on Highway 7 and drive 17 miles to Elbe and Highway 706. Turn right (east) on Highway 706 and drive to Ashford; continue for six miles to the resort on the right.

Contact: Mounthaven Resort, 360/569-2594, www.mounthaven.com.

44 BIG CREEK

🚶 ≈ 🛶 🏊 🐕 ♿ 🚐 ⛺

Scenic rating: 8
in Gifford Pinchot National Forest

Map 5.2, page 302

This camp is useful as an overflow spot for Mount Rainier Sound and for those who want to avoid driving their RV on the windy park roads. It is set along a stream next to a rural residential area in a forest setting made up of Douglas fir, western hemlock, western red cedar, and big-leaf and vine maple.

Campsites, facilities: There are 24 sites for tents or RVs up to 40 feet long. Picnic tables and fire rings are provided. Drinking water, firewood, and vault toilets are available. A camp host is on-site. Some facilities are wheelchair accessible. Leashed pets are permitted.

Reservations, fees: Reservations are accepted at 877/444-6777 ($10 reservation fee) or www.recreation.gov ($9 reservation fee). Single sites are $18 per night, double sites are $30 per night, $9 per night for each additional vehicle. Open May-mid-September.

Directions: On I-5, drive to Exit 68 (south of Chehalis) and U.S. 12. Turn east on U.S. 12 and drive 62 miles to Packwood and Forest Road 52/Skate Creek Road. Turn left (northwest) and drive 23 miles to the campground on the left.

Contact: Gifford Pinchot National Forest, Cowlitz Valley Ranger District, 360/497-1100, www.fs.usda.gov or www.hoodoo.com.

45 COUGAR ROCK

Scenic rating: 9

in Mount Rainier National Park

Map 5.2, page 302

Cougar Rock is a national park campground at 3,180 feet elevation at the foot of awesome Mount Rainier. To the east lies the Nisqually Vista Trail, a beautiful 1.2-mile loop trail. It begins at the visitors center at Paradise and provides stellar views of Mount Rainier and the Nisqually Glacier. Fishing tends to be marginal. As in all national parks, no trout are stocked, and lakes without natural fisheries provide zilch. Nearby Mounthaven Resort offers winter activities in Mount Rainier Park, such as cross-country skiing, snowshoeing, and innertube sledding down slopes.

Campsites, facilities: There are 173 sites for tents or RVs up to 35 feet and five group sites for tents only that accommodate up to 24-40 people each. Picnic tables and fire rings are provided. Restrooms with flush toilets, drinking water, a dump station, and an amphitheater are available. A general store is located two miles away at Longmire. Some facilities are wheelchair accessible. Leashed pets are permitted.

Reservations, fees: Reservations are accepted at 877/444-6777 or www.recreation.gov ($9 reservation fee). Sites are $20 per night, plus a $25

per vehicle park entrance fee. Group sites are $60 per night. Open late May-late September.

Directions: From Tacoma, drive south on I-5 for five miles to Highway 512. Turn east on Highway 512 and drive two miles to Highway 7. Turn right (south) on Highway 7 and drive to Elbe and Highway 706. Continue east on Highway 706 and drive 12 miles to the park entrance. Continue 11 miles to the campground entrance on the left (about 2 miles past the Longmire developed area).

Contact: Mount Rainier National Park, 360/569-2211, www.nps.gov/mora.

46 OHANAPECOSH

Scenic rating: 8

on the Ohanapecosh River in Mount Rainier National Park

Map 5.2, page 302   **BEST (**

This camp is set at an elevation of 1,914 feet at the foot of Mount Rainier, though old-growth Douglas firs screen the view. It is also set along the Ohanapecosh River, adjacent to the Ohanapecosh Visitor Center, which features exhibits on the history of the forest, plus visitor information. A 0.5-mile loop trail leads from the campground, behind the visitors center, to Ohanapecosh Hot Springs. The Silver Falls Trail, a three-mile loop trail, follows the Ohanapecosh River to 75-foot Silver Falls. Warning: Do not climb on the wet rocks near the waterfall; they are wet and slippery. Note that Stevens Canyon Road heading west and Highway 123 heading north are closed by snowfall in winter.

Campsites, facilities: There are 188 sites for tents or RVs up to 32 feet and two group sites for up to 25 people each. Picnic tables and fire rings are provided. Flush and vault toilets, drinking water, and a dump station are available. An amphitheater is nearby. Some facilities are wheelchair accessible. Leashed pets are permitted in camp, but not on trails.

Reservations, fees: Reservations are accepted

at 877/444-6777 or www.recreation.gov ($9 reservation fee). Sites are $20 per night, plus a $25 per vehicle park entrance fee. The group site is $60 per night. Some credit cards are accepted. Open mid-May-September.

Directions: On I-5, drive to Exit 68 (south of Chehalis) and U.S. 12. Turn east on U.S. 12 and drive 72 miles (7 miles past Packwood) to Highway 123. Turn left (north) and drive 6.5 miles to the Ohanapecosh entrance to the park. As you enter the park, the camp is on the left, next to the visitors center.

Contact: Mount Rainier National Park, 360/569-2211, www.nps.gov/mora.

47 LA WIS WIS

Scenic rating: 9

in Gifford Pinchot National Forest

Map 5.2, page 302

This camp is ideally located for day trips to Mount Rainier and Mount St. Helens. It's set at an elevation of 1,400 feet along the Clear Fork of the Cowlitz River, near the confluence with the Ohanapecosh River. Trout fishing is an option. The landscape features an old-growth forest of Douglas fir, western hemlock, western red cedar, and Pacific yew, with undergrowth of big-leaf maple. A 200-yard trail provides access to the Blue Hole on the Ohanapecosh River, a deep pool designated by an observation point and interpretive signs. Another trail leads less than 0.25 mile to Purcell Falls. The entrance to Mount Rainier National Park is about seven miles south of the camp.

Campsites, facilities: There are 122 sites for tents or RVs up to 40 feet long, including a few double sites, and the Coho Group site. Picnic tables and fire rings are provided. Flush and vault toilets, drinking water, garbage bins, and firewood are available. Some facilities are wheelchair accessible. Leashed pets are permitted.

Reservations, fees: Reservations are accepted at 877/444-6777 ($10 reservation fee) or www.

recreation.gov ($9 reservation fee). Single sites are $20 per night, double sites are $38 per night, $10 per extra vehicle per night, the group site is $90 per night. Open late May-early September, weather permitting.

Directions: On I-5, drive to Exit 68 (south of Chehalis) and U.S. 12. Turn east on U.S. 12 and drive 69 miles (about 6 miles past Packwood) to Forest Road 1272. Turn left and drive 0.5 mile to the campground on the left.

Contact: Gifford Pinchot National Forest, Cowlitz Valley Ranger District, 360/497-1100, www.fs.usda.gov or www.hoodoo.com.

48 WHITE PASS

Scenic rating: 7

on Leech Lake in Wenatchee National Forest

Map 5.2, page 302

This campground on the shore of Leech Lake sits at an elevation of 4,500 feet and boasts nearby trails leading into the Goat Rocks Wilderness to the south and the William O. Douglas Wilderness to the north. A trailhead for the Pacific Crest Trail is also nearby. Beautiful Leech Lake is popular for fly-fishing for rainbow trout. Note that this is the only type of fishing allowed here—check regulations. No gas motors are permitted on Leech Lake. White Pass Ski Area is located across the highway, 0.2 mile away.

Campsites, facilities: There are 16 sites for tents or RVs up to 20 feet long. Picnic tables and fire grills are provided. Vault toilets, garbage bins, and firewood are available. There is no drinking water. A store and ice are located within one mile. Boat-launching facilities are nearby. No gas motors on boats are allowed; electric motors are permitted. Leashed pets are permitted.

Reservations, fees: Reservations are not accepted. Sites are $8 per night, $5 per night per additional vehicle. Open mid-May-mid-September, weather permitting.

Directions: On I-5, drive to Exit 68 (south of

Chehalis) and U.S. 12. Turn east on U.S. 12 and drive 81 miles (1 mile past the White Pass Ski Area) to the campground entrance road on the left side. Turn left (north) and drive 200 yards to Leech Lake and the campground.

Contact: Okanogan-Wenatchee National Forest, Naches Ranger District, 509/653-1401, www.fs.usda.gov.

49 DOG LAKE

Scenic rating: 5

on Dog Lake in Wenatchee National Forest

Map 5.2, page 302

Set on the shore of Dog Lake at 3,400 feet elevation is little Dog Lake Campground. Fishing can be good for native rainbow trout, and the lake is good for hand-launched boats, such as canoes and prams. Nearby trails lead into the William O. Douglas Wilderness.

Campsites, facilities: There are eight sites for tents or RVs up to 24 feet long. Picnic tables and fire grills are provided. Vault toilets and garbage bins are available. There is no drinking water. No horses are allowed in the campground. Leashed pets are permitted.

Reservations, fees: Reservations are not accepted. Sites are $8 per night, $5 per extra vehicle per night. Open mid-May-early September, weather permitting.

Directions: On I-5, drive to Exit 68 (south of Chehalis) and U.S. 12. Turn east on U.S. 12 and drive 84 miles (3 miles past the White Pass Ski Area) to the campground entrance road on the left side.

Contact: Okanogan-Wenatchee National Forest, Naches Ranger District, 509/653-1401, www.fs.usda.gov.

50 CLEAR LAKE NORTH

Scenic rating: 7

on Clear Lake in Wenatchee National Forest

Map 5.2, page 302

This primitive campground is set along the shore of Clear Lake at an elevation of 3,100 feet; it gets relatively little use. A 5-mph speed limit keeps the lake quiet and ideal for fishing, which is often good for rainbow trout. It is stocked regularly in the summer. Clear Lake is the forebay for Rimrock Lake. Swimming is allowed.

Campsites, facilities: There are 33 sites for tents or RVs up to 22 feet long and three double sites. Picnic tables and fire grills are provided. Vault toilets and garbage service are available. There is no drinking water at Clear Lake North, but there is drinking water at Clear Lake South Campground. Boat docks and launching facilities are nearby. Some facilities are wheelchair accessible. Leashed pets are permitted.

Reservations, fees: Reservations are not accepted. Sites are $10 per night, $5 per extra vehicle per night. Open mid-May-mid-November, weather permitting.

Directions: From Yakima, drive northwest on U.S. 12 for 17 miles to the junction with Highway 410. Turn west on U.S. 12 and drive 31 miles to Forest Road 1200. Turn left (south) and drive 0.25 mile to Forest Road 1200-740. Continue south for 0.5 mile to the campground.

Contact: Okanogan-Wenatchee National Forest, Naches Ranger District, 509/653-1401, www.fs.usda.gov.

51 CLEAR LAKE SOUTH

Scenic rating: 7

in Wenatchee National Forest

Map 5.2, page 302

This campground (elevation 3,100 feet) is located near the east shore of Clear Lake, which is the forebay for Rimrock Lake. Fishing and swimming are recreation options. For winter travelers, several Sno-Parks in the area offer snowmobiling and cross-country skiing. Many hiking trails lie to the north.

Campsites, facilities: There are 22 sites for tents or RVs up to 22 feet long. Picnic tables and fire grills are provided. Drinking water, vault toilets, and garbage bins are available. Downed firewood may be gathered. Boat-launching facilities are nearby. Some facilities are wheelchair accessible. Leashed pets are permitted.

Reservations, fees: Reservations are not accepted. Sites are $10 per night, $5 per extra vehicle per night. Open mid-May-mid-November, weather permitting.

Directions: From Yakima, drive northwest on U.S. 12 for 17 miles to the junction with Highway 410. Turn west on U.S. 12 and drive 31 miles to Forest Road 1200. Turn left (south) and drive one mile to Forest Road 1200-740. Continue south and drive 0.25 mile to the campground.

Contact: Okanogan-Wenatchee National Forest, Naches Ranger District, 509/653-1401, www.fs.usda.gov.

52 SILVER BEACH RESORT

Scenic rating: 8

on Rimrock Lake

Map 5.2, page 302

This resort along the shore of Rimrock Lake is one of several camps in the immediate area. It's very scenic, with beautiful lakefront sites. Hiking trails, marked bike trails, a full-service marina, a sandy swimming beach, and a riding stable are close by.

Campsites, facilities: There are 46 sites with full or partial hookups and 20 sites with no hookups for tents or RVs up to 40 feet long. Some sites are pull-through. There are also three cabins with kitchens and 16 motel rooms. Picnic tables and fire pits are provided. Restrooms with flush toilets and coin showers, a café, convenience store, dump station, bait and tackle, propane gas, ice, a playground, boat

docks, launching facilities, and boat and personal watercraft rentals are available. Some facilities are wheelchair accessible. Leashed pets are permitted.

Reservations, fees: Reservations are accepted. Sites are $20-35 per night, $10 per extra vehicle per night. Some credit cards are accepted. Open year-round, with limited winter facilities.

Directions: From Yakima, drive northwest on U.S. 12 for 40 miles to the resort on the left.

Contact: Silver Beach Resort, 509/672-2500, www.silverbeach.biz.

53 INDIAN CREEK

Scenic rating: 7

on Rimrock Lake in Wenatchee National Forest

Map 5.2, page 302

Fishing, swimming, and waterskiing are among the activities at this shorefront campground on Rimrock Lake (elevation 3,000 feet). The camp is adjacent to Rimrock Lake Marina and Silver Beach Resort. This is a developed lake and an extremely popular campground, often filling on summer weekends. Fishing is often good for rainbow trout. The treasured Indian Creek Trail and many other excellent hiking trails about 5-10 miles north of the campground lead into the William O. Douglas Wilderness.

Campsites, facilities: There are 38 sites for tents or RVs up to 45 feet long. Picnic tables and fire grills are provided. Drinking water, vault toilets, and garbage bins are available. Downed firewood may be gathered. A camp host is onsite. A café, store, ice, boat docks, launching facilities, and rentals are nearby. Leashed pets are permitted.

Reservations, fees: Reservations are accepted at 877/444-6777 ($10 reservation fee) or www.recreation.gov ($9 reservation fee). Sites are $20 per night, $10 per extra vehicle per night. Open mid-May-mid-September, weather permitting.

Directions: From Yakima, drive northwest on U.S. 12 for 17 miles to the junction with

Highway 410. Turn west on U.S. 12 and drive 20 miles to Rimrock Lake and the campground entrance at the lake.

Contact: Okanogan-Wenatchee National Forest, Naches Ranger District, 509/653-1401, www.fs.usda.gov or www.hoodoo.com.

54 PENINSULA

🕺 🚴 🏊 🎣 🚌 ❄️ 🐕 ♿ 🚐 ⛺

Scenic rating: 7
on Rimrock Lake in Wenatchee National Forest

Map 5.2, page 302

Fishing for silvers and rainbow trout, swimming, and waterskiing are all allowed at Rimrock Lake (elevation 3,000 feet), where this shorefront recreation area and camp are located. The lake is stocked regularly in summer and is popular, in part because of the nearby boat ramp. This camp is one of several on the lake. A point of interest, the nearby emergency airstrip here features a grass runway. A nearby Sno-Park offers wintertime fun, including cross-country skiing and snowmobiling.

Campsites, facilities: There is a dispersed camping area for 60 tents or RVs up to 20 feet long. Picnic tables are provided. Vault toilets and garbage bins are available. There is no drinking water. Boat docks and launching facilities are nearby. Some facilities are wheelchair accessible. Leashed pets are permitted.

Reservations, fees: Reservations are not accepted. Sites are $8 per night, $5 per night per additional vehicle. Open May-mid-November, weather permitting.

Directions: From Yakima, drive northwest on U.S. 12 for 17 miles to the junction with Highway 410. Turn west on U.S. 12 and drive 22 miles to Forest Road 1200. Turn left (south) and drive three miles (across the cattle guard) to Forest Road 711. Turn right (west) and drive a short distance to the campground.

Contact: Okanogan-Wenatchee National Forest, Naches Ranger District, 509/653-1401, www.fs.usda.gov.

55 SOUTH FORK GROUP CAMP

🚴 🏊 🚌 🐕 ♿ 🚐 ⛺

Scenic rating: 8
in Wenatchee National Forest

Map 5.2, page 302

South Fork Group Camp is set at 3,000 feet elevation along the South Fork of the Tieton River, less than one mile from where it empties into Rimrock Lake. Note that fishing is prohibited to protect the bull trout. By traveling a bit farther south on Tieton River Road, you can see huge Blue Slide, an enormous prehistoric rock and earth slide that has a curious blue tinge to it. Note: In 2009, a fire burned south of this area.

Campsites, facilities: There is one group site for tents or RVs up to 40 feet long that accommodates up to 80 people. Picnic tables and fire grills are provided. Vault toilets are available. There is no drinking water and garbage must be packed out. Some facilities are wheelchair accessible. Leashed pets are permitted.

Reservations, fees: Reservations are accepted at 877/444-6777 ($10 reservation fee) or www.recreation.gov ($9 reservation fee). The site is $60 per night. Open May-mid-November, weather permitting.

Directions: From Yakima, drive northwest on U.S. 12 for 17 miles to the junction with Highway 410. Turn west on U.S. 12 and drive 22 miles to Forest Road 1200. Turn left (south) and drive four miles to Forest Road 1203. Bear left and drive 0.75 mile to Forest Road 1203-517. Turn right and drive 200 feet to the campground.

Contact: Okanogan-Wenatchee National Forest, Naches Ranger District, 509/653-1401, www.fs.usda.gov.

56 IRON CREEK

Scenic rating: 7

in Gifford Pinchot National Forest

Map 5.2, page 302

This popular U.S. Forest Service campground is set along the Cispus River near its confluence with Iron Creek. Trout fishing is available. The landscape features primarily Douglas fir, western red cedar, and old-growth forest on fairly flat terrain. The camp is also located along the access route that leads to the best viewing areas on the eastern flank for Mount St. Helens. Take a 25-mile drive to Windy Ridge Vista Point for a breathtaking view of Spirit Lake and the blast zone of the volcano.

Campsites, facilities: There are 80 single sites and 18 double sites for tents or RVs up to 40 feet long. Picnic tables and fire rings are provided. Drinking water, vault toilets, firewood, and an amphitheater are available. A camp host is on-site. Some facilities are wheelchair accessible. Leashed pets are permitted.

Reservations, fees: Reservations are accepted at 877/444-6777 ($10 reservation fee) or www.recreation.gov ($9 reservation fee). Sites are $20-38 per night, $10 per extra vehicle per night. Open mid-May-early September, weather permitting.

Directions: From Chehalis, drive south on I-5 for 10 miles to Exit 68 and U.S. 12. Turn east on U.S. 12 and drive 48 miles to Randle and Highway 131. Turn south on Highway 131 and drive one mile (becomes Forest Road 25). Continue south on Forest Road 25 and drive nine miles to a fork. Bear left at the fork, continue across the bridge, turn left, and drive two miles to the campground entrance on the left (along the south shore of the Cispus River).

Contact: Gifford Pinchot National Forest, Cowlitz Valley Ranger District, 360/497-1100, www.fs.usda.gov or www.hoodoo.com.

57 TOWER ROCK

Scenic rating: 5

in Gifford Pinchot National Forest

Map 5.2, page 302

Tower Rock Campground along the Cispus River is an alternative to nearby Iron Creek and North Fork. It has shaded and sunny sites, with lots of trees and plenty of room. The camp is set fairly close to the river; some sites feature river frontage. It is also fairly flat and forested with Douglas fir, western hemlock, red cedar, and big-leaf maple. Fishing for trout is popular here.

Campsites, facilities: There are 22 sites for tents or RVs up to 40 feet long. Picnic tables and fire grills are provided. Drinking water, vault toilets, and firewood are available. Leashed pets are permitted.

Reservations, fees: Reservations are accepted at 877/444-6777 ($10 reservation fee) or www.recreation.gov ($9 reservation fee). Sites are $18 per night, $9 per extra vehicle per night. Open mid-May-mid-September, weather permitting.

Directions: From Chehalis, drive south on I-5 for 20 miles to Exit 68 and U.S. 12. Turn east on U.S. 12 and drive 48 miles to Randle and Highway 131. Turn right (south) on Highway 131 and drive one mile to Forest Road 23. Turn left on Forest Road 23 and drive eight miles to Forest Road 28. Turn right and drive two miles to Forest Road 76. Turn right and drive two miles to the campground entrance road on the right.

Contact: Gifford Pinchot National Forest, Cowlitz Valley Ranger District, 360/497-1100, www.fs.usda.gov or www.hoodoo.com.

58 NORTH FORK, ELK, BEAVER, AND BEAR GROUP

🥾 🚴 🛶 🐴 🚙 ⛺

Scenic rating: 6

in Gifford Pinchot National Forest

Map 5.2, page 302

This campground offers single sites, double sites, and group camps, with the North Cispus River flowing between the sites for individual and group use. Campsites are set back from the river in a well-forested area, however some trees have weak roots; campsites may be periodically closed to remove diseased trees. A national forest map details the backcountry access to the Valley Trail, which is routed up the Cispus River Valley for 16.7 miles. This trailhead provides access for hikers, bikers, all-terrain vehicles, and horses. If you explore Road 2300-083, 15 miles west, you will find Layser Cave, a Native American archaeological site that is open to the public. The elevation is 1,500 feet.

Campsites, facilities: There are 33 sites for tents or RVs up to 31 feet long, including a few multi-sites, and three group camps that accommodate up to 35 people each. Picnic tables and fire grills are provided. Drinking water, vault toilets, garbage bins, and firewood are available. Leashed pets are permitted.

Reservations, fees: Reservations are accepted at 877/444-6777 ($10 reservation fee) or www.recreation.gov ($9 reservation fee). Single sites are $18 per night, double sites are $34 per night, $9 per extra vehicle per night, and group sites are $75-100 per night. Open mid-May-mid-September, weather permitting.

Directions: From Chehalis, drive south on I-5 for 10 miles to Exit 68 and U.S. 12. Turn east on U.S. 12 and drive 48 miles to Randle and Highway 131. Turn right (south) on Highway 131 and drive one mile to Forest Road 23. Bear left and drive 11 miles to the campground on the left.

Contact: Gifford Pinchot National Forest, Cowlitz Ranger District, 360/497-1100, www.fs.usda.gov or www.hoodoo.com.

59 BLUE LAKE CREEK

🥾 🚴 🛶 🐴 ♿ 🚙 ⛺

Scenic rating: 7

near Blue Lake in Gifford Pinchot National Forest

Map 5.2, page 302

This camp is set at an elevation of 1,900 feet along Blue Lake Creek. With access to a network of all-terrain vehicle (ATV) trails, it is a significant camp for ATV owners. There is nearby access to 16.7-mile Valley Trail. This camp is also near the launch point for the 3.5-mile hike to Blue Lake; the trailhead lies about a half mile from camp.

Campsites, facilities: There are 11 sites for tents or RVs up to 30 feet long. Picnic tables and fire rings are provided. Vault toilets and garbage bins are available. Drinking water is not always available, so bring your own. Firewood can be gathered outside of the campground area. A camp host is on-site. Some facilities are wheelchair accessible. Leashed pets are permitted.

Reservations, fees: Reservations are accepted at 877/444-6777 ($10 reservation fee) or www.recreation.gov ($9 reservation fee). Sites are $16 per night, $8 per extra vehicle per night. Open mid-May-mid-September, weather permitting.

Directions: From Chehalis, drive south on I-5 for 10 miles to Exit 68 and U.S. 12. Turn east on U.S. 12 and drive 48 miles to Randle and Highway 131. Turn right (south) on Highway 131 and drive one mile to Forest Road 23. Turn south and drive about 10 miles to the campground on the left.

Contact: Gifford Pinchot National Forest, Cowlitz Ranger District, 360/497-1100, www.fs.usda.gov or www.hoodoo.com.

 ADAMS FORK

🚶 🚴 🏊 🏕 🚐 ⛺

Scenic rating: 7

in Gifford Pinchot National Forest

Map 5.2, page 302

Adams Fork Campground is set at 2,600 feet elevation along the Upper Cispus River near Adams Creek and is popular with off-road vehicle (ORV) enthusiasts. There are many miles of trails designed for use by ORVs. A trail just 0.5 mile away leads north to Blue Lake, which is about a five-mile hike (one-way) from the camp. Most of the campsites are small, but a few are large enough for comfortable RV use. The area has many towering trees. The Cispus River provides trout fishing.

Campsites, facilities: There are 22 single sites and one double site for tents or RVs up to 22 feet long. A group camp accommodates 20-50 people. Picnic tables and fire grills are provided. Drinking water and vault toilets are available. Firewood may be gathered outside the campground area. Leashed pets are permitted.

Reservations, fees: Reservations are accepted at 877/444-6777 ($10 reservation fee) or www.recreation.gov ($9 reservation fee). Single sites are $16 per night, the double site is $30, the group site is $35-45 per night, $8 per extra vehicle per night. Open May-mid-September, weather permitting.

Directions: On I-5, drive to Exit 68 (south of Chehalis) and U.S. 12. Turn east on U.S. 12 and drive 48 miles to Randle and U.S. 131. Turn right (south) and drive one mile to Forest Road 23. Turn left (southeast) and drive 18 miles to Forest Road 21. Turn left (southeast) on Forest Road 21 and drive five miles to Forest Road 56. Turn right on Forest Road 56 and drive 200 yards to the campground on the left.

Contact: Gifford Pinchot National Forest, Cowlitz Valley Ranger District, 360/497-1100, www.fs.usda.gov or www.hoodoo.com.

61 OLALLIE LAKE

🚶 🚴 🏊 🎣 🏕 🐾 ♿ 🚐 ⛺

Scenic rating: 9

on Olallie Lake in Gifford Pinchot National Forest

Map 5.2, page 302

Located at an elevation of 4,200 feet, this campground lies on the shore of Olallie Lake, one of several small alpine lakes in the area fed by streams coming off the glaciers on nearby Mount Adams (elevation 12,276 feet). Trout fishing is good here in early summer. The campsites are situated close to the lake and feature gorgeous views of Mount Adams across the lake. Several of the campsites are small, and there is one larger area with room for RVs. A word to the wise: Mosquitoes can be a problem in the spring and early summer.

Campsites, facilities: There are eight single sites and one double site for tents or RVs up to 22 feet long. Picnic tables and fire rings are provided. Vault toilets are available, but there is no drinking water. Firewood may be gathered outside the campground area. Boat-launching facilities are nearby, but gasoline motors are prohibited on the lake. Some facilities are wheelchair accessible. Leashed pets are permitted.

Reservations, fees: Reservations are not accepted. Sites are $12 per night, $6 per night per additional vehicle. Open June-September, weather permitting.

Directions: From Chehalis, drive south on I-5 for 10 miles to Exit 68 and U.S. 12. Turn east on U.S. 12 and drive 48 miles to Randle and U.S. 131. Turn right (south) and drive one mile to Forest Road 23. Turn left (southeast) and drive 29 miles to Forest Road 2329. Turn left (northeast) and drive one mile to a junction with Forest Road 5601. Bear left and drive 0.5 mile to the campground on the right.

Contact: Gifford Pinchot National Forest, Cowlitz Valley Ranger District, 360/497-1100, www.fs.usda.gov or www.hoodoo.com.

62 TAKHLAKH LAKE

Scenic rating: 9

on Takhlakh Lake in Gifford Pinchot National Forest

Map 5.2, page 302

This campground is situated along the shore of Takhlakh Lake—one of five lakes in the area, all accessible by car. It's a beautiful place, set at 4,500 feet elevation, but, alas, mosquitoes abound until late July. A viewing area (Mount Adams is visible across the lake) is available for visitors, while the more ambitious can go berry picking, fishing, and hiking. This lake is much better than nearby Horseshoe Lake, and the fishing is much better, especially for trout early in the season. The Takhlakh Meadow Loop Trail, a barrier-free trail, provides a 1.5-mile hike. This is a very remote area, so don't expect cell service.

Campsites, facilities: There are 54 sites for tents or RVs up to 40 feet long. Picnic tables are provided. Vault toilets and garbage bins are available. There is no drinking water. Firewood may be gathered outside the campground area. A camp host is on-site. Boat-launching facilities are available in the day-use area, but gasoline motors are prohibited on the lake. Some facilities are wheelchair accessible. Leashed pets are permitted.

Reservations, fees: Reservations are accepted at 877/444-6777 ($10 reservation fee) or www.recreation.gov ($9 reservation fee). Single sites are $18 per night, double sites are $30 per night, $9 per night for each additional vehicle. Open mid-June-late September, weather permitting.

Directions: From Chehalis, drive south on I-5 for 10 miles to Exit 68 and U.S. 12. Turn east on U.S. 12 and drive 48 miles to Randle and U.S. 131. Turn right (south) and drive one mile to Forest Road 23. Turn left (southeast) and drive 29 miles to Forest Road 2329. Turn left (northeast) and drive 1.5 miles to the campground entrance road on the right.

Contact: Gifford Pinchot National Forest, Cowlitz Valley Ranger District, 360/497-1100, www.fs.usda.gov or www.hoodoo.com.

63 CAT CREEK

Scenic rating: 5

in Gifford Pinchot National Forest

Map 5.2, page 302

This small, rustic camp is set along Cat Creek at its confluence with the Cispus River, about 10 miles from the summit of Mount Adams. The camp, which features a forested setting, gets a lot of all-terrain vehicle (ATV) use. A trail starts less than one mile from camp and leads up along Blue Lake Ridge to Blue Lake. The area has many towering trees and the Cispus River provides trout fishing.

Campsites, facilities: There are five undefined sites for tents or RVs up to 15 feet long. Picnic tables and fire grills are provided. Vault toilets and firewood are available. There is no drinking water and garbage must be packed out. Firewood may be gathered outside the campground area. Some facilities are wheelchair accessible. Leashed pets are permitted.

Reservations, fees: Reservations are not accepted. There is no fee for camping. Open June-mid-September, weather permitting.

Directions: On I-5, drive to Exit 68 (south of Chehalis) and U.S. 12. Turn east on U.S. 12 and drive 48 miles to Randle and U.S. 131. Turn right (south) and drive one mile to Forest Road 23. Turn left (southeast) and drive 18 miles to Forest Road 21. Turn left (southeast) on Forest Road 21 and drive six miles to the campground on the right.

Contact: Gifford Pinchot National Forest, Cowlitz Valley Ranger District, 360/497-1100, www.fs.usda.gov.

64 HORSESHOE LAKE

Scenic rating: 9

on Horseshoe Lake in Gifford Pinchot National Forest

Map 5.2, page 302

This camp is set on the shore of picturesque, 10-acre Horseshoe Lake. The campsites are poorly defined, more like camping areas, though some are close to the lake. A trail runs partway around the lake and is open to mountain bikers and horseback riders (who occasionally come from a nearby camp). Fishing for trout is just fair in the lake, which is stocked infrequently. The water is too cold for swimming. A trail from the camp, about a three-mile round-trip, goes up to nearby Green Mountain (elevation 5,000 feet). This is a multi-use trail that ties into the High Lakes Trail system. Another trail heads up the north flank of Mount Adams. Berry picking is an option in the late summer months.

Campsites, facilities: There are 10 sites for tents or RVs up to 16 feet. Picnic tables and fire rings are provided. Vault toilets are available. There is no drinking water and garbage must be packed out. Firewood may be gathered outside the campground area. Primitive launching facilities are located on the lake, but gasoline motors are prohibited on the water. Leashed pets are permitted.

Reservations, fees: Reservations are not accepted. Sites are $12 per night, $6 per each additional vehicle. Open mid-June-late September, weather permitting.

Directions: From Chehalis, drive south on I-5 for 10 miles to Exit 68 and U.S. 12. Turn east on U.S. 12 and drive 48 miles to Randle and U.S. 131. Turn right (south) and drive one mile to Forest Road 23. Turn left (southeast) and drive 29 miles to Forest Road 2329. Turn left (northeast) and drive seven miles (bearing right at the junction with Forest Road 5601) to Forest Road 078. Turn left on Forest Road 078 and drive 1.5 miles to the campground on the left.

Contact: Gifford Pinchot National Forest,

Cowlitz Valley Ranger District, 360/497-1100, www.fs.usda.gov or www.hoodoo.com.

65 KEENE'S HORSE CAMP

Scenic rating: 7

in Gifford Pinchot National Forest

Map 5.2, page 302

This equestrians-only camp is set at 4,200 feet elevation along the South Fork of Spring Creek on the northwest flank of Mount Adams (elevation 12,276 feet). The Pacific Crest Trail passes within a couple miles of the camp. Several trails lead from here into the backcountry and to several alpine meadows. The meadows are fragile, so walk along their outer edges. Nearby Goat Rocks Wilderness has 50 miles of trails open to horses; other trails meander outside the wilderness boundary.

Campsites, facilities: There are 16 sites in two areas for tents or RVs up to 22 feet long. Picnic tables and fire grills are provided. Vault toilets, water troughs, a mounting ramp, manure bins, hitching facilities (high lines), and stock water are available. There is no drinking water. Firewood may be gathered outside the campground area. Some facilities are wheelchair accessible. Leashed pets are permitted.

Reservations, fees: Reservations are accepted at 877/444-6777 ($10 reservation fee) or www.recreation.gov ($9 reservation fee). Sites are $14 per night, $7 extra vehicle fee. Open mid-June-late September.

Directions: On I-5, drive to Exit 68 (south of Chehalis) and U.S. 12. Turn east on U.S. 12 and drive 48 miles to Randle and U.S. 131. Turn right (south) and drive one mile to Forest Road 23. Turn left (southeast) and drive 18 miles to Forest Road 21. Turn left (southeast) on Forest Road 21 and drive five miles to Forest Road 56. Turn right on Forest Road 56 and drive five miles to Forest Road 5603. Turn right and drive five miles to Forest Road 2329. Turn right and drive two miles to the camp on the right.

Contact: Gifford Pinchot National Forest,

Cowlitz Valley Ranger District, 360/497-1100, www.fs.usda.gov or www.hoodoo.com.

66 KILLEN CREEK

Scenic rating: 7

near Mount Adams in Gifford Pinchot National Forest

Map 5.2, page 302

This wilderness trailhead camp is ideal as a launch point for backpackers. The campground, set along Killen Creek at the foot of 12,276-foot Mount Adams, marks the start of a three-mile trail that leads up the mountain and connects with the Pacific Crest Trail. It's worth the effort. The Killen Trail goes up to secondary ridges and shoulders of Mount Adams for stunning views. Berry picking is a summertime option.

Campsites, facilities: There are nine sites for tents or RVs up to 22 feet long. Picnic tables and fire grills are provided. Vault toilets are available, but there is no drinking water. Garbage must be packed out. Firewood may be gathered outside the campground area. Leashed pets are permitted.

Reservations, fees: Reservations are not accepted. Sites are $12 per night, $6 extra vehicle fee. Open June-mid-September, weather permitting.

Directions: On I-5, drive to Exit 68 (south of Chehalis) and U.S. 12. Turn east on U.S. 12 and drive 48 miles to Randle and U.S. 131. Turn right (south) and drive one mile to Forest Road 23. Turn left (southeast) and drive 29 miles to Forest Road 2329. Turn left (northeast) and drive six miles to Forest Road 073. Turn left (west) and drive 200 yards to the campground.

Contact: Gifford Pinchot National Forest, Cowlitz Valley Ranger District, 360/497-1100, www.fs.usda.gov or www.hoodoo.com.

67 WALUPT LAKE

Scenic rating: 8

on Walupt Lake in Gifford Pinchot National Forest

Map 5.2, page 302

This popular spot, set at 3,900 feet elevation along the shore of Walupt Lake, is a good base camp for a multi-day vacation. The trout fishing is often good here; check regulations. But note that only small boats are advisable here because the launch area at the lake is shallow and it can take a four-wheel-drive vehicle to get a boat in and out. A small swimming beach is nearby. In addition, several nearby trails lead into the backcountry and to other smaller alpine lakes. One trail out of the campground leads to the upper end of the lake, then launches off to the Goat Rocks Wilderness; it's an outstanding hike, and the trail is also excellent for horseback rides.

Campsites, facilities: There are 34 sites for tents or RVs up to 22 feet long and 10 walk-in sites. Picnic tables are provided. Drinking water and vault toilets are available. Fire rings are located next to the campground. There is primitive boat access with a 10-mph speed limit; no waterskiing is allowed. Leashed pets are permitted.

Reservations, fees: Reservations are accepted at 877/444-6777 ($10 reservation fee) or www.recreation.gov ($9 reservation fee). Sites are $18-34 per night, $9 per night for each additional vehicle. Open mid-June-mid-September.

Directions: On I-5, drive to Exit 68 (south of Chehalis) and U.S. 12. Turn east on U.S. 12 and drive 62 miles to Forest Road 21 (2.5 miles southwest of Packwood). Turn right (southeast) and drive 20 miles to Forest Road 2160. Turn left (east) and drive 4.5 miles to the campground.

Note that floods in 2017 caused some road damage. Check with the ranger station for updates.

Contact: Gifford Pinchot National Forest,

Cowlitz Valley Ranger District, 360/497-1100, www.fs.usda.gov or www.hoodoo.com.

Cowlitz Valley Ranger District, 360/497-1100, www.fs.usda.gov or www.hoodoo.com.

68 WALUPT HORSE CAMP

Scenic rating: 7

near the Goat Rocks Wilderness in Gifford Pinchot National Forest

Map 5.2, page 302

This camp is for horse campers only and is set about one mile from Walupt Lake, which is good for trout fishing and has a 10-mph speed limit for boats. Several trails lead from the lake into the backcountry of the southern Goat Rocks Wilderness, which has 50 miles of trails that can be used by horses; other trails meander outside the wilderness boundary. If you have planned a multi-day horse-packing trip, bring in your own feed for the horses. (Feed must be pellets or processed grain and only certified "weed-seed-free" hay is allowed.)

Campsites, facilities: There are nine equestrian sites for tents or RVs up to 22 feet long. Picnic tables and fire grills are provided. Drinking water, vault toilets, and firewood are available. Garbage must be packed out. A horse ramp and high lines are available. Leashed pets are permitted.

Reservations, fees: Reservations are not accepted. Single sites are $16 per night, multi-sites are $30 per night, $8 extra vehicle fee. Open June-late September, weather permitting.

Directions: On I-5, drive to Exit 68 (south of Chehalis) and U.S. 12. Turn east on U.S. 12 and drive 62 miles to Forest Road 21 (2.5 miles southwest of Packwood). Turn right (southeast) and drive 20 miles to Forest Road 2160. Turn left (east) and drive 3.5 miles to the campground on the right.

Note that floods in 2017 caused some road damage. Check with the ranger station for updates.

Contact: Gifford Pinchot National Forest,

69 CLOVER FLATS

Scenic rating: 8

near the Goat Rocks Wilderness

Map 5.2, page 302

Clover Flats Campground is located in the subalpine zone on the slope of Darland Mountain, which peaks at 6,982 feet. Trails connect the area with the Goat Rocks Wilderness, six miles to the west. This is a popular area for winter sports.

Campsites, facilities: There are nine sites for tents or RVs up to 24 feet. Picnic tables, fire grills, and tent pads are provided. Vault toilets and drinking water are available. Garbage must be packed out. Some facilities are wheelchair accessible. Leashed pets are permitted.

Reservations, fees: Reservations are not accepted. There is no fee for camping, but a Discover Pass is required. Open year-round, weather permitting; snow limits access except mid-July-October.

Directions: From Yakima, drive south on I-82 for two miles to the Union Gap exit. Take that exit and turn right on East Valley Mall Road. Drive one mile to 3rd Avenue. Turn left and drive 0.25 mile to Ahtanum Road. Turn right (west) and drive 20 miles to Tampico and Road A-3000 (North Fork Road). Turn right (west) and drive 9.5 miles to the Ahtanum Camp. Continue to a junction with A-2000 (Middle Fork Road). Bear left and drive nine miles to the camp on the left. Note: The last few miles of Road A-2000 are very steep and unpaved, with a 12 percent grade. Only high-clearance vehicles are recommended.

Contact: Department of Natural Resources, Southeast Region, 509/925-8510, www.dnr.wa.gov.

70 TREE PHONES
[icons]

Scenic rating: 7

on the Middle Fork of Ahtanum Creek

Map 5.2, page 302

Forested Tree Phones Campground is set along the Middle Fork of Ahtanum Creek at an elevation of 4,800 feet. It is close to hiking, motorbiking, and horseback-riding trails. A shelter with a wood stove is available year-round for picnics. During summer, there are beautiful wildflower displays.

Campsites, facilities: There are 12 sites for tents or RVs up to 40 feet. Picnic tables, fire grills, and tent pads are provided. Drinking water and vault toilets are available. A 20- by 40-foot snow shelter and hitching rails are also available. Stock are not permitted to drink from the creek. Some facilities are wheelchair accessible. Leashed pets are permitted.

Reservations, fees: Reservations are not accepted. There is no fee for camping, but a Discover Pass is required. Open year-round, weather permitting (heavy snows are expected late November-March).

Directions: From Yakima, drive south on I-82 for two miles to the Union Gap exit. Take that exit and turn right on East Valley Mall Road. Drive one mile to 3rd Avenue. Turn left and drive 0.25 mile to Ahtanum Road. Turn right (west) and drive 20 miles to Tampico and Road A-3000 (North Fork Road). Turn right (west) and drive 9.5 miles to the Ahtanum Camp. Continue to a junction with A-2000 (Middle Fork Road). Bear left and drive six miles to the camp. Note: Only high-clearance vehicles are recommended.

Contact: Department of Natural Resources, Southeast Region, 509/925-8510, www.dnr.wa.gov.

71 GREEN RIVER HORSE CAMP
[icons]

Scenic rating: 8

in Gifford Pinchot National Forest

Map 5.2, page 302

This premier equestrians-only horse camp is set on the Green River near an area of beautiful, old-growth timber. The campsites, however, are in a reforested clear-cut area with trees about 25-40 feet tall. The camp features access to great trails into the Mount St. Helens blast area. The lookout from Windy Ridge is one of the most drop-dead awesome views in North America, spanning Spirit Lake, the blast zone, and the open crater of Mount St. Helens. The campground features high lines at each site, and the access is designed for easy turning and parking with horse trailers.

Campsites, facilities: There are eight sites that can accommodate up to two trailer rigs or three vehicles each. Picnic tables, fire grills, and high lines are provided. Vault toilets are available. No drinking water is provided, but it is available five miles north at Norway Pass Trailhead. Stock water must be hand-carried from the river; however, new facilities are currently under construction. Garbage must be packed out. Some facilities are wheelchair accessible. Leashed pets are permitted.

Reservations, fees: Reservations are not accepted. There is no fee for camping. Open mid-May-November, weather permitting.

Directions: From Chehalis, drive south on I-5 for 10 miles to Exit 68 and U.S. 12. Turn east on U.S. 12 and drive 48 miles to Randle and Highway 131. Turn right (south) and drive one mile (becomes Forest Road 25). Continue south and drive 19 miles to Forest Road 99. Turn right (west, toward Windy Ridge) and drive 8.5 miles to Forest Road 26. Turn right (north) and drive five miles to Forest Road 2612 (gravel). Turn left (west) and drive about two miles to the campground entrance on the left.

Note that winter storm damage led to a

temporary closure of the access road. Check with the ranger station for updates.

Contact: Gifford Pinchot National Forest, Mount Adams Ranger District, 509/395-3402, www.fs.usda.gov.

72 LEWIS RIVER HORSE CAMP

Scenic rating: 7

in Gifford Pinchot National Forest

Map 5.2, page 302

During summer, this camp caters to equestrians only. The camp is not particularly scenic, but the area around it is: There are six waterfalls nearby on the Lewis River. There are also many trails, all of which are open to mountain bikers and some to motorcycles. The spectacular Lewis River Trail is available for hiking, mountain biking, or horseback riding, and there is a wheelchair-accessible loop. Several other hiking trails in the area branch off along backcountry streams.

Campsites, facilities: There are nine sites for tents or RVs up to 35 feet long. Picnic tables and fire rings are provided. A composting toilet is available. There is no drinking water and garbage must be packed out. Horse facilities include high lines, mounting ramp, stock water, and three corrals. Some facilities are wheelchair accessible. Leashed pets are permitted.

Reservations, fees: Reservations are not accepted. Sites are $5 per night. Open May-November, weather permitting.

Directions: From Woodland on I-5, take Exit 21 for Highway 503. Drive east on Highway 503 for 23 miles to the Highway 503 spur. Drive northeast on the Highway 503 spur road for seven miles (becomes Forest Road 90). Continue east on Forest Road 90 for 33 miles to Forest Road 93. Turn left and drive a short distance to the campground (along the Lewis River) on the right.

Contact: Gifford Pinchot National Forest,

Mount Adams Ranger District, 509/395-3402, www.fs.usda.gov.

73 LOWER FALLS

Scenic rating: 10

in Gifford Pinchot National Forest

Map 5.2, page 302   BEST (

This camp is set at 1,400 feet elevation in the primary viewing area for six major waterfalls on the Lewis River. The spectacular Lewis River Trail is available for hiking or horseback riding, and it features a wheelchair-accessible loop. Several other hiking trails in the area branch off along backcountry streams. The sites are paved and set among large fir trees on gently sloping ground; access roads were designed for easy RV parking. Note that above the falls, the calm water in the river looks safe, but it is not! Stay out. In addition, the Lewis River Trail goes along cliffs, providing beautiful views but potentially dangerous hiking.

Campsites, facilities: There are 42 sites for tents or RVs up to 60 feet long and two group sites for up to 20 people each. Picnic tables and fire grills are provided. Drinking water and composting toilets are available. Some facilities are wheelchair accessible. Leashed pets are permitted.

Reservations, fees: Reservations are accepted at 877/444-6777 ($10 reservation fee) or www.recreation.gov ($9 reservation fee). Single sites are $15 per night, double sites are $30 per night, $5 per extra vehicle per night. Group sites are $35 per night. Open May-November, weather permitting.

Directions: From Woodland on I-5, take Exit 21 for Highway 503. Drive east on Highway 503 for 23 miles to the Highway 503 spur. Drive northeast on the Highway 503 spur for seven miles (becomes Forest Road 90). Continue east on Forest Road 90 for 30 miles to the campground (along the Lewis River) on the right.

Contact: Gifford Pinchot National Forest,

Mount Adams Ranger District, 509/395-3402, www.fs.usda.gov.

74 TILLICUM

🏃 🚵 🏊 ⛵ 🏠 🐕 ♿ 🚐 ⛺

Scenic rating: 8

near Meadow Lake in Gifford Pinchot National Forest

Map 5.2, page 302

This pretty camp is primitive but well forested, and within walking distance of several recreation options. A 4.5-mile trail from the camp leads southwest past little Meadow Lake to Squaw Butte, then over to Big Creek. It's a nice hike, as well as an excellent ride for mountain bikers. This is a premium area for picking huckleberries in August and early September. The Lone Butte area about five miles to the south provides a side trip. There are two lakes nearby, Big and Little Mosquito Lakes, which are fed by Mosquito Creek. While we're on the subject, mosquito attacks in late spring and early summer can be like squadrons of World War II bombers moving in. The Pacific Crest Trail passes right by camp.

Campsites, facilities: There are 24 sites for tents or RVs up to 18 feet long. Picnic tables and fire grills are provided. A vault toilet and garbage service are available. There is no drinking water. Some facilities are wheelchair accessible. Leashed pets are permitted.

Reservations, fees: Reservations are not accepted. Sites are $5 per night. Open June-late September, weather permitting.

Directions: From Vancouver, Washington, on I-205, take Highway 14 and drive east for 66 miles to Highway 141. Turn left (north) on Highway 141 and drive 25 miles to Trout Lake and County Road 141 (Forest Road 24). Turn left (west) and drive two miles to a fork. Bear left at the fork and drive 20 miles (becomes Forest Road 24) to the campground on the left.

Contact: Gifford Pinchot National Forest, Mount Adams Ranger District, 509/395-3402, www.fs.usda.gov.

75 MORRISON CREEK

🏃 🏠 ♿ 🏠

Scenic rating: 7

in Gifford Pinchot National Forest

Map 5.2, page 302

Here's a prime yet little-known spot. This camp is located along Morrison Creek at an elevation of 4,600 feet, near the southern slopes of 12,276-foot Mount Adams. The area is still recovering from a severe fire in 2012 and there is not much shade. Nearby trails will take you to the snowfields and alpine meadows of the Mount Adams Wilderness. In particular, the Shorthorn Trail is accessible from this campground.

Campsites, facilities: There are 12 sites for tents only. Picnic tables and fire rings are provided in some sites. Vault toilets are available, but there is no drinking water. Garbage must be packed out. Some facilities are wheelchair accessible. Leashed pets are permitted.

Reservations, fees: Reservations are not accepted. There is no fee for camping. Open late June-late September, weather permitting.

Directions: From White Salmon, take Grangeview Loop Road to W. Jewett Boulevard/WA-141. Turn right on WA-141 and drive 21.4 miles to the campground.

Alternately, from Hood River, Oregon, drive north on Highway 35 (over the Columbia River) to Highway 14. Turn left and drive two miles to Highway 141-A. Turn right (north) on Highway 141-A and drive 20 miles to County Road 17 (just 200 yards east of the town of Trout Lake). Turn right (north) and drive two miles to Forest Road 80. Turn right (north) and drive 3.5 miles to Forest Road 8040. Bear left (north) and drive six miles to the campground on the left.

Note: The access road is rough and is not recommended for RVs, motor homes, or trailers.

Contact: Gifford Pinchot National Forest, Mount Adams Ranger District, 509/395-3400, www.fs.usda.gov.

76 ISLAND CAMP

Scenic rating: 8

on Bird Creek

Map 5.2, page 302

Island Campground sits in a forested area along Bird Creek and is close to lava tubes and blowholes. A strange one-foot-wide slit in the ground (too small to climb into and explore) can be reached by walking about 0.75 mile. Bird Creek provides a chance to fish for brook trout in late spring. In the winter, the roads are used for snowmobiling. A snowmobile shelter with a wood stove is available year-round for picnics.

Campsites, facilities: There are six sites for tents or RVs up to 16 feet. Picnic tables, fire grills, and tent pads are provided. Vault toilets are available, but there is no drinking water. Garbage must be packed out. Some facilities are wheelchair accessible. Leashed pets are permitted.

Reservations, fees: Reservations are not accepted. There is no fee for camping, but a Discover Pass is required. Open May-October, with limited winter access.

Directions: From Yakima, drive south on I-82 for 15 miles to U.S. 97. Turn south and drive 49 miles to Goldendale and Highway 142. Turn right (west) and drive 10 miles to Counts Road. Turn right (northwest) and drive 26 miles to Glenwood; continue for 0.25 mile to Bird Creek Road. Turn right and drive 0.9 mile to K-3000 Road (still Bird Creek Road). Turn left, drive over the cattle guard, and drive 1.2 miles to Road S-4000. Turn right and drive 1.3 miles to Road K-4000. Turn left and drive 3.4 miles to Road K-4200. Turn left and drive 1.1 miles to the campground entrance on the left. Turn left and drive 0.25 mile to the campground.

Contact: Department of Natural Resources, Southeast Region, 509/925-8510, www.dnr.wa.gov.

77 BIRD CREEK

Scenic rating: 7

near the Mount Adams Wilderness

Map 5.2, page 302

Bird Creek Campground is set in a forested area of old-growth Douglas fir and ponderosa pine along Bird Creek. This spot lies just east of the Mount Adams Wilderness and is one of two camps in the immediate area. (The other, Island Camp, is within three miles. It is also a primitive site, but it features snowmobile trails.)

Campsites, facilities: There are 12 sites for tents or RVs up to 22 feet and one group camp for tents or RVs up to 35 feet that can accommodate up to 25 people. Picnic tables, fire grills, and tent pads are provided. Pit and vault toilets are available, but there is no drinking water. Garbage must be packed out. Some facilities are wheelchair accessible. Leashed pets are permitted.

Reservations, fees: Reservations are not accepted. There is no fee for camping, but a Discover Pass is required. Open May-mid-October, weather permitting.

Directions: From Yakima, drive south on I-82 for 15 miles to U.S. 97. Turn south and drive 49 miles to Goldendale and Highway 142. Turn right (west) and drive 10 miles to Counts Road. Turn right (northwest) and drive 26 miles to Glenwood. From the post office in Glenwood, continue 0.25 mile to Bird Creek Road. Turn right and drive 0.9 mile. Turn left (still Bird Creek Road), cross the cattle guard to Road K-3000, and drive 1.2 miles to Road S-4000 (gravel). Turn right and drive 1.3 miles to Road K-4000. Turn left and drive two miles to the campground on the left.

Contact: Department of Natural Resources, Southeast Region, 509/925-8510, www.dnr.wa.gov.

78 CAMP KALAMA RV PARK AND CAMPGROUND

Scenic rating: 6

on the Kalama River

Map 5.3, page 303

This campground has a rustic setting, with open and wooded areas and some accommodations for tent campers. It's set along the Kalama River, where salmon and steelhead fishing is popular. A full-service marina is nearby. Note that some sites are filled with monthly renters.

Campsites, facilities: There are 118 sites with full or partial hookups (20, 30, and 50 amps) for RVs of any length and 50 sites for tents. Some sites are pull-through. Picnic tables and fire pits are provided. Restrooms with flush toilets and coin showers, drinking water, cable TV, Wi-Fi, propane gas, two dump stations, general store, café, banquet room, firewood, coin laundry, ice, boat-launching facilities, a beach area, and a playground are available. Some facilities are wheelchair accessible. Leashed pets are permitted.

Reservations, fees: Reservations are accepted. RV sites are $36 per night, tent sites are $23 per night, $2.50 per person per night for more than two adults, $5 per night per extra vehicle, and $1 per pet per night. Weekly and monthly rates are available. Some credit cards are accepted. Open year-round.

Directions: From the north end of Kalama (between Kelso and Woodland) on I-5, take Exit 32 and drive south on the frontage road for one block to the campground.

Contact: Camp Kalama RV Park and Campground, 360/673-2456 or 800/750-2456, www.kalama.com/~campkalama.

79 COLUMBIA RIVERFRONT RV PARK

Scenic rating: 8

near Portland

Map 5.3, page 303

Columbia Riverfront RV Park is located directly on the Columbia River, north of Portland. That means it is away from freeway noise, airports, and train tracks. Quiet? Oh yeah. The park encompasses 10 acres and boasts 900 feet of sandy beach, perfect for fishing for steelhead or salmon and beachcombing.

Campsites, facilities: There are 76 sites with full hookups for RVs up to 78 feet; some sites are pull-through. Picnic tables are provided, but only beach sites have fire rings. Drinking water, restrooms with flush toilets and coin showers, a park store (with groceries, propane, and ice), horseshoe pits, Wi-Fi, cable TV, coin laundry, swimming pool (seasonal), and a playground are available. Some facilities are wheelchair accessible. Leashed pets are permitted, with breed restrictions.

Reservations, fees: Reservations are recommended. Sites are $48-61 per night.

Directions: From I-5 in Woodland, take Exit 22 and turn south onto Dike Access Road. Drive two miles on Dike Access Road to the T intersection and turn left onto Dike Road. Drive one mile on Dike Road to the campground on the right.

Contact: Columbia Riverfront RV Park, 360/225-2227 or 800/845-9842, www.columbiariverfrontrvpark.com.

80 PARADISE POINT STATE PARK

Scenic rating: 8

on the East Fork of the Lewis River

Map 5.3, page 303

Paradise Point is named for the serenity that once blessed this area. Alas, it has lost much of that peacefulness since the freeway went in next to the park. To reduce traffic noise, stay at one of the wooded sites in the small apple orchard; the sites in the grassy areas have little noise buffer. This park covers 88 acres and features 1,680 feet of river frontage. The two-mile hiking trail is good for families and children. Note that the dirt boat ramp is primitive and nonfunctional when the water level drops; it is recommended for car-top boats only. Fishing on the East Fork of the Lewis River is a bonus.

Campsites, facilities: There are 58 sites for tents or RVs up to 50 feet long (no hookups), 18 sites with partial hookups (30 and 50 amps) for tents or RVs up to 40 feet long, nine hike-in/bike-in sites, and two yurts. Picnic tables and fire grills are provided. Restrooms with flush toilets and coin showers, drinking water, a dump station, firewood, an amphitheater, and summer interpretive programs are available. A primitive, dirt boat-launching area is located nearby on the East Fork Lewis River. Some facilities are wheelchair accessible. Leashed pets are permitted.

Reservations, fees: Reservations are accepted at 888/226-7688 or https://washington. goingtocamp.com ($8-10 reservation fee). Sites are $20-45 per night, hike-in/bike-in sites are $12 per night, $10 per extra vehicle per night, yurts are $45-59 per night. Some credit cards are accepted. Open year-round, with some sites closed October-April.

Directions: From Vancouver, Washington, drive north on I-5 for 15 miles to Exit 16 (La Center/Paradise Point State Park exit). Take that exit and turn right. Almost immediately at Paradise Park Road, turn left and drive one mile to the park.

Contact: Paradise Point State Park, 360/263-2350; state park information, 360/902-8844, http://parks.state.wa.us.

81 BATTLE GROUND LAKE STATE PARK

Scenic rating: 8

on Battle Ground Lake

Map 5.3, page 303

The centerpiece of this state park is Battle Ground Lake, a spring-fed lake that is stocked with trout but popular for bass and catfish fishing as well. Underground lava tubes feed water into the lake, which is similar to Crater Lake in Oregon, though smaller. The park covers 280 acres, primarily forested with conifers, in the foothills of the Cascade Mountains. There are 10 miles of hiking trails, including a trail around the lake, and an additional five miles of trails open to horses and bikes; a primitive equestrian camp is also available. The lake is good for swimming and fishing, and it has a nice beach area; boats with gas motors are not allowed. If you're traveling on I-5 and looking for a layover, this camp, just 15 minutes from the highway, is ideal. In July and August, the area hosts several fairs and celebrations. Like many of the easy-access state parks on I-5, this one fills up quickly on weekends.

Campsites, facilities: There are 25 sites for tents or RVs up to 35 feet long (no hookups), six sites with partial hookups (50 amps) for RVs, 15 primitive hike-in sites, one group site for 25-32 people, a horse camp for 10-16 people, and four cabins. Picnic tables and fire grills are provided. Restrooms with flush toilets and coin showers, drinking water, a dump station, a store, firewood, a seasonal snack bar, sheltered picnic area, amphitheater, summer interpretive programs, a playground, horseshoe pits, and an athletic field are available. Boat-launching facilities and rentals are nearby. Carts are provided to tote your gear the 0.25-0.5 mile to the primitive sites. Some facilities are wheelchair accessible. Leashed pets are permitted.

Reservations, fees: Reservations are accepted at 888/226-7688 or https://washington.goingtocamp.com ($8-10 reservation fee). Sites are $20-45 per night, hike-in sites are $12 per night,

$10 per night per extra vehicle, cabins are $45-79 per night. Some credit cards are accepted. Open year-round.

Directions: From I-5 southbound, take Exit 11; from I-5 northbound, take Exit 9. Drive to the city of Battle Ground (well marked); continue to the east end of town to Grace Avenue. Turn left on NE Grace Avenue and drive three miles (a marked route) to the park.

Contact: Battle Ground Lake State Park, 360/687-4621; state park information, 360/902-8844, http://parks.state.wa.us.

82 SUNSET FALLS

Scenic rating: 9

in Gifford Pinchot National Forest

Map 5.3, page 303

This campground is located at an elevation of 1,000 feet along the East Fork of the Lewis River. Fishing, hiking, and huckleberry and mushroom picking are some of the favored pursuits of visitors. Scenic Sunset Falls is located just upstream of the campground. A barrier-free viewing trail leads to an overlook.

Campsites, facilities: There are 18 sites for tents or RVs up to 22 feet long. Picnic tables and fire grills are provided. Vault toilets and garbage service are available. There is no drinking water. Some facilities are wheelchair accessible. Leashed pets are permitted.

Reservations, fees: Reservations are accepted at 877/444-6777 ($10 reservation fee) or www.recreation.gov ($9 reservation fee). Sites are $12 per night, $6 per extra vehicle per night. Open year-round.

Directions: From Vancouver, Washington, drive north on I-5 about seven miles to County Road 502. Turn east on Highway 502 and drive six miles to Highway 503. Turn left and drive north for five miles to Lucia Falls Road. Turn right and drive eight miles to Moulton Falls and Old County Road 12. Turn right on Old County Road 12 and drive seven miles to the National Forest boundary and the campground entrance on the right.

Contact: Gifford Pinchot National Forest, Mount Adams Ranger District, 509/395-3402, www.fs.usda.gov.

83 COLD CREEK CAMP

Scenic rating: 6

on Cedar Creek

Map 5.3, page 303

The late Waylon Jennings once told me that few things worth remembering come easy, right? Well, sometimes. First, don't expect to find a "cold creek" here. There just is no such thing. And second, the directions are complicated. This campground is set in a forested area with plenty of trails nearby for hiking and horseback riding. The camp gets minimal use. A large shelter is available at the day-use area.

Campsites, facilities: There are eight sites for tents or RVs up to 20 feet long, including one group camp for up to six people. Picnic tables, fire grills, and tent pads are provided. Vault toilets are available. There is no drinking water, and garbage must be packed out. A camp host is on-site. Some facilities are wheelchair accessible. Leashed pets are permitted.

Reservations, fees: Reservations are accepted at 360/577-2025. There is no fee for camping, but a Discover Pass is required. Open year-round with a seven-day stay limit, weather permitting.

Directions: From Vancouver, Washington, drive north on I-5 to Exit 9 and NE 179th Street. Turn east and drive 5.5 miles to Highway 503. Turn right and drive 1.5 miles to NE 159th Street. Turn left on NE 159th Street and drive three miles to 182nd Avenue. Turn right and drive one mile to NE 139th. Turn left and drive eight miles (becomes Rawson, then Road L-1400) to Road L-1000. Turn left and drive four miles to the campground entrance road. Turn left, past the yellow gate, and drive one mile to the camp.

Contact: Department of Natural Resources, Pacific Cascade Region South, 360/577-2025, www.dnr.wa.gov.

84 ROCK CREEK CAMPGROUND AND HORSE CAMP

Scenic rating: 6

on Rock Creek

Map 5.3, page 303

This camp is located in a wooded area along Rock Creek. It is popular among equestrians and mountain bikers, especially on weekends, because of the Tarbell Trail, a 25-mile loop trail that is accessible from the campground and goes to the top of Larch Mountain (this road becomes Rawson, then L-1400).

Campsites, facilities: There are 19 sites for tents or RVs up to 20 feet long. Picnic tables, fire grills, and tent pads are provided. Vault toilets, a horse-loading ramp, stock water, and corrals are available. There is no drinking water, and garbage must be packed out. There is a camp host on-site. Some facilities are wheelchair accessible. Leashed pets are permitted.

Reservations, fees: Reservations are not accepted. There is no fee for camping, but a Discover Pass is required. Open year-round with a seven-day limit, weather permitting.

Directions: From Vancouver, Washington, drive north on I-5 to Exit 9 and NE 179th Street. Turn east and drive 5.5 miles to Highway 503. Turn right and drive 1.5 miles to NE 159th Street. Turn left on NE 159th Street and drive three miles to 182nd Avenue. Turn right and drive one mile to NE 139th (Road L-1400). Turn left and drive eight miles (road becomes Rawson, then L-1400) to Road L-1000. Turn left and drive 4.5 miles (passing Cold Creek Campground after three miles) to Road L-1200/Dole Valley Road. Turn left and drive 200 yards to the campground on your right.

Contact: Department of Natural Resources, Pacific Cascade Region South, 360/577-2025, www.dnr.wa.gov.

85 REED ISLAND BOAT-IN

Scenic rating: 10

on Reed Island

Map 5.3, page 303

Where else can you have your own personal island? Only in Washington, that's where. Reachable only by boat, this 510-acre marine park is part of the Columbia River Water Trail. Activities include boating, bird-watching, and picnicking, and there is a heron rookery on the southwest side of the island.

Campsites, facilities: There are two primitive sites for tents only. Picnic tables and pedestal stoves are provided. There is no drinking water or toilets. Garbage must be packed out. Leashed pets are permitted.

Reservations, fees: Reservations are not accepted. Sites are $12 per night. Open year-round.

Directions: From the Port of Camas, head east on the Columbia River for approximately three miles. Signs on the southwest end of the island indicate where the campsites are located.

Contact: Reed Island State Park, 360/902-8844, http://parks.state.wa.us.

86 DOUGAN CREEK

Scenic rating: 7

near the Washougal River

Map 5.3, page 303

This small, remote campground is located on Dougan Creek, where it empties into the Washougal River. Heavily forested with second-growth Douglas fir, it features pretty sites with river views.

Campsites, facilities: There are seven sites for tents or RVs up to 20 feet long. Picnic tables, fire grills, and tent pads are provided. Vault toilets are available. There is no drinking water, and garbage must be packed out. Some facilities are wheelchair accessible. Leashed pets are permitted.

Reservations, fees: Reservations are not accepted. There is no fee for camping, but a Discover Pass is required. Open year-round, weather permitting.

Directions: From Vancouver, Washington, on I-205, take Highway 14 and drive east for 20 miles to Highway 140. Turn north on Highway 140 and drive five miles to Washougal River Road. Turn right on Washougal River Road and drive about seven miles until you come to the end of the pavement and pass the picnic area on the left. The campground is 0.25 mile beyond the picnic area.

Contact: Department of Natural Resources, Pacific Cascade Region South, 360/577-2025, www.dnr.wa.gov.

87 BEACON ROCK STATE PARK

Scenic rating: 8
in Columbia River Gorge National Scenic Area

Map 5.3, page 303   BEST (

This state park features Beacon Rock, the second-largest monolith in the world, which overlooks the Columbia River Gorge. Lewis and Clark gave Beacon Rock its name on their expedition to the Pacific Ocean in 1805. The Beacon Rock Summit Trail, a 1.8-mile round-trip hike, provides excellent views of the gorge. Beacon Rock State Park covers nearly 5,000 acres and includes 9,500 feet of shoreline along the Columbia River and more than 22 miles of nearby trails open for hiking, mountain biking, and horseback riding. An eight-mile loop trail to Hamilton Mountain (2,300 feet elevation) is one of the best hikes, featuring even better views than from Beacon Rock. Rock climbing is excellent here, with the climbing season running mid-July-January. Fishing for sturgeon, salmon, steelhead, smallmouth bass (often

excellent), and walleye is available in season on the Lower Columbia River below Bonneville Dam; check regulations.

Campsites, facilities: There are 26 sites for tents or small RVs (no hookups), five sites with full hookups (30 amps) for RVs up to 40 feet, two equestrian sites with high line, and one group site for up to 200 people. Picnic tables and fire grills are provided. Restrooms with flush toilets and coin showers, drinking water, picnic areas, and a playground are available. Boat docks and launching facilities, moorage, and boat pumpout are also available. Some facilities are wheelchair accessible. Leashed pets are permitted.

Reservations, fees: Reservations are not accepted for family sites but are required for the group camp at 888/226-7688 or https://washington.goingtocamp.com ($8-10 reservation fee). Sites are $20-45 per night, equestrian sites are $12 per night, $10 per night per extra vehicle. The group site is $140 per night (30-person minimum). The boat launch fee is $7, with daily mooring $0.70 per foot ($15 minimum). Open April-October, with two sites available year-round.

Directions: From Vancouver, Washington, take Highway 14 and drive east for 35 miles. The park straddles the highway; follow the signs to the campground.

Contact: Beacon Rock State Park, 509/427-8265; state park information, 360/902-8844, http://parks.state.wa.us.

88 CULTUS CREEK

Scenic rating: 7
in Gifford Pinchot National Forest

Map 5.4, page 304

This camp is set at an elevation of 4,000 feet along Cultus Creek on the edge of the Indian Heaven Wilderness. Situated amid gentle terrain, the sites are graveled and level. The camp is popular during the fall huckleberry season, when picking is good, but gets light use the rest of the year. Nearby trails lead into the back-country, which has numerous small meadows and lakes among old-growth stands of fir and pine. Horse trails are available as well. Access to the Pacific Crest Trail requires a two-mile climb.

Campsites, facilities: There are 50 sites for tents or RVs up to 32 feet long. Picnic tables and fire grills are provided. Vault toilets and fire-wood are available. There is no drinking water, and garbage must be packed out. Some facilities are wheelchair accessible. Leashed pets are permitted.

Reservations, fees: Reservations are not accepted. Sites are $10-20 per night, $5 per night per additional vehicle. Open late June-late September, weather permitting.

Directions: From Vancouver, Washington, on I-205, take Highway 14 east and drive 66 miles to State Route 141-A. Turn left (north) on State Route 141-A and drive 28 miles (becomes Forest Road 24); continue two miles to a junction. Turn right (staying on Forest Road 24) and drive 13.5 miles to the campground.

Contact: Gifford Pinchot National Forest, Mount Adams Ranger District, 509/395-3400, www.fs.fed.us.

89 LITTLE GOOSE HORSE CAMP

Scenic rating: 5
in Gifford Pinchot National Forest

Map 5.4, page 304

Located near Little Goose Creek (between Smokey Creek and Cultus Creek Campgrounds), this camp has sites ranging from good to poor and is lightly used in fall. Note that the access road is paved but rough and not recommended for RVs or trailers; campers with horse trailers must drive slowly. (The camp sits close to the road and is sometimes dusty.) Several trails lead out from the campground. Huckleberry picking is quite

good in August and early September. The elevation is 4,000 feet.

Campsites, facilities: There are eight sites for tents or RVs up to 24 feet long and three sites for campers with stock animals. Picnic tables and fire grills are provided. Vault toilets are available. There is no drinking water and garbage must be packed out. Leashed pets are permitted.

Reservations, fees: Reservations are not accepted. There is no fee for camping. Open late June-late September, weather permitting.

Directions: From Vancouver, Washington, on I-205, take Highway 14 east and drive 66 miles to State Route 141-A. Turn left (north) on State Route 141-A and drive 28 miles (becomes Forest Road 24); continue two miles to a junction. Turn right (staying on Forest Road 24) and drive eight miles (one mile past Smokey Creek) to the campground.

Contact: Gifford Pinchot National Forest, Mount Adams Ranger District, 509/395-3400, www.fs.usda.gov.

90 SMOKEY CREEK

Scenic rating: 7
in Gifford Pinchot National Forest

Map 5.4, page 304

This primitive, little-used campground is set in an area of old-growth Douglas fir along Smokey Creek. A trail leading into the Indian Heaven Wilderness passes near the camp. Berry picking can be good here in summer and early fall. The elevation is 3,700 feet.

Campsites, facilities: There are three sites for tents only. Picnic tables and fire rings are provided. Pit toilets are available. There is no drinking water, and garbage must be packed out. Leashed pets are permitted.

Reservations, fees: Reservations are not accepted. There is no fee for camping. Open July-late September, weather permitting.

Directions: From Vancouver, Washington, on I-205, take Highway 14 east and drive 66 miles to State Route 141-A. Turn left (north) on State Route 141-A and drive 28 miles (becomes Forest Road 24); continue two miles to a junction. Turn right (staying on Forest Road 24) and drive seven miles to the campground.

Contact: Gifford Pinchot National Forest, Mount Adams Ranger District, 509/395-3400, www.fs.usda.gov.

91 PETERSON PRAIRIE AND GROUP

🏃 ❄ 🏕 🚐 ⛰

Scenic rating: 8

in Gifford Pinchot National Forest

Map 5.4, page 304

Here's a good base camp if you want a short ride to town as well as access to the nearby wilderness areas. Peterson Prairie is a prime spot for huckleberry picking in the fall. A trail from the camp leads about one mile to nearby ice caves; a stairway into the caves provides access to a variety of ice formations. An area Sno-Park with snowmobiling and cross-country skiing trails is open for winter recreation. The elevation is 2,800 feet.

Campsites, facilities: There are 21 single sites and six double sites for tents or RVs up to 32 feet long and two group sites for 20-50 people. Picnic tables and fire grills are provided. Drinking water, vault toilets, and firewood are available. A camp host is available in summer. Leashed pets are permitted.

Reservations, fees: Reservations are accepted at 877/444-6777 ($10 reservation fee) or www.recreation.gov ($9 reservation fee). Single sites are $16 per night, double sites are $30 per night, $8 per extra vehicle per night. The group site is $75 per night. Open May-mid-September, weather permitting.

Directions: From White Salmon, take Grangeview Loop Road to W. Jewett Boulevard/WA-141. Turn right on WA-141 and drive 26 miles to Carson Guler Road/NF Development Road 24. Follow Carson Guler Road/NF Development Road 24 two miles to the campground.

Alternately, from Hood River, Oregon, drive north on Highway 35 (over the Columbia River) to Highway 14. Turn left and drive two miles to Highway 141-A. Turn right (north) on Highway 141-A and drive 25.5 miles to Forest Road 24 (5.5 miles beyond and southwest of the town of Trout Lake). Bear right (west) and drive 2.5 miles to the campground on the left.

Contact: Gifford Pinchot National Forest, Mount Adams Ranger District, 509/395-3400, www.fs.usda.gov or www.hoodoo.com.

92 TROUT LAKE CREEK

🏃 🏊 🏕 🚐 ⛰

Scenic rating: 7

in Gifford Pinchot National Forest

Map 5.4, page 304

This spot makes a popular base camp for folks fishing at Trout Lake (five miles away). Many anglers will spend the day at the lake, where fishing is good for stocked rainbow trout, then return to this camp for the night. Some bonus brook trout are occasionally caught at Trout Lake. The camp is set along a creek in a forest of Douglas fir. In season, berry picking can be good here.

Campsites, facilities: There are 17 sites for tents or RVs up to 28 feet. Picnic tables and fire rings are provided. Vault toilets are available. There is no drinking water, and garbage must be packed out. Leashed pets are permitted.

Reservations, fees: Reservations are not accepted. Sites are $10-20 per night, $5 per night per additional vehicle. Open mid-May-mid-September, weather permitting.

Directions: From White Salmon, take Grangeview Loop Road to W. Jewett Boulevard/WA-141. Turn right on WA-141 and drive 22 miles to Trout Creek Road/Trout Lake Creek Road. Turn right on Trout Creek Road/Trout Lake Creek Road and drive four miles to National Forest Development Road 010. Take a slight right and drive about 0.5 mile to the campground on the left.

Alternately, from Hood River, Oregon, drive north on Highway 35 (over the Columbia River) to Highway 14. Turn left and drive two miles to Highway 141-A. Turn right (north) on Highway 141-A and drive 25 miles north to Forest Road 88. Turn right and drive four miles to Forest Road 8810. Turn right and drive 1.5 miles to Forest Road 8810-010. Turn right and drive 0.25 mile to the campground on the right. Note that the access road is rough.

Contact: Gifford Pinchot National Forest, Mount Adams Ranger District, 509/395-3400, www.fs.usda.gov.

93 PARADISE CREEK

Scenic rating: 9
in Gifford Pinchot National Forest

Map 5.4, page 304

This camp is located deep in Gifford Pinchot National Forest at the confluence of Paradise Creek and the Wind River. It gets light use despite easy access and easy RV parking. The well-shaded campsites are set among old-growth woods, primarily Douglas fir, cedar, and western hemlock. Lava Butte, located a short distance from the camp, is accessible by trail; the 1.2-mile round-trip hike from the campground provides a good view of the valley. Fishing is closed here. The elevation is 1,500 feet.

Campsites, facilities: There are 42 sites for tents or RVs up to 40 feet long. Picnic tables and fire grills are provided. Drinking water, vault toilets, and firewood are available. A camp host is on-site. Some facilities are wheelchair accessible. Leashed pets are permitted.

Reservations, fees: Reservations are accepted at 877/444-6777 ($10 reservation fee) or www.recreation.gov ($9 reservation fee). Sites are $18 per night, double sites are $34 per night, $9 per extra vehicle per night. Open mid-May-mid-September, weather permitting.

Directions: From Vancouver, Washington,

take Highway 14 east and drive 50 miles to Carson and the Wind River Highway (County Road 30). Turn left (north) on the Wind River Highway and drive 20 miles to the camp on the right.

Contact: Gifford Pinchot National Forest, Mount Adams Ranger District, 509/395-3400, www.fs.usda.gov or www.hoodoo.com

94 FALLS CREEK HORSE CAMP

Scenic rating: 5
near the Pacific Crest Trail in Gifford Pinchot National Forest

Map 5.4, page 304

Falls Creek sits at the threshold of a great launch point for hiking, horseback riding, and mountain biking. The camp is set along Race Track Trail, adjacent to the western border of Indian Heaven Wilderness. A wilderness trailhead is available right at the camp. There are 90 miles of trail for horses and hiking and 40 miles for mountain bikes. Although this is a multiple-use campground, the sites are small and the turnaround is tight for RVs.

The camp has been intermittently closed due to trees hazards, so call to confirm availability before heading out.

Campsites, facilities: There are four sites for tents or RVs up to 15 feet long. Picnic tables and fire grills are provided. Pit toilets and a loading ramp for horses are available. There is no drinking water and garbage must be packed out. Some facilities are wheelchair accessible. Leashed pets are permitted.

Reservations, fees: Reservations are not accepted. There is no fee for camping, but a free wilderness permit is required; a self-issued permit is available at the trailhead. Open mid-June-November.

Directions: From Vancouver, Washington, on I-205, take Highway 14 and drive east for 50 miles to Carson and the Wind River Highway (County Road 30). Turn left (north) on the

Wind River Highway and drive 9.5 miles to Forest Road 6517. Continue 1.5 miles to Forest Road 65. Turn left and drive 15 miles to the campground on the left.

Contact: Gifford Pinchot National Forest, Mount Adams Ranger District, 509/395-3400, www.fs.usda.gov.

95 CREST HORSE CAMP

Scenic rating: 6
in Gifford Pinchot National Forest

Map 5.4, page 304

Crest Horse Camp is a small, primitive, multiple-use camp set near the Pacific Crest Trail, adjacent to the eastern boundary of the Indian Heaven Wilderness. It is an excellent jumping-off spot for wilderness treks with horses or other stock animals. The camp features a forested setting, primarily second-growth Douglas fir. Adjacent to the camp is the Big Lava Bed, a volcanic flow known for its lava tubes and lava tube caves.

Campsites, facilities: There are three sites for tents or RVs up to 16 feet long. Only one back-in is allowed at this site; other vehicles must park on the road. Picnic tables and fire pits are provided. A vault toilet and a loading ramp and high lines for horses are available. There is no drinking water and garbage must be packed out. Some facilities are wheelchair accessible. Leashed pets are permitted.

Reservations, fees: Reservations are not accepted. There is no fee for camping. Open mid-May-mid-October, weather permitting.

Directions: From Vancouver, Washington, take Highway 14 east and drive 50 miles to Carson and the Wind River Highway (County Road 30). Turn left (north) and drive nine miles to Forest Road 6517. Turn right (east) on Forest Road 6517 and drive 1.5 miles to Forest Road 65. Turn left (north) on Forest Road 65 and drive about 10 miles to Forest Road 60. Turn right and drive two miles to the camp on the right.

Contact: Gifford Pinchot National Forest, Mount Adams Ranger District, 509/395-3400, www.fs.usda.gov.

96 GOOSE LAKE

Scenic rating: 8
on Goose Lake in Gifford Pinchot National Forest

Map 5.4, page 304

This campground is set along the shore of beautiful Goose Lake at an elevation of 3,200 feet. Though the lake is quite pretty, the camp itself is set well above the lake and is not as nice; it can also be crowded in summer. Trout fishing and berry picking are available and a 5-mph speed limit is enforced on the lake. Adjacent to the camp is the northern edge of Big Lava Bed, a volcanic flow known for its lava tubes and lava tube caves.

Campsites, facilities: There are 18 walk-in sites for tents only situated on a hillside, though the sites themselves are level. Roadside parking is available. There is also one site for RVs up to 18 feet, though the road is rough. Picnic tables and fire rings are provided. Vault toilets and firewood are available, but there is no drinking water. A camp host is on-site. A boat ramp is nearby. Leashed pets are permitted.

Reservations, fees: Reservations are not accepted. Sites are $10 per night, $5 per extra vehicle per night. Open mid-May-mid-September, weather permitting.

Directions: From Vancouver, Washington, on I-205, take Highway 14 east and drive 50 miles to County Road 30/Wind River Road. Turn left and drive six miles to Panther Creek Road and Forest Road 6517. Turn right on Forest Road 6517 and drive 10 miles to a four-way intersection called Four Corners. Turn right on Forest Road 60 and drive 10 miles to the campground on the left.

Contact: Gifford Pinchot National Forest, Mount Adams Ranger District, 509/395-3400, www.fs.usda.gov.

97 BEAVER

Scenic rating: 7

in Gifford Pinchot National Forest

Map 5.4, page 304

This is the closest campground north of Stevenson in the Columbia Gorge. Set along the Wind River at an elevation of 1,100 feet, it features pretty, shaded sites. The campsites are paved, and a large grassy day-use area is nearby. Hiking highlights include two nearby trailheads. Two miles north is the trailhead for the Trapper Creek Wilderness with 30 miles of trails, including a loop possibility. Three miles north is the Falls Creek Trail. No fishing is permitted.

Campsites, facilities: There are 18 sites for tents or RVs up to 25 feet long, five double sites, and one group site for up to 40 people. Picnic tables and fire grills are provided. Drinking water, firewood, and flush and vault toilets are available. A camp host is on-site. Some facilities are wheelchair accessible. Leashed pets are permitted.

Reservations, fees: Reservations are accepted at 877/444-6777 ($10 reservation fee) or www.recreation.gov ($9 reservation fee). Sites are $20 per night, double sites are $34 per night, $10 per extra vehicle per night. The group site is $100 per night. Open early May-late September.

Directions: From Vancouver, Washington, take Highway 14 east and drive 50 miles to Carson and the Wind River Highway (County Road 30). Turn left (north) and drive 12 miles to the campground entrance (five miles past Stabler) on the left.

Contact: Gifford Pinchot National Forest, Mount Adams Ranger District, 509/395-3400, www.fs.usda.gov or www.hoodoo.com.

98 PANTHER CREEK

Scenic rating: 8

in Gifford Pinchot National Forest

Map 5.4, page 304

This campground is set along Panther Creek in a second-growth forest of Douglas fir and western hemlock, adjacent to an old-growth forest. The sites are well defined, but despite a paved road to the campground and easy parking and access, it gets light use. The camp lies 3.5 miles from the Wind River, an option for those who enjoy fishing, hiking, and horseback riding. The Pacific Crest Trail is accessible from the adjacent Panther Creek Horse Camp. The elevation is 1,000 feet.

Campsites, facilities: There are 33 sites for tents or RVs up to 25 feet long, including six double sites, and one equestrian site with a stock loading ramp at the adjacent horse camp. Picnic tables and fire rings are provided. Drinking water, pit toilets, garbage bins, and firewood are available. A camp host is on-site. Some facilities are wheelchair accessible. Leashed pets are permitted.

Reservations, fees: Reserve at 877/444-6777 or www.recreation.gov ($9-10 reservation fee). Single sites are $18 per night, double sites are $34 per night, $9 per extra vehicle per night. The horse site is free. Open mid-May-mid-September.

Directions: From Vancouver, Washington, take Highway 14 east and drive 50 miles to Carson and the Wind River Highway (County Road 30). Turn north and drive nine miles to Forest Road 6517 (just past Stabler). Turn right (east) on Forest Road 6517 and drive 1.5 miles to the campground entrance road on the right.

Contact: Gifford Pinchot National Forest, Mount Adams Ranger District, 509/395-3400, www.fs.usda.gov or www.hoodoo.com.

99 OKLAHOMA

Scenic rating: 7

in Gifford Pinchot National Forest

Map 5.4, page 304

Pretty Oklahoma Campground is set along the Little White Salmon River at an elevation of 1,700 feet. Located close to the Columbia River Gorge, it features a paved road all the way into the campground and easy RV parking. The camp features some open meadow, but is generally flat and gets light use. Fishing can be excellent in this area and the river is stocked in the spring with rainbow trout.

The camp was named after the large influx of homesteaders that moved into the area around 1893. They were likened to the "Oklahoma Boomers" of the great land rush two years earlier.

Campsites, facilities: There are 13 single sites and one double site for tents or RVs up to 40 feet long. Picnic tables and fire rings are provided. Drinking water and vault toilets are available. Some facilities are wheelchair accessible. Leashed pets are permitted.

Reservations, fees: Reservations are accepted at 877/444-6777 or www.recreation.gov ($9-10 reservation fee). Single sites are $16 per night, double sites are $30 per night, $8 per night for each additional vehicle. Open mid-May-mid-September, weather permitting.

Directions: From White Salmon: Take N. Main Avenue to E. Jewett Boulevard. Turn left on E. Jewett Boulevard and drive 0.5 mile to SE 6th Avenue/Dock Grade Road. Turn right on SE 6th Avenue/Dock Grade Road and drive 0.8 mile to Lewis and Clark Highway/WA-14W. Turn right on Lewis and Clark Highway/WA-14W and drive 1.5 miles to Cook Underwood Road. Turn right on Cook Underwood Road and drive 8.3 miles to Willard Road. Turn right on Willard Road and drive two miles to Oklahoma Road. Turn right on Oklahoma Road and drive five miles to National Forest Development Road 18/Oklahoma Road. Turn right on National Forest Development Road 18/ Oklahoma Road and drive three miles to the campground on the left.

From Hood River, Oregon: Drive north on Highway 35 for one mile over the Columbia River to Highway 14. Turn left on Highway 14 and drive about five miles to Cook and County Road 1800. Turn right (north) and drive 14 miles (becomes Cook-Underwood Road, then Willard Road, then Oklahoma Road) to the campground entrance at the end of the paved road.

Contact: Gifford Pinchot National Forest, Mount Adams Ranger District, 509/395-3400, www.fs.usda.gov or www.hoodoo.com.

100 MOSS CREEK

Scenic rating: 7

in Gifford Pinchot National Forest

Map 5.4, page 304

This campground is set at 1,400 feet elevation, about one mile from the Little White Salmon River. Although it's a short distance from Willard and Big Cedars County Park, the camp gets light use. The river provides good fishing prospects for trout in the spring, usually with few other people around. The sites are generally small but are shaded and still functional for most RVs. The road is paved all the way to the campground.

Campsites, facilities: There are 17 sites for tents or RVs up to 40 feet. Picnic tables and fire grills are provided. Drinking water, vault toilets, and firewood are available. A camp host is available in the summer. Some facilities are wheelchair accessible. Leashed pets are permitted.

Reservations, fees: Reservations are accepted at 877/444-6777 ($10 reservation fee) or www. recreation.gov ($9 reservation fee). Sites are $16 per night, $8 per night for each additional vehicle. Open mid-May-mid-September, weather permitting.

Directions: From White Salmon: Take N. Main Avenue to E. Jewett Boulevard. Turn left on E. Jewett Boulevard and drive 0.5 mile to SE 6th Avenue/Dock Grade Road. Turn right on SE 6th Avenue/Dock Grade Road and drive 0.8 mile to Lewis and Clark Highway/WA-14W. Turn right on Lewis and Clark Highway/WA-14W and drive 1.5 miles to Cook Underwood Road. Turn right on Cook Underwood Road and drive 8.3 miles to Willard Road. Watch for the fish hatchery, then turn right on Willard Road and drive two miles to Oklahoma Road. Turn right on Oklahoma Road and drive 1.3 miles to the campground on the left.

From Hood River, Oregon: Drive north on Highway 35 for one mile over the Columbia River to Highway 14. Turn left on Highway 14 and drive about five miles to Cook and County Road 1800. Turn right (north) and drive 10 miles (becomes Cook-Underwood Road, then Willard Road, then Oklahoma Road) to the campground entrance on the right.

Contact: Gifford Pinchot National Forest, Mount Adams Ranger District, 509/395-3400, www.fs.usda.gov or www.hoodoo.com.

101 COLUMBIA HILLS STATE PARK

🏃 🏊 🚤 🎣 🚐 ⛺

Scenic rating: 10

near the Dalles Dam

Map 5.4, page 304

The 338-acre park boasts 7,500 feet of Columbia River shoreline. It also adjoins the 3,000-acre Dalles Mountain Ranch State Park. Horsethief Lake, created by the Dalles Dam, covers approximately 100 acres and is part of the Columbia River. Horsethief Butte, adjacent to the lake, dominates the skyline. The bloom of lupine and balsamroot in mid-April creates stunning views. Rock climbing in the park is popular, but the river canyon is often windy, especially in late spring and early summer. Most people find the place as a spot to camp while driving along the Columbia River Highway. There are hiking trails and access to both the lake and the Columbia River. The boat speed limit is 5 mph, and anglers can try for trout and bass. Guided tours on weekends feature pictographs and petroglyphs; reservations are required at 509/439-9032.

Campsites, facilities: There are eight sites with partial hookups (15 amps, converters available) for tents or RVs up to 30 feet long, four walk-in tent sites, two platform tent sites, and two hike-in/bike-in sites. Picnic tables and fire grills are provided. Drinking water, restrooms with flush toilets and coin showers, firewood, a dump station, a horseshoe pit, and a picnic area are available. A store is within three miles. Boat-launching facilities are located on both the lake and the river. Leashed pets are permitted.

Reservations, fees: Reservations are accepted at 888/226-7688 or www.goingtocamp.com. Sites are $20-45 per night, $12 per night for primitive sites and the hike-in/bike-in site, $10 per extra vehicle per night. Open April-late October.

Directions: From Dallesport, drive east on 6th Avenue to Dallesport Road. Turn left on Dallesport Road and drive 2.3 miles to Lewis and Clark Highway/WA-14E. Turn right at Lewis and Clark Highway/WA-14E and drive four miles to the campground on the left.

Alternately, from The Dalles in Oregon, turn north on Highway 197, cross over the Columbia River, and drive four miles to Highway 14. Turn right (east) and drive two miles to Milepost 85 and the park entrance on the right.

Contact: Columbia Hills State Park, 509/767-1159; state park information, 360/902-8844, http://parks.state.wa.us.

SOUTHEASTERN WASHINGTON

The expansive domain of southeastern Washington is a surprise for many newcomers. Instead of the high mountains of the Cascades, there are rolling hills. Instead of forests, there are miles of wheat fields. Instead of a multitude of streams, there are giant rivers like the Columbia and the Snake. Just one pocket of mountains and a somewhat sparse forest sit in the southeast corner of the state, in a remote sector of Umatilla National Forest. More than 200 years ago, the Lewis and Clark Expedition routed through this area. Today, major highways like I-82 and U.S. 395 link the region to other destinations. A network of camps is set along these highways, including RV parks created to serve the needs of travelers. Of the area parks, the state parks offer the best campgrounds.

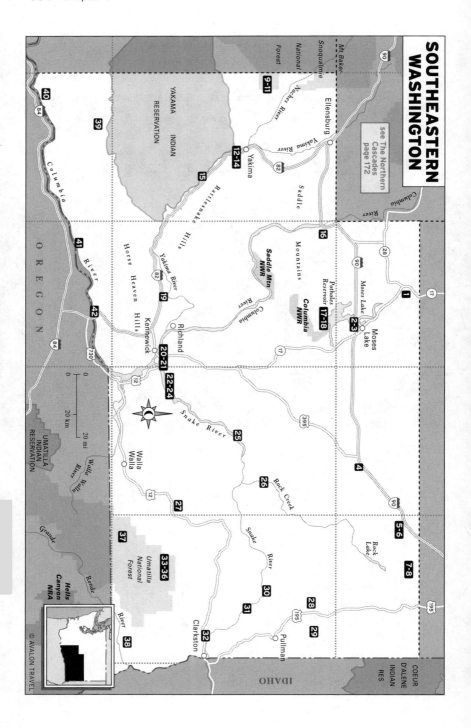

1 OASIS RV PARK AND GOLF

🏊 🚣 🎿 🐕 🚴 🚐 ⛺

Scenic rating: 5

near Soap Lake

Map page 354

This area can be extremely warm and arid during the summer months, but, fortunately, Oasis RV Park offers shaded sites. There are two fishing ponds at the resort: One has crappie, while the other is for kids and has trout and bass. There is also a nine-hole golf course at the park. Mineral baths are located just a few miles north.

Campsites, facilities: There are 12 sites for tents only and 69 sites with full or partial hookups (30 amps) for tents or RVs of any length. Some sites are pull-through. Picnic tables are provided. Restrooms with flush toilets and coin showers, cable TV, Wi-Fi, a playground, horseshoe pits, picnic area, a nine-hole golf course, an 18-hole miniature golf course, dump station, a store, propane, coin laundry, ice, a seasonal heated swimming pool, and a youth fishing pond are available. A café is located within one mile. Some facilities are wheelchair accessible. Leashed pets are permitted.

Reservations, fees: Reservations are recommended. RV sites are $25-33 per night, tent sites are $22 per night, $5 per night per extra vehicle. Some credit cards are accepted. Open year-round.

Directions: From Spokane, take I-90 west to the Moses Lake exit and Highway 17. Turn northeast on Highway 17 and drive 32.7 miles to the Y junction with Highway 282. Take Highway 282 and drive four miles to Highway 281/283 (a stoplight). Turn left and drive 1.9 miles to the park on the right (just before reaching the town of Ephrata).

Contact: Oasis RV Park and Golf, 509/754-5102 or 877/754-5102, http://oasisrvandgolf-course.com.

2 LAKEFRONT RV PARK

🏊 🚣 🚐 🐕 🚐

Scenic rating: 5

near Moses Lake State Park

Map page 354

This park sits a short distance from Moses Lake State Park, which is open for day-use only. The primary appeal is Moses Lake, Washington's largest freshwater lake, where you will find shady picnic spots with tables and fire grills, beach access, and moorage floats. Waterskiing and personal watercraft are allowed on the lake. Bird hunting is popular in season. Sand dunes are located a few miles away and can be used for all-terrain-vehicle (ATV) activities.

Campsites, facilities: There are 50 sites with full hookups (30 amps) for RVs of any length; half of the sites are long-term rentals. Some sites are pull-through. Picnic tables are provided. A restroom with flush toilets and showers, coin laundry, cable TV, dump station, and boat docks and launch are available. A store and restaurant are located within one mile. Leashed pets are permitted with certain restrictions.

Reservations, fees: Reservations are accepted. Sites are $35 per night. Open year-round.

Directions: From Spokane, drive west on I-90 to Moses Lake and Exit 176. Take that exit to Broadway, turn right, and drive 0.75 mile to Burress Avenue. Turn left (west) on Burress Avenue and drive one block to the park.

Contact: Lakefront RV Park, 509/765-8294.

3 WILLOWS TRAILER VILLAGE

🐕 🚴 ♿ 🚐 ⛺

Scenic rating: 5

near Moses Lake State Park

Map page 354

One of two campgrounds in the area, Willows Trailer Village has grassy, shaded sites, horseshoe pits, barbecues, and a recreation field.

Most recreation opportunities can be found at Moses Lake, including picnicking, beach access, waterskiing, and moorage floats. Bird-watching and sand dunes for ATV riding are nearby. Note that there are some permanent site rentals at this RV park, but a landscape barrier separates them from the other sites.

Campsites, facilities: There are 20 sites for tents and 68 sites for RVs of any length; all RV sites are pull-through and most have full hookups (30 and 50 amps). Picnic tables are provided. A restroom with flush toilets and coin showers, propane, a convenience store, ice, coin laundry, playground, and horseshoe pits are available. There is also a hair salon on-site. Some facilities are wheelchair accessible. Leashed pets are permitted.

Reservations, fees: Reservations are accepted. Sites are $28.50-34.50 per night, $3 per person per night for more than two people. Open year-round.

Directions: From Spokane, drive west on I-90 to Moses Lake and Exit 179 and Highway 17. Turn south on Highway 17 and drive 2.5 miles to Road M SE. Turn right and drive 0.5 mile to the park on the left.

Contact: Willows Trailer Village, 509/765-7531.

4 FOUR SEASONS CAMPGROUND & RESORT

🏊 ⛵ 🚤 🐕 🚐 ⛺

Scenic rating: 7

on Sprague Lake

Map page 354

This campground along the shore of Sprague Lake, one of the top fishing waters in the state, has spacious sites with plenty of vegetation. The fishing for rainbow trout is best in May and June, with some bass in spring and fall. Because there is an abundance of natural feed in the lake, the fish reach larger sizes here than in neighboring lakes. Walleye up to 10 pounds are taken here. Crappie and catfish are also abundant, with a sprinkling of perch and bluegill. In

late July-August, a fair algae bloom is a turnoff for swimmers and water-skiers.

Campsites, facilities: There are 38 sites with full or partial hookups (30 and 50 amps) for RVs of any length; some sites are pull-through. There are also four cabins. Tent camping is allowed when space is available. Picnic tables and fire pits are provided. Restrooms with flush toilets and coin showers, drinking water, a dump station, firewood, ice, a convenience store with fishing tackle, a fish-cleaning station, and a small basketball court are available. Boat and fishing docks, launching facilities, slips, and rentals are nearby. Leashed pets are permitted.

Reservations, fees: Reservations are accepted. RV sites are $34 per night, tent sites are $23 per night, cabins are $90-100 per night, $5 per night for more than four people, $2 per night for extra vehicle, $1 per night per pet. Open mid-April-mid-October, weather permitting.

Directions: From Spokane, drive west on I-90 for 35 miles to Exit 245. Take Exit 245 and drive south to 4th Street. Turn right and drive one block to B Street. Turn left and drive two blocks to 1st Street. Turn right and drive one mile through the town of Sprague to a Y intersection (from here, the resort is six miles away). Continue (over the railroad tracks and then under I-90) to Lake Road. Turn left and drive (parallel to the freeway) until the road bears to the right to Bob Lee Road. Turn left on Bob Lee Road and drive (over I-90) to the resort.

Contact: Four Seasons Campground and Resort, 509/257-2332, www.fourseasonscampground.com.

5 SPRAGUE LAKE RESORT

⛵ 🚤 🐕 🚣 ♿ 🚐 ⛺

Scenic rating: 5

on Sprague Lake

Map page 354

This developed campground is located on the shore of Sprague Lake, about 35 miles from Spokane. It offers a pleasant, grassy setting with about 50 cottonwood and native trees on the property. Sprague Lake is one of the top fishing waters in the state—look for rainbow trout, bass, walleye, crappie, catfish, perch, and bluegill. A late-summer algae bloom tends to leave swimmers and water-skiers landlocked.

Campsites, facilities: There are 50 sites for tents and 31 pull-through sites with full or partial hookups for RVs of any length. Picnic tables and fire grills are provided. Restrooms with flush toilets and coin showers, drinking water, a small store, coin laundry, Wi-Fi, ice, firewood, a playground, boat docks, launching facilities, and rentals are available. Some facilities are wheelchair accessible, including a paved area lakeside for fishing. Leashed pets are permitted.

Reservations, fees: Reservations are accepted. RV sites are $37 per night, tent sites are $29 per night, $2 per person per night for more than two people. Weekly and monthly rates are available. Open April-November.

Directions: From Spokane, drive west on I-90 to the Sprague Business Center exit. Take that exit to Sprague Lake Road and continue two miles to the resort on the left (well signed).

Contact: Sprague Lake Resort, 509/257-2864, www.spraguelakeresort.com.

6 KLINK'S WILLIAMS LAKE RESORT

Scenic rating: 6

on Williams Lake

Map page 354

This family-oriented resort is set on the shore of Williams Lake, which is less than three miles long and is popular for swimming and water-skiing. The resort has a swimming area with a floating dock and slide. This lake is also one of the top fishing lakes in the region for rainbow and cutthroat trout. Rocky cliffs border the lake in some areas. Note that about 100 permanent residents live at the resort.

An option for a side trip is Turnbull National Wildlife Refuge, an expanse of marsh and pine that is a significant stopover point for migratory birds on the Pacific Flyway. This is a prime spot and only a 30-minute drive out of Spokane, yet it is relatively unknown.

Campsites, facilities: There are 60 sites with full or partial hookups (30 and 50 amps) for RVs of any length, 15 sites for tents, and seven log cabins. Picnic tables and fire grills are provided. Restrooms with flush toilets and coin showers, drinking water, Wi-Fi, propane, a dump station, firewood, a general store, bait, tackle and fishing licenses, café, restaurant, ice, a playground, covered pavilion for group use, boat docks, launching facilities, and boat rentals are available. Some facilities are wheelchair accessible. Leashed pets are permitted.

Reservations, fees: Reservations are recommended. Sites are $40-45 per night, cabins start at $115 per night (two-night min.), moorage is $10 per night. Weekly rates are available. Some credit cards are accepted. Open mid-April-October.

Directions: From Spokane, drive west on I-90 for 10 miles to Exit 270 and Highway 904. Turn south on Highway 904 and drive four miles to Cheney and Cheney Plaza Road. Turn left (south) on Cheney Plaza Road and drive 12 miles to Williams Lake Road. Turn right (west) and drive two miles to the resort on the left.

Contact: Klink's Williams Lake Resort, 18617 W. Williams Lake Rd., Cheney, 509/235-2391, www.klinksresort.com.

7 BUNKER'S RESORT

Scenic rating: 8

on Williams Lake

Map page 354

Bunker's Resort is set on the shore of Williams Lake. The lake is stocked with rainbow, cutthroat, and triploid trout; fishing season is from the last Saturday in April through September. Waterskiing, wakeboarding, and personal watercraft are allowed; swimming is also popular.

Campsites, facilities: There are six sites with full or partial hookups (30 amps) for RVs up to 34 feet long, eight tent sites, and four cabins. Picnic tables and fire pits are provided. Restrooms with flush toilets and coin showers, drinking water, propane, remove dump station, a restaurant, convenience store, bait and tackle, ice, boat and fishing docks, launching facilities, and boat rentals are available. Some facilities are wheelchair accessible. Leashed pets are permitted.

Reservations, fees: Reservations are accepted. RV sites are $30-40 per night, tent sites are $30 per night, cabins are $95-125 per night. Some credit cards are accepted. Open mid-April-September.

Directions: From Spokane, drive west on I-90 for 10 miles to Exit 270 and Highway 904. Turn south on Highway 904 and drive six miles to Cheney and Mullinex Road. Turn left (south) on Mullinex Road and drive 12 miles to the resort.

Contact: Bunker's Resort, 509/235-5212 or 800/404-6674, www.bunkersresort.com.

8 HAUSE CREEK

Scenic rating: 7
on the Tieton River in Wenatchee National Forest

Map page 354

Several creeks converge at this campground along the Tieton River (elevation 2,500 feet). The Tieton Dam, which creates Rimrock Lake, is located just upstream. Hause Creek is one of the larger, more developed camps in the area. Willows Campground provides a primitive alternative.

Campsites, facilities: There are 42 sites for tents or RVs up to 30 feet, including a few multi-family sites. Picnic tables and fire grills are provided. Drinking water, flush toilets, firewood, and garbage bins are available. A camp host is on-site. Boat docks, launching facilities, and rentals are located on Rimrock Lake. Some

facilities are wheelchair accessible. Leashed pets are permitted.

Reservations, fees: Reservations are accepted at 877/444-6777 ($10 reservation fee) or www.recreation.gov ($9 reservation fee). Sites are $18 per night, $35 per night for multi-family sites, and $9 per extra vehicle per night. Open late May-September, weather permitting.

Directions: From Yakima, drive northwest on U.S. 12 for 17 miles to the junction with Highway 410. Turn west on U.S. 12 and drive 22 miles to the campground on the left.

Contact: Okanogan-Wenatchee National Forest, Naches Ranger District, 509/653-1400, www.fs.usda.gov.

9 WILLOWS

Scenic rating: 5
on the Tieton River in Wenatchee National Forest

Map page 354

This primitive, beautiful, and easily accessible camp can be found on the Tieton River at 2,400 feet elevation. Rimrock Lake to the west provides many recreation options, and hiking trails leading into the William O. Douglas Wilderness are within driving distance.

Campsites, facilities: There are 13 sites for tents or RVs up to 35 feet and one site for tents only. Picnic tables and fire grills are provided. Drinking water, pit toilets, firewood, and garbage service are available. Some facilities are wheelchair accessible. Leashed pets are permitted.

Reservations, fees: Reservations are accepted at 877/444-6777 ($10 reservation fee) or www.recreation.gov ($9 reservation fee). Sites are $14 per night, $7 per night per extra vehicle. Open mid-May-September, weather permitting.

Directions: From Yakima, drive northwest on U.S. 12 for 17 miles to the junction with Highway 410. Turn west on U.S. 12 and drive 16 miles to the campground on the left.

Contact: Okanogan-Wenatchee National

Forest, Naches Ranger District, 509/653-1400, www.fs.usda.gov.

10 WINDY POINT

Scenic rating: 5

on the Tieton River in Wenatchee National Forest

Map page 354

This campground, located along the Tieton River at an elevation of 2,000 feet, is more isolated than the camps set westward toward Rimrock Lake. Drinking water is a bonus. Fishing access is available.

Campsites, facilities: There are 10 sites for tents or RVs up to 37 feet. Picnic tables and fire grills are provided. Drinking water and vault toilets are available. Garbage service and firewood are available nearby. Some facilities are wheelchair accessible. Leashed pets are permitted.

Reservations, fees: Reservations are accepted at 877/444-6777 ($10 reservation fee) or www.recreation.gov ($9 reservation fee). Sites are $14 per night, $7 per extra vehicle per night. Open mid-May-September, weather permitting.

Directions: From Yakima, drive northwest on U.S. 12 for 17 miles to the junction with Highway 410. Turn west on U.S. 12 and drive nine miles to the campground on the left.

Contact: Okanogan-Wenatchee National Forest, Naches Ranger District, 509/653-1400, www.fs.usda.gov.

11 CIRCLE H RV RANCH

Scenic rating: 8

in Yakima

Map page 354

This pleasant, centrally located, and clean park with a Western flavor has comfortable, spacious sites among ornamental trees and roses. Nearby recreation options include an 18-hole golf course, hiking trails, and marked bike trails.

Campsites, facilities: There are 69 sites with full hookups (20, 30 and 50 amps) for RVs of any length and 12 tent sites. Some sites are pull-through. Picnic tables and barbecues are provided. Restrooms with flush toilets and showers, a recreation hall, coin laundry, Wi-Fi access, clubhouse, playgrounds, horseshoes, a tennis court, tetherball, volleyball, and basketball, an 18-hole miniature golf course, and a seasonal heated swimming pool are available. Propane, a store, casino, and shopping center are located within one mile. Mini storage units are available for a fee. Some facilities are wheelchair accessible. Leashed pets are permitted.

Reservations, fees: Reservations are accepted. Sites are $28-35 per night, $4 per person per night for more than two people. Some credit cards are accepted. Open year-round.

Directions: In Yakima on I-82, take Exit 34 West and drive one block to South 18th Street. Turn right (north) and drive 0.25 mile to the campground on the right.

Contact: Circle H RV Ranch, 1107 S. 18th St., Yakima, 509/457-3683, www.circlehrvranch.com.

12 TRAILER INNS RV PARK/YAKIMA

Scenic rating: 7

in Yakima

Map page 354

This spot has many of the luxuries you'd find in a hotel, including a pool, spa, on-site security, and a large-screen TV. An 18-hole golf course, hiking trails, marked bike trails, and tennis courts are close by. Local pond fishing, as well as fishing in the Yakima River, is available. It's especially pretty in the fall when the sycamores turn color. The region has become known for its wineries and breweries. A variety of fresh produce is available in the local area in season.

Campsites, facilities: There are 135 sites for

tents or RVs of any length (15, 30, and 50 amp full hookups). Some sites are pull-through. Picnic tables are provided and some sites have gas barbecues. Restrooms with flush toilets and showers, cable TV, Wi-Fi, propane, a dump station, a recreation hall, coin laundry, ice, an indoor heated swimming pool, a whirlpool, TV room, dog walk, enclosed barbecue area (no open fires permitted), and a playground are available. A store and café are within one block. Some facilities are wheelchair accessible. Leashed pets are permitted.

Reservations, fees: Reservations are accepted at 800/659-4784. RV sites are $30-58 per night, tent sites are $28 per night, $5 per person per night for more than two people, and $5 per extra vehicle per night. Weekly and monthly rates are available. Some credit cards are accepted. Open year-round.

Directions: In Yakima on I-82, take Exit 31 and drive south for one block on North 1st Street to the park on the right (west side of the road).

Contact: Trailer Inns RV Park, 1610 N. 1st St., Yakima, 509/452-9561 or 800/659-4784, www.trailerinnsrv.com.

13 YAKIMA SPORTSMAN STATE PARK

Scenic rating: 8

on the Yakima River

Map page 354   **BEST (**

Yakima Sportsman State Park is a popular layover spot for visitors attending events in the Yakima area. Campsites and picnic areas are shaded, thanks to the park's location on the Yakima River floodplain. There is a fishing pond for children (no anglers over age 15 are allowed), access to the river for adult anglers, and an unpaved roadway on the river dike for hikers and horseback riders. A put-in for kayaking and rafting is an approximately 20-minute drive away. No swimming is allowed. Nearby recreation options include bird-watching, an 18-hole golf course, and hiking trails.

Campsites, facilities: There are 30 sites for tents and 37 sites with full hookups (50 amps) for RVs up to 60 feet; some sites are pull-through. There is one group site for tents only that accommodates up to 100 people. Picnic tables and fire grills are provided. Restrooms with flush toilets and coin showers, a dump station, firewood, playground, horseshoe pit, and picnic shelter are available. A store and ice are within one mile. Some facilities are wheelchair accessible. Leashed pets are permitted.

Reservations, fees: Reservations are accepted in peak season only at 888/226-7688 or https://washington.goingtocamp.com ($8-10 reservation fee); sites are first-come, first-served in winter. Sites are $25 per night, $10 per extra vehicle per night. Some credit cards are accepted. Open year-round.

Directions: In Yakima, drive on I-82 to Milepost 34 and the Highway 24 exit. Turn east on Highway 24 and drive one mile to Keys Road. Turn left and drive 0.75 mile to South 33rd Street. Turn left and drive approximately 300 feet to the park entrance on the left.

Contact: Yakima Sportsman State Park, 509/575-2774, http://parks.state.wa.us.

14 GINKGO PETRIFIED FOREST/WANAPUM STATE RECREATION AREA

Scenic rating: 7

on the Columbia River and Wanapum Lake

Map page 354

The site of an ancient petrified forest, Ginkgo Petrified Forest State Park is a National Natural Landmark. This fossilized forest is set along Wanapum Lake along the course of the Columbia River. Ginkgo is a huge park, covering 7,740 acres and surrounding the 27,000 feet of shoreline of Wanapum Lake. The park features an interpretive center and trail.

Although completely separate, Wanapum

State Recreation Area is linked to Ginkgo Petrified Forest State Park. Camping, however, is permitted only at the Wanapum Recreation Area, which is three miles south of I-90. Recreation options include hiking (three miles of trails), swimming, boating, waterskiing, and fishing. There are also several historical Civilian Conservation Corps structures from the 1930s. The Wanapum campground is set up primarily for RVs, with full hookups, restrooms, and showers. Note that the park always fills up during the Gorge concert season.

Campsites, facilities: There are 50 sites with full hookups (30 amps) for RVs up to 50 feet long. Picnic tables and fire grills are provided. Restrooms with flush toilets and coin showers and firewood are available. Boat docks, launching facilities, a museum, a swimming beach, and a picnic area are nearby. Some facilities are wheelchair accessible. Leashed pets are permitted.

Reservations, fees: Reservations are accepted in season at 888/226-7688) or https://washington.goingtocamp.com ($8-10 reservation fee). Sites are $30-45 per night, $10 per extra vehicle per night. Open March-October, weather permitting.

Directions: From Ellensburg, drive east on I-90 to the Vantage Highway/Huntzinger Road (Exit 136). Take that exit, turn south on Huntzinger Road, and drive three miles to the campground on the left.

Contact: Wanapum State Recreation Area, 509/856-2700, http://parks.state.wa.us.

15 POTHOLES STATE PARK
🚶 ♨ 🚐 🐕 🛶 ♿ 🚍 ⛰

Scenic rating: 8

on Potholes Reservoir

Map page 354   BEST (

This 640-acre park is set on Potholes Reservoir (also known as O'Sullivan Reservoir) with 6,000 feet of freshwater shoreline—fishing is a highlight. Trout, walleye, bass, crappie, and perch are among the species taken here.

Waterskiing and hiking (on one mile of hiking trails) are other recreation options. A side trip to the Columbia National Wildlife Refuge, located two miles southeast of the park, is recommended. Note: Do not confuse Potholes Reservoir with the Potholes Lakes, a 30- to 45-minute drive away.

Campsites, facilities: There are 61 sites for tents or RVs up to 50 feet long (no hookups), 55 sites for tents or RVs up to 50 feet long (30 amp full hookups), five cabins, and a group site for up to 50 people. Picnic tables and fire grills are provided. Restrooms with flush toilets and showers, a dump station, a playground, volleyball courts, firewood, and a sheltered picnic area are available. Boat-launching facilities and rentals are nearby. Some facilities are wheelchair accessible. Leashed pets are permitted.

Reservations, fees: Reservations are accepted at 888/226-7688 or https://washington.goingtocamp.com ($8-10 reservation fee). RV sites are $25-45 per night, tent sites are $12 per night, cabins are $45-79 per night, $10 per night per extra vehicle. Call for group rates. Open year-round.

Directions: From I-90 at Moses Lake, take Exit 179 and Highway 17. Turn south and drive nine miles to Highway 262. Turn right (west) and drive 11 miles to the resort on the southern shore of Potholes Reservoir (well signed).

Contact: Potholes State Park, 509/346-2759, http://parks.state.wa.us.

16 MAR DON RESORT
🚶 🚲 ♨ 🛶 🚤 🐕 🛶 ♿ 🚍 ⛰

Scenic rating: 7

on Potholes Reservoir

Map page 354

This resort is located on Potholes Reservoir and provides opportunities for fishing, swimming, and boating. A marina, tackle, and boat rentals are all available. Hiking trails and marked bike trails are close by. Many visitors find the café and cocktail lounge a nice bonus. The Columbia National Wildlife Refuge is located nearby to the south and provides exceptional bird-watching; pelicans and kingfishers are common, and bald eagles and migratory sandhill cranes are often seen as well.

Campsites, facilities: There are 88 sites for tents or RVs of any length (no hookups) and 187 sites with full or partial hookups for tents or RVs of any length; some sites are pull-through. Three rental homes, nine cottages, and a bunkhouse are also available. Picnic tables and fire rings are provided. A restroom with flush toilets and coin showers, drinking water, propane, a dump station, a small convenience store, a boutique, coin laundry, ice, Wi-Fi, a playground, fish-cleaning station, boat moorage, boat rentals, and launching facilities are available. Some facilities are wheelchair accessible. Leashed pets are permitted with breed restrictions.

Reservations, fees: Reservations are accepted. RV sites are $27-47 per night, tent sites are $20-42 per night, $10 per extra vehicle per night, $5 per extra person per night, $4-10 per pet per night. Rental homes are $130-175 per night, cottages are $130-220 per night, the bunkhouse is $40-60 per night. Winter rates are available. Some credit cards are accepted. Open year-round.

Directions: From Highway 17 in Moses Lake, drive south nine miles to Highway 262. Turn right (west) and drive 10 miles to the resort on the southern shore of Potholes Reservoir.

Contact: Mar Don Resort, 509/346-2651 or 800/416-2736, www.mardonresort.com.

17 BEACH RV PARK

Scenic rating: 8

on the Yakima River

Map page 354

This park along the shore of the Yakima River is a pleasant spot with spacious RV sites, a large grassy area, and poplar trees and shrubs that provide privacy between many of the sites. Note that Beach RV is the only park in the area that has tent camping available. Fishing for bass and trout is available in season. Nearby recreation options include an 18-hole golf course and a full-service marina, both within 12 miles.

Campsites, facilities: There are 100 sites with full hookups (20, 30 and 50 amps) for RVs of any length, including some pull-through sites, and 25 sites for tents. Picnic tables are provided; fire pits are provided in the tent area only. Restrooms with flush toilets and free showers, cable TV, Wi-Fi, and coin laundry are available. Propane, a dump station, a store, and a café are located within one mile. Boat-launching facilities are nearby. Leashed pets are permitted.

Reservations, fees: Reservations are accepted. RV sites are $35 per night, tent sites are $22 per night, $4 per person per night for more than two people, $2 per night per extra vehicle. Weekly and group rates available. Some credit cards are accepted. Open year-round.

Directions: From Pasco, drive west on U.S. 12 past Richland and continue eight miles to Exit 96 and the Benton City/West Richland exit. Take that exit and drive one block north to Abby Avenue. Turn left (west) and drive 1.5 blocks to the park.

Contact: Beach RV Park, 509/588-5959, www.beachrv.net.

18 GREENTREE RV & MOBILE HOME PARK

Scenic rating: 6

in Pasco

Map page 354

This shady park in urban Pasco is close to an 18-hole golf course, hiking trails, and a full-service marina. The Franklin County Historical Museum, which is located in town, and the Sacajawea State Park Museum and Interpretive Center, located three miles southeast of town, both offer extensive collections of Native American artifacts. Note that most sites are filled with monthly rentals.

Campsites, facilities: There are 40 sites

with full hookups for RVs up to 40 feet. A coin laundry is available, but there are no toilets. A mini storage facility is on-site. Propane, a store, café, and ice are located within one mile. Boat docks, launching facilities, and rentals are nearby. Some facilities are wheelchair accessible. Leashed pets are permitted, with certain restrictions.

Reservations, fees: Reservations are accepted. Sites are $20 per night. Weekly and monthly rates are available. Open year-round.

Directions: In Pasco on I-82, take Exit 13 onto 4th Avenue and continue a short distance to the park entrance driveway on the right.

Contact: Greentree RV & Mobile Home Park, 509/547-6220.

19 ARROWHEAD RV PARK

Scenic rating: 5

near the Columbia River

Map page 354

Arrowhead provides a decent layover spot in Pasco. The park has both trees and grassy areas. Nearby recreation options include an 18-hole golf course, a full-service marina, and tennis courts. Some sites are filled with monthly renters.

Campsites, facilities: There are 80 sites for tents or RVs of any length (20, 30, and 50 amp full hookups) and a large grassy area for tents. Some sites are pull-through. Picnic tables are provided. Restrooms with flush toilets and showers, drinking water, Wi-Fi, and coin laundry are available. A store and café are located within walking distance. Some facilities are wheelchair accessible. Leashed pets are permitted, with certain restrictions.

Reservations, fees: Reservations are accepted. Sites are $30-40 per night, $7 per person per night for more than two people. Open year-round.

Directions: In Pasco on U.S. 395 North, take the Kartchner Street exit, turn east, and drive a short distance to Commercial Avenue. Turn

right (south) and drive 0.25 mile to the park entrance on the right.

Contact: Arrowhead RV Park, 509/545-8206.

20 PALOUSE FALLS STATE PARK

Scenic rating: 10

on the Snake and Palouse Rivers

Map page 354   BEST (

This remote state park is well worth the trip. Spectacular 198-foot Palouse Falls is a sight not to miss. A 0.25-mile wheelchair-accessible trail leads to a waterfall overlook. The park is set at the confluence of the Snake and Palouse Rivers, and it does not receive heavy use, even in summer. The park covers 1,282 acres and features a waterfall observation shelter, shaded picnic facilities, historical displays, and an abundance of wildlife.

Campsites, facilities: There are 11 primitive sites for tents only. Picnic tables and fire grills are provided. Drinking water (in summer), pit toilets, and a picnic area are available. Some facilities are wheelchair accessible. Leashed pets are permitted.

Reservations, fees: Reservations are not accepted. Sites are $12 per night, $10 per extra vehicle per night. Open year-round, weather permitting, with limited winter facilities.

Directions: From Starbuck, drive northwest on Highway 261 for 15 miles (crossing the river) to the park entrance and Palouse Falls Road. Turn right and drive to the park.

Contact: Palouse Falls State Park, 360/902-8844, http://parks.state.wa.us.

21 WINDUST

Scenic rating: 6

on Lake Sacajawea

Map page 354

With no other campgrounds within a 30-mile

radius, Windust is the only game in town. The camp is located along the shore of Lake Sacajawea near the Lower Monumental Dam on the Snake River. The park covers 54 acres. Swimming, waterskiing, and fishing are popular.

Campsites, facilities: There are 24 sites for tents or RVs of any length (no hookups). Picnic tables and fire grills are provided. Flush toilets are available May-September, and pit toilets are provided the rest of the year. Drinking water, garbage bins, dump station, a playground, and a swimming beach are available nearby. No alcohol is permitted. Boat docks and launching facilities are nearby. Some facilities are wheelchair accessible. Leashed pets are permitted.

Reservations, fees: Reservations are not accepted. There is no fee for camping. Open mid-May-early September.

Directions: From Pasco, drive east on U.S. 12 for 2.5 miles to Pasco/Kahlotus Highway. Turn east and drive 28 miles to Burr Canyon Road. Turn right on Burr Canyon Road and drive 5.2 miles to the park (from the north, Burr Canyon Road becomes Highway 263).

Contact: U.S. Army Corps of Engineers, Walla Walla District, 509/547-2048, www.nww.usace.army.mil.

22 FISHHOOK PARK
🏊 🚣 🚐 🦌 🎣 ♿ 🚐 ⛰️

Scenic rating: 6

on Lake Sacajawea

Map page 354

If you're driving along Highway 124 and you need a spot for the night, check out this wooded camp along the Snake River. It is a nice spot within a 46-acre park set on Lake Sacajawea, which is a dammed portion of the Snake River. The park provides some lawn area, along with places to swim, fish, and water ski. A one-mile walk along railroad tracks will take you to a fishing pond. This park is popular on summer weekends.

Campsites, facilities: There are 11 walk-in

tent sites, 41 sites with partial hookups for tents or RVs of any length, and two group tent sites that can accommodate up to 16 people. Some sites are pull-through. Picnic tables and fire grills are provided. Drinking water, restrooms with flush toilets and showers, a dump station, and playground are available. Boat docks, launching facilities, a swimming beach, and group picnic shelters that can be reserved are nearby. Some facilities are wheelchair accessible. Leashed pets are permitted.

Reservations, fees: Reservations are accepted at 877/444-6777 or www.recreation.gov ($10 reservation fee). Walk-in tent sites are $10-24 per night, sites with hookups are $12-30 per night, $4 per night per additional vehicle, the group tent site is $22 per night. Open mid-May-September. Park gates are locked 10pm-6am.

Directions: From Pasco, drive southeast on U.S. 12 for five miles to Highway 124. Turn left (east) and drive 18 miles to Fishhook Park Road. Turn left on Fishhook Park Road and drive four miles to the park.

Contact: U.S. Army Corps of Engineers, Walla Walla District, 509/547-2048, www.nww.usace.army.mil.

23 LEWIS AND CLARK TRAIL STATE PARK
🥾 🚣 ❄️ 🦌 🚐 ⛰️

Scenic rating: 8

on the Touchet River

Map page 354

Lewis and Clark features an unusual mixture of old-growth forest and riparian habitat, with ponderosa pine and cottonwood amid the prairie grasslands. The park is set on 37 acres with frontage along the Touchet River. Fishing for rainbow trout and brown trout can be excellent here. An interpretive display explains much of the history of the area. A seasonal Saturday evening living-history program depicts the story of Lewis and Clark and the site's history here on the original Lewis and Clark Trail. In winter, cross-country skiing and snowshoeing are good here. Note: If it's getting late and you need to stop, consider this camp because it's the only one within 20 miles.

Campsites, facilities: There are 24 sites for tents or self-contained RVs up to 28 feet, four primitive hike-in/bike-in sites (Apr.-Oct.), two teepees, and two group sites for up to 100 people each. Picnic tables and fire grills are provided. Restrooms with flush toilets and coin showers, firewood, and a dump station are available. Two fire circles, an amphitheater, interpretive programs, a picnic area, badminton, a baseball field, and a volleyball court are available nearby. A store, café, and ice are located within four miles. Leashed pets are permitted.

Reservations, fees: Reservations are accepted May-September at 888/226-7688 or https://washington.goingtocamp.com ($8-10 reservation fee). Sites are $12-40 per night, $10 per extra vehicle per night. Call for group and teepee rates. Open April-mid-September.

Directions: From Walla Walla, drive east on U.S. 12 for 22 miles to Waitsburg. Bear right on U.S. 12 and drive east for 4.5 miles to the park entrance on the left.

Contact: Lewis and Clark Trail State Park, 509/337-6457, http://parks.state.wa.us.

24 PALOUSE EMPIRE FAIRGROUNDS & HORSE CAMP

Scenic rating: 6

west of Colfax

Map page 354

The camp consists primarily of a large lawn area with shade trees. It is set just off the road, but the highway noise, surprisingly, is relatively limited. All sites are on grass. The park covers 47 acres, with paved trails available around the adjacent fairgrounds. This area is agricultural, with rolling hills, and it is considered the "Lentil Capital of the World." With wash racks, corrals, arenas, and water troughs, the camp encourages horse campers to stay here. It fills

up for the Whitman County Fair in mid-September. They turn back the clock every Labor Day weekend with the annual Threshing Bee, where there are demonstrations of historical farming practices dating back to the early 1900s, including the use of draft horses.

Campsites, facilities: There are 60 sites with partial hookups for tents or RVs of any length. Large groups can be accommodated. Restrooms with flush toilets and showers, drinking water, and a dump station are available. Restaurants, gas, and supplies are available 4.5 miles away in Colfax. Some facilities are wheelchair accessible. Leashed pets are permitted.

Reservations, fees: Reservations are accepted for groups only. RV sites are $20 per night, tent sites are $10 per night; there is no charge for horse stalls. Open mid-April to mid-November.

Directions: From Colfax and Highway 26, drive west on Highway 26 for 4.5 miles to the fairgrounds on the right.

Contact: Palouse Empire Fairgrounds & Horse Camp, Whitman County, 509/397-6263, www.palouseempirefair.org.

25 CHARBONNEAU PARK

Scenic rating: 6

on the Snake River

Map page 354

This shorefront campground is the centerpiece of a 244-acre park set along the Snake River, just above Ice Harbor Dam. Named one of America's Top 100 Family Campgrounds, it is a good spot for fishing, boating, swimming, and waterskiing. An overflow camping area provides a backup if the numbered sites are full. No alcohol is permitted. At Lake Sacajawea, the dam's visitors center (open daily April-October) features exhibits and a view of a salmon fish ladder.

Campsites, facilities: There are 52 sites with full or partial hookups for tents or RVs up to 45 feet. Some sites are pull-through. Picnic tables and fire grills are provided. Restrooms with flush toilets and showers, a dump station, pay telephone, playground, and volleyball court are available. A camp host is on-site. A marina with boat docks, launching facilities, a marine dump station, a swimming beach, fishing tackle, seasonal snack bar, ice, and a day-use area and picnic shelters are nearby. Some facilities are wheelchair accessible. Leashed pets are permitted.

Reservations, fees: Reservations are accepted at 877/444-6777 or www.recreation. gov ($10 reservation fee). Sites are $12-30 per night. Open April-October with full facilities; there are limited facilities and no fee the rest of the year.

Directions: From Pasco, drive southeast on U.S. 12 for five miles to Highway 124. Turn left (east) and drive eight miles to Sun Harbor Road. Turn left (north) and drive two miles to the park.

Contact: U.S. Army Corps of Engineers, Walla Walla District, 509/547-2048, www.nww.usace. army.mil.

26 HOOD PARK

🏃 🏊 🛶 🎣 🐕 🚴 ♿ 🚐 ⛺

Scenic rating: 6

on Lake Wallula

Map page 354

This 99-acre developed park on Lake Wallula provides access for swimming and boating. Some sites are situated near the shoreline, and shaded sites are available. No alcohol is permitted. There are hiking trails throughout the park, along with stocked fishing ponds. Other recreation options include basketball and horseshoes. McNary Wildlife Refuge is right next door, and Sacajawea State Park is within four miles.

Campsites, facilities: There are 46 sites, some with partial hookups (30 and 50 amps), for tents or RVs of any length. Picnic tables and fire grills are provided. Drinking water, restrooms with flush toilets and showers, a dump station, a playground, horseshoe pits, a basketball court,

swimming beach, covered picnic area, and an amphitheater are available. A restaurant and convenience store are located within two miles. Boat docks and launching facilities are nearby. Some facilities are wheelchair accessible. Leashed pets are permitted.

Reservations, fees: Reservations are accepted at 877/444-6777 or www.recreation.gov ($10 reservation fee). Sites are $22-26 per night on weekends, $4 per night per additional vehicle, $8 per night for boat camping and in the overflow area. Open May-September.

Directions: In Pasco, drive southeast on U.S. 12 for five miles to the junction with Highway 124. Turn left (east) on Highway 124 and drive to the park entrance on the left (just before the town of Burbank). Drive 0.5 mile to the gate entrance.

Contact: U.S. Army Corps of Engineers, Walla Walla District, 509/547-2048, www.nww.usace. army.mil.

27 KAMIAK BUTTE COUNTY PARK

🏃 🐕 🚴 ♿ 🚐 ⛺

Scenic rating: 8

east of Colfax

Map page 354

This quiet and peaceful park gets medium use. Kamiak Butte is a National Natural Landmark with more than five miles of wooded hiking trails. The 3.5-mile Pine Ridge Trail is part of the national trails system, and hikers can obtain excellent views of the Palouse region by walking to the highest point at 3,641 feet. The park gate closes at dusk each night and reopens at 7am.

Campsites, facilities: There are seven sites for tents or RVs up to 18 feet long (no hookups). Overflow camping for RVs of any length is available in the parking lot. Picnic tables and fire grills are provided. Drinking water (mid-April-mid-October) and vault and pit toilets are available. A playground, picnic area, amphitheater, and group facilities that can be reserved are available. Some facilities are wheelchair accessible. Leashed pets are permitted.

Reservations, fees: Reservations are not accepted. Sites are $15 per night, $5 per night per extra vehicle. Open year-round, with limited winter facilities.

Directions: From Colfax, drive east on Highway 272 for five miles to Clear Creek Road. Turn right and drive seven miles to Fugate Road. Turn right and drive 0.5 mile to the park entrance on the left.

Contact: Whitman County Parks and Recreation, 509/397-6238, www.whitmancounty.org.

28 BOYER PARK AND MARINA

🏃 🚲 🏊 ⛴ 🏕 🐕 ♿ 🚐 ⛺

Scenic rating: 7

on Lake Bryan on the Snake River

Map page 354

This 99-acre park on the north shore of Lake Bryan is located two miles from the Lower Granite Dam. It features 3.5 miles of trails for hiking and biking, and the lake is popular for waterskiing and fishing for sturgeon, steelhead, and salmon. Most campsites are shaded, and all are paved and bordered by a grassy day-use area. The landscape is flat and open, and it gets hot here in summer. The camp is well above the water level, typically about 100 feet above the lakeshore. The camp commonly fills on summer weekends.

Campsites, facilities: There are 48 sites with full or partial hookups for tents or RVs up to 70 feet, seven sites for tents, and four cabins. Group camping is also available. Picnic tables and fire grills are provided. Restrooms with flush toilets and coin showers, drinking water, and a dump station are available. A coin laundry, covered shelters, a swimming area, snack bar, restaurant, convenience store, ice, and gas are available. A marina, fuel dock, fishing licenses, boat docks, a boat launch, moorage, and a marine dump station are nearby. Some

facilities are wheelchair accessible. Leashed pets are permitted.

Reservations, fees: Reservations are accepted at 509/397-3208 ($10 reservation fee). Tent sites are $18 per night, $9 per night per additional tent. RV sites are $37-45 per night, $4 per night for extra person, $8 per night per extra vehicle; moorage is $15-45 per day. Cabins are $60-75 per night. Winter rates are available. Some credit cards are accepted. Open year-round, with limited winter facilities.

Directions: From U.S. 195 at Colfax, turn southwest on Almota Road and drive 17 miles to the park and campground.

Contact: Boyer Park, 509/397-3208; Port of Whitman County, 509/397-3791, www.portwhitman.com.

29 WAWAWAI COUNTY PARK

🏃 ⛴ 🏕 🐕 ♿ 🚐 ⛺

Scenic rating: 7

on Lower Granite Lake

Map page 354

This park covers 49 acres and is set near the inlet to Lower Granite Lake, about 0.25 mile from the lake. The camp itself is situated on a hillside, and all sites are paved. Some sites have views of a bay, but not the entire lake. Tree cover is a plus. So is a 0.5-mile loop trail that leads to a bird-viewing platform, and a diverse mix of wildlife and geology, making interpretive hikes with naturalists popular. One strange note: An underground house built in 1980 has been converted to a ranger's residence. This camp often fills on summer weekends. No campfires are permitted during the summer season.

Campsites, facilities: There are nine sites for tents or RVs up to 24 feet long (no hookups). Some sites are pull-through. Picnic tables and fire grills are provided; fires are restricted in Hells Canyon mid-April-mid-October. Drinking water (mid-April-mid-October) and pit toilets are available. A group picnic shelter that can be reserved and a boat launch are nearby. Some facilities are wheelchair accessible. Leashed pets are permitted.

Reservations, fees: Reservations are not accepted. Sites are $15 per night, $5 per extra vehicle per night. Open year-round, with limited winter facilities.

Directions: From Colfax, drive south on U.S. 195 for 15 miles to Wawawai-Pullman Road (located just west of Pullman). Turn right (west) and drive approximately 9.5 miles to Wawawai Road. Turn right on Wawawai Road (signed) and drive 5.5 miles to the park.

Contact: Wawawai County Park, Whitman County Parks and Recreation, 509/397-6238, www.whitmancounty.org.

30 CHIEF TIMOTHY PARK

Scenic rating: 8

on the Snake River

Map page 354

This unusual park is set on an island composed of glacial tills in the Snake River; it is accessible by car over a bridge. The park covers 282 acres with two miles of shoreline and features a desert landscape. There are 2.5 miles of hiking trails, plus docks for boating campers and a beach area. Water sports include fishing, swimming, boating, waterskiing, and sailing. Outfitters in Clarkston will take you sightseeing up Hells Canyon.

Campsites, facilities: There are 70 sites, including 33 sites with full or partial hookups (30 amps), for tents or RVs up to 60 feet. There are also two primitive sites for tents and four camping cabins. Some sites are pull-through. Picnic tables and fire pits are provided. Restrooms with flush toilets and coin showers, dump station, a picnic area, a small store, firewood, ice, a playground, volleyball court, and horseshoe pits are available. A camp host is on-site. Boat docks and launching facilities, a swimming beach, and beach house are available. Some facilities are wheelchair accessible. Leashed pets are permitted.

Reservations, fees: Reservations are accepted. RV sites are $29-40 per night, tent sites are $24 per night, $5 per night per extra vehicle, cabins are $75 per night. Some credit cards are accepted. Open May-October, weather permitting; walk-in camping is permitted in November.

Directions: From Clarkston on the Washington/Idaho border, drive west on U.S. 12 for seven miles to the signed park entrance road on the right. Turn right (north) and drive one mile to the park, which is set on a bridged island in the Snake River.

Contact: Chief Timothy Park, 509/758-9580, www.sunrisereservations.com.

31 TUCANNON

Scenic rating: 8

in Umatilla National Forest

Map page 354

For people willing to rough it, this backcountry camp in Umatilla National Forest is the place. It has plenty of hiking, fishing, and hunting, all in a rugged setting. The camp is set along the Tucannon River, which offers a myriad of recreation options for vacationers. It is popular from early spring (the best time for fishing) through fall (when it makes a good hunting camp). In summer, several nearby ponds are stocked with trout, making it a good family destination. There is some tree cover. The elevation is 2,600 feet.

Campsites, facilities: There are 15 sites for tents or RVs up to 21 feet long and two sites for tents only. Picnic tables and fire grills are provided. Vault toilets are available, but there is no drinking water. Garbage must be packed out. Two covered shelters are available nearby. Some facilities are wheelchair accessible. Leashed pets are permitted.

Reservations, fees: Reservations are not accepted. Sites are $8 per night, $5 per night per additional vehicle. Open year-round, weather permitting.

Directions: From Clarkston, drive west on U.S. 12 for 37 miles to Pomeroy. Continue west for five miles to Tatman Mountain Road (signed for Camp Wooten). Turn left (south) and drive 19 miles (becomes Forest Road 47). Once inside the national forest boundary, continue southwest on Forest Road 47 for four miles to the campground on the left.

Contact: Umatilla National Forest, Pomeroy Ranger District, 509/843-1891, www.fs.usda. gov.

32 ALDER THICKET

Scenic rating: 7

in Umatilla National Forest

Map page 354

This is probably the first time you've heard of this place. Hardly anybody knows about it, including people who live relatively nearby in Walla Walla. It is set at an elevation of 5,100 feet, making it a prime base camp for a back-country hiking adventure in summer or a jumping-off point for a hunting trip in the fall. This is a primitive camp, but it's great if you're looking for quiet and solitude.

Campsites, facilities: There are five sites for tents or RVs up to 21 feet long. Picnic tables and fire grills are provided. Vault toilets are available, but there is no drinking water. Garbage must be packed out. Some facilities are wheelchair accessible. Leashed pets are permitted.

Reservations, fees: Reservations are not accepted. There is no fee for camping. Open mid-May-mid-November, weather permitting.

Directions: From Clarkston, drive west on U.S. 12 for 37 miles to Pomeroy and Highway 128. Turn south and drive seven miles to a fork. At the fork, continue straight to Forest Road 40 (15 miles from Pomeroy to the national forest boundary) and drive 3.5 miles to the campground on the right.

Contact: Umatilla National Forest, Pomeroy Ranger District, 509/843-1891, www.fs.usda. gov.

33 BIG SPRINGS

Scenic rating: 8

in Umatilla National Forest

Map page 354

This camp is set at an elevation of 5,000 feet. In the fall, primarily hunters use Big Springs; come summer, this nice, cool site becomes a possible base camp for backpacking trips. Although quite primitive with little in the way of activity options, this is a perfect spot to get away from it all. It's advisable to obtain a U.S. Forest Service map.

Campsites, facilities: There are six sites for tents or self-contained RVs up to 16 feet and two sites for tents only. Picnic tables are provided. Vault toilets are available, but there is no drinking water. Some facilities are wheelchair accessible. Leashed pets are permitted.

Reservations, fees: Reservations are not accepted. There is no fee for camping. Open mid-May-mid-November, weather permitting.

Directions: From Clarkston, drive west on U.S. 12 for 37 miles to Pomeroy and Highway 128. Turn south and drive 25 miles to Forest Road 42 (to the Clearwater Lookout Tower). Turn left and continue on Forest Road 42 for five miles to the campground entrance road (Forest Road 4225). Turn left and drive to the campground at the end of the road.

Contact: Umatilla National Forest, Pomeroy Ranger District, 509/843-1891, www.fs.usda. gov.

34 TEAL SPRING

Scenic rating: 8

in Umatilla National Forest

Map page 354

The views of the Tucannon drainage and the Wenaha-Tucannon Wilderness are astonishing from the nearby lookout. Teal Spring Camp is set at 5,600 feet elevation and is one of several small, primitive camps in the area. Trails in the immediate area provide a variety of good day-hiking options. Hunting is popular in the fall.

Campsites, facilities: There are three sites for tents or RVs up to 35 feet and four sites for tents only. Vault toilets are available, but there is no drinking water. Picnic tables and fire grills are provided. Garbage must be packed out. Some facilities are wheelchair accessible. Leashed pets are permitted.

Reservations, fees: Reservations are not accepted. There is no fee for camping. Open late May-mid-November, weather permitting.

Directions: From Clarkston, drive west on U.S. 12 for 37 miles to Pomeroy and Highway 128. Turn left (south) and drive 25 miles to Forest Road 42 (to the Clearwater Lookout Tower). Turn left and continue on Forest Road 42 for one mile to the campground entrance road. Turn right and drive 200 yards to the campground.

Contact: Umatilla National Forest, Pomeroy Ranger District, 509/843-1891, www.fs.usda. gov.

35 GODMAN

Scenic rating: 8

near the Wenaha-Tucannon Wilderness in Umatilla National Forest

Map page 354

This tiny, little-known spot bordering a wilderness area is set at 6,050 feet elevation and features drop-dead gorgeous views at sunset, as well as a wilderness trailhead. It is used primarily as a base camp for backcountry expeditions. A trailhead provides access to the Wenaha-Tucannon Wilderness for both hikers and horseback riders. Horse facilities are available 0.2 mile away. There are also opportunities for mountain biking, but note that bikes are forbidden past the wilderness boundary. A bonus here is a two-story cabin, the Godman Guard Station. The cabin has a propane stove, refrigerator, heater, and electricity, but there is no indoor restroom. It is available year-round,

but is accessible only by snowmobile in the winter months.

Campsites, facilities: There are eight sites for tents or RVs up to 16 feet long, plus one cabin that can accommodate up to eight people. Picnic tables and fire grills are provided. Vault toilets and a group picnic shelter are available, but there is no drinking water. Garbage must be packed out. Facilities, including hitching rails and a spring, are available nearby for up to six people with horses, with an additional fee for more than six. There is also a barn about 200 yards up the hill. Some facilities are wheelchair accessible, but assistance may be required. Leashed pets are permitted.

Reservations, fees: Reservations are not accepted for campsites. The Godman Guard Station can be reserved at 877/444-6777 or www.recreation.gov. ($10 reservation fee). There is no fee for camping. The cabin is $60-75 per night. Open mid-June-late October; cabin is available year-round.

Directions: From Walla Walla, drive northeast on U.S. 12 for 32 miles to Dayton and North Fork Touchet River Road. Turn right on North Fork Touchet River Road and drive 14 miles southeast to the national forest boundary; continue to Kendall Skyline Road. Turn left (south) and drive 11 miles to the campground on the left.

Contact: Umatilla National Forest, Pomeroy Ranger District, 509/843-1891, www.fs.usda. gov.

36 FIELDS SPRING STATE PARK

Scenic rating: 8

near Puffer Butte

Map page 354

Not many people know about this spot, yet it's a good one, tucked away in the southeast corner of the state. This 825-acre state park is located in the Blue Mountains, set in a forested landscape covering Puffer Butte, with views of

Oregon, Idaho, and the Grande Ronde. Basalt dominates the landscape. Two hiking trails lead up to Puffer Butte at 4,500 feet elevation, providing a panoramic view of the Snake River Canyon and the Wallowa Mountains. The park is noted for its variety of birdlife and wildflowers, and there are seven miles of mountain-biking trails, along with three miles of hiking trails. In winter, non-motorized recreation opportunities include cross-country skiing (groomed trails), snowmobiling, snowshoeing, and general snow play; warming huts are available. There is also a retreat center with lodges that can be reserved. Two day-use areas with boat launches, managed by the Department of Fish and Wildlife, are within about 25 miles of the park.

Campsites, facilities: There are 20 sites for tents or RVs up to 30 feet (no hookups), one cabin, two tepees, and two lodges for 12-20 and 20-80 people respectively. Picnic tables and fire grills are provided. Drinking water, restrooms with flush toilets and coin showers, firewood, a dump station, two picnic shelters, two sheltered fire circles, a playground, horseshoe pits, a softball field, and volleyball courts are available. Some facilities are wheelchair accessible. Leashed pets are permitted.

Reservations, fees: Reservations are accepted at 888/226-7688 or https://washington.goingto-camp.com ($8-10 reservation fee). Sites are $20-35 per night, $10 per extra vehicle per night. Call for tepee, lodge, and cabin rates. Open year-round, with limited winter facilities.

Directions: From Clarkston, turn south on Highway 129 and drive 30 miles (just south of Rattlesnake Pass) to the park entrance on the left (east) side of the road.

Contact: Fields Spring State Park, 509/256-3332, http://parks.state.wa.us.

37 BROOKS MEMORIAL STATE PARK

Scenic rating: 7

near the Goldendale Observatory

Map page 354

Brooks Memorial State Park sits near the South Yakima Valley at an elevation of nearly 3,000 feet. The campground is located on the Little Klickitat River amid the pines of the Simcoe Mountains. The park's 700 acres include nine miles of hiking trails, and occasionally excellent fishing for trout. You can extend your trip into the mountains, where you'll find open meadows with a panoramic view of Mount Hood. Nearby side trips include the Goldendale Observatory and a replica of Stonehenge on State Route 14. Note that the Yakama Indian Nation is two miles north.

Campsites, facilities: There are 22 sites for tents or RVs (no hookups), 23 sites with full hookups (50 amps) for RVs up to 30 feet, and a group site for 20-50 people. Picnic tables and fire grills are provided. Restrooms with flush toilets and coin showers, a dump station, and a playground with horseshoe pits and volleyball court are available. A sheltered picnic area, ball field, and store are nearby. Leashed pets are permitted.

Reservations, fees: Reservations for single sites can be made at 888/226-7688 or https://washington.goingtocamp.com ($8-10 reservation fee). Sites are $20-45 per night, $10 per extra vehicle per night. Call for group rates. Open year-round, with limited winter facilities.

Directions: From Toppenish, drive south on U.S. 97 for 40 miles to the park on the right (well signed).

Contact: Brooks Memorial State Park, 509/773-4611, http://parks.state.wa.us.

38 MARYHILL STATE PARK
🏃 🏊 ⛵ 🚣 🏕️ 🐕 ♿ 🚐 ⛺

Scenic rating: 8
on the Columbia River

Map page 354

This 99-acre park has 4,700 feet of frontage along the Columbia River. Fishing, waterskiing, and windsurfing are among the recreation possibilities. The climate here is pleasant March-mid-November. Two interesting places can be found near Maryhill: a full-scale replica of Stonehenge, located on a bluff overlooking the Columbia River about one mile from the park, and the historic Mary Hill home, which is open to the public. Mary Hill's husband, Sam Hill, constructed the Stonehenge replica.

Campsites, facilities: There are 50 sites with full hookups (30 and 50 amps) for RVs up to 60 feet long, 20 tent sites, two hike-in/bike-in sites, and one group camp for up to 200 people. Picnic tables and fire pits are provided. Restrooms with flush toilets and showers, a dump station, and a picnic area with covered shelters are available. A café and store are within one mile. Boat docks and launching facilities are nearby. Some facilities are wheelchair accessible. Leashed pets are permitted.

Reservations, fees: Reservations are accepted and are required for the group camp at 888/226-7688 or https://washington.goingto-camp.com ($8-10 reservation fee). Sites are $25-45 per night, $12 per night for hike-in/bike-in sites, $10 per extra vehicle per night. The group camp is $79-561 per night. Some credit cards are accepted. Open year-round.

Directions: From Goldendale and U.S. 97, drive 12 miles south to the park on the left.

Contact: Maryhill State Park, 509/773-5007, http://parks.state.wa.us.

39 CROW BUTTE PARK
🏃 🏊 ⛵ 🚣 🏕️ 🐕 ♿ 🚐 ⛺

Scenic rating: 8
on the Columbia River

Map page 354

How would you like to be stranded on a romantic island? Well, this park offers that possibility. The park is set on an island in the Columbia River and is the only campground in a 25-mile radius. Sometimes referred to as the "Maui of the Columbia," the park covers 1,312 acres and has several miles of shoreline. It is set on the Lewis and Clark Trail, with the camp situated in a partially protected bay. The highlight of 3.5 miles of hiking trails is a mile-long path that leads to the top of a butte, where you can see Mount Hood, Mount Adams, and the Columbia River Valley. Waterskiing, sailboarding, fishing, swimming, and hiking are among the possibilities here. One downer: Keep an eye out for rattlesnakes, which are occasionally spotted. The Umatilla National Wildlife Refuge is adjacent to the park and allows fishing and hunting in specified areas. Note that this former state park is now run by the Port of Benton.

Campsites, facilities: There are 50 sites for tents or RVs up to 90 feet long (20, 30, and 50 amp full hookups) and one primitive group camp for tents only that accommodates up to 100 people. Some sites are pull-through. Fire grills and picnic tables are provided. Restrooms with flush toilets and coin showers, a sheltered picnic area, a swimming beach, and a dump station are available. Boat-launching and moorage facilities are nearby. A concession stand is open on weekends. Some facilities are wheelchair accessible. Leashed pets are permitted.

Reservations, fees: Reservations are accepted. RV sites are $32 per night, tent sites are $17 per night, $5 per extra vehicle per night, boat launch is $5 per day. The group site is $80 per night. Open mid-March-October.

Directions: From the junction of I-82/U.S. 395 and Highway 20 at Plymouth, just north of the Columbia River, turn west on State Route

14. Drive to Paterson and continue west for 13 miles to the park entrance road at Milepost 155 on the right. Turn right and drive one mile (across the bridge) to the park on the island.

Contact: Crow Butte Park, Port of Benton, 509/875-2644, www.crowbutte.com.

40 PLYMOUTH PARK

Scenic rating: 7

near Lake Umatilla

Map page 354

Plymouth Park is a family- and RV-style campground set near Lake Umatilla on the Columbia River. The 112-acre park is not located on the shore of the lake, rather about a quarter-mile drive from the water. The camp has tree cover, which is a nice plus, and it fills up on most summer weekends. Each campsite has a tent pad.

Campsites, facilities: There are 32 sites with partial hookups (30 and 50 amps) for tents or RVs up to 40 feet. Most sites are pull-through.

Picnic tables and fire grills are provided. Restrooms with flush toilets and showers, drinking water, a dump station, playground, and coin laundry are available. A boat dock, boat launch, swimming areas, and covered picnic shelters are available nearby. A store and a restaurant are within five miles. Some facilities are wheelchair accessible. Leashed pets are permitted.

Reservations, fees: Reservations are accepted at 877/444-6777 or www.recreation.gov ($10 reservation fee). Sites are $15-27 per night, $5 per night per extra vehicle. Some credit cards are accepted. Open April-October.

Directions: From Richland and I-82, drive south on I-82 for about 30 miles to State Route 14. Turn west on State Route 14 and drive two miles to the Plymouth exit. Take that exit and drive south 1.5 miles to Christy Road; turn right and continue 200 yards to the campground entrance on the left.

Contact: U.S. Army Corps of Engineers, Walla Walla District, 541/506-7818, www.nww.usace.army.mil.

RESOURCES

NATIONAL FORESTS

The U.S. Forest Service provides many secluded camps and allows camping anywhere except where it is specifically prohibited. If you ever want to clear the cobwebs from your head and get away from it all, this is the way to go.

Many Forest Service campgrounds are remote and have no drinking water. You usually don't need to check in or make reservations, and sometimes there is no fee. At many Forest Service campgrounds that provide drinking water, the camping fee is often only a few dollars, with payment made on the honor system. Because most of these camps are in mountain areas, they are subject to winter closure due to snow or mud.

Dogs are permitted in national forests with no extra charge. Always carry documentation of current vaccinations.

Northwest Forest Pass

A Northwest Forest Pass is required for certain activities in some Washington national forests and at North Cascades National Park. The pass is required for parking at participating trailheads, non-developed camping areas, boat launches, picnic areas, and visitors centers.

Daily passes cost $5 per vehicle; annual passes are $30 per vehicle. Combined recreation passes for Washington and Oregon are also available. You can buy Northwest Forest Passes at national forest offices and dozens of retail outlets and online vendors. Major credit cards are accepted at most retail and online outlets and at some Forest Service offices.

More information about the Northwest Forest Pass program, including a listing of retail and online vendors, can be obtained at www.fs.usda.gov.

An Interagency Pass is available for $80 annually in lieu of an Northwest Forest Pass. The America the Beautiful Pass is honored nationwide at all Forest Service, National Park Service, Bureau of Land Management, Bureau of Reclamation, and U.S. Fish and Wildlife Service sites charging entrance or standard amenity fees. Valid for 12 months from the month of purchase, the America the Beautiful Pass is available at most national forest or grassland offices or online at http://store.usgs.gov.

National Forest Reservations

Some of the more popular camps, and most of the group camps, are on a reservation system. Reservations can be made up to 240 days in advance and up to 360 days in advance for groups. To reserve a site, call 877/444-6777 or visit www.recreation.gov. The reservation fee is usually $10 for a campsite in a national forest, but group site reservation fees are higher. Major credit cards are accepted.

National Forest Maps

National Forest maps are among the best you can get for the price. They detail all backcountry streams, lakes, hiking trails, and logging roads for access. They can be obtained online at www.nationalforestmapstore.com.

Forest Service Information

Forest Service personnel are most helpful for obtaining camping or hiking trail information. Unless you are buying a map or Adventure Pass, it is advisable to phone in advance to get the best service.

For specific information on individual national forests, contact the following offices:

Colville National Forest
765 South Main St.
Colville, WA 99114
509/684-7000
www.fs.usda.gov/colville

Gifford Pinchot National Forest
1501 E. Evergreen Blvd.
Vancouver, WA 98682
360/891-5000
www.fs.fed.us/giffordpinchot

Mt. Baker-Snoqualmie National Forest
2930 Wetmore Ave.
Everett, WA 98201

425/783-6000 or 800/627-0062
www.fs.usda.gov/mbs

Okanogan-Wenatchee National Forest
215 Melody Ln.
Wenatchee, WA 98801
509/664-9200
www.fs.usda.gov/okawen

Olympic National Forest
1835 Black Lake Blvd. SW
Olympia, WA 98512
360/956-2402
www.fs.usda.gov/olympic

Umatilla National Forest
Pomeroy Ranger District
71 West Main St.
Pomeroy, WA 99347
509/843-1891
www.fs.usda.gov/umatilla

Walla Walla Ranger District
1415 West Rose St.
Walla Walla, WA 99362
509/522-6290
www.fs.usda.gov/umatilla

STATE PARKS

The Washington State Parks system provides many popular camping spots in spectacular settings. The camps include drive-in numbered sites, tent spaces, and picnic tables, with restrooms provided. Reservations are often a necessity during the summer. Although some parks are well known, there are still some little-known gems in the state parks system where campers can enjoy seclusion, even in the summer.

State Park Reservations

Many of the state park campgrounds are on a reservation system, and campsites can be booked up to nine months in advance at these parks. Reservations can be made at 888/CAMP-OUT (888/226-7688) or at http://washington.goingtocamp.com. Major credit cards are accepted for reservations, and credit cards are accepted at some of the parks during the summer. A $8-10 reservation fee is charged. The reservation fee for group sites is $25.

Washington State Parks and Recreation Commission
P.O. Box 42650
Olympia, WA 98504-2650
360/902-8844
http://parks.state.wa.us

NATIONAL PARKS AND RECREATION AREAS

The national parks and recreation areas in Washington are natural wonders, ranging from the spectacular Mount Rainier National Park to the lava-strewn Mount St. Helens National Volcanic Monument to the often fog-bound Olympic National Park. Reservations are available at some of the campgrounds at these parks and recreation areas.

For information about each of the national parks in Washington, contact the parks directly:

Lake Roosevelt National Recreation Area
1008 Crest Dr.
Coulee Dam, WA 99116
509/754-7800
www.nps.gov/laro

Mount Rainier National Park
55210 238th Ave. East
Ashford, WA 98304
360/569-2211
www.nps.gov/mora

Mount St. Helens National Volcanic Monument
42218 NE Yale Bridge Rd.
Amboy, WA 98601
360/449-7800
www.fs.usda.gov/giffordpinchot

Mount St. Helens Visitor Center
360/274-0962

North Cascades National Park
810 State Route 20
Sedro-Woolley, WA 98284
360/854-7200
www.nps.gov/noca

Olympic National Park
600 E. Park Avenue
Port Angeles, WA 98362
360/565-3130
www.nps.gov/olym

DEPARTMENT OF NATURAL RESOURCES

The Department of Natural Resources manages more than five million acres of public land in Washington. All of it is managed under the concept of "multiple use," designed to provide the greatest number of recreational opportunities while still protecting natural resources.

The campgrounds in these areas are among the most primitive, remote, and least known of the camps listed in this book. The campsites are usually free, and campers are asked to remove all litter and trash from the area, leaving only footprints behind. Due to budget cutbacks, some of these campgrounds have been closed in recent years; expect more closures in the future.

In addition to maps of the area it manages, the Department of Natural Resources also has Washington public lands maps, U.S. Geological Survey maps, and U.S. Army Corps of Engineers maps. For information, contact the Department of Natural Resources at its state or regional addresses:

State of Washington Department of Natural Resources
1111 Washington St. SE
P.O. Box 47000
Olympia, WA 98504
360/902-1000
www.dnr.wa.gov

Northeast Region
225 South Silke Rd.

Colville, WA 99114
509/684-7474

Northwest Region
919 N. Township St.
Sedro Woolley, WA 98284
360/856-3500

Olympic Region
411 Tillicum Ln.
Forks, WA 98331
360/374-2800

Pacific Cascade Region
601 Bond Rd.
P.O. Box 280
Castle Rock, WA 98611
360/577-2025

Southeast Region
713 Bowers Rd.
Ellensburg, WA 98926
509/925-8510

South Puget Sound Region
950 Farman Ave. N.
Enumclaw, WA 98022
360/825-1631

U.S. ARMY CORPS OF ENGINEERS

Some of the family camps and most of the group camps operated by the U.S. Army Corps of Engineers are on a reservation system. Reservations can be made up to 240 days in advance and up to 360 days in advance for groups. To reserve a site, call 877/444-6777 or visit www.recreation.gov. The reservation fee is usually $10 for a campsite, but group site reservation fees are higher. Major credit cards are accepted.

Walla Walla District
201 North 3rd Ave.
Walla Walla, WA 99362-1876
509/527-7020
www.nww.usace.army.mil

OTHER VALUABLE RESOURCES

Tacoma Power
3628 S. 35th St.
Tacoma, WA 98409
253/502-8690 or 800/752-6745
www.mytpu.org

U.S. Geological Survey
650/853-8300 or 888/ASK-USGS (888/275-8747)
www.usgs.gov

Washington Department of Fish and Wildlife
Natural Resources Building
1111 Washington St. SE
Olympia, WA 98501
360/902-2200
http://wdfw.wa.gov

Washington State Department of Transportation
www.wsdot.wa.gov

Index

Acknowledgments

The following state and federal resource experts provided critical information and galley reviews regarding changes in reservations, fees, directions, and recreational opportunities. We are extremely grateful for their timely help and expert advice.

U.S. Forest Service

Nan Berger, Colville National Forest, Newport Ranger District
Eric McQua, Colville National Forest, Republic Ranger District
Wendy Zoodsman, Colville National Forest, Sullivan Lake Ranger District
Carmen Nielsen, Colville National Forest, Three Rivers Ranger District
Cheryl Mack, Gifford Pinchot National Forest
Amber Malandry, Gifford Pinchot National Forest, Cowlitz Ranger District
Julie Knutson and Byron Carlisle, Gifford Pinchot National Forest, Mount Adams Ranger District
Diane Tharp, Gifford Pinchot National Forest, Mount St. Helens National Volcanic Monument
Shayla Hooper, Mt. Baker/Snoqualmie National Forest, Darrington Ranger District
Ann Dunphy, Mt. Baker/Snoqualmie National Forest, Mt. Baker Ranger District
Pam Young, Mt. Baker/Snoqualmie National Forest, Skykomish Ranger District
Nikolai Ferrell, Mt. Baker/Snoqualmie National Forest
Carol Bow, Okanogan-Wenatchee National Forest
Linda Belcher, Christina Perez, Rena Rex, Kelly Underwood, Okanogan-Wenatchee National Forest, Chelan Ranger District
Kim Larned, Okanogan-Wenatchee National Forest, Cle Elum Ranger District
Monte Bowe, Okanogan-Wenatchee National Forest, Entiat Ranger District
Terri Halstead, Okanogan-Wenatchee National Forest, Lake Wenatchee Ranger District
Mary Anderson, Okanogan-Wenatchee National Forest, Leavenworth Ranger District
Kathy Corrigan, Okanogan-Wenatchee National Forest, Methow Valley Ranger District
Kevin Hill, Mike Rowan, Okanogan-Wenatchee National Forest, Naches Ranger District
Joseph Cox, Okanogan-Wenatchee National Forest, Tonasket Ranger District
Mary Spear, Olympic National Forest
Debbie Schreuer, Olympic National Forest, Hood Canal Ranger District
Molly Erickson, Mary O'Neil, Olympic National Forest, Pacific Ranger District
Ruth Forcier, Umatilla National Forest, Pomeroy Ranger District

U.S. Army Corps of Engineers

Kathy Johnston, Central Ferry Park
Wayne O'Neal, Chief Timothy Park
Jesus Navarro, Walla Walla District

National Parks

Lorie Carstensen, Lake Roosevelt National Recreation Area
Mindy Garvin, Daniel Keebler, Mare Staton, Mount Rainier National Park
Aaron Pouliot, North Cascades National Park
Benjamin Komar, Josh McLean, Kirran Peart, Olympic National Park

State Parks

Katie Brieoff, Linda Burnett, Angela Harper, Virginia Painter, Washington State Parks
Morris Shook, Alta Lake State Park
Breeanne Jordan, Beacon Rock State Park
Kathy Stermolle, Belfair State Park
Nancy Wallwork, Brooks Memorial State Park
Dolores Delk, Camano Island State Park
Tracy Zuern, Cape Disappointment State Park
Fritz Osborne, Columbia Hills State Park
Ryan Layton, Conconully State Park
Don Robertson, Curlew Lake State Park
John Wennes, Daroga State Park
Douglas Hinton, Dosewallips State Park
Peggy Russell, Fay Bainbridge State Park
Shaun Bristol, Fields Spring State Park

Brett Bayne, Fort Casey State Park
Lori Bond, Fort Flagler State Park
Susan Thomas, Fort Worden State Park
James Mitchell, Ginkgo-Wanapum State Park
Candace Rodda, Grayland Beach State Park
Reuben Stuart, Ike Kinswa State Park
Roy Salisbury, Illahee State Park
Chris Patterson, Jarrell Cove and Hope Island State Parks
Kristie Cronin, Joemma Beach State Park
Karlene Herron, Kanaskat-Palmer State Park
Vern Matzen, Kitsap Memorial State Park
Matthew Smith, Kopachuck State Park
Carina Silva, Lake Chelan State Park
Teri Milbert, Lake Easton State Park
Brian Hageman, Lake Sylvia State Park
Gary Lentz, Lewis and Clark Trail State Park
Roy Torgerson, Manchester State Park
Kim Shupe, Maryhill State Park
Jim Schmidt, Ocean City State Park
Marlene Jeffries, Osoyoos Veterans Memorial Park
Daniel Cox, Pacific Beach State Park
Cynthia Brown, Potholes State Park
Becky Meyer, Potlatch State Park
Dave Rush, Rainbow Falls State Park
Lori Cobb, Riverside State Park
William Hoppe, San Juan Marine Area
Brad Muir, Seaquest State Park
Arnold Hampton, Schafer State Park
Teresa McCullough, Sequim State Park
Patty Anderson, South Whidbey State Park
Tina O'Brian, Spencer Spit State Park
Stacy Czebotar, Twanoh State Park
Dennis Mills, Twenty-Five Mile Creek State Park
Tyler Vanderpool, Twin Harbors State Park

Matt Morrison, Wenatchee Confluence State Park
Bryce Erickson, Yakima Sportsman State Park

State Department of Natural Resources

Brett Walker, Northeast Region
Jim Cahill, Stan Kurowski, Candace Johnson and Christ Thompsen, Northwest Region
Cathryn Baker, Olympic Region
Nick Cronquist, Brian Poehlein, Pacific Cascade Region
Erin Kreutz, Mike Williams, Southeast Region
Nancy Barker, Karen Robertson, Jesse Sims, South Puget Sound Region

Other

Cathy Mether, Mike Miller, City of Auburn
Tracey Paddock, City of Chehalis
Lori Peña, Clallam County
Blanca Anderson, City of Entiat
Rhonda Dow, Shawn DuFault, Kaly Harward, HooDoo Recreation
Randy Juette, Naches Valley Chamber of Commerce
Hank Nydam, City of Oak Harbor
Ron Curran, Pend Oreille County Public Works
Erin Grasseth, Port of Wahkiakum No. 2
Jackie Boplin, Quinault Nation
Kyle Peninger, Skagit County
Marcie Allen, Linda McCrea, Joe Miller, Snohomish County
Jeanne Blackburn, Wenberg County Park
Janel Goebel, Terry Jeffries, Ernie Miller, Whitman County Parks and Recreation
Gale Bridges, Tisa Pelletier, Trish Stanfield, Tacoma Power

States & Provinces

WASHINGTON
MATTHEW LOMBARDI

OREGON
JUDY JEWELL & W.C. McRAE

BRITISH COLUMBIA
ANDREW HEMPSTEAD

Regions & Getaways

OLYMPIC PENINSULA
JEFF BURLINGAME

COASTAL OREGON
W.C. McRAE & JUDY JEWELL

VICTORIA & VANCOUVER ISLAND
ANDREW HEMPSTEAD

Cities

SEATTLE
ALLISON WILLIAMS

PORTLAND
HOLLYANNA McCOLLOM

VANCOUVER
CAROLYN B. HELLER

Road Trips & Outdoors

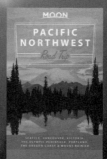

75 GREAT HIKES SEATTLE

OREGON CAMPING
TOM STIENSTRA

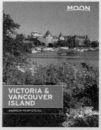

PACIFIC NORTHWEST Road Trip

SEATTLE, VANCOUVER, VICTORIA, THE OLYMPIC PENINSULA, PORTLAND, THE OREGON COAST & MOUNT RAINIER

We've got you covered, PNW!